EMILY RATEPAYERS 1867

VERULAM

Scale 40 Chains = 1in

David Mulcahey | Denis Donohue | Eugene Henelly | William McConnell / Richard Maginnis | Richard S. | 1

Robert Winn / enis Scully | Widow Donohue | Thomas Winn | Joseph McConnell / William Magahay | James Magahay | Robert Wilson / James Moore / David Kennedy | Benjamin White / James Hennedy / John Jim Reid | 2

enis Scully / rich O'Hara | Matthew Connell | William O'Neill | William Pigott | Samuel Herr / John Ashmore | Wm. Maghan | David Kennedy / David Davidson / John Smith | David Hennedy / William Thurston | 3

ohn nody / John Connors | John and Phillip Brady Jno Connell | Edmond Pigott | William Pigott / Patrick O'Grady | Widow Peel | Henry Padget / William Ashmore | James Waters / John H. Cassidy | 4

rles Lucas / ssey | William Lehane | John Lucas | William Pigott / Alexander McDonald | | Michael Callaghan / James Johnson | William Campbell / Thomas English | 5

n O'Leary / olomon owney | John Johns Fitzgerald | Thomas John / David Rolam / Alexander McDonald | Thomas Harrington / Martin Harrington / John Callaghan | Michael Callaghan / Robinson John Smith | William Sanderson / John Murdock | 6

ry ary | John Fox / Patrick Fox | James Fox | John Fox | Patrick Houlihan / Denis Houlihan | Robert Wilson / Robert Wilson | Patrick McMullen / William McMullen | William / John Murdock | 7

rich agan / Charles Lucas | William Houlihan | Patrick Corbett / Simon Harrington | Michael Caisey / Martin Harrington | Patrick Meehan | Thomas Counery / James Kelly | John Cullon | George Doyle / William McMullen | 8

hael pers pers | William Lehane / Edward O'Neill | Wm. Lehane | Thomas Corbett / Thomas Houlihan | William Dwyer / Michael | Henry Padget | James Campbell | 9

elius William / ynn Houlihan | Michael Guiry / William Ryan | Theophilis Ryan / Thomas Houlihan | Michael Meehan / John Mason | Marsh | Robert Hill / Marsh | William Parker / Robert English | 10

urice / Patrick Clancy | Owen O'Brien / Meredith | Marsh | Marsh | Marsh | Marsh | 11

ry / rria ☒ | Owen O'Brien / Owen O'Brien ☒ | Widow Flynn ☒ / Michael Sowers | Marsh ☒ XII | Marsh ☒ XIII | Marsh XIV | 12

ard / issey | John Callaghan / Widow Callaghan | Thomas McCarthy | Michael O'Neill | Patrick Collins / Benjamin Madigan / James Madigan | Patrick Murtha | Peter Murtha | Marsh | 13

an / rney | Edward Morrissey | Patrick Fitzpatrick / Edward Morrissey | Thomas Flynn | Joseph Sandy | Martin Dorgan | William / Thomas Herlihey Hawkey | Peter Murtha | James Dorgan / Henry Simpson | Marsh | 14

hn / mith Clancy | Maurice Flynn | Thomas Garrett Guiry | John Guiry | Joseph / Z.Guiry Sandy | Jeremiah Herlihey / James Burns | Timothy Dorgan | William McFeeters | 15

emiah Shea / chael Lehane | David Begley / Denis Begley | Patk Guiry Patk Guiry | Garrett Guiry / Martin Dorgan | Patrick / Timothy Crimeh | Patrick Down | Patrick Burke | Timothy Dorgan | T. Flynn Jer Dorgan Thomas | 16

Michael Lehane | Timothy Morrissey | Patrick Guiry / Timothy Morrissey | Patrick Guiry | Garrett Guiry | Francis Duffy | John Shiels | George Stewart | John McFeeters | 17

Timothy Morrissey | Widow Hennessey | Michael Hennessey | Connell William Lundy | David / Maurice Fitzgerald Samuel Ellery | John Moore / David Rowan | John O'Neill / John O'Neill | 18

William Richardson | John McCarthy / Thomas Brenan | Samuel Cottingham / David Daniel White | James Crimen | Henry Traynor | George Stewart | 19

rtin uliffe | Marsh | John Fitzgerald | John Harrington / Patrick Jim Herlihey | Widow Donovan / John King | Thomas Brenan | James Cormick | 20

illiam / livan Sullivan | Andrew Sullivan | Marsh | Richard Owens / John Sullivan | Martin Crowley / Patrick Brenan | Timothy Crowley | James Dolan | 21

rrich chey / James charly Flaherty | Mrs. Bn. Flaherty | Marsh | Marsh | John Jim Collins | Bernard Gilleece | W. Harrington Hugh Harrington | 22

chael nessey Hickey | John Hickey | David Travis | Richard Davidson | Marsh | Marsh | Bernard Gilleece | 23

Emily Lake
Marsh

LILIES
AND
SHAMROCKS

William Shakespeare: *"There is a history in all men's lives."*
Peter McArthur: *"The true spirit of Canada is the spirit of the pioneers*
    . . . where there had been a wilderness, they made a land of homes."
Stephen Leacock: *"I did not realize that the old grave among the brambles*
    at the foot of our farm was HISTORY."

Pioneer gravestones in Henderson Cemetery, on the Knight farm,
Lot 13, Concession 2, Emily Township.

". . . . . those fields of ripening grain,
Bright homes where once was wildness sere,
Provide the strong—the deathless—strain
Of homage to the PIONEER."

(From a poem *"The Pioneers"* by F. M. DelaFosse, chief librarian of
    Peterborough for many years.)

LILIES
AND
SHAMROCKS

A HISTORY OF EMILY TOWNSHIP
COUNTY OF VICTORIA, ONTARIO
1818-1973

HOWARD T. PAMMETT, M.A.

PREPARED FOR THE
EMILY TOWNSHIP HISTORICAL COMMITTEE

Printed by
John Deyell Co.
Lindsay, Ontario

TABLE OF CONTENTS

AUTHOR'S PREFACE

The proposal for a history of Emily Township began in the excitement of preparations for celebration of Centennial Year 1967, and in that April a committee was organized to begin gathering material and other basic research in various areas. The original committee consisted of Simon Connell (chairman), Mrs. Helen Connell, Harry Jackson, Mrs. Olive McCall (secretary), Mrs. Beryl Clark, Mrs. Mary Harrington, Mrs. Yvonne Lowes, Wilfred McMullen, Mrs. Winnifred McMullen, John Bent, Lowry McQuade, Alvin Franks, Chester Best, and Lloyd Ashmore; representing all parts of the township. Of these, John Bent, Chester Best and Lowry McQuade have passed on. In 1967 (while working in Ottawa) I agreed to assist the committee, having helped with the Douro Township history published that year. Since that time others have joined the committee—John Hollingshead and Ronald Pogue, representing the township council which has supported and financed the project.

The magnitude of the task ahead in 1967 can only be seen after 7 years' work, and only those who have participated in such a local community enterprise can appreciate its problems and complexities, its puzzles and rewards— the innumerable trips and interviews and meetings, the collection and correlation of reminiscences and reports, pictures and maps and other materials required, as well as the copying of council minutes, searching of newspaper files, thousands of hours of reading and annotating and typing—not only in all parts of Emily itself, but in Peterborough, Omemee, Lindsay, Toronto and Ottawa—which continued right up to the end.

Many people gave generously of their time and their collected memories of various aspects and areas of Emily through the generations, but the responsible duty of the committee and the author was to arrange and sift the vast collection of data, and to produce from it as complete, accurate and interesting a history as possible. We hope we have been successful in this task, which was from first to last a voluntary, co-operative and remunerative effort—not remunerative in money, but rather in satisfaction at the preservation (between covers) of the story of a typical Central Ontario rural township, in transition through the triumphs and tribulations, the prosperous and depressing periods, of 155 years. A special word of appreciation should go to the late C. H. Williamson, author of *Omemee: Mississauge Camp Site to Ontario Village* (Peterborough 1968) and to his executors, for permission to use any of the material he collected to write his warm history of his beloved Omemee. The author's thanks go also, for aid provided without stint, to the staffs of the Trent University Archives, Ontario Archives, Public Archives of Canada, and the County Councils of Victoria and Peterborough; and to Mrs. Valda Honour who typed the manuscript, to Mrs. Marianne MacKenzie who helped in proof-reading and indexing, and to others who assisted in the extensive editorial work. The Committee and the author are indebted to two Emily residents for the fine art-work in the book—for the jacket design and the township crest to Mrs. Dorthea Weise, and for the end-paper maps, front and back, to Mrs. Erika Hollingshead.

As author, I would like to explain several features of the book: (1) Much detailed information about particular groups, families, activities and incidents was worth recording for those specially interested, and has been placed in appendixes which are listed; (2) The notes on each chapter have been placed at the end of the chapter, rather than as footnotes on each page, or all together at the end of the book; (3) No bibliography of sources or further reading has been placed at the end, for various reasons, but every source used or quoted has been given as accurately as possible in the text, appendices and notes. Similarly, credit has been given wherever possible for each picture or other illustration, in a bracket under each; (4) Because of the many hundreds of family names that occur throughout, no index of them would be feasible; there are lists of names in various appendices. If readers note surnames spelled in various ways, this is because in pioneer times people frequently altered their names, and they were written and printed in several variations, especially in the first few decades when most people had little schooling. The index at the back of the book is a subject index only.

Finally, I would like to close with a double dedication of this book: (a) a GENERAL dedication to the Emily settlers who began creating this pioneer community in the backwoods in 1819-26, and their descendants through 5 or 6 generations who led hard-working, law-abiding, quiet, neigh-bourly and essentially unspectacular anonymous lives in the township, and also to their present-day descendants who remain in the same rural way of life, and often on the same land, still cherishing the memory of their fore-fathers who came out from "the auld sod", Ireland . . . and (b) a PARTIC-ULAR dedication to Leo Peter McGillen of Peterborough, who gave encouragement and advice while this history was being researched and written —boyhood friend in Ashburnham, enthusiast for the Kawartha outdoors, noted writer, journalist and broadcaster on sports, recreation, wild life and conservation, the best type of Irish Canadian—who died unexpectedly in October 1973, as I was writing the last chapter of the Emily History. Only a few weeks before his sudden death, he was discussing with youthful enthusiasm the prospects of organizing a mass excursion of district Irish Canadians back to Ireland in 1975, to celebrate the 150th anniversary of the Peter Robinson emigration of 1825, on which I had written my Master of Arts thesis in Canadian History at Queen's University almost 40 years ago (and which he was constantly urging me to have reprinted in hard covers). The Kawarthas have been fortunate in having native sons of the high calibre of Pete McGillen, and his work should be remembered.

November 17, 1973

INTRODUCTION

When Emily Township was surveyed 155 years ago, it was an average township of about 100 square miles and 69,000 acres in area, rectangular 8½ by 12 miles, 14 concessions deep, north-northwesterly from the Cavan boundary. The drainage pattern for its streams, running mostly northeasterly, was determined by the rolling drumlin hills forged in the glacial ages. Emily was central in the Kawartha Lakes region, which was central in the upper Canadian frontier north of the Lake Ontario strand and just south of the Pre-Cambrian Shield. After the war with United States ended in 1815, there was talk in government circles for a few years of moving the capital from York to this sheltered fertile area 30 miles north of Lake Ontario, which was taken from the Mississauga Indians by the 1818 "Treaty of Surrender". Certainly, by 1818 influential leaders in Upper Canada were convinced that the region should be secured with loyal British settlers, gentry and half-pay officers among an industrious peasantry, before the Yankees made aggressive raids northward again. After three decades, only about 4,000 settlers were located in the lakefront townships of Northumberland and Durham Counties (Newcastle District), and to the north the newly-acquired Indian lands stretched endlessly through a largely unexplored and unsurveyed wilderness up over the Shield to the Ottawa-Nipissing fur route, and farther into the wilderness beyond to Hudson Bay. Through this region the Upper Canada planners projected the Trent-Simcoe waterway to the Upper Lakes, with unexcelled water transportation, limitless pine forests, fertile millions of acres for profitable land speculation, plentiful water power for mills, and (not least) exceptional scenery and outstanding sporting pleasures with Indian guides over a wide network of lakes and streams for the upper classes of Upper Canada and British visitors.

Thus in 1818 Emily Township was on centre stage, and Major Samuel Wilmot, Deputy-Surveyor-General (who in the few previous years had surveyed other townships near Rice Lake) was instructed to survey the new township north of Cavan. It was named in honour of Emily, sister of the Duke of Richmond, Governor-General of Canada 1818-19 . . . and it was only a coincidence that John Beverley Robinson, new Attorney-General of Upper Canada, who married in 1817, had a daughter Emily somewhat later . . . and that John's older unmarried brother, Peter Robinson, placed more of his 1825 Irish settlers in Emily Township than anywhere else. Another interesting coincidence is that the Irish Diocese of "Emly" (from the Gaelic word "Imleach") with its cathedral, village and populous farming region in Limerick and Tipperary, was a focal point for land and "tithe" troubles in the 18th and early 19th centuries, especially in the 1820s. As an Irish wit would say: "Coincidences sometimes alters cases"!

This then is the story of Emily, a typical rural township in central southern Ontario, first to be surveyed and settled in what later became Victoria County. Its unique features will emerge in the chapters and appendices that follow.

LIST OF MAPS AND ILLUSTRATIONS

LIST OF MAPS AND ILLUSTRATIONS (cont.)

Part I: Pioneer Emily
to 1950

EMILY BEFORE WHITE SETTLEMENT

After four glacial ages that covered a million years, the Emily landscape that developed about 12,000 years ago was far different from the land that had existed before, but not so different from what the Indians and settlers of 1818 A.D. saw . . . or what we see now. The bedrock of Trenton limestone, shale and sandstone, which rose from the primeval ocean floor, contained marine fossils, that are occasionally still found in rocks. However, the pressure of the quarter-mile-thick Pleistocene glaciers and their erosive action as they advanced south and retreated north four times, with tropical intervals of 120,000 to 300,000 years, compacted and planed the bedrock into its modern shape.

As the last glacier retreated slowly north-northeast across modern Ontario, about 12,000 years ago, it left behind Lake Iroquois, a larger Lake Ontario with a bay extending up to a larger Rice Lake. Lake Iroquois waters lapped against the Oak Ridge Moraine, the height of land just south of Emily Township, stretching from south of Rice Lake through Manvers and Cavan, to the south of Lake Simcoe and on westward. The Moraine was composed of boulder clay, sand and gravel, deposited by the melting water of the glacier edge. As the glacial ice thinned and melted over a thousand years, the land lifted about 400 feet, and the retreating ice edge left behind drumlins and eskers running southwest to northeast in the glacial path. The 4,000 drumlin hills of the Kawarthas, of which at least a hundred are in Emily, are oval hills of glacial deposits with smooth convex contours, 60 to 80 rods wide, 50 to 100 feet high (before erosion) and averaging half a mile long. The eskers are knobby gravel ridges of various sizes, composed of glacial till deposited in the ice crevasses and tunnels—one very noted esker is the Omemee Esker, running about twelve miles from near Bethany to Pigeon Lake near Fee's Landing, crossing Highway No. 7 a mile west of the village of Omemee and the county road two miles north of Omemee. There a branch esker runs six miles northward through Downeyville.

The waters of huge Lake Algonquin (covering the area from Lake Superior to Lake Simcoe) at that stage poured in a mile-wide torrent along Sturgeon-Stoney Lake valley, over the edge of the granite Laurentian Shield and down the Indian River valley into Lake Iroquois. The streams of the Emily district made their way north and east into this Algonquin River, carving out their own valleys. After many years, as the glacier retreated northward, the land tilted and lifted, and the Algonquin waters poured down the Otonabee River basin. Finally, after another thousand years or more of land-raising and shifting, the waters of the Upper Lakes were diverted down the Erie-Niagara basin where they still flow. The Kawartha watershed from Scugog to Haliburton, with its thousands of lakes and streams, drained down the Otonabee and Indian Rivers to Rice Lake and the Trent much as the first Indians saw them several thousand years ago. The whole ecology of the region including Emily Township—the hills, valleys, waterways, soils, vegetation and animal life—can only be explained by the glacial ages and what men have done to the virgin wilderness of the post-glacial period, in the last two thousands years, and particularly the last 155 years of white settlement.[1]

In the Emily region, the typical bedrock was then within two to four feet of the surface, and with much limestone rubble rising through the soil. The oval drumlins still crowd together, and the intervening valleys have swampy bottoms with slowly-flowing streams because of the northward warping of the land, as explained above. The calcareous stony grey-brown soil (called Otonabee loam) between and along the drumlins and eskers (after the bigger stones are piled or built into fences or houses) lends itself to contour plough- ing on gentler slopes, leaving the steeper areas to pasture or forest, to control erosion. When swampy margins or beaver meadows are drained, a rich sandy loam of grey-brown colour is widespread, suitable for a wide variety of crops and easy to cultivate. This is the predominant soil in southern Emily. Other types of imperfectly-drained thinner sandy and clay loams are found increasingly toward the north part of Emily, with a thin layer of rich organic matter often only one to two feet deep above bedrock (one of these is even called "Emily loam" by the soil experts)—in high rainfall seasons they yield good crops of spring grain, but they are mainly productive of clover and timothy hay, ensilage corn, and pasture grasses. Tile drainage and a complete fertilizer mixture often improve production on these soils, but some small areas of sandy outwash over heavy clay do not grow crops economically, and are useful only for woodland and permanent pasture.[2]

The hillsides and plains of Emily were mostly covered with hardwoods —oak, ash, maple, walnut and birch—and in the swampy lowlands with coni- ferous and other softwoods such as pine, hemlock, cedar and sumach. The large Cavan swamp just to the south—over 3,000 acres on the site of a glacial lake—was full of willow, dogwood, poplar, spruce, and many types of fruit-bearing bushes, as well as varieties of orchids, cattails, some wild rice, and other exotic water plants. The mammals of the township included deer, wolves, raccoons, beavers, skunks, muskrats, mink, rabbits and hares, and porcupine, while the warm shallow waters teemed with salmon, trout, varieties of bass, maskinonge, pickerel and about 25 other species. Over 200 species of birds were found, including waterfowl in the swampy areas and along the streams, and most are still there; migratory birds such as geese and ducks swarmed in their millions to darken the skies spring and autumn. To the early Indian newcomers, this must have seemed a paradise, at least for the season May to October. As they were non-agricultural, the mean annual precipita- tion of over 30 inches would not be of much significance to the Indians, except to keep the streams flowing and the flora and fauna flourishing; how- ever, the warmer summers and milder winters of the Kawartha watershed would be welcome relief to natives whose ancestors and grandfathers had suffered in the rigorous climate of the Laurentian Shield between the Yukon and Lake Nipissing in their migrations.[3]

Anthropologists now believe the first humans came down into the Simcoe-Haliburton region before 3,000 B.C., and they were surely in the Kawarthas 4,000 years ago. Those called the Hopewellian Mound Builders of the Middle Woodland period were widespread by the time of Christ, and began their Serpent Mound burial places on Balsam Lake and at the Otonabee mouth about a century later. These people clothed themselves in hides and furs, and lived in wigwams covered with skins and birchbark, and travelled in canoes of the same materials. They hunted, fished, gathered wild fruits, roots and berries, wove mats and cloth from grasses, as the Indians have done in the Kawarthas ever since. No doubt some family groups came up the streams from Pigeon and Chemong Lakes into Emily, to live quietly in safety, remote from the main water routes.

These peaceful aborigines were pushed northward about 1,000 A.D. by the warlike Iroquois, who claimed central Ontario as their hunting grounds. Through six centuries the Kawarthas were an area of conflict between the Ojibways, Hurons and Algonquins pushing southward and the Iroquois surging north each spring and summer, competing for the deer, fish and water-fowl for food, the wild rice harvests of Rice Lake and other harvests, the birchbark for canoes and wigwams, flintstone for arrowheads and spear-points, shells for wampum, grasses and roots for matting, and other necessary products of the lakes from Rice to Stoney to Scugog to Balsam. Large migra-tory groups, accompanied by young warriors, would portage and canoe into the Kawarthas from northwest and southeast, to the larger camping-grounds on Balsam, Scugog, Stoney and Rice Lakes. Smaller family parties would canoe up the little streams, like those in Emily Township, to camp through the summer and autumn months, harvesting nature's abundance . . . and some-times dying there if discovered by an enemy war-party. Before the ice and snow of winter froze water transportation, the Iroquois withdrew to their villages around Quinte and south of the St. Lawrence, while the northern tribes withdrew to their permanent villages on Georgian Bay, Lakes Simcoe and Nipissing and the upper Ottawa River.

After 1600 A.D. the warfare became fiercer, when the French armed the northern tribes, and the English and Dutch armed the Iroquois, with rifles, steel tomahawks and spears, and other weapons, each side seeking control of the fur trade of the Upper Lakes. Champlain promoted this rivalry on his famous trip in 1615 A.D. with a large Huron war-party from Georgian Bay down the Simcoe-Trent waterway, to attack the Iroquois villages south-east of Lake Ontario. He wrote later "All these tracts were in former times inhabited by savages, who were subsequently compelled to abandon them from fear of their enemies . . . many tribes go to these regions for their winter supply". He was enthusiastic about the beauties of the Kawarthas, and their abundance of game and fish. The French and Hurons, defeated and dis-couraged, followed the same route northward in the ice and slush of November 1615, enroute back to Georgian Bay. Incidentally, these French may have been the first white men to glimpse Emily Township, even from a distance, for it is probable that they used the Pigeon-Buckhorn-Chemong canoe route when proceeding southward, and returning in November may have portaged across from the south end of Chemong Lake to Pigeon Lake; we may even surmise that they camped overnight and hunted food around Frank Hill or Emily Provincial Park before proceeding northwest! Anyhow, it is doubtful if any French explorers or traders ventured into the Kawarthas in the next hundred years, as Iroquois war-parties raided up through the district frequently to destroy the Hurons and their allies around Georgian Bay and Lake Simcoe.

Until 1700 A.D., the Iroquois ruled the Kawarthas unopposed, with permanent villages at the Bay of Quinte, at Kentsio on the northeast shore of Rice Lake, and on the Indian and Moira Rivers. They built 'long houses' of tree-branches, covered with large sheets of bark and woven grasses and vines, and they planted crops such as corn, squash, beans, and possibly potatoes. In the autumn they harvested wild rice and berries and fruits, snared ducks and geese, salted fish and smoked deer and bear meat, tanned hides and dressed furs. Grimmer hunting parties of painted warriors paddled northward to Lake Simcoe and Georgian Bay to raid the Algonquins and Ojibways, after the Hurons were driven away in 1648-49. The French tried desperately to keep open the Ottawa-Nipissing-Georgian Bay fur route and Governor Frontenac built Cataraqui at Kingston in 1673 to intimidate the Iroquois, but the latter held the Kawarthas with little opposition. This is the reason that Iroquoian artifacts are the large majority throughout the region. Watson Kirkconnell in his Victoria County History described 55 Iroquoian sites in the county, though none is listed in Emily Township; no doubt others have been washed away by erosion, or buried by the swampy windfalls of three centuries, or covered by rising waters.

The Mississaugas originated near Sault Ste. Marie, where the French had a trading post, and were mainly Ojibways with some Algonquin and Chippewa connections. By 1700 A.D. they were fighting the Iroquois war parties around Georgian Bay and Lake Simcoe, and seeking to expand into the rich Kawartha hunting grounds. The account which we have is from the Mississauga point of view, and describes their advance around 1740, armed by the French, driving the enemy south from Lake Simcoe and down through the Kawarthas, with bitter fighting especially at Little Lake (Peterborough) and along Rice Lake. By 1744 the Iroquois village of Kentsio on Rice Lake had disappeared. The story was handed down by the old people for 160 years— in 1904 Chief Paudash of the Rice Lake Mississauga Band narrated the whole account, and concluded "The Mississaugas then returned and, seeing that the land conquered from the Mohawks, who had dispossessed the Hurons, was full of game and an excellent hunting ground, they came down from Lake Huron and settled permanently in the valleys of the Otonabee and the Trent. . . ."[4]

The Mississaugas were neutral in the French-British war which concluded in 1763 when Canada became a British colony. By 1784 and 1788 treaties the Mississaugas had to cede the land along Lake Ontario from Toronto to Brockville, as far north as Scugog, Rice and Rideau Lakes; and Loyalists fleeing from Yankee persecution began the settlement of Upper Canada along the St. Lawrence and Lake Ontario, establishing Smith's Creek (Port Hope) at the mouth of the Ganaraska in 1778, and Cobourg on its sheltered harbour in 1798. Herkimer's trading post on Rice Lake at the mouth of the Otonabee was begun in 1793, and by 1800 there were flourishing trading posts at Quinte, Windsor (Whitby), and Scugog (Port Perry). The natives became increasingly dependent on these to trade their furs and skins for guns and ammunition, metal objects (pots, knives, axes, needles, traps), also ribbons, beads, and, unfortunately, liquor.

Like the earlier Algonquians, the Mississaugas were more primitive and less settled than the Iroquois they displaced. They had semi-permanent villages of small family clans scattered through the Kawarthas, whose brush shelters and corn fields they came back to occasionally, especially in winter; but for most of the year they broke up into family groupings and wandered to isolated camping places on remote lakes and creeks, to hunt and fish and gather roots and fruits through the warmer months. They canoed sporadically from the rice beds of Rice Lake to the blueberry harvests of the upper lake islands, from the wildfowl hunting in spring to the deer and bear hunting of autumn, the trapping of beaver and otter and mink, the gathering of birch-bark and grasses, the pauses to smoke meat, dry roots, cure skins and furs—all the preparations for winter along the lakes from Scugog to Cameron to Katchewano. They were peaceful and not particularly industrious, pleasant and helpful to strangers (including the white settlers and traders), especially indulgent toward their young children, and looking after their sick and crippled old people until the time came to take them into the remote forest retreats for burial. Their main troubles came when they gathered for religious rites or near the trading posts, when dancing and drinking bred quarrels and fighting disrupted long established family customs and rituals.

We shall see more of the life of these Indians, including the effects of white trading and settlement, in later chapters. One of the small Mississauga clans were called the Omimis, the Pigeon Indians, who were still wandering along Pigeon and Emily Creeks and the adjacent lakes when the first white settlers came.[5]

NOTES

[1]For further reading on this early period, the following are important:
  (a) Chapman & Putnam *The Physiography of Southern Ontario,* Toronto 1966.
  (b) C. P. Gravenor *Surficial Geology of the Lindsay-Peterborough Area &c.,* Ottawa 1957.
  (c) D. F. Hewitt *Geology and Scenery—Peterborough, Bancroft & Madoc Area* Toronto 1969.

[2]Gillespie & Richards' government publication *The Soil Survey of Victoria County,* 1957 gives much more interesting information about Emily soils, and a detailed soil map.

[3]Trent University Occasional Paper No. 1 (Department of Geography). *The Geography of the Peterborough Area,* Peterborough 1972.

[4]There is much background reading on the Indians of the Kawarthas, including
  —*Otonabee Region Conservation Report,* 1964—Chapter 1.
  —Wright *The Ontario Iroquois Tradition,* National Museum, Ottawa, 1966.
  —Edmison & Pammett *Through the Years in Douro,* 1967.
  —Morris *Indians of Ontario,* Ontario Dept. of Lands & Forests, 1943.
  —*Peterborough, Land of Shining Waters,* 1967, Chapter 1.
  —Guillet *The Valley of the Trent,* 1957, Section 1.

[5]The *Dictionary of Ojibway Indian Language,* Toronto 1907, gives the word "Omimi" as meaning wild pigeon or turtle-dove.

CHAPTER TWO

GOVERNMENT ACTION: INDIAN LAND SURRENDER AND EMILY LAND SURVEY 1818

Governor John Graves Simcoe in 1792 divided the Province of Upper Canada into 19 counties, of which two were Northumberland and Durham; ten years later they became the Newcastle District, for better administration of the settlers pouring in from the United States. The District consisted of "the counties of Northumberland and Durham, with all the land in their rear, confined within their extreme boundaries, produced north 16 degrees west, until they intersect the northern limits of the province. . . ."

Settlers were coming into the Hope, Hamilton and Clarke lakefront concessions before 1800, but there was much absentee ownership, with few people moving northward into the bush. As late as February, 1817, when Charles Fothergill of Port Hope rode to Rice Lake, he noted: "There is one farm farther back than six miles from Lake Ontario in this direction—an Irishman of the name of Goheen lives upon it. Beyond this house a wild but very picturesque and even beautiful forest and difficult to make out a road." This was along the Indian portage trail up the Ganaraska River and over the ridge to the west end of Rice Lake. Cavan and Manvers Townships were surveyed 1816-17, and in 1816 John Deyell started his first district tavern on the Cavan-Monaghan boundary trail a few miles north of Rice Lake, where he had a farm; soon afterward he built the first grist mill on the site of Millbrook in Cavan. Monaghan was surveyed 1817-18, and again in 1821, as York, Cobourg and Port Hope businessmen and officials became interested in promoting the Trent-Simcoe waterway; in 1845 Monaghan was divided into North and South Monaghan Townships.

The war of 1812-15 with the United States, and the Napoleonic War that ended in 1815 at Waterloo, stimulated the British and Canadian governments to solve their military and economic problems by encouraging landless and poverty-stricken peasants from the rural counties of Ireland, Scotland and even England to emigrate, by the offer of cheap passages and free lands in Canada. Jobless soldiers crowding home after twenty years of war in Europe, retired half-pay officers of Army and Navy, farm labourers unemployed when prices fell and their employers turned to sheep growing, all the surplus population of the British Isles, began pouring across the Atlantic in the uncomfortable sailing-ships that had taken square timber and other products eastward to British ports. A. C. Buchanan, the British agent at New York, encouraged thousands of these, especially Protestant Irish, to come to Canada instead of going westward in the United States, by cheap or even free transportation overland to Upper Canada, to settle the frontier counties against the continued threat of invasion from the United States. Other thousands who landed at Quebec and Montreal were sent by boat to Kingston and schooner to Ontario lake ports for the same purpose. Of these multitudes, in the decade 1815-25, a large number were put ashore at Trenton, Cobourg, Port Hope and Whitby to settle in the frontier townships of the Kawarthas.

A petition to the Legislative Assembly dated November 11, 1817, from 186 people in the Newcastle District, stated: "At present the District consists of only 8 inhabited townships, three of which are very thinly settled . . . much too thinly inhabited. . . . The whole amount of the inhabitants by the Town Clerks' Returns of 1817 being 4063." The next year, October 1818, another Newcastle petition said "that owing to the want of a road from the settled parts of the townships of Hope and Hamilton to the new settlements now forming in Cavan and Monaghan and the other townships thereunto adjoining, the inhabitants in those townships suffer a great many privations and inconveniences." They asked for a sum of money toward the opening of the road along the Hope-Hamilton and Cavan-Monaghan boundaries, "and building bridges and causeways thereon"; it is pleasant to record that the Assembly in the next month voted £250 for this Cavan-Monaghan road, which was improved in the next two years, in time for the entry of the Protestant Irish and others who swarmed into Cavan and Monaghan and southern Emily by 1824.

The surveyors running boundary lines and blazing trees in the Newcastle townships mentioned above found the Indians suspicious, as they did not understand the need for map-making and official boundaries. One trader warned the surveyors that they would run into trouble if they extended their work beyond a line from Lake Scugog to Rice Lake. Yet in 1816-17 the Government went ahead with its plans to lay out more townships—Manvers, Cavan, Monaghan, Emily, Smith, etc—and only in November 1818 did they gather the Mississauga chieftains at Smith's Creek (Port Hope) to make a treaty by which the Indians surrendered the region northward of Northumberland and Durham. One can picture the scene in the little village of about 100 inhabitants on its pleasant bay, with one or two mills and taverns, and the gathering of the chief village personages (Walton, Choate, Riordan, Fothergill, Ward, Boulton, Sculthorp, Butcher, and so on) to meet the government delegation from York, led by William Gruet, J. Givens and William Hands of the Indian Department, who had come by schooner for the ceremony.

The chiefs of the six Kawartha Mississauga tribes—Eagle, Crane, Reindeer, Pike, Snake and White Oak—were in the forefront, and crowding behind them hundreds of curious but bashful tribesmen of all ages, some of them newly-decorated with bright dresses and shirts and head-dresses from the trading-post. They did not realize that they were surrendering the whole Kawartha district, nearly two million acres, to the Great White Father, in return for an annual grant of about $3,500, which at the time amounted to $9 or $10 per Indian. A codicil "clarified" the grants by limiting them to the lifetime of the living tribesmen.[1] As added benefits the Indians had the right to live, hunt and fish on any unsettled lands in the area, and were promised tribal reservations when they settled permanently. But even there they were cheated, being given a total of about 6,700 acres in reserves at Alnwick on the Trent, Rice Lake, Mud (Chemong) Lake, and Scugog . . . while their former enemies, the Iroquois Mohawk tribe, were given one large reserve of

92,700 acres on Bay of Quinte! Some families refused to settle on the reservations, moving permanently into the northern wilderness, and in a few cases settled among the white people and competed for a livelihood, with some trade or equal skill . . . a few even worked for the traders to lure the Indians with liquor and rob them of fair prices for their furs and skins.

The diary and letters of Surveyor Samuel Wilmot concerning his survey of Emily Township are preserved in the Ontario Archives at Toronto. Part of the township was surveyed between October 18 and December 31, 1818. Wilmot's diary for Sunday, October 18 lists his survey party: Jacob Lavin, Lewis Manor, Baptist La Fleur, Charles La Roye, Joseph Richardson, Francis Tashie, Joseph Hill, John Hill, Thomas Needy, Adron Green. Most of the next week Wilmot was completing other reports, while "men getting provisions in readiness . . . employed a waggon and got the Provisions packed up into bags and purchased leather for shoepacks for the men." On the 25th he went to Rice Lake, spending $4 to transport his party and provisions from Smith's Creek, and ran into his first problem, as the canoe and boat he had used previously (in surveying Smith Township) were being used to take trading goods to "the Carrying Place" (the site of Peterborough) and by "the English emigrants settling in Smith who were employed in moving their baggage and families." He sent men to bring back "the large canoe" and then had to repair it, but enroute up the Otonabee on the 31st the "rotten heavily-loaded canoe" broke apart.

After great exertions, the party moved their supplies to the Peterborough site, and "proceeded along the Boundary line between Smith and Monaghan three miles with very heavy packs . . ." (in other words, they went over the hills out Parkhill Road West to the Emily Township boundary (Highway 7B). Their survey of Emily began on November 3rd, at the second concession, "and laid off lots of 29c. each which I then divided into 100 acres to No. 18." By the 6th he was "to the east boundary of Manvers" and returning he planted "posts at the corner of each 100 acres on each side of the allowance for a Road as per instructions." The next few days were spent marking lots along the 2nd and 3rd concessions, and on the 11th he wrote: "Produced the western boundary of this township from the N.E. corner of Manvers N.N.W. to the 5th concession, allowing 70C. 40L. including roads for each concession. . . ." By the 19th he had laid out the 5th and most of the 4th concession and wrote "All day in swamp, opened 5 lots. One lot and 4 chains to the river impassable, which I was obliged to make a floating bridge about 10C. below the line" (this was probably near the west end of Chemong Lake). On November 21st he "produced the eastern boundary from the (lake?) to the intersection of the 6th concession line" and on Monday the 23rd sent the men, probably south into Cavan, for more provisions. Their return on the 24th heralded "the first day clear of clouds since this month began", but they laid out the east boundary northward in the next few days "the depth of 2½ concessions, bad swamps". By the 28th they had taken the eastern boundary to "the 12th concession terminating at a river in a very large marsh at present impassable." (where later the floating bridge crossed

Diary for the Survey of the
Township of Emily
in the year of [our Lord] ...
the District.
                Sunday 18th 1818.
Surveying Party Jacob
Lewis, Lewis Manor,
Baptist La Fleur, Charles
La Rouge, Joseph Richardson
Francis Pashu, Joseph
Hill, John Hill, Thomas
Nudy, Aaron Green
                Monday 19th
Making out a Plan
of the Townships of Smith
& Street of Communication
at Clarke
                Tuesday 20th
Do . . . . oo . . . . oo
                Wednesday 21st
men getting oxen in
readiness

to let the compass o[ ] the
corner of each lot between
the planting of the posts
which give a direction
for the division line of the
lots
                Sunday 8th
Completed ... the 2nd
line & ... the 3rd Con.
3 Miles by planting two
rows of ... at the corner
of each lot
                Monday 9th
Continued in 3rd Con.
to No. 6.
                Tuesday 10th
Completed the 3rd Con. to the
termination of No. ... the
western boundary to be
produced
                Wednesday 11th
Produced the western Boundary
this Township from the

Pages from the Diary of Samuel Wilmot re Emily Township Survey 1818.
(Crown Lands Papers, Ontario Archives)

the river). The last few days of November were spent surveying the 7th and 8th concessions.

December opened with snow, and they were on the 12th concession, waiting for ice to form so that they could get across Emily Creek; the weather was "clear and cold" and one of the men went through into the water, so that on the 4th they went to work on the west boundary, marking it out to the 10th concession next day. On Sunday, December 6, Wilmot noted in his diary: "A very heavy snow storm during the night. The trees and limbs falling in every direction, every bush and trees 10 or 12 inches diameter was bent to the ground by the weight of snow;" this made their boundary-marking northward difficult next day "through a solid body of snow." On the 8th he commented: "Continued the 11 con. 6 lots. it will appear singular to the Settlers of this Township to see the Trees from 50 to 60 feet high with their tops loped off which was bent down by the wight of snow." By the 11th they had reached the Pigeon Creek, and then for several days worked along the 9th concession, and by December 21 "completed chaining the 6th con. to the eastern boundary." They then set out for the Lake Ontario front to make out their reports on work done and spend the holiday season, which lasted until the end of December.

On December 31st Wilmot sent his plan and notes to the Surveyor-General at York and wrote: "The quality of the land whereon there is maple, oak, elm and beech timber is exceedingly good, but the township is very much cut to pieces with bad swamps and a river that takes its rise in Manvers, presses diagonally through the township from the 2nd concession on that (west) boundary to the 12th concession on the east boundary, with immense marshes on each side. This river is navigable for boats from Mud Lake to the township of Manvers. . . ." The rest of Wilmot's Survey Diary, for the first part of 1819, is unfortunately unavailable, but on March 31, 1819, he sent the rest of the township survey to his superior in York, with the comment: "A very small proportion of the township will answer for settlement; very well-watered but much broken with . . . large swamps, except a few front concessions".

By late 1819 government contracts were let for surveying townships to the north (Verulam, Fenelon, etc.) and to the east (Otonabee, Asphodel, etc.)—these were let to friends of the Family Compact such as Zaccheus Burnham of Cobourg, who received 4½ or 5% of the lands surveyed as payment, and usually gave ½% of this to the surveyor who did the actual work. As Wilmot was a government official this system was not used in the Emily survey. The customary way of surveying and opening a township for settlement was standardized. One-seventh of the lots were withheld as Clergy Reserves and the same amount as Crown Reserves, scattered through the township. Concessions were 100 chains or 1¼ miles apart, fronting on road allowances 60 feet wide. Every fifth lot-line at right angles was also a road allowance, of 60 feet near the front and 40 feet wide near the rear of the township. The ordinary 100-acre half-lot had a 30-chain frontage on the road and a depth of about 135 chains, back-to-back with a similar lot on the next concession; but some lots were longer and narrower, and some "broken lots" on lakes and streams had smaller acreage. When the surveyor was careless or inefficient, much confusion and litigation resulted, since lots might be larger or smaller than 100 acres, with boundaries badly marked, with swamps or hills, and road allowances in zigzag fashion, with lot corners and crossroads not meeting squarely . . . this was especially true when surveying was done in winter, and when lots were not laid out systematically from front to rear concessions, as happened in Emily. When roads were not promptly cleared and used, the settlers often fenced them off with their fields and were very reluctant to consider them public thoroughfares a few decades later.[2]

NOTES

[1]The full text of the Kawartha Land Surrender, from *Canada: Indian Treaties and Surrenders 1680-1890,* vol. 1 (1891) is given in Appendix I. The Mississaugas are called Chippewas in the document.

[2]Some interesting sample pages from Wilmot's survey diary are given in Appendix II.

PIONEERS IN EMILY (1819-1825)

On July 15, 1819, Smith's Creek was officially renamed Port Hope, and became the Durham port of entry for customs and settlement purposes, as well as the post office and administrative centre for Durham County and the new townships to the north.

The tradition related in Kirkconnell's Victoria County History and others is that David Best, a Protestant Irishman, came via Cobourg or Port Hope with a larger party into Cavan, and in 1819 ventured north to Lot 20, Concession 2, Emily, where he did some slashing of trees, and may even have erected a rude shanty, before returning to Cobourg for the winter. This was near the later flag stop on the Peterborough-Omemee branch railway line called Best's Station, and just east of Orange Corners.

The Newcastle District Land Board, meeting in Cobourg, and consisting of government-appointed leading district gentry, began making land grants in Emily at their meeting of June 9, 1819. These grants, mostly half-lots of 100 acres, were made by location-ticket, subject to settlement duties being performed within a few years, and application made for deed, with fee based on acreage, supported by an affidavit signed by a Justice of the Peace (or Magistrate) that the settlement duties had been completed.

The actual Land Board records (preserved in the Ontario Archives) show that by the end of 1819 forty-four settlers had been granted 100-acre lots on the first six concessions of Emily, between Lots 8 and 23. Seven of these were allowed to change their lots (some of them within a month), mostly because the lot granted was swampy, but one because his lot was less than 100 acres—the board carelessly granted these poor lots later to other settlers. But the significant fact is that many of the 44 grantees must have gone into Emily that year to inspect their lots, measure their size, see what the land was like for farming, and even start the slashing of trees, etc. Of the 44, 31 were from Ireland, 7 from U.S.A., 2 from Scotland, 1 from England, 1 from Germany, and only 2 born in Upper Canada. Over half (28) were in their twenties, 13 in the age group 30 to 49, 2 of 60 years, and 1 of 71 years. In addition, one woman, Catherine Smith, was given a full lot (200 acres) being Lot 14, Concession 2, as the daughter of a United Empire Loyalist.[1]

It is probable, of course, that some of these 44 grantees never went into Emily to settle, and others (especially the younger ones without capital) worked in Lake Ontario towns, or on public works or farms, to earn money and to meet possible brides, going occasionally to their lots to build shanties, cut roadways, clear fields, and other settlement duties, for the first few years. Incidentally, at the August 1819 Land Board Meeting, a grant was made to David Best, born in Ireland, age 51, arrived Quebec July 7, 1819, granted the west half of Lot 12, Concession 1. The very next entry shows a grant to his cousin David Best the second, age 49, arrived Quebec the same date, who was granted the east half of Lot 12, Concession 1. They were granted east and

LOCATION TICKET.

LAND BOARD,

DISTRICT OF NEWCASTLE.

John Hall —— born in *Ireland* —— of the age of *fifty* —— years, having *Came from Dunoon & follows far* and petitioned to become a settler therein, has been examined by us, and we being satisfied with his character and of the propriety of admitting him as a Settler, and having administered to him the Oath of Allegiance, do assign to him *fifty* Acres of Land, being the *North East half fifty*

Acres of Lot No. *Eight* —— in the *Second* Concession of the Township of *Emily* in the said District, subject to the following Settling Duties required by an Order in Council, of Five Acres cleared and fenced, along the length of the front adjacent to the Road, for every hundred Acres granted: a Dwelling-house of sixteen feet by twenty in the clear, and one half of the Road cleared in front and rear of each Lot: the whole to be performed within eighteen months. (And it is to be observed, that clearing one half of the Road, and cutting down, without clearing, one chain in depth from the Road along the front of each Lot, shall be considered a part of the five acres per hundred required for settlement duty.) And upon his giving satisfactory proof of having performed the same, he will be entitled to receive a Grant to him and his heirs *further*

Hamilton, *30th*
August —— 1820

By Order of the Board,
M. F. Whitehar
Clk. to the Board.

Richard Beardman
Walter Boswell
John Burn

The Settlement Duty performed as certified
by M.L.B. Inspector District of Newcastle

GRANT to *John Hall (an Emigrant Settler from Ireland)*

part of the Township of *Emily* in the County of *Durham* in the District of *Newcastle Upper* all that parcel of Land

in the Township of *Emily* in the County of *Durham* in the District of *Newcastle*; being

the North East Quarter of Lot Number *Eight*

in the *Second* Concession that is to say

Commencing in front of the said Lot

Lot No. 849 —— Concession on the Centre Johnson

then North *16* degrees —— minutes West *34* chains *70* Links

more or less, to the allowance for Road in the rear of the said Concession

then South *74* degrees —— minutes West *14* chains *50* Links between Lots No.

then South *16* degrees —— minutes East *34* chains *70* Links

more or less, to the allowance in front of the eighth Concession

then North *74* degrees —— minutes East *14* chains *50* Links

more or less, to the place of beginning

containing —— *50* —— Acres more or less.

For which an allotment of —— *7* —— Acres and —— *seventy* in the *forty*

is made for a Protestant Clergy, in Lot No. *three* in the *Second* Concession of the said Township of *Emily*

containing —— *50* —— acres of Land

for —— *50* —— acres of Land under the Regulations of

The Land Board of the District of Newcastle
Order in Council of the 30 day of August 1820
Under the Administration of His Excellency Sir Peregrine Maitland K.C.B. & Governor

Fred. Ridout
Surveyor

S.G.O. fiat No.
Description Number *L.B. 59*
Warrant No.
C.O. No.
R.G.O. No. *A.A. 91*
A.G.O. No. *6140*
Settlement Duty Performed

Location Ticket of John Hall on Concession 2, Emily, in 1820 with Certificate of Settlement Duties 1823, and particulars on back side of Ticket.

(Crown Lands Papers, Ontario Archives)

west halves of the lot though all other grantees were given the south (front) or north (rear) half of a lot.[2]

Kirkconnell's account (page 16) continues: ". . . before his [Best's] return in 1820, Humphrey Finlay and his wife came in and located, thus earning their later title of 'King and Queen of Emily'. In the autumn of 1820 Maurice Cottingham, his sons William and Samuel, and one James Laidley, pushed in farther through the pathless forest to Pigeon Creek, which they bridged by felling two oak trees into it from opposite sides. Beside the stream, about where Omemee now stands, they did a little underbrushing and clearing, but retreated to Cavan for the winter". The section on early Emily in the MacDonald *Atlas of Canada* 1881 (Victoria County edition) adds interesting imaginative details—that a child was born to the Finlays in Cavan on their way into Emily, who was first child in the township—that James Laidley and S. Cottingham built a 12 x 14 shanty on the Omemee site "roofed with cedar slabs . . . built on the deep and crusted snow which had to be shovelled out to lay the floor of split cedar"—that they planted corn and potatoes and a little wheat (from which they raised 6 bushels, the first Emily crop).

The Land Board records for 1820 give a more concrete story; the Board turned their main attention to Emily in June, having spent the earlier months granting lands in Otonabee and Smith Townships. But for an accurate picture we should first examine an important document (reproduced herewith) which was the *first* census of Emily Township, prepared April 7, 1820, by John Huston, Surveyor, Militia Officer and Justice of the Peace in Cavan Township.

The Census shows 35 people living in Emily at April 7, being 10 men, 6 women, 10 boys and 9 girls. The largest family was Henry Jackson's, on the south half of Lot 18, Concession 2—in fact the Jackson family of 9 could claim to be a quarter of the population of Emily! David Best (1st) and David Best (2nd) each had a family of 6 persons. Henry Marshel, with wife and two children, may have been John Marshall, granted the south half of Lot 10, Concession 1 in the previous December. William Lee with wife, and Nathan Lee, bachelor, were the father and son named Lees granted the south half of Lot 18 and the north half of Lot 17, Concession 3, in December; in June, 1820, they returned their tickets "for the whole of Lot 17 in Concession 3 and proved it to be a swamp", and were given in exchange the whole of Lot 18 in the first concession, Nathan the east half, William the west half, on the condition that settlement duties would be performed in one year. James Tigort was in fact James Taggart, who had been given the south half of Lot 12, Concession 3. Hugh Collins was Hugh Collum, given the north half of Lot 12, Concession 2. Robert Bealy was Robert Baity (probably Beatty) given the north half of Lot 20, Concession 1. Last but not least, Humphery Finlay with wife and two children was the 33-year-old Irishman who in October 1819 had been granted the south half of Lot 15, Concession 1.

The Land Grant records confirm that in August, 1820 "Morris Cottram" (age 41) was given the northwest quarter of Lot 6, Concession 3; his son Samuel (age 21) was given the southwest quarter of Lot 6, Concession 4; and his son William (age 21) the northeast quarter of Lot 6, Concession 3,

An Enumeration for the Township of Emily Johnson 1820

Names							
Wm Jones							
John Thornton							
Morris Cottingham							
David Armstrong							
Wm R. Taylor							
Leonard Henderson							
Hugh Coleman							
George Dickson							
John Dickson							
William Fee							
Jno. Trotter							
Robt. Jackson							
David Belford							
James Tysett							
Robt. Mitchell							
David Best							
Humphrey Finley							
David Best							
Wm Henderson							
Robt. Mitchell							
Henry Jewison							
Robert Marshall							

2 2

Census of the Township of Emily for the Year 1820

	Men	Women	Boys	Girls
William Lee	1	1		
Felton Lee	1	1	1	
Henry Marshal	1	1		
James Sigart	1	1		
Hugh Collins	1	1		
Robert Braly	1	1	3	
Henry Jackson	1	1	1	1
Humphrey Finley	1	1	1	2
David Best	1	1	2	1
David Best	1	1	3	
	10	6	10	9

Males — 10
Females — 6
Boys — 10
Girls — 9
Total 35

Taken April 27th 1820

Census Roll of Emily Township 1820. (Ontario Archives)

in September. James Laidley (or Ladley) (age 21) was given the southwest quarter of Lot 21, Concession 4. But this was in fact only the beginning: 95 grants of land were made in Emily in 1821, a few of half-lots (100 acres) but nearly all of quarter lots (50 acres); also one Land Board member, John Burn of Hope Township, was granted four lots (800 acres) for his services. In addition, 8 former grantees were allowed to change their lots, because the earlier ones were unsuited for farming. As in 1819, the great majority of grantees were from Ireland; actually, many were Protestant Irish from Armagh, Fermanagh and Cavan in Northern Ireland, specially directed to Cavan and Emily in Upper Canada by the British agent in New York or the Upper Canada officials on entry . . . some of them had landed in Quebec or New York only a week or two before applying for land at Cobourg. Among them are some of the names listed by Kirkconnell (page 16) though he placed them in 1821.

One other interesting family group from Ireland might be mentioned: William Fee (age 36) given the south half of Lot 12, Concession 5; Thomas Fee (age 21) the north half of the same lot; and Henry Fee (age 26) the north half of Lot 7, Concession 3—there is no explanation why they were granted 100 acres each like the 1819 grantees, when nearly all others were given only 50 acres.[2] An ex-private of the Royal Scots (born in France) was given a lot, also an ex-marine from Ireland. Five Englishmen received grants, 2 Scots, 1 Yankee and 1 German. As in the previous year, the majority (57) were in their twenties, with 25 in the middle years, and 10 aged 50 years and over (age was not listed for a few grantees). By the end of 1820, then, the population of Emily was around one hundred—men, women and children.

1821 was an active year in the district, as settlers poured in at Cobourg and Port Hope. In March the new townships (Cavan, Emily, Ops, etc.) were attached officially to Durham County for administrative purposes such as assessment and taxation. Similarly the new eastern townships (Monaghan, Otonabee, Asphodel, etc.) were attached to Northumberland. Toward the end of the year it was announced that land grants would commence in the 8 newly-surveyed northern townships—Fenelon, Verulam, Harvey, Douro, Dummer, Belmont, Burleigh and Methuen—but it was difficult enough to settle in southern Emily and its vicinity, without plunging another twenty miles into the wilderness, and little settlement to the north began until the thirties.

In Emily and Cavan, John Huston was appointed to certify that settlement duties had been performed, indicating that a few settlers were progressing toward acquiring deeds for their lands. The first Assessment Roll was prepared by assessors Christopher Knowlson and Henry Spinks[3] and lists 22 actual settlers: William Jones, John Thornton, Morris Cottingham, David Armstrong, Richard Taylor, Francis Henderson, Hugh Column, George Dickson, John Dickson, William Fee, Thomas Trotter, Robert Jackson, David Belford, James Tygett, Thomas Michell, David Best, Humphrey Finlay, David Best (2nd), William Henderson, Robert Michell, Henry Jackson and Christopher Marshall. Their lots are designated, and the amount of land they had cleared (which ranged from 2 to 10 acres). There were no horses, and only 3 oxen (one owned by Hugh Column and two by C. Marshall). There were 17 cows and 3 young cattle. In these conditions, it was remarkable that 16 settlers had cleared some of their land—probably by using muscle-power and hitching up their cattle to pull away the tree-limbs for burning, and to drag logs to the site of the shanty, and to begin some primitive ploughing. Fortunately no taxes were levied in the township for several years.

Sixty-eight land grants were given in Emily in 1821, nearly all 50-acre quarter-lots, and two-thirds to Irish immigrants. There were grants also to 19 born in U.S.A., 3 born in Upper Canada, 1 in Lower Canada (Quebec), 1 in England. A bare majority (37) were in their twenties, 22 of middle years, and the rest 50 years and over. Also five previous grantees were allowed to exchange unsuitable lots. Late this year the first two deeds were issued for ownership of lands in Emily, with reservation to the Crown of Mines of gold and silver, and white pine timber. These were to Hiram Ash, yeoman, the front or south half of Lot 13 in Concession 2, being 100 acres; and to Catherine Smith of Hamilton Township, "wife of John Smith and daughter of Baltus Hanes of the same place, a United Empire Loyalist"—given the whole of Lot 14 in Concession 2, being 200 acres.

The granting of lots in Emily tapered off in 1822, 1823-1824 and the first half of 1825, for two reasons: (a) the number of individuals landing in the district to seek land declined, and (b) the Land Board showed an interest in sending more newcomers into Smith, Otonabee, Ops and Mariposa. In 1822 there were only 20 grants in Emily, and three of these (including 2 women) were given 200-acre lots by special order of the Lieutenant-Governor, no reason being noted. The 1822 Emily Assessment Roll, prepared by George Dixon and William Holroyd, showed 54 settlers on lots, mostly with families, and each with from 1 to 10 acres cleared. There were 2 horses (owned by Thomas Michel and Wm. Bradley), and 7 oxen (W. Holroyd, Chris. Marshel and John Mitchell each owned 2, and Morris Cotnam 1). In the township were 49 milch cows, and 25 horned cattle 2 to 4 years old. Emily had no gristmills, no sawmills, no houses of squared or hewn timber or frame, and no shops, or post offices. It did have a township clerk, William Holroyd, who compiled the census: 153 inhabitants, being 61 males over 16, 32 females over 16, 31 boys and 29 girls under 16 years.

The Upper Canada *Gazette,* official government paper at York, had an article May 16, 1822, "On the State of the Colony" which made an interesting comment on Emily settlement: "In the new settlements of the District of Newcastle, there are many individuals who have abundance, and to spare, upon the smaller grants, who have not yet been 3 years in the province; and it is not many days since we saw a man of Emily . . . native of Cumberland in England, who arrived in this country IN A PENNYLESS STATE little more than 2 years ago; yet we had the pleasure of seeing this man with a heavy load of wheat for sale, at Port Hope, 30 miles distant from his residence in Emily, which he had brought down in a sleigh with a yoke of oxen of his own, as part of a quantity of produce which he had over and above what he

LOCATION TICKET.

LAND BOARD,

DISTRICT OF NEWCASTLE.

John Mitchel, Senior _____ born in *Ireland*

_____ of the age of *Fifty Six* _____ years, having *came to this Province in July last* _____

and petitioned to become a settler therein, has been examined by us, and we being satisfied with his character and of
the propriety of admitting him as a Settler, and having administered to him the Oath of Allegiance, do assign to him

Fifty _____ Acres of Land, being the *North*
East Fifty acres _____
of Lot No. *Fifteen* _____ in the *first*
Concession of the Township of *Emily*

in the said District, subject to the Settling Duties required
by the Order in Council of the 20th of October, 1818, of
Five Acres cleared and fenced, along the length of the front *4 chains*
deep adjacent to the Road, for every hundred Acres granted; a
Dwelling-house of sixteen feet by twenty in the clear, and
one half of the Road cleared in front and rear of each Lot:
the whole to be performed within Eighteen Months. And
upon his giving satisfactory proof of having performed the
same, he will be entitled to receive a grant to him and his
heirs, *Gratis* _____

R. Henry

Jas. ?

Hamilton, 9th
August ____ 182 *0*
By Order of the Board,
M. F. Whitehead

Elias Jones

_____ Clk. to the Board.

*I do hereby Certify that I have Examined the North East
Fifty acres of Lot Number Fifteen in the first concession of the
Township of Emily Granted to John Michael Senior met the
following Settlement Duties are Performed on said Fifty acres
viz. There are three acres chopped a Building Erected on this
Improvement of Sixteen by Twenty feet in the Clear and the
Road in front of said Improvement is cleared Two Rods
wide —*

John Huston

Location Ticket 1820 and Certificate of Settlement Duties 1822 John Mitchel Senior,
Concession 1, Emily Township. (Top: Crown Land Papers, Ontario Archives)
Bottom: Huston Papers, Trent University Archives)

required for seed, and for his next year's consumption; he added that he owed no man a shilling, and told us 'with joy sparkling in his 'een' that he thanked God he was now at his ease for life. . . . Such a look of content and honest satisfaction and joy as he gave us, would be a dagger to men like Gourlay. . . ."[4] This was most probably the William Holroyd mentioned above as assessor who also had two oxen, and had been settled in June 1820 at age 45 on the southeast quarter of Lot 20, Concession 3. It will be noted that he bypassed the Deyell mill in Cavan and took his grain to Port Hope, where he obtained a better trade or even cash money for it.

A few other interesting items round out 1822: The Upper Canada *Gazette* in August printed a list of letters remaining in the Port Hope post office, of which 4 were for Emily residents: David Best, Royal Colum, Andrew Holmes and James Moore—the same month Adam Scott, the miller at Scott's Plains (site of Peterborough) was named agent for the Upper Canada *Gazette & Weekly Register* for Emily and Smith Townships. Possibly a few prosperous settlers subscribed to the newspaper in the next few months, and word reached the 4 addressees in time for them to get their letters and read the news from home before Christmas! Finally, 10 more settlers received deeds for their land in 1822—John Mitchell, Sr., John Mitchell, Jr., Roswell Belnap, Benjamin Barris, James Holmes, Robert Savey, James Jones, Thomas Cliff, James Moore and William Holroyd—these, with the 2 in 1821, comprise an "Honour Roll" of the 12 first landowners in Emily Township.[5]

In 1823 only 18 land grants were made in Emily, and one of these was a full lot (200 acres—Lot 1, Concession 2) to Simeon Wright, son of a United Empire Loyalist. As previously, most grantees (14) were Irish, and most were middle-aged. The Assessment Roll prepared in March by John Thornton and Thomas Mitchell may have been incomplete, as it covered only 49 settlers, with 5 oxen, 49 milch cows and 44 young cattle; two settlers had each 10 acres cleared, but little progress was indicated. On the other hand, the census prepared by Henry Sherin, titled "town clerk", showed 187 inhabitants: males over 16—58; males under 16—45; females over 16—44; females under 16—40; servants nil.

The stagnation continued in 1824, when only two grants were made, in February, to an Irishman and an Englishman each aged 45; and in March 1825 only one grant to an Englishman, John Mitchell, aged 33, the last grant before the township was set aside for the influx of Peter Robinson's Irish settlers. In 1824 there were two censuses, Henry Sherin's showing 190 inhabitants, and the other by John Mitchell and Thomas Fee showing 185.

One romantic tale started in the 1881 *Atlas* (Victoria County edition) and repeated since, can be corrected at this point: "In 1824 the first district tax was levied on the township and collected by S. Cottingham, who carried the amount ($4) to the District Treasurer at Cobourg, receiving as his percentage one shilling. He had paid several shillings of the amount out of his own pocket. The following year another collector had $6 to account for, and he is said to have seized a woman's irons for an amount due." In actual fact, the Tax Payment Register for Newcastle District (now in Ontario

Deed of Samuel Cottnam to southwest quarter of lot 6, con. 4, in June 1824.
(Emily Township Records)

Archives) shows that in 1823, 72 properties in Emily paid taxes, all in the first 8 concessions; and without doubt as the administrative machinery began to function the taxes collected (in pounds, not dollars) rose steadily through 1824 and 1825. Samuel Cottingham is not listed as paying taxes in 1823, though "Morris and William Cotnam" did!

A map of Emily Township as it was in April 1825, showing lands granted and actual settlers, would indicate the patchy unplanned development that, with lack of roads, shops and mills, had hampered progress—a complaint common to every frontier township in the Newcastle District. Even the road from Port Hope up the Hope-Hamilton, Cavan-Monaghan boundaries toward Emily was still only a promise. In five years about 250 land grants had been made, almost all in the front 7 concessions; and about 20 had been allowed to exchange unsuitable lots for better ones. Over 75% of the lots on the first 6 concessions had been granted, with Clergy and Crown reserves scattered throughout the granted lots, half-lots and quarter-lots. Yet the 1825 assessment and census rolls, prepared by assessors James Moore and James Laidly, showed only 45 locations, with 216 inhabitants. There were 69 males over 16 years; 48 females over 16; 47 males under 16; and 52 females under 16 years. Two families (William Holroyd and Joseph Porter) totalled 10 persons each; William Laidley's family had 9; and 4 families had 8 each: William Thornton, David Best senior, Edward McCawl (McCall) and Thomas Mitchell. Other progress was rapid—there were now 6 horses in the township, 34 oxen, 71 milch cows, and 69 young cattle. William Holroyd (with 8 children) had 19 acres cleared, David Best Sr. (with 6 children) had 16 acres cleared, and Thomas Fee had 14 acres. In fact David Best Sr. was about the most prosperous man in Emily, with 16 of 100 acres cleared on the west half of Lot 12, Con. 1, and 1 horse, 2 oxen, 3 milch cows and 5 young cattle. David Best Jr. on the east half of the lot was close behind, with 9 acres cleared, 2 oxen, 2 cows and 14 young cattle. Maurice Cottingham (or Cotnam) on the northeast quarter of Lot 6, Con. 3, had 7 acres cultivated out of 50, with 2 horses, 2 oxen, and 4 milch cows. Far down the list came Humphrey Finley, titled 'king of Emily', on Lot 15, Con. 1, with 6 of 100 acres cleared, and 3 cows and 3 young cattle in his stable. Plenty of children husky enough to work meant potash and grain to trade for oxen and cattle, which in turn meant more acres cleared as the seasons rolled by, producing more potash and grain to trade. But there was no gristmill nearer than Deyell's in Cavan or Scott's in Monaghan, (in spite of the stories that have been told about Maurice Cottingham and Omemee).

It was estimated later by Robinson, in his evidence before the Emigration Committee of the British Parliament in 1826, that nearly 100 Protestant Irish from Northern Ireland had been sent by Buchanan in New York for settlement in Cavan, Monaghan and south Emily up to early 1825. As mentioned before, many of these worked for £2 or £3 a month and provisions

See Opposite: 1819 Map of Emily Township front seven concessions, with names of lot-holders up to 1827 written on each lot. (Ontario Archives)

on lake schooners, on canals, in York brickyards, etc., especially the younger men, before coming with their savings to buy oxen and cattle and supplies at Port Hope, and head inland to clear their lots and begin the hard work of farming, with or without a bride. Those who settled in southern Emily formed an industrious loyal basic strata on which the government planned to build, with the influx of assisted Irish immigrants under Peter Robinson in 1825, a prosperous township on the west side of the important Trent-Simcoe water-way in the decades ahead. Linked to this in the minds of some officials and capitalists were more mercenary considerations—the profits to be made from land speculation, from water transportation, from banks and mills and shops and inns along the main routes, and profitable government contracts for those with influence in the right quarters.

NOTES

[1]A list of Land Board grants in Emily 1819 to 1825 will be found in Appendix III.

[2]An interesting account of the family's early struggles, composed by David Best's son William in 1876, will be found in Appendix IV.

[3]This first Emily Assessment Roll 1821 is reproduced as an illustration.

[4]Charles Fothergill, editor of the Upper Canada *Gazette* and government printer, was formerly of Port Hope and much interested in Newcastle District development; in 1822 he published his booklet *A Sketch of the Present State of Canada,* full of advice for prospective emigrants to Canada, both those with capital and the less affluent, and boosting the attractions of the new townships north of Port Hope and Cobourg: "We are quite satisfied that the District of Newcastle offers the finest field for enterprise and merits more attention from Emigrants than any other part of Canada." He estimated a new settler could do very well with about £50, to build a roomy log house (£7½), seed and tools (£4), yoke of oxen (£15), a cow, sow and two ewes (£4½), a good log barn (£5), 2 iron kettles (£3), an ox-sleigh (£1½), and necessary furniture (£10)—and in addition get 5 acres cleared, fenced and sown for £15 if he could not do it himself—of course many settlers, especially from Ireland, started with much less.

[5]A list of these first 12 Emily landowners will be found in Appendix V.

CHAPTER FOUR

ASSISTED IRISH IMMIGRANTS SETTLED BY PETER ROBINSON (1825-26)

The background factors in the British plan for assisted emigration of indigent Irish peasantry to Upper Canada—the strains and stresses, the land troubles and starvation and injustices in southern Ireland—have been studied and written about elsewhere in some detail—also particulars of Peter Robinson's supervision of the selection, transportation, financing, feeding and settlement of the Irish in the Kawartha townships—with all its achievements and mistakes, its errors and omissions, its triumphs and failures.[1] The proposal to bring in and settle over 2,000 experienced Irish "farmers", with their supplies and equipment and food provided by the British government for a year or two, was greeted with enthusiasm by the Government of Upper Canada, even after the limited success of Robinson's smaller experimental Irish settlement near the Ottawa River in 1823. But in Upper Canada the 1825 project was rightly seen as a tremendous boost to the development of the important Trent-Scugog-Simcoe area north of Lake Ontario, and an asset to the future prosperity of all Upper Canada.

Out of 50,000 applications in south Ireland, Robinson in April and May 1825 selected 307 families containing 2,024 persons, mostly recommended by a few large landowners in Cork County, with a few from Kerry, Limerick, Tipperary, etc.—385 men, 325 women, 726 boys under 21 and 588 girls under 21 years. Robinson bent his instructions somewhat, by choosing 80 heads of families who were not experienced farmers, but tradesmen from shoemakers to coopers to carpenters, and was very wise in taking these along for frontier settlement, as we shall see later in Emily. The 9 naval transports sailed from Cork between May 10 and 25, and arrived at Quebec June 12 to July 5. There were few deaths or desertions, and after a steamer ride to Montreal, they were brought by York boats to Kingston, accompanied by naval surgeons from the transports. Their movement was mentioned in the Quebec, Montreal and Kingston newspapers, among reports about riots and robberies in Ireland, a devastating heat wave in Lower Canada, and a blazing comet seen in the sky each evening.

The ship surgeons were responsible to convey the emigrants upriver to Prescott, in the absence of Robinson, who had gone to London, sailed to New York, gone around by Niagara and York, gone inland from Cobourg to check the routes and townships north of Rice Lake, and finally arrived at Kingston about August 10 to take charge of the expedition. One surgeon went on with them to Kingston, where no plans at all had been made for their arrival, beyond appointing an official to keep an eye on them. The emigrants arrived July 2 to 30, and were deposited in army tents on the marshy flats at the river mouth beside Lake Ontario. There were now 1,942 emigrants, subtracting deaths, a few allowed to stay in Lower Canada, and 67 allowed to join relatives on the Ottawa—and adding births plus a few Irish allowed to join in Lower Canada. The July heat and plague of mosquitoes and flies at Kingston resulted in much ague, dysentery and malaria,

Hon. Peter Robinson, Superintendent of the 1825 Assisted Emigration from Ireland to Upper Canada, and later Commissioner of Crown Lands for Upper Canada.
(Peterborough Centennial Museum)

with over 300 sick and 33 deaths before Robinson's arrival. The fever and ague attacked most new arrivals in Upper Canada, and most who survived became immune after a year or two, except those settled in or near low-lying areas.

Robinson, realizing the need for haste, immediately took the first steamer-load of his settlers to Cobourg, 92 miles away, and began hiring ox-carts and buying provisions to be taken over the hills on the rough road to Sully (Harwood), a hamlet on Rice Lake. With weekly trips from Kingston, the remainder were brought to Cobourg by the middle of September and as each group came ashore, they were started on the walk to Sully. Three large punts were also dragged from Cobourg to Sully, where Robinson had a scow 60′ by 8′ constructed to get his people and supplies up the Otonabee to Scott's Plains, rowed by 8 or 10 sturdy Irish. By the end of October, after about 60 trips from Sully, he had all his settlers at Scott's Plains . . . allowing for a few deserters and others, the total was now approximately 1,900 Irish. Robinson reported in the next March that he had settled 1,878 in the district —621 men, 512 women and 745 children. In rude temporary huts made from mill slabs, bark and sods, westward toward the Cavan-Emily road behind Scott's mill and the government offices, the Irish settled down to wait for allocation to their backwoods lots. They were fed generously and Scott improved the occasion by starting a crude distillery and trading the "poteen" —one gallon for a pound of meat or flour. This doubtless put an added glow of colour on the autumn woods around, as the settlers explored their new wilderness surroundings. As Frances Stewart commented in *Our Forest Home*: "Their huts look very odd, being made with poles standing up, boughs or branches of trees interwoven and mud plastered over this. They live in these till log shanties are ready for their families. . . . Doctor Reade has come as the emigrants' doctor [and] is liked among the poor Irish. . . ."

Robinson settled most of his Irish newcomers on lots between mid-October and the end of November, before the heavy snows—one of the most serious criticisms of his project is that they should have been on their lands in June or early July, rather than having to hibernate from November to April before doing more than cutting a few trees. All heads of families, and most boys 18 years and over, were given 100-acre lots, so that while about 287 families were settled, 408 locations were made—these included a few widows, some under-age sons, and men betrothed to daughters of Irish emigrants (some may have been ship stowaways, or joined enroute up to Cobourg). Even a few sons and sons-in-law who left that winter to work elsewhere were later given lots (by Robinson as Commissioner of Crown Lands 1827 on—as late as 1836). A few men changed names between Cork and Scott's Plains, to add to the confusion, and even a few young district settlers married the newly-arrived "colleens" and were rewarded with 100-acre lots. There were other infractions of the original Government regulations which need not be detailed here. Roads were hastily hacked out from Peterborough, including one southwest to Monaghan, Cavan and Emily, and teams of oxen (plus a few horses) hired from former settlers to transport baggage and utensils. District axemen were also hired to build shanties for the newcomers—two men could build one in a day, and were paid $10. A few of the Irish who could wield an axe with experience put up their own shanties and were paid the same.

The 408 locations in the Kawartha district were as follows: Emily 142, Ennismore 67, Otonabee 52, Douro 60, Asphodel 36, Smith 33, Marmora 11 and Ops 7. Incidentally, up until 1827 Ennismore was known as "the Gore of Emily." Over half the Irish locations were in Emily Township and Emily Gore.

John Huston of Cavan, previously mentioned, now re-enters the story more prominently.[2] Peter Robinson wrote him from Smith September 22, 1825, asking if he would locate the "Irish Emigrant Settlers" in Emily and requesting an immediate answer. Two days later Robinson wrote him: "I should be glad that you would immediately begin to locate the emigrants in Emily. I shall send a small party to Cottenhams to meet you on Monday morning and by one of them the numbers of the vacant lots and such other information as I possess." On the 26th Robinson sent the list of vacant and reserve lots from the 6th to 14th concession[3], on which was a scribbled list of 13 preferred 100-acre lots: No. 2 in Con. 6; east half 8, Con. 8; Lot 7, Con. 8; Lot 6, Con. 8; north half 3, Con. 7; north half 1, Con. 8; south half 1, Con. 9; north half 2, Con. 8; west half 3, Con. 9 and east half 6, Con. 9. Attached was a list of 18 Irish in the first party, to be located in their order on the memorandum, viz.: Zachariah Lowes, Richard Sullivan, Michael Sullivan,

(A)

Smith Sept 22 1825

Sir

If you are not otherwise engaged, I should be glad to employ you to locate the Irish emigrant settlers on the vacant lots in Emily — It is necessary that I should immediately know whether you can undertake this service, and I will pay any price you may choose to — send your answer by

I am Sir
Your most Obdt
Servt
P. Robinson

Mr Huston
D.S.

(B)

... going with Mr Huston into Emily
24 October 1825

Axemen:
Benjamin Phillips
Silas Meade
James Brown

Settlers Names
1 Jas Flaherty
2 Pat Flaherty
3 Martin McAuliffe Jr
4 Michael McAuliffe
5 Margaret McAuliffe
6 John Brien + Family
7 John Carew + Family

James Flaherty — North Half 22 in 9 Con
Pat Flaherty — South 23 in 9
Martin McAuliffe Jr — East 20 in 9
Mick McAuliffe — West 20 in 9
John Brien — North 19 in 7
John Carew — East 18 in 7

(A) Robinson's letter to Huston Sept. 1825 asking him to settle the emigrants in Emily township.
(B) Robinson's Memorandum October 1825 re one party of Emigrants to Emily.
(Huston Papers, Trent University Archives)

Richard Lowes, Richard Walsh, Morris Fitzgerald, Michael Lowes Jr., Robert Wynne, Henry Wynne, Michael Lowes, Adam Shouldess, Samuel Corneille ("sick"), Thomas Groves, Edmund Gillman ("Cobourg"), Richard Wynne, John Morrisey and John Hodge ("sick"). His letter ended with specific instructions: "It is my wish that no one of the settlers should be placed on a bad lot, or on one that he could not make his living off of . . . to ensure the latter, I think it requisite that there should be from 30 to 40 acres of good land on each lot and where you find this to be the case, the person whose turn it may be to be located must not be allowed to refuse it".

The next group listed as "Going with Mr. Huston into Emily 24 Octr. 1825" consisted of Benjamin Phillips, Silas Meade and James Brown, axemen, the first two rationed for 10 days, Brown for 6 days; with them went seven settlers, rationed for 10 days (with lots listed): James Flaherty—north half 22 in 9 con.; Patrick Flaherty—south half 23 in 9 con.; Martin McCauliffe Jr. —east half Lot 20 in 9 con.; Michael McCauliffe—west half Lot 20 in 9 con.; Margaret McCauliffe (no lot given); John Brien and family—north half Lot 19 in 7 con.; and John Carey and family—east half Lot 18 in 7 con. A week later Timothy Sheehan carried a letter from Robinson at "Monaghan" instructing Huston to place him if possible on the west half of Lot 12 in the 10th Concession. Until the water routes froze up, these parties went by government scow from the Chemong end of the Communication Road around by Lakes Chemong, Buckhorn and Pigeon, up Pigeon Creek, as far as "Cotnam's Landing", the site of Omemee village; possibly a few went by boat directly across Chemong Lake to its west end, into the eastern part of Emily (as they did also into Ennismore). From Pigeon Lake or Creek they could go directly west into the northern concessions. It is doubtful if any went by water along Emily Creek, in that early period. The government scow made regular trips until freeze-up to "Cotnam's Landing" with settlers, supplies and rations, to be distributed by Huston from his central base, probably at Cotnam's.

Only too soon, Robinson on November 2 wrote: "As the season is so far advanced as to give no reasonable cause to expect that the families can be sent by water, it might be well that the men should go in a party of ten or twelve, each party with one axeman of the country, and underbrush their acres . . . so that they might be prepared for the winter. . . ." The axemen in each party would also aid settlers in putting up their shanties and Huston was told to engage "Cottenham or any other person to assist." In locating the Irish, Huston was advised: "Should any of this party wish to exchange lots to be near each other you may allow them, but I would not propose it to them." In the next week, Robinson sent John Collins and his large family with provisions, and Flaherty's wife and two children with them ("the husband and sons are already with you"), with two axes and bearing half a pound of tea for Huston. Robinson wrote: "With respect to building the shanties, I quite approve of your getting them done by contract and I wish you to engage enough men to house the people located in Emily with as little delay as possible—I shall continue to send out provisions and families until the ice sets in. The people who have come in (to Scott's Plains) seem in good spirits and much pleased with their land—and I am in hopes you will get on very well with them. James Cunningham . . . a decent industrious man . . . has the number of his lot—east ½ of 22 in 7th con. His family will be sent out the next trip of the scow."

Huston prepared an interesting list of 79 "old settlers" on the first four concessions who might be employed—a list which contains the names of six "emigrants" who had been allowed to settle there; on the 3rd concession: George Miller, Adam Shouldis, Jno. Lancaster and Jno. Driskel (Driscoll); on the 4th concession: George Miller and Samuel Gordon. The list includes a few marked "over 60"—William Lee on 1st concession, Royal Collum and Jas. Jones on 2nd concession, Mitchell Seegin on 3rd concession, Wm. Ladely on 4th concession (plus John Dixon—"maimed"). His paylists in the Trent Archives are too detailed to quote here, but give particulars of old settlers and Irish emigrants paid for work performed, and the rations of flour and pork they received, through late October and the month of November. Doubtless the neighbourly co-operation and warm friendships between Protestant "old settlers" and Irish Catholic newcomers throughout Emily began in this period. The north Cavan people also shared in some of the prosperity, besides employment as axemen—Robinson informed Huston by letter November 26th that John Deyell of Cavan had been hired to furnish beef for the Irish settlers in Emily and has it already "stored at David Armstrong's (Lot 13, Con. 4, Emily). . . . Mr. Ritchie goes out for the purpose of regulating the issue of provisions and takes with him the Books shewing the quantity each Family is entitled to . . . can afford you a good deal of assistance. A few Emigrants go with Mr. Ritchie to be located by you in Emily. . . . I send four axemen with them, to be under your orders."

Huston's papers marked "Locations in Emily Nov. 1825" are in places indecipherable and faded, but full of interest. There are details of the first road he built that month with his axemen: "Road from the 5 con. to the 10 con. on the Hard Land. . . . Commence at the S.W. angle of Lot No. 6 in the 5 con. then N. 16° W. across the 5 and 6 con. to the N.W. angle of Lot No. 6 in the sixth concession. Then N. 14° W. to the centre of the south half of Lot No. 8 in the 9th con. in front, then north 14° E. to the southeast angle of Lot No. 9 in the 10th con. then N. 74° east to the line of road to the King's Warf." There are particulars of about 110 locations he made that month, and the type of land on the lots, and the provisions issued to the settlers; but they are altered, crossed out and revised endlessly as the newcomers examined the lands, measured them, and tried to improve their choice. For example, William Cotter, given the west half of Lot 22, Con. 7, was later at his request given the south half instead; the south halves of Lots 18 and 19, Con. 8, were reserved as "a mill seat"; Jonathan Leary, given the south half of Lot 1, Con. 10, was lucky—"70 acres good land examined by himself"; Dennis Fitzpatrick, given the east half of Lot 13, Con. 10—"examined by himself—55 good acres"; Tim Collins was given the south half Lot 6, Con. 11 and Jas. Sheney the north half—they later changed to the west and east halves of the

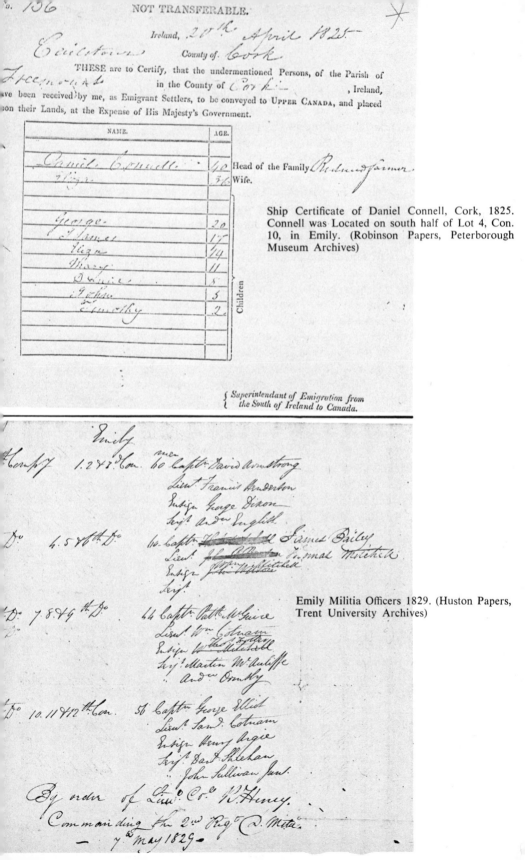

No. 136

NOT TRANSFERABLE.

Ireland, 28th April 1825.

County of Cork

THESE are to Certify, that the undermentioned Persons, of the Parish of
in the County of Cork , Ireland,
have been received by me, as Emigrant Settlers, to be conveyed to UPPER CANADA, and placed
upon their Lands, at the Expense of His Majesty's Government.

NAME.	AGE.	
Daniel Connell	40	Head of the Family
Mary	36	Wife.
George	20	
James	17	
Eliza	14	
Mary	11	
Denis	5	
John	5	
Timothy	2	

{ Superintendant of Emigration from
the South of Ireland to Canada.

Ship Certificate of Daniel Connell, Cork, 1825. Connell was Located on south half of Lot 4, Con. 10, in Emily. (Robinson Papers, Peterborough Museum Archives)

Emily.

Comp.y 1. 2 & 3 Con. 60 Capt.n David Armstrong
Lieut. Francis Henderson
Ensign George Dixon
Serjt. Andw English.

Do. 4. 5 & 6th Do. 60 Capt. James Bailey
Lieut. Thomas Mitchell
Ensign Wm Mitchell
Serjt.

Do. 7. 8 & 9th Do. 44 Capt.n Patk. McGuire
Lieut. Wm Cotnam
Ensign Wm Mitchell
Serjt. Martin McAuliffe
„ Andw Ormsby

Do. 10. 11 & 12th Con. 56 Capt.n George Elliot
Lieut. Saml. Cotnam
Ensign Henry Argie
Serjt. Davd Sheehan
„ John Sullivan Jun.

By order of Lieut. Col. W. Henry.
Commanding the 2nd Regt. D. Mil.
— 7th May 1829.

Emily Militia Officers 1829. (Huston Papers, Trent University Archives) same lot; Jonathan Finn started clearing on the west half of Lot 15, Con. 11 and later found he should have been on the east half; Owen Madigan was located on the west half Lot 14, Con. 13: "60 good acres, examined by himself." Apparently that month no settlers were put on Concession 14.[2]

Robinson kept in touch by frequent letters to Huston, forwarded with families who often made their own way by trail. One December note read: "Timothy Ryan, bearer of this, says that his lot is bad and he is desirous of getting the lot Daniel Fitzpatrick and son were located on. They refused it as bad and have given it up. If you have not promised it to any other person, I wish you to let him have it. . . . By the next trip of the scow I will send you a good stove and crosscut saw." A note from J. Smith Jr. in "Superintendent's Office" requested Huston on December 30 to have shanties built for Owen Kelly on S. half Lot 15, Con. 11 and Patt. Shea on west half Lot 16, in 8 Con., adding "Dennis Fitzpatrick may have the east half of Shea's lot if good (land)." Notes of Dec. 31st asked Huston to deliver a barrel of flour to John Connell and one to John Sullivan "out of the Public Stores in your charge." To add to Huston's troubles, George Boulton of Cobourg on December 6 and 16 requested him to send a return of the Militia of Cavan and Emily, "at least of all the males from 16 to 60 . . . we wish to know how many to put in a Company . . . mention the people of each concession separately." Boulton and Henry, Cobourg magnates, journeyed to Scott's Plains in January, 1826, to visit Robinson, and then came out to Emily to talk to Huston before returning via Cavan to the lakefront; no doubt they were preparing for the Governor's visit soon after.

The original plan had been to give the emigrants rations for 12 months, up to July 1826, but because of their late arrival on their lands the emigrants had no crops and little money by then; Robinson continued the rations until November 24, 1826, about 18 months after departure from Cork. The scale, as shown in Robinson's records, was (with many exceptions): Men and boys 14 years and over—1 lb. flour and 1 lb. pork daily; women and girls 14 years and over—1 lb. flour and ½ lb. pork daily; children 7 to 13 years— ⅓ lb. of each daily; children up to 6 years—¼ lb. of each daily. Often fresh beef was substituted for salt pork, and potatoes for flour. Undoubtedly the rations were much too plentiful, and discouraged the Irish from hunting the game, fish and edible plants and fruits abundant all around in the woods and streams . . . no doubt some did hunt fresh food, and sell the rations for whisky and other luxuries and necessities. As one emigrant said: "Some of us . . . had brought our ancient flint-locks and muskets with us. But sport lost half its charm when we were confident that there were no vigilant keepers around with an eye for poachers, but where we were free to shoot all we could. . . ." The same loquacious Irishman said: "We received also a cow, an axe, an auger, a handsaw, a hammer, 100 nails, 2 gimlets, 3 hoes, a kettle, a frying-pan, an iron pot, 8 quarts of Indian corn to plant, and 5 bushels of seed potatoes. . . ." Most families with children received a couple of blankets as well. The number of oxen distributed is not clear, but generally a pair of those bought late in 1825 to help transport families and supplies out to the townships was given to each community, for common use in their heavy work —hauling supplies from the depots, dragging stumps out of the road allowances and fields, raising shanties and stables, etc.

The tools—auger, saw, axe, hammer, gimlet, etc.—were put to work immediately in building log shanties, about 20 by 12 feet with roof of hollowed-out quarter logs, which the settlers made weather-tight by stuffing cracks with mosses, mud, grasses and even leaves in mixture. The hearth was often a few large stones with a hole in the roof above to let out the smoke, until a chimney could be built. Sods around the base kept out the winter winds until a wooden floor could be put in, and the tools were handy to build partitions, bunkbeds and furniture as well, to carve out ox-yokes, sleighs, buckets, hayforks, harrows, feed troughs and many other necessities. No doubt they learned many skills from the experienced earlier settlers and probably traded extra rations for better equipment and clothing. When they were sick or cold, they went to see Doctors Reade or Connin in Scott's Plains and were given medicines and blankets. Robinson stayed there until February 1826, and came back frequently through 1826, always ready to listen to complaints, troubles and problems and to help to the best of his ability—and the Government stores.

Governor Maitland with John B. Robinson, Colonel Talbot and a large party of officials and notables, visited Scott's Plains early in February 1826, to inspect the Irish settlement. At a banquet there, attended by Frances Stewart, Samuel Strickland and others, the name "Peterborough" was bestowed on the infant village, after which several petitions were presented— the earlier settlers felt most the need of a good grist-mill built by government, while the Irish emigrants felt most seriously the need of a priest and a school; incidentally the Upper Canada Government in a real demonstration of energy satisfied all these requests within a few months, ensuring that the district would strongly support the Government party in the test with Mackenzie's radicals a decade later. Next day Governor Maitland and party went by sleigh to Chemong Lake, across the ice into Ennismore, and there met settlers from all parts of Ennismore, Emily and Ops, who also asked the Governor for a priest and a teacher. The party then went down through Emily and Cavan to Lake Ontario. The first Roman Catholic priest was Father Crowley, who lived at the corner of George and Charlotte Streets in Peterborough and celebrated mass in one of the Government cabins nearby; he was aided during 1826 by Father Ahearn and they were responsible for the whole northern part of the Newcastle District. Father Crowley was granted lots in the town and district and stayed until 1833. The first district school was held in the log Anglican Church in 1826 by Rev. Samuel Armour, (behind the present Central Public School in Peterborough) and was naturally of little use to the children of settlers in Emily Township.

A complete list of the Irish settled in Emily by families and location will be given later[4], so that here only a few interesting particulars will be given

Pioneer Log Shanty of the 1820's, with roof of hollowed half-logs laid alternately. John McCrea Model (Royal Ontario Museum)

Interior of pioneer home before 1860, serving as kitchen, living- and dining-room. John McCrea Model. (Royal Ontario Museum)

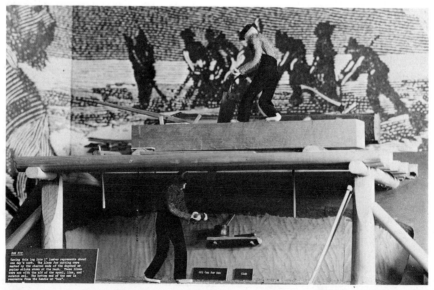

Pioneer sawpit for sawing logs into lumber with vertical saw (the man above worked harder, but the man below suffered more!) John McCrea Model (Royal Ontario Museum)

about their first year of backwoods life, to November 1826. Contrary to the accounts which have stated that the Irish emigrants were placed on the northern concessions, apart from the Protestant Irish and others located 1819-25 in the south concessions, the fact is that 37 of Robinson's newcomers were located in the south, where often the lands were more fertile and closer to mills, churches, etc. A few of these were Protestants brought out in the 1825 emigration: John Blackwell, wife and 8 children, on south half Lot 17, Con. 1; Tobias Switzer, wife and 7 children, south half Lot 18, Con. 5; Thomas Groves, mother, 2 brothers and 1 sister, north half Lot 17, Con. 7. Early newcomers like the Shouldess men, the Lowes, Gordons and others also settled there, after working for Huston from October 1825 on as supply-carriers, shanty builders, road-cutters, etc. Quite a few of these in the south were placed on lands granted earlier to locatees who apparently never settled on their land. Of the other 105 locations, only 23 were made on the 7th and 8th concessions and the balance between the 9th and 12th concessions, with none on the 13th and 14th concessions. Except for those who picked lots along the eastern boundary (from present Fowler's Corners to Frank Hill and northward east of Pigeon River), most were taken to examine their lots and settle on them from Huston's depot at Cottenham's Landing (the present Omemee) northward on his rough road toward Downeyville, which angled northeast to the front of the 11th concession. Bart. Downie was settled on the east half of Lot 6, Con. 9, later called Downie's Cross.

Another interesting fact is that over one-third of the Irish settlers were given the east and west halves of 200-acre lots, though the large majority of earlier locations had been on south and north halves of lots. Huston may have allowed newcomers to examine their lands and pick the 100 acres with most good farming acreage, avoiding the drumlin hills and the swamps; but often relatives were located on the two halves of a lot and worked them together. There were endless variations—for example, Owen Maddigan, widower of 60 years with 8 children, including 5 sons eligible for lots and a daughter Mary, age 22. At the depot, oldest "son" Michael (age 29) suddenly was renamed Bartholemew Kenely, married Mary and was given a separate lot. Sons James, Benjamin, Owen and Denis were also given lots and when the father died, younger son Matthew was given his lot—yet of all these lots, only two were later patented.

The hardships of life in that first year of settlement, even when aided by a paternal government, can hardly be imagined now. Their undernourished condition in Ireland, then 18 months on naval rations, the long delays before getting to their lands, were compounded by a strenuous winter in primitive shanties, and left the Irish victims of ague and malarial fever through 1826. Quinine was unknown and the doctors prescribed camomile, for fevers of all kinds; from earlier settlers (and the Indians) the Irish learned of local remedies such as wild sarsaparilla, peppermint and tansy, taken with a stiff dose of whisky, which either killed or cured! Clearing and draining low-lying land also helped diminish the fever danger. In May 1826 Dr. Reade in Scott's Plains was replaced by Dr. Dowsley, who did not stay long, and then came Dr. Roddy, who remained a year or two. In Cavan was Dr. Hutchison, who moved to Peterborough in 1830. As will be seen from the appendix later, there were fortunately few deaths in Emily, and they were about balanced by births up to Nov. 1826. Usually when the head of the family died, the widow had sons to carry on, or, in a few cases, she remarried—as when Jeremiah Ahern (age 40) died in Emily Dec. 30, 1825, after infant daughter died October 13, leaving widow Johanna (age 22) alone on the lot. Widow Hannah Lowes (age 37) whose husband George had died enroute and whose son Zachariah vanished, was left with two small children in Emily and "married 28th March to James Best, an old settler," according to Robinson's report.

Another danger was the numerous ferocious bears, attracted by the fish and fruit of the lower levels, as well as by the pigs which the Irish soon obtained. When the settlers went to their fields, or on trips to the depot or to town, they had to take their smaller children with them. Those moving through the bushes and trees at night carried burning pine torches to scare off the bears. One tale is common everywhere, of the small children hiding in a hollow tree or log when lost in the woods, while bears prowled all around. Babies were usually taken out to the fields while everyone else worked at clearing and burning, seeding and harvesting; the babies were in cradles made of hollowed logs, placed in a furrow close to mother, while father kept his axe or musket handy. Until the Irish had skill and time to build solid stables, their calves, pigs, sheep and other stock were never safe from hungry bears, even after the fields and roadways were cleared of trees and bushes.

Robinson reported to the British Government in November 1826 on the progress made by his Irish settlers and this is very informative about Emily. Listed as "working at his trade", in addition to the farmers, were: Daniel Finnegan, blacksmith; Jeremiah Driscoll, mason; Andrew Ormsby, shoe-maker; George Ormsby, shoemaker; Tobias Switzer, wheelwright; Timothy Cronin, "keeping a school"; Jeremiah Boland, mason; Edmond O'Donnell, mason; William Fitzgerald, shoemaker ("working at his trade in Cavan"); James Hurley, carpenter; Patrick Ryan, schoolmaster; Moses Begly, black-smith; Bart. Kennelly, tailor, and Richard Owens, carpenter. There were also half a dozen "labourers". Doubtless all of these plied their trades for their neighbours, including the two schoolmasters. Moses Begley and James Hurley were working in Peterborough; James Sherrick and Owen Maddigan worked in summer on the Welland Canal; about 30 located settlers were stated to be sick during that year, of ague or other illness. In addition to the school-masters listed above, Patrick Baragy, on east half Lot 5, Con. 9, resumed his teaching career soon after settlement (though listed by Robinson as a "farmer"). Michael Flynn on the south half of Lot 10, Con. 9, operated a "halfway house" on the Huston road, where travellers could stop for a meal and to feed their animals—the road was later extended to King's Wharf and north toward Bobcaygeon; at the south end of the road, near the Huston depot, the Cottinghams started an inn, being at the crossroads of this north-south road (leading through Cavan to Port Hope) and east-west from Peterborough out toward Mariposa. There were still no mills or stores in Emily, but peddlers were coming north from Port Hope either on foot or horseback, Patrick Tobin and Dennis Driscoll licensed "to travel on foot", Henry Griswold and Samuel Peck licensed "to travel with one horse". Close behind them were the circuit-riding preachers, as we will see later.

Robinson's tables in November, 1826, as mentioned, list 142 locations, totalling now 604 people. They had cleared 315½ acres and harvested 22,200 bus. potatoes, 7,700 bus. turnips, 3,442 bus. Indian corn; 2,800 lbs. maple sugar had been made in the spring; 44½ bus. wheat were sown that autumn (1826). In addition to livestock given to them, they had purchased for themselves 6 oxen, 10 cows and 47 hogs. For over 50 of the locatees, who had cleared no land and produced nothing, various excuses were given: they lived with father, brother or son; they had been sick all summer; they were working at a trade or out of the township, etc. But the statistics were proof of the industry of the majority, who had cleared an average of 3½ acres per farm and harvested crops sufficient to keep them comfortably when government rations stopped. After all, the 1826 Assessment Roll indicated that among the "old settlers" some of whom had been on their lots for 6 or 7 years, the average of cleared and cultivated land was only about 6½ acres. When the younger sons matured and began clearing their own lots, when the sick became healthy and could swing an axe and drive a plough, when the men away working came back with oxen, cattle, tools and cash in their pockets, the Irish emigrant settlement developed even more rapidly, as later chapters will demonstrate.

It was evident that the Irish emigrants adapted quickly to the challenges of the pioneer backwoods life and most worked hard to make prosperous farms for their children. Numerous observers and writers in the next two decades praised their industry, loyalty and peacefulness as citizens of Upper Canada. Robinson appended to his 1826 report various testimonials and declarations, including one signed by 85 Irish emigrants settled by him in Emily, Smith and Ennismore, dated "Emily, Dec. 20, 1826", which stated: ". . . most humbly beg leave to express to Your Lordship our deep sense of Gratitude to His Majesty's Most Gracious and Bountiful Government for the cheerful competency we now enjoy in this happy portion of His Majesty's Dominions. Having now resided about a twelve-month on our lands, we have every reason to be thankful for the excellent locations assigned us. . . . We take this opportunity of expressing to Your Lordship how much of Gratitude we owe to the Honorable Peter Robinson our Leader our Adviser our Friend since we have been under his direction, particularly for his exertions in administering to our comfort during a season of sickness and privation. . . ."

Governor Maitland sent the same message earlier to the British Government, when reporting after his trip to name Peterborough. "With respect to the Emigrants of 1825 I cannot perceive that the difference of religion has occasioned or is likely to occasion any disagreeable occurrences among themselves or between them and the other settlers. On the contrary, though they are in general Roman Catholics, they are kindly received by the Irish Protestants settled in the adjoining township. . . ."

NOTES

[1]H. T. Pammett "The Emigration from Ireland to Upper Canada under Peter Robinson in 1825" (Queen's University M.A. Thesis, 1934) and a summary article in *Ontario History,* 1936. Recent studies have included Dr. John Manion's Ph.D. Thesis at University of Toronto in 1968 comparing the Irish assisted settlement in Upper Canada, New Brunswick and Newfoundland, and Guy Ferguson's Honour Thesis at Trent University 1972 "The Peter Robinson Emigration of 1825 and Some Factors Influencing the Location of Emigrants". The original Robinson Papers and Reports about the scheme are now in the Peterborough Centennial Museum Archives.

[2]Some of John Huston's survey and militia papers are in the Ontario Archives, Toronto. His personal papers, including many dealing with the Robinson settlement, surveying, militia matters and administration of justice, have recently been given to Trent University Archives, Peterborough. The firm of Pierce Surveyors, Peterborough, also have some original Huston survey papers.

[3]Robinson's list of vacant and reserved lots in Emily will be found in Appendix VI.

[4]A detailed list of the Irish settlers by family and location will be found in Appendix VII.

THE FIRST DIFFICULT YEARS (1826-31)

Emily's population rose drastically to a total of 837 in 1826: 196 males 16 years and over; 182 females 16 and over; 243 males under 16 and 216 females under 16.[1] But three-quarters of these were Irish newcomers, who paid no taxes that year. The 1826 Assessment Roll showed that the "old settlers" were also increasing and prospering, partly because of the Robinson imigration. It covered 59 located lots, with 4,142 acres uncultivated and 381 acres cultivated. All houses were shanties of logs, one storey, with no more than one fireplace per shanty; the assessed settlers owned 7 horses, 48 oxen, 149 milch cows (doubled in one year) and 99 young cattle. Property was valued at £2,011 and rates collected were £10 1s. 3d[1]. The assessors found no grist or sawmills or merchants' shops in the township—this contradicts the stories in the 1881 Atlas and later that Morris Cottingham started his gristmill and that son Samuel opened a shop in 1826, on the Omemee site. Samuel may have been connected with Huston's depot for Irish emigrant supplies and rations, but no shop was assessed or licensed that year in Emily. Two innkeepers were licensed—James Laidley on S.E. ¼ Lot 4, Con. 4 and "Morris Cotnam" on N.W. ¼ Lot 6, Con. 3. Also licensed that year were a foot peddler, Dennis Driscoll, and an auctioneer, Samuel Peck, who may have done business in Emily, travelling from Port Hope.

The Government decided in 1826 to end all free land grants in Upper Canada and to begin land sales, except for the Clergy and Crown reserves. This was one result of the Irish settlement, since district gentry like Burnham, Boulton, Stewart and Rubidge noted that the value of the lands they owned in the district doubled by the end of 1825, especially as the Governor and his officials recommended British gentry and retired officers with capital to settle along the Trent-Sturgeon waterway with its thousands of industrious "peasants" and its prospects of profitable development. The Surveyor-General late in 1825 ordered John Huston of Cavan and four other surveyors to make separate evaluations of the Newcastle townships and report to the District Land Board, which was to weigh their reports and decide on a reasonable price per acre for land in each township. Huston reported early in 1826: "Emily is well watered and settled, with good land; fine millsites [but] no mills; values 6s. and 4s. (late sales in desirable situations) and 3s. 9d. The greatest encouragement to settle new townships is MILLS. A grist and sawmill erected in this township would increase the value of lands one-fourth." Richard Birdsall thought Emily had "generally good land with water advantages," like Smith, but valued it as 3s. 9d. for best land, 3s. for good and 2s. for rest. H. Erwing also thought the Emily land good, but valued it at 2s. 6d. for good land, 2s. for average. Isiah Merriman was even lower, at 2s. 3d., 2s. and 1s. 9d. per acre. Samuel Wilmot, who had originally surveyed Emily, gave his opinion of Cavan lands but not of Emily. On these estimates, the Newcastle Land Board (Elias Jones of Cobourg, chairman) struck an average and commented: "EMILY: generally good, well settled and watered —values 4s., 3s. 6d. and 3s. 3d. per acre. This township has been settling since 1819; it has no church but the clergyman of Cavan Township (Anglican) occasionally does duty there." These were lower than the values placed on land in Cavan, Monaghan and Smith, but higher than others like Asphodel, Otonabee, Mariposa, Ops and Fenelon.[2]

Late in 1826 two militia grants were made in Emily—800 acres to John Burn, captain in the 1st Durham Militia (who as a Land Board official was given 800 acres in 1820) and 100 acres to G. Gifford, a private in the same Durham Militia. These were the last, as on Oct. 31, 1826, the Governor ordered the Surveyor-General to suspend all locations in Emily, Smith, Douro and Dummer. Soon afterwards (March 1827) the area known as "Gore of Emily" was renamed Ennismore Township. As further means to keep the Peterborough area firmly under the paternal control of the Family Compact party in the government, Peter Robinson was made Commissioner of Crown Lands and Surveyor-General of Upper Canada in 1827, a post he held for nearly ten years. Robinson was now in his forties and in poor health, but continued to handle a flood of letters of solicitation from his Irish settlers concerning their numerous problems. He placed Alexander McDonell, nephew of Bishop McDonell, as his land agent for the Peterborough District, receiving regular reports from him thereafter.

The tightening bureaucratic grip soon became evident. The Upper Canada *Gazette* of Feb. 7, 1828, contained notice of the first Sheriff's Sale in Emily—the northeast quarter of Lot 19 in 3rd concession Emily "with the building thereon erected, belonging to Thomas Moore", in a suit by Edward Smith, to be sold by Sheriff Conger at Cobourg on May 24th. The Ontario Archives has "A Schedule of Lands in Township Emily for which Descriptions were issued previous to 14th July 1828", but this covers lots only from concessions 1 to 8 (totalling 185); Deeds for lands were already being issued in Emily and the Surveyor-General's Office and Crown Lands Department kept separate files thereafter on every lot in the township. Their records indicated that in Emily (up to 1828) 176 persons had been located on 18,016 acres and that 185 persons had been granted 11,750 acres. There were hundreds of Sheriff's sales in 1829 and 1830 in the district, but none advertised in Emily, which proves that the settlers were industriously clearing their lands, selling their produce and doing their settlement and militia duties. The second Sheriff's Sale in Emily occurred Dec. 24, 1831, when 200 acres in Lot 10, Con. 7, belonging to James Murray and Darby Dwyer, were sold at the suit of John Brown, by Sheriff Ruttan.

Settlement duties were altered in November, 1830, to require: "The locatee shall clear thoroughly the half of the road in width opposite the front of his lot, by burning or totally removing all timber, wood and underwood of every kind therefrom. He shall cut down the stumps for the space of 10 feet from the centre of the road so low that a waggon wheel may easily pass over anything that stands within that space and sow with grass seed the road so cleared." Other duties were that some person be resident on the lot for two years, or alternatively the timber cleared wholly from the front of the lot for the space of one chain (66 feet)—this was to accommodate those who

were away working, or had more than one lot. If proof of duties being completed was not forthcoming within 2½ years of location, the lot would again
be open for new location. In September, 1831, a list was prepared of 30
lots in Emily on which no settlement duty had been proven (including the
very first locatee in Emily, June 1819—S. Peacock); the list is mainly on the
front 8 concessions and apparently Robinson's 1825-6 settlers were not
covered. With another bureaucratic twist, the Government in May 1832
abolished all settlement duties, requiring only residence, but a number of the
lots listed as above were sold off in a large Sheriff's Sale in 1832.

In fact, roads cleared by settlers were unsatisfactory and mostly impassable, except for people on foot, horseback or oxcart. This task was hated by
settlers busy on their own lands, with many sick or working away from home
at times, and no one did the road-clearing along ungranted and reserve lands.
Those settled along navigable waters preferred water transport and by 1830
steamboats were planned on Rice and Chemong Lakes; but for Cavan and
Emily residents, especially in swampy lowlands, improved roads were im-
perative to allow them to get out to markets, shops and mills. A start was
made after 1820 on the Boundary Road, but again in 1826 a petition went
from Cavan, Emily, Monaghan and Smith to the Legislature to grant money
"to complete the road along the Boundary Line, from the S.E. corner of
Cavan to the waters of Pigeon Lake." The government was slow to respond
—in March 1829 £337 10s. was voted and Commissioners appointed to
build the Boundary Road as petitioned, but work was only begun in May 1831
and completed the next year. Meanwhile, since more funds were available
after the system of land sales began 1827 under Robinson's control, tenders
were called in 1829 to build a bridge across "Pigeon Creek" near Cotnam's
Landing (the Omemee site) and this was supervised by John Huston. Huston
was also ordered in April 1831 to mark out and construct the "gravel middle
road" from Hope through Cavan, "and between Lots 12 and 13 in the Township of Emily", at cost £300—this became known as the Emily Road.

Up the trails into Cavan and Emily before 1830 travelled foot peddlers
like Michael Donohue, Patrick Farrall, Patrick Tobin, John McMicklass and
Patrick Turnley, with others on horseback (paying double license £10)—
Dennis Riorden and Samuel Peck. In 1831 the foot peddlers were Jacob
Jacobs, Thomas Tozer and Wm. Waddel, while on horseback went Patrick
Tobin, John Griffin and Oliver Bonny. Post-offices were opened in 1830 at
Cavan, Monaghan and Peterborough, and soon after stage-coaches and freight-
wagons began rolling north from Port Hope and Cobourg over the improved
roads, to profit from the backwoods trade.

By 1830 few Emily farmers had to carry their grain and potash to Port
Hope, unless they wanted to visit the fashionable shops there.[3] By 1830
several mills were operating in Cavan (plus 5 stores, 2 distilleries and a
church); there were fine government-built mills at Peterborough, with a variety
of shops; the Purdys were building a mill at the Lindsay site; and a couple of
small mills had started in Smith and Monaghan. In Emily the situation was
vague—repeated accounts, from the 1881 Victoria *Atlas* onward, have stated

that William Cottingham, aided by a man named Myles, built a mill at the Omemee site 1825-6, with millstones made from stones cut nearby and in 1826 started a store nearby—these are local legends, but are inaccurate.[4] The Emily Assessment Rolls (*U. C. Assembly Journal* Appendices) and other authorities list no mills in Emily until 1828, when the first is mentioned. In 1827 it was reported that a small gristmill was built on the north half of Lot 19, Con. 4, on a creek running into Chemong Lake; this lot was granted to G. Gifford, private in the 1st Durham Militia—just by coincidence, the mill was financed by Captain Baldwin and Thomas Ward, Port Hope magnates, who probably arranged the 1826 grant to Gifford. This was a poor mill with one pair of stones and was operated by James Tiggert (or Tiggett, or Taggart) an early Emily settler (on lease or for wages); there is a hint that one "William Cotteram" had an interest in this mill—perhaps he learned his trade there. When Baldwin built a better mill on Pigeon Creek, this one stopped running; Dennehy in his 1840 survey of south half Lot 18, Con. 4, said the south end was all swampy "and drowned with the old dam of Tiger's Mill." In 1850 Wm. Cottingham claimed that he owned "the mill privilege at the head of Mud Lake."

The Emily Assessment Rolls prove that from 1828 through 1831 there was only one grist-mill licensed in Emily, Col. Baldwin's, and no sawmill, shop or distillery. There is an interesting letter of Adam Scott's to Peter Robinson, written from Emily, June 8, 1829, which is worth notice; Scott after 1827 operated a small mill in Cavan Township. He wrote about a "transaction" between Baldwin and a James Barry re "the 18 and south ½ of 19th Lots in 8 Con. of Emily which was as Baldwin stated granted him on condition of erecting a mill thereon." The deal involved, according to Scott, complicated trading of acreage elsewhere for the 300 acres in Emily, "by Baldwin giving him a crank and saw for a sawmill and Baldwin to pay for the other C[100?] acres and Barry agreed to perform the settlement duty by building the mill." Scott was asked to design "a description of iron that was wanted"; probably Barry complained to him when Baldwin asked him for "power of attorney" papers and sent a man named Morison to do settlement duty on the lots "on which the mill is building." Apparently the scheme fell through, as no sawmill appears on Emily Assessment Rolls until 1832; but Baldwin (first as Captain, later as Colonel) was on the Emily scene for some years, one of the new breed trying to make quick profits from land and mill speculation.[5]

The table on page 43 indicates that the five years after Government aid was stopped were a difficult period for the Irish emigrants, who had to live on their own resources, and for the other settlers who had done so from the first. In the year up to the 1827 census, the population dropped 78, mostly due to deaths among the women and children. Yet land clearance doubled, and doubled again by 1831; for this hard work, oxen were clearly better than horses and increased to 156 by 1831. Milch cows increased to provide milk for the young, while young cattle increased to 183 in 1829 and then fell off, probably found unprofitable. Assessed values rose 75% in the five years and district and provincial taxes proportionately. Houses of hewn timber and

EMILY CENSUS AND ASSESSMENT RETURNS
(U.C. LEGIS. ASSEMBLY APPENDICES)

	1827	1828	1829	1830	1831
Males 16 and over	197	197	212	226	232
Females 16 and over	162	159	167	169	183
Males under 16 years	218	216	231	227	248
Females under 16 years	182	193	184	196	206
TOTAL POPULATION:	759	765	794	818	869
Persons Assessed	140	144	. . .	172	184
Uncultivated land (in acres)	11808	11833	16694	14867½	15664½
Cultivated land (in acres)	682	718	910	1063½	1295½
Horses	4	9	15	19	24
Oxen	80	102	131	127	156
Milch cows	177	190	200	208	227
Young cattle	49	51	183	128	95
Assessment	£3982/8	£4361/12	£5321	£5618/6	£6644/8
Total rates	£19/1/1	£20/17/11	£28/14/10	£29/6/8	£34/6/5

frame, and some of two storeys, were beginning to appear in the northern townships by 1831, especially if close to sawmills; one hewn timber house was built in Emily in 1829, the only one for several years. Nobody north of Rice Lake was taxed up to 1831 for "a pleasure wagon or gig".

The British government set out in 1828 to find out whether Irish assisted emigration was worth repeating, and sent a questionnaire which Peter Robinson had completed by a few in the townships around Peterborough. Patrick Ryan of Emily completed his reply June 9, 1828, giving his views. He stated that "Previous to my emigration, I was Clerk in the Mercantile Department", and on the voyage had with him £5 sterling. He added "I have not been able yet to build a comfortable house. I have but a Temporary Dwelling and offices, 7 acres of land cleared and fenced, a Yoke of Oxen, Two Cows and Hogs . . . my two brothers have as much cleared land each as I, but not as much Stock." His family was now four persons and none had died since Quebec. Re state of health, he stated "In a very bad state. They were afflicted during the last year with the Ague and Dysentery, which are common to this climate." To the question about produce or livestock to dispose of, above what was required for the family, he answered: "I had none to dispose of and if I had there is no Market within 30 miles, nor passable roads even there." To the question about food for his family, he replied: "Chiefly Potatoes, Milk and Butter, Bread and Flesh Meat." He was not very pleased with his situation and felt his "comfort and happiness" had not improved by coming to Canada, but hoped by "Perseverance and Industry" to bring better times. He strongly recommended any emigrants in government projects to accept assistance to come to Canada, even if it had to be repaid, but this repayment should be "in the produce of the Soil, and to have Government Stores and agents convenient to receive said Produce." This was the attitude of an emigrant who had prospered more than the average, though the transition from mercantile clerk to backwoods farmer must have been difficult (on the south half Lot 7, Con. 10, for which he obtained his fiat or deed April 26, 1834).

Guillet's *Pioneer Inns and Taverns* (vol. IV) states "The first school in Emily Township was in Williamstown [Omemee] in a room in Cotnam's Tavern. It was opened in 1836 and among the early teachers were Captain M. Handcock and another old soldier, John Henderson. . . ." In fact, of course, since several schoolmasters were among the Irish settlers, there were small schools held in homes much earlier. The Common-School Returns (*U.C. Assembly Journal,* 1828) list two for 1827: in Emily: Mr. T. Mitchell with 21 pupils and Mr. P. Baragy with 41 pupils, each given £12½ salary—they taught reading, writing, arithmetic, grammar, catechism, etc. and used such texts as Mavor and Fenny's Spelling Book, Murray's Grammar and English Reader, and Gough's Arithmetic. In 1828 the same two teachers had 23 and 36 pupils respectively, but each teacher was allowed only £8 from district funds. By 1830 there were four schools in Emily: P. Baragy with 33, T. Mitchell with 26, R. Sullivan with 20, and J. Stacks with 20 pupils, a total of 99 pupils. In fact Emily was foremost in education among townships north of Rice Lake by Dec. 1830: populous Cavan had 4 schools but only 82 pupils, Smith had 3 schools with 70 pupils, and other townships only had one small school each. The teachers received £8 each from district funds, but were no doubt given fees or goods by parents to supplement this. They had few texts and no maps or other aids; instead of slates or paper they used birchbark, on which they wrote in charcoal. Most children attended no school and those who attended had to do so when weather and work at home permitted. Children matured early in the backwoods and did adult work from the age of ten, particularly when sickness and absence of parents required their help. But reading and writing and arithmetic were of value to those who hoped to prosper in the decades ahead, and devoted teachers inspired intelligent students.

Early inns and taverns are difficult to mark definitely, since numerous settlers put up weary travellers and gave food to man and beast, without any license; on the new Emily and Boundary Roads and on the road from Peterborough, this might become a profitable business. Thomas Dixon, granted the southeast quarter of Lot 11, Con. 4, in 1820, petitioned in 1830 for an innkeeper's license, which would permit him to sell liquors; he wrote "having commenced keeping entertainment for Travellers about 3 months since and finding that petitioner could obtain such custom from the publick as would be useful to his welfare." He went on to claim that "being placed between two tavern keepers, they prejudiciously and maliciously entered a complaint against Petitioner stating that a quarrel took place at his house" which he denied without avail. His petition was signed by 95 settlers, headed by "Humphry Finly, king of Emily" and "Patrick Connel, king of Opps", but even so it was refused. Yet in 1832 William and Morris Cotnam were given separate innkeepers' licenses, at least one of which was on the Omemee site, as noted above.

Out of numerous examples, two letters to Robinson are given in part to illustrate the problems referred to him. The first from Peterboro, 1 July 1828, was written by his agent, A. Macdonell: "In my last I mentioned my intention to visit Emily and Ennismore, which I am sorry to say was not productive of obtaining as many answers to the Queries as I could have wished, the people having principally gone to the Canals to work. . . . In my visit to Emily I was much pleased to find people in good spirits with prospect of an abundant crop; they have considerably increased their improvements which look very neat; a few however are likely to give the ensuing Quarter Sessions some business: Collins, Lyne and Sullivan have long been at variance, which has at last ended in a battle, and parties at instance of Collins, the long man at the King's Wharf, who is a troublesome fellow, have all been bound over. I made every enquiry into the matter and proposed a plan to them of settling their difficulties, to which they agreed. I had consequently written to the Magistrates before whom they were taken, of the circumstances, who approved of the measure, but to my astonishment, Collins has this moment appeared and says that nothing but the law will satisfy him, consequently several poor families will have to attend at Hamilton [Cobourg] from the interior of Emily."

The second, from John Callaghan of Emily, written Feb. 13, 1830, is given in parts: "I have wrote to your Honour on October last the same week after being with you, about my son Besness at Nigara and my other son that went to the States of Pensel Vine [Pennsylvania] and remained there till all the people were getting very sike and he left it and come over to Nigara to his Brother and gave him $30 to send home to his father and went from that to Kingston Canall and stapt there for some time . . . and was at home when I came down from York and he told me he had given Jerry 30 daller to send it to me which I did not get . . . and I was told he had given it to the Judge of Kings Bence the day of his triall. . . . I depend in your Honour that you will get him [out] of being fined and I know very well that your Honour can dow it that the Governor will do [it] for you . . . and the attorney-General. . . . His mother is these 6 months in very bad steate of helt and if she know that he was to be whipt she wold lose her life and also if he is whipt that all my childer will goe way from me. . . ." This shows some of the problems of the emigrants in keeping track of their wandering sons and their anxiety to keep them down on the farm, preferably on a neighbouring lot.

No attempt was made in early census returns to list the people by religion, but in this period in Emily about half were Roman Catholics. These found it hard to go to Peterborough to worship, but the priest there made occasional trips through Smith, into Ennismore, Emily and Ops, with services in homes enroute. The backwoods life made almost impossible the necessary rites of regular confession, abolution before death, etc., but babies could be baptized when the priest visited the area and couples could go to Peterborough to be married. Bishop Alexander McDonell, in a letter of Feb. 19, 1827, from "Peterboro on the Rice Lakes", after touring through the Irish settlements, assured Earl Bathurst, British Colonial Secretary, that "both the Irish emigrants sent out by Govert. and those who had found their way to the province by their own exertions are coming on better than any other class of settlers . . . [some] who have not been upon their lands more than 3 to 5 years, showed me from 200 to 300 bushels of wheat of the last harvest's growth and from 17 to 24 head of black cattle of an excellent breed; but what

I found more gratifying and of more importance to themselves was that in the whole course of my travells I did not meet with a single individual sick or indisposed . . . the sum of £750 which your Lordship has been so good as to grant from the proceeds of the Canada Company for the maintenance of Roman Catholic clergymen will do a great deal, but a provision for schoolmasters is no less necessary . . . if the Irish emigrants be kept under the control and direction of proper pastors and teachers their Loyalty and grateful attachements to the British Govert. for the favors that have been conferred on them will prove the strongest line. . . ." McDonell's request for priority financial aid included two priests in Ennismore and Ops, to supplement the work of the priest in Peterborough, also a school in Ennismore.

St. John's Anglican Church in Ida, Cavan, was established 1819 and an item in the *U.C. Journals* Jan. March 1828 notes "Rev. J. Thompson at Cavan has charges at Monaghan and Emily which are visited occasionally." Rev. Samuel Armour, Church of England minister at Peterborough and headmaster of the Grammar School there, had charges in Monaghan, Smith and Otonabee—when he retired from Peterborough in 1832, he served the Cavan and Emily parish for many years, until a separate Emily parish was formed. However, even earlier the Methodists were preaching in Cavan and Emily; Sanderson stated that in 1823 "the Smith's Creek preachers (S. Belton and Jos. Atwood) were extending their bounds northward as far as Omemee, with rich spiritual rewards".[6] In 1824 Rev. Anson Green made itinerant rounds through 12 townships with 30 preaching places, prayer meetings and family visitations. In the next two years most attention was devoted to converting the Rice, Mud and Scugog Lake Indians and by 1827 the Cavan Methodist preacher, James Norris, looked after Rice Lake circuit also. In 1828 Rev. H. Biggar reported that Methodist members in Cavan and Emily had risen from 96 the previous year to 194; by 1830 the Cavan Methodist Society had 132 members, including Emily, and next year Rev. Gilbert Millar was reported as riding circuit regularly north into Emily to preach. The Methodists, however, had no church in Emily yet, nor had any other denomination; besides home meetings, the Methodists favoured large outdoor camp meetings.[6]

The papers of John Huston,[7] Cavan Justice of the Peace, Militia Officer and Surveyor contain some revealing documents on the stresses and strains of Emily life in those years. Huston was adjutant of the 2nd Durham Militia and on July 9, 1828, the Colonel, W. Henry of Port Hope, wrote chiding him for planning "an Orange meeting on the 12th preparatory to coming forward to the election". He pointed out that the Governor strongly disapproved of such "Party meetings" and added: "it certainly is the Interest of both Parties to live in Peace and brotherly feelings. . . . The party feelings should be buried in oblivion. . . ." In Emily there were four militia companies and at May 7, 1829 they were commanded as follows: *7th Company* (1, 2 and 3rd con.) 60 men—Captn. David Armstrong; *8th do.*)4, 5 and 6th con.) 60 men—Captn. Bailey; *9th do.* (7, 8 and 9th con.) 44 men—Captn. Patrick McGuire; *10th do.* (10, 11 and 12th con.) 56 men—Captn. George Elliot. The force of 220 men was officered by "old settlers", though some of the sergeants were Robinson settlers. Huston was given charge of the militia training and Col. Henry by letter May 14, 1830, ordered him to summon them on June 4 at 10 a.m. "for training with arms"—the Cavan Companies at Hutchinson's Tavern, the Emily Companies "at the most central part of that Township, that is all the men over 18 and under 40; should Major Boulton or myself not be in Emily to take the Command, it will devolve on the senior Captain of the Emily Companies." Each captain was also to send in a return of men absent without leave from the training.

L. O. L. No. 41 Emily was formed 1830 (among the first 59 lodges in Canada formed that year). Among members were Magees, Moores, etc.— although the warrant was not issued until 1847.

Dr. John Hutchison of Peterborough, formerly of Cavan, wrote Huston July 5, 1830, much perturbed at news that the Orangemen of Cavan were coming in procession to Peterborough on July 12th. On behalf of the Peterborough magistrates he urged Huston to prevent this parade: "such exhibitions can now and in this country serve no good but, on the contrary, tend to perpetuate that religious feud which has so long destroyed the peace of your native Isle. . . . For heaven's sake why transplant that rancorous party feeling to this peaceful country, where no earthly distinction is made between Catholic and Protestant . . . the Magistrates here will be prepared to use the most energetic measures to prevent any interruption to the public peace." His concluding paragraph is on another topic: "I have not yet visited the site of the bridge in Emily—was told by the neighbours that it was impossible and impolitic to enter upon the work [until] the waters had farther subsided—but I will see it soon and communicate to you my ideas."

A petition to the District Magistrates in January 1831, signed by Thos. Mitchel, John Collum and Francis Henderson of Emily, shows another source of strife. They claimed that when the people assembled on January 3 after a public notice, to elect local officers, "a dispute arose between the old and new setlers respecting the election of the Town Clerk . . . there was a majority in favour of one of the new setlers; the old setlers were quite indignant at this and insisted they should have a man from among themselves." They claimed that every year "the most lucrative situation[s] being given to the old setlers, viz—clerk, collector, and the assessors, notwithstanding that it is generally acknowledged that the major part of the new settlers are more competent to hold such situation . . . this disagreement was premeditated by the old settlers in tearing down the Warrant signed by Dr. Hutchison and Mr. Maguire and opening the meeting with the Warrant signed by Messrs. Brown and Huston which your petitioners are informed was illegal and contrary to law. Your petitioners after having elected Town Clerk by a large majority were even denied the books and records of the Town by the old Clerk and a number of others and even a pen and ink or a sheet of paper, and even ordered to the barn by the landlord of the Inn who was quite displeased because his brother-in-law was not elected." Unfortunately the outcome is not disclosed.

Huston wrote indignantly to Robinson early in July, 1831, after Pat Maguire, J.P. had written Robinson. Huston claimed "If there is any display of Protestants and Orangemen walking in procession on the 12th inst. the cause must be attached to Mr. Maguire and him only. He has roused that religious fiend which has so long destroyed the peace of unhappy Ireland which here ought to rest obscure. . . ." In his view Maguire had goaded both sides to dispute, pretending to support each in turn. "The Catholics of Emily, Ops and Cavan will not be drove to quarrel with the neighbours the Protestants (;) some of the Catholics told me after the last town meeting in Emily that they were encouraged by Mr. Maguire so to do but they would not, others said they were sorry for what had happened." This religious squabbling, condemned by the Governor and the whole administration, infected the militia also. William Lyon Mackenzie published in his *Colonial Advocate* in June 1831 an item from the new Port Hope *Telegraph* weekly, about a battle at militia camp near Peterborough that month "between the Orangemen and the Catholics" which led to action by the magistrates. An affidavit sworn by Robert Mitchel of Emily, at Peterborough Dec. 6, 1831, stated that he had obtained a Judgment in January 1829 against William Cotingham, that the latter had paid the sum over to Patrick Maguire soon afterwards, and was now forced to sue Maguire to obtain his Judgment with costs. The interesting thing is that in the 9th Militia Company, Maguire was Captain, Wm. Cotnam was Lieutenant, and an Ensign Wm. Mitchell was moved over to the 8th Company during this dispute, to join Lieutenant Thomas Mitchell.

More important in the history of Emily in 1831 was the Millersmith settlement in the north west corner, from Concessions 11 to 14.[8] They sailed from Liverpool in June, some of them ex-soldiers, and proceeded together upcountry to Port Hope, inland up the Otonabee to Peterborough, and by water around Chemong and Pigeon Lakes to King's Wharf at the east end of Con. 14, Emily. Among them were six families of Millers and Smiths, with Kennedys, Bentleys, McMullens and Cullons. "Here they built wigwams of Cedar, spruce and balsam boughs for their families, while the menfolk came around by Downeyville to the lots assigned to them"—between Lots 5 and 8 on Concessions 13 and 14. While the men were building shanties on the lots assigned, their families suffered from fever and ague, and one of John Kennedy's children died at King's Wharf and was buried at Downeyville (later moved to a family cemetery on their farm). By Nov. 2 they were in their own shanties, of logs with roofs of hollowed logs laid alternately over and under, like the 1825 shanties, and with doors and windows covered with blankets or quilts until doors and shutters could be fashioned. It was a winter of deep snow, and only through the warmhearted aid of the Downeyville settlement did they get through the winter and start farming next spring. We shall see something of their early struggles in the next chapter—one interesting fact is that Katherine Miller, who was 10 years old when they emigrated, later worked for the Langtons on Sturgeon Lake, and is mentioned several times in Anne Langton's book *A Gentlewoman in Upper Canada* (1950) as the maid Kitty; she narrated the story of the settlement's early life before her death in 1911.

Several writers from Britain, visiting Upper Canada, came to Newcastle District around 1830-2, and mentioned Emily Township in their subsequent books, sometimes imaginatively, but not always accurately. To close this chapter, a paragraph is quoted from H. Picken *The Canadas* (London 1832), which is about the best description:

"EMILY is settled, through a few of the first concessions, by emigrants from the north of Ireland, thence to the rear by those of 1825. The roads are yet new but improving; in the latest settlements but partially opened. The soil is generally good, sandy loams in the hills, on the flats and in the valleys clayey loam; the township is for the most part level, and has numerous swamps, especially towards the rear, and on the line of Pigeon Creek, which traverses the township. Beaver meadows are frequent in this, and are also met with in the other townships in this range; they are very serviceable to the new settler. There are two good sawmill sites in this township; one reserved by government on south half 18th and 19th in 8th concession; a second on 6th in 10th concession. A small gristmill is being built on 19th in 4th concession.† It is probable, however, that excepting for the home use of settlers, the produce will be generally taken to Peterborough, from the excellent mills there and other conveniences. To that place a road has been opened, and the magistrates of Hamilton‡ having lately granted £30 to aid the inhabitants, it will soon be improved. By the line of Pigeon Creek, the settlers in Emily may pass by water to Mud Lake, within 7 or 8 miles (by a good road) of Peterborough, and by this route many of Mr. Robinson's emigrants, and their provisions, were conveyed."

†—Baldwin's first mill, as described above.

‡—this was Cobourg, in Hamilton Township, capital of the Newcastle District.

NOTES

[1]Ontario Archives Document, Assessment on Rateable Property in District of Newcastle 1826, and Appendices to *Journals of Upper Canada Assembly* (Jan. March 1828).

[2]Public Archives of Canada: CO 47, Canada Miscellania, vol. 115, "Surveyors' Reports on Townships 1826: Upper Canada".

[3]Old-timers' romantic tales of carrying grain from Emily as far as Kingston (usually on their backs), to be ground, can be treated as fables.

[4]Wm Cotnam was given a distiller's license in 1827, but apparently not renewed in following years.

[5]For more about Baldwin's mill ventures, see Chapter 6.

[6]Sanderson *The First Century of Methodism in Canada* Toronto 1908; also Carroll *Case and his Contemporaries.* Toronto 1867; Playter *"History of Methodism in Canada"* Toronto 1862; and Rev. Anson Green *"Life and Times"* Toronto 1877.
One source says that in the early years they met in a building on the N.W. corner of Lot 13, Con. 2, owned by Francis Henderson.

[7]See Note 2 in Chapter Four, concerning the Huston papers.

[8]Most of the information in this section was provided by Mr. W. N. McMullen; supplemented by a Lindsay news clipping of Nov. 3, 1939.

CHAPTER SIX

TWO DECADES OF TROUBLES AND TRIUMPH
(1832-50)

Nicholas Davin in *The Irishman in Canada,* 1877, made an important point: "There are two aspects to the Irish emigration to Canada. What the Irishman has done for Canada is the first. The second is not less important, what Canada has done for the Irishman." In the next few chapters on the progress of Emily Township from pioneer backwoods settlement to flourishing rural township, we will see many examples of both these important aspects of sound social and economic development. As Davin pointed out: "Men have come here [to Canada] who were unable to spell, who never tasted meat, who never knew what it was to have a shoe to their foot in Ireland." The short-sighted snobs in the British Islands and in Canada despised them and predicted they would all end in the United States or in jail; history has shown that they helped to develop their new country by their co-operative industry, just as the country shaped and matured them into prosperous, orderly and well-rounded citizens from coast to coast. The people and the country each helped the potentialities of the other. Some Peterborough area "gentry" urged that the Irish be scattered among English and Scottish settlers who would show them good examples of industry and perseverance; but Robinson wisely ignored this in some townships; and in fact the Irish progressed just as industriously and peacefully as their neighbouring Scots and English on the land, whether they were the majority as in Douro, Ennismore and Emily, or a minority as in Asphodel, Smith and Otonabee. All settlers (except those with capital and large land grants) shared the same backwoods problems—lack of roads, of cash, of schools, of mills, of churches, etc.; and all shared the same benefits —plenty of fuel, fish, food and fresh unpolluted air and water, religious and social freedom, and reliance on their own hard work, honesty and neighbourly sharing of troubles and pleasures. In a bush settlement 15 to 30 miles from all amenities—when a house burned, a child was sick, a person died, a building was to be put up, a harvest was to be gathered, etc., the neighbours rallied around, regardless of race, creed or political convictions. Co-operation was a necessary way of life for the survival of all.

A severe economic depression in the mid-thirties over Europe and North America, plus a cholera epidemic and other troubles in Europe, brought a flood of new settlers into the Newcastle District, whose population rose 500% in 15 years. In the period 1832-1850, Emily's population rose from 1,095 to 2,461.[1]

About 10,000 acres of land passed into private ownership in these 20 years in Emily—mostly by land sales, held in early years in Peterborough, but later at "Cottingham's Mills" in Emily. Until he retired, Robinson was lenient to his Emily Irish, allowing changes from poor lots to better land, holding lots for men working away, and granting 50-acre lots to some indigent newcomers, with payment spread over long periods. As we shall see, some Clergy Reserves were sold off and some granted to churches and clergy in the township. Some settlers bartered, sold, bought, leased, abandoned and reclaimed lots recklessly. Deals with speculators often led to lawsuits. One fact stands clear in the following table: the great industry of the average settlers in clearing land, with more oxen and horses and tools, with more sawmills to buy logs and gristmills to buy grain, more roads to mills, and more money in pocket:

LANDS HELD IN EMILY[2]

	1832	1841	1851
Uncultivated (in acres)	22,365	27,278	21,093
Cultivated (in acres)	1,413	4,133	12,224
	23,778	31,411	33,317

Among the participants in this progress, in 22 or 23 years since settlement, were the Irish 1825 settlers. A British Government Emigration document, 1848, reported on 122 of their lots still in their hands, totalling 13,800 acres of which 12,200 acres were patented. Among the most successful were listed: Wm. Mulcahey (family 5) with 65 acres cleared, 2 horses, 4 cattle; John Hogan (family 8) with 40 acres cleared, 3 cattle; Abraham Groves (family 4) with 40 acres cleared, 2 horses, 4 cattle; Thomas Carew (family 8) with 40 acres cleared, 2 horses, 3 cattle; John Geary (family 3) with 40 acres cleared; Pat Callahan (family 5) with 50 acres cleared, 2 horses, 2 cattle; and Bart Kenely (family 9) with 40 acres cleared, 1 horse, 1 cow. Numerous others had 20 to 35 acres cleared and as much livestock. About a third of the lots had a non-relative as "in occupation", indicating the owners were leasing, possibly having bought other property. Another quarter of the lots were marked "no assessment" and with no assessor's report on improvements, indicating that they were not being occupied or worked, possibly held for the sons to grow up and farm them; on only one lot, that of Patrick Walsh, is there the notation "Gone to the United States."

An interesting trade of January 3, 1832 is among the Huston papers: David Thornton of southeast quarter Lot 9, Con. 4, with Andrew Ormsby of west half Lot 3, Con. 5—to take effect the following October 1 after Thornton had reaped his crop; the advantage seems to have been with Thornton, trading 50 acres for 100, and also "Andrew Ormsby agreed to pasture 15 sheep for . . . the years 1832 and 1833 for said David Thornton."

Even in late 1831, A. McDonell, Robinson's agent in Peterborough, was arranging surveys of lots on which settlement duties were undone and district taxes had not been paid, assessing their value. In Aug. 1833 the papers advertised 61 lots in Emily on concessions 1 to 7, mostly of 50 acres, for tax arrears from 8s. to £1/8/5 (this last a 100-acre lot, south half of Lot 7, Con. 5) and the sale was held February 1834. A list in July 1835 advertised 8 Emily lots for sale, all of 50 acres, the sale to be Feb. 5, 1836, 10 a.m. at "Cotnam's Mills". The Canada Company in April 1836 advertised for sale ten lots in Emily. In April 1839 over 100 lots forfeited for tax arrears since

WILLIAM the FOURTH, by the Grace of GOD, of the United Kingdom of Great Britain and Ireland, King, Defender of the Faith.—To all to whom these Presents shall come——**GREETING:**

Know Ye, That We, of our special Grace, certain Knowledge and mere Motion, have given and **Granted,** and by these Presents do give and **Grant** unto

Richard Owens

heirs and assigns for ever: **All** that parcel or tract of **Land,** situate in our said Province, containing by admeasurement be the same more or less, being

Together with all the Woods and Waters thereon lying and being, under the reservations, limitations, and conditions, hereinafter expressed; which said butted and bounded, or may be otherwise known as follows: that is to say,

To have and to hold, the said parcel or tract of Land, hereby given and granted, to him the said *Richard Owens* heirs and assigns for ever; saving, nevertheless, to Us, our Heirs and Successors, all Mines of Gold and Silver that shall or may be hereafter found on any part of the said parcel or tract of Land hereby given and granted as aforesaid; and saving and reserving to Us, our Heirs and Successors, all White Pine Trees, that shall or may now or hereafter grow or be growing on any part of the said parcel or tract of Land hereby granted as aforesaid. **Provided Always,** that no part of the parcel or tract of Land hereby given and granted to the said and heirs, be within any reservation heretofore made and marked for Us, our Heirs and Successors, by our Surveyor General of Woods, or his lawful Deputy, in which case, this our grant for such part of the Land hereby given and granted to the said heirs for ever, as aforesaid; and which shall, upon a survey thereof being made, be found within any such reservation, shall be null and void, and of none effect, any thing herein contained to the contrary notwithstanding. **Provided also,** that the said heirs or assigns, shall and do within three years, erect and build, or cause to be erected and built; in and upon some part of the said parcel or tract of Land, a good and sufficient dwelling house, the said heirs or assigns, not having built, or not being in his or their own right, lawfully possessed of a house in our said Province, and the therein, or cause some person to be therein resident, for and during the space of three years, then next ensuing the building of the same. **Provided also,** that if at any time or times hereafter the Land so hereby given and granted to the said heirs, shall come into the possession and tenure of any person or persons whomsoever, either by virtue of any Deed of sale, conveyance, enfeoffment, or exchange; or by gift, inheritance, descent, devise, or marriage, such person or persons shall within twelve months next after his, her, or their entry into and possession of the same, take the oaths prescribed by Law, before some one of the Magistrates of our said Province, and a certificate of such oath having been, so taken, shall cause to be recorded in the Secretary's Office of our said Province. **In default** of all or any of which conditions, limitations and restrictions, this said grant, and every thing herein contained, shall be, and We hereby declare the same to be null and void, to all intents and purposes whatsoever; and the Land hereby granted, and every part and parcel thereof, shall revert to, and shall become vested in Us, our Heirs and Successors, in like manner as if the same had never been granted, any thing herein contained to the contrary thereof in anywise notwithstanding. **And whereas,** by an Act of the Parliament of Great Britain passed in the thirty-first year of the Reign of the late King George the Third, entitled "An Act to repeal certain parts of an Act passed in the Fourteenth year of His Majesty's Reign, entitled 'An Act for making more effectual provision for the Government of the Province of Quebec, in North America, and to make further provision for the Government of the said Province," it is declared, "that no grant of Lands thereafter made, should be valid or effectual, unless the same should contain a specification of the Lands to be allotted and appropriated solely to the maintenance of a Protestant Clergy within the said Province, in respect of the Lands to be thereby granted". **Now Know Ye,** that we have caused an allotment or appropriation of

GIVEN under the Great Seal of our Province of Upper Canada: **Witness** our trusty and well-beloved

this day of in the year of our Lord One Thousand, Eight Hundred and Thirty and in the year of our Reign.

Deed of Richard Owens to south half lot 18 in Con. 12, Emily, Aug. 1834.

I certify that *John Blackwell*

one of the Irish Settlers of 18*25* is now residing on *the e South half*

Lot No. *Seventeen* in the *first* Concession, in the

Township of *Emily* in the *New Castle* District, and

that he has cleared thereon *Thirty* Acres.

A. McDonell

Peterboro' 24th day of *October* 1833.

I certify that there is a house erected & about fifteen acres
cleared on lot 17 in the 7th Concesesr of Emily which had been
granted to Mr Groves who died there. his eldest son Thos
Groves has gone to the States & fixed there — his Second son
Abraham has had possession of the lot & worked upon
it since his brothers departure & now wishes that it may
be granted to his brother James a boy 16 years old who has no lot
con . . . . line in front of the lot has been cleared on . . . . . .
. . . . . 7th Jany 1834

C Baldwin

CERTIFICATES OF SETTLEMENT DUTIES PERFORMED IN EMILY:
(1) A. McDonell re John Blackwell's lot on con. 1 in 1833
(2) C. Baldwin re Thomas Groves' lot on con. 7 in 1834.
(Crown Lands Papers, Ontario Archives)

1832, or no settlement duties performed, on all concessions were for sale, and another sale list of August 1839 had 12 lots. Again in 1840 a sale was held in August of 5 forfeited lots in Emily. In February 1842 Clergy Reserve lots in Emily, sold for unpaid balances owing, totalled 2,600 acres and brought £1,265. In August, 1843, over 60 Emily lots were advertised, to be sold April 1844. In Sept. 1846 the District Treasurer offered 7 Emily lots on which taxes were overdue, often paltry sums. This was a period of depression, unrest and speculation all over Upper Canada, far more apparent in other areas than in Emily. Some lots in Emily were purchased by outside speculators (including Baldwin, Bethune, Boulton and Burnham from the Lake-ports), while many Emily farmers bought better lots to move to, or for their sons growing up, their daughters getting married, etc.

Huston was kept busy surveying and valuing lots prior to these sales; for example, in April 1835 he reported on (1) east half 16th lot in 5th con.— concession line and south end swampy, north end good land with maple, beech, basswood and ironwood, worth 8s. 9d. per acre; (2) lot 9 in 5th con. partly swamp with some "knowls", principally marsh adjoining Pigeon Creek, worth 8s. 9d. per acre; (3) 10th lot on 4th con.—the land ascends to a hill then slowly down to north end of lot where is some swamp; maple, beech, basswood, pine and ironwood; 10 acres improved by George Dixon; worth 12s. 6d. an acre.

Thomas Dennehy surveyed about 100 lots in July 1840, covering all concessions[3], and his comments are of general interest. Distances were given to the nearest mills—those in the south from Best's mill in Cavan or Cottingham's on Pigeon River, those in the middle concessions from Cottingham's or from Baldwin's mill farther down Pigeon River; those in the west from Purdy's mills at Lindsay, and those in the north from Need's mill at Bobcaygeon. Several protested to Dennehy that they had sent money to Toronto, but the bureaucrats were slow in sending deeds. In several other cases, ownership was disputed—on the north half of Lot 21, Con. 4, when locatee J. Driscoll died, his widow married twice more and went to live at Mud (Chemong) Lake, but still argued ownership with Alex. Brennan, the occupant, though it was a poor lot two-thirds swampy; another poor lot, north half of Lot 19, Con. 6, was disputed by two locatees, John Shouldis and James Reed, though none of it was cleared and neither lived on it. A lot of special interest was part of Lot 11, Con. 6, west of Pigeon River, given to George Cowan, 4 miles from a mill, good soil but partly swampy; this was the site later of Cowan's Bridge, but he was unhappy with it and demanding a new lot in exchange.

On the north half of Lot 17, Con. 7, Thomas Groves had 40 acres cleared; the soil was sandy loam and value 8s. an acre, and only a half-mile from Baldwin's Mills; but Groves refused the northwest quarter as marshy, and demanded the government give him the southeast quarter instead, being excellent hardwood land.[4] On the west half of Lot 16, Con. 8, there was a squatter, Wm. Barret; the lot was mostly marsh, with about 5 acres of hardwood and only 2 or 3 acres cleared; the locatee, Pat Shea, before he died had moved to the adjoining Clergy Reserve lot in Con. 9 and cleared about 25 acres, and his son Cornelius was claiming it instead. Nearby, on north half Lot 14, Con. 9, Edward Morrisey had 10 acres cleared; the clay soil was excellent and the lot well placed, 8 miles from Cottingham's and 2¼ miles from Baldwin's Mills. On the north half of Lot 17, Con. 11, John Sheehan had clay loam on the north part and swamp on the south; he was 2 land carriage miles from Verulam Mills and 10 by water. On the east half of Lot 8, Con. 14, with 8 acres cleared, locatee John McMullin had good clay soil upon limestone gravel, with much maple and beech; he was 10 miles from Cottenham's or Purdy's Mills and the land worth 10s. an acre. After Dennehy's report was received, some of these lots were reassigned or sold off, where the locatees did not pay the fees and taxes due; others, of course, were deeded to the occupants who farmed them.

Robinson's image as the sympathetic "father" of his 1825 settlers resulted in a deluge of hundreds of letters in his ten years as Commissioner of Crown Lands, many from Emily and mostly about land troubles; this habit carried on after his 1836 retirement. Richard Sullivan (west half Lot 2, Con. 6) wrote in July 1834 that "he was in close custody of the sheriff" for £12/10 in taxes which he was unable to pay; "I have young cattle to cover the amount but unable to sell them as money is scarce in the country." He pleaded for his land deed as "Mr. Boulton of Port Hope will lend me the money with the deed as security. . . . By doing so you will save my wife a long fitaguing journey."

Even more pressing was Adam Shouldis (or Shouldice) who wrote Robinson Aug. 7, 1833: "When I was in York I signed a Proposal for a Broken Front ajoined to my Land of 16 acres for the purpose of a Road from my House to Peterborra. . . . That verrey day Mr. Mudge offered me the above 16 or any lot I could shuse for 4s. per acre and 7 yrs. for the Payment as being a solder. . . . Now Sir I request it at 10s. per Acer as we cannot fly over the Trees. We are living on the north end of 22 in 3rd. . . . I hope you will grant it to Me as having so many Boys still unsettled and my other Sun (Son?) will be out next Spring and I want land for 5 Boys. . . . All my Famulley requests your Kindness in this Matter and shall ever Pray for your Good Helth. . . ." He wrote again in 1842 as "a true Protestant and an old soldier for 18 years" and claimed he was in 1825 given Lot 22, Con. 3 being "a broken lot of 60 acres and a second spot of 11 acres and 29 still due" and had 3 boys still unsettled; in the Huston papers is a draft letter stating that Huston "was present at a conversation between Alex. McDonell Esq. and Adam Shouldis of Emily, at Peterboro. . . . Mr. Shouldice was soliciting part of a lot in Smith Township adjoining Mud Lake," while McDonell insisted there was no such lot; this resulted in Huston surveying the area, result unknown. Again in 1845 the persistent Shouldis, at age 71, wrote Crown Lands protesting that his son had been given the north half of Lot 19, Con. 6, Emily in 1825 by Robinson, but "was a cripple and had to live with parents or brothers," and now the government was selling his lot off; the situation was complicated since John, the son, was living in Mariposa with a brother.

Timothy Dorgan, in July 1839, petitioned the Governor (with a supporting affidavit), stating that when he came out with Robinson in 1825 he brought "a full cousin, as a son, by name Daniel Mahony . . . he was located on a half of Lot 14, 11th con . . . went out to earn about 12 years ago and did not return since, nor no acct. from him, but Pettner. was informed that he died. He ordered said petitioner to do settlement duties on said lot and if he did not return that he might have the land for his trouble." Dorgan claimed he cleared 10 acres about 1833 and on applying to Robinson, had his eldest son's name put on the lot. "Puttner. has a large family 5 boys and 4 girls, and he is not able to buy land for any of his sons . . . 3 of his boys says that if they dont get said lot after all their labour that they will go elsewhere to do for themselves." The Council approved, but for some reason no action was taken; a note on the document read: "I cannot find that the name of Petnr's son was placed on the land." Again on May 31, 1847, Daniel Dorgan petitioned, asking that Clergy Reserve lot (north half of Lot 16, Con. 13) adjacent to his own would be valuable to him; he was on south half of Lot 15, Con. 13 patented to John Dorgan, his father now deceased, but he had 6 brothers and they needed more land. Dennehy the surveyor had surveyed the lot recently, and he asked to be permitted to buy it at 8s. an acre. Dennehy's survey indicated the lot was unoccupied and unimproved and not worth the upset price of 8s. an acre, being half swampy, with bad roads and 12 miles from Cottingham Mills. The Crown Lands Department decided Dorgan had no better claim than anyone else, and put the lot up for sale at 8s. an acre; let us hope the anxious Dorgan managed to buy it.

Henry Sherin, schoolmaster, who came to Emily in 1824, was located in 1827 on the north half of Lot 17, Con. 3; in 1829 he gave his brother 50 acres of it. In his letter to the Crown Lands Department March 10, 1840, he claimed a dwelling house, barn and sheds, with 30 acres improved; he also claimed he had been "living on the southeast quarter of the lot since 1822," that his sons were chopping 10 acres more and he hoped "to send for deed this last winter but the wheat done so bad in this part of the country this last harvest that I have been disappointed, having a large family to support, a wife, 6 boys and 2 girls". He had asked George Boulton, Durham member of the Legislature, to intercede; the last act of this drama was issuance of the deed Feb. 17, 1848. Another kind of claim was that of John Owens who wrote from Emily Feb. 8, 1848, saying that Mr. Hall had awarded him damages £37/10 for flooding due to the raising of Pigeon Lake waters and that the amount was too little but he needed the money. "I and my family have suffered so much by sickness these six months past that dire necessity compels me to accept the offer." He also wanted to know what had been done with John Sullivan's claim at King's Wharf for losses due to rising water in the area.

Sheriff's sales of settlers' property to satisfy taxes, fees, debts and judgments were held after official notices had been printed, mostly for Emily at Cotnam's Mills (the family officially changed their name from Cotnam to Cottingham by 1840). For more serious cases, that could not be handled

Settlement Patterns in Emily Township 1819-1838 (H. T. Pammett)

R—Lots given to Robinson settlers 1825 (with some trading of lots, grants to sons etc.)
L—Location tickets given to settlers for 50 or 100 acre lots, 1819-25 (with a few of 200 acres)
C—Crown Land sales by Canada Company &c. 1827-38 (some bought by former settlers)
x—marks Crown and Clergy Reserves—church glebes marked by cross (Anglican on con. 4 and Roman Catholic on con. 10)
(Some early roads are marked, and Cottingham's Mills or Metcalfe Village;
D.C.—Downey's Cross; **K.W.**—King's Wharf; **C.B.**—Cowan's Bridge; **F.C.**—Fowler's Corners)

by local justices of the peace, prisoners and defendants had to go before a Circuit Court held at Cobourg. Sheriff's sales at Cotnam's Mills were advertised for Feb. 7, 1834 and Feb. 4, 1836. On Apr. 20, 1839, Chris. Knowlson against John Sanderson re the southwest quarter of Lot 1, Con. 4, Emily; July 14, 1839: T. Benson against Robt. Sheppart deceased re quarter acre in Williamstown and other property of deceased; Sept. 5, 1840: H. Smith against Edmond Dwyer re north half Lot 12, Con. 10 and west half Lot 10, Con. 11, Emily. When the new Colborne District was organized, with Peterborough as its centre, the Colborne Sheriff, W. S. Conger, carried on: August 24, 1844: James McCutcheon against Hugh Collum re north half Lot 2, Con. 2, Emily "which property together with all buildings and erections thereon I shall offer for sale"; Dec. 7, 1844: James McCutcheon against Bart. Kenaly re Lot 1, Con. 11; April 2, 1845: John Carrall against Adam Shouldis the elder and sons Samuel, William and George re north half of Lot 23, Con. 4, Emily; Aug. 14, 1845: John Hartnet against Bart. Pieket (or Pickel) re west half Lot 5, Con. 11, Emily. Sheriff Conger only differed in preferring to hold most such lawsuits and sales at the new courthouse in Peterborough.

Water navigation continued to be very important in the Emily area throughout the pioneer period. A. McDonell, government land agent at Peterborough (who was aided by Charles Rubidge as immigration agent in the thirties) continued to bring thousands of incoming settlers for Emily and Ops up the Otonabee to Peterborough, by wagon to Mud (Chemong) Lake, by government scow around and up Pigeon River to King's Wharf or Cotnam's Landing, and on by bush-road to their lots. Dozens of petitions were sent from Newcastle District urging improvement of Trent waterway navigation (some with Emily signatures), and the government made a beginning 1832-7 with the Baird survey, the building of Bobcaygeon lock and dam and some other work—unfortunately during the Mackenzie rebellion 1837-38, the diversion of attention to the Welland Canal and the rising speculation in plank roads and iron railways persuaded the government to drop the Trent waterway for fifty years. As Anne Langton noted in her Journal in 1841: "(Governor) Lord Sydenham . . . does not patronize water communication, expecting railways to supersede everything." Among projects dropped were, unfortunately, "expending a sum of money on Pigeon River in removing temporary obstructions from its mouth to Cotnam's Mills in township of Emily", as well as improving the Peterborough-Chemong road, building a lock at Purdy's Mills, etc.

The same Kingston *Chronicle* that is quoted above (Feb. 1834) stated in August 1833 that "the steamboat 'Sturgeon' is now receiving her Engine at the village of Bridgenorth" and would ply the waters around as far as Fenelon and Purdy's Mills (Lindsay). The account continued: "The 'Sturgeon' will also during the high waters occasionally descend Pigeon River through the heart of the well-settled township of Emily as far as Norman's Mills [sic], stopping at the King's Wharf, Russel's Wharf and Baldwin's Mills." The 'Sturgeon' was launched the next month, a little scow-like craft that could steam 6 or 7 knots an hour; it puffed its way up Chemong Lake to the amazement of the Indians, "who cried 'Shemong! Shemong! (Canoe! Canoe!)' with repeated discharges of firearms". There is no record that the steamer did sail up the meandering swampy Pigeon River, especially after mill-dams were built along it to hold back water and impede the passing of all boats except the light canoes and punts of Indians and settlers. Bethune of Port Hope, who built both the 'Sturgeon' and the Bridgenorth village site, went bankrupt about 1840.

The accompanying table indicates how difficult it is to get an accurate picture of pioneer mills, shops and other enterprises in Emily.[5] By 1840 gristmills were being assessed at £150 each (additional for more than one pair of stones), sawmills at £100 (additional for more than one saw) and merchant shops at £200 each, which made business very risky when money was scarce, crops uncertain, water-levels fluctuating and trade often unprofitable.

Emily	Gristmills	Sawmills	Merchants' Shops	Distilleries
1832	1	1	1	0
1833-4	2	2	0	0
1835	2	2	3	0
1836	3	2	3	0
1837-8	3	2	3	0
1838-9	3	2	4	0
1840	1	1	4	0
1841	2	2	2	1
1842	2	2	2	1
1843	2	2	2	1
1844	3	2	2	1
1845	2	2	4	1
1846	1	1	5	1
1847	0	1	3	1
1851 (census)	1	2	—	1

The Montreal *Gazette,* advertising in August 1833 the launching of the 'Sturgeon' and the prospects for "uninterrupted steam navigation for 80 miles", also on Aug. 10 commented "Emily contains a population of 1,295 souls, principally Protestant Irish [on] excellent land. . . . There are 2 sawmills and 1 gristmill in the township." William Cotnam built grist and saw mills on his lot probably in 1831-2, beside Pigeon River, with a log dam packed with earth to hold back the floodwaters and provide an even flow for his "under-shot" waterwheel. The grist mill had one pair of stones which even by 1851 could grind only ten barrels of flour daily, and the sawmill had one rather awkward up-and-down saw, worked by waterpower. The second sawmill, assessed in 1833, was that of James Ivory, built near Cotnam's and "Evidently near the King Street bridge," according to Williamson's *Omemee.* Apparently Cotnam also had some interest in the first mill at the head of Chemong Lake, as mentioned in the last chapter.

Colonel Baldwin, who had planned the above-mentioned mill, acquired the reserved Government millsite on the south half of Lots 18 and 19, Con. 8, and by 1833 had a gristmill operating there. John Langton, writing in October 1833 in *Early Days in Upper Canada* said: "Purdy's mills have, I should imagine, the largest mill-dam in the world. It raises the water seven feet . . . destroys seven millsites and overflows 11,000 acres of land. Last year the dam gave way and the water was six months in running out, raising the waters of our lakes so high that for five weeks Col. Baldwin's Mills, 40 miles off by water (on Pigeon Creek in Twp. of Emily) were stopped from working. . . ." In a letter of Aug. 12, 1835, he added: "Emily is a much older settled township. . . . The land is fair and upon the whole it is a thriving township though some of the later settlers are yet but wretchedly off. It boasts of two mills, Cottenham's and Col. Baldwin's, both on Pigeon Creek, a village rising at the former, 2 or 3 pretty good taverns in different parts and a good road to Port Hope." But Baldwin the speculator found the profits insufficient—the *Toronto Patriot* of Jan. 7, 1840, carried an advertisement for the sale of his 300 acres, with his fine building including "an excellent saw and grist mill."[6] However, he was claiming flood damages for the mills a decade later.

It is possible that James Lawson bought the Baldwin Mills and moved them one concession south, since in 1839-40 he was assessed for saw and gristmills on Lot 18, Con. 7. Also in 1840 David Best was reported to have a sawmill on Lot 12, Con. 1, which may have been used only occasionally. The drop in assessed mills in 1840 and 1846-7 may have been due to the twin perils of flood and fire, which often put pioneer mills out of operation. An item in the Kingston *Chronicle,* May 31, 1845 (reprinted from the Peterborough *Chronicle)* noted: "FIRE: We regret to learn that the Carding and Fulling Mill of Mr. Richard Lambert, Emily, was accidentally destroyed by fire on Sunday morning about 2 a.m. Mr. L. had just returned from the States with some new cards, which were to have been in full operation yesterday, but which, with every item belonging to the concern, were reduced to ashes. Our correspondent also informs us that it was with some difficulty that the adjoining grist-mill of W. Cottingham, Esquire, which was full of grain, was saved." Lambert's mill was probably not rebuilt, as the 1851 Census listed only saw and grist-mills in Emily. Curiously enough, Sandford Fleming's map of Colborne District, drawn in 1848, showed 11 mills in Cavan and no schools, while for Emily it showed not one mill, but recorded 13 schools! But numerous pioneer industries flourished (in leanto or outbuilding) without being assessed or recorded—blacksmiths, coopers, asheries, carpenters, tanners, ironworkers, wagonmakers, etc.—incidentally, the distillery assessed from 1841 on was probably the anonymous one mentioned in Williamson's *Omemee,* on Distillery Creek southwest of Omemee village; a foundry operated on the site a generation later. We have no reports on the potency of the beverage distilled there.

Cottingham waged an interesting legal fight for a decade after 1841 to get compensation from the Board of Works for losses sustained due to government works, mostly the dam at Buckhorn: "The Buckhorn dam is

what backs us up . . . there is no way of letting the water off." By contrast,
the Bobcaygeon works caused no problem and raised the lakes only 8 inches.
"There is scarcely any fall from my tail-race to Buckhorn water . . . indeed
all the bridges and swamps and in many cases the roads in Emily, Ennismore
and Smithtown are wasted by the water raised by that one dam." In 1843 he
estimated his total loss for 4 years at £1,096/10, including 52 days the
mills were totally stopped; "the gristmill totally stopped or grinding only one
bushel per hour . . . the sawmill totally stopped that had done 2,000 feet per
day." An engineer surveyed the situation for the Board in August 1844 and
estimated damages at £679 including flooded lands around; after a flood of
correspondence Cottingham accepted the £679 sum. "I never would have
consented to take so small a sum as this if my circumstances was such as
would enable me to repair my Mills without it . . . it has destroyed the health
of this village and the surrounding settlements." He had two runs of stones
in his gristmill and was planning to put in a third with "a packer, cooker and
elevators," but had to give up his plans because of lack of waterpower. "The
wheels and pinions of first quality . . . the stones excelled in their kind one
pair being Burrs . . . a great quantity of castings, an excellent smut machine
all lie in the mill unused." His claims were backed by masses of statistics, a
testimonial signed by nearly 100 Emily settlers, another by James Cunningham, local schoolmaster, and one from Thomas Need, J.P., eminent Bobcaygeon millowner.

By 1850 Cottingham was also claiming £150 damages for his mill
privilege "at the head of Mud Lake. . . . I can prove it is a better mill
privilege than one that Col. Baldwin has in this township for which he claims
damages." He claimed he had helped build it, then had left it idle for a time,
and now wanted to build a mill on it. Again a flood of testimonials declared
that the mill "at the head of Mud Lake a little west of Lancaster's bridge . . .
the only Grist Mill we had in the township for several years" had been ruined
by the Buckhorn dam, "which took away the Bridge on the Publick highway
close to the Mill dam and stopped the publick from travelling that way for a
very long time." One letter of Dec. 14, 1850 by William Ivory asserted that
"he had the privilege of the Carding and Fulling Mill rented from William
Cottingham" in Metcalfe village, and that he estimated the damages at
Cottingham's Mills in Metcalfe were £1,000 and including his other properties more than £2,000. Among those backing Cottingham's claims were
Chris. Knowlson, J.P.; Dr. John Irons; Wm. Hilliard and Wm. Beatty,
merchants; John Goodliffe, carpenter; V. Matchett and Wm. Matchett and
Richard Everett, merchants; Wm. Ivory, clothier; David Harkness, innkeeper; Geo. Beatty, carpenter; Hiram Graham, millwright; Wm. Saunby,
miller; Thomas Bell, gent., and dozens of farmers. Cottingham's arguments
were consistent: "I have spent over £600 making alterations and my Metcalfe
gristmill grinds only 2 or 3 bushels an hour where it used to grind 8 bus.
. . . there being no mills nearer than Lindsay, Peterboro or Cavan. My other
mills, that is my sawmill, my carding and fulling mill, have of course been
injured in an equal degree with the Flowering mill." If he raised his mill-dam

We the undersigned hereby certify that in our candid opinion the mill privilege belonging to William Cottingham Esquire in the village of Metcalfe in this township would be worth over six thousand pounds cy, were it not injured by backwater and we are well assured that a great amount of damage has been done to the said mill privilege by the said backwater — We further state our conviction that the backwater has seriously injured the surrounding country inasmuch as the mills are thereby rendered incapable of performing all the milling required in the locality — though now grinding with three runs of burr stones — and as the amount of work required to be performed by the said mill is rapidly increasing the inconvenience will be more felt as other mills being in the neighbourhood

Emily 4 Oct 1850

Hiram Graham
Millwright —
George Bealty
Carpenter —
James Laidly Farmer
Arthur McQuade Farmer
Edwd Blackwell

John Goodliffe Carpenter

John Ross M.D
William Hilliar
Merchant
P. Matchett Merchant
William Matchett Merchant
Richard William Enett
Merchant
Thomas Bell Junr

William Bealty
Merchant

Petition from Emily 1850 re Flooding of Cottingham Mill Property at Metcalfe by Trent Works. (Trent Canal Papers, Public Archives of Canada)

even one foot it would flood many hundreds of acres of farmland upstream, and the stagnant waters would be unhealthy, as well as flooding the road from Peterborough to Lindsay. Such persistence certainly justified full compensation.[7]

As we have seen previously, land travel to and in Emily developed very slowly, because of its many hills, swamps and streams. Nearly every visitor and writer condemned the roads north of Lake Ontario as the worst feature of the district and travelled by boat wherever possible. Road clearances uncleared or grown wild, flooding creeks, and stumps left standing, made even the strongest oxcarts slow down to a few miles' travel in a full day. When money was granted for improving roads, gangs were hired to cut off trees, stumps and bushes, level off rough spots and fill holes with stones and logs, with log culverts to cross creeks and layers of logs in the worst swamps; but within a few months the roads were as bad as ever, especially in spring floods and rainy periods. Very little ditching, draining or grading was attempted, until after 1850, when crushed gravel was used to make main roads firmer and more durable. According to Simon Connell: "The many creeks that intersected the roads were crossed by log bridges; a crib of logs was built on each side and filled with stones, then several large cedar logs were laid across the stream with the ends resting on the stone-filled cribs. These were the beams for the bridge and were floored with logs flattened on the top and placed crossways on the beams. Most bridges had a bypass where in hot summer weather travellers could drive their horses down through the stream, give them a drink and wet the wheels of their vehicles, causing the wood to expand and thus tightening the iron tires."

In 1832 Huston was still working on the middle road into Emily between Lots 12 and 13. An Emily petition, signed by E. McGibbon and others, asked for money to build a road into the north concessions, to supplement the old settler trail from Downey's Cross to King's Wharf and north along the west shore of Pigeon Lake; again in 1833 petitions asked for a road from Concession 4 through Downey's Cross to Sturgeon Lake and Verulam, and for improvement of the road from Deyell's Mills in Cavan north into Emily. Adam Shouldis' letter of 1833 to Robinson talked of "the road from my house to Peterburra," along which so many new settlers trudged both ways; this was gradually improved, and in 1835 Huston was expending a grant of £50 to extend it from Williamstown into Ops to Purdy's Mills.[8] Due mainly to Robinson's influence, that year a total of £375 was granted for area roads (including the £50 above): £100 for a bridge near Col. Baldwin's Mills over Pigeon Creek, £50 to open a road north of Con. 3 between Lots 6 and 7, £75 for a road from the Emily-Smith border north to Pigeon Lake, £50 to improve the middle road through Cavan and £50 on a road from Con. 9, Monaghan, to the Emily-Smith boundary. The commissioners to spend these grants included Col. Baldwin, John Huston, David Armstrong, Sam. Cottingham, Thos. Mitchell, John McCall, John Thompson and R. Sillicoe.

But in 1836 the petitions continued: Wm. Cottingham and 125 others asked aid for a bridge over Pigeon River at Williamstown; John Darcus, J.P. and 29 others of northeast Emily asked road aid; Henry Hughes and 182 others of Emily asked road aid; Charles Knowlson and 130 others of Emily asked road aid; John McCall and 64 others asked that the Cavan-Emily boundary road be opened; Thomas Reed and 63 others of Emily, Verulam and Fenelon asked for a bridge over Emily Creek and a road north into Verulam. Due to unsettled times (and Robinson's death) most of these were ignored; but in 1838 the government noted that no accounting had yet been received for £75 spent in 1834 on the road from Cavan-Emily boundary north to Pigeon Lake, and in 1840 James Mitchell complained to Toronto that he had never been paid the balance due on his contract for building a Pigeon River bridge. With the Colborne District centred at Peterborough, the Peterboro-Metcalfe-Lindsay road became increasingly important, for both business and for incoming settlers looking at lands in Mariposa and Ops. John Davidson of Lindsay in 1846 was advertising in the Peterborough *Gazette:* "STAGE CONVEYANCE! New stage from Lindsay to Peterboro, Log House Inn, Lindsay whence it will leave every Monday and Friday at 9 a.m., and the Albert House, Peterboro, at same hour on Tuesdays and Saturdays." But in 1848 a report on the Peterborough-Lindsay road stated that while £250 had been appropriated, no work had been done yet to improve it. Again in 1849 a petition went from Emily, Ops and Verulam urging erection of a bridge across Pigeon River in north Emily. But little was done to improve road travel until county and township administrations took control, levying local taxes for such local improvements.

After getting licenses at Port Hope, the peddlers continued to pack their goods into Emily and neighbouring townships in the thirties—on foot Wm. Maddell, John Tate, Robert Sheppard, Alfred Carpenter, John Clagg, Samuel Fowles; on horseback C. W. Bonny. Then in May 1837 B. Bletcher of Port Hope began running daily stages north to Bewdley to meet the steamer which plied up to Peterborough; he also had waggons "to convey families, baggage and merchandise" on regular service by road through Cavan and Monaghan to Peterborough; his agent in Emily was Christopher Knowlson. Samuel Cottingham had an inn license at Williamstown in 1836. When David Armstrong in February, 1837, requested renewal of his inn license, his testimonial from Huston and Knowlson said "he has kept an Inn there (in Emily) for a number of years and we have never heard of any complaints against him with regard to accommodation for travellers and believe he keeps an orderly house" (this was renewed again in 1838). Similarly, Thomas Dixon on Lot 11, Con. 4, Emily, in March, 1837, requested renewal of his license "to keep a public Inn and house of entertainment" (and again in 1838 supported by testimonial signed by four Justices of the Peace). In January, 1838, Thomas Mitchell of Williamstown village applied for a license "to keep a public Inn and house of entertainment". Along with the applications above, in the Huston papers, are copies of the licenses granted for 1838 to Thomas Mitchell and David Armstrong, costing £10 each, on condition that each "shall not suffer or use any unlawful games within his house and shall keep good order, and observe all such rules and regulations . . . for the observance of innkeepers". Yet in March 1846 the Peterborough *Gazette* stated that of 20 inn licenses in the new Colborne District, only one was in Emily (at Metcalfe), and there was not one license to sell beer and ale in Emily. The same paper in December 1846 advertised a "new stage conveyance" to operate twice a week from Lindsay to Peterborough and return, via Metcalfe village.

From April, 1842, Wm. Weller of Cobourg was operating daily stage coaches Cobourg to Peterborough and return, via the Cavan-Monaghan boundary road, and a scheme was promoted to build a toll-paying plank road from Cobourg to Peterborough. A Legislative Committee heard evidence on the scheme, including the fact that since 1820 nearly £1,000 had been spent on roads north toward Emily, Smith and Monaghan. E. Fowke and M. Whitehead of Port Hope agreed that the people in Durham rear townships were opposed to a toll road: "Emily and Cavan have the largest population of the rear townships and about 19 in 20 favor the old route . . . the new road would not accommodate them as well as the old road to Port Hope." George Hughes of Emily said: "The general feeling where I reside is alarm at the large outlay . . . and heavy tolls which would necessarily be demanded. . . . Signers of the petition in rear townships are strongly in favor of the old route. . . ." These opponents preferred an extended road as far as Bobcaygeon to service a Durham County population of 11,083, rather than one which would chiefly benefit the Northumberland population of 4,208. In turn, the Port Hope promoters began scheming a toll road of plank from that town to Bewdley; in 1848 they were trying to form a joint stock company to make a plank road along the Middle Line Road through Cavan. In 1849 the project grew into "a gravel or plank road to Millbrook and extended through mid-Cavan to Metcalfe in Emily," capital £15,000 in 3,000 shares of £5 each. Perhaps it is as well that the scheme was stillborn, as it would never have been profitable—even though it would have been ideal for Emily's first "pleasure waggon" assessed from 1845 on at £15!

Even earlier, in July 1832, Port Hope promoters were applying for a permit to construct a railroad from that town to Bewdley on Rice Lake. By 1847 this had grown into the "Peterboro & Port Hope Railway" whose Engineer's Report, Aug. 28, 1847, is worth noting. The cost was estimated at £57,936/12/3 with many optimistic statistics about the possible profit; but of special interest is a map showing a "practicable line of railway to Lakes Simcoe and Huron" from Peterborough, cutting across Emily from the end of Chemong Lake to Con. 8 in the west. This extension line will also be found on Fleming's 1848 map. The Port Hope *Advertiser* of Nov. 13, 1847, reported, "A public meeting in the village of Metcalfe, township Emily, on Nov. 4 which passed a resolution in support of the Peterboro & Port Hope Railway, urging the duty of farmers to take shares in the railway". For various reasons, mostly lack of local subsidies, the railway when built a decade later did not pass through Emily or Peterborough, but it is interesting to conjecture how differently the township might have developed if it had. For years the possibility was strong, as seen by an order of Feb. 1, 1854, from the Secretary of the Peterboro & Port Hope Railway Company, to pay £37, 10s. to Thomas Rowan "for right-of-way on the north half Lot No. 2, 1st concession, Emily," which shows that a route farther south was also under consideration.

Through the 1820s and 1830s Cavan and Emily were firmly attached to the Family Compact government, through the Robinsons, through Port Hope financiers like George Boulton, and the local officials like Huston and Knowlson. They led the Cavan-Emily militia, and there were even attempts to march the men to Port Hope under their officers to vote in crucial elections like that of 1836, as well as a flurry of government activity to get all possible land deeds sent to settlers in time for them to vote. Opposition to the Government clique was mostly in towns, led by such men as Fothergill, Gilchrist and Hall. Governor Sir John Colborne in 1834 visited the district, circling around Emily from Cavan to Peterborough to Chemong and Curve Lakes and up to Buckhorn, Bobcaygeon and Fenelon. He observed the waterway construction at the Otonabee, Bobcaygeon and Buckhorn, before returning through the eastern townships to Rice Lake. He encouraged high hopes in the district for rapid development of the Trent-Simcoe waterway. One result was an 1835 petition signed by nearly 1,000 in the rear townships (including Emily) asking establishment of a separate district centred on Peterborough. A second result we have seen—some government money that year for roads and bridges (totalling £2,350 in the district, including £375 for Emily), but a flood of petitions in 1836 for road aid met with little response from the new administration of Governor Head.

The First Emily Post Office was set up August 6, 1836, at Williamstown, probably in the store of Josias L. Hughes, though he was not appointed postmaster until Jan. 30, 1838; his sureties for £200 were Wm. Cottingham and George Dixon. For the year ending July 31, 1838, the revenues of the office grossed £23/4, with net £18/1/4, about the same as the new Lindsay Post Office, but only half that of Cavan. Obviously few people in Emily wrote letters and received even fewer (since postage was paid on receipt of mail). As a result, Hughes' salary, with commissions, was £5/13 in the year to July 31, 1840, and two years later was only up to £7/5.[9] Probably Robert Grandy, who was clerk in Hughes' store from 1838, did the postal work. Mail was brought by horseback up to Cavan and Emily weekly, and later more often; with it came Port Hope, Cobourg and even Toronto papers, published weekly. Unfortunately, the Hughes family were fond of speculation—Josias was buying and selling land, and Thomas was listed in 1838 as the only district stockholder in the Toronto Farmers' Joint Stock Company. Thus in the Peterborough *Gazette* of Aug. 15, 1846, appeared: "IN BANKRUPTCY: Josias Hughes of township of Emily, Colborne District, merchant . . . first meeting of creditors at Courthouse, Peterborough 26th August at 11 a.m. W. S. Conger, Sheriff." When Hughes left town, Robert Grandy took over as postmaster. Oddly enough, another notice was appearing in the same Peterborough newspaper that summer: "NOTICE: All persons are hereby cautioned not to purchase or give value for two notes of hand drawn by me in favour of Mr. Wm. Cottingham of Emily, each of the sum of £23 2s. 6d., falling due respectively on 29th July and 29th October next, as I shall not pay the sums, having received no value for them. Wm. Mepsted, Ops." Hughes and Cottingham were the Emily representatives on the first Colborne District Council, in 1841!

Most of our information about the 2nd Durham Militia Battalion (Cavan and Emily) comes from the John Huston papers, as he was battalion adjutant. In May 1832 he was ordered to gather at Hutchinson's Inn in Cavan on June 4 at 10 a.m., "all men under 60 years", with fines for those who did not appear. The men over 40 were called out specially to form two new companies for whom the government would give arms, and Huston was asked to nominate someone as captain of the new Emily Company. In September, 1835, Huston was ordered to assemble the Cavan militia on October 26, and the Emily men October 27, at 10 a.m. "armed and equipped as the law directs for training at Williamstown in Emily." A paylist prepared by Huston is headed "Captain William Cottingham's Company who marched from Emily toward Toronto to quell the rebels until countermanded by express from H.E. the Lt. Governor on duty from 7th December 1837;" this gives the officers: Capt. Wm. Cottingham, Lt. Samuel Cottingham, Ensign Henry Argue, Sgt. John Sullivan, Sgt. Daniel Sheehan, Henry Tims, Charles Hamilton and Bugler John McMullin; unfortunately the only men listed are some Ops volunteers, not the Emily Company. Then January 9, 1838, Huston ordered Capt. Thomas Mitchell, Williamstown, Emily, to form a volunteer company "to take the command of them as their Captain and with them this day march for Toronto."[10]

The Mackenzie rebellion scare was soon over, but later in 1838 there were threats of raids from the United States plotted by Mackenzie. Nov. 9, 1838, Huston was ordered to assemble his Cavan and Emily Companies, "from 16 to 60 years of age . . . with Government arms and accoutrements," the Emily division at Williamstown on Nov. 29, where Col. Boulton would attend. Capt. Elliott in Cavan and Capt. Cottingham in Emily were each authorized to raise a company of 100 volunteers from the militiamen, each with two lieutenants, one ensign and three sergeants. These volunteers were to be prepared to march to the lakefront or to Toronto when required. The Cobourg *Star* said (Dec. 11): "Major Elliot marched into Cobourg on Saturday last with near 100 fine fellows from Cavan, volunteers for 6 months, to be stationed here. Another hundred are expected shortly (from Emily)." The Peterborough *Sentinel* ten days later said, "Thomas Murphy of Ops marched into town the other day at the head of a remarkably fine body of Robinson's emigrants who had volunteered under his command from Emily." Huston in April, 1839, in a letter to the Lt.-Governor, General Arthur, took credit for raising the 90 volunteers in Cavan and Emily, and asked that they be kept on strength for 18 months instead of 6 months. In a militia reorganization of July, 1839, new regiments were to be organized, and Emily and Ops militia were placed under Lt.-Col. John Logie (formerly of the Royal Marines) of Ops Township. And as a humorous ending, James Magee of Emily made an affidavit Feb. 24, 1840, swearing that he had gone to Cobourg with Huston's Durham Volunteers, had left his "musquet" with William Reed there when going home on furlough, and "after the Durham Volunteers had been disembodied, he, the deponant, received from said Wm. Reed a musquet but not the one first given him." We shall never know whether Mr. Magee finally got his own musket back again.

The Act establishing the Colborne District, with Peterborough for the district town, was adopted in the Legislature in March 1837; it separated 18 townships plus the rear seven concessions of Monaghan from Newcastle District; Emily, Ops, Verulam, Fenelon, Mariposa, Eldon, Bexley and Sommerville were included, but not Cavan. The significance for Emily was that it was to be administered from Peterborough, after two decades of rule from Port Hope and Cobourg. The Act was approved May 31, 1839, and there was some opposition; the Peterborough *Sentinel* in September 1839 criticized political frauds over road and bridge contracts in the area and said mysteriously: "Look at the Emily Job!!" But finally on October 14, 1841, the Act was proclaimed as in effect. In January, 1842, the Government decided to inaugurate local township administrations for township business such as roads, schools and licensing, paid for by levying local taxes. By township meeting three Wardens were elected: Jos. L. Hughes, postmaster; Wm. Cottingham and Dennis Hullihan, of whom the first two were also township representatives on the District Council. Chris. Knowlson was first Township Clerk, Hugh Collum was Collector and James English elected Assessor. The meeting also elected pathmasters and poundkeepers, and the council was empowered to pass simple bylaws on local matters. Kirkconnell and Williamson repeat the statement (in the 1881 *Atlas*) that the township accounts for the period 1843-9 showed total expenditures of £8 currency, which if true means that all officials served without pay and no money spent on roads and bridges. The Kingston *Herald* on June 13, 1843, carried a glowing article on the Colborne District, with its "beautiful lakes", its growing capital, Peterborough, with 2,000 inhabitants, fine public building, "the best Court House and Gaol in Canada, a stone Episcopal Church, a large stone Catholic chapel, a Church of Scotland Meeting House, two Methodist chapels. . . ." The population of 16,000 spread over 18 townships were said to have a promising future, with fertile crop lands and a most promising timber trade, and the article ended "large quantities of choice land are still for sale here, by Government and by private individuals."

When the Reform government called an election in 1844, a bitter contest ensued over the implementation of Lord Durham's proposals for responsible government. In Durham County, the Reform candidate was J. Smith and the Tory candidate J. Williams. The Toronto *Examiner* of April 17, 1844, reported a meeting of reformers in Emily on March 25 to form a Reform Association Branch and to endorse the movement to responsible government in Canada. John Lane was Chairman, P. Ryan, secretary, and the movers of resolutions were J. Dwyer, D. Paquette, M. Lehane, Michael Collins, David Owen, Mr. Connell and D. Houlihan.[11] In October, however, the Tory candidate Williams won by a large majority, and at a victory dinner in Port Hope "David Smart of Port Hope officiated as President and George Hughes of Emily as Vice-President. . . ." Perhaps this reconciled the Emily Reformers to their inclusion in the Colborne District, particularly as the Government promptly (Feb. 1845) redefined the electoral ridings, placing Emily and other rear townships in a new Peterborough Riding with other townships of the Colborne District. Another Act in March, 1849, transformed the Colborne District into the United Counties of Peterborough and Victoria; Victoria was to include the townships of Emily, Mariposa, Ops, Ennismore, Eldon, Fenelon, Bexley, Verulam and Somerville—Ennismore was later moved into Peterborough County. Emily was second in population and prosperity among the Victoria townships. Finally, in March 1850, an application was made to the Legislature for a bill to form a new township out of the four rear concessions of Emily Township, and the part of Verulam Township south of Sturgeon Lake, and the part of Harvey Township west of Pigeon Lake—this intriguing scheme was obviously not successful, but it indicated local discontent.

Government journals provide a clearer picture of early Emily schools than local legend. In 1832 two teachers received government grants: T. Mitchell and George Hamilton, each with 21 pupils. In 1833-4 teachers given grants were: George Hamilton (24 pupils), Stewart Pogue (21), William Hall (20), Joseph Cunningham (20), and James McClatchley (20)—they taught reading, writing and arithmetic, using the Testament, a speller and an English reader. By 1835 there were nine teachers receiving grants, all born in Ireland: William Hall (23 pupils), Robert Wade (39), Thomas Donihue (21), George Hamilton (34), John Dwyer (26), Robert Brown (27), Michael Buck (26), Richard Sullivan (28) and Pat Baragy (27)—251 pupils, who were taught mostly in homes, in addition to a few who went to town or Cavan schools; plus some for advanced learning in Grammar Schools at Cobourg and Peterborough. For example, John Dwyer taught in his log cabin on Lot 8, Con. 14, in Millersmith community. We have noted other early settlers who had teaching experience, who may have taught their own and neighbouring children, and doubtless some mothers started their children in simple spelling, reading, writing and figuring, when isolated from schools.

The *Victoria Atlas,* 1881, stated briefly that the first school was built about 1835 on a corner in Williamstown, later occupied by Bradburn's Hotel, and that among the earliest teachers were James Laidley and Captain Handcock. This story was repeated by Kirkconnell and others later. Williamson in his *Omemee* found it hard to reconcile the reminiscences of Omemee "old-timers" who each claimed to have studied in the first Victoria County school—one in a log school taught by James Laidley on the site of the United Church manse, another in a log shanty on the "Glebe lot", perhaps east of Crawford's Hill, and again in a log house built about 1840 on Queen Street. The most factual accounts were printed by J. C. Hodgins, long-time Department of Education official, after gathering massive data from files and school officials and teachers, in *Documentary History of Education in Upper Canada,* 1894 and *Establishment of Schools in Ontario,* 1910.[12] The first account by a teacher stated explicitly: "The first Public School opened in what is now the County of Victoria was opened in Township Emily on the S.E. corner of Lot 10, Con. 3, then known as the Clergy Reserve Lot . . . an old log shanty about 20 by 12 feet covered with elm bark, a flat roof, it had neither window, floor or fireplace or stove. The school was opened in June 1834 and lasted 3 or 4 months until the days got too cold for the pupils to sit without a fire. The teacher . . . was an old British soldier named Hamilton . . . he drifted to Emily where he took up the land granted him as a discharged soldier . . . he was engaged to teach . . . at the rate of $8 a month." The second section began: "The next school in that neighbourhood was taught in the village then known as Williamstown, now Omemee. The teacher was Mr. William Bamford, son of a retired Methodist preacher. . . . The School was opened late in the Fall and was kept open 6 months. The House was the Barroom of an old Tavern . . . the school opened in 1835 and continued in operation until the spring of 1836 . . . The next school in Omemee was taught by another old ex-British officer, Captain Handcock . . . also in the barroom of an unused Tavern belonging to a member of the same family of 'Cotnum'. . . . This school lasted until 1837. The next school in the village was held in a 1-story frame building . . . the teacher also an old soldier . . . his name was John Henderson . . . called 'Uncle Johnnie' by everyone. . . ." In his second book, Hodgins added another account: "In the year 1837 Mr. Geo. Hughes settled in Omemee and opened a school for his grandchildren, the sons of J. L. Hughes and Wm. Cottingham and other pupils, and he taught until the year 1843 . . . soon after a log school house was built on what was called the Distillery Road, and a man named Captain Handcock, who had been in the Army, became Master of the School. After a time Mr. R. Grandy (father of the present Richard Grandy postmaster at Omemee) was chosen to succeed Captain Handcock, and for many years taught the public school. . . ." Because of their interest, these accounts are given in full in an Appendix.

In the 1838 Journals, only five teachers are listed, four born in Ireland: H. Heaney, William Huggins, Patrick Maloney and William Bamford (the last aged 19); the fifth teacher was Matthew Handcock, born in England— the number of pupils was not given. Then in 1839 the list contained six: P. Mallon (21 pupils); William Branford (or (Bamford) (25); H. J. Heaney (28); William Higgins (22); John Henderson (29); Matthew Handcock (28). Each teacher was granted £8 government aid, plus whatever fees the parents would pay; they used Murray's English Reader and English Grammar, Mavor's Speller, Walkingame's Arithmetic, and Goldsmith's Geography. Then in 1844 Dr. Egerton Ryerson was appointed Superintendent of Education in Canada West, and began a complete reorganization of the educational system, starting the training of teachers, setting up a standard curriculum and text-books, etc. The Journals report that in 1844 Emily had six schools, open on the average 5½ months a year, with 217 pupils attending out of 817 children of the age 5 to 16 years; the Emily schools were visited 21 times by the district superintendent, Dr. Burnham of Peterborough, who complained bitterly of the enormous distances he had to travel on his duties; he graded the Emily schools as "good"; the teachers were paid a total of £113/8/6. With the Ryerson regulations (including compulsory schooling) becoming effective the improvement is noticeable in the year Aug. 1845 to Aug. 1846: Emily School sections 16, number of schools open 11, average time open 9 months, children taught 480, children of school age in township 943, total paid teachers £132/3, visits by school superintendents in year 26. The Peterborough *Gazette* in Feb. 1846 had an advertisement for the first time: "Wanted a competent teacher in Emily—liberal salary paid."

By 1847, the government report showed in Emily 14½ school sections, with 11 schools in operation; of 1,061 children of school age, 548 were at school, plus 70 pupils over 16 years of age. The schools were open 8 months and the teachers were paid £413/10, an average annual salary per teacher £37/12/6; the legislative school grant was only £90/2/5 of this.[13] The 1850 school figures are much the same: 1,078 children of school age, and 527 attending school (286 boys, 241 girls). All 13 of the schools were of log, and all one-room; 8 were in good repair with suitable desks; but only one school had a privy. One school was new in 1848 and another in 1850. The schools now were heated in winter, and even a few in the township had maps and globes; slates and exercise books were coming in, with lead pencils and some homemade quill-pens for use with homemade ink (or ink bought in stone crocks from the pharmacist). But today's children would shudder at the pioneer hardships of school in those days.

We have few clues to the level of general learning and culture in the backwoods townships of Colborne District in pioneer days. No newspapers were published in Emily, but no doubt some families subscribed to Toronto, Port Hope, Cobourg and Peterborough weeklies, and passed them around or read them aloud in neighborhood gatherings, especially in times of crisis. For lack of news early newspapers printed serially whole books by Scott, Dickens, Disraeli and others; they also imported books and gave them to new subscribers or sold them cheaply to readers. Mechanics' Institute libraries started in Port Hope and Cobourg in the forties, and in Peterborough soon after 1850; and some literary clubs circulated books, though there were no public libraries. Professional men and "gentry" settlers often had a few volumes on their shelves. Later some religious denominations promoted church magazines to fill the need for inspirational reading, and farm organizations started weeklies and monthlies for their members, but these were apt to be specialized. There were few glass windows in pioneer homes, and no coal-oil lamps until the 1860s—thus on long winter evenings reading was difficult by the light of the fireplace, or homemade lard lamps and candles. One interesting fact illustrates the cultural level and reading habits of district towns and townships—the list of subscribers to the *Victoria Magazine,* founded by Susanna Moodie in Belleville (she was formerly in Douro), which flourished briefly 1847-8—the magazine had 18 subscribers in Peterborough town, 3 in Otonabee, 1 in Ops, 3 in Cavan, and 12 in Emily—"Geo. Beatty, Ebenezer Moore, Henry Finch, H. Jones, Mr. Galbraith, Mr. English, Miss Jones, Miss

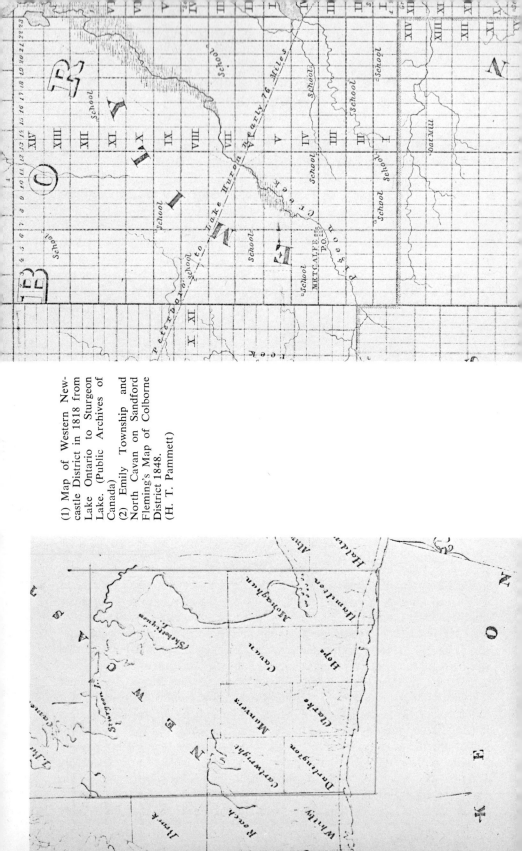

(1) Map of Western Newcastle District in 1818 from Lake Ontario to Sturgeon Lake. (Public Archives of Canada)
(2) Emily Township and North Cavan on Sandford Fleming's Map of Colborne District 1848.
(H. T. Pammett)

Jane Ladley, Robt. Grandy, C. Knowlson, Mrs. Henry Hate, and Mrs. Wm. Cottinhard" (this was doubtless Mrs. Wm. Cottingham).[14]

Church publications help to give us insight into religious developments in Emily, including the Cobourg *Church* weekly (of the Church of England), whose Emily agent was postmaster J. Hughes. It is the fashion in some modern sociological writing to denigrate the clergy of the established churches, allegedly full of class prejudices from the British Isles and alien to rough back-woods society, and to conclude that they therefore neglected the pioneer settlers and left them to evangelical circuit-riders, often from the United States, with their emotional revivals and demagogic camp meeting pyrotech-nics. The actual situation in Emily does not substantiate this thesis, as we shall see.

The task was immensely difficult, as Strickland, Stewart, Langton and others pointed out in their books—there were only two or three Anglican clergy to look after their people in 18 or 20 townships. Bishop McDonell had the same problem when he sought more government aid for his Roman Catholic flock in the region. Lack of money, bad roads, and settlers scattered thinly, miles apart in some areas, made it necessary to defer church-building and hold services in any large log building where a clergyman could gather a few people together. Some of these buildings were used by all denominations, such as the one on the Henderson farm, later called the Middle Line Church, and Robinson's supply depot at Williamstown where Cottingham later started a store. The Anglican clergy in Peterborough and Cavan, and other local clergy were endowed with lots to help finance churches; and Rev. J. Crowley, Roman Catholic priest, was in 1827 given lots in 4 townships (including Lot 5, Con. 10, Emily) for the same purpose, as well as a lot in Peterborough. The Clergy Reserves were meant to provide funds for construction of churches and payment of ministers, at first for the Church of England, but later broadened to aid all established churches. Some Reserves were sold or rented after 1832, but the sharing of the proceeds caused much conflict, until the Clergy Reserves were secularized in 1854, the proceeds to be used for education. Since the Clergy Reserves were $\frac{1}{7}$ of surveyed land widely scattered, they totalled about 9,000 acres in Emily, of which 2,000 acres were being offered for sale in 1850.

Rev. Samuel Armour, when he moved from Peterborough to Cavan in 1832, laboured to cover a broad parish stretching north to the lakes and west to Scugog and Mariposa, aided by the retired Rev. Thompson (who died in 1844). Anglican services were held in Williamstown in a log school on Sturgeon Street, until in 1835 a parish committee started a frame church at the north end of Division Street, amid a burying-ground used for 40 years. Though Rev. Armour continued his tours, church funds in 1837 financed a Travelling Missionary, Rev. Chas. Wade, who recorded on his first visit to Emily in November preaching in a log school on the 2nd concession, and later in Williamstown to a congregation upwards of 100 persons. Two years later he was succeeded by Rev. George Street, whose journals like Rev. Wade's were printed in the *Church* weekly.[15] Rev. Street rode a black horse "on whose back I made many weary pilgrimages through Emily on my way to the back lakes." In July he preached to about 250 persons in a school, with the overflow crowd seated outside the windows, and added, "A good frame for a church has been erecting and nearly roofed"—this was St. John's Church on Concession 2, completed in 1840. He also encouraged the building committee in Williamstown, led by W. Cottingham and J. Hughes, who finished the frame of Christ Church there in 1840.

The *Church* stated in Nov. 1839: "We trust that before many months a resident minister will be appointed to Emily—where the Church population is very numerous [and] a neat sacred edifice in the course of completion. . . ." The weekly that year optimistically claimed 803 Anglicans in Emily, but in fact the District Census showed 784 in 1839, down to 714 in 1840 and up to 770 in 1841 (when the population was 1,851). Bishop Strachan visited Cavan and Peterborough in July 1840, and no doubt was briefed on Emily, for church funds were allocated and Rev. Street stationed there as Missionary, and then as Rector, serving the two Emily churches and also Ops Township. He came with his bride to a cottage near Cottingham's millpond, and in the 15 months he spent in the parish, started a Sunday School with about 40 children, baptized 93 persons and performed ten marriages. Though his own parishioners were "almost to a man staunch Protestants and Orangemen," he discouraged religious feuding and Orange Parades and "stirring up bad blood." Decades later he recounted how he had travelled through the bush a dozen miles to "a large Roman Catholic settlement" on school business, where he met Rev. Father Fitzpatrick, "the good-natured priest", whose "ready Irish wit" at the parents' meeting in a cow-house brought success in getting a school organized. He wanted to build a log house on the glebe lot (Lot 10, Con. 4) which might later be the kitchen for a parsonage, but Bishop Strachan disapproved.[16]

After a short interval, in Sept. 1841 the Bishop arranged for Rev. William Shaw, just graduating at the Cobourg College, to replace Street, and instructed Shaw "to go to Emily to get acquainted with your people." In 1842 the Church Society formed a Newcastle-Colborne branch, whose committee included from Emily Rev. Shaw, the two church wardens, plus George Hughes, Richard Marmion and Gerard Patterson. Rev. Shaw returned to England in 1845 for his health, and was succeeded in Emily by Rev. Robert Harding, "lately Travelling Missionary in Newcastle and Colborne Districts" who was ordained at Toronto in October; he remained in Emily for 12 years, and was very popular there. A new stone rectory was built in 1843 just east of Williamstown, on Crawford's Hill. On Lot 22, Con. 6, the Boate family in 1845 donated a site for a church and burial ground on which a squared timber church 36' by 30' was built in 1845, consecrated as St. James Church, with a driving-shed on the southeast corner. With Christ Church, Metcalfe, and St. John's Church, it formed the parish of Emily, which by 1851, according to the Census, consisted of 1,094 persons.

The Roman Catholics were the next largest group, increasing from 387 in the 1839 census, to 639 in 1841, and up to 1,044 in the 1851 census; of those who entered Emily after the Irish famine 1846-9, a majority were

Roman Catholics who settled mostly in the north concessions. The Canada Company gave Rev. J. Crowley of Peterborough the deed for the south half of Lot 5, Con. 10, for the sum of £25 in 1830 and this glebe was transferred some years later, after he left the area, to the Roman Catholic Church. In 1835 Father Hugh Fitzpatrick had a log church built on the lot, which was blessed by the Bishop and given the name St. Luke's, near Downey's Cross (the later Downeyville). Father John Butler, who served in Peterborough for 19 years before his death in 1853, came to Emily regularly for services, including baptisms, marriages and burials, aided occasionally by Father Fitzpatrick, appointed to Lindsay parish in 1840. It is recorded that he built a little "log priest's house" at Downey's Cross about 1841. The Roman Catholics of course often visited the lovely stone St. Peter's Church built in 1837-8 after the first small frame church in Peterborough burnt down, or went to the log church built in Lindsay in 1841; but not until Father John Bourke came to Downeyville in 1852 did they have their own parish priest to help them plan for the future. Father Bourke held services at King's Wharf and Ennismore also.

The Presbyterians of Emily totalled 121 in 1839, 230 in 1841, and 261 in 1851, and they found it difficult, therefore, to built a church. Yet, like the Anglicans, they were credited with three churches in the 1851 Census, while the Roman Catholics and Methodists had one each. The first Presbyterian congregation was led by the two David Bests (from County Armagh, Ireland) who worshipped during the 1820s in a small log school at the southwest corner of Concession 2 and the Middle Road, where the Emily Presbyterian Cemetery still is. David Best donated ten acres where by 1830 a log house was built for visiting preachers like Rev. Douglas, Lawrence and Cassiday, who served other congregations in Cavan, Ops and west Emily. The first actual church is said to have been erected in 1835 on a lot donated by William Thornton about two miles west of Williamstown, near the Ops boundary, though this also was used as a school on weekdays. When Rev. Douglas accepted a charge in Centreville, Cavan, he continued to visit Emily, as did Rev. John Roger of the Church of Scotland congregation in Peterborough, whose St. Andrew's Church there, built of stone in 1836, was used by Presbyterians of east Emily. The Emily charge (including Ops) was also served through the 1830s by clergy from Whitby and Port Hope. As Williamson says, "Their Sabbath services depended on visits by neighbouring ministers, and their religious life was developed by family worship, and meetings for social worship and fellowship under the supervision of Elders." In Sept. 1842, Rev. James Dick of Edinburgh became pastor, residing on the Best glebe-lot and serving all Emily and Ops congregations. In the great schism of 1844 with the Church of Scotland, the Emily charge like most in Canada West supported the Free Presbyterian Church of Canada. When Rev. Dick left in 1848, the next year Rev. John Ewing of Antrim, Ireland, accepted the call and served in the parish for 44 years, surely a record of service. Some old-timers still recall him, as he travelled through Emily and Ops, by horseback and later with horse and buggy.

The Methodists of Emily by census count were 99 in 1839, doubled to

193 by 1841, and up to 330 in 1851. Their first reported meeting place in the late 1820s was a log building on the northwest corner of Frank Henderson's Lot 13, Con. 2, where a burying-ground spread around it—it became known later as Magog (or Middle Road) Methodist Church. In Omemee the Methodists like most others met in Cottingham's store, while log schools or barns were often used elsewhere, unless meetings were outdoors. As mentioned before, preachers rode in from Port Hope, like Rev. C. Vandusen, who on June 20, 1832 wrote: "After much prayer for a revival we commenced a protracted meeting in Emily. The chapel not being large enough, we preached in the open air. About 150 professed justification by faith, nearly half of whom have united with our society." But a bitter quarrel among Methodist sects, partly due to British-U.S. differences, split the Port Hope circuit; there was a clash of Irish Methodists, called Ryanites, with Ryerson Methodists "in Emily in the Cavan Circuit", as described in the *Christian Guardian,* May 1, 1833; Rev. Jos. Stinson and others spent most of their time with the Rice Lake and Mud Lake Indians and on the Peterborough circuit during the next few years.

In 1836 the Cavan and Peterborough circuits were united, but perhaps because of the above-mentioned controversy, Emily was ignored—the church histories and memoirs by Carroll, Sanderson and others never mention Emily until about 1861. A group of Williamstown Methodists in 1836 under trustees J. L. Hughes, George Dixon, W. Hanna and Robert Sherin began a frame church on a lot acquired from the Cottinghams, where the modern United Church is. This was opened for worship in 1840, probably by Rev. James Norris of Cavan. Beside the church was a burying-ground, and one of the first buried there was Maurice Cottingham, pioneer settler. Williamson in his *Omemee* has a good drawing and description of the church, which after 1850 became the centre of the Metcalfe Methodist circuit, stretching from Dunsford to Cavan to Manvers. Incidentally, and in conclusion, the Almanacs and Gazetteers of the period provide little or inaccurate information about churches in Emily: Smith's 1846 *Canadian Gazetteer* listed no clergy in the township; Scobie's 1850 *Canadian Almanac* mentioned the Anglican Rev. R. Harding, but no others; Smith's *Canada, Past, Present & Future* [1851] said only: "There are two churches in Emily, Presbyterian and Roman Catholic." As there were 3 sects of Methodists and 3 sects of Presbyterians in Canada West, their confusion is perhaps understandable.

Perspective on progress in Emily can be obtained by some highlights and interesting anecdotes and details on pioneer life through these two decades. For example, people began to build better homes—in the thirties there was one house of square-hewn timber in the township, but by 1847 there were ten such 1-storey and two-storey houses; frame 1-storey houses rose in number from one in 1832 to 10 by 1840 and to 17 by 1847, while frame 2-storey homes began in 1836 and totalled five by 1847. The first stone house is recorded in 1839, and there were 4 by 1847, of which one may have been 2-storey. Part of the slow growth was because hewn timber 1-storey houses were assessed at £20 extra, and 2-storey at £30; frame 1-storey

Original House on Lot 20, Con. 2
built c. 1830 (Lyle Faulkner)

Log House, Lot 17, Con. 1, built c. 1830
(Ernie McCall)

Harrington House, North Emily, with
fireplace, built c. 1840 (S. J. Connell)

Log House, Lot 5, Con. 7 built c. 1840
(Sam Fitch)

O'Neill House — Lot 18, Con. 14 built
c. 1840 (Donald O'Leary)

Log House — E½ Lot 10, Con. 14, built
c. 1840 (W. McMullen)

Log barn north of Omemee (from Rempel's Building with Wood, by permission)

Log barn on Lot 22, Con. 7 — (Beryl Clark)

Log barns, Lot 19, Con. 11 — (built in courtyard plan)
(John Perdue)

houses at £35; brick or stone 1-storey at £40, and any 2-storey frame, brick or stone at £60, with £4 to £10 added for every fireplace after the first one. By the 1851 census, Emily had 8 stone houses, none of brick, 35 frame, 300 of logs, and 87 listed as "shanties", probably the original small ones. There were 430 houses for 432 families, with 5 vacant and 9 just "building". The same Census listed 8 church buildings, 8 shops, 7 inns and taverns, 10 schools, and no public buildings in Emily.

Smith's *Canadian Gazetteer,* 1846, described Emily: "a township in Colborne District, bounded on the east by Ennismore and Smith; on the north by Verulam; on the west by Ops; and on the south by Cavan. In Emily 35,357 acres are taken up; 5,399 of which are under cultivation. This is a good township and is well settled by a mixed population, principally Irish Protestants. It has a good mill stream running through it; and a small settlement called Metcalfe (so named 1844) is situated in its southwest corner. There are two grist and two sawmills and one distillery in the township. 4,100 acres of Crown lands are open for sale at 8s. per acre. The only postoffice is Emily, J. L. Hughes, postmaster. Number of common schools 12. Magistrates include J. L. Hughes and Wm. Best; Coroner Christopher Knowlson."

Lakefront and Peterborough newspapers gave items on pioneer crops worth noting: July 4, 1833: "From every part of Newcastle district the most pleasing accounts of flourishing crops, especially wheat . . . The dry early spring and subsequent genial showers have been favourable to spring grain and clothes meadows and pastures with luxuriant herbage." Sept. 5 and 12, 1835: "We are sorry to hear that the wheat crop in the back country . . . is likely to fall far short of expectations. . . . The late rains prevented the reaping of many ripe fields . . . the weather has been extremely variable and unfavourable to the farmer. . . . The oats crop appears to be particularly abundant and extensive fields of it still uncut. . . ." July 8, 1837: "The crops in the rear townships said to be promising; most of the fall wheat looks thriving; spring wheat never was in better condition. Early potatoes will be fit for digging in a fortnight. . . . Hay crops are likely to turn out well." July 26, 1843: "The hay is nearly all cut, quality good, quantity great, and weather favourable; of wheat and other grain the prospect of abundant harvest never more cheerful." August 4, 1846: "The wheat crop throughout the back country is particularly fine; in Emily, Ops and Mariposa it is unusually heavy, yielding on average more than of late years. Potatoes also are looking well, and in a journey of 30 miles back, we did not hear a single complaint." June 16, 1849: "It is with great pleasure we are able to state that crops throughout the district look most promising." July 24, 1849: "Swindlers at work in back townships buying horses . . . paying farmers with flash notes of Montreal Citizens' Bank, no such bank existing. . . . Fall wheat is luxuriant and healthy . . . spring wheat suffered from want of rain; potatoes abundant with no sign of rot; hay is an extra abundant yield this summer."

Farmers usually bartered their grain at the mill, getting half the flour, made the same deal for their logs at the sawmill, took their skins to the tanner and with the leather made a deal for boots with the shoemaker. The

Two styles of constructing corners on pioneer log building — 1. Square notch
2. Dovetail (S. J. Connell)

Early Downey house (log at right) with a
frame Shoemaker's shop attached (at left)
E½ Lot 6, Con. 9 (Gene Downey)

Pioneer Fireplace in north east Emily

Sullivan timber frame house built c. 1850
N½ Lot 21, Con 12
(a former stage-coach inn) (Steve Sullivan)

Stone House, Lot 23, Con. 2, built 1846
(a former stage-coach inn)
(M. Bowen)

(Though these pictures are from Canadian government pamphlets for assisting new immigrants in 1863 and 1880 respectively, they provide some insight into the situation of pioneer backwoods settlers in Emily Township several decades earlier.)

family's other needs such as mocassins, harness and belts were made at home. Those who raised sheep (or obtained wool by trading with neighbours) spun it into yarn for stockings, shawls, sweaters, dresses, trousers and underwear for everyday wear. Store-bought clothes were worn on festive occasions only and lasted a lifetime. Hard currency was very scarce in pioneer Emily, and men were glad to hire out for farm work or labouring jobs at £1 or £2 a month with board, though skilled men like coopers and masons got 4s. to 6s. a day, and carpenters 3s. or 4s. In the 1830s oxen cost £15 a pair, and horses much more. Blacksmiths charged 5s. to 7s. to shoe a horse. To take farm produce to Peterborough, Cavan or Port Hope over bush trails was an endurance test. At first the men carried their grain, potash, potatoes and other produce on their backs or on a yoke; with the first oxen, they sometimes used a small tree with branched top, the trunk being the yoke and with a box on the branches to carry their produce out to store or mill, and their purchases home, with the baby sitting in the middle. Then came the homemade jumper, a box-body with flat wooden runners, followed by the ox-cart with wooden wheels roughly hewn, 8" wide and 4' in diameter —before 1850 prosperous farmers had better carts and even wagons, with iron tires, especially those living near the improved roads, or those with horses.

Prices as quoted in the Peterborough and Lakefront weeklies remained fairly constant through the period 1832-50: fall wheat 3s. 9d., oats 1s. 3d., beef or pork about 6d. a pound, maple sugar the same, eggs 6d. a dozen, fowl 1s. a pair. On the other side, by contrast, store prices were high: a suit £8 to £10, common boots 12s. 6d., ladies' slippers 8s., cotton stockings 2s. to 5s. a pair, tea 2s. to 5s. a pound, Scotch or Irish whisky 8s. but Canadian whisky 2s. a gallon, sugar 6d. a pound, tobacco 5s. a pound, chocolate 1s. a pound, a good horse £25 but a serviceable one £10, a single sleigh £7 to £20, a wagon £10 to £12, 10s., chairs 4s. to 12s., chest of drawers £4, bedstead £3, wallpaper 1s. 9d. to 3s. 6d. a roll. No wonder most farmers made as many of their needs as possible, and traded work or produce for most of the balance. The luxuries—from brandy to oysters to fancy carriages and mahogany furniture—they did without. The numerous Emigrant Guides were full of advice on these matters, warning emigrants that good glasswear, crockery, furniture and clothes were expensive and scarce in Canada, and to bring what they could from home.

Durham and Northumberland Fairs were held from 1830 and the first agricultural shows at Cavan and Peterborough were in 1837; the few records do not indicate any Emily prize-winners, but the Peterborough *Sentinel* reported in December, 1838, "The fairs at Peterboro and Cavan this month were well attended, and the show of cattle at both good, but money scarce. The breed of horses in the back country is decidedly improved and we feel confident that in Cavan, Emily and this neighbourhood strong and active horses could be found. . . . A fine horse, which was brought up from the front to the Cavan fair to challenge the whole back country, was beaten by a young horse belonging to Widow McCall of Emily. . . ." (Beaten in the show-ring probably, not on the race-track!). Concerning Emily itself, the *Centennial Yearbook* of the Ontario Association of Agricultural Societies, telling of Ontario fairs and exhibitions 1792 to 1967, states: "EMILY: This Society was organized in the early 1840s and there is record of a fair at Omemee prior to 1854. . . . Wm. Cottingham says 'My brother-in-law, Mr. Hughes, and I started the first Agricultural Society in this back country . . . uphill work as the farmers were few and far between.' . . ." The book has a list of township societies in 1854, including Emily, Ops, etc.

Clearing land was the first preoccupation of the first generation in Emily, in all seasons. Until chemical dyes were invented, and whale oil first used for soaps (in the late 1840s) potash and pearlash obtained by burning their trees was an important "cash crop"; every acre of timber cleared produced 250 pounds of ash worth up to £2 at the store or ashery. Bees were organized with all the neighbourhood people and their oxen, in teams competing to clear an acre fastest; the best timber was piled separately—pine for lumber, oak for pipe-staves, cedar for fence-rails, etc. Other bees were held for building, stumping, fencing, maple-sugarmaking, ploughing, haying, harvesting and barn-raising. For the women there were quilting and soap-making bees, for the youth corn-husking and apple-paring bees (sometimes called "kissing bees"). The women competed in preparing food for the hungry—Mrs. Stewart in 1841 mentioned a feast of roast pig, cold ham, boiled mutton, fish, potatoes, beans, carrots, rice and bread puddings, currant and gooseberry tarts. When the work and eating were done, there were foot-races, jumping, pole-vaulting, wrestling, weight-lifting, and ridgepole-walking. District gentry unanimously condemned bees (while using them) because of drinking, fighting and the general tone of equality predominant, but they were a vital and necessary form of pioneer community co-operation and involvement. They were also proof of neighbourly aid whenever a family was inflicted with sickness or death, and in fact they have persisted throughout the 150 years since, in emergencies.

The rest of this chapter will be a general roundup of events and activities on a wide spectrum by years, to give a third dimension to the description of pioneer Emily:

1831-2: Twelve years after they surrendered their lands, the Mud and Rice Lake Indians were petitioning Peter Robinson to preserve their hunting-grounds for them and stop "white men making depredations on our hunting grounds." Mrs. Stewart called them "strange wild forest savages . . . long black hair hanging loose and matted" and lamented their tendency to get drunk, but John Langton was probably nearer the truth when he called them "a most peaceable, sober set of men . . . strong and active, always willing to accompany the white man to the chase; but neither entreaties, bribes nor threats will induce them to help him in his farm or garden. . . ." The government responded to Indian entreaties by setting up, in July 1832, reservations at Mud Lake and Rice Lake although the Indians did not like living and farming on small confined settlements, preferring to roam the lakes and streams (including Pigeon and Emily Creeks). Moreover, the New

England Company of Methodist missionaries was put in charge of the reservations, to Christianize and settle the Indians into farming. One result was that
by 1850 there were only 52 at Chemong or Curve Lake reservation and 134
at Rice Lake; the rest roamed freely, living in wigwams instead of log shanties,
worshipping Manitou in the woods instead of in church, fishing, hunting and
trapping as their forefathers had done. But by 1850 they were forced to go
northward into the wilderness.

1833: The Huston papers contain an affidavit (July 22, 1833) by John
Rowley of Ops, who swore that "John Mahar of Emily, labourer, did on Fri.
21st June commit an assault upon him . . . by giving him a severe blow and
nocking him down and afterwards made several attempts to strike and ill-
treat him at Emily. Deponant prayeth that Justice may be done to him." It
would be interesting to hear full details of this quarrel, and its outcome.

1834: Mossom Boyd, later a leading lumberman at Bobcaygeon, came to
Upper Canada at age 19 in 1834, and reminiscenced 43 years later: "[I] took
passage on the only steamboat on Lake Ontario and met on board old Cottingham who told me all about these back lakes. . . . I accordingly got off at
Port Hope & went with him in his spring waggon to Omemee where his
father had a small sawmill & gristmill. He lived in a little log shanty . . .
the town at that time consisted of the mills and 3 or 4 other buildings. . . . A
small boy was sent to conduct me by a path through the woods to King's
Wharf where Pigeon Creek bridge is now . . . the river winding back &
forth across the wide marsh. John Sullivan's log shanty was the only building.
It was called King's Wharf because here all the provisions, etc. for Robinson
Emigrants were landed for Ops, Emily, etc. [I] then travelled with a group
of half-drunk surveyors toward Bobcaygeon. . . ." Boyd had many business
dealings with Emily settlers and merchants later, as we shall see.

The Port Hope *Warder* noted in May: "MELANCHOLY DEATH OF
3 CHILDREN: Last week Francis Taylor of Emily whilst planting potatoes
in a field some distance from his house had three children consumed by fire.
. . . Mr. and Mrs. Taylor left 4 children in the house; the eldest sometime
afterwards went out to the field, saying he had put the other 3 to sleep and
locked the door . . . [when] the house was discovered on fire, Mr. and Mrs.
Taylor rushed to the scene with a hope of saving their children but such was
the rapidity of the flames that in an instant all was consumed. . . . This
should be warning to parents not to leave their children in a house without
some mature person with them."

1835: Port Hope *Warder*: "A coroner's inquest was held on the 6th
September by Chris. Knowlson Esq., on the body of John Welsh (or Welch)
of township Emily, aged 2 years 3 months. The verdict of the jury was that
deceased came to his death by the influence of ardent spirits administered by
his father, mother and one M. Lucas . . . the child was in perfect health but
his parents (like too many others) seemed to feel no harm could result from
allowing infants to sip that deleterious drug, whisky . . . it was immediately
taken ill, and one (of them) thought giving a little more would tend to its
recovery . . . more of the poison was given, and in a short time it was evident

that its existence was terminated." Such poisonings were common in the next few decades, as U.S. patent medicines poured over the border, full of alcohol and opium—Dr. Jonathan Moore's Essence of Life, curing whooping cough, quinsy, rickets, consumption, gout, rheumatism, catarrh, etc.; Moffatt's Life Pills and Phoenix Bitters, to cure all from blindness to horsesickness; Dr. Spohr's Health Elixir for colds, aches, pains and dyspepsia; Ray's Liniment for piles, dropsy, sores, rheumatism; Vegetable Pulmonary Balsam for coughs, colds, asthma, consumption, etc; and many more .

1836: The Kingston *Chronicle* in March reported: "Married at Port Hope on the 17th inst. by Rev. A. Bethune, James Smith, Esq., Barrister, to Mary Anne Jane, eldest daughter of John Henderson of Emily Township, late of Kilkenny, Ireland."

1837: Upper Canada *Herald,* May 16: "MARRIED: at Emily on Wed. the 12th inst. by Rev. S. Armour, Thomas Crawford, merchant, Williamstown, to Miss Aphra Marmion, eldest daughter of Richard Marmion of said township."

William McConel of Emily made affidavit before J. Huston, J.P. on March 9, swearing that his goods had been stolen "one tub, 2 lbs. tea, 1 pair women boots, one comb check glass and putty all amounting to £1 10s. feloniously stolen, taken and carried away off a 'slay' from before the store of Howard & Thompson at Millbrook . . . he doth suspect that some person in or about the said village of Millbrook had taken stolen and carried away . . . prayeth that Justice may be done."

In August, the Toronto *Constitution* noted: "The largest procession and assemblage of Orangemen ever known before in the Newcastle District took place in Cavan, July 12. . . . Members of 13 lodges met at Millbrook, mustered from Hope, Hamilton, Clarke, Darlington, Monaghan, Manvers, Ops, Emily and Smith, and after indulging pretty freely in whiskey, playing party tunes, displaying their flags, etc. they dispersed. . . ." (The Assembly prohibited Orange parades for a time after 1840).

1838: The Huston Papers have two interesting letters from Samuel Cottingham to John Huston in February: alleging "that Mr. Greerson brake in my house on the 28th November and I think I aught to acquaint you as a magistrate for the language he used to the woman and laid hands to hir which frighted hir a good deal. I want to take every necessary steps of the law. . . . I expect to be at your house the last of next week or if you could send me word with Mitchell when I might see you." Next day he wrote again: "It was a Capus that James Chambours from Peterboro served me with but his name was not in it. . . . Edward Greerson Broke in my house the same night which was 28th November last we think it was between 12 and 1 oclock he laid hands to the woman in hir bed whare she had a young Child the only ones in the house with the exception of the two little girls. The Caparis was from Toronto for the amount of £15. . . . Mr. Ed. Greerson did not attempt to take me but I offerd him Beal and Security for the amount due. . . ." This indicates some problems in the Cottingham businesses at Williamstown, in those years.

A warrant was issued to William English, constable, by Richard Marmion, J.P., dated Emily, August 23, 1838, to arrest James Shield on a complaint of Abraham Hartley, "for that he the said James Shield on 22nd day of August . . . did bite off part of the nose of said witness Abraham Hartley and also bit him on his face in several places, and also threatened to take out the eyes of said Abraham Hartley the younger and put them in his pocket. . . ." A subsequent note indicates that James Shields was sent to jail for the offence; it would be most interesting to know more about the background of this curious incident.

1839: The Peterborough *Sentinel* reported in January: "On the night of the 26th ult. the house of a most respectable settler, Samuel Mitchell, Emily, was burned to the ground. The father, mother and 10 children with difficulty escaped an awful death, and were exposed during the rest of the night to an intense severity of frost from which they have all suffered. All their clothing, furniture, &c. together with winter provisions were destroyed. The mother and one child are not expected to survive. . . . An appeal to the public in their behalf we understand is about to be made and we feel confident it will not be made in vain."

In 1839, three frame houses were assessed in Emily—only one of these has been determined, the 1½ storey frame house built that year by John Mitchell on north half Lot 15, Con. 1. There was at least one stone house assessed that year also, but the earliest to be determined was James Evens' one-storey stone house built in 1842 on south half Lot 9, Con. 2.

1840-2: Samuel Strickland in his 1854 book mentioned an undated incident in Emily which might be described here: "The person . . . resided in the township of Emily, and had been all the summer working at his trade in the village of Bowmanville, to earn money sufficient to pay for his land. . . . As the cold weather has set in, he determined to return home and chop all the winter on his farm." After crossing Darlington and Manvers for about 25 miles, he could get home in half the time by roundabout roads; but after ten or twelve miles he had to struggle through a snowstorm amid swamps and ridges. He spent a bad night in the swamps, then found he was circling on his own tracks. On the second night when lying down he heard a cock crow, and was found in the morning badly frozen and died a week later, in spite of the care of Dr. Hutchison of Peterborough.[17]

We might place here also an anecdote that happened to one of the Magees, whether to John Magee who settled on concession 1 in 1839 or to one of his sons later. The story goes that one Sunday he told his family to walk on toward church and he would catch up later, but before leaving the house he heard a disturbance and, investigating, found a bear in the pigpen. When he tried to drive it off with an axe, the bear knocked it from his hands, picked him up in his paws, and carried him into the woods. But the little family dog nipped at the bear's heels, and the bear had to drop Mr. Magee to swing at the annoying dog, which managed finally to drive the bear off into the woods. Mr. Magee picked himself up, tended to his clothes and cuts at the house, and hastened after his family to church, to thank God for his many mercies, including his own lucky escape.

In the history of Millersmith which appeared in a Lindsay paper Nov. 3, 1939, reference is made to the deaths of Hugh and John Miller in 1840 or 1841: "with malarial fever, caused by the water being dammed at Bobcaygeon, and it flooded the swamps along Emily Creek. At one time, while the fever rages, there was only one man—John Cullen—able to go to all the homes and bring in a pail of water and wood, and help make them as comfortable as possible. Later Agnes and James dies of Scarlet Fever. Six of the Millers are buried on the Miller property. . . . John Miller died in 1852, his wife shortly before that."

1843: The Cobourg *Star* (Feb. 9) carried disastrous news, repeated in other papers: "MELANCHOLY ACCIDENT: a most grievous and heart-rending accident which occurred on the night of Monday last at Williamstown, Emily Township, when the house of Wm. Cottingham, Esq., was destroyed by fire and two of his children burned to death; the particulars of the accident we have not heard. . . . Since the above was in type we have received not only confirmation but a horrible addition, dreadful to state, that 4 of Mr. Cottingham's children and two servant girls were burned to death—in all 6 lives lost—this is a most appalling calamity." Williamson in his *Omemee* gives full particulars, including the parents' attempts to rescue the children, resulting in their own severe burns. Every article in the house was burned, including Cottingham's records and accounts. The house is thought to have been on the south side of King Street near the southwest corner of George Street. The Colborne District Council adopted a message of condolence sent to postmaster Hughes, Cottingham's brother-in-law, to be given to him.

The same papers in March carried a cheerier item: "MARRIED: on the 15th inst, at Emily Church, by Rev. Wm. Shaw, Hugh Grey Hamilton, Esq. of Cobourg, from County Leitrim, Ireland, to Mary Jane, only child of Robert Dickson, Esq., of Dicksonville, Canada, formerly of Fermanagh, Ireland." Bishop Strachan, Anglican Bishop of Toronto paid his first visit to Emily Church Sept. 3.

1844: Montreal *Gazette,* Jan. 18: "At a public meeting of the inhabitants of Williamstown, Emily Township, it was resolved that the name of the village should be changed to Metcalfe, in honour of His Excellency the Governor-General, and in 'cordial approbation' of his conduct."

The Upper Canada *Herald* on Aug. 27 quoted from the Port Hope *Gazette* the following: "ACCIDENT: a young man, Robert Wilson, age 18, was drowned in the millpond of Wm. Cottenham, of Emily, on Friday the 9th inst. The lad had walked out on the logs that floated in the pond and, probably not knowing how readily they whirl underfoot when incautiously stepped upon, he was thrown into the water. He seized the logs however, which whirled from his grasp, and being no swimmer he went to the bottom. Several good swimmers, attracted by the cries of a woman who saw him go down, were immediately on the spot, but due to the depth of water, 14 feet, and the uncertainty of the place where he sank, half an hour elapsed before the body was taken from the water. . . . By the exertions of Josiah Hughes, who dived to the bottom several times, the body was brought to the bank; Dr. W. M. Smith, who was on the spot, tried to restore animation without success. An inquest by C. Knowlson, Coroner, returned a verdict of accidental death."

Mossom Boyd of Bobcaygeon, who took over Need's Mills there, began selling planks and flooring to Emily residents in 1844—some of his customers were George Harkness, Moses Twomey, Joseph Lowes, Michael McAuliffe, Ann Lowes, Denis Sullivan, Chris. Switzer, Adam Shouldis, James Reid, John McCarroll, and James Best. In 1844 Samuel Wright bought 1,064 ft. lumber for £1/11/10; in 1845 Ed. McCaul bought 1,208 ft. for £1/16; in 1846 Mrs. Lowes bought 346 ft. lumber for flooring for 10s. 4d.; in 1847 Geo. Westall bought 448 ft. lumber for 13s. 5d.—this was probably delivered by steamer and scow to King's Wharf, or part way up Pigeon Creek, or to the end of Chemong Lake, and thence by wagon to the site. It may have been better grade pine lumber than the local mills could produce, or better finished, or sold at a lower price. A receipt signed by George Hughes, clerk, reads: "Emily, 6th Oct. 1845, Recd. from Mossom Boyd Esq., £1 12s. 6d. costs on his several suits in the 4th Division Court of the Colborne District to date." Perhaps he had difficulty collecting, since several of the accounts have "bad debt" written on them.

1845: Montreal *Gazette* of March 1: "MARRIED: at Cobourg on the 5th ult, by Rev. T. Alexander, Mr. Henry Hale of Emily Township to Ann, daughter of David Brodie, Esq., of Cobourg."

A farewell may be made at this point to John Huston of Cavan, who had much to do with pioneer Emily, as he died in Cavan, May 18, 1845, at age 55; his daughter Jane married William Cottingham and is buried in the Cottingham family plot, Lady Eaton Cemetery, Omemee. He worked to the last, as in Dec. 1844 he surveyed the Clergy Reserves in Emily Township.[18] His field notes commenting on the development of these lots are full of interesting detail.

Port Hope *Gazette* of June 17: "A BOY KILLED: On the 11th inst. the son of Mr. Elsworth, who lives within 4 miles of Metcalfe, Emily, was killed by the fall of a tree. It appears that the unfortunate lad who was about 5 years old had just run out to where his father was chopping, and was crushed beneath the very tree that was felled by his father's hand."

1846: Montreal *Gazette* of Feb. 6: "MARRIED: at Christ Church, Metcalfe, Emily, on the 7th ult. by Rev. R. Harding, Mr. Charles Hale of Peterboro to Anna, daughter of Geo. Hughes, Esq., Emily."

Toronto *Examiner* of Aug. 12: "Last Saturday night the Musquitoes were so bad at Rice and Mud Lakes that the people in their vicinity were obliged to leave their houses and roam about the fields till morning."

Kingston *Patriot* of Dec. 11: "Died: at Emily, Colborne District, on 17th November, Samuel, youngest son of Dr. John Irons, aged 6 months and 8 days."

1847: The Irish famine and plague of 1846-8 was deeply felt in Colborne District, and a fund was raised to send relief. In addition, by 1847 hundreds of Irish, mostly penniless, poured off the boats at Cobourg and Port Hope and came north, some to join relatives, others publicly supported. One tragic result was the death of Dr. John Hutchison of Peterborough, who had lived for some years in Cavan and had served some early settlers there, who often continued as his patients. Toronto *Banner,* Aug. 20, quoting from Peterborough *Gazette* "DIED on the 1st August, of typhus fever caught while in attendance at the Emigrant Sheds, John Hutchison, MD, aged 50 years . . . the assiduous and meritorious attention bestowed by this gentleman on the unfortunate immigrants . . . required more than ordinary medical skill and attention. . . . From a visit to the temporary hospital he returned home under symptoms of disease which rapidly developed into the worst type of Typhus Fever, terminated fatally . . . all who were able to be present made a point of joining the melancholy procession to the graveyard. . . ."

1848: Peterboro *Dispatch,* Nov. 23: "FIRE: We regret to learn that a very serious accident by fire occured at the village of Metcalfe, on Thursday, by which the Clothing Works of Mr. Ivory were consumed together with a large quantity of cloth and wool belonging to the neighbouring farmers. The fire seems to have broken out during the absence of the men at breakfast, and had made so much progress before it was discovered as to render fruitless all attempts to save any portion of the property. Loss estimated at £375. No insurance."

1849: Cobourg *Church* of July 12: "Bishop Strachan, Lord Bishop of Toronto, will be present for confirmations in Cavan's two churches July 31 and Aug. 1, and at Emily Church Aug. 1, at 2 p.m."

As Pete McGillen wrote in the 1940s: "Few juvenile crimes in the long history of Ontario can match in depravity an almost century-old murder of a beautiful 5-year-old child by her foster brother age 10", which occurred in Emily in the autumn of 1849. Margaret O'Connor was adopted by Thomas and Eliza Rowan, and soon became a family pet loved by all, except another adopted child, George Green, aged 10 or 11, placed on the Rowan farm by Rev. Mr. Dick, after a period in the Presbyterian manse—the boy had to work around the farm, and conceived a fierce jealousy of little Margaret. When the Rowans went on Oct. 26 to a plowing bee at the farm of Samuel Hannah a mile away, George was left to dig potatoes, and Margaret left with him to help put them in the wheelbarrow. The whole sad story of how George rushed over to tell them Margaret had been killed by a bear, and how he himself was revealed to have done it with the hoe, and his trial at Peterborough, and conviction for murder in May 1850 (and sentence to be hanged) has been written about extensively in law journals; the sentence was commuted to life imprisonment in Kingston penitentiary, but the boy died soon after.[19]

The pioneers depended mainly on homemade remedies in time of illness, and of necessity learned the best remedies from the Indians and from earlier settlers, since often no doctor could be obtained for days or weeks. Herbs were collected, tied in bundles, and hung up to dry, both for cooking and for healing. Hoarhound plants were boiled, the liquid sweetened and made into syrup, and used for colds. The roots of ginseng made an excellent tonic.

Catnip plants when cooked and mixed into a syrup were given to infants with colic. Poultices were made from mullein and plantain leaves, and even from egg-shell lining. Clear vinegar was taken for arthritis. Honey-comb was chewed to cure hay-fever, and for other similar troubles. Olive oil mixed with turpentine was rubbed on to cure bronchitis, and mustard plasters were the standard remedy for chest colds. A brew of hemlock leaves and bark was recommended by Indians to cure scurvy. Compare with these the quack medicines loaded with alcohol and opium which were widely advertised and sold in every store, and often bought by credulous people: Clockeners Vegetable Pills to cure all from Dyspepsia to Consumption, Gout to Gravel, Scrofula to Scurvy; Dr. Vaughn's Lithostriptic Mixture "the great infallible American Remedy for kidney, liver and all diseases, jaundice, ague, fevers, dropsy, gravel, etc."; Dr. Christie's Galvanic Belt, Bracelets and Necklace and Magnetic Fluid, for nervous diseases, fits, lumbago, paralysis, epilepsy, gout, apoplexy, heart palpitations, liver complaints and rheumatism; Urquhart's Jamaica Sarsaparilla for rheumatism, indigestion and syphilis; Wistar's Balsam of Wild Cherry for worms, colds, constipation and "almost every other disease"; Ayer's Cherry Pectoral "the Children's Panaccea for stomach, bowels, kidneys, skin and circulation"—and many more. Some of them even warned people on the label to "beware of imitations and counterfeits"; there was of course at that period no government control on such shameless exploitation.

NOTES

[1] A table of population and assessment statistics will be found in Appendix VIII.

[2] Based on District Assessment Rolls which ended in the late 1840s, and on 1851 Canada census, two points are worth noting:
   (a) In the 1851 Census lands uncultivated were called "wood and wild land", while lands cultivated were divided into those under crop (7,277 acres in Emily) those under pasture (4,863 acres in Emily), and gardens (84 acres in Emily);
   (b) The 1851 total of lands in private ownership also indicates that almost half the land in Emily was still in Crown possession.

[3] About half the Dennehy Survey (on 49 lots) is given in Appendix IX.

[4] C. Baldwin, the mill-builder, had certified about this lot January 4, 1834: "I certify that there is a house erected and about 15 acres cleared on lot 17, 7th concession, granted to Mrs. Groves who died there. Her eldest son Thomas has gone to the States and fixed there. Her second son Abraham has had possession of the lot and worked up on it since his brother's departure and now wishes that it may be granted to his youngest brother James who is 16 years old and has no land. The concession line in front of the lot has been cleared on Groves' side." Again in 1836 James Groves was petitioning Robinson to get the southwest quarter of this lot, as he was now 21 and had no land and "will have to become a wanderer if not granted land." His mother was a widow and his brother had the adjoining lot, and James was the only child unprovided for.

[5] Based on Newcastle and Colborne District Assessment Rolls (Ontario Archives).

[6] Toronto *Patriot,* Jan. 7, 1840: "IN TOWNSHIP EMILY: lot 18 and south half 19 in 8th con.—300 acres; these lots are situated on Pigeon Creek, navigable from the Lake 6 miles beyond the lots, and on which it is intended to run a steamboat. There is on them a clearing of over 30 acres, with log house and new frame barn 30 by 60 ft.

18 ft. high, divided into a mow of 26 feet, thrashing floor of 20 feet, and stable with 6 stalls, 14 ft.; also an excellent saw and gristmill—the gristmill is 3 stories high, having one run of stones and fitted for reception of two. There is a quantity of pine on one lot, and abundance in the neighbourhood which could be floated to the mill; the sod is an excellent sandy loam."

[7]This correspondence is preserved in the Trent-Newcastle waterways files, Department of Railways and Canals, now in the Public Archives of Canada. Cottingham was granted compensation of £339/10 in 1847, but probably nothing more.

[8]Some of Huston's field notes on constructing this road are preserved in the Huston papers at Trent University.

[9]Upper Canada Journals 1846—Report of Inquiry into Post Offices.

[10]Capt. Mitchell was elected to form this volunteer company of forty because, as Col. Henry wrote to Huston, "Capt. Thos. Mitchell has already come forward with his Company to offer their services. They will be the first placed upon the list of Volunteers".

[11]The text of the newspaper item is given in Appendix X.

[12]The three excerpts from Mr. Hodgins' books are given in Appendix XI.

[13]Fleming's 1848 map of Emily shows the position of 13 schools, 7 of them in the south 4 concessions.

[14]The *Victoria Magazine* 1847-8, edited by Susanna and J. W. D. Moodie, reprinted in book form, Vancouver 1968.

[15]Two excerpts from these Missionary Journals will be found in Appendix XII.

[16]An interesting letter of Rev. Shaw, 1844, about this glebe lot is reproduced in Appendix XIII.

[17]This excerpt from Strickland's book is given in full in Appendix XIV.

[18]Biographical Notes on John Huston's life have been collected in Appendix XV.

[19]The chapter "When a Child was Sentenced to the Gallows" in Hassard's *Famous Canadian Trials*, 1924, will be found in Appendix XVI.

Part II: Victorian Emily
(1850-1900)

CHAPTER SEVEN

THE SECOND GENERATION (1850-1875)

The simple population figures for Emily present an enigma: 1851—2,763; 1861—3,923; 1871—3,790; 1881—2,876. Why did the population soar almost 1,200, then drop 133, and then drop over 900? Only a wide-ranging study of Emily's development can explain the phenomenon, which happened in other district townships predominantly rural. The first fact to be established is that in 1851 over half the people in Emily were born in Canada—1,600 to be exact. The origins of the others were: England and Wales 44, Scotland 31, Ireland 1,062, U.S.A. 21, others 5. It is significant that about half the Emily population in 1851 had been born in the township and had grown up there, the *second generation* residents. Those born in the first years on backwoods farms, up to 1830, were now marrying and beginning to raise families, accounting for much of the increase in the 1850s. Similarly, the abrupt decrease in Emily's population 1871-1881 can be mostly explained by the fact that Metcalfe village, which changed its name to Omemee in the 1860s, had over 600 inhabitants by 1870, and incorporated as a separate village in 1874. It reached its peak of about 800 people in 1878, and was down to 744 in the 1881 census, and not included in Emily population; numerous Central Ontario villages incorporated in that decade, dazzled by the largely illusory "advantages" of separate status. For Emily, as we shall see, the separation curtailed its progress in the decades to 1900, although the two municipalities co-operated in many spheres, sometimes of necessity.

Another fact that marks the end of Emily's pioneer days by 1850 was that about half the land was in private ownership, and much of the rest not arable. The 1851 census showed 33,317 acres held, of which 12,224 were under cultivation (7,277 in crops, 4,863 in pasture, 84 in gardens) while 21,093 acres was wood and wild lot. The lands privately owned, and the acreage cultivated, grew slowly after 1858, so that young people growing up after 1860 began to look to the northern townships for farmlands, and after 1885 to the western prairies. A birdseye view of Emily in 1851 is in Smith's *Canada, Past, Present and Future*: "From Peterborough to Metcalfe, in the township of Emily, is about 14 miles. The country is hilly and the soil gravelly. Through the front of Smith and Emily, on the road to Metcalfe, most of the settlers are Protestant Irish, with a few English; they have good farms, generally well-cleared. In the back of the townships the settlers are principally Irish Catholics. The village of Metcalfe is situated on Pigeon Creek, where there is a fall of about 6 feet, and contains a gristmill with 3 runs of stones, a sawmill, carding and fulling mill, distillery, tannery and post office. There are two churches, Presbyterian and Roman Catholic. The township of Emily is improving. . . . From Metcalfe to Lindsay is about 14 miles. A large portion of the road is level, and the soil of clay, with a few small swamps by way of variety. . . ." In listing district merchants, etc., Smith mentioned at Metcalfe only two: "Wm. Cottingham, miller, lumber merchant, carder and fuller" and "Mr. Beatty, merchant". Crown Lands in Emily were 5,300 acres, Clergy Reserves 2,000 acres.

The townships of Colborne District had little power except to elect a few officials to handle district grants for schools and roads, and to assess for taxes and regulate fences and wandering livestock. Change was obviously needed, and the municipal reforms of 1850 abolished district governments, set up the United Counties of Peterborough and Victoria, and gave far more local responsibility to elected township councils, whose reeves and deputy-reeves in turn made up County Councils. The first Emily Council elected consisted of William Cottingham, Chris. Knowlson, William Buck, Thomas Fee, and Michael Lehane. At their first meeting on Jan. 20, 1850, they elected Cottingham reeve; in February, Bylaw no. 1 appointed Robert Grandy as clerk; Thomas Matchett as treasurer; Dr. Irons as school superintendent; James and Isaac English and Michael Collins as assessors; John Collum as tax collector; Thomas Crawford and Henry Sherin as auditors; John and George Miller and Thomas Evans as township wardens; plus 55 highway overseers (also called pathmasters), 7 pound-keepers and 18 fence-viewers. Grandy and Irons were paid £5 each for the year, and the treasurer received 3% of money paid out, but the rest were either unpaid, or in the case of pound-keepers received fees for services. The township bylaws and council minutes contain a wealth of interesting facts about Emily through the years; even by 1860 there were 93 bylaws, and by 1875 a total of 148.[1] In 1851 Arthur McQuade became tax collector. William Cottingham, incidentally, was not only Reeve of Emily 1850 to 1872, and Reeve of Omemee in 1874, but also Warden of United Counties of Peterborough and Victoria 1852 to 1858, and of Victoria County separately in 1865, a tribute to his ability and leadership.

Early bylaws defined the duties of officials such as assessors, and the rules to be followed in collecting and handling taxes and other moneys. For example, the treasurer was told how and when to collect taxes, to allow 30s. off for each wolf a taxpayer killed, how to proceed against those neglecting or refusing to pay taxes, including seizure and sale of delinquent property—the tax collector's salary was £10 a year; he like the treasurer had to post a surety bond yearly—in 1858 Thos. Matchett was bonded for £500 and Arthur McQuade for £250—in 1863 their bonds were $2,000 and $1,000 respectively, and also Wm. Cottingham for $1,000. The 1850 taxes totalled only £200—£150 for schools and £70 for township administration including salaries. In Dec. 1850 Council decided to pay themselves 5s. each a day for meetings. An amusing incident occurred when by Bylaws 22 and 23 they provided that their meeting-place in 1851 should be David Harkness' Inn in Metcalfe, and he to get £3 10s. to cover use of the room, fire and candles in the year—but the new Council on Jan. 27, 1851, promptly repealed this by Bylaw 24, with meetings to be at Edward Blackwell's Inn in Metcalfe. Later that year they reversed themselves, when a bylaw to raise £275 in taxes was repealed, and the taxes again set at £200; also they appointed 56 overseers of highways, 18 fence-viewers, 9 pound-keepers, 3 town wardens and 2 auditors, and increased salaries of main officials.

In 1852 taxes went up—£50 15s. 3d. for county, £85 for schools, and £140 for "improvement of roads and bridges, salaries of tcwnship officials

No. 7

A By Law to define what animals shall
not be allowed to run at large and to establish the
height and description of fences. —
Be it enacted that all Entire Horses, Bulls, Boars
Rams and breachy cattle shall be kept up and
shall not be allowed to run at large and that all
Hogs and Horses be kept up from the first day of
April until the first day of November and that
each animal so found running at large shall be
liable to a fine of 9/6 for the first time offering for
and 5/- for the second one and so on and that the
height of fences be 4½ feet sufficiently made and
of good material. —
And be it further enacted that the said
fine or fences shall be collected in a summary
way agreeable to a By Law of the Municipality
of Emily —

February 9th 1850   William Coffey han
                                        Townreeve

No 25

A By Law to authorise the
Inspectors to grant certificates
to certain persons to keep Inns
within the Municipality of Emily

And be it therefore enacted by the
Authority of the Municipality of Emily
and It is hereby enacted by the authority
aforesaid that the Inspectors do grant
Certificates to the following persons to keep
Inns within the Municipality of the same.

Viz Francis Best, David Harkness,
Edward Blackwell, Robert Henderson
Isaac English, James Collins and Mary
Ann Davidson —

                                Signed C Knowlson
Passed 27th February 1851   Chairman pro tem.
                                        Robert Grandy
                    No 29   Clerk

Two early Bylaws of Emily Township Council, 1850 and 1851.

and contingent expenses"; next year only £70 was levied for schools, but because of county levies the taxes rose again. In 1854 taxes soared to £700, due mostly to county debentures and other levies, and license fees were levied on inns, shops, auctioneers, taverns, and peddlers to provide more money without placing the whole load on property. By 1857 it was necessary to pay the clerk £20, assessor and collector the same, treasurer £12, 10s., auditors £2 each. Thus in 1858 taxes were up to £1,000: £288, 10s. for county; £107 for schools; £200 for township salaries and expenses and £404 for roads and bridges; that year the license inspector was paid "$40 per annum" (the first mention of dollars), and there were 60 highway over-seers (who were also fence-viewers), and 11 pound-keepers. Incidentally, from 1857 on bylaws were all signed by reeve and clerk at "Council Chambers, Omemee", being the first use of the name 'Omemee'.

In 1859 the township was divided into 5 wards for elections: WARD ONE: part of first 3 concessions from lots 1 to 9 inclusive, at Old School House near David Balfour's—Returning Officer Robert Grandy; Ward TWO: from line between lots 9 and 10 on con. 1 north to intersect Pigeon River, then north along river to sideline between lots 16 and 17, then southeast between said lots to front of 1st concession—at Schoolhouse no. 8—R. O. Arthur McQuade; WARD THREE: from con. 1 between lots 16 and 17 northwest to intersect Pigeon River, then northeast along river to east boundary of Emily at Ennismore, then east to front of 1st concession—at Schoolhouse no. 13—R. O. David Storey; WARD FOUR: from front of con. 4 between lots 9 and 10 along concession front to Ops boundary, then northwest along boundary to front of con. 10, then northeast along concession line to Pigeon River and southwest along river until it intersects sideline between lots 9 and 10, then south to place of beginning—at Schoolhouse no. 5—R. O. Wm. Curry; WARD FIVE: on west boundary in front of lot 1, con. 10, then northwest along boundary to Verulam boundary, then northeast along boundary to Pigeon River, then southwest along river until it intersects the 4th concession line, then northwest along this to place of beginning—at house of Michael Walsh—R. O. Michael Walsh. Needless to say, these wards or divisions were altered and adjusted many times in the next 100 years, as population changed.

In the 1860s taxes continued to rise, from $3,100 in 1861 ($1,023 for county; $273 for debenture tax; $600 for schools; $638.77 for county roads; $565.23 for township purposes), up to $5,500 in 1869 ($4,031 for county; $600 for schools; $869 for township expenses). Fortunately for Ontario, this was a period of rising prosperity and higher farm prices, due to expanding markets in Europe, faster new steamships, and civil war in the United States. In 1866 the 5 wards were rearranged into 4 electoral divisions, and then in 1870 into 3, and again in 1874 (after Omemee separated) into 5 divisions. In 1867 councillors voted themselves expense money ranging from $25 to $28 a year, and in 1875 this was stabilized at $2 a day when attending council, plus "mileage for attending"; in the latter year taxes totalled $6,000 for the first time: $4,467 for county, $500 for schools, and $1,033 for township expenses, including roads and bridges. There were 90 pathmasters (who served also as fence-viewers) and 11 pound-keepers by 1875; Thomas Stephenson was reeve that year; Robert Ford, Wm. Adams, Wm. Mills and Wm. Mitchell councillors; Robert Grandy clerk; Thomas Matchett treasurer; Michael Costello collector; plus assessors, auditors, license inspectors, court constables, school trustees, and returning officers.

Roads were a chief concern of local councils—the county re township boundary roads and main highways, the township re improvement of concession roads and bridges—in the early 1850s there were 55 Emily township road overseers appointed, and as many county road overseers, and by 1875 these numbers had nearly doubled. In 1850 Council defined the duties of the highway overseers, and assessed statute labour to be performed by every ratepayer on roads, based on his assessment—under £25 two days; £25 to £50—three days; and so on up to 12 days' labour if assessed £400 to £450, and for every £100 above £500 another day. Any person owning a cart, wagon or team (oxen or horses) had to work on roads at least three days. Statute labour could be commuted for 2s. 6d. a day, which the overseer was authorized to spend on the local road. There were special road grants from the county in 1850 to open up the Cavan/Emily boundary line, the Emily/Smith boundary line, the road between concessions 1 and 2, the 8th concession line, the 6th concession line which went through Carey's swamp, the road between Cowan's Bridge and the Middle (10th con.) line, the Scully swamp road, etc. In December, 1851, the main problem was protection of Metcalfe sidewalks from "person or persons riding or driving any horse, mare, gelding, oxen or other cattle along said sidewalks", and also persons who cut or carried away part of said sidewalks—fines to range from 2s. 6d. to 20s. In 1852-3 new roads were being built—on 7th concession, south to north between lots 16 and 17 in front and angling northwest to rear between lots 17 and 18, 50 ft. wide; through 12th concession between lots 13 and 14 northwesterly, 50 feet wide; through lot 18 in concession 6, 40 feet wide; in 7th concession between lots 9 and 10, angling east to middle road at Cowan's Bridge, then northwest to east bank of creek, then southwest across creek on lot 9, 40 feet wide. In 1854 also the county granted £25 to the Metcalfe-Downeyville road and "thence to Sergeant Miller's northward", on condition the township spent the same sum.

Road regulations were stiffened in 1855, with fines for those refusing statute labour (who could now commute same for 5s. a day) and for overseers who neglected their duties. In the next two years more new roads were started—"the travelled road through the swamp in concession 4 commonly called Middle Line, to be 66 ft. wide", and a new road around the hills on the first 3 concessions from Cavan boundary to Ops boundary, an improved gravel road 66 feet wide crossing the Middle Line beyond con. 2, requiring purchase of 6.28 acres from H. Best, Wm. Kells, James Fee and John Storey. The County Council granted £40 for 4th line road from the Smith boundary to David Armstrong's, £35 to lower Crawford's Hill near Metcalfe and the Metcalfe bridge, £20 on the Metcalfe-Downeyville road, called "the mail road", and another £30 to extend it to the southeast corner of Verulam, £10 on Cowan's Bridge, and £10 on the Cavan/Emily boundary road. Appointed in Emily to spend the county grants were: Bartholemew Kinnelly, Thomas Jackson, Humphrey Finley, Robert Hayes, Joseph Windren, John Murdock, Francis Best and Andrew Fowler. Again in 1858 the county, in addition to small sums on boundary roads, granted £25 for Omemee bridge, £100 for the west quarterline from Cavan to Verulam, and £50 on the Middle Emily line (Cavan to Verulam).

The township in 1860 raised $970 plus $230 provincial grant for roads, such as the new one around Dickson's Hill on the north end of lot 15, con. 4, 66 ft. wide; another between lots 18 and 19 in con. 14 and northward between lots 17 and 18 to the Verulam boundary, 40 ft. wide; and between lots 15 and 16 in con. 13 to centre, then easterly and northeast through lot 17 and part of 18 to its north limit, 66 ft. wide. Through the 1860s the United Counties (and from 1863 Victoria county) spent more on roads in Emily, with little new construction by the township—the main north-south and east-west roads, Cowan's Bridge, the road from King's Wharf to Bobcaygeon, from Best's Tavern in Emily into Peterboro, Lindsay to Downeyville and other travelled roads. In 1875 the county was spending $421 on Emily roads, plus $200 to repair Cowan's Bridge, while the township spent about $400. Every year Emily council had problems with people who farmed road allowances, blocked roadways, erected illegal fences, etc. In 1862, for example, a road was surveyed through McGibbin's lot on con. 13, title to be bought "at same price James Madigan got for his land . . . and that Ira Spencer do get an Order for $21 being the balance for building a bridge known as Pogue's Bridge on the boundary . . . and that Saml. Brown be notified to remove his fence from the road allowance on con. 1 or law proceedings will be taken." In 1863 James Magahay (McGahey) was given $20 for "causewaying over 30 rods" of corduroy road through a swamp on lot 1, con. 13; and Duncan McDonald was allowed to cut cedar for railwood on the concession line at north end of lot 5, con .11 "which he occupies". Settlers along the new roads made money by selling gravel and timber for roads, culverts and bridges— John Carew in 1867 sold 130 loads of gravel to the pathmaster at 5c a load!

With improving roads came better mail deliveries, and prepaid postage stamps increased letters also. Postmaster Grandy at Emily in 1852 was paid only £10, 7s. 3½d. Wm. Bletcher of Port Hope, stagecoach-owner, had the contract 1853-57 for £75 yearly to take mail to Emily—north on Monday, Wednesday and Friday, south on Tuesday, Thursday and Saturday. Downeyville Postoffice was established Nov. 6, 1852, with Michael Lehane postmaster; he also contracted to handle mail between Downeyville and Bobcaygeon by horseback or sleigh, for £13 per annum, each Saturday. Jeremiah McCarthy was new Downeyville postmaster May 1, 1864, and then Michael O'Neill April 1, 1872 until 1875. From 1856, J. Findlay (or Finley) carried the mail Bobcaygeon to Downeyville and return; this service was doubled to twice-weekly from June 1857, at contract price £34 yearly. In this period also, A. English was carrying mail between Downeyville and

Omemee by horseback, wagon or cutter, twice-weekly, for £11, 5s. yearly,
later raised to £15. R. W. Shaw carried mail 6 times weekly between
Omemee and Peterborough in 1857 for £76, 12s. 7d.; but next year when the
railway came, this was cancelled. In 1858 the Omemee postmaster was paid
£28, 9s. 3½d., and the Downeyville postmaster £4, 6s. 8d.—postoffices
were in stores, since no official could live on this salary. In 1860, the Omemee
Postoffice was authorized to sell the new money orders, and a postoffice opened
earlier at Henderson's Corners, with postmaster R. Morton, was closed as it
was considered unnecessary.

Business picked up in 1861—the Omemee Postoffice sold one money
order of $38.50 payable in Canada, and one more of $24.45 payable in
United Kingdom. Robert Shaw in 1861 got the contract to carry mail from
Omemee Postoffice to the railway station, 1¼ miles, on foot, 12 times weekly,
at $156 a year, until 1865. Robert Grandy had the contract to carry mail
twice-weekly between Omemee and Downeyville (Tuesday and Saturday)
for $64 yearly, and in 1862 he also got the job of carrying mail Omemee to
Willocks via Downeyville 12½ miles, Wednesday and Saturday each week
for 4 years, at $140 yearly. In 1865 Edward Hanna took over the mail route
from Omemee Postoffice to rail station, for $104 a year; and the Downeyville
to Dunsford route was added by Grandy to his Omemee-Downeyville route at
an extra $70 a year. Money order business was booming; Omemee Postoffice
in the year ending June 30, 1867, issued 102 orders valued at $160.03. In
July, 1868, a postoffice savings-bank was opened at Omemee and within a year
had two accounts totalling $171, being a local substitute for a saving-bank. In
the year ending June 30, 1870, Omemee postoffice issued 89 money orders
totalling $5,221.70 and cashed 23 with value $716.20. That year Michael
O'Neill took over the three times weekly mail route between Downeyville
and Omemee, $97 a year for four years. Frank Hill Postoffice under Thomas
Franks was opened January 1, 1872, and the Omemee postmaster was paid
$165.50, the Downeyville postmaster $29.50. Finally, in 1873, Robert Grandy
took over delivery of mail to Omemee rail station from his postoffice, 18
times weekly, $104 a year, on a four-year contract raised to $150 in 1875;
and in 1875 M. Tracey took over the Downeyville-Omemee route at $75 a
year, still 3 times weekly.

Land was the main basis of taxation, and increasing land speculation and
usage of marginal lands, coupled with flooding due to the building of Trent
navigation dams, led to many complaints to government departments and
lawsuits. In 1851 G. Shouldice was granted £35 damages for drowned land
on north half lot 21, con. 4, and sold it later to William Hughes who tried
(unsuccessfully) to collect damages in 1863. In 1852 Owen Callaghan was
on the west half lot 4, con. 6, being "a poor man with 8 children", and
steadily improving the property, according to a testimonial from Postmaster
Grandy; yet Daniel Scully was trying to get the lot, "a rich young man who
has plenty without taking the land poor Callaghan is living on"; by November
Callaghan had paid for the lot and received his deed from Walter Crawford,
Crown Land agent at Peterborough, but in 1855 he sold the lot for
£217 10s. to Wm. Lang of Emily.

	Taxable Real Property	Aggregate Value before Equalization	Total Taxes	Number of Ratepayers
1851	33,317 acres	£72,301	£200	344
1862	61,349 acres	$452,697	$3,800	592
1875	58,965 acres	$707,580	$6,000	564

Notes on table:

1. Vacant or non-resident property (taxed at a lower rate) was over half in 1851, but was down to 1,500 acres in 1875.

2. A small amount of personal property was taxed in addition to real property.

3. The separation of Omemee in 1874 is evident in taxable property and number of ratepayers, though not in aggregate value and in total taxes.

In March 1854, Thomas Dennehy, P.L.S., surveyed drowned lands on lots 15 and 16, con. 7, owned by J. McDonald, Denis Carrol and Thomas Trotter; he found that the flooding also extended across lots 15 and 16, con. 8, close to the millpond of the old Baldwin Mill, but his report does not indicate whether any damages were paid. In 1861 Wm. Reynolds complained about north half lot 3, con. 6, where he and his father before him had cleared and improved; but now his father was "a drinking man" and three speculators were trying to oust him and get the lot—he appealed to the Crown Land Agent "as a brother Orangeman" to postpone any sale of the lot. James Dunsford, M.P., wrote in Jan. 1862 to the Commissioner of Crown Lands concerning the north half lot 2, con. 8, where the Wynde family, he asserted, had been placed in 1825—Henry Wynde had been the 1825 locatee but had never applied for a deed and was now an old man, having cleared 60 acres; in 1861 the government had sold the lot to Robert and Daniel Wynde, his nephews, who threatened to dispossess their uncle; the decision on this dramatic case is not on file. The Cottingham flood claim surfaced again in 1862, when Wm. Cottingham with Dunsford's aid tried to get additional compensation from the Board of Works on his lot 7, con. 3, because of public works at Buckhorn Rapids; he complained that the Buckhorn millowners put "boards on the dam then throwing the water still higher, if this is continued I might as well give up my mill property". Even with new wheels and machinery "I cannot do as much business as on former occasions, and it is exactly so with the Sawmill, we can do little or nothing in the spring and also when we have heavy rainfalls—in dry weather the water is so low that we are scarcely able to do anything. . . ." The investigation showed that in 1851 he had been awarded £550, "in full satisfaction and discharge of above claim & also of all damage or injury by said Buckhorn dam & works that may hereafter be occasioned to him," so they denied any further compensation.

By the 1851 census, Emily residents had 599 bulls, oxen or steers; 941

milch cows; 626 calves or heifers; 577 horses; 3,397 sheep; and 2,129 pigs. One of Council's most serious problems was to keep these from wandering, hence the annual appointment of poundkeepers and fenceviewers. In 1850 the poundkeepers were: Charles Hartley, John McGee (or Magee), Wm. Herlihey, Luke Connell, Thomas O'Brien, James Boate and Thomas Dwyer; the fence viewers were Edward Hanna, Thomas Trotter, Samuel Magee, Thomas Crawford, Adam Thornton, Francis Henderson, George Miller, David Rowan, Wm. Laidley, Wm. Lang Jr., James Laidley, John Kearns, Martin McCauliffe, Wm. Doran, John Miller, Wm. Lehane, Michael Collins and James Balfour. By Bylaw 5, each pound-keeper was to set up enclosures for stray animals, and charge poundage: 1s. a day for a horse, 9d. for an ox, 7½d. for a cow, 6d. for young cattle, 3d. for a pig, 1d. for a sheep, plus same amount for food and water; if not collected by owner within 48 hours paying fees, notices were posted publicly for 15 days, and the animals sold to highest bidder, with fees for sale, and surplus given to owner if known. Bylaw 7 specified that all lot fences were to be at least 4½ feet high of good durable material, and all "intire horses, bulls, boars, rams and breachy cattle" prohibited from running at large April 1 to November 1, with owner fined 2s. 6d. for first offence, 5s. for second offence, etc. An 1855 bylaw prohibited all animals from running at large December 1 to April 1 also, with fine 2s. plus costs and poundage charges. By 1862 the problem of dogs chasing and killing sheep became acute, and a bylaw imposed a tax of $1 on each dog or bitch kept by a ratepayer, over the first one, plus a fine of $1 on any dog running at large "without a proper muzzle on him or her"—also anyone seeing a dog running at large unmuzzled was authorized to shoot it—this, and the worrying of sheep by dogs, caused much quarrelling and "taking to court" in the next four decades, as well as heavy compensation charges annually paid by Council for sheep killed or maimed. From about 1868, the fence-viewing duties were taken over by highway overseers; in 1874, the pound-keepers were: Geo. Harkness, Andrew Fowler, John Fee, Wm. Franks, Jos. Sanderson, Jacob McBrien, Dan. Winn, Wm. Richardson, John Callaghan, James Crimin, and Wm. McMullen (apparently appointed for a four-year period).

The related problems of inns and taverns, liquor and morals, worried Emily council incessantly through this generation, reflecting, of course, a general concern in the township. The shift from Harkness' Inn to Blackwell's Inn for township meetings in January 1851 was an indication. Shortly after, Bylaw 26 limited "inns and houses of public entertainment" to 7 in the township, "where spirituous or malt liquors shall be sold"; each was to be licensed, with fee £4 in or near Metcalfe, £3 10s. near the Emily-Cavan boundary, and £3 at Downey's Cross. Each was to have "a comfortable dwelling-house with at least 3 furnished bedrooms" extra to those used by the Innkeeper's family, and rules for reception of travellers, provision of stable stalls, water supply, etc. The door was to be locked at 11 p.m. with no more drinking, no selling of liquor to intoxicated persons, "no profane swearing, immodest or disloyal songs or tales . . . no slight of hand, tumbling, rope-

No. *9*   *Inn-keeper's License for the Year 18—* *on the last day of February 1852*

PROVINCE OF CANADA.   COUNTY *of Peterborough.*

HIS EXCELLENCY THE RIGHT HONORABLE JAMES, EARL OF ELGIN AND KINCARDINE, *Baron Elgin, K. T., Governor General of British North America, &c., &c., &c.*

TO ALL WHOM THESE PRESENTS MAY CONCERN:

This License is granted to *Mary Ann Davidson*
of the Town*ship* of *Emily*
County of in the *Peterborough* County
in that part of the Province heretofore called Upper Canada, INN-KEEPER, to keep the House known by the sign
of *Mrs. Davidson's Hotel* situated *in the village of Metcalfe* as an Inn,
or other House of Public Entertainment, and to sell therein by Retail, Wine, Brandy, Rum, or other Spirituous Liquors.
This License to be in force until the first day of *February* one thousand eight hundred and fifty *two*, and
no longer; and provided that the said *Mary Ann Davidson* shall, during the continuance of
the said License, maintain and keep good order in the said Inn, or House, and duly observe all such rules, regulations,
matters and things respecting Inns, or other Houses of Public Entertainment, as by any Act or Acts made, or to be
made, by the Provincial Parliament, are, or shall be enacted and declared.

Given under my Hand, at *Metcalfe* this *Eighth* day of
March one thousand eight hundred and fifty *one*.

By His Excellency's Command,

Lewis   Deputy Inspector General.

RECEIVED from the said *Mary Ann Davidson*
the sum of *Four Pound 3/9*
being the Duty payable on this License.   Lawful money of the Province,

Thomas Milburn
Inspector of Licenses
County of Peterborough

County License 1851-52 for Mary Davidson's Inn at Metcalfe Village, Emily Township.
(Mrs. M. Bowen)

Arthur McQuade, born in Ireland 1817, died in Emily Township 1894; prominent in community affairs and politics, and Member of Parliament 1874-82.

dancing, card-playing or any kind of gambling whatever", subject to fines from 5s. to £5. Bylaw 27 required innkeepers to post £40 security, prohibited selling liquor on the Sabbath except to travellers, also no sale to any person under 16 years of age. The next two bylaws appointed inn inspectors to issue licenses, and prescribed their duties—the licenses granted were to: Francis Best, David Harkness, Edward Blackwell, Robt. Henderson, Isaac English, James Collins, and Mary Davidson. Bylaw 30 amended the above to allow 9 inns and taverns selling liquor, the new ones to Michael Lehane (Downeyville) and David Armstrong. But in 1852 new bylaws restricted the licenses to 7, and three months later allowed an 8th—Hardis Alwill's Inn in Metcalfe; then bylaw 42 authorized 7 "temperance hotels" in Emily at license £1 5s., with most of the above regulations, and an absolute prohibition on any sale or use of liquor under penalty £10.

But next year (1853) the system was revised and regulations stiffened— tavern licenses were limited to five—F. Best, Robt. Henderson, Edward Blackwell, David Harkness, and Michael Guiry (Downeyville). Each inn in Metcalfe village was to have for travellers 4 well-furnished bedrooms, a sitting room and a dining room besides the barroom, plus good stabling for 8 horses "with sufficiency of provender and water", sheds for 6 teams and a good enclosed yard. At Downeyville and along the Emily-Smith boundary road each inn was to have 3 bedrooms for travellers, a sitting room besides the barroom, stabling for 6 horses, sheds for 4 teams, and an enclosed yard. The earlier rules were retained, and in addition innkeepers were accountable for the safety of travellers and their baggage, were to close the barroom on Sunday, were forbidden to allow any intoxicated person to leave the premises, but to take care of him "until he became sober", and themselves were to be "of good moral character". In 1854, each inn or tavernkeeper selling liquor was required to pay £6 12s. 6d. in fees, (soon increased to £10), each storekeeper retailing liquor and wine £7 11s. 9d., or selling ale and beer only £2 13s. 9d. Next year licenses were extended to Robt. Henderson, Richard Owens (at King's Wharf) and Benjamin Madigan, and the last two exempted from the regulations about bedrooms and stabling.

Troubles persisted, and in 1856 Council had to pass a bylaw about disorderly and/or intoxicated persons disturbing council meetings, with fines and imprisonment for offenders. The 1857-8 Directory mentioned 3 hotels in Metcalfe, and in Downeyville 1 hotel and 1 saloon. Bylaw 79 in 1858 appointed a license inspector, with sureties of £150, at salary $40 a year, to inspect and license all inns, saloons, beerhouses, and temperance houses and "report if they are conducted in orderly manner." Next year the scale of licenses was set at: $40 for taverns in villages, and saloon or shop licenses; $30 for taverns outside villages; $12 to sell ale and beer; $4 for temperance houses—the rules now forbade selling liquors between 7 p.m. Saturday and 8 a.m. Monday except to bonafide travellers staying at an inn.

The new wave of Victorian morality, including temperance, across Canada West, is summed up in Bylaw no. CLXII adopted by the Council of United Counties of Peterborough and Victoria June 30, 1860, entitled "A

Bylaw for the Preservation of Public Morals", applicable in Emily. All business was prohibited on Sunday (except for works of necessity, charity, mails and sale of drugs and medicines), also all games, races, dances, profane music, fishing, hunting, or any other sport—even carrying a fishing-rod or net or trap or gun on Sunday was subject to fine. Seven days a week it was prohibited to sell or give liquor to any child or servant, to post or circulate "any indecent placards, writings or pictures", to write the same on wall or fence, to utter obscene or insulting language in public, to appear drunk or disorderly in public, to indulge in any immoral or scandalous behavior in public, to bath in any waters near a house or public highway between 6 a.m. and 8 p.m. "unless provided and clothed in a proper bathing dress, sufficient to prevent any indecent exposure", or even to allow any stud horse to perform in any exposed place! Seven days a week it was unlawful to disturb any church service or "social and intellectual entertainment", to conduct a "tippling house", or a "house of ill-fame", or to have any horse race for money, or to hold any circus or exhibition for profit, or to conduct any bowling alley or gambling house, any roulette table "and other devices for gambling"—fines up to $50 or 20 days in gaol "with or without hard labour".

This atmosphere was reflected in Emily Bylaw 94, January 1861, to regulate licensing of taverns and other places selling liquors. Taverns and wholesale venders were licensed unless a petition signed by 30 resident electors was opposed, but only in a proportion no greater than 1 license for every 250 persons resident. No licenses at all were to issue for ale or beer-houses "or other house of public entertainment". The former rigid rules were maintained for places licensed, plus requiring them to close Monday to Friday at 7 p.m. instead of 11 as before, with severe penalties for infractions. A new "lockup house" was built in 1862 at Omemee to hold offenders, and that year inn and tavern licenses were: at Omemee $40, Downeyville $40, Fowler's $35, Henderson's $35, Callaghan's (King's Wharf) $30, Cowan's Bridge and others $25—these rates continued for several years. In 1865 Emily Council was in legal trouble for passing a bylaw (which does not appear in the existing Minute-book) prohibiting issuing of licenses for sale of any ardent spirits in Emily, on the grounds that "the bylaw was not prepared in conformity with the prohibitory Duncan Act of 1864". The Council replied to the writ "This Council is of opinion the Duncan Bill does not go far enough to prohibit the use of intoxicating liquors in general and liquor is used as freely in this municipality as before its passing"—but Council had to back down. By 1867 Emily Council limited the number of taverns and vendors licensed to ten: 4 in Omemee and 3 in Downeyville at $40 fee, 1 at John Callaghan's and 1 at McColl's (known as Fowler's Corners) at $35 fee, and 1 at Ben. Madigan's at $30; shop licenses were $40 each. In 1868 there were 8 tavern licenses in the township, according to the Ontario Government Journals. One other faint echo of the 1860 County bylaw occurred in 1872, when Emily adopted a bylaw to prohibit all billiard tables and gambling in the township. However, the temperance forces were gathering their strength for a powerful campaign before 1875.

Another major concern of county and township councils after 1850 was the improvement and upgrading of education, both common and grammar school— from building and equipment to books and teacher training—the Canadian government was little concerned, beyond giving small grants for education and setting up Toronto Normal School, but the Ontario government after Confederation (1867) took more interest, since education was a provincial responsibility. In 1851 there were 1,078 children of school age (5 to 16 years) in Emily, of whom 527, about half, were at school for 8¼ months—286 boys and 241 girls. There were 14 school sections, but only 12 schools open. The total spent on education was £309, 11s. 4½d. of which teachers were paid £265, 4s. 10d.—the township raised by taxes £85, and the legislative grant was £85, 7s. 3½d., and the parents in the sections had to find the rest, by fees or otherwise. Thomas Benson was District school superintendent at £130 a year, but he complained to the Council of the immense distances to be covered, which ate up £70 of his salary in 1851 and again in 1852, when he resigned from poor health; most of Council wanted township superintendents, though Warden Cottingham disapproved, but the change was made and Dr. John Irons of Metcalfe was appointed school superintendent for Emily and Ennismore.

Meanwhile the Emily Council had its school problems—Bylaw 15 in 1850 levied the sum of £5, 7s. 10½d. "for following repairs to s.s. 13 viz laying and jointing upper floor, building chimney, making seats & desks; providing 500 ft. lumber, 15 lbs. nails, 250 bricks, 2 elbows for stove, drawing said lumber & paying Geo. Miller sum of 27/6 due to him for work by section." Bylaw 20 the same year added £2, 10s. to collector's roll in favour of Wm. Laidley "to remunerate him in part for loss sustained in burning of schoolhouse in section S.S. 2 Union School (with no. 10 Ops) . . . to be collected off the inhabitants resident within S.S. 2." On July 8, 1851, Bylaw 35 was passed to levy £17 for a schoolhouse in s.s. no. 6; "materials necessary for the erection of said schoolhouse shall be received by the Trustees at fair & current price delivered by any of the inhabitants compelled to assist by law in the erection of the same."—this is an example of a building-bee for erection of a schoolhouse, the material not mentioned.

The first township bylaw in 1854 (no. 56) united s.s. 10 and 14 into one school section, "it having at the annual school meeting in January held in the section been unanimously agreed upon by the ratepayers thereof." This was a depression year, when tax allotment for schools was only £70 and grant about the same. Dr. Irons was still school superintendent, and placed by county council on the Board of Examiners for common-school teachers in Lindsay (Victoria) district. Emily had its first superannuated teacher, Gideon Gibson, born in Ireland, age now 69, retired of age and infirmity after 19 years teaching; size of pension not stated, but probably microscopic. In 1855 Metcalfe (Omemee) Grammar School was established by the County Council on June 23 (Bylaw XCIII), with trustees: Rev. Harding, Rev. Ewing, Rev. Briden, Dr. Irons, Wm. Cottingham, Chris. Knowlson, T. Matchett, Rev. Bourke; in following years the trustees changed, but in 1857 the Council noted "no school yet in operation."

Appendix 16 of the Legislative Journals 1856 contained statistics on Emily education in 1855 worth recording—of 1,070 children of school age, 784 were in school, plus 31 pupils over 16 years of age, being 537 boys and 278 girls; among these were 2 deaf and dumb children, and 2 blind. Of the Emily population, only 15% were unable to read and write, very creditable since for Victoria County the illiteracy was 23%. There were 13 school sections, with 12 schools open—of these 8 were free schools, the rest charging fees. The schools had been established: 1 in 1830, 1 in 1831, 1 in 1834, 2 in 1838, 1 in 1844, 2 in 1845, 1 in 1846, 1 in 1847, 2 in 1848. Of the teachers, 11 were male, 1 female—3 Anglican, 4 Roman Catholic, 1 Presbyterian and 4 Methodist. Only 1 teacher had been trained in Normal School, with provincial certificate; 1 had a first class certificate, 5 2nd-class and 5 3rd-class. The highest salary paid was £100, the lowest paid a male teacher £48, male without board £65, female teacher without board £36. Of the 12 schools, all were of logs, and open 9 months a year. There were 67 visits: 1 by school superintendent, 1 by a clergyman, 9 by magistrates, and 56 by trustees. The rest of the survey covers textbooks used, etc.; incidentally, there were only 3 maps and 5 blackboards in Emily. Textbooks and a few maps were allocated to schools from a central school repository in Peterborough (and later when Victoria county separated in 1863, from a similar building in Lindsay).

In 1856 the tax levy for common schools in Emily was up to £100, and Rev. Harding was appointed Emily school superintendent, succeeded later in the year by Rev. Wm. Braiden (or Bredin) who served through 1857. Bylaw 77 authorized the Reeve to sign a quit-claim deed of the land now occupied by the school no. 4 at Downeyville, to Bartholemew Downey, being part of north half lot 6, con. 9. in lieu of another site purchased from Downey for a new school to be built. The Omemee *Warder* of Feb. 20, 1857, carried an advertisement by John Irons Jr., Secretary of the School Board: "SCHOOL TEACHER WANTED: a firstclass teacher is required for the Amalgamated Grammar and Common School in the village of Omemee, township Emily, to whom a liberal salary will be paid." (The Weekly Toronto *Globe* and the *Journal of Education* were asked to copy). The Assembly Journals reported that one of 3 schools in Victoria chosen to receive government libraries was S.S. 4, Emily, given 54 volumes. Next year a fuller report on books sent to Emily schools, for free public use, was tabled: with a legislative grant of £50 and local council vote of £50, a total of 748 volumes had been sent: 104 history, 59 zoology, 18 botany, 16 natural phenomena, 16 physical science, 9 geology and minerology, 14 natural philosophy, 5 chemistry, 3 agricultural chemistry, 51 practical agriculture, 75 manufactures, 44 literature, 69 voyages, 105 biography, 148 tales (fiction), 12 for teachers— the number of volumes taken out in the last year 179, the number of inhabitants reading 153. These volumes in local schools were the beginning of free public libraries in the rural areas of Emily. In 1858 also Emily had its second superannuated teacher, Matt. Handcock, born Ireland, age 70, after 22 years teaching—"commenced teaching in Emily 1835 and taught in Emily, Cavan and Manvers to Dec. 31, 1856—carried King's Colours at battle of Lundy's Lane"—pension £33 plus subscriptions £23—certified by Dr. Irons, Wm. Cottingham, Rev. R. Harding, etc.

The tax levy for common schools was still only $438 in 1859, $500 in 1860, and stood at $600 a year through 1861 to 1873, falling in 1874-75 to $550 (with government grant rather lower). Rev. John Goodfellow, school superintendent 1858 to 1861, was replaced next year by Rev. Noah Desbrow. In 1859 Bylaw 90 divided S.S. no. 6, taking away the north part to be called S.S. 15 (composed of all the part of concessions 13 and 14, and also the north half of con. 12, from Emily Lake marsh easterly to Pigeon River marsh) the schoolhouse to be erected on the rear of lot 19 in con. 13. Omemee Grammar School was now operating, with 1860 Board of Trustees: Wm. Cottingham, Thomas Matchett, Wm. Turner. Wm. Beatty, Wm. Curry, Dr. Irons, Rev. Leich, Rev. Goodfellow, Rev. Ewing and Rev. Coyle.

We are able to get an interesting insight into an 1860 Emily school from the Visitors' Book of United Sections nos. 10 and 14 kept by the teacher, Wm. J. Webster.[2] In March he wrote: "School visited by Mrs. W. Best— scholars solved different questions in Arithmetic. Scholars addressed on different subjects by Mrs. Best." An April 5 entry reads: "Examined Mr. Webster's School in reading, spelling, arithmetic and the elements of Geography and was pleased with their advancement in knowledge and general proficiency. John Goodfellow S.S." Others who visited that year were Thos. Jackson, trustee; Sam Endicott, trustee; James Henderson; Mr. McCague; plus another visit by John Goodfellow October 22. The accounts for 1860 are revealing: RECEIPTS: government grant $24.70, local grant $20.00; subscription $20.50; on property $236.38—total $301.58. EXPENSES: Teacher's salary $260.00; Section 14 expenses $6.17; Seats in no. 10—$25.55; clerk and corporate seal $1.50—total expenses $33.22 plus teacher's salary; BALANCE ON HAND $8.36. The trustees "moved and carried that 2½ months be' taught in Sect. no. 14 and 9½ months the remainder of the year in no. 10". At the Ratepayers' Annual meeting in 1861, chaired by Thomas Magee, the trustees reported; Thomas Jackson was elected new trustee. A motion read: "in consideration of Mr. Brady giving the site for the Brick Schoolhouse and for certain annoyances which he experiences from the same, he be exempted from paying more than $3 school taxes during each year of his encumbrance of the place on which he resides and be allowed to send one child for the aforesaid consideration". The school fees were set at $2.50 per child attending, or 25c per month. Another motion, to separate the two school sections, was defeated. W. H. Hill was teacher in 1862, and visitors wrote in the book of their pleasure with the conduct of the school, including on July 17: "Rev. N. Desbrow visited the school today and expressed himself pleased with the manner the school is conducted, etc. W. H. Hill". The 1861 and 1862 school accounts are confused, but the teacher was paid $204 per annum.

By 1864 s.s. 14 was separated, as the Annual Meeting in January 1864 was "held in s.s. 10 and part of no. 17 in Cavan", with Thomas Magee, chairman. Wm. Burns and Geo. Evans were elected new trustees. A motion

MINUTE BOOK OF TRUSTEES S.S.10, Emily
Receipts and Expenses—1860 and 1867 (Mrs. N. McBain)

Government Grant for 1860 $24.70

Local   "   "   "   20.35

Subscription   20.50

On property   236.38

$301.58

Teachers Salary for 1860   260.00

Balance on hands after Teachers Salary   41.58

Expenses of Sect 14   6.17

Expenses for Seats on No 10   25.55

For cordwood deal and Cloth   1.50

Total Expenses $33.22

Balance on hands   8.36

It was moved and carried that
2½ months be taught in Sect No 14
& the Remainder of the year in No 10

Emily November 20th 1867
Receipts of School Section No 10
and part of 17 Cavan

Government in Emily $18.69

do   pt of 17 Cavan   2.10

Local Grant Supposed to be   20.00

40.79

Expences

Teachers Salary   140.00

Books   2.25

To Grundy   2.00

Cards for School   .50

Chalk Crayons   .50

To 1½ Cord of Wood   3.75

To Glass   .20

Putty   .5

To Mending the Stove   1.00

1 Burner   .25

1 Elbow for Stove pipe   .25

1 Broom   .25

151.09

carried that the school be "free", but every parent sending children to school provide "half a cord of wood cut for the stove". In 1866 this was defined as "half a cord of stovewood for every child" . . . those persons who do not bring their quantity of wood will be obliged to pay at rate of 3s. 9d. per half cord". Sixteen fathers are listed, and their allotment 14 cords to be delivered. The teacher, R. H. Johnston, received $175 in 1865 but only $153.86 in 1866, and the 1867 accounts indicated he got only $140, with total school expenses for the year $151.00 (including $2.25 for books, 20c for window-glass, $1 for mending the stove, 25c for a broom, and 25c for a stovepipe elbow). The 1869 Annual Meeting, with H. Moore chairman, elected Alex Findley and John Mitchell trustees for three-year term; each parent was required to furnish a cord of wood delivered at the school or in default to pay $2.25 for each child. The School Superintendent, J. H. Delamere, visited the school on March 22 and wrote: "Visited school in s.s. 10 today, found it in good working order, examined the several classes and found the Pupils well advanced in their studies. . . . The teacher, Mr. Wm. Elliott, seemed to devote his best attention to the work of imparting information to his pupils." Elliott's salary was $210, and including salary the total year's expenses were only $224.30.

In 1865 the Assembly received a petition from Wm. Lehane and others of Emily township, "that the Separate School law may be so amended as to secure for them efficient schools and educational institutions." Perhaps as a result, Emily Council decided to hold a meeting in Town Hall open to the public on July 4 "to remodel the school sections and wards", but the only recorded result was Bylaw 107 early in 1866 to unite part of Union S.S. 2 to Union S.S. 1 and to separate Union S.S. 2 from no. 9 of Ops township. The Omemee *"Warder"* Nov. 3, 1865, had an item from Wm. Curry, secretary: "SCHOOL TEACHERS' EXAMINATION: The Junior Western Board of Public Instruction of Victoria will meet in the School House, Omemee, for the purpose of examining Teachers, 15th December, 1865. . . . Applicants for third-class certificates will be required to be posted up in books mentioned in the programme." Omemee Grammar School, which began classes in 1860, by 1866 had 51 students, who paid no fees; the building was frame, and the headmaster was listed as John Shaw, paid $600 in 1866—the Grammar School had started in 1860 with 21 students which increased yearly, but attendance was poor—in 1866 average attendance was only 21 out of 54; by 1868 when there were 82 students and two teachers, AVERAGE attendance was only 27.[3]

Bylaw 116 in 1867 approved levying the sum of $400 on ratepayers in S.S. no. 12 to erect a new school, either frame or brick. Then in 1868 a new red brick school was erected in S.S. no. 13, on the northwest corner of the present L. Wright's property; this school served the community for about 55 years, with rows of double seats, and extra seats along the walls when attendance rose toward 75 (such as annual meetings). The last School Superintendent, John Delamere, in his report in 1871 chided the parents for not sending their children regularly to school, adding "The people of this community do not seem to read much." Perhaps this did not apply in S.S. 10, where N.W. Will visited May 10, 1871 and wrote: "Visited this school taught by Mr. Geo. Balfour and was well pleased at the manner he conducted the classes, and the general conditions in the school." On May 19, Henry Sherin Jr. (teacher in S.S. no. 14) visited S.S. 10 and wrote: "Visited this school taught by Mr. Balfour today and found great signs of intellectual progress, good conduct, etc., etc., etc." The teacher's salary was $200, and other expenses in the year only $23.40. In 1872 the teachers's salary was only $180, and other expenses $9.80 (including repairing pump $1, balance on map $1.50, and stovepipe elbow 30c). S.S. no. 10 had its first lady teacher, "Miss Stevenson", in 1872, and she was only paid $130 in 1873, and apparently replaced by Miss Tully later that year. At the annual meeting in 1873, S.S. no. 10 and S.S. no. 14 were united and to be known as S.S. no. 10, and they purchased the school site. Also that year council bylaws authorized trustees of S.S. no. 6 to raise a loan of $600 to buy a site and build a schoolhouse, loan to be paid off in 5 years; and authorized the trustees of S.S. no. 15 to raise $450 to buy a site, build a school and enclose the land with a fence.

Starting in 1872, J. R. Knight became Common School Inspector for East Victoria, including Emily, replacing the township superintendents, and reporting yearly to the County Council. His 1873 report showed that Emily, which in 1855 had 12 log schools and none brick or frame, now had 6 brick, 2 frame and 6 log; the next year there were 2 more brick and 1 more frame schools, and by 1875 the township had 8 brick, 3 frame and only 2 log schools. Only 3 of the schools were fenced. Of 15 teachers (3 in Omemee) 7 were male and 8 female, 2 with 2nd-class certificates. 13 3rd-class. There were 1,181 children of school age in 1874, of whom 1,047 attended school, but average attendance was only 372. Three new schools had been built 1873-4 in Emily in S.S. 6, 11 and 15, and a new one building in S.S. 7— but he added "In township Emily very few of the schools are in an efficient state. I attribute this, to a great extent, to the low standard of admission to the Omemee High School. Scholars have been admitted who should have attended the Public Schools at least another year. . . ." A table in his 1875 report gives details of each of 10 schools reporting with number of parents and children attending school. It was obvious that the parents and trustees were trying hard to improve the school buildings, but the onus was on the provincial government and local councils to provide much more money to upgrade teacher training and salaries, books and equipment, and other facilities.

A few more incidents from county and township minutes and bylaws are introduced at this point, before proceeding to other aspects of Emily development. Indigent persons were looked after by small grants—Widow McBrien $10 in 1862, and again in 1864, Cornelius Russell $5 in 1864; then in 1865 Owen Casey $5 as "he is in poor health and very hard up", and $5 to Michael Nicholson "as we understand he is in a starving condition"— in 1865 Nicholson was also given $10.50 for clothing. In Nov. 1863 Council granted a sum to build a sidewalk from Orange Hall to the Grammar School in Omemee, and in May 1864 granted $100 to purchase a weigh scale for the use of merchants and farmers "to be placed in some convenient place in the village." In April 1865, Mr. Laskin (or Laslin) was given a $3 refund "that he paid Mr. Grandy for the use of the Town Hall to hold a Concert, he having taught the children of Omemee gratis at his Singing School." Late in 1866 David Hartly's tender was accepted for $500 to build a drill hall for the militia in Omemee (the government to pay half the sum), and to be completed by Jan. 1, 1867. In 1873-4 much turmoil was stirred up by Mr. Cottingham's motion in County Council to allow Omemee to incorporate, and a committee was set up to define the village boundaries. Bylaw 149 authorized incorporation, stating the population was over 750, and of these 150 had petitioned for separate status; the area was to be 496 acres in lots 4-8 of con. 4 and parts of lots 4-8 of con. 3. Emily Township protested in 1874 that this took $9,000 off the taxable property of that township. including acreage at $12 an acre, and $\frac{1}{3}$ of the personal property. It was agreed that the Town Hall remain Emily property, which caused friction in later years.

Militia matters were prominent in Emily 1860 to 1871, with Fenian scares after the U.S. Civil War, and then the Riel Rebellion in Manitoba. The first Battalion Victoria Militia was commanded by Col. Edward Davidson, and when he retired in 1858 by Colonel Wm. Cottingham of Omemee— other officers from Emily were Majors Francis Henderson and Chris. Knowlson (the former 1852, the latter 1858), Captains Charles Hamilton and Ed. Davidson (both 1855), and Capt. Charles Hartley (1858), also Capt. John Sullivan who died 1858; and Wm. Davidson (made lieutenant 1856 and captain 1860); Lieut. Thomas Matchett and Lieut. Edward Hanna (both 1856), and Lieut. Wm. Matchett (1860); and Ensigns Humphrey Finley and John Murdock (1856), John English (1858) and Thomas Lehane. Capt. James Durnsford moved to Emily from Peterborough, and John McFeeters became Lieutenant 1858; Ensigns Wm. Irons, A. McQuade and Thos. Stephenson (1861)—the battalion surgeon was Dr. John Irons until his death in 1855, and the adjutant from 1858 was Lieut. Thomas Bell of Emily.[4] By 1862 the Battalion had 22 officers, 15 sergeants, 510 men and a reserve of 107. As the Fenian scare spread, by 1865 Victoria had an Active Militia Battalion of 795 men organized, of whom 135 volunteers were from Emily, to meet any attack across Lake Ontario. Nov. 3, 1865, the Omemee *Warder* had an editorial and a long article headed "The Fenians to Invade Upper Canada". But in 1866 some men from Cavan and Peterborough County were called for frontier duty to combat raids, though none from Victoria County.

By 1868 with reorganization, the South Victoria Reserve Militia Battalion, under Col. Cottingham, had a total of 3,720 men in 9 companies, plus 93 enrolled in the volunteers—no. 5 company with Omemee headquarters had about 400 personnel. In 1869 the Emily reserve totalled 771, of whom 317 were unmarried men 18 to 29 years, and there were 50 men from the township in the volunteers, and one sailor. From 1871 this was part of the 45th West Durham Battalion with no. 5 Company at Omemee (724 men), and in 1874 they went to camp at Cobourg June 22 for 12 days for drill, target practice, etc. With the crisis fading, Capt. Cottingham of Omemee in 1875 took 2 officers and 34 men to camp at Cobourg, June 14 to 25, the rest having harvest leave. There is no record to show that any Emily men (unless among the volunteers on active service) fired a shot at the enemy during either the Fenian raids or the Riel Rebellion.

Elections in the Peterborough/Victoria Riding (including Emily) caused some interesting situations. In 1851 John Langton, staunch Conservative, ran against James Hall, and Emily voted 178 for Langton, 100 for Hall. On Dec. 21 Langton wrote Thomas Need, back in England, giving particulars of the election (which he won) crediting his win on the backing of the "Orangemen, Church of England, Methodists, Irish Presbyterians and Old Kirk, against Free Church, Catholic, Baptist, etc. . . . [In Emily] the desertion of the Catholics was severely felt here, otherwise I should have had 200 majority".[5] Most of the Peterborough townships favoured Hall, who lost by 100 votes. Charles Vizard wrote to Langton from Emily on Nov. 22: "Dear Langton: Finley wishes me to inform you that Alex. Brannon and Thos. Brannon intend to vote on neither side at the Election and he thinks that if you would send a couple of Notes for him to send to them they would be induced to vote for you." In the 1854 election Mr. Smith (Liberal) won over Mr. Boyd (Conservative), though Emily voted Smith 95 and Boyd 150; by this time Victoria was a separate Riding. In 1858, Emily voted 297 for Cameron (Conservative), 170 for Laing (or Lang) (Liberal), and 4 for McLaughlin— Cameron won. In 1862, Emily voted 247 for Jas. Dunsford (who won), 222 for Cameron—total 469 out of 543 eligible voters, an admirable proportion.

Confederation 1867 brought the same political excitement and debating in Emily as in all Ontario, and Victoria County was divided into North and South Ridings. For the Canadian Parliament, Geo. Kempt (Liberal) won the riding of Victoria South over H. Cameron (Conservative); Emily voted 148 for Kempt, 253 for Cameron. In the 1871 Census, the riding was slightly realigned, and Chris. Knowlson of Omemee was Census Commissioner in Victoria South. Next year in an upset George Dormer (Conservative) won over John McLennan (Liberal); when the Macdonald government was upset in 1873 over the CPR scandal, a new election was held, and Arthur McQuade (Conservative) of Omemee and Emily, defeated John McLennan—Emily's 4 polls gave McQuade 439 of the 537 votes cast (of 666 eligible voters);[6] he was re-elected in 1878. For the first Ontario Legislature in 1867, Thomas Matchett of Omemee (Liberal) won by acclamation as the first local member.[7] Matchett, who had lived in Omemee area for 40 years, was County Treasurer. In 1871 Samuel Wood (Liberal) won over Matchett, and repeated his win in 1875, defeating Wm. Cottingham (Conservative). When Wood was made Provincial Secretary, he had to contest his riding again, and this time defeated A. Hudspeth, who had no party label. In 1871 the Emily polls voted: Matchett 438, Wood 21; in 1875 (first election)

Emily voted: Cottingham 254, Wood 135; in 1875 (2nd election) Emily
voted: Hudspeth 283, Wood 125. Omemee village, which now had a separate
poll, voted also heavily against Wood.

The Fourth Division Court met quarterly at Omemee Town Hall on the
Assize Court Circuit to try civil and criminal cases too serious for the local
magistrates to handle. But Emily, and indeed the whole Kawartha area, had
one of the lowest crime records consistently in Ontario. Minor offenders
were put in Omemee lockup for a few days, or for more serious misde-
meanours into Peterborough or (after 1863) Lindsay County jail for a few
weeks or months. But through this Victorian era while the population of
Kingston Penitentiary rose into the hundreds, there were seldom more than
3 to 6 prisoners from Peterborough and Victoria Counties. The pioneer traditions of hard work, neighbourly co-operation (rather than feuding), family
control of the shiftless and quarrelsome, and regular church-going lasted much
longer in rural areas like Emily than in the larger towns. A few examples
will suffice—Feb. 24, 1854, magistrates Cottingham and Knowlson put
Patrick Goggan (age 25) in jail for 10 days on a charge of lunacy; on Nov.
10, Cottingham committed Wm. Strickland to jail for 6 months for assault;
on July 22, 1856, Knowlson sentenced Henry Moon (age 45) to 14 days
for non-payment of debts, and discharged Bridget O'Brien (age 23) who
had been charged with larceny; on Nov. 8 Knowlson gave Martin Tinne (age
20) two months for assault, and on Dec. 16 gave Robert McConnell (age 14)
1 week for assault. Since many of the cases (usually estimated at about half)
that came before the justices were caused by intoxication, it is understandable that in 1858 Knowlson and others of the Emily Division of the Sons of
Temperance sent a petition to the Government urging the passing of a
prohibitory liquor law!

There were other law-cases also: in March 1857 John Kells, merchant
at Metcalfe, was declared bankrupt and jailed—he had 14 creditors, debts
£1,477, assets £429. In Oct. 1859 Denis Callahan of Emily petitioned
against Michael Lehane, magistrate, to the Canadian Provincial Secretary,
claiming that Lehane was unqualified as he was bankrupt and unfit
to administer justice; the petition went to John A. Macdonald, who
recommended no action on vague allegations which required no attention.
"If Mr. Lehane acts as a Magistrate without being duly qualified according
to law, the proper course for the petitioner is to proceed against him
in some Court of competent jurisdiction for having done so."[8] In 1865
the case of Ford v. Cottingham, re illegal voting in ward 1, Emily Township,
went up to the Provincial Appeals Court; John McNeily, Wm. Clark, Thos.
Baldwin, Robt. White, Wm. and James Anderson, James and David Balfour,
Matt. Larmer, Alex. Scott, Wm. Cottingham and Alex. Shannon were alleged
to have voted without being freeholders—but James English, township
assessor in 1864, testified to refute the allegations, and the case was dismissed.
However, most court-cases continued to be minor, as in March 1864:
Justices Wm. Cottingham, Thos. Matchett, Thos. Stephenson and Chris.
Knowlson sentenced Samuel Wilson to a $1 fine for one assault charge and

25c for another, Francis Fitch to a 50c fine for assault & misdemeanour, R. Hungerford to 10 days for assaulting a bailiff, and Denis Maguire to $30 or 30 days for 3 charges of selling liquor without a license. The Emily magistrates have been mentioned above—other similar officials were the Coroners: in 1867, R. Henderson, J. G. Potts, Geo. Morris and Dr. Wm. Black, of whom by 1872 only Geo. Morris and Wm. Black were acting.

The churches, as the community conscience, continued and intensified their crusade against the allied evils of liquor and crime. The four main denominations by census totalled:

	1851	*1861*	*1871*	*1881* (excluding Omemee)
Church of England	1094	1278	1039	608
Church of Rome	1044	1517	1292	1139
Methodist	313	655 (4 sects)	971 (3 sects)	751
Presbyterians	261	451 (3 sects)	474 (2 sects)	365

(In each census also there were 2 or 3 dozen who belonged to small denominations, or had no specific church, or refused to state their religion).

For the Anglicans, the 1850s were a period of growth but also strife. In 1856, when Dr. John Irons and Wm. Matchett were churchwardens, the Bishop wrote them stressing the need to provide £50 annually as promised to Rev. Harding, and if this could not be done the priest would be removed and the parish returned to the status of a travelling mission; later Bishop Strachan wrote Harding to regret that the people were "behaving very ill", and suggesting he take another parish or mission. So Rev. John Hickie arrived in 1857, and promptly aroused trouble by his evangelical "Low Church" doctrines, which he even put into a pamphlet "A Defense of the 'Gospel Church' and 'Vindication' " which, interestingly enough, was for sale (price 25c) at "Mr. Hickie's Store, Omemee"—perhaps he stayed in town and started a shop. Williamson in *Omemee* gives full details of the Church Commission under Archdeacon Bethune which arrived in 1859 to investigate, the conviction of Rev. Hickie and locking of the church doors, which were then unlocked by the congregation for Rev. Hickie to hold service. Hickie blamed the incident on Wm. Turner, storekeeper and Church Warden, whose children had been reprimanded for bad behaviour in Sunday School. However, the wrath of the ancient Bishop Strachan (now 80) was visited upon Rev. Hickie, who was replaced in 1859 by Rev. Thomas Leach; when he resigned in 1860, Rev. Noah Disbrow came, remaining until 1869. Bishop Strachan wrote two letters in July 1860, first asking Disbrow to act with prudence in choosing a churchwarden "acceptable to the congregation" and avoiding party feeling, and to be on friendly terms with Mr. Nelson (or Neilson) "who has behaved with so good a spirit on this occasion"; his second letter to Chris. Knowlson thanked him for his "wise and Christian conduct in agreeing to the arrangement about churchwardenship suggested by Archdeacon Bethune".

Rev. W. H. Jones served the Anglican parish 1869-74, and was followed by Rev. Richard Harris who stayed until 1881. Before Rev. Jones left, the task began of tearing down Christ Church, Omemee, now too small, and laying the cornerstone of the new larger structure, in a ceremony led by Rev. Jones, and Churchwardens Arthur McQuade, MP, and Isaac McNeely, June 12, 1874. The frame church on a stone foundation cost about $3,000, and was opened for worship January 1875 with the attendance of several neighbouring clergy—it faced east and west with main entrance at the base of a square tower at the southwest corner, "of Gothic Architecture" and capable of seating 250 persons in the nave. Next June 18, Rev. Harris married Miss Olivia Cottingham in the church; she was given by Thomas Matchett, her uncle, as her father Squire Wm. Cottingham had recently died. There is little news in this period about St. John's and St. James' Churches in Emily, also served by the clergy above mentioned; they were probably aided by the rural deans on occasion, particularly in the 1870s by Rural Dean Allen.

Father John Bourke was appointed to the Emily parish in 1852 as first resident Roman Catholic priest, and held services at King's Wharf and in Ennismore also. His main challenge was the influx of Irish immigrants and growth of the faithful, whose numbers soared 50% in the 1850s. When Father Bernard Coyle came in 1858, therefore, a new much larger frame church, about 75 ft. by 40 ft., to hold 250 people, was built on the site of the present St. Luke's Church at Downeyville. Father Coyle served for two decades in a parish expanding northward, visiting Bobcaygeon and Kinmount to look after Emily men who went to work in lumber mills and shanties, or to start new farms along the Colonization Roads leading north. This Emily parish was between the populous Peterborough parish, and the growing Lindsay parish, where a new brick church was erected in 1859. Fortunately, the laborious trips over rough bush trails on foot or horseback, prior to 1850, had, in this generation, become easier and quicker over improved gravel roads where a horse and buggy could be used, in most of Emily if not in the northern townships.

An interesting anecdote is recorded in the history of the Fitzgerald family, by Rev. M. Fitzgerald of San Francisco, concerning William Fitzgerald, 48 years old when he came to Emily with the Robinson Emigration, accompanied by sons Michael, Maurice, Richard and Thomas. After his son Michael's death in 1857, and feeling himself bereft of family and friends, old "Daddy Bill" bought a solid granite tombstone which he placed in his log cabin, where over the months he chiseled on it the following heartfelt message: "In Memory of William Fitzgerald, native of Liscarroll, Ireland, not dead yet and whose age at this day, Nov. 10, 1857, is 80 years—Here lies Daddy Bill, in this cold grave laid, forsaken by all his friends. May the Lord have mercy on him." The tombstone still stands in Downeyville cemetery, among others of historic interest.

Anecdotes about Father Coyle still circulate in Downeyville parish a

Humphry Finley and his wife Elizabeth (one of the first families in Emily Township)
(Bruce Finley)

Rev. Bernard Coyle, P.P., Downeyville,
c. 1860 — (Hubert Flood)

William (Captain) King of King's Wharf
(Hubert Flood)

atherine Miller came from Ireland to
orth Emily in 1831 when 10 years old—
died 1911 (W. McMullen)

Mrs. McCarrell, one of the Peter Robinson
settlers in east Emily (S. McCall)

SOME EMILY PIONEERS

century later, and bring further stories about the strong-willed priest in any local gathering. He was very much opposed to Sunday dancing and entertainment, and knowing about the pioneer custom of holding a square dance whenever a new barn or house was completed, he kept himself informed whenever there was a building-bee; then when the music and singing were at their loudest on a Sunday afternoon, Father Coyle would appear dramatically in the doorway, waving his buggy-whip, and would chase old and young to the rafters or across the surrounding fields, warning all and sundry to show up at confession without delay. Another story is still told of a noted rivalry between the "fisticuff" champions of Downeyville (one of the Mulcaheys) and of King's Wharf (one of the Hennesseys) about 1870; after challenges had passed back and forth for weeks, and local interest was at its height, a match was finally arranged for a quiet Sunday afternoon in a meadow near King's Wharf, and all the men and boys gathered from far and near for the most exciting spectacle since the last circus came to the district. The match was at its climax, but still undecided, when Father Coyle's buggy was seen racing down the nearby road and across the field. He was waving his whip and shouting at the Sabbath-breakers to get away home and pray for their souls. The whole crowd scattered into the nearest woods in record time, led by the two champions, Mulcahey and Hennessey, leaving the victory to Father Coyle. It should be noted also that during Rev. Coyle's ministry the St. Patrick's Society was active in the Downeyville area, holding parades and celebrations every March on St. Patrick's Day, until it was dissolved by the Bishop on the grounds that it promoted unnecessary religious dissension.

In south Emily the Presbyterians worshipped in the log structure, surrounded by the Presbyterian Cemetery, secured from Henry Best on Concession 2. Here the first frame church was built in 1853 at cost $1,650, the minister living nearby on a glebe of 10 acres donated by David Best. The old log church at Omemee was also by 1859 found unsuitable for a growing congregation, and a new lot secured from the Railway, just west of the railway tracks and north of King Street; a roughcast frame church was erected and opened for service in Feb. 1860, with planks across cedar blocks for seats until proper closed pews could be built. The Springville Presbyterian charge opened a preaching station in the house of Andrew Fowler on Con. 4 at the Smith-Emily boundary, in August 1865; Mr. Fowler also offered a site where a frame church 30 by 40 feet was built on Lot 23, Con. 4, for $675, with opening services Jan. 25, 1866. In 1872 this Lakevale Church was separated from Springville and added to the charge of Omemee and Mount Pleasant, with Rev. Ewing holding regular services in all three churches (as mentioned previously, he served the charge from 1849 until his death in 1893).

When Metcalfe was renamed Omemee in 1857, the Metcalfe Methodist Mission became the Omemee Circuit, covering all Emily township, plus parts of north Cavan and Manvers, and south Verulam as far as Dunsford. Cornish's *Handbook of Canadian Methodism* (1867) listed the ministers

St. James Anglican, East Emily, built 1900

St. John's Anglican, (Orange Corners)
built 1888

Communion set from Lebanon
Methodist Church S½ Lot 6,
Con. 1 — before 1900 —
(Irvine Connell)

St. Luke's, Downeyville
built 1858

Altar from first log church,
Downeyville
1835-1858—(James Piggott)

Presbyterian Church, Fowler's Corners
built 1866

Salem North Emily 1899 — 1970

EMILY CHURCHES

who served, with membership: 1850-51 Rev. John Sanderson (150), 1852-3 Rev. John Osborne (180), 1854 Rev. L. Vanderburg (126), 1855-7 Rev. Wm. Briden (142), 1858-61 Rev. John Goodfellow (158), 1861-63 Rev. Henry McDowell and Isaac Welden (143 up to 208), 1864-5 Rev. Sam. Phillip, J. C. Wilson and Wm. Barker (224), 1866 Rev. Wm. Scott and Jas. McClung (226), and 1867 Rev. Wm. Burns and Joseph Hall (230). In addition to services twice daily in Omemee, there were regular services at Middle Road, Third Line, Bethel, Ops, Lebanon, Mt. Horeb, and Orange Line school. The Circuit was governed by the Quarterly Board, about 12 men from various congregations, presided over by the Minister, to arrange payment of salaries and expenses, collection of money from members, appointing church officers, arranging Sunday Schools and special events, etc. Sales, teas, lectures and picnics were held to raise money for expenses. For example, Williamson quotes 1860 payments to Rev. Goodfellow totalling $609, of which $28 was for wood, $68 for keeping a horse, $6 for horseshoeing, etc. In 1862 the Omemee caretaker was paid $40 a year to attend all services, making fires one hour before service and ringing bell 15 minutes in advance, sweeping and dusting weekly, keeping lamps in good order, and washing the whole church four times yearly.

In this period to 1875, the Methodist Episcopal Church was a frame building on Sturgeon Street near the present St. Andrew's Church; the New Connexion Methodists had a red brick church at southwest corner of George and Rutland Streets, opposite the Orange Hall. The New Connexion united with the Wesleyan Methodists in 1875, so the old church was moved south, and the new white brick church 35 by 60 feet on stone foundation, with 50 ft. spire, was opened and dedicated Dec. 10, 1875 (the old church ended its career, oddly enough, as the Bradburn Hall or Opera House, until torn down in 1910). Bethel Methodist (later United) Church has records beginning 1854, when the Quarterly meeting was held, Rev. Vanderburg and Rev. Musgrove presiding; the meeting gave the Minister £108 that year. In 1862 William Mills deeded a lot to the church where the frame building was erected, and used for 30 years (later used as L.O.L. Lodge). The Lebanon Methodist Church was built in 1862 on south half Lot 6, Con. 1, and closed about 1921.

In conclusion, the Almanacs of the period (though often inaccurate and incomplete) give names of Methodist preachers in the Emily Circuit that are worth noting: 1851: T. McMullen; 1855: John Sanderson; 1858: W. Briden, S. Lyon; 1861: John Goodfellow, R. Earl; 1864: John Laird, Henry McDowell, J. Sparrow, G. Buggin; 1871: Wm. Andrews, Jas. Norris, G. Buggin, W. M. Pomeroy. Some preachers complained they were moved so much that they never became really acquainted with their flock and their problems, while others said that with the building of churches and the decline of outdoor camp meetings, some of the evangelical enthusiasm had gone from southern rural circuits. Sanderson in his 1910 book quoted an 1861 report on Victoria County: "The religious condition of the people is not less than 100% better than it was 2 years ago. . . . It is the glory of our missionaries to follow the woodman's axe. . . . This county has been a terror to some of our young men. . . ." The church's main missionary thrust was into the bush settlements along the colonization roads north from Fenelon, Bobcaygeon, Burleigh and Buckhorn.

Emily interdenominational Cemetery was opened in 1872, a mile or so east of Omemee, and the cemeteries in the village were closed with removal of some of the remains to the new burying-grounds. The Lindsay 'Post' of Nov. 5, 1875, in describing the plans for the new Methodist church, and the enlargement of the parsonage nearby, added "Removal of the dead from the churchyards to the cemetery has commenced." However, the Roman Catholics retained their cemetery at Downeyville, and the Presbyterians theirs in south Emily, but few traces remain of some of the smaller pioneer cemeteries, except a few broken stones.

At this point we might note some of the references to Emily (and Omemee) in the Almanacs, Directories and Gazetteers of the period, before going on to economic and general development. The *1851 Canada Directory* listed Metcalfe as 15 miles from Peterboro, with stage fare 2s. 6d., and township population 2,461; the main citizens were listed: R. Grand, postmaster; Wm. Beatty, Wm. Hilliard, W. and T. Matchett, and M. Parker, general storekeepers; Chris. Knowlson, merchant and insurance agent; Wm. Sannley, miller; Ed. Blackwell, Mrs. Davidson, David Harkness, innkeepers; Dr. John Irons; Gabriel Balfour, Henry Finch, John Goodliffe, Ab. Hayland, carpenters; William Cottingham, J.P.; Wm. Davey and Wm. Woods, blacksmiths; plus Anglican and Wesleyan clergy.

The *Peterborough & Victoria Directory 1858* described Downeyville as: Popul. 100, 3 stores, 1 hotel, 1 saloon, 2 shoemakers, 2 blacksmiths, 1 millinery shop, 1 R.C. church (Rev. Coyle); M. Lehane, J.P., postmaster and general store; Michael Walsh, grocer; Michael Collins, storekeeper. Omemee was growing: Popul. 500-600; flouring and gristmill with 3 run of stones; sawmill; carding and fulling mill; grammar school, 15 stores, 2 bakeries and groceries, 2 taverns, 1 temperance hotel, 3 saloons; the Omemee "Warder" published by Jos. Cooper; in addition to more innkeepers, storekeepers, carpenters and blacksmiths as listed above, there were now Jas. Clarke, stationmaster; Sam. Cottingham, grocer and baker; Chester Dies, teacher; Andy English, bailiff; John Hanna, cooper; Charles Hartley, temperance hotelkeeper; James Ivory, carder and fuller; George Lamb, tanner; Wm. Matchett, notary public; John Might, saddler and harnessmaker; John Newman, waggonmaker; Mrs. Odell, teacher; Wm. Sherwood, shoemaker; Ralph Simpson, cooper; Wm. Thompson, tailor; Hart William, sawyer; Jas. Whitson, cooper; Wm. Simpson, shoemaker, etc. The 1858 Directory also listed Emily magistrates: Wm. Best, Wm. Cottingham, David Best, C. Buck, C. Knowlson, and John McNeely. Thomas Matchett was clerk of the Division IV Court meeting at Omemee. The Postoffices listed were Omemee and Downeyville, also Henderson's Corners (with postmaster R. Morton and mail from Peterborough by horseback through Ennismore Tuesday and Friday). Emily's farmlands were valued at $6.66 an acre, and average farm production per acre was given: wheat 15 bus., barley 24 bus., rye 16¼ bus.,

DIRECTORY OF THE UNITED COUNTIES OF PETERBOROUGH & VICTORIA
1858 published in Peterborough, pages 38-39.

THE VILLAGE OF OMEMEE,

The principal village in the township of Emily, is situated on Pigeon River, which, besides supplying it with Hydraulic power, promises to be an important inlet for the produce and lumber of the northern townships. It has one excellent flouring and grist mill, with three run of stones; a very good saw mill, and a carding and fulling mill, all worked by water power. It contains two churches — an Episcopalian and Wesleyan; a grammar school; fifteen stores — some of them very good ones; two bakeries and groceries; two taverns, and a temperance hotel; three saloons; and blacksmiths, coopers, waggon makers, shoe makers, tailors, carpenters, harness makers, and dress makers, in fair numbers. Omemee boasts a very excellent newspaper the "Warder," published by Mr. Joseph Cooper. It is on the line, and is one of the most important stations, of the Port Hope, Lindsay and Beaverton Railroad; and should the inhabitants be successful in procuring Government assistance to dredge and improve the navigation of Pigeon River — now capable, when the water is high, of floating a steamer to the village — there is little doubt that it will become a town of very great importance. It has a daily mail from Port Hope, Peterborough, and Lindsay. The population is between 500 and 600.

Andrew, G. & H., blacksmith
Balfour, Gabriel, carpenter
Banners, William, baker
Beatty, George, carpenter
Beatty, William, general store
Bell, Thomas, shoemaker
Black, Wm., druggist, &c
Blackwell, Mrs., hotel keeper
Bradburn, James, general store,
Bradburn, Stewart, general store
Clarke, James, station master
Cooper, Joseph, proprietor and publisher of "Warder,"
Clarke, James, station master
Cottingham, Samuel, grocer and baker
Cottingham, William, millowner, and Warden United Counties of Peterborough and Victoria.

Curry, William, general store
Dies, Chester, teacher
Ellery, Samuel, sawyer
English, Andrew, bailiff
English, James, township assessor
English, Samuel, carpenter
English, William,   do
Equitable Insurance Company, Thos., Matchett, agent
Goodfellow, John, Rev., Wesleyan
Goodliffe, John, carpenter
Grandy, Robert, post master
Graves, Giles, carpenter
Hale, Charles, general store
Hanna, John, cooper
Hickie, John Rev., Church of England
Hartly, Charles, temperance hotel
Hartly, David, carpenter

39

Hamilton, Hugh, tavern keeper
Heffner, F. W., tailor
Henderson, John, grocer
Henderson, Robert, hotel keeper
Hungerford, Richard W., bailiff
Hyland, Abraham, carpenter
Irons, John, M.D., physician
Ivory, James, carder and fuller
Knowlson, Christopher, J.P., general store, and agent Provincial Insurance Company
Lamb, George, tanner
Lunnis, John, miller
Lytle, Robert, carpenter
Mars, Wm., N., general store, ashery
Matchett, Thomas, clerk of Division Court, secretary-treasurer Emily Branch Bible Society, township treasurer, agent for Equitable Insurance Company, and commissioner for taking affidavits in Queen's Bench, County Court and Court of Chancery
Matchett, William, notary public

Morgan, Miss, general store
M'Gaffney, Bernard, mason
M'Gowan, John, blacksmith
M'Neely, John, president Emily Bible Society
M'Quade, Arthur, township collector
Might, John, saddler and harness maker
Morrison, George, grocer & baker
Neil, William, blacksmith
Newman, John, waggon maker
Odell, Mrs., teacher
Sherwood, William, shoemaker
Simpson, Ralph, cooper
Simpson, William, shoemaker
Stevenson, Thomas, general store
Thompson, Wm., tailor
Tanner, William, general store
Thornton, David, general store
William, Hart, sawyer
Wood, William, general dealer and blacksmith
Whitson, James, cooper

THE VILLAGE OF DOWNEYVILLE:

A small village in the township of Emily, situated on lots 6 and 7, on the 9th and 10th concession. It has three stores, one hotel, one saloon, two shoe shops, two blacksmiths' shops, one milliner's shop, and one church—Roman Catholic. It is about 8 miles from Lindsay. Population about 100.

Coile, Rev. Mr., Roman Catholic
Collins, Michael, general store
Lehane, M., J.P., post master, and

general dealer
Walsh, Michael, grocer

oats 25½ bus., peas 12 bus., Indian corn 21 bus., potatoes 43⅓ bus., turnips 161¾ bus.

The *Victoria County Directory 1869-70* stated: "Omemee is a village in township Emily, situated on Pigeon River, 10 miles from Lindsay. The Port Hope, Lindsay and Beaverton Railway has a station a short distance out of the village. . . . At present it contains two civil and one military organization, viz. 2 lodges of the Orange body, nos. 114 and 666, both holding weekly meetings in a fine hall built by them in 1859 of roughcast at the cost about $500; also one Volunteer Infantry Company under command of Capt. W. H. Cottingham. The public buildings are: a town hall built of brick about 1856, costing $1,600, and a United Grammar and Common School of wood built in 1860, at about the same cost; a company drillshed of wood built 1867 costing nearly $600; and the following churches: a Church of England of wood, built about 1833, at cost about $800; a Canada Presbyterian of roughcast erected 1860, cost about $700; one Episcopal Methodist of wood, erected 1863, at about same cost; a Wesleyan Methodist of wood built 1835, at the cost $800; and a New Connection Methodist of brick built 1861, at cost about $1,000. The manufactories are: 1 gristmill, 1 sawmill, 1 woolen and carding factory, 2 tanneries, 1 foundry, together with the usual number of mechanics, several general stores, 3 hotels, etc. There is published here every Friday . . . the Omemee *Standard,* J. H. Delamere being editor and publisher. Daily mail and money order office. Population about 600."[9]

An unusual view was that of the *Mercantile Agency Reference Book, Jan. 1872* which listed all businesses by financial capital and credit, ranging from A1 down to K3½: Omemee was covered by the following: Wm. Beatty, G.S., E1½; Wm. Black, physician, K; Catherine Blackwell, tavern, K3; Mrs. Bradburn, tavern, G2½; Jos. Campbell, tinsmith, K3; W. Clark, tavern, H3; John Comstock, K; Vincent Cornell, physician, K; Wm. S. Cottingham, D.G., H3; Wm. Cottingham, mills, D1½; W. Curry, G.S., K; Fred Dawson, ashery, H3; Chester Dies, tanner, K; Wm. Dornan, blacksmith, K3½; Wm. Elliott, saddler, K3½; Isaac English, Groc., K; John English, wagons, K3; John Hanna, cooper, K3½; James Ivory, fulling and carding, F2; Jos. Keele, boots and shoes, G2; Thos. Kennedy, blacksmith, K3; Thos. Kennedy, Jr., groc., K; C. Laidley, shoes, H3; Geo. Lamb, tanner, G2½; W. N. Mars, groc., K3; Matchett and McNeillie, drugs, etc., F2; McBrien, John, shoes, K3½; John McCrae, cabinetware, K3½; Isaac McNeely, G.S., F2; Wm. Miller, tailor, K3; Geo. Morrison, groc., H2½; Wm. Neal, blacksmith, H3; Dr. Geo. Norris, drugs, H3; Henry O'Dell, watches, K; E. Peplow, gristmill, K; John Read, G.S., K; A. Redmond, Sr., tailor, K; Jas. Richardson, groc., K3½; Wm. Sherwood, shoes, K; Thos. Stephenson, G.S., G2½; D. Thornton, Jr., G.S., K3; Thos. Thompson, pumps, K3½; Jas. Wallace, foundry, K3; E. C. Williamson, harness, K3; John Williamson, groc. and tailor, K; Mrs. Wm. Wood, G.S., H3. (G.S. in the above means "general store"). It is obvious that to the mercantile fraternity, including wholesalers and salesmen, Omemee merchants and businessmen were operating mostly on very shaky capital and credit ratings. This was not too promising for its success as a separate incorporated village.

Lovell's *Gazetteer* in 1873 had only brief references: "Downeyville: a post village in Victoria county, 6 miles from Omemee. Popul. 80", and "Omemee: a flourishing post village of county Victoria, on Midland Railway, 33 miles from Port Hope. It contains 3 churches, a Montreal Telegraph office, a printing-office issuing a weekly newspaper, an iron foundry, a tannery, saw, grist and woollen mills, and about 20 stores. Popul. 600". Since these were 1871 census population figures, the indication was that Emily was still about 82% rural.

The improvement of Emily roads by county and township action had already been outlined. The Peterborough *Weekly Dispatch* of Jan. 30, 1851, said: "Mail stage leaves Commercial Hotel, Peterboro, Monday and Thursday mornings for Emily, Lindsay and 4 Corners, Mariposa, return trips Tuesday and Friday mornings. Sleighing on this line is generally firstrate and the hotels very good." By 1853 Wm. Bletcher of Port Hope ran stages to Metcalfe Monday, Wednesday and Friday with mail, returning Tuesday, Thursday and Saturday. Another route of growing importance was north from Fowler's Corners, across Pigeon River near its mouth (where a floating bridge was built in 1869) and north to King's Wharf and Bobcaygeon—a weekly stage ran on this route between Peterborough and Bobcaygeon by 1870. But there was growing dissatisfaction with the difficulties of getting goods into Emily and produce outward to markets by waggons for about 8 months and by sleighs in winter. The solutions widely discussed were railway construction and steamboat navigation, both of which have been briefly mentioned in earlier chapters. It is interesting that the Omemee *Warder* in Oct. 1856 was advertising Henderson's Hotel at Metcalfe as "the Stage Office", but in the same paper William Simpson of Metcalfe called his inn the Railway Hotel.

A fever of railway speculation by local magnates, playing off Montreal and Toronto financiers, sponsored and chartered a dozen schemes in this period to push rails north from Belleville, Cobourg, Port Hope, Whitby, Oshawa and Toronto to exploit what Lacroix's *Canadian Guide* (1873) called "shipment of immense quantities of lumber, sawn and square . . . annually taken from the almost illimitable forests which stretch away to the rear . . . extensive trade in grain and flour, the produce of the fine agricultural country . . .", plus untold mineral wealth on the Laurentian Shield. Toronto interests were determined to exploit this country by the waterway from Georgian Bay via Welland to Lake Ontario, and by railways north from Toronto into the Simcoe-Haliburton country, and therefore opposed Trent waterway construction and engineered the separation of Haliburton County in 1874. But businessmen of Belleville, Cobourg, Port Hope and Whitby, with some spasmodic aid from Montreal and British capital, pushed their rails north with great difficulty to Peterborough, Lakefield, Chemong, Lindsay, Port Perry and even farther toward the back country.

The first of these projects to affect Emily was the reorganized Port Hope, Lindsay and Beaverton Railway, which obtained a loan of £30,000 from the Grand Trunk and $920,000 in municipal bonuses (or subsidies). Contractors Tate and Fowler began building in 1854, using a gravel roadbed two feet deep,

No. 6. TIME TABLE, **No. 6.**

TAKES EFFECT ON MONDAY, MAY 27th, 1872.

TRAINS MOVING NORTH.

MILES	STATIONS	No. 1 BEAVERTON MAIL	No. 3 LAKEFIELD MAIL	No. 5 BEAVERTON MIX'D	No. 7 LAKEFIELD MIXED	No. 9 WAY FREIGHT
66	+ Beaverton, Arr.	12.30 P.M.		8.00 P.M		
58	† Woodville	12.10		7.30d / 7.18a		
54	* Oakwood	11.53		7.00		
49	* Cambray	11.41		6.42		
43	† Lindsay	11.25d / 11.20a		6.20d / 6.00a	8.40 A.M	
38	* Kelly's	11.08		5.38	8.20	
33	* Omemee	10.58		5.20	8.05	
38	* Franklin	10.43		4.55d / 4.35a	7.42	
6	* Brunswick	10.38		4.27	7.35	
4	† Bethany	10.33		4.29	7.27	
0	† Lakefield		12.40P.M		7.00 P.M	
1	† Peterboro'		12.00d / 11.40a		6.20d / 6.00a	
4	* Fraserville		11.16		5.36	
	† Millbrook	10.15d / 10.10a	11.00d / 10.50a	3.50d / 3.30a	5.20d / 5.02a	7.00d / 6.50a
4	* Summit	9.58	10.35	3.12	4.45	6.30
10	† Campbell's	9.46	10.18	2.50	4.25d / 4.10a	6.10
9	* Perrytown	9.43	10.14	2.45	4.05	6.03
5	* Quay's	9.35	10.04	2.35	3.55	5.52
0	† Port Hope, Dep.	9.20 A.M	9.45A.M	2.15 P.M	3.35P.M	5.30A.M

TRAINS MOVING SOUTH.

MILES	STATIONS	No. 2 BEAVERTON MAIL	No. 4 LAKEFIELD MAIL	No. 6 BEAVERTON MIX'D	No. 8 LAKEFIELD MIXED	No. 10 WAY FREIGHT
0	† Beaverton, Dep.	3.00 P.M.		7.00 A.M.		
8	† Woodville	3.25		7.30a / 7.42d		
12	* Oakwood	3.37		8.00		
17	* Cambray	3.49		8.18		
23	† Lindsay	4.05a / 4.10d		8.40a / 9.00d		11.40A.M
28	* Kelly's	4.22		9.22		12.02
33	† Omemee	4.35		9.40		12.20
38	† Franklin	4.47		10.00		12.43
40	* Brunswick	4.52		10.08		12.52
42	† Bethany	4.57		10.15a / 10.33a		1.10
0	† Lakefield		1.50 P.M		5.20 A.M	
9	† Peterboro'		2.30a / 3.00d		5.55a / 6.10d	
16	* Fraserville		3.24		6.32	
48	† Millbrook	5.15a / 5.20d	3.40 / 3.50	10.55a / 11.15d	6.50 / 7.00	1.35a / 1.55d
52	* Summit	5.30	4.04	11.33	7.17	2.15
56	† Campbell's	5.43	4.22	11.53	7.37	2.35a / 2.50d
57	* Perrytown	5.46	4.26	11.58	7.42	2.55
61	* Quay's	5.54	4.36	12.08	7.53	3.06
66	† Port Hope, Arr.	6.10 P.M.	4.55 P.M	12.30P.M	8.15 A.M	3.30P.M

* Platform Stations, Trains stop on Signal only. † Telegraph Stations. ☞ HEAVY FIGURES denote Train Crossings. The figures set opposite the Stations indicate the leaving time of Trains. Trains must start promptly on time. Should any Employee not fully understand this Time Table, or Special Rules on the back, it will be his duty to apply to the head of his department for information. Trains run by Port Hope time, which is 20 minutes slower than Grand Trunk time.

DESTROY FORMER TIME CARDS.

H. G. TAYLOR, *Supt. of Motive Power and Trains.*

culverts of masonry and heavy iron rails of wide gauge (5½ ft. apart)—by 1855 they had passed Millbrook and were crossing the millpond south of Omemee by a wooden bridge; since Emily had refused a subsidy, the line had been shifted south, and cut across one corner of the township, with the station 1¼ miles west of Omemee village. By Dec. 1856 the rails reached Reaboro, and the first train ran from Port Hope to Lindsay in Oct. 1857, with much enthusiasm on all sides, although due to depression the company was already bankrupt and unable to pay the contractor. However, the line from Millbrook to Peterborough was finished in 1858, and trade picked up after 1860 to make the line prosperous. A PHI&B advertisement said "The route traversed by the line . . . has no superior in the province as a grain and cattle producing country", and talked of the vast quantities of timber and mineral wealth, the fine chain of navigable waters with their hydraulic power, etc. The rail charges were 21c a ton-mile for general merchandise, 4c a ton-mile for wheat and flour, special agreed rates for lumber, 3c a mile for passengers, 2c a mile for immigrants. Williamson quotes John McCrea about the shortage of rolling-stock in the early days, when excursions were carried on flat-cars with balsam fences around, and temporary seating in the open air, amid sparks and smoke from the wood-burning locomotives; but later they purchased more passenger and freight cars.

In Feb. 1861 the Montreal Telegraph Company put their posts along the rail lines from Port Hope to Millbrook, via Omemee to Lindsay, and Millbrook to Peterborough, sending their first telegrams on these routes in April. By 1865 the railway had a service once daily each way in 3½ hours Port Hope to Lindsay, and twice daily in 2½ hours on the Peterborough line, and these did not change in the next few years. Emily Council complained in 1867 that the rail crossing near Omemee on Concession 4 was very unsafe for teams, and demanded the railway improve it. After weathering the difficult depression years 1866-69, the railway was reorganized as the Midland Railway, and built the line north from Peterborough to Lakefield, and by 1871 had its extension Lindsay to Beaverton in operation. In 1871, according to the *Lacroix Guide,* the line brought south to Port Hope 1,676,922 cu. ft. square timber, 65,520,000 b.m. ft. sawn lumber, 382,533 bus. grain, etc. An 1872 timetable shows three southbound trains through Omemee—at 4:35 p.m. the "Beaverton Mail", at 9:40 a.m. the "Beaverton Mixed", and at 12:20 p.m. a "Way Freight"; northbound were the same three at 10:58 a.m., 5:20 p.m. and 8:05 a.m. respectively. According to the 1881 Victoria Atlas, a meeting was called to promote the railway in 1855 or 1856 in which the name 'Omemee' was suggested as more attractive for the railway stop, and was adopted; later, after some pressure, Omemee incorporated separately and the railway agreed to build a new station freight depot, etc. within village limits, the village paying $2,000 and James Laidley providing the land, north of King Street. The Atlas adds: "A great deal of grain is shipped from Omemee and it is generally a good market. Travelling buyers purchase butter, pork, hay, &c. . . ."

A few other rail schemes through and near Emily may be briefly mentioned. The Grand Junction Railway was chartered in 1852 as a Grand Trunk subsidiary to build north from Belleville, west to Peterborough, through central Emily north of Omemee, and on to Lindsay and Toronto. The *Lacroix Guide* 1873 had a map showing this projected line, though by then the promoters talked of running their trains from Omemee to Lindsay over the Midland line, and later dreamed of a line through Ennismore, north Emily, Verulam, and Fenelon to Lake Huron. Finally in the 1880s the Grand Junction did reach Peterborough, but soon became a GTR branch. The Peterborough & Chemong Railway (a branch of the Cobourg & Peterboro Railway) was chartered in 1855 and by July 1859 had four miles of track from Ashburnham to Chemong Lake north of Bridgenorth—however, it was used for freight almost exclusively, and was never profitable, going bankrupt in 1877.

Strangely enough, the only time the Emily Council voted a subsidy was in April 1872, when they decided to give a bonus of $30,000, repayable at low interest, to the Bowmanville, Lindsay and Bobcaygeon Railway—perhaps fortunately, the railway was never built. Then in 1872 the Omemee, Bobcaygeon & North Peterboro Railway was chartered—one promoter was George Cox, Peterborough businessman, who later got into the Midland management and became a Toronto financial tycoon. Harvey granted a $10,000 subsidy to the OB&NPR, and other towns and townships, but not Emily or Omemee. After long complicated financial manipulations, exposed in an Ontario Sessional Return in March 1874, the Grand Junction gave up its rights west of Peterborough to the Midland, and the OB&NPR became the Midland Extension Railway, empowered to build from Omemee to Bobcaygeon and northward—however, these powers lapsed in March 1876, with no company organized, no stock issued, and not a foot of rail laid. Emily was left for a decade with only the Port Hope to Lindsay Midland line across its southwest corner.

Meanwhile, in Sept. 1857 Toronto papers were quoting the Omemee *Warder*: "Mr. E. Haycock, C.E., had reported that the obstructions to steamboat communication on Pigeon River between Omemee, Bobcaygeon and the adjacent back country are slight & can easily be removed at no great outlay. Mr. Haycock reports there are 2 points that particularly require dredging—one about 116 rods long near Muskrat Island, the other 113 rods near Grape Island. In both cases the material to be removed is an accumulation of clay material, no roots or stumps interfering." This was reinforced with petitions early in 1858 from Emily Council, and from groups headed by M. Walsh and Wm. Cottingham, for government aid to improve the navigation of the Pigeon River to Omemee. But political turmoil and the division of powers at Confederation in 1867 delayed government aid, and in 1869 Cottingham was urging Victoria Council to support a memorial to the Ontario government for a grant to improve navigation: "That navigation of the Pigeon River for a small sum would enable steamers of light draft to run up-river as far as Omemee and connect with the railway to Port Hope and Lindsay . . . that a steamboat is now ready to be put on that route as soon as said improvement can be made." County and township councils combined to clear away the remains of Baldwin's dam on the lower river, and to build a floating bridge lower down which could be moved to allow steamboats to pass (at lots 22-23, con. 12).

On Feb. 2, 1871, the Trent Works Superintendent wrote: "I see by the newspapers that the Ontario Govt. have included in the Estimates a sum to improve Emily Creek to get up to Omemee." (He obviously meant Pigeon River, but enclosed with his report a map also marking it as Emily Creek). The Ontario Journals 1871-2 reported: "IMPROVEMENT of Navigation of Pigeon River: An appropriation of $5,000 was made toward this work in 1871, and a contract let to Thos. Walters; removing logs, roots, sunken timber, &c. by steam dredge and 4 men, $20 per diem; Dredging clay, sand, gravel &c. in the bed of the river at 30c per cu. yard. The work was commenced in October, and following expenditure to close of 1871: Payments to contractor $1,020.00; Payments for Surveys & Superintendence $507.40— total $1,527.40. The balance of $3,772.60 will be required for this work in 1872." The 1873 Journals reported in 1872 that another $1,623.25 had been spent to open a 50-foot channel 5 feet deep up to Omemee, adding "it is now navigable for small steamers from its outlet in Pigeon Lake to lot 7 in con. 4, Emily, although there are a few points where the length of navigation could

be materially reduced by making new cuts." The balance of the original
$5,000 was spent in 1873, dredging, removing logs and sunken timber, etc.
The 1874 report concluded "the channel is not likely to be much used except
for transit of logs and other timber to the mills at Omemee."

This pessimism was echoed in the 1881 Victoria Atlas: "Six years ago
government spent $5,000 in dredging Pigeon Creek, and an engineer has
again been examining it with a probable view to keeping its navigation open.
The township at one time built a stationary bridge across the stream, about
5 miles below Omemee, but Government forced its removal and the substitu-
tion of a swing bridge. A steamboat for some time ran on the creek up to
Omemee; but business was not sufficient to sustain the enterprise. Last year
(1880) the building of a small steamer at Omemee was advocated, but the
project fell through." The small steamer mentioned has not been identified,
but it may have been one of these, all built before 1868: "Mary Ellen" (31
tons) on Lake Scugog; "Ontario" (38 tons); "Anglo-Saxon" (38 tons);
"Scugog" (49 tons) built at Bridgenorth; "Ogemah" (79 tons) built at Fenelon Falls; and "Ranger" (53 tons) built at Lindsay. Some of the other smaller
ones operating in the western lakes in the 1870s, mostly paddlewheelers, were
"Samson" (30 tons), "Novelty" (67 tons), "Lady Ida" (18 tons), and
"Ranger" (58 tons). But heavy timber scows required wider deeper channels,
and the tourist trade had not yet been developed, so that only an occasional
steamboat came to Omemee.

Inadequate transportation and water-power inhibited the growth of industry, as it also hampered the prosperity of the whole township. By census
returns, Emily produced in 1851 about 56,000 bus. wheat, up to 130,000 bus.
in 1861, down to about 72,000 in 1871, and up to 95,000 bus. in 1881. Yet
the only mill was Cottingham's gristmill in Omemee which in 1861 produced
10 barrels of flour a day, and by 1858 could grind only 250 bus. wheat a day.
Even when rebuilt and improved in 1872, the mill was clearly insufficient, and
most Emily grain had to be shipped out, for sale to dealers, or to be ground at
Bobcaygeon, Lindsay, Peterborough, etc. Similarly in timber production—
there were two sawmills in Emily in 1851, one being the Cottingham mill at
Metcalfe—but their combined cut in 1851 was 4,000 feet daily; by 1858
there was only the Cottingham mill with one saw, cutting 2,000 feet lumber
a day.

The energetic Mossom Boyd of Bobcaygeon was not only buying grain
in north Emily and taking it by wagon or boat to Bobcaygeon to be milled;
he was also before 1850 buying timber in Emily, moving it to Bobcaygeon to
be cut in his mill, and selling the lumber back to Emily residents. For
example, the Boyd Papers contain a series of indentures dated 1851 by
which the owners agree to sell Boyd all the elm timber on their lots for price
either 1s. 4d. to 1s. 10d. per tree, or for £1 10s. for all elm on the lot—
James Collins, south half 7, con. 10; Thomas Donan, east half 5, con. 6; Wm.
Irwin, lot 9, con. 7; Wm. Warner, N.E. quarter 10, con. 4; Margaret Belford,
north half 6, con. 6; James Connell, lot 9 east half, con. 10; Thos. Henesy,
west half 17 and 18, con. 10; Thos. Rowan, lot 2, con. 1; James Oliver, north

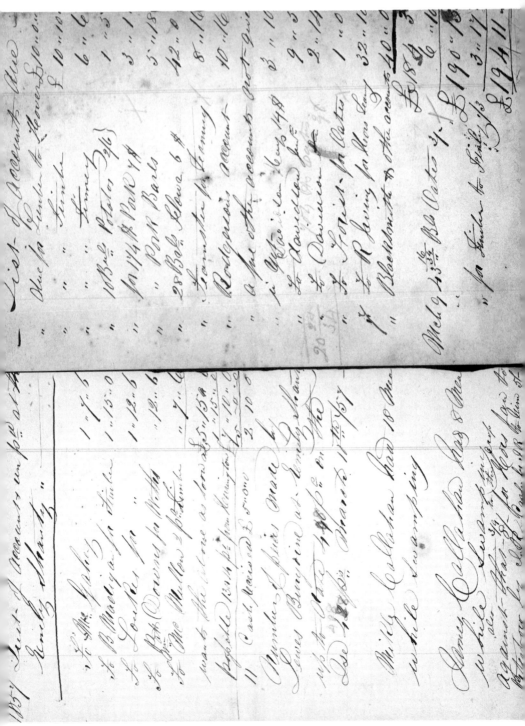

BOYD LUMBER CO. ACCOUNTS FOR LUMBER SHANTY IN NORTH EMILY 1857. (S. Boyd)

half 8, con. 7, etc. Some of these contained the owner's permission "to permit M. Boyd to draw it on most convenient route through his premises, M. Boyd to engage that no damage be done either to fences, building or crop." A Boyd note to W. Irwin in July 1852 said: "We made 69 pieces of elm on your land containing nearly 3,000 ft. which comes to £4 10s. Be pleased to sign the following receipt . . ." and Irwin in Peterborough signed for 70 Elm trees on lot 9, con. 7. A faded note dated Metcalfe, June 14, 1851, lists Francis Adams, con. 1, lot 1; Oliver Warner, con. 4, lot 10; also "Arthur McQuade", Hanna and Evers, to be paid 1 shilling for each tree "that is fit for Lumber"; the note ends mysteriously: 'Church Lot I spak the . . . and I think you can get it."

Boyd even had a lumbering shanty in Emily—one account reads: "1851 Emily, M. Boyd in acct. with John Toole & sons—to David Toole, carrying 1 load by waggon from Ed. Blackwell's tavern to my house, of shanty things for Mr. Lambert 2s. 6d. 1852—To David Toole, carrying 2 loads one from the shanty on my land, lot 4, con. 2, one from village, both to Ellsworth Shanty, Emily—7s. 6d." This account goes on to record loads of wheat "delivered to Duncan McDonald at Metcalfe Mills, at 3s. per bushel." Boyd had an account with "Arthur McQuade" in 1851 for 80 pieces of elm at 1. 10d., 5 tons of hay at 35s., 209 lbs. of Pork at 22s. 6d. per cwt., 61 bus. oats at 1s., etc. total £29 3s. 2d.; these were shanty supplies and services, and there were similar accounts with McQuade in 1852-54. In 1852 the Boyd foreman bought from N. Parker "1 large tin teapot for shanty 2s. 4d.", from W. Hilliard gloves, axes and chains costing £4 9s., from Michael Lehane of Downeyville 22 yrds. tartan plaid for shirts costing 6s. 1d., etc. One bill from M. Lehane to Jas. Lambert, foreman, in Feb. 1852 requested payment of £6 3s. 2d. on amounts owed by shantymen Jas. Doolin, John Doolin, Geo. Edgley, Matt. Casey, Pat Malligan, Victor Murray, Thos. Mushie and Jos. Billoe—no doubt mostly Emily workers. An undated account from this period headed "Acct. of Expenses of Elm Timber made at Pigeon Creek" totalling £192 11s. 9d. has such items as "Cook's wages £3 2s. 8d.", "potatoes from Stinson 8s. 11d.", "J. Sanderson's wages for 1 month 4 days —£3 9s. 4d.", "To use of oxen and horses—R. Hunter £3 14s., Robt. Owens £1 12s. 6d., James Dorgan £1 2s. 6d.", etc.[10]

Mossom Boyd owned the north half lot 16, con. 12 from 1859 for at least 15 years, receiving county tax bills ranging from $4.01 to $17.39. He received an angry letter from Jer. Scully of Emily, dated Oct. 25, 1867, for the use of his team to draw timber to the lake and rafting it (probably for towing to Bobcaygeon), against which was a bill for lumber purchased from Boyd, worth $14. By agreement of Feb. 2, 1871, Thos. McAuliff (or McCauliff) agreed to sell Boyd 400 basswood logs or more of 13 ft. length and 22 ins. diameter "free from rot knots doze or shakes, no log to be less than 13 ins. diameter to be delivered safely in good sufficient booms at Grenadier Island or Collins Landing on Pigeon Lake to be put into the water . . . at rate of $1 per log." On Apr. 12, 1872, Boyd paid $10.24 to Pat O'Hara of Downeyville "for drawing 4,800 logs from Scully's." But Boyd's

Lumbering in North Emily in the 1860s. (H. T. Pammett)

main interests now were in Harvey and northward—in 1871 he bought 8 tons of hay at $19 a ton from Tim. Dorgan of Emily "to be delivered at Squaw River, Harvey." He was, however, selling lumber in Emily through Isaac McNeely of Omemee—in July, 1874 he wrote McNeely "I send you this day per steamer 'Lady Ida' 3,500 ft. 1½ ins. siding, 6,000 ft. 1¼ ins. flooring, 5,000 ft. strip, 10,000 ft. cull, 1,500 ft. 2 ins. plank; I also ship on same scow on top of your lumber, 8,000 ft. cull strip for Mr. Thos. Stephenson . . . marked his name with red chalk. You will please get the scow unloaded and returned here as quickly as possible . . ." John Rea of Omemee wrote Boyd Oct. 9/74 "I am going to buy some lumber this winter to build barns. I want to know what you charge for your cull lumber that you sold last winter for $5 per thousand . . . (I want) 20 or 30 thousand delivered at Omemee or Lindsay and if you could not deliver it let me know what you will charge at the Mills for it."

References have been made to other small industries and businesses in Emily. Thanks to Williamson's *Omemee,* we have information about several Omemee industries besides Cottingham's Mills, in this period. James Ivory's mill near King St. Bridge made sash, doors, shingles, &c.; the Lindsay *Post* of Aug. 27, 1875 reported its burning: "It was impossible to arrest

its destructive career until the entire establishment . . . were one mass of
flames. . . . Mr. Kincaid's residence and sash & door factory and the river
bridge were in imminent danger but through a well-ordered effort on the
part of the villagers they were saved together with about a thousand cords of
shingle batts. The loss to Mr. Ivory will not fall much short of $10,000
covered by insurance of about $4,000. . . . The fire is supposed to have
originated in the boiler room." Ivory died soon after and J. J. English built
a mill on the site 1877-78. J. Evans started a foundry in 1874 on the old
distillery site, with water-power from the dam, to make farm machinery, etc.
George Lamb's tannery began in 1852 in a log building and was rebuilt in the
1860s, and Chester Dies (former teacher) started a small tannery on an
island north of the gristmill. James Lewis and George English had shops to
build wagons and carriages on Sturgeon Street—perhaps these shops turned
out some of the 84 "pleasure carriages" worth $5,618 recorded in Emily in the
1861 census. By 1875 also Samuel English was making improved grain cradles
near his brother; these were fastened to scythes for hand-reaping of grain. As
recorded in the Directories, there were also blacksmiths who made horse-
shoes, hinges, spades, scoops, forks, tongs, &c., and coopers who made tubs,
buckets, barrels, firkins, &c. Fred Dawson and John Wolstenholme had
asheries in Omemee, buying ashes from farmers and making potash, pearlash
and soft soap; "ashes at 15c a bushel were paid for with cakes of dark laundry
soap" (Williamson). Carpenter shops, making furniture, cabinet-ware and
even contracting to erect houses, were kept in Omemee by C. Balfour, H.
Finch, J. Goodliffe, A. Hoyland, J. McCrae, etc., and Thos. Thompson made
pumps in 1872. James Ivory, the miller, was also listed in the 1872 Mercantile Reference Book as operating the fulling and carding factory; Wm.
Elliott made saddles, and Jos. Campbell was a tinsmith—there were also
several boot and shoemakers, and tailors.

Other tradesmen were scattered throughout the township—Downeyville
in 1858 had 2 shoemakers, 2 blacksmiths and a milliner. At the Lebanon
settlement on lot 6, con. 1, there was at one time a small sawmill; also the
Gordon family had a store, Wm. Mulligan wove carpets, John Newman made
wagons and did blacksmithing. Moses Begley did blacksmithing and wood-
working on south half lot 16, con. 10, for many years. Simon Perdue had a
blacksmith shop on north half lot 18, con. 11, and was followed by his son
John. J. C. Leary had a blacksmith shop near King's Wharf, later operated
by his son John—the hamlet of King's Wharf with its postoffice, general store,
blacksmith shop, school and half-dozen houses has disappeared gradually
since 1914. In the Millersmith community, Alex Cullen had a blacksmith
shop on lot 7, con. 13, and Mr. Courtney made his own looms and did weaving on lot 8, con. 12. Mr. Bird on lot 6, con. 14, installed a pit-saw and sawed
lumber. John Cullen made boots and shoes on lot 8, con. 13. Wm. Callaghan
on lot 6, con. 13, dammed up a small creek for power to cut lumber and
make shingles and chop grain; later he used steam-power for this work, and
it is said he also had a still to make whisky.

A few others were travelling craftsmen who did blacksmithing and

custom-iron work, such as Alex Feir—his papers 1867-81 have been preserved by J. R. F. Johnson of Emily, and include bills and other records
of Omemee, Mt. Pleasant, Ops, and various other points in the region. One
of his early accounts with Isaiah Best 1867-69 has items like: repairing smut-
machine $4.00; making a sleigh-shoe $1.25; a turning shaft with couplings,
bolts and wheel $5.00; one dansil $2.50; 1 gate and flange $4.50—the total
bill for 3 years was $80.50—at that time when finances were handled in
leisurely manner such accounts were allowed to run for one to three years
before payment was demanded. Best, incidentally, offset against the account
one quarter of beef $6.00 and $50 cash paid before bill was presented. In
1872-75 Feir had accounts with E. H. Grandy of Omemee, Jos. Keelie,
James Ivory, D. Thornton, I. McNeely, James Evans and others. In 1875 he
purchased machinery for a job from the Wm. Hamilton foundry in Peterborough, costing $273.40. Another craftsman who did custom-work for his
neighbours was James Fowler, settled on lot 23, con. 3, Emily (Fowler's
Corners) who July 8, 1865, received notice from the agent of the Port Hope,
Lindsay & Beaverton Railway at Peterborough that his new corn-machine
had arrived, weight 1,400 lbs., cost of transit $5.28—this was probably a
grain-reaper, and would be drawn from town to Fowler's Corners by a team
of horses, ready for use in the harvest.

EMILY TOWNSHIP:	*1851*	*1861*	*(Census)*	*1871*	*1881*
Occupiers					
(10 acres and under)	5	11		62	34
(11-20 acres)	3	5			61
			combined	100	
(21-50 acres)	50	97			
(51-100 acres)	152	258		221	176
(100-200 acres)	16	79		98	138
(Over 200 acres)	6	19		33	40
	232	469		514	449
Total Agricultural Land	22,197	51,066		52,001	54,507
Cultivated	9,156	24,116		30,937	35,419
Crops	5,657	14,555		25,577	29,369
Pasture	3,476	9,280		4,899	5,461
Gardens and Orchards	23	281		461	589
Wood and Wild	13,041	26,950		21,064	19,088

Some farming trends can be seen in the above table. The small lots, usually
close to villages, increased as well-to-do business and professional men built
their country estates (preferably by river or lake)—by horse and buggy on
improved roads they could easily get into town daily to the shop, office or
mill. The small farms of 50 to 100 acres increased at first and then fell off,
while those over 100 acres continued to increase. When sons moved away or
neighbours sold out, it was convenient to farm 200 or 300 acres with the new

farm machines and more horsepower. Pastureland more than doubled 1851
to 1861 as did cattle, and then fell off sharply as grain-farming proved more
profitable than cattle-raising. The steady increase of gardens and orchards,
averaging finally over an acre per farm, show the growing appreciation of
vegetables and fruit in the farm diet. After 1851 the number of oxen declined
quickly and with more money farmers bought horses—the 1851 census
showed 336 horses on 232 farms—the 1861 census showed 815 horses plus
324 colts and fillies, used to power the new hay-rakes, grain-reapers, &c.
Sheep and pigs both doubled 1851 to 1861, but declined somewhat afterwards. These farms required more labour, and when the Government in 1870
obtained municipal returns of immigrant labour that could be used in the
next season, Emily Council replied that the township could make use of 100
labourers, 13 mechanics and 50 female servants.

It will be noted that croplands increased fivefold 1851 to 1881, and
some general trends can be highlighted, though changes in census factors
sometimes confuse the picture.[11] Wheat acreage was at first over 50% and by
1881 only 35% of cropland—the crop was 56,045 bus. in 1851, and more
than doubled to 1861 (33,510 bus. winter and 99,950 bus. spring wheat)—
though acreage continued to rise, the crop in 1881 was smaller, and almost
all spring wheat (699 bus. winter, 94,423 bus. spring wheat). Oat crops
rose even more sharply (from 47,753 bus. in 1851 to 165,166 bus. in 1881),
potatoes from 17,147 bus. to 60,860 bus., and barley from 884 bus. to 64,839
bus. As the table will show, there were also steady increases in production
of peas, turnips and other roots, carrots, etc. Hay more than doubled, from
1,219 to 3,136 tons. Worthy of special note is the large and growing production (in which the womenfolk had a major part) of homemade wool, flannel,
butter, cheese, maple sugar, barrelled beef and pork, etc. Much of this was
traded to storekeepers, or sold at town markets, or for cash to regular
customers, while the barrelled meat went mostly to rail and other construction
jobs, or to lumber-camps northward.

Out of many details buried in the township census returns, a few might
be mentioned—for example, the average Emily family in 1851 was 6-plus
persons, in 1861 up to 8-plus, in 1871 down to 6 persons, and in 1881 down
to 5-plus persons—can this be explained by young people marrying after
1870 and moving to town or to free lands on the Colonization Roads northward, or were families (now out of the pioneer stage) having fewer children,
or were more succumbing to epidemics such as diphtheria and scarlet fever,
since more children now went regularly to crowded country schools? The
1851 census stated births at 99 and deaths 27, with two persons over 80
years of age—there were also 26 widowers and 46 widows. In 1861, births
were 163 and deaths 37—there were 15 people 80 to 90 years old, and two
over 90—also 47 widowers and 76 widows; in this year also there was one
negro in Emily, but not a single Indian. Illiteracy was very low, only 142
adults being unable to read and write. In 1871, there were 14 people 80 to
99 years old, and one female over 100, also 39 widowers and 101 widows;
and in Emily was recorded one hired man! In 1881, there were only 37

widowers, 77 widows, but now 9 hired men. The number of Canadian-born rose steadily from nearly 58% in 1851 up to over 83% in 1881, and this with other factors (one of which was Canadian Confederation) brought a decline in racial and religious differences and frictions, and increased a common concern with politics, tariffs, transportation, farm prices, and other matters which influenced depression or prosperity, for everyone in the township.

	Census 1851	1861	1871	1881
Families	432	459	636	501
Houses: inhabited	430	568	634	500
vacant	5	7	51	16
building	9	11	34	8

This table provides a fascinating insight into living habits in Emily. There were no brick houses in 1851, but 4 in 1861; there were 8 stone houses in 1851 (of which the first in 1842 was built on the south half lot 9, con. 2, by James Evens (or Evans, 1 storey) and 11 by 1861. Frame houses, 35 in 1851, had gone up to 92 in 1862.[12] In 1851 the census-takers counted 300 log houses and 87 "shanties", but in 1861 they marked 461 log houses only, probably including some shanties. The paradox of 568 inhabited buildings and only 459 families in 1861 is hard to explain, unless with the large families some of the children slept out in the old log cabin behind the new frame, brick or stone house. The sudden increases by 1871 of houses vacant and building are also puzzling, but certainly an indication of more prosperity. Unfortunately the census figures after 1861 do not indicate the type of houses, but no doubt brick and frame houses increased steadily, with a few more stone ones also, as log cabins were either torn down or used for the pigs, chickens, machines and storage. Incidentally, Emily was one of the leading district townships in construction of frame, stone and brick houses, quite a few of them from timber, stone and brick-clay found on the premises.[12]

In this period 1850-75 life on farm and in town became steadily more comfortable. Wells were dug and pumps installed. New sewing and knitting machines allowed women to make underclothes, socks, shirts and dresses at home more easily—cottons and homespun flannel were 40c-50c a yard, and fulled cloth 80c a yard; by 1875 factorymade clothing was coming into the stores also. The village milliners and dressmakers helped in making "Sunday-best" hats and clothing for the women while men purchased a "Sunday-best" suit for $4-$6, which lasted with care a lifetime (and the funeral after)—by 1875 all clothing had increased 25% (except the factory-made), and tailor-made suits cost double the above prices. Similarly, moccasins and shoepacks could be made at home, or bought for $1 to $1.25 (a pair), while the local shoemaker provided sturdy working boots for $4 to $5 a pair; factorymade children's shoes sold for 80c or $1 a pair, but those made by the local shoe-maker, while costing more, could be handed down to younger children as the older ones grew out of them; the young men and town-dwellers also bought

Ruth House — N½ Lot 20, Con. 5 — stone part built c. 1850 — (Ed Ruth)

Stone House — Lot 20, Con. 1, built c. 1850 (Nelson McConnell)

Brick House of Scully family — Lot 2, Con. 7, built c. 1855 (bricks made on the farm). This was the first brick house built by a Peter Robinson, settler. (John Peeters)

One of the first brick houses built with homemade bricks, c. 1850 — (W½ Lot 20, Con. 3) — (Ray Storey)

Timber frame house — Lot 19, Con. 2, built c. 1850 (Earl McCall)

Parish House, Downeyville, built 1880 (Francis Campa)

fancy fine-leather shoes for $5-$7 a pair, for special occasions. Other signs of the more comfortable life were kerosene lamps and lanterns, after oil was discovered in 1859—by 1870 kerosene fell to 35c a gallon, and lamps and lanterns sold for 50c to 60c. Pewterware and steel cutlery gradually replaced woodenware in homes, and occasionally, as for the wedding of a favourite daughter, imported china, silverware, stuffed parlour furniture, glass chandeliers, etc.

Wages held steady in the 1850s, rose in the 1860s, and fell again in the depression years after 1872—skilled craftsmen such as mechanics, black-smiths, carpenters found jobs at $25 to $50 a month, and construction and lumbercamp labourers at $15 to $20; wages for farm help averaged (with board and lodging) $8 to $15 a month for men, $2 to $8 for women and boys. Wheat, which was 85c to 95c a bushel in the 1850s, rose in the next decade to $1.25 a bushel. In the 1870s spring wheat rose from 65c to 90c a bus., while fall (or winter)wheat was 75c to $1.05 a bus. by 1880. Oats and barley sold at 40c-45c a bus. in the 1850s and 1860s, and barley remained at that, while oats fell to 35c in the 1870s. Potatoes remained stable at 40c-50c a bushel, peas at 50c-70c a bushel. Hay rose from $10-$12 a ton up to $14 a ton in the 1860s, and then fell to $8-$11 a ton. Flour rose steadily from $2.25 a barrel (100 lbs.) up to $8 a barrel by 1875, with exports to Europe growing. While butter rose from 10c to 15c a pound 1850 to 1875, cheese fell in the same price-range. Honey and sugar prices were about the same in the period, 12c to 17c a pound, and maple syrup at 90c a gallon. Some other prices fluctuated, especially things the farmer bought: tea was 75c to $1.25 per lb. and coffee 25c per lb., candles 10c to 16c per lb., tobacco 25c to 35c per lb., teakettles 60 to 75c each, whisky 20c to 40c a gallon, gunpowder 65c per lb., trace or halter-chains 40c to 50c, a broad axe about $4, an ordinary axe, hayfork or spade $1 to $1.25, a scythe $2.25. A plough cost $24 in 1860, but only $10 by 1875, while a good wagon was $55 in 1860, down to $45 in 1875. Dressed lumber was $10 per M in the 1850s, down to $6 by 1870, and to $5 in 1875. Horses were $70 to $125 in the 1860s, and down only slightly in the next decade, while cows were steady at $25 to $40 depending on breed, condition, etc.

Emily fairs were held at Metcalfe as early as 1854 by the township society, organized in the 1840s—among the sponsors and officers were Wm. Cottingham, J. Hughes, C. Knowlson, and R. Grandy. In addition to classes for exhibitors in grains, vegetables, livestock, poultry, honey, homemade farm tools, harness, wagons and cradles, &c., the farm-women showed in classes for homespun cloth, knitted goods, preserved vegetables and fruit, bread, eggs, painting on wood and linen, and other fancy work. After 1867 the Ontario government reorganized agricultural societies by electoral ridings, and Emily became a branch of the Victoria South (later East) Agricultural Society, which each year received a grant of $700 (later revised upward). In 1868 the Emily Branch had 7 members—receipts were $191.25 and expenses $166.31, of which $111.25 was for fair prizes (over half for livestock), and $39.60 for farm publications circulated among members. Membership was

$1 per farm, and was the same in 1870, with receipts $206.24 and expenses $171.58. The 1873 Report mentioned a Spring Show (probably at Lindsay) for livestock, and the Fall Show October 6-7 much improved over the previous year, except in wheat exhibits: "fall wheat . . . a general failure throughout the Riding from the effects of winter killing", but all other grain showed quality unexcelled. In fruit also, due to "long severe drought which prevailed all summer", the exhibits were very inferior, and most apples infested with codling moth worm. The report noted and encouraged efforts to organize community cheese factories, and experimental or model farms in each riding, to aid in improvement of farm production.

The 1874 Report was full of praise for Emily: 178 members, receipts $398.22, expenses $397.91 (of which $245.25 for Fair prizes). "This Society held two exhibitions in 1873, each at Omemee. . . . The Spring Show was for entire horses and bulls. . . . The entries were large, and the display the finest ever held by this society. . . . The entries for the Fall Show were greatly in advance of any previous year. . . . The total number of entries 566, an increase of 202 over 1872. . . ." Entries in horses, cattle, sheep and pigs, poultry, grain and dairy produce, fruit, root crops and vegetables "very fine, surpassing any display ever held here. In ladies' work, curiosities, flowers, and fine arts . . . the display very fine, being the great attraction of the indoor exhibition. . . ."

In addition to fairs and an occasional concert or parade in Omemee, most social activities in Emily were connected with the local churches and schools, or bees and other events in Millersmith, Lebanon, Downeyville and other rural communities. The Emily Branch of the Sons of Temperance, led by Rev. Ewing and C. Knowlson, petitioned 1858 on for a total prohibition of liquor, and this campaign gathered strength in the next two decades. The officers of the Emily Branch, Canadian Bible Society, were listed in the 1857-58 Directory as John McNeely, president, and Thomas Matchett, secy. treasurer (Matchett was township treasurer and court clerk); the Omemee *Warder* Feb. 20, 1857, had a long account of a Bible Society meeting a week earlier at Omemee Town Hall: ". . . the Emily Branch of the Bible Society is in its infancy . . . the meeting was chaired by Gabriel Balfour"; on this occasion, the lecturer, Mr. Johnston from Toronto, described the operations of the Bible Society in Ireland, and emphasized that Canada would only prosper with the spread of the Gospel.

The same *'Warder'* issue announced a "Grand Orange Soiree . . . Orangemen of the District of Omemee will give a Grand Soiree in aid of the fund for finishing the Parsonage in this Parish—in the Town Hall, Omemee, on Thursday, 26th February. . . . A good Brass Band will be in attendance." We learned earlier of the Cavan and Emily Orange activities in the 1830s, which were discouraged for a time after the 1837 Rebellion by a government prohibition on factional processions. However, the Protestant Irish who emigrated from north Ireland, and those who moved to Emily from other parts of Canada, brought Orange membership certificates, resulting in the formation of the first Orange Lodge no. 294 in 1841 by James Balfour at

Metcalfe. The warrant was reissued to John Mills in 1851, and soon after the lodge was moved to a log building near Bethel Methodist Church. The Lodge's earliest surviving minute book is dated 1866, when initiation fee was $1 and annual fee the same—it is significant that the lodge's early rules firmly prohibited use of liquor at meetings or parades, and required members to show co-operation and friendship toward Roman Catholic neighbours, stressing the positive belief in British Crown and democratic traditions, rather than negative religious factionalism. The second Lodge in Emily, no. 41, at Orange Corners, was organized June 19, 1847, at the home of Francis Best, and officers elected: James Moore, Master; John Nous, Deputy; Ed. Blackwell, Treasurer; and Francis Galbraith, Secretary. In 1867 the Lodge's officers were Thos. Magee, Master; Andrew Fowler, chaplain; James Mitchell, Deputy; Samuel McCormack, Secretary. In 1875, when Thomas Magee was still Master, the Lodge decided to build their Hall, and with members helping at a building bee, the new frame Hall was opened late in 1876. Ladies' auxiliaries were still in the future, but a district lodge, centred in Lindsay, was formed 1854, and the Grand Lodge of Ontario East met there in 1864.

Mr. Richard Howden, born in Fermanagh, Ireland, in 1844, and brought to Canada two years later, grew up in Cavan, and in 1885 married Celia Latchford of Emily and farmed there until 1922—they were interviewed in 1934 when retired to Omemee, and the newspaper headline designated him as "Last of the Cavan Blazers", and also an Orangeman since the age of 15. The expert on the Cavan Blazers was E. S. Clarry, who wrote in the Millbrook *Mirror-Reporter* Nov. 18, 1943, and was copied in other papers. The name was given to a group of youths mostly on 9th to 11th concessions Cavan, but occasionally from south Emily, who for the period 1845-1870 carried on reckless pranks and mischievous acts, grossly exaggerated then and since by local rumor and newspapers. In a period when there was little organized social and sports activity for young people, youths gathered in the evenings at crossroads, barnyards or saloon to expend excess energy in horseplay or devilment, or storytelling about local feuds and quarrels. When the 1846-48 fever epidemic was especially severe in the swampy area, west of Springville, some youths began going out on moonlit nights to help by reaping the crops for the sick, and when one stern father locked a girl in her bedroom to force her to marry an old man instead of her sweetheart, the Blazers helped her down a ladder and away to Peterborough with her swain to be married. Other pranks were to hang a cowbell on the wires in front of a church where the parson preached too long, and to put a miser's wagon on the ridgepole of his barn. On one occasion they were said to have brought Father Butler from Peterborough to the bedside of a dying Catholic, but they were also accused of burning the buildings of some disliked Catholics, and fomenting fights at St. Patrick's Day parades in town. In fact every theft of a pig or chicken for a midnight feast, every Halloween prank, every cutting of cows' tails and other mischief, every barn-fire in the whole district, was thenceforth blamed on the Cavan Blazers, though often the work of tramps or gypsies, or passing workmen. When sports and more wholesome recreation were promoted after

1870, the actual deeds of the Cavan Blazers gradually ceased, though perpetuated and inflated in story. Their ties with Orangeism and anti-Catholic feuding were always largely fictional.

Four 1874 items from the Lindsay *Post* are connected to the above: (1) In January, the Loyal Orange District Lodge of Emily elected its officers: T. Stephenson, Master; Wm. Adams, Deputy; Rev. Jas. Norris, Chaplain; Dr. G. A. Norris, Treasurer; John Shaw, Secretary—also L.O.L. 114 of Omemee elected Wm. Adams, Master; Wm. Neill, Deputy; Wm. Balfour, Chaplain; Wm. Lang, Treasurer; and John Shaw, Secretary. (2) In January also, the Sons of Temperance, no. 182, elected officers: John Shaw, Miss M. Ivory, Thomas Savage, Miss A. Peplow, etc. (3) In May, a meeting was held to reorganize the Cricket Club, electing J. Shaw, president; W. C. Penton, vice-president; C. Bent, captain; W. Beatty, secretary; T. Savage, treasurer. (4) On June 19, the paper stated: "The Young Men's Christian Association have prospered so well (in Omemee) that they find the hall in which they hold their meetings far too small, and are about going into a new hall, and intend to have reading-room and library attached. The beneficial effects of the society are quite apparent, judging from the number of young men that attend, and also the young ladies." That summer the paper also reported the sadness in Omemee and all Emily at the retirement of Colonel Cottingham to Lindsay, after 55 years as a pioneer leader in industry and community affairs; he died in Lindsay in May, 1875, marking the end of an era.

Until a local paper was started, local events were printed only when they were reported to outside papers. The *Church* July 7, 1853 wrote: "MARRIED: at residence of the bride's father on 22nd June, by Rev. Robert Harding, Emily, Mr. Richard Everett of Cavanville, merchant, to Miss Mary Jane Knowlson, 2nd daughter of Christopher Knowlson, Esq, Metcalfe."; and two years later reported that Bishop Strachan would visit Emily for confirmations on July 16. On. Aug. 14, 1855, the Toronto '*Leader*' quoted a Port Hope paper: "We regret to learn the store of Thos. Matchett, Metcalfe, was totally destroyed by fire on the 2nd inst. The whole stock was consumed, with exception of about £65 worth. Mr. M's loss is mostly covered by insurance, £600 on stock and £150 on building. How the fire originated is not known." However, in Nov. 1856 Jos. Cooper began printing the *Metcalfe Warder* each Friday (7s. 6d. in advance, 10s. otherwise) at his book and job printing office, and one of the first local items (reprinted in a Toronto paper) was "FIRE: we learn that an uninhabited house in Metcalfe, property of W. Laidley, was partially burned on the 28th ult." Next year this paper blossomed out in four pages as *"THE WARDER, or Omemee, Emily and County of Victoria Weekly Gazette"* and we are fortunate that a copy of the Feb. 20, 1857, issue has been preserved.

Among the front page business cards, Chris. Knowlson is prominent as a dealer in dry goods, groceries, medicines, drugs and chemicals, also issuer of marriage licenses, commissioner for oaths, and insurance agent. Wm. Cottingham, county warden, and commissioner of oaths; Dr. Irons; Thomas Bell, commission agent; McKay & Redmond, tailors; R. W. Hungerford, auctioneer & land agent; Wm. Matchett, grocer and general merchant;—these shared space with some Peterborough, Lindsay and Toronto businessmen. Among hotels advertising were Edward Blackwell's Metcalfe Hotel, Henderson's Hotel and Stage Office, Catherine Collins' Agricultural Hotel at Downeyville, and William Simpson's Railway Hotel, Metcalfe. Henderson's New Livery Stable at Metcalfe advertised rental and sale of "double and single horses and carriages", as well as horses for sale "at all hours for cash and cash only." As usual, most of the front page was devoted to articles, fiction and poetry from British sources. The second page continued the news from Europe and United States, with a description of the Bible Society meeting, and news about Cottingham's new and improved Grist-Mill just completed, built by Mr. Davis, millwright—"our farmers will no longer have to trudge to other townships to get their milling done." J. Might of Omemee advertised fine lines of saddles, harness, bridles, trunks etc. W. L. McCallum, at James English's New House for 2 weeks only, was prepared to take "Ambrotype Likenesses" at very low prices—these were early forerunners of the photograph. John Hanna was advertising for a good journeyman cooper "to whom the highest wages will be paid", and the publisher wanted an apprentice printer with some experience. Wm. Fraser cautioned anyone from cutting timber or trespassing on lot 4, in 3rd con. Emily, and Ed. Blackwell likewise on the property of Matt. Ruttan in Omemee Village, "or removing wood therefrom without permission." John McNeely was offering for sale 200 acres, being lot 3, con. 12, Emily. Dr. Irons wanted a first-class teacher for Omemee Amalgamated School "to whom a liberal salary will be paid." Michael Buckley was selling a fine farm, north half lot 13, con. 9, Emily, terms £50 down.

Some of the largest advertisements were on page 3. Wm. Turner of Omemee "the best place to trade in Victoria" had dry goods, groceries, wines and liquors, glassware, china, boots, shoes &c. James Bradburn had as wide a stock, also readymade clothing, blankets, carpeting, oilcloth, rubber shoes etc. in his enlarged store. C. Knowlson had a wide complete assortment of goods, and Thomas Matchett likewise, including "almost all the popular Patent Medicines of the day." Jos. Cooper not only sold a newspaper and printed forms, but paper, ink, pens, wax, pipes, brooches, tooth and nail brushes, glass ornaments, rings, decanters, combs, violin strings, purses, and "an assortment of Room Paper in every variety." W. M. Marrs was buying ashes in quantity "at the old stand, belonging to Thos. Matchett, formerly used as an Ashery". S. B. Chandler, surgical & mechanical dentist, notified readers that he had taken rooms in Omemee, and had with him a good watchmaker who would repair watches and jewelry, as well as selling watches, gold and silver chains, brooches, earrings, and all types of jewelry. Especially interesting was an advertisement by Francis Henderson who was selling his "Clover Hill Farm" of 800 acres, lots 13 and 14, con.2 and 3, Emily, where he had resided over 30 years, "having decided to retire from Farming avocations . . . located on the middle road—the Port Hope Stage traversing on the side, and Peterboro Stage on the end, daily. . . . There is a nice Frame-House 30 x 40, splendidly finished; frame-barn, sheds, stables—an

The Warder,

OR. OMEMEE, EMILY, AND COUNTY OF VICTORIA WEEKLY GAZETTE.

TERMS: 7s. 6d. IF ADVANCE]   MAN'S NOBLEST MOTIVE IS THE PUBLIC GOOD.   [10s. IF OTHERWISE.

VOLUME I.]   OMEMEE, CANADA WEST, FRIDAY, FEBRUARY 20, 1857.   [NUMBER 16.

Montage of Some Interesting Items in
Omemee-Emily Warder, Feb. 20, 1857

Orchard that speaks loud for fruits of all sorts. 90 acres well cleared and fenced under very best cultivation with 20 acres fall wheat; and for convenience of wood and water cannot be beaten . . . will dispose of one lot or both as option of purchaser may decide." The last page had more poetry, general articles "lifted" from journals, and a variety of long and misleading patent medicine advertisements.

In June, 1857, Cooper was proud to announce: "BIRTH on 23rd June, in Omemee, Emily, to Emily, wife of Joseph Cooper, proprietor of the *Warder,* a daughter". In Dec. 1858, the *Warder* reported: "We regret to learn a most melancholy accident occurred in township Emily on Friday evening last. John Cassidy of 14th conc. was attending a threshing machine during the day, and when about to leave, early in the evening went in search of his fork, which he was told was on the other side of the machine. As he was going to where the fork lay, his coat caught in the machinery, dragging him in and so mutilating him that in 2 or 3 hours he died. Mr. Cassidy was a respectable farmer advanced in age, and leaves a wife and grownup family to mourn his untimely end." More cheerful was a March 1859 item: "MARRIED: in Omemee on 16th ult., by Rev. Mr. Hickle, Mr. James Bowis of township Galway to Miss Jane Harkness of Emily."; and the following reprinted in Peterboro *Review,* Dec. 1862: "MARRIED: by Rev. John Carrol in Smith township, Dec. 23, 1862, Mr. John James Mitchell of Emily to Miss Ruth Milburn, daughter of Thomas Milburn of Smith."

By 1863 and 1865, judged by copies which have survived, the *Warder* had declined in qualtiy; the first page in July 3, 1863, had the same format, mostly poetry and fiction from Europe, with small business cards of Wm. Cottingham, Dr. George Norris, Dr. W. A. Black, Dr. P. Davison, and Dr. Geo. Potts—all of Omemee (Potts and Norris being coroners also). Page 2 had general U.S. and outside articles, with a birth announcement of a daughter to Wm. Cottingham. Page 3 had a few local business cards: Jos. Campbell was selling stoves at Omemee Tin Store, also tin, sheet iron and copperware; G. Morrison of Omemee sold dry goods, groceries, crockery, spices, confectionery and choice fruits; Wm. Currie was selling spring and summer dry goods, boots and shoes, groceries &c. for cash; John Madden advertised his farm for sale a quartermile from Pigeon River—150 acres, 120 of which under cultivation, being the s.½ lot 12 in con.8 and west part of lot 13 in con. 8 (50 acres)—"a good road—the middle line—runs between the 2 lots." I. McNeely's Store at Omemee had just received their new Summer Goods. On page 4 Thomas Eley advertised clockmaking, repairing and engraving at Omemee, while Comstock & Shannon at Omemee Carriage Factory were making wagons, carriages, gigs, buggies, sulkies &c. "in the latest style", also horseshoeing and general jobbing "cheap for cash, produce taken in exchange." The PH.L & B. Railway was advertising that their mail train now left Omemee at 10:25 a.m. and arrived Port Hope 1:10 p.m., back at 3 p.m. arriving Omemee 5:55 p.m. Otherwise, three-quarters of these two pages were devoted to long patent medicine advts. offering "Health, Happiness and Long Life" for buying and consuming Dr. Buchan's Vegetable

Medicines and Sarsaparilla Pills, Canadian Pain Destroyer, Henry's Vermont
Liniment (for everything from toothache to diarrhea), Clarke's Celebrated
Female Pills, Bryan's Pulmonic Wafers, Herrick's Sugar Coated Pills ("the
Great Healer of Mankind—children cry for them!") and a dozen more quack
medicines.

The *Warder* of Nov. 3, 1865 on page 1 carried cards of Dr. George
Norris, Dr. W. A. Black, Wm. Cottingham, and Jos. Keele of Omemee ("fresh
arrivals of Boots & Shoes"). Wm. Beatty merchant, of Omemee, was willing
to rent his store and dwelling. T. D. Collins and T. H. Lehane of Downeyville
advertised a farm for sale, east half of lot 6 in con. 5 "all good hardwood" in
Fenelon township. On page 2 Thomas Evans published a letter to Arthur
McQuade contradicting a false report circulated by Evans "that you had
purchased wheat and exhibited it at the County Fair in Lindsay on 17th
inst. and getting the prize therefor . . . without any foundation whatever",
and apologizing to McQuade. But except for a few more district advertisements, and a bit about the Fenian scare, the rest of the paper was devoted to
patent medicine advertisements. The price was down to $1 a year, and the
next step was in sight—in 1867 Cooper moved his paper to Lindsay after a
fire destroyed his plant, and it flourished as the Victoria *Warder,* Conservative
organ. In 1869 J. H. Delamere started the *Omemee Standard* about which
little is known; it survived several years, but no copy has been found—in
1874 an Omemee correspondent wrote: "Our local newspaper is dead,
sure." With Toronto, Port Hope, Lindsay and Peterborough papers coming
into Emily by rail and mail daily, small local papers then and later found it
very difficult to survive or prosper.

Many other local events, important at the time, could be described. In
1865 a fire swept across north Emily, and dozens were burnt out; stories are
told of babies put out in cradles or 'democrats' far out in a ploughed field,
to avoid the roaring blaze caused by a long drought. Again in 1874 bush
fires burned farm buildings on con.13 and 14 in Emily. In Sept. 1871 the
Emily Presbyterian Session book, kept by Wm. Best, clerk, recounted a
dramatic quarrel: "the complaint of Jos. McGill against Wm. Roan for making false statements before a Magistrate upon oath—adjourned to Oct. 2 that
Roan might be able to get his witnesses. Mrs. McGill's evidence: said she
heard loud talk and went to the door, saw Wm. Roan jump off the waggon,
heard him tell Jos. McGill he could kick him . . . did not see who struck
first . . . she asked son Joseph would he stand and see them kill each other . . .
saw Roan's eye bleeding and some swelled . . . says that he Joseph was
whiting his scythe when Roan left the waggon. . . ." The quarrel blew up over
Roan's promise to thrash McGill's grain and then delaying. "Roan said that I
might go to the Devil, both me and my thrashing, you ugly Ape . . . he
challenged me to fight and got off the waggon . . . he came up to me and
struck at me, I then struck him and knocked him down, my son Joseph
caught me by the arm and pulled me back . . . Roan got up, he went to the
waggon and got a piece of board and Joseph took it from him. . . ." Roan's
version was of course quite different, saying he was winning the fight until
McGill's son also piled onto him, but that he, Roan, finally won the fight.

Roan went to Squire Dick to swear an affidavit, denying most of the aggression. The Session found both parties much to blame, and both behaving "most unChristianlike". Thomas Best, a Presbyterian Church Elder for over 30 years, died in 1874, and Wm. Best, who served as clerk in the Session above, also a Church Elder for 36 years and a temperance leader, died in 1879.

John Bent, J.P., tells how his father Charles when he first came to Canada in 1873 at age 17 went to work for Thomas Matchett (who in 1865 bought the Hinds property, lot 7, con.4, close to the village). At that time "a family of five generations of the Pigeons lived in a wigwam back in the bush. Sally Pigeon was 92 and her mother Phoebe was well over 100. Very soon the tribe was all moved to the Indian Reserve, on the water joining Chemong and Buckhorn Lakes. A few years later Chief Pigeon died. My father told me some 200 Indians paddled up the Pigeon River and buried their dead chief's body on the north bank, just outside the village, in his canoe, with all the things he would need in the Happy Hunting Grounds. . . . Later my father bought the farm. It is now mine . . . I would like to see a plaque placed in the little Omemee Park, in the village that once belonged to his tribe, and bears his name. It would be very fitting alongside the cenotaph bearing the names of the World War heroes of the community." This is a fitting conclusion to the story of the first 57 years of white settlement in Emily. The changes in Emily township since 1818 had indeed been vast, by 1875, but the changes in the 98 years to follow were even greater, as we shall see.

NOTES

[1] Lists of early bylaws, and chief officials, will be found in appendixes, and one or two bylaws may be illustrated.

[2] Now in the possession of Mrs. Mildred McBain (nee Magee) of Peterborough.

[3] Ontario Legislative Journals, 1868-69, appendix no. 41. A more cheerful report appeared in the 1873 Journals, stating that Omemee High School, built and opened in 1860, had a frame building valued at $2000 and a playground of one acre, with 18 maps, 2 globes, and a library valued at $500. Standards in the school were improving, and of its graduates in 12 years—6 had entered mercantile life, 5 farming, 9 professions and 2 teachers.

[4] Some Registers of Officers of the Upper Canada Militia, 1812-58, including Peterboro, Durham & Victoria Regiments, Public Archives of Canada.

[5] The original is in the Need Papers, now in the Ontario Archives.

[6] A paragraph from N. Davin "The Irishman in Canada" (1877) (page 350) concerning Mr. McQuade will be found in Appendix XVII.

[7] Kirkconnell in "Victoria Centennial History" lists Matchett as a Conservative, but the Ontario Centennial History of Electoral Districts 1867-1967 lists him as a Liberal.

[8] Volume II, "The Letters of Sir John A. Macdonald 1858-61" Public Archives 1969.

[9] Further quotation from this important Directory is impossible, as no copy could be located, among Mr. Williamson's records or elsewhere; a map showing 1867 Emily ratepayers has been substituted, from information compiled by L. McQuade.

[10] An interesting 1857 List of Accounts at Emily Shanty will be illustrated.

[11] A comparative table from Census returns will be found in Appendix XIX.

[12] Particulars of the first frame, stone and brick houses in Emily, prepared by Simon Connell, will be found in Appendix XX.

[13] The front page of this Feb. 20, 1857 "Warder" will be shown as an illustration, with some items in a montage.

EMILY ON A PLATEAU (1875-1900)

For Emily this is a period which economists call a "plateau"—population declined slowly according to the census: *1871*: 3790; *1881*: 2876; *1891*: 2603; *1901*: 2304.[1] On the economic side, however, it was a period of relative prosperity—Emily pulled out of a period of poor crops (1872-75) and depression (1873-79), into rising production and prices, until the next depression (1893-97) sent assessment, production and prices tumbling down again:

	1875	*1882*	*1891*	*1900*
No. of ratepayers	564	708	865	845
Property Assessment (before equalization)	$744,500	$1,175,134	$1,007,586	$950,596
Total Taxes (twp. & county)	$6000	$6760	$6400	$9909.32

It was a generation when the average Emily family decreased from 5.7 in 1881 to 4.8 in 1901. Farm machines were bought in increasing numbers, the average farm became larger, and by 1900 there were only 10 working oxen left in Victoria County, probably nearly all on the northern frontier. The introduction gradually of phonographs, telephones, and bicycles in the 1880s, and by 1900 the coming of electric power, automobiles and the wireless, had noticeable effects on rural young people, and helped to lure youth into the towns. The first mail order catalogues (both Eaton's and Simpson's) in the 1880s had enormous results for all merchandising, and doubled mail deliveries in the period, besides providing basic family reading, first in the kitchen and later in the outdoor privy. The lure of new homesteads on the Colonization Roads into Haliburton, and work in the lumber shanties and river-drives, were after 1885 transformed into the lure of railway construction to the Pacific, prairie farms of a thousand acres, and a quick fortune in the Klondike goldfields, for the younger generation growing in Emily. For the first time, hiring help for farm operations, especially in harvest-time, became an important question on many Emily farms, although neighbourhood "bees" continued in some parts.

The township council of 1876 was: Reeve Thos. Stephenson (re-elected each year to 1880), and Councillors Wm. Adams, John Bailey, John Mitchell and Dennis Scully.[2] The paid officials were R. Grandy, clerk, $125 p.a.; W. Curry, treasurer, $60; Geo. Magee, assessor, $90; M. Costello, collector, $100; two auditors received $6 each, and a medical health officer $5 per annum. In 1877 when M. Costello died, James Lehane became collector at $90, and in 1878 Wm. Curry replaced Thomas Matchett as treasurer. In 1880 David Storey became collector, in 1881 James Sherin, in 1884 Isiah Thornton, in 1889 J. J. Magee, and in 1890 Charles Corneil (for 20 years). Pat Flynn became assessor in 1882, in 1893 Josiah Mitchell, in 1895 C. Corneil (also collector), in 1900 William Patrick. By 1890 salaries were:

clerk $175, treasurer $75, assessor $70 and collector $100 per annum; by 1900 these salaries were: clerk $185, treasurer $85, assessor $50 and collector $105. The first road engineer, Michael Deane, was appointed in 1887, salary not given; in 1896 the medical health officer, Dr. Cornwall, resigned, and the new one, Dr. B. Bradd, had the salary of $10 per annum; Dr. George Cameron replaced him in 1900. Emily up to 1875 was the township with second highest assessment in Victoria, next to Mariposa; however, by 1900 when William Adams was reeve, Emily was fourth after Ops, Mariposa and Lindsay town. But unlike some other municipalities, Emily in the early part of the period had no funded or debenture debts, and acquired little before 1900.

Emily levied $500 a year for roads and bridges up to 1877, supplemented by government grants. When Ontario divided the Municipal Loan Fund among municipalities in 1876, Emily received the enormous sum of $6640.75 from it, which was used in the next few years for wholesale improvement of roads and bridges throughout the township. Omemee obtained $1191.25, used to erect a railway siding into the village. In 1877 Michael Deane P.L.S. was employed to survey a new road 3 rods wide on the north half lot 21, in con. 12 "toward the old established road leading to the Floating Bridge", and the old road on lot 21 was closed. The road levy was doubled to $1000 from 1878 to 1895, and by an 1881 bylaw statute labour was changed: property assessed at $500 required 3 days' work on roads, $900— 4 days, $1500—5 days, $2200—6 days, and each additional $1000 one more day of statute labour; provision was made to commute this labour for cash payments. In 1884 Victoria Council gave $712 to Emily for roads, plus $100 to build a north approach to the Pigeon River Floating Bridge; Victoria also agreed to aid in a new iron one-span bridge about 60 feet long across the river in Omemee village. In 1887 Emily Council appointed the first road engineer, Michael Deane—his first job was to widen the road through lot 21 in con.13 "which is part of the public highway between Peterborough town and Bobcaygeon village"; this 30-foot road was now insufficient for increased traffic, and was widened to 66 feet. In 1890 a district road built in 1842 was closed, from rear of lots 4 and 5 in con.5 south to centre of concession, then east to road allowance between lots 6 and 7. A few other pioneer roads, now unused or unsuitable, were also closed in the period—through lots 18 and 19 on con.11, through lots 17 and 18 in con.14, through north half lot 17 in con.13, etc.

Victoria Council in 1891 on motion of McQuade and Switzer from Emily sent a memorial to the Ontario Public Works Department to have a swing rebuilt in Cowan's Bridge, and in 1892-93 gave small grants to aid in repairing Pigeon Floating Bridge and Cowan's Bridge; then in 1900 Council studied a motion of Reeve Adams and Dennis Scully for a grant of $700 to aid Emily in "providing a high level steel Cowan's Bridge to permit the passage of steamers", but no more was heard of this proposal. We shall learn more about Pigeon River navigation later. Emily was levying about $1500 a year by 1900 for roads and bridges, with added grants from county and province to meet the demands of steadily growing road traffic, at all seasons of the year. The Ontario Government by 1900 was urging local authorities to commute all statute labour and to increase dollar expenditures on roads; the 1914 Ontario Roads Report showed that while in ten years up to 1896 statute labour in Emily had given work valued at $23,440 (e.g. in 1893, 2382 days of statute labour worth $1738), tax levies had raised for roads and bridges only $14,813, varying from a high of $2188 in 1890 to a low of $576 in 1895; in 1897 the tax levy was $1173, and in 1898 $1602, quite inadequate to maintain good roads.

In 1876 County Council required Emily to have a special vote in north-west Emily (north of con.7 and west from Middle Road) to pay toward the county $85,000 bonus to the Whitby, Port Perry and Lindsay Extension Railway, claiming that section would benefit from the railway. The vote Feb. 25, 1876, was held at J. O'Leary's dwelling in Downeyville and at Kelley's School, and was favourable, since from 1877 on that area paid additional taxes of $706 toward the bonus. In 1880 County Council started a judicial inquiry about alleged fraud by Reeve T. Stephenson of Emily in handling a grant for work on Cowan's Bridge, on grounds the actual cost in 1878 was $1999.66, while the account submitted to County totalled $2600—the next year, after the judge found serious irregularities, Victoria Council censured Stephenson's conduct as fraudulent. Growing awareness of the tourist trade in Victoria is found in an 1885 petition to Ottawa for an extended closed season during the spawning of maskinonge and bass, up to June 15, and an 1887 petition to Toronto asking a closed game season Dec. 1 to Oct. 15 (next year) since deer, moose and other game animals were being rapidly exterminated. County Council noted in 1890 that of 39 persons wholly sustained by charity, only one was in Emily, and of 126 others getting casual aid, only 4 were in Emily, indicating the obvious thrift and self-reliance in that township. Reeve McQuade of Emily was elected warden that year, and in Jan. 1894 County Council passed a motion of regret on his death, remembering his service over two decades on township and county councils, and his two terms as Member of Parliament.

Emily Council was concerned with livestock running at large, due to heavier road traffic. In 1879 Council banned hogs from being loose outside barnyards "except they have good noserings". Bylaw 189 in 1879 fixed the height of "lawful fences" of wood at 4½ feet, and of wire 5 feet, with stone base 2 feet, or a rail on top—the wire spaces were to be not more than 6″ at the bottom and 9″ above. Bylaw 191 introduced stringent rules to prevent animals running at large, and regulating the duties of pound-keepers: "no horn beast, no bull, stag, boar, ram or breachy cow, ox or young cattle or any poultry . . . during any period of the year, and no pig between Apr. 1 and Dec. 1" to be loose on public property. Pound-keepers were to keep a register of animals in custody, with a schedule of fines and legal charges for daily poundage, advertising &c. payable by owner. Again in 1885 rules were tightened about proper dimensions and care of all fences. Earlier, in 1882, Council worried about steam-shovels tearing up roads when moving, and heard complaints that the shovels had been actually working on Sunday! In 1883 Council was still paying 5c a load for gravel, paying M. McElwain $7.90 for 158 loads. In 1884 the "old township hall" in Omemee was leased for 99 years to Thos. Blackwell, David Corneil, John Ingram and Robt. Lytle, for $300 payable over 4 years, lessees to keep the hall insured, and allow township to use it for meetings and elections. Finally, in 1899, Council Bylaw 291 indicated that modern times had arrived—it authorized contractor J. Culverwell of Toronto "for the purpose of transmitting electricity from a certain waterpower to the town of Lindsay and other places . . . to erect, place & maintain poles, wires & appliances upon, through, under and along streets, squares & other public roads or places in the township"; no fee or rental was mentioned, but the township inspector paid by the company would ensure there would be no injury to public and private property or persons.

For 20 years 1876 to 1895, Emily Council levied $500 rates annually for schools, to supplement government grants and local fees; this rose to $1800 a year 1896 to 1900. In 1875 there were 8 brick, 3 frame and 2 log schoolhouses in Emily, value $8150. Inspector Knight's report stated: "In Emily a site has been purchased and fenced in no. 7. A frame schoolhouse is to be erected this summer; I was in hopes the building would be of brick, and heating arrangements in the basement . . . but the Trustees were unwilling. . . . In no. 5 the building is out of repair and to build would probably be cheaper than repairing. In no. 4 at Downeyville the school is too small, and the Trustees have promised to make preparations for building . . . a brick schoolhouse in 1876. . . . Fences . . . were erected this year in Nos. 9 and 13 Emily . . . and a privy in No.4, Emily". The 1876 expenses in S.S.10 were at a new high of $2088.80, of which $278 was for the teacher's 1875 salary and $305 for 1876, also about $1370 for building a new brick schoolhouse (of which $1100 was borrowed). One of the early pupils in the new school, Walter Magee, recalled in the 1960s that it had double seats, and extra seats around the wall—when attendance grew to 70 in winter months, ranging from 7 to 20 years, some smaller ones had to sit on the front platform near the teacher. The Inspector in 1877 joyfully reported: "The last log school in Emily will disappear in 1877", noting that all Emily schools were now valued at $11,396. That year S.S.3, Millersmith, erected a new red brick school within a fence on the site of the old log school (which became a woodshed), on lot 7, con.13—this new school was used for 90 years.

Thus by 1880 all Emily schools were of brick or frame, with 803 children of school age, of whom 782 were enrolled in schools; the frame schools were in S.S.5, 7 and 15. In the 13 school sections, trustees in the previous year (1879) had expended $5046.39, including grants and fees, and the average Emily teacher had 4½ years' experience. County Council intervened to aid Samuel Mulligan, who had taught 1879-81 in S.S.8 and 9, Emily, and then in 1882 had attended Ottawa Normal School to get a 2nd-class certificate, but was failed without being given any explanation. Late in 1883 the Inspector informed Council that the Ontario Department indicated "he had failed in aptitude to teach", which seemed peculiar to his friends and students in Emily, who had thought him a good teacher. Omemee High School, which in 1877 had only 52 students, was up to 74 in 1878 and 72 in 1879—John Shaw was headmaster with an assistant teacher; the frame school, erected in 1860, had 31 maps and 3 globes. The 1881 Victoria Atlas commented: "The High School under direction of Mr. John Shaw, M.A. . . . is united with the Public School, there being 3 subordinate teachers. The District includes a part of Emily near the village, the township paying its share . . . last year $534.85. The school has a good standing. Of the School Sections in Emily, Nos.1 and 2 are united with the Grammar School; 10 and 14 are joined as one; two are united with Cavan sections; and the remaining 11 have houses and teachers independently." The Ontario Journals in 1882 reported that in Dec. 1879 at Omemee High School Entrance 29 were examined of whom 23 passed, and in June 1880 26 were examined of whom 20 passed, much above the provincial average (though down somewhat in 1881). The East Victoria Teachers' Association held a convention in 1881 at Omemee. By 1881 Omemee High School had 78 students, and the average cost per pupil was $23.93, no fees being required.

School Inspector Knight reported in June 1883 on an Arithmetic test he gave in each school in Emily, and the percentage who passed: No.3—teacher Eliza Gertley—68%; No.4—Robt. Killaby—66%; No.5, Eliza Blackwell— 45%; No.6, Margaret Morrison—56%; No.7—John Collins—59%; No.8, Geo. Mills—41%; No.9—Geo. Lamb—41%; No.10, Jas. Smyth—46%; No.11—Walter Elliott—78%; No.12—Pat. Meagher—58%; No.13—Wm. Smith—57%; and No.15—teacher Miller Murdock—56%. It will be noted that 9 of 12 teachers were still men. Knight also reported on the school blackboards, finding those in S.S.4, 7, 9, 11 and 15 fairly good, the rest inferior. Emily had 904 pupils, down from 952 in 1879. His 1884 report on each of the 12 Emily schools and the Omemee Public School is even more interesting.[3]

The 2-storey frame structure in Omemee, housing the Public School on ground floor and High School above, was enlarged by addition of wings in 1875-76; it was attended by nearby Emily pupils as well as village children, and the inspector urged a new building, preferably of brick. Williamson in *Omemee* quotes the dramatic news-story of its burning late in Oct. 1884, from a fire left burning in a hall stove, the loss about $4000, though some furniture, books and maps were taken out. A nearby house was also burned, and the Orange Hall, old Methodist Church, and drill-shed across the street were only saved by "untiring exertion". In 1885 John English got the contract to build a new frame school on the site, costing $2844, heated by woodburning stoves again—then in 1903 a furnace was installed in the cellar, and promptly in Feb. 1904 the scholars had to be evacuated while the school burned down again, loss about $2500. The Inspector called the new 1885 school "fairly commodious", and High School enrolment rose from 24 in 1884 to 52 in 1885(25 boys, 27 girls) with principal J. S. Tanner, M.A., salary $800 a year. But the poverty of teaching aids is shown by valuation of library $41, apparatus $76, and maps and charts $32. In the period 1887-89 the headmaster was John McGregor M.A. (salary $800) and assistant Alfred Orr (salary $600) and enrolment by 1890 was 59: Form I—50; Form II—7; Form III—2; it is obvious that few graduated and went on to university or the professions. The cost per pupil at this High School fell from $43.50 in 1884 to $36.82 in 1889. One insight into the mediocre public school teaching in the area, and the difficulty of getting into high school, is the record of High School Entrance examinations at Omemee H.S.: 1883-4: 43 tried examinations, 12 passed; 1884-5: 42 tried, 18 passed; 1885-6: 63 tried, 21 passed; 1886-7: 48 tried, 26 passed; 1887-8: 49 tried, 25 passed; 1888-9: 48 tried, 25 passed; 1889-90: 59 tried, 24 passed—these were about average for all rural districts in Central Ontario, and help to explain why the majority of farm children left school at the end of Fourth Book.

Inspector Knight strove incessantly to get trustees to improve school conditions with fenced lots, better heating equipment, lighting, hygienic facilities, etc, and better teachers' salaries, and to get teachers to improve their certification and training, and make school more attractive and rewarding to the children. At S.S.10, for example, in 1881 total expenses were only $429.93, of which teacher's salary was $400; in 1887 their agreement with new teacher Wm. Blackwell of Lindsay (holder of a 3rd class certificate) called for salary $375 a year, signed by trustees Henry Jackson, Henry Head and George Rutherford; he had also to keep the schoolhouse clean, and heated in winter. The main expenditures were buying wood (about $2 or $3 a cord), cleaning well and repairing pump $3, insurance $6.50, a new homemade blackboard $4, building porch $30, and the yearly items like chalk, brooms etc. Knight's 1893 report to the trustees of S.S.10 comments: "Schoolhouse—woodwork needs painting; door of porch should be nailed on. Furnishings: repairs to blackboard needed. Outside condition (fences, well &c): repairs to privy needed. Standing of pupils: fair to good. Discipline & management: fair. General progress: several pupils not supplied with books." At S.S.3, a new picket fence in 1883 cost $37.30 (including $12 for labour), but this was not durable, and a new board fence in 1892 cost $38.50, followed in 1901 by a wire & picket fence along the front for $28.52.

Arbour Day each June was spent in cleaning up the schoolyard, and in the 1880s 40 or 50 trees were planted yearly around Emily schools. But the Inspector criticized each year two negative factors: (1) over half the Emily teachers changed schools yearly, (2) average attendance was only about 45% due to long distances and winter snowdrifts, harvest work, etc. He was pleased that late in 1891 the S.S.9 trustees had repaired and improved their school greatly. In fact, his 1891 report comparing Emily schools in 1871 and 1891 is worth reproduction.[3] In 1893 the Inspector commented on the serious epidemic of diphtheria in the area, which closed one school in Emily, also the S.S.11 teacher was seriously ill; he was critical that at Omemee the 1892-3 Entrance Examinations showed 13 passing out of 31 writing. He applauded improvements in upkeep of buildings, equipment and grounds, and the teaching of reading, grammar and writing, but criticized slow progress in arithmetic, history and geography. Again he noted in 1895 that while Emily had 602 public school pupils, average attendance was 277 or 46%, one of the lowest in the county, while in Omemee average attendance was 66%, one of the highest—he blamed bad roads, sickness, parental indifference and farm work.

In his 1897 report the Inspector conceded that most trustees tried hard to improve their schools, but made one exception: "The school in S.S.3, Emily, midway between Dunsford and Downeyville, is one of the worst. Last September I reported to the Trustees: 'Repairs to walls inside & out needed. Woodwork needs painting. Walls & ceiling need whitewashing. Window-blinds needed. Stovepipes need cleaning. Repairs & cleaning to out-buildings needed.' When I visited the school a few days ago, I found things in still worse condition. The floor had holes in several places, the only chair was scarcely safe to sit upon, and the walls were going to decay for want of repairs. The scholars, I understand, suffered much from cold during the last winter." He ended by hinting that the teacher's salary was rather high, and some of it might have been better spent on repairing the school itself. His 1898 report noted falling school enrolment in Emily, stating: "Epidemic diseases, such as diphtheria, measles and mumps are very prevalent, reducing attendance and sometimes necessitating the closing of schools." But next year he reported: "Two new schoolhouses are being erected, in East Victoria, one in S.S. no. 12, Emily, known as Scully's . . . out of 9 teachers absent from the 82 teachers in the inspectorate, at the Lindsay convention, was Mr. Hooper of Emily, assisting in the celebration of his father's golden wedding . . . also Mrs. McCarroll of Emily." Incidentally, the only Emily bylaw of the period devoted to schools was no. 294 in 1899, raising a loan of $800 to erect a new school in S.S.12, to be paid off in 8 years. By 1900, Henry Hooper, teaching at S.S.10 (Orange Corners) for $400 a year, had organized a football team and also a campaign by which the children raised money to buy a fine bell for the school, which rang at 9 a.m., 12 noon, 1 and 4 p.m.

There was little interest in militia and military matters in Emily in this period. Capt. W. Cottingham's no.5 Company of the 45th Battalion (West Durham) comprising 2 officers and 42 men, mustered at Omemee July 1, 1876, for 8 days of drill, manual and firing exercise and skirmishing; the inspecting officer termed them "fair" when he inspected them on July 10. The government was economizing on militia funds, and only in 1880 was a camp held: "The 45th Battn. of which companies came from Fenelon, Omemee and Lindsay, went into camp at Bowmanville on 23rd June and was inspected by me on the 30th . . . cost of rations at camp 18c per head daily." In 1883 Col. Villiers compained that the 45th and some other battalions "came to Cobourg camp in weak numbers . . . on account of late harvests and high wages the officers found it impossible to take the men out of the field"; his report that year described Omemee drill-shed as erected 1868, 90 by 50 ft, with armoury 12 by 22 ft, on lot 6, George Street. By 1885 No. 5 Company was led by Capt. James Evans and Lieut. James

Thornton—for the Northwest Rebellion campaign that year, a company of volunteers from the 45th Battalion was mobilized in Lindsay under Major John Hughes, totalling 47 men, according to Kirkconnell; they served in a district force of 400 under Col. Williams of Peterborough, and fought at Batoche, but it is not known if any Emily men were among the contingent.

Victoria Council urged in 1888 that the government establish a battalion of active militia in the County, centred at Lindsay, but nothing was done. The Militia report for 1891 stated: "Omemee drill-shed is in very bad state and should be repaired at once, otherwise the building will collapse." In 1894 a full-scale Rifle Range was constructed for the 45th Battalion, and every few years in June or July an 8-day camp was held at Gananoque, Kingston, Barriefield etc. to which the Emily company entrained for a "holiday" of drilling, target-shooting and skirmish exercises. In the heavy snows of the winter 1895-96 the drill-shed did collapse, and its contents were stored in Evans' foundry; Cols. Cotton and J. Hughes inspected the wreckage in February, and after getting tenders had a small armoury erected on the site. No militia from the Kawartha district were included in the 1897 Canadian contingent of 202 sent to London for the Queen's Diamond Jubilee Parade; however in that year the 45th was transferred to Victoria County as the 45th Victoria, and Lt. Col. Sam Hughes, tempestuous Lindsay editor and political figure, became its commander. He offered in 1898 to raise 1000 men in Victoria to serve in the Sudan under Lord Kitchener, and renewed his campaign in 1899 when the Boer War broke out, alienating the Canadian commanders by his demands; finally he served with the British forces in a minor role, and 14 men from the 45th Victoria Regt. volunteered with the Royal Canadian Regiment and saw action in South Africa—it is not known if any of the 14 men were from Emily township.[11] However, Lady Eaton in 'Memory's Wall' mentions that her mother, Mrs. John McCrea, led a group of Omemee women who knitted and gathered comforts to send to the "men who had joined up and left for South Africa", and no doubt other district groups did the same.

Arthur McQuade's electoral victory in 1874 was repeated in the 1878 federal election, when Emily gave him 311 votes and 131 for Connolly (Liberal). In a closer race, Dundas (Cons.) won Victoria South in 1882 over Needlar, with Emily voting 320 for Dundas, 156 for Needlar. In 1887 Adam Hudspeth (Cons.) won over Wm. Lounsborough narrowly, and Emily (which now had 6 polls) gave Hudspeth 440 votes, his opponent 261; due to irregularities, a by-election was held a month later, with much the same result. Charles Fairbairn (Cons.) won the by-election in 1890 after Hudspeth's death, and again in the 1891 election won over Walters— narrowly—but Emily supported him with 443 votes, to 287 for Walters; again due to irregularities a by-election was necessary, and Fairbairn won it in 1892. When the Laurier Liberal tide came in, Geo. McHugh finally won Victoria South for the party, against Dr. Vrooman (Cons.), in 1896, but the 6 polls in Emily and Omemee remained in the Tory fold, 358 for Vrooman, 302 for McHugh. In the 9th General Election, 1900, Laurier stayed in power, but in Victoria South Vrooman won over McHugh, with Emily voting 295 for Vrooman, 293 for McHugh. Since Sam Hughes was the Conservative winner in Victoria North, "the county turned entirely blue again in 1900", in Kirkconnell's words.

The provincial scene was different—we have noted that Wood (Liberal) won over Cottingham, and then over Hudspeth, in 1875. In 1879 Hon. S. C. Wood (Provincial Secretary) won narrowly over W. L. Russell (County Warden), with Emily voting emphatically 293 for Russell, 146 for Wood. Again in 1883 D. J. McIntyre (Lib.) won over Chas. Fairbairn (Cons.), with Emily voting 279 for Fairbairn, 182 for McIntyre—the separate Omemee poll was also strongly for the Conservative. The ridings were juggled in 1885, and the new Victoria East Riding consisted of Emily, Omemee, Verulam, Bobcaygeon and some of the northern townships formerly in North Victoria Riding—in 1886 John Fell (Conservative M.L.A. in North Victoria) won it easily against Geo. Bick, Liberal, with Emily voting 248 for Fell, 203 for Bick. In 1890 Fell won a narrow victory over J. B. Campbell, and Emily voting 184 for Campbell, 178 for Fell; Campbell was supported by the Patrons of Industry, a farmers' organization, which explains his strong backing. In 1894 John Carnegie (Cons.) won over Wm. Thurston, with Emily voting 256 for Carnegie, 212 for Thurston; Carnegie won in 1898 by increased majority over J. Austin, with Emily on the bandwagon, 323 votes for Carnegie, 204 for Austin (and Omemee even more strongly pro-Carnegie).

One other political issue in Emily as in other parts of Ontario should be mentioned, the campaign for prohibition of importation, manufacture and sale of intoxicating liquors. The Ontario Dunkin Act 1854 allowed municipal local option, but in any case Emily Council was hostile, and the Act was useless to curb the problem. The Sons of Temperance and the new Women's Christian Temperance Union campaigned for total prohibition. Then the Canada Temperance Act (or Scott Act) 1878 provided for local option all across Canada—this was approved in July 1885 in a plebiscite in Victoria by a large majority, but in Emily, of 641 voters on the lists, only 289 voted, 111 for the Act, 178 against it. Licenses to sell liquor in Emily in taverns and shops (excluding hotels) declined from 4 in 1875 to 2 in 1879, and none by 1885—in other words, Emily people were of moderate views, and felt no need for a tavern at every main crossroads, but still did not approve of prohibition. But in 1893 Emily Council again sent a petition to the Ontario government for a total prohibition on liquor, indicating growing temperance feeling. As enforcement of the Scott Act proved ineffective, again in 1898 a national vote was held—Victoria and Peterborough Counties voted strongly for prohibition, and this time Emily voted 165 for, 69 against, in a light vote. However, no government action resulted for a couple of decades, as support in most provinces was doubtful or apathetic.

The growing reliance of rural families on mail-order is shown when in 1875 Omemee postoffice issued $17,787.35 in money-orders, and cashed $853.80 of same; strangely, this was larger than Lindsay or Peterborough, which issued $16,231.97 and $17,134.20 respectively in money-orders; northern hamlets like Minden were even higher, showing the lack of retail outlets, for the variety of merchandise that farm people now required. The big spring and fall orders to Eaton's or Simpson's were major events on Emily farms in this period, and the arrival of the mysterious parcels even more so, though there was no rural mail delivery yet. In 1876 M. Tracey had the contract to carry mail Downeyville to Omemee 3 times weekly, for annual fee $75, and R. Grandy continued the contract between Omemee and the rail station (1¼ miles) 18 times weekly, annual fee $150. By 1880 Grandy was paid $196 yearly for this job, and B. Downey carried mail Downeyville to Omemee 3 times weekly for annual fee $80; also D. Fowler had the contract to carry mail from Fowler's Corners to Peterborough twice weekly, annual fee $95. The gross revenue of Downeyville postoffice in 1880 was $66, and postmaster's salary $30—the postmasters there were Michael Tracey 1876-82, Michael Lehane (4 months in 1882), Tracey again 1883-86, Mrs. Hannah Tracey 1886-1901. At Frank Hill postoffice the postmaster was George Franks 1876-86 and Christopher Lowes 1886-1908. When the King's Wharf postoffice was established in May 1882, James Leary became postmaster, and served until 1914 when it was closed, with the coming of rural mail delivery.

The 1887 Postal Guide thus showed 4 postoffices in Emily: Omemee— R. Grandy; Downeyville—Mrs. H. Tracey; Frank Hill—C. Lowes; King's Wharf—J. Leary. In addition, the Fowler's Corners office (in Smith township) with John Williamson postmaster, Dunsford to the north, Ennismore to the east, Lindsay to the west, and Millbrook to the south, provided service for some Emily people nearby. The only postoffice with savings bank facilities and money-order service was that at Omemee, and even there people were often tempted to put cash in a letter and mail it off—in 1880, for example, H. Higinbotham of Omemee sent a registered letter to Lyman Boos, Toronto, containing $30, and it arrived without the money; in Jan. 1886 Miss C. B. Fagan of Downeyville sent $1 cash in a letter to Thos. Coffee of London, but it was never received (and believed lost or stolen at Blackwater Junction on the Midland Railway). By 1890 Grandy was getting $250 to carry the mail 24 times weekly between Omemee postoffice and the rail station, and B. Downey $160 for carrying mail 6 times weekly Downeyville to Omemee; Omemee postoffice issued 701 money orders valued at $11,445.37, and its gross revenues were $1,138.40. In the year ending June 30, 1895, Downeyville postoffice had revenue $16.10 and postmaster's salary was $20; at Frank Hill postoffice, revenue $7, salary $12; at King's Wharf postoffice, revenue $42, salary $20—these were typical of a hundred in crossroad stores through the district.

In the following year, C. Chambers had the contract to carry mail 1½ miles 6 times weekly from Fowler's Corners to "Best's Railway Station" in Emily, annual fee $90. A storm blew up in the Postal Department in April 1896 because the Downeyville-Omemee contract was let in 1883 to J. Morrisey at $160 per annum, transferred to B. Downey in 1884 at the same rate, and renewed up to 1894 at that rate. The trouble was that tenders by O. O'Connor at $140 and H. Tracey at $150 in 1894 were not even considered, and Charles Fairbairn, M.P., was asked by Mrs. Tracey to intercede; in March 1894 Vinc. Cornwall of Omemee wrote Fairbairn: "Mr. B. Downey wishes me to write you requesting you to call personally upon the Postmaster-General and ask him to give instructions to renew the contract at the present rate—$40 every 3 months. I need hardly tell you that Downey is an intelligant man, and *one of the very few friends we have in that quarter . . .* I cannot urge you too strongly to exert yourself on his behalf . . . he has always been faithful and we should take care of him. . . ." Two weeks later the Postmaster-General assured Fairbairn that Downey's contract had been renewed for 4 years. This example of political patronage was revealed when the Liberal government took power in 1896. The last mail contracts recorded in the period, in Emily, were in 1898-99 to C. Lowes, carrying mail Ennismore to Frank Hill 6 miles once weekly for annual fee $66, and to J. C. Leary carrying mail 9 miles twice weekly from Ennismore to King's Wharf and return, fee $75 (this contract was turned over to J. Moffitt March 31, 1899).

Another sector in which political pressures had considerable influence was the development of navigable waterways and railways, increasingly vital to improve business and industry. Victoria Council petitioned the Ontario Government in 1881 for improvement of Pigeon River navigation up to Omemee, including removal of "large quantities of sawlogs, tanbark, cedar, &c. put into the stream"; this was repeated in an 1886 petition. But the Ontario authorities claimed Ottawa had jurisdiction, and the Trent Waterway staff were more interested in the Canal route, now being strongly urged by the Trent Canal Association. On Feb. 10, 1886, a big meeting was held in Peterborough, with representatives from the whole district, to promote the Trent Valley Canal, and one delegate was T. H. McQuade, reeve of Emily, others being from as far away as Rama, Trenton and Midland. McQuade and I. McNeely of Omemee were among the hundred signatures on a Memorial to the Governor-General urging completion of the Canal. The raising of Buckhorn Dam 1886-87 led to numerous claims for flood damage from Emily in the next few years—Wm. Robert McQuade (n.w. ¼ lot 12, con. 6), $57; Timothy Crowley (e. ½ lot 19, con. 11), $30; Robert Perdue (s. ½ lot 21, con. 12), $60; Henry Fitzgerald (n. ½ lot 20, con. 11), $65; Robt. and Ann O'Donaghue (lot 23, con. 11), $66; Patrick Duffy (n. ½ lot 15, con. 8), $93; Patrick O'Leary (lots 16 in con. 8 and 9), $70; Michael Lowes (n. ½ lot 17, con. 7 and s. ½ lot 17, con. 8), $80. Most were calculated at $2 or $2.50 per acre per year when flooded, and a small sum for any crop destroyed—the valuator declared them to be mostly "moderate and justified". Some claims were accompanied by neat maps of the flooded acreage, and other details. The problem continued after 1900.

Peterborough and Victoria Counties shared the annual costs of keeping the Pigeon River Floating Bridge in repair, which in 1892-3 was $947, and in the latter year Peterborough decided to abandon its share of this arrangement, and petitioned the Ontario Government to this effect, repeated in 1894 with the proposal that a Corporation take the bridge over and charge a toll for passage; needless to say, this was not done. With construction and maintenance costs of the Trent-Simcoe waterway escalating, the Canadian government also refused any funds for side-streams like Pigeon River; their 1892 Report on Canals did list some of the flood claims mentioned above. The Federal Fisheries supervisor in the area did report that year that "There are no fishways yet, but there should be one at Omemee on Pigeon Creek. The mill-owners are doing their best to carry out the regulations regarding disposal of their rubbish (but) some were dumping sawdust too near the water's edge." The Trent Superintendent mentioned incidentally in his 1896 report that: "Emily Creek was deepened and straightened in order to allow barges to go further up into Emily township for the shipping of grain, etc.", with no other details; this would be helpful for the Millersmith and Downeyville areas.

The period closed as it began: Victoria Council in 1898 petitioned the Minister of Railways and Canals in Ottawa "that Pigeon River, tributary to Trent waterway navigation, extends to the village of Omemee, with a navigable channel the whole distance and much money spent on dredging . . . that navigation is entirely impeded by the stationary structure known as Cowan's Bridge, about 5 miles northeast from Omemee . . . the means of preventing construction of large sawmills and other important manufactories in said village of Omemee . . . a large grain centre and an important feeder to traffic on the Trent Valley Canal . . . that a swing bridge be constructed across said Pigeon River in lieu of the stationary bridge and at the same point." Just to play safe, next year they sent the same petition to the Ontario Minister of Public Works, but with no better result. Thus in 1900 when Emily proposed a county grant of $700 to erect a high level steel bridge "to permit passage of steamers" at Cowan's, county council gave it some study, but took no further action.

We have noted that Emily Council in 1877 raised a bonus for the Whitby & Port Perry Extension Railway to Lindsay, by levying on northwest Emily, on the rather dubious grounds that it would be helpful to that section. Another newly-chartered project, the Huron & Quebec Railway, in 1877 announced it would build through Ennismore, Emily, Smith, Cavan, Mariposa, Ops, and other district townships, providing of course that any township wanting the line would come up with a large bonus—which none of them did, so the line was not built. An Ontario report on rail accidents 1874-77 gave details of only one in Emily on the Midland: "Feb. 10, 1876, Seven cars on mixed train ran off the track about 2½ miles north of Omemee. Cause—broken rail. Cars loaded with grain in bulk. Three cars badly damaged. Line blocked for 21 hours, daytime." Throughout this period the Midland operated 3 trains through Omemee each way daily, "2 mixed and 1 express" as they were rather fancifully called. Their 1881 report showed a profitable year, including the "amalgamation" of the Grand Junction, Victoria, Whitby, Port Perry and Lindsay, and other lines; grain shipments from the district were up, with less flour made locally, and sharp increases were noted in lumber and

square timber exports, likewise shingles, etc. There was much building of
facilities at Midland, Peterborough, Port Hope, Chemong branch, etc. but
in the Emily-Omemee section, just one item: "Omemee & Peterboro extension $1,958.18", plus $14.50 spent on slight repairs to the 100-ft. trestle
bridge at Cottingham's Creek. Among long lists of, facilities along the lines
(telegraph and flag stations, engine and repair shops, turn-tables and water
tanks, round houses and freight warehouses, wharves, etc.) only two are
listed in Emily—at Omemee a telegraph office and a freight-house less than
100 feet long.

To the fury of Port Hope, George Cox of Peterborough, Midland
President, began scheming in 1881 to change the traffic flow, which had
poured down from Lindsay and Peterborough to Port Hope. The Peterborough
Review in July said that the Midland was asking Peterborough for a $40,000
bonus to build the "missing link" to Omemee, and in return Midland head
offices and workshops would be moved up to Peterborough; at a Peterborough
meeting in August Cox also promised that trains would start from that town,
and daily service increased; also the engines were being converted to burn
coal instead of wood in future. In Jan. 1882 tenders were called to build the
Omemee link, and by April 100 men were at work, under contractor J.H.
Beemer; immediately they ran into great difficulties in building over the
"roller-coaster" drumlins, swamps and creekways of the area. According to
Williamson, this meant "a number of curves, together with the bridging the
wide and deep valleys, and crossing a swail at Lily Lake"; Doube's (Buttermilk) valley was bridged by a wooden trestle 1,500 ft. long, 70 ft. above the
valley, and Tulley's farther east with a trestle 700 ft. long and 40 ft. high—
later Doube's was partly filled by a causeway, and Tulley's completely filled.
The Lindsay *Post* reported Oct. 19: "On Monday Oct. 8 the first train of cars
was successfully taken over the big bridge across Buttermilk Valley on the
'missing link', Engineer W. Pilling, Conductor Ed. Pymn, Fireman H.
Maloney being the heroes. The speed made when crossing was about 4 miles
per hour. The bridge is pefectly safe and stood the great strain without a
quiver."

The Lily Lake swail swallowed endless hundreds of tons of fill; according
to Kirkconnell, "in the swamp west of Peterborough, the 'sinkhole' had a
prodigious appetite—trees, logs, stones, and gravel disappeared . . . even after
the rails were laid, a train of cars left out on the new roadbed during construction vanished overnight and was never recovered!" There were labour
troubles also—in July 1883 a battle lasting several days was fought with
revolvers and knives between Italian workers striking over a wage cut and
Irish immigrant labourers who wanted to stay at work, centering on Sherin's
Cut, 2 miles east of Omemee, but with skirmishes east and west. The first
train went from Peterborough to Omemee and on to Toronto November 2,
1883, and as the Toronto *Mail* reported Nov. 27: "Regular train service over
the missing link Omemee to Peterborough began yesterday."[4]

Other than a new railway bridge and a new station at the Junction just
north of Omemee, the main advantage of the new line was to permit Emily
people to build up their milk business to Toronto a while later, and to get out

to Peterborough and Toronto to shop more easily. The other link built from Manilla to Blackwater Junction diverted much of the rail traffic away from the Omemee area, and indeed most railway extensions in this period benefited nobody much except the investors. To counter the Grand Trunk schemes, the Canadian Pacific backed a new venture, the Lindsay, Bobcaygeon & Pontypool Railway, chartered in 1890 to build from Lindsay northeast to Bobcaygeon and onward; one of the sponsors, Mossom Boyd of Bobcaygeon, worked to get bonuses from Ops, Emily, Verulam, Lindsay, Manvers, etc. but had little success in those depression years—in his railway notebook Emily was listed for a bonus of $4,000 repayable in 20 years at 5% interest, but Emily Council proved unreceptive. It is interesting that School Inspector J. Knight wrote Boyd Feb. 22, 1893, urging him to run the rail line east from Lindsay just north of the north branch of Emily Creek south of Emily Lake through northwest Emily, and then swinging northeast through Verulam to Bobcaygeon; accompanying his neat map, he listed his arguments: "1. The land would be cheaper to purchase. 2. The road will be more cheaply constructed as it avoids high land. 3. The road will be easier to run as it will be more level. 4. It will be as short as any route likely to be taken. 5. It will interfere less with navigation. 6. It will serve a section of country badly off for means of communication. 7. It will bring people to Lindsay who now go to Peterborough. 8. It will require less switching at Bobcaygeon. 9. It will interfere less with travelled roads and save accidents." When the railroad was built in the next decade, it went of course straight to Dunsford, bypassing Emily township, but it is intriguing to speculate on the result if Emily had voted a large bonus and the rail line had been built across north Emily.

We have noted above the battle of the temperance forces, mostly centred in the churches, against liquor—an 1881 report, noting the decline in liquor licenses, stated: "The custom of drinking at bees is now done away with and is seldom practised at sales. . . . When the railway went through, the navvies did a lot of drinking. . . ." In the decades to come, the churches had another problem to face, the decline of congregations inevitable when the population decreased, as seen in Census statistics:

EMILY (without Omemee)	1881	1891	1901
Church of England	608	580	435
Church of Rome	1139	1048	946
Methodists	751	779	704
Presbyterians	365	189*	173*

(*in 1891 there were 7 others in Emily, including 1 member of the Salvation Army; in 1901, there were 46 others, including 14 Salvation Army) (to the above for church purposes we should add: Omemee members of the denominations: 1891: 189 Anglicans, 7 Roman Catholics, 331 Methodists, and 116 Presbyterians, plus 44 others including 38 Salvation Army; 1901: 130 Anglicans, 20 Roman Catholics, 345 Methodists and 76 Presbyterians, plus only 3 others, all Salvation Army).

Rev. R. H. Harris, who married Squire Cottingham's daughter in 1875, remained rector of Christ Church (Omemee) and St. John's and St. James' in Emily until 1881; he was followed by Rev. W. T. Smithett who served until his death in 1887. After a short vacancy, Rev. W. H. French arrived in time to open the new brick St. John's Church at Orange Corners. Mr. Magee, who was present, wrote later: "The present church was opened in Dec. 1889. I well remember it, the largest gathering I ever saw around the scene. The church, school and Orange Hall were all full, waiting to be served at a big supper held in the present schoolhouse." Rev. W. McCan became Rector in 1892, and organized the Women's Auxiliaries to help in parish work at the three churches, the first president being Mrs. Thos. Stephenson. Isaac McNeely, storekeeper, and churchwarden at Christ Church, died that year, and his relatives in his memory built a belfry with fine bell, topped by a spire, on the church. During the rectorship of Rev. E. Langfeldt (1898-1901), the parish bought the old Cottingham lot on King Street, and built a new rectory on it to replace the old stone rectory over Crawford's Hill; Dr. Langfeldt left in 1901 to go to St. Luke's, Ashburnham, but his successor, Rev. J. H. Teney, carried through the plan to move Christ Church on rollers to the new site south of King Street, where it was reopened Nov. 3, 1901. St. James' Church near Chemong Lake was also, in 1900, rebuilt in brick, and moved a short distance to the southwest corner of the lot, better to serve parishioners in that rural area. Lady Flora Eaton in *Memory's Wall* has some reminiscences of church events in the 1890s, such as picnics in McGee's Grove west of Omemee, picnic suppers, and excursions down the river, or by train to Lindsay and steamer to Sturgeon Point, or Bobcaygeon. She remembered in amusement that Sunday School attendance always increased in December before the annual Anglican Christmas Tree, then increased again as the Methodist Sunday Schools prepared for Anniversary festivities in January.

The Roman Catholics, largest denomination in Emily, had a special problem in this period, as their only church was in Downeyville, and yet the young people were spreading to farms (and to Omemee) some distance away; however, with better roads, families were able to come even ten miles in democrat or buggy for church services. Father M. E. Connelly succeeded Father Coyle in 1879, and the Downeyville parish house was built 1880. In 1886 the church was renovated with a 50 x 20 ft. chancel, to which was added a 20 ft. vestry to complete the cruciform edifice, which was redecorated and covered with brick as at present. Father C. Bretherton served the parish 1894-1905. This would be the appropriate place to mention Fergus Patrick McEvay, born in Downeyville in 1852, educated there and at Lindsay, who after higher education at St. Michael's in Toronto and other colleges entered the priesthood in 1882. Father McEvay will be remembered as rector of St. Peter's in Peterborough 1887-99; he was then consecrated Bishop of London, and in 1908 became fourth Roman Catholic Archbishop of Toronto, dying at an early age in 1911.

We have already described the new Methodist Church built in Omemee in 1875, 60 x 35 ft. with a belltower and 50 ft. spire; in 1889 the church was renovated with new pews and pulpit, and a basement furnace for winter warmth. As in earlier times, the ministers changed frequently; Williamson in 'Omemee' lists them fully. They also served the smaller churches at Lebanon, Bethel, etc. In Nov. 1892 Rev. C. Thompson dedicated the new brick Bethel Methodist Church, organist and choirmaster being Mrs. and Mr. W. C. Switzer. Apparently the old Omemee Circuit was reorganized about 1874-5, and the Salem Methodist Church in the Millersmith community was made part of Lindsay East Circuit, with Dunsford, Fenelon, &c., to make the minister's task easier, with Rev. Cathcart followed by Wilkinson, Loyeland, Powers, and others. Then in 1887 a new Dunsford Church was built and Salem included in this new mission circuit, with Rev. Thomas, Saunders, Metheral, and Kenny. The red brick church was on the north side of Con. 14 road, and Mrs. J. A. Elliott remembered the 6 windows, the coaloil lamps on brackets along the walls and behind the pulpit and organ, the stove in the aisle, etc. In 1899 a new white brick church was built south of the road on a site donated by Mr. and Mrs. John Smith, when Rev. Kenny was minister, the cost being $700—trustees then were John Ashmore, Jas. Patrick, Jas. Kennedy and Geo. Kennedy. Mrs. Jas. Elliott Sr. kept the 12 lamps shining in the new church as in the old, for the grand sum of $7 a year.

William Best, Clerk of Presbyterian Session and a church Elder for 36 years, died in 1879. Perhaps coincidentally, the frame Presbyterian Church in south Emily was torn down the next year, and rebuilt with brick veneer in Mt. Pleasant, where it is still used. In Omemee the congregation decided in 1889 to build a new church, a pleasant brick building on Sturgeon Street; according to the Omemee *Herald*; "The members are to be congratulated on the success with which they have met in the erection of such a beautiful and substantial sacred edifice." Here also the lighting was by 5 large hanging oil lamps suspended from the roof, supplemented later by bracket lamps around the walls and one in the vestibule. A new improved organ replaced the smaller one bought in 1880, which went to the Sunday School. After Rev. Ewing resigned in 1893, Rev. Tanner served until 1899, to be followed by Rev. Kannawin—by 1900 the debt on the church was paid off, and a manse built next door for the Minister. About Lakevale Presbyterian Church at Fowler's Corners, served by the clergy from Omemee, there is little news except that in 1876 they agreed that the congregation should stand when singing henceforth, and in 1889 the church was repaired with a new driving-shed, and in 1898 the Ladies Aid Society was formed.

S. E. Clark in *Church and Sect in Canada* (1946) noted: "The Salvation Army came to Canada in 1883, and by Nov. 1, 1884 had local corps in Lindsay, Omemee, &c." Williamson describes their early meetings, when there was some hostile reaction in Omemee during their meetings at the village hall, and their marches through the streets. Late in 1884 they leased the old township hall and fitted it up as Salvation Army Barracks, holding regular meetings and making numerous converts in Omemee and neighbourhood; it will be noted that in the 1891 census they had 39 adherents, and in 1901 only 14 are listed, indicating the fading away of the faithful, which soon led to disbanding of the local Barracks. Lady Eaton in 'Memory's Wall' described how her kindly family took pity on the friendless outside officers of the Salvation Army working in the district; "often on Sunday two or three of their young officers would come to dinner or supper with us." In rural and village areas where family and church ties were strong, there was evidently little need for the dramatic evangelism of the Army.

Another religious organization which made its modest contribution in these decades was the Upper Canada Bible Society, whose Omemee Branch in 1889 reported $57.58 in subscriptions; the Branch president that year was G. Balfour, and the Society held occasional meetings in Methodist or Presbyterian churches, set up exhibits at agricultural fairs, and sold Bibles door to door in villages and through the countryside; it had some small support outside Omemee in Emily. The Sons of Temperance were also waging war on 'Demon Rum' right up to 1900, with some success.

We have noted that L.O.L. #41 at Orange Corners opened their new frame Hall in 1876. Prominent in the work of this lodge were names such as Finley, Magee, Fowler, McCall, Jackson, Elliott, Hooper and Faulkner; for example, Frederick Magee was master in 1890 and Walter Magee in 1900. Lorne Lodge no. 375 of the Masons was established at Omemee in 1879 with 9 charter members, and grew steadily in membership. The Lindsay *Post* noted, July 20, 1877: "About 500 Orangemen and Orange Young Britons commemorated the 12th at Omemee by a fine parade through the streets to the music of fife and drum. . . . The streets were lined with visitors from the surrounding country. . . . Speakers of the day in Mrs. English's Grove were the Grand Chaplain of Ontario East, Rev. J. Norris, Rev. R. H. Harris, Rev. John Ewing, Rev. J. Chapman, and G. Balfour, Master of #113; Mr. Thos. Stephenson, District Master, acted as chairman. The best of order and sobriety prevailed. . . ." Next year on Nov. 1 they reported: "The Glorious Fifth is to be observed by members of LOL and OYB Lodges of the village by an evening procession and a grand supper." Williamson quotes the report on the 1880 July 12 parade, when 7 LOL lodges and 2 OYB lodges paraded and dined, with "a large turnout of the yeomanry of Emily, Ops and Manvers", also of the local politicians and clergy.

In an age before organized team sports, before easy access to urban entertainment by radio, television and automobile travel, before the wartime parading of uniformed soldiers behind bands setting off to Europe or Africa, such gatherings and parading satisfied a basic social need, which for other groups was met by building bees, church concerts and picnics and excursions, agricultural fairs and exhibitions. For women also, smaller families and more labour-saving devices increased the need for more outside group activities, when the new brick or stone home had been redecorated and embellished, and the flower and vegetable gardens established; so ladies' auxiliaries were begun at churches and lodges and societies, so agricultural fairs added new classes of ladies' exhibits, and church choirs and Sunday Schools augmented their female participation. Any worthy cause from liquor prohibition to child health to musical concerts to missionary knitting relied more and more on zealous woman supporters. It is significant, for example, that in this generation 1875 to 1900 the number of women in teaching, nursing, church work and Sunday Schools became the large majority, though they left the men to do most of the parading behind bands, running for public office, competing in athletics, racing horses and showing cattle, and other outward symbols of leadership. We shall see more indications of these trends later in the chapter, as well as some other changes in aspirations and life-styles among the young people brought up on the farms of Emily township, unsettled by more news of the outside world, cash wages in lumbering and river-driving, rail construction on the prairies where there were millions of fertile acres to farm, and finally the lure of Klondike gold . . . why dig out potatoes on the family farm when a chap can dig nuggets from the Yukon hillsides as big as potatoes? (or so the Toronto papers said!)

One sign of the times was greatly increased governmental and parental concern over health of the young, and avoidance of epidemics—no longer were families resigned to having 10 or 15 children and being able to raise 4 or 5 to adulthood, or, when the partner died of pioneer hardships, remarrying 2 or 3 times with new broods of children to replace those who had died or gone away. Even up until about 1890 being township medical health officer (at salary $5 or $10 a year) meant only a few routine sanitary inspections, or looking after the rare individuals living on welfare. A questionnaire from the Ontario Board of Health in May 1883 and the Omemee district replies have some interest, indicating there were no village or township Boards of Health, and no bylaws regulating disposal of garbage and excreta, nor on distance of privies from wells, and no concern about drinking water being from streams where infection was present; no attempt was yet made to isolate and placard homes where there were infectious diseases, nor to request medical certificates before readmission of children to school "where contagious diseases have existed in the family". Further, there were no local inspections of slaughter-houses or other food sources where infections might breed, or of workers in same. Yet diphtheria deaths in Victoria were heavy in 1882, 1883 and 1885, and railway labourers and immigrants were being blamed for bringing in smallpox and other diseases.

Doctors who served the Omemee and Emily communities in this period, driving endless miles up and down concession lines in all weather, included Dr. Norris (1861-1886), Dr. Cornwall (1875-1915), Dr. Higginbotham (1886-95), Dr. Cochrane (1892), Dr. Bradd (1894), Dr. Thompson (1890-91), and Dr. Cameron (1897-1906). Dr. Cornwall lived in a large white house just east of Omemee, and was active in community church, council and school affairs. Dr. Higginbotham operated a drug store. Dr. Cochrane sold his practice to Dr. Bradd who later sold it to Dr. Cameron, who was a popular Master of the local Masonic Lodge for two years—Dr. Cameron's son studied medicine, rose to the post of Deputy-Minister of Health for Canada, and after a long career retired to Ashburnham where he still lives.

Emily was fortunately healthy during the 1880s, and the first report by its M.H.O., Dr. V. Cornwall, appears in government records for 1889: "General health . . . has been exceptionally good. In the south portion of the township we had one severe case of diphtheria; but with complete isolation and efficient disinfection the disease was confined to the person first attacked . . . who made a good recovery." In 1892, however, the Inspector urged the need to supply physicians with blank forms to report infectious diseases, and said isolation had been used on 2 diphtheria and 4 scarlet fever cases in Emily. Again in 1892 he reported sanitary conditions good in Emily, and no infectious diseases, but in 1894 expressed some concern that local statistics showed the birthrate in the district at least twice the death-rate, but in Emily the reverse was true—the birthrate 5.5 per 1,000, the deathrate 8.5 per 1,000.[5] Dr. Cornwall reported that year that Emily still had no sanitary inspector; there had been 8 diphtheria cases and 6 typhoid, none isolated nor houses placarded—all families had their own milk cows, and there were no dairies in the township, nor any slaughter-houses. In 1895, however, Dr. Cornwall reported that isolation and placarding was being used on 14 diphtheria cases and 3 scarlatina; but there was no compulsory vaccination, and no children had been vaccinated that year—there were 602 school children in 12 one-room schools in the township; it was a rural township with no factories or mills or institutions, where families used well water and disposed of their own garbage.

Next year (1896) the situation was worse, when Dr. F. Bradd reported 5 cases of scarlatina and 12 of diphtheria (of which 5 died); these were isolated at home, as there was no convenient hospital, and the homes disinfected afterwards; there was still no programme of vaccination in schools, nor any use of diphtheria antitoxin. At last in 1897 an Emily Board of Health was set up (R. Grandy, secretary), and when in 1898 Dr. G. Cameron took over as Medical Health Officer, he had one typhoid and 2 tuberculosis cases to handle (both the latter died); he also reported an unlicensed slaughterhouse in the township. 1900 was a good year, with only one diphtheria case in Emily, and no problems. Some of the general statistics for Victoria County are worth noting, as they apply in Emily: in general it was a healthy county, being mostly rural; the birthrate was down 50% from 1851, but was still higher than the provincial level. The average Victoria age at death in 1882 was 35 while the provincial average was 28.2 years, and Victoria's rose to 40 by 1900. Victoria's deathrate was 8.9 per 1,000 population in 1881, well below the provincial level, though it rose over 10. per 1,000 in 1883, 1884, 1885, 1892, 1893, and 1897 on, up to a towering 13.2 deaths per 1,000 in 1900 (when the provincial rate was 13.5). The province began in the late 1890s to organize local health services, sanitary regulations and inspections, vaccination of children, and other preventive health measures, to meet the growing threat. Emily was healthier than most of Victoria, having only 1 or 2 villages, as farm families prepared most of their own food right on the farm with little chance of pollution, using water from their own wells, and buying little outside produce, with few outside sources of infection.

By 1901 the census recorded 66,310 acres occupied in Emily, and of this about half was cultivated, a slight drop in acreage from 1881, due to population reduction, but with hired help and more machines, production actually increased in the period in the crops where market demand and price was high. Another way to gauge farmland use was by the local assessment, since of "acres resident", 60 to 65% was cultivated in the late Victorian period:

	1875	1883	1891	1900
Acres resident assessed	57,465	58,364	59,237	59,630
Acres non-resident assessed	1,500	1,526	600	200

The printed census figures on agricultural production by townships unfortunately ceased in 1891, but they show that in the 1880s wheat acreage in Emily fell nearly to the 1871 level, while production of wheat was slightly more than 1881 (of this, fall wheat rose from 699 bus. to 5,334 bus. in the 1880s). Oats production in 1891 soared to 205,221 bus., barley was up slightly and rye down slightly, peas up slightly, potatoes down slightly; hay, turnips and various root crops were up 50 or 60% over 1881, and buckwheat up from 472 bus. to 14,079 bus. These can be related to district market prices; the following are some farm prices as quoted in local papers and fluctuated according to supply, up in winter and spring, down in summer and autumn:

	1876	1882	1886	1894	1897
Wheat (bus.)*	90c-$1	85c-$1.35	79c-$1	55c	75c-81c
Oats (bus.)	38c	41c-42c	28c-29c	32c-34c	21c-23c
Barley (bus.)	45c	51c-70c	40c-54c	35c-40c	22c-30c
Rye (bus.)	40c	53c-80c	—	—	40c
Buckwheat (bus.)	—	—	—	40c-41c	25c-26c
Peas (bus.)	65c	73c	54c-57c	54c-59c	40c-48c
Potatoes (bag)	70c-$1	60c-$1	70c	50c-60c	25c-35c
Flour (cwt.)	$5-$6	$4.50-$5	$4	$2.50	$2.75
Hay (ton)	$9-$12	$9-$10	$8	$7-$8	$7-$10
Apples (bag)	40c-75c	60c-80c	$1	75c-$1.25	50c-$1
Eggs (doz.)	10c-20c	16c-24c	18c-20c	14c-15c	14c-17c
Butter (lb.)	16c	13c-16c	15c-18c	19c-24c	16c-20c
Beef (lb.)	5c	5c	4c	3c-6c	5c
Lamb & Mutton (lb.)	7c	8c-12c	8c	6c-8c	6c-9c
Pork, Ham & Bacon (lb.) 6c-8c		7c-12c	7c	3c-6c	7c-8c
Cheese (lb.)	12c	16c	13c	11c-12c	8c
Honey & Maple Sugar (lb.) 11c		15c	16c	8c-10c	8c

*(fall wheat a bit higher than spring wheat)

This table indicates that there was relative prosperity and rising prices in the 1880s, but depression was evident again in the period 1893-97, with slight rises to end the century. The record of livestock production in Emily (compiled from county assessments) can also be correlated with the above:

	Cattle	Sheep	Hogs	Horses
1871	2062	2663	1154	782
1877	969	1926	996	764
1882	902	1271	715	731
1891	2197	2213	1027	1192
1895	2629	1980	1031	1423
1900	3051	1537	1162	1222

It will be noted that depression and low prices in the 1870s had a marked effect in cutting down livestock production; but the sound steady growth in the 1880s provided a firm economic base, so that when depression came again in the 1890s, it had little effect except upon sheep production (when wool and mutton prices fell, due to huge Australian and New Zealand production for the British market). From 1880 on, the northern lumber shanties provided a steady market for Emily cattle, hogs and horses.[6]

By 1880 the old stump fences were largely replaced in Emily by split cedar rail fences, and some farmers were even building dry stone fences, elegantly topped by wire; the first barbwire fences came in by 1880 also, to keep "breachy" livestock off the roads. Some were clearing off all the trees, and draining their swampland, and the water-table was dropping; those digging wells now had to do down to 20 feet to find water, on average, and there were wells drying up in drought years. Nearly all farmers had horse-drawn rakes, reapers, seeders, etc., and the first binders and steam-threshers were in use by 1885, about the same time as the potato beetle coming in from Colorado. There were few breeders of thoroughbred cattle in Emily, though the Bureau of Industries in 1883 mentioned John Bailey and David Corneil, Sr., of Omemee as owners of Durhams, and Eugene Shine of Downeyville as owner of Ayrshires. An 1884 Ontario report on medal-winning farms mentioned a gold-medal farm in Mariposa and a silver-medal farm in Smith—on his train-ride between them, the inspector commented: ". . . until Omemee was reached . . . the land appears fairly good and well suited to agricultural purposes. From Omemee to Peterborough . . . decidedly uneven and not such as would be easy to operate self-binders and sulky-ploughs. . . ." The same year an Ontario Forestry report quoted W. C. Switzer of Emily on wind-breaks: "for maples take them from soil as much as possible like the soil you are going to plant them in. As soon as the weather gets warm in spring after planting, put some long manure or wet straw round them with a few stones on top." John Fowler, who farmed near Fowler's Corners, gave a receipt Sept. 2, 1885, as follows: "I have this day received from Mr. C. W. Amstrong of Derry West 2 bus. of "Reliable" Fall wheat which I agree to sow on good high land, to harvest when ready, and to thresh on or before the last week in August 1886, and to deliver at Omemee Station all yield over 20 bus. to the acre, to Edward Finney, who acts as Agent for Mr. Armstrong,

Pioneer Snake Fence

Pioneer Stump Fence

Wartman Square Brace Fence

Stone Fence

HE WARTMAN SURFACE SQUARE BRACE FENCE POST.

PATENTED 24TH APRIL, 1893.

CEIVED from Mr............ ....of the Township of

....in the County of...the sum of

....Dollars
                                                                                                        100

the right to use "THE WARTMAN SURFACE SQUARE BRACED FENCE POST" on his farm of

.....................Acres in the said Township of.............................. ......being composed of

....................of Lot No ....in the...................Concession of the said Town-

p and on no other place, and for which said right this receipt is his title.

ted this ....day of...................... A. D. 190

....
Assignee of the said Patent Right for the said Township

Order Form for Patent Fence — (Milburn Hutchinson)

to visit and look after the crop, see grain weighed, &c. I further agree to clean the growing crop of all obnoxious weeds." One would like to know how this experiment with a new type of seed worked out.

The Emily Branch of the Victoria South Agricultural Society, in its 1877 report noted that it had 154 members, and a prizelist of $121.50 for livestock and $136.75 for grains and general exhibits; "many of the most intelligent & progressive farmers in Emily consider it their duty to take an active part". They noted benefits from their Spring and Fall Fairs in improvement of livestock, use of artificial manures, and regular crop rotation, and hoped to purchase a Fair-grounds shortly. In 1879 their two Shows were also successful, but the directors deplored the lack of a suitable show-ground and a market in Omemee, and the poor grain harvests and low prices. In 1880 again they deplored "the small yield of spring wheat which averaged not more than 10 bus. an acre . . . compensated in some degree by the very good price. . . . Fall wheat, however, was an excellent yield; it averaged fully 30 bus. to the acre, in some cases as much as 50 bus. . . . Coarse grains such as barley, oats, etc. were an excellent crop. . . ." The Emily Society went into a decline with membership halved, and the Ontario Agricultural Reports do not mention Emily again except occasionally: in the 1886 Crop Report, W. Sullivan of Emily was quoted: "Fall wheat in very poor condition generally, but on flat sheltered land it is good; badly killed by frosts in exposed lots, supposed to be in January after a heavy thaw."; in 1888 the first cheese factory in Emily was reported, operated at Downeyville, with Eugene Shine secretary. One other unusual feature is that, in Agricultural & Arts Associations, Farmers' Institutes, and Associations of dairymen, sheep-breeders, swine-breeders, fruitgrowers, beekeepers, poultry and pet raisers, shorthorn breeders, cheese and creamery associations, etc., which began to proliferate in the 1880s, usually covering Ontario, no officers or members are listed from Emily; it is apparent that Emily farmers were not joiners of provincial associations in specialized types of farming, nor convinced that they could farm better by reading literature and attending Conventions, to hear speeches and discuss problems.

In the 1890s the Ontario Agricultural Department scattered gold, silver and bronze medals on model farms from Fenelon to Asphodel, with much publicity, and quoted local speakers on dairy-farming, apple-growing, under-draining, etc. but never a mention of Emily. The Emily Cheese Factory at Downeyville was reported in 1892, with J. C. Lucas, secretary; next year it was listed as a Creamery or butter-factory, with C. F. Revill, manufacturer. In 1893 also at a Fruitgrowers' Association convention in Peterborough, a Guelph professor mentioned in passing that Victoria was a very poor fruit-growing county, having only 1,525 acres of orchard, and in Victoria, Emily was one of the lowest, with only 152 acres of orchard. As might be expected, Northumberland and Durham Counties were far ahead of the northern counties in fruitgrowing. The Downeyville factory was again producing cheese (not butter) in 1894, with Wm. Cook, proprietor, and another one close by at Dunsford; it burned down in Nov. 1895, when J. Lucas was secretary, but was rebuilt as the "Maple Leaf Cheese Factory" in 1896, with John Reid, secretary; there was now a second cheese factory at Omemee, H. Stephenson, secretary. County Cheese Boards were set up at Lindsay and Peterborough, and the government provided an inspector-instructor in cheese-making who visited the two Emily factories three times in 1897, to improve cheese quality, and to increase delivery of good quality milk at factory. Thus Emily ended the 19th century as an average farming township, total acreage 61,581, cleared 39,716, woodland 1,375, waste 17,680; with only a couple of working oxen left, compared to 1,222 horses for use in fields and on roads, and looking ahead to the rapid changes brought by steampower, gasoline and electricity.

The Emily Fall Exhibitions continued right up to 1900, at Omemee, and we are fortunate to have copies of the programmes, printed at the Omemee 'Mirror', beginning Oct. 8 and 9, 1895: Officers: Isaac Fee of Emily, pres.; Eugene Shine, Downeyville, vice-president; O. G. Williamson, Omemee, sec. treas.; directors: W. R. McQuade, J. Blackwell, Wm. Deyell, Thos. Graham, Hiram Corneil and A. Faulkner, all of Emily; I. W. Wilson, Omemee; Michael Clancey, Downeyville; Wm. Cunningham, Reaboro. The classes were listed, with advertisements from Omemee, Lindsay and Peterborough sprinkled among them: Class A—draught horses; Class B—agricultural horses; Class C—carriage horses; Class D—cattle; Class E—sheep; Class F—swine; Class G—poultry; Class H—grain and seed; Class I—roots, &c. Class J—vegetables; Class K—fruit; Class M—general manufactures; Class P —agricultural implements; Class R—dairy produce; Class S—fancy work; and special prizes for 12 largest hen eggs, best team of drawing horses, baby show, best lady rider on horseback, girls' race under 10 years, and best collection of old books. In 1896 the EAS Officers were mostly the same, with W. Stinson replacing I. Wilson of Omemee, and 3 new Emily directors: Geo. McQuade, E. Storey and R. E. Ford, also J. Beatty of Omemee. The Fair was Sept. 28-29, with note "The Society Dinner will be held at the Omemee House at 11 o'clock on 2nd day of show". Admission was 25c adults, 15c children 10 to 15 years, younger children free. A warning notice read: "Any person exhibiting any animal or article not their own, and found out, their names will be published." The prize classes were the same, and the special prizes: for 12 largest hen eggs, for best apple pie, for ladies' bicycle race, for best team of drawing-horses, for best team of walking horses, for best lady driver, for men's bicycle race; there were also boys' and girls' races "for valuable prizes." The Lindsay 'Post' described the festive appearance of the fairgrounds in McQuade's field just east of Omemee: "a large tent designated the main building, surrounded by half a dozen small ones. . . . This village of tents presented quite an attractive appearance, located in the centre of the ring on which the horses were speeded and judged. . . . The Citizens' Band played several selections during the afternoon."

The next Exhibition at Omemee, Oct. 4 and 5, 1897, listed the officers: Pres. G. McQuade of Emily, Vice-pres. E. Shine of Downeyville, Secretary O. Williamson of Omemee, and Treasurer T. Stephenson of Omemee; the

---

PRIZE LIST.

CLASS A, B, C.

HORSES.

CLASS A—DRAUGHT HORSES.

	FIRST	SECOND
For the best heavy draught team, 1st, pair of best all wool pants, presented by Oak Hall Clothing Co., Peterboro, value....	$4 00	$2 00
Mare and Foal......	2 00	1 00
Two year old Gelding or Filly........	2 00	1 00
One year old Gelding or Filly........	1 50	1 00

CLASS B. AGRICULTURAL HORSES.

	FIRST	SECOND
Span Agricultural Horses, 1st one potato scuffler, by Massey, Harris Co. Ltd., Toronto, J. Maitland, Agt., Omemee, value	9 00	2 00
Agricultural Mare and Foal,..........	2 00	1 00
Two year old Gelding or Filly........	1 50	1 00
One year old Gelding or Filly........	1 50	
2nd, Condition powders, by Dr. Waldon, value		1 00

CLASS C—CARRIAGE HORSES.

	FIRST	SECOND
Span Carriage Horses, 1st prize, a large, handsome negotent engraving in massive gold frame, presented by Grafton & Co., Clothing Manufacturers, Peterboro.....		2 00
Carriage Mare and Foal, 1st by Jas. O'Shea, Peterboro.......	2 00	1 00
Two year old Gelding or Filly...........	1 50	1 00

CLASS C—CARRIAGE HORSES Cont.

	FIRST	SECOND
One year old Gelding or Filly,............	1 50	1 00
Single Horse in harness, 15¾ hands high and over, 1st whip, by B. Shortly, Peterboro, value...........	2 00	1 00
Single Horse in harness, under 15¾ hands high, 1st whip, by Peterboro Hardware Co., Peterboro, value	2 00	1 00
Single Horse in harness, 3 years old, speed considered, 1st pair pants, by H. McLean, Mt. Pleasant, value..........	2 00	1 00

CLASS D,

CATTLE.

	FIRST	SECOND
Thoroughbred Cow with pedigree, 1st goods by Fairweather & Co., Peterboro, value..	$2 00	$1 00
Milch Cow, grade....................	1 00	75
Thoro'bred 2 year old Heifer, with pedigree	1 00	75
Two year old Heifer, grade............	75	50
Thoro'bred one year old Heifer, with pedigree, 1st pr. boots, by R. Neill, Peterboro	1 50	75
One year old Heifer, grade...........	75	50
Thoro'bred Heifer Calf, with pedigree	1 00	75
Heifer Calf, grade	75	50

CLASS E, SHEEP.

LEICESTER.

	FIRST	SECOND
Aged Ram, 1st Weekly Examiner, 1 year by J. R. Stratton, Peterboro		75
Shearing Ram....................	1 00	75
Ram Lamb, 1st, 50 lbs. flour, by J. W. Brisbin, Peterboro...........		75
Pair Aged Ewes.......................	1 00	75
Pair Shearling Ewes	1 00	75
Pair Ewe Lambs	1 00	75

COTSWOLDS.

	FIRST	SECOND
Aged Ram, 1st, Weekly Review 1 year, by F. H. Dobbin, Peterboro,.............		75
Shearing Ram.......................	1 00	75
Ram Lamb	1 00	75
Pair Aged Ewes.....................	1 00	75
Pair Shearling Ewes	1 00	75
Pair Ewe Lambs	1 00	75

FINE WOOLS.

	FIRST	SECOND
Aged Ram, 1st Weekly Review one year by F. H. Dobbin, Peterboro................		75
Shearling Ram.......................	1 00	75
Ram Lamb	1 00	75
Pair Aged Ewes......................	1 00	75
Pair Shearling Ewes	1 00	75
Pair Ewe Lambs	1 00	75

CLASS F.

SWINE.

IMPROVED YORKSHIRE.

	FIRST	SECOND
Aged Boar, pedigree................	$1 00	50
Boar, under 6 mos., pedigree...........	1 00	50
Aged Sow	1 00	50
Sow, under 6 months................	1 00	50

CHESTER WHITE.

	FIRST	SECOND
Aged Boar with pedigree, 1st Victoria Warder 1 year, by Major S. Hughes, Lindsay,....		50
Boar, under 6 mos., pedigree...........	1 00	50
Aged Sow	1 00	50
Sow under 6 months................	1 00	50

BERKSHIRE.

	FIRST	SECOND
Aged Boar, with pedigree, 1st Watchman 1 year, by G. Lytle, Lindsay............		50
Boar, under 6 mos., pedigree...........	1 00	50
Aged Sow	1 00	50
Sow under 6 months...............	1 00	50

POLAND CHINA.

	FIRST	SECOND
Aged Boar, with pedigree...........	1 00	50
Boar, under 6 mos., pedigree...........	1 00	50
Aged Sow	1 00	50
Sow, under 6 months..............	1 00	50

TAMWORTH.

	FIRST	SECOND
Aged Boar, with pedigree	1 00	50
Boar, under 6 mos.,..............	1 00	50
Aged Sow......................	1 00	50
Sow, under 6 mos................	1 00	50

directors were: W. McQuade, I. H. Fee, Wm. Deyell, Thos. Graham, T. B. Laidley, Evans Storey and R. Ford, all of Emily; Dr. F. Bradd of Omemee; Jos. Brown of Reaboro. The prize classes were the same, and the special prizes for best team of drawing horses, best lady driver, ladies' and men's bicycle races, boys' and girls' foot races, and open tug-of-war. The 1900 Exhibition, held Oct. 3 and 4, at Omemee, listed the same officers and directors, except that F. Cann and T. W. Blackwell replaced two Emily members, and there was no Reaboro director. The prize classes were the same still, but the special prizes showed the new urge to entertain outsiders: speeding in the ring, a mix-up, best lady driver, fat man's race, sawing wood race, best baby under 1 year, young lady with best display of canned fruit grown by herself, etc. The prizes were modest, ranging from 50c to $3 in main classes, 25c to 50c in minor classes, and remained the same up to 1900; the classes give a fascinating insight into the special interests of farm men and women, from the thoroughbred livestock to the finest exhibits of grain and roots and fruits; Class M was for lumber wagon, single buggy, cutter, household furniture, farm and carriage harness, rag carpet, handmade boots, woolen socks and mittens, homemade bread, pies, cakes, &c.; in Class R, farm-wives competed with homemade cheese and butter; in Class S (Fancy Work) they competed in 44 sections from fancy knitting to pencil drawing, from silk quilts to crazy patchwork, from table drapes to oil paintings.[7]

In addition to the skilled craftsmen scattered through Emily as mentioned in the last chapter, a few others in the period might be mentioned: John McMullen threshed grain in north Emily with a horse-powered machine, and later James McMullen used a portable steam thresher; William Callaghan threshed with a traction engine, and the Bell brothers. Other early threshers in middle Emily were Bob Stinson, George Windrem, Bob Courtney, Tom Rowan, and Pat and Bill Callaghan. Charles Revill made cheese at Downeyville in the 1890s, as did Mr. and Mrs. John Reid. Early blacksmiths in Downeyville were Dennis O'Leary, George Clark, Tom Tully, and Pat and Jim Callahan. James Leary had a shop at King's Wharf and hired a helper until his son John learned the trade. Simon Perdue had a smithing shop in the 1890s on lot 18, con. 10. Their price to remove a shoe and replace it was 10c, or to put on a new shoe 20c; some of them also made sleigh runners, chains and ironwork, logging hardware, etc. John Fowler of Fowler's Corners had a bill with Jacob Isbister, local blacksmith, which ran from Oct. 26, 1883 to May 20, 1884, totalling $7.65, including such items as "2 new shoes 60c; new double clives 50c; 3 links whiffeltry 25c; 4 shoes set 40c; claw hook repair 15c." A travelling blacksmith, already mentioned, Alex Feir of Ops and Emily, has left accounts as late as 1888 for ironwork done in Omemee and Emily, and his accounts with local merchants for supplies—in 1880, for example, he bought a 3,000-lb. waterwheel from Geo. Needler of Millbrook, brought it by railway to Omemee, and installed it for an unknown client; and in 1883 brought from Toronto by Midland 2 millstones (weight 3,370 lbs.) plus machinery to be installed for an Omemee client, freight bill $10.44. Between such jobs he did blacksmithing, and several of his bills covering a year or two of work (shoeing, bands on wheels, welding, springs for shingle saw, replacing king bolt, &c.) are in the collection—the prices are remarkably moderate—putting handle on gang plough 75c, 3 shoes set 30c, placing hinges 20c, putting 3 keys in mower 30c, 3 six-inch bolts 25c, etc.

Another Emily industry, lumbering, is mentioned in a list of properties for sale by Adamson & Co. of Hamilton in Feb. 1880: "PARCEL 209: $700 will buy 50 acres of good land, known as the Thos. Dwyer lot, heavily timbered with beech, maple, elm, some hemlock, and a few acres of choice cedar & tamarac, being s.w. quarter lot 17, con. 12, township Emily, near village of Downeyville. The timber will more than pay for the lot. Terms easy." This was the type of land transaction that was profitable for sawmillers like Mossom Boyd of Bobcaygeon and Wm. Cottingham of Emily. Boyd's agent at Omemee was Isaac McNeely, and the Boyd accounts are full of items showing a busy trade along Pigeon River—in 1876, May 12 to 24, he sent 337,790 feet of siding, plank, strip, culls, &c. valued at $1,947.05 to McNeely "delivered on scows at Omemee Wharf." A telegram from McNeely in Omemee, May 22, to Boyd in Bobcaygeon, read "Impossible to unload in time for Boat. Scows must wait." Later in May he wrote ". . . the scows you forwarded on 12th are now delivered safe to 'Novelty' steamer. Planks & inch boards have not arrived & are much enquired after." Boyd wrote S. Cottingham Apr. 9, 1877: "Capt. Lane of my steamboat 'Novelty' has just handed me his bill against you for towing sawlogs to Omemee for you on 28th May, 1876, amount $12 which will thank you to remit as promised him." Two months later McNeely wrote Boyd about "the burning of the only Planing Mill in this place on 4th ult." but "a planing mill will soon be in operation again, which will improve the lumber business". July 3, 1877, Thomas Fee of Lindsay wrote Boyd: "I am sending my boat up Pigeon Creek for shingle-bolts and if you want any scows sent up to Omemee we will tow them up for you & take lumber in payment." The Lindsay 'Post' reported May 3, 1878: "Upwards of 100,000 ft. lumber were towed up Pigeon River this last week from Bobcaygeon for John Kincaid, builder." and three years later, Apr. 29, 1881: "The steamer 'Maple Leaf' will shortly begin towing sawlogs for John Kincaid from Sandy Pt. on Pigeon Lake to his mill in Omemee village."

Boyd had a lime kiln also at Bobcaygeon, and an account sent James Balfour of Omemee June 5, 1878 read: "By steamer 'Lady Ida' I sent you 20 bbls. lime $10, 1,000 ft. plank $9,"; Balfour's account had risen to $348.32 for such material, and he had paid on account $100. McNeely sold about 135,000 ft. lumber for Boyd on commission in 1879, but as some of it had been in his yard since 1876, it was not a profitable venture for Boyd, who began selling to others in Omemee—Henry Toole, J. Evans, &c. John Lang of Omemee in 1883 wrote asking an agreement to sell all Boyd lumber in Omemee, but Boyd refused as his mill output was all taken. There were also difficulties in sending scows up Pigeon River, as Boyd wrote J. Morrison of Omemee Apr. 20, 1883: "I cannot deliver your lumber at Omemee as my

boat and scows are too large to go up the creek . . . I could let you have
the 5 ins. and 6 ins. strip and a 11 width lumber & lath, providing you can
get some boat & scows to take it, or else you might apply to S. Walker at
my Lindsay yard & have it shipped from there by rail." Robert Wilson on
Mar. 11, 1886, wrote Boyd "I am thinking of starting a lumberyard at my
residence Cowans Bridge as it is the centre of a fine farming Community
where a lot of lumber & shingles & lath are used, and as owners of
lumberyards in Omemee charge so high for it, the farmers go to Lindsay &
Peterboro for what they need; it would be very handy for you to unload scows
at the bridge and for me to draw to my yard. . . ." Boyd agreed to provide him
with some lumber to get started, though he warned again "our boat & scows
are too large to navigate your river, but there are other smaller boats you
can get with their scows to tow the lumber up." Through the 1890s Boyd
stopped shipping lumber up Pigeon River to Omemee, and advised all who
ordered to get it shipped by train from his Lindsay yard. On Aug. 23, 1892,
he submitted a quotation for lumber to repair the Pigeon Creek Bridge, price
$99, "to be delivered on scow at our Little Bob yard." The Lindsay *Post*
noted Dec. 24, 1897: "LUMBERING: The Parkin-Nichols lumber camp
at Cowan's Bridge is in full swing, and employs quite a few from Omemee and
vicinity"; this was on land owned by Thomas Matchett of Lindsay.

Boyd's other business connections in Emily are interesting. In 1888-90
his stallion "Clovis" was on tour through the township, and receipts are on
file for "keep of stallion" from J. D. O'Brien of Downeyville; Peter Murtha,
King's Wharf; John Fee, Omemee; James Bell, Dunsford, etc. Then in 1900
his Suffolk Punch stallion "Tumbrel" was making the tour, and we shall have
more details in the next chapter. In 1893 Boyd wrote Eugene Shine of
Downeyville about plans for his Lindsay, Bobcaygeon and Pontypool Railway,
"I have written Dennis Scully, Wm. Lehane and James O'Brien asking them
kindly to come into Lindsay and attend the public meeting on 14th inst. for
the purpose of assisting us in showing the people of Lindsay that a large part
of the grain & other produce which should naturally come to Lindsay,
being nearest market, is each year going to Peterboro and elsewhere . . . if
you will be good enough to attend the meeting along with them I will be
much obliged." (We learned earlier that Boyd rejected Inspector Knight's
proposal to route the railway through northern Emily).

Finally, Emily farmers were keen to sell supplies to the Boyd lumber
shanties, and some of their sons to get jobs in the Boyd camps. A note to
Dan. Crimmins, Downeyville, Jan. 4, 1878, read: "I am now hiring teams
& can find sleighs & chains; I can take your team if they are good &
heavy and if you come at once." Sam. Webster of Omemee wrote Nov. 18,
1878: "I am informed you are at the Lumbering business this Winter again
. . . if you want a man send me word and what Wadges you are giving for
men."; a week later Robt. Grandy of Omemee wrote a postcard to Boyd:
"David McKinley, baker, son-in-law of Mrs. Jas. English, has requested
me to write to know if you want a cook for one of your shanties." A note of
Jan. 6, 1892, to Wilby Sherman, lot 15, con. 9, Emily, at Downeyville P.O.

stated: "Mr. Connell tells me you were in about a week ago asking about work in the woods. . . . Can you come in time to start back early Mon. morning with a team & at the wages we are paying, $16 a month." Jan. 2, 1893, Carnaby Thurston of Downeyville wrote "Mr. Boide sir: I have some hay to part with and if you neede some i will give it to you and take lumber in payment if it suites you; the lumber i want is for outbuildings mostly . . . Pleas answer soon for i would like to draw while the roads is good state prise you give for hay." Boyd wrote Jas O'Brien of Downeyville Mar. 15, 1894: ". . . We are overstocked with horses but are buying stripper cows at 2½c a pound live weight & if you have any will take them against your promissory note of $49.00." There are many notes and postcards to and from Emily on such matters in the Boyd records—in 1897 Thos. Walker of Omemee wanted to trade his heavy team for a lighter team, and in 1898 D. M. Costello of Downeyville wanted to know if the Boyd Company wanted any hay (he was told they would buy what he had at $8 a ton).

Usually some lumberjacks paid off at Kinmount, Fenelon or Bobcaygeon after a winter in the shanties lost their cash by drinking and gaming in local hotels and saloons, and a gang would start off on foot via Dunsford and King's Wharf toward Peterborough and the route homeward. When they raided hen-roosts and root-cellars enroute through Emily and Ennismore, or tried to sleep in farm barns along the road, the resulting moonlit skirmishes, both verbal and fistic, enlivened many spring nights in the area, though seldom ending in law-court. Both the Irish farmers and the Irish, English and French-Canadian shantymen preferred a settlement by fist or axe-handle, and a brisk "argument" down a mile or two of country road, with no hard feelings afterward. There was another side to the story—over the decades, hundreds of Emily men went into northern lumber-shanties in the winters, and drove logs down the rivers in spring; some of these occasionally brought a chum back to the farm from the shanty or log-drive, to meet the family, and some of the outsiders married Emily girls and settled down nearby to farming or a trade—the 1901 census, for example, shows 14 French-Canadians in Emily.

Edith Fowke, noted collector and publisher of Ontario folksongs, found one still sung locally about the death of Bob Cottingham (or Cunningham) and Bill Dunbar, drowned at "Gannon's Narrows at the foot of Pigeon Lake" on an 1894 log-drive; Dunbar was "foreman for Mossom Boyd". Another local song was even more closely tied to Omemee and Downeyville, though originating in Vermont and sung all over the eastern lumbering regions; it was called "The Backwoodsman" and was sung for Mrs. Fowke by Calvin Kent of Haliburton.

The Almanacs, Atlases and Gazetteers of the period have some limited value as giving short items about local villages and officials, clergy and professional men. *The Canadian Legal Directory* 1878 listed Omemee-Emily coroners: George Potts, George Norris and Chris. Knowlson. The Victoria County Atlas 1881 listed the prominent men of Emily, meaning those who bought a copy of the Atlas.[8] The *Canadian Almanac* 1881 mentioned only the following Emily clergy: R. H. Harris (Anglican), M. Connelly of

THE BACKWOODSMAN

1. It's as well as I remember, 'twas the year of 'forty-five.
   I thought myself so thankful for to find myself alive.
   I harnessed up my horses, and I joined the Super crew,
   And I went a-hauling cordwood as I often used to do.

2. I might have hauled one load, I might have hauled four.
   I went down to Omemee, and I couldn't haul no more.
   The barroom it was open, the liquor flying free,
   And I drank one glass, another filled for me.

3. Oh, I met an old acquaintance, I dare not tell his name.
   He was going to a ball at night; I thought I'd do the same.
   He was going to a ball at night, the music sweetly played,
   And the boys and girls all danced till the breaking of the day.

4. Oh, I put the saddle on my arm, I struck out to the barn.
   I saddled up the old gray nag, not thinking any harm.

   I saddled up the old gray nag, I rode away quite still,
   And I never halted till I got to Downeyville.

5. Oh, when I got to Downeyville the night was far advanced.
   I got up on the floor, thought I'd have a little dance.
   The fiddler he was rested, and his arms were stout and strong,
   Played "The Bluebells of Ireland" for four hours long.

6. Oh, my father followed after me, I heard the people say.
   He must have had a spyglass, or he'd never have found the way.
   He peeked in every keyhole where he could see a light
   Till his old gray locks was covered with the dew of the night.

7. Oh, come all you old married men, I think you've danced enough.
   Let us spend a half an hour, and we'll get a cash account.
   We'll go home to our plows and whistle and we'll sing,
   And you'll never catch us out on a spree like this again.

8. Oh, come all you old women who tell your tales about,
   I pray you tell no tales on me, I'm bad enough without.
   I pray you tell no tales on me—I'm sure it's not the first.
   If the truth was only known, I'm sure I'm not the worst.

One of the Songs sung by Kawartha Lumbermen in the Late 19th Century. (Courtesy of Edith Fowke "Lumbering Songs from the Northern Woods" Austin 1970.)

Downeyville (Roman Catholic), Ed. Barrass and J. Norris (both Methodist);
Rev. J. Ewing (Presbyterian) was now at Mt. Pleasant. The *Ontario County Gazetteer* 1885 gave only a mention of Downeyville (pop. 40), Frank Hill (pop. 25), King's Wharf (population not given), and Omemee (pop. 744). The 1887 *Postal Guide* listed 4 postoffices in Emily, including Omemee (p.m. Robt. Grandy), Frank Hill (p.m. Chris. Lowes), King's Wharf (p.m. Jas. Leary), Downeyville (p.m. Mrs. Hannah Tracey), with others nearby at Fowler's Corners in Smith, Lindsay in Ops, and Dunsford in Verulam; the only postoffice savings bank was at Omemee, useful since there was no other bank in Omemee or Emily. The *Farmers' Classified Business Directory of Durham, Northumberland, Peterborough & Victoria* 1887 gave a complete listing of all propertyowners in Emily and Omemee; the entry for Downey-ville was: "Popul. about 100—Callaghan, P&W. blacksmiths; Crowley, Wm., livestock; Flynn, Timothy, livestock; Scully, Dennis, livestock; Reid, John, cheesemaker; Tracey, Mrs. H., general store & postmistress." For Frank Hill, no population was given, and only Thomas Lowes, postmaster, named; also for King's Wharf, where only J. C. Leary, postmaster, was named. Omemee was flattered with a population of about 900, and all merchants and tradesmen listed, from John Calder, publisher of *'Omemee Herald',* to John Young, hotelkeeper.[9]

The *Canadian Almanac* 1891 listed clergy: W. H. French (Anglican), Omemee, and Wm. Johnston and M. Sexsmith (Methodists), Omemee; Wm. Miller of Omemee was an officer of the Grand Lodge of Masons, and J. O. McGregor principal of Omemee High School. The 1896 *Almanac* listed W. McCann (Anglican) of Omemee, and N. Hill (Methodist), also Father C. Bretherton (Roman Catholic), Emily. The Lovell *Gazetteer of British North America* 1895 stated "Downeyville is a postvillage 5½ miles from Omemee, with 1 Roman Catholic Church, 1 cheese factory & 2 stores; population 80. Frank Hill is a postoffice 6 miles from Best's Station, population 25. Omemee is a flourishing village on Pigeon River and on the Midland division GTR with 3 churches, telegraph, express and telephone offices, a printing office issuing weekly newspaper, 1 iron foundry, saw and flour mills, about 15 stores, 2 hotels, sash & door factory and 1 bank. Population 687." One final reference-book is of interest—Dun & Co. *Mercantile Reference Book* 1898, which graded all businesses in North America on financial standing (Aa with over $1 million down to M with less than $500 assets) and in credit rating (from A1 down to 4); in Omemee (popul. 687) there were 36 merchants and tradesmen listed from W. Curry, general store (F3) as highest, down to 13 customers at the bottom with M4, e.g. John McCrea (father of Lady Eaton) furniture and undertaking (M4). Downeyville was mentioned for Henry Matthews, general store (M4); Fowler's Corners for James Fowler, implement agent (H3½) and Moses Ruth, general store (M4); Frank Hill was not listed, but King's Wharf had James Leary, groceries (M). Downeyville, Fowler's Corners and King's Wharf were each given a population of 25 people!

After Alexander Bell invented the telephone in 1876, it soon spread

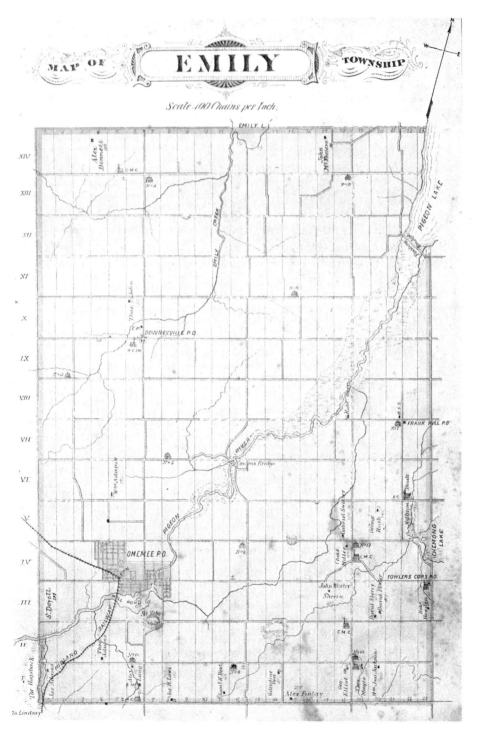

Map of Emily Township in 1881 Victoria County Atlas: (Names on Map are of people who subscribed to buy copies of Atlas)

into the Kawartha district, used chiefly for long-distance calls, over the wires of the telegraph system. In December, 1877, Mossom Boyd of Bobcaygeon, who already had a telephone link between his home and mills, talked for the first time over the new telephone line via Dunsford to Lindsay. Bell Telephone Co. of Canada was incorporated in 1880, and by 1883 had lines from Port Hope via Millbrook and Omemee to Lindsay (along the Midland); that same year the telephone was working from Port Hope to Peterborough, and a preliminary line rigged along the rail-line from Peterborough to Omemee, and on to Lindsay—this line was improved with iron wire between 1893 and 1903. A few offices, mills and stores bought a telephone and had a wire rigged to the main line, but to most people the telephone remained a spectacular novelty, used rarely for a critical call to a distant relative; the Lindsay *Post* recorded in Feb. 1884 that D. McKinley played his mouthorgan over the telephone in Waugh's Grocery, Omemee, and "entertained audiences in Peterborough, Port Hope, Toronto and intermediate points. . . . He played some 60 tunes but still the heartless people of Peterborough wanted more", indicating an endurance inconceivable today, especially at present long-distance rates! T. A. McPherson handled the long-distance telephone office at Omemee in the 1890s, and by 1904 had 13 local subscribers in the area (only 2 of these in homes).

With children growing up who received more thorough education, a need was felt in many homes for more reading than was provided by the books that the authorities had put in school libraries, and the family Bible and the mail-order catalogues. Agitation began in 1876 to get for Omemee a Mechanics' Institute branch, which would receive a government grant to provide a lending library, a public reading-room, and trades instruction for workingmen, partly financed by an annual fee; it was not started until about 1890, and in 1892 the village council gave it a grant of $25; a news report in 1893 stated that the reading-room was largely patronized, occupying the top floor of a main street store. It was used by Emily families who could borrow books on trips to town, and by students attending school in Omemee. They could also subscribe to the Omemee *'Herald'* started by J. A. Calder in his printshop on King Street; it was described as "an 8 page journal, neat and spicy, in the Conservative interest", and continued to publish weekly until destroyed in the big Omemee fire of 1891. Next year J. H. Hand began publishing the Omemee *'Recorder',* claiming to be non-political, but after a libel suit in 1893 Hand moved away from Omemee. Then Lane & Richards of Peterborough began the Omemee *'Mirror'* in December 1893, and lasted to 1903 when Richards moved it to Millbrook, calling it the *'Millbrook & Omemee Mirror'.* Williamson in his book *Omemee* gives an entertaining series of quotations from local papers in the period 1877 to 1906.

The names of Emily pioneers and community leaders who died in this period are a roll-call of those who gave an inspiring example in development of a prosperous township, which includes: William Cottingham 1875, Rev. Bernard Coyle c.1878-79, Christopher Knowlson 1880, Samuel Cottingham 1884, Dr. George Norris 1886, James Laidley 1889, Samuel English 1890,

James Fee 1891, Isaac McNeely 1892, Arthur McQuade 1894, Rev. John Ewing 1897, Robert Grandy 1899, and Thomas Matchett 1900. To them can be dedicated a little poem written by Martin Carroll of Downeyville in November 1898:

"Our years are like the shadows
On sunny hills that lie,
Or grasses in the meadows
That blossom but to die—
A sleep, a dream, a story,
By strangers quickly told,
An unremaining glory
Of things that soon are old.
Lord, crown our faith's endeavour
With beauty and with grace,
Till clothed in light forever
We see Thee face to face—
A joy no words can measure,
A fountain brimming o'er,
An endless flow of pleasure,
An ocean without shore."

An event long remembered was the North Emily fire of 1881, recorded by an old-timer long afterward: "August 31 began as another hot dry day, weather that had prevailed for several months. About 9 a.m. the west wind began to increase. A small fire had been burning in a swamp in northeast Ops for most of the summer, and fanned by the wind it began to burn vigorously, within an hour crossing into Emily on concessions 12 and 13 for about 4 miles by noon, until stopped by Emily Creek. On its path of destruction, from a half to over a mile wide, lay 7 barns and 3 dwellings in ashes, all their crops and woodlands and many livestock. Mr. McGahey rescued a pen of pigs from his burning barn, only to find their burnt carcasses later in a drainage ditch. Some settlers saved their homes by using quilts and blankets from the beds to spread on the roofs after soaking in water. Martin Harrington had recently purchased a dress suit, a considerable investment in those days. When the fire approached he rushed in and removed it, placing it in a field nearby for safety; but when the excitement was over the house was saved intact, but not the suit—the fire had passed over it and left only a handful of blackened metal buttons."

The government reported yearly on fires by townships for a few years, and it is clear that Emily was not addicted to the carelessness that often causes fires: in Dec. 1886 there was one fire, caused by chimney sparks, loss $528; in 1887 there were 2 small fires; in Mar. 1888 there was a fire due to defective chimney, loss $5; in Dec. 1891 one fire caused by defective chimney, loss $200; in 1892-93 none were reported in Emily. By contrast Omemee had a few fires every year, some recorded in Williamson's *'Omemee'*,

John Dovey built the first log hotel at
Downeyville about 1840
(Victor Callaghan)

Hubert Elliott --- teacher in Millersmith
School for many years. (Mrs. W. Thurston

Frank Fitch, wife and niece,
c. 1910 — (Harry Jackson)

James Patrick and his wife Eliza
McMullen (the first white child
born in Millersmith settlement)
c. 1900 (W. McMullen)

Neil Powers — aged
Feb. 14, 1974
(Mrs. C. Harringt

Robert Casey — South Emily Fence
Builder (Olive McCall)

William O'Brien driving a car on his
birthday, 1948 (Mrs. F. Morrissey

SOME OUTSTANDING EMILY RESIDENTS

such as Aug. 1888 when the G.T.R. Junction station burned down; then in Aug. 1891 there was a big fire burning down half the business section, loss $7,173.23; and again in Nov. 1892 another big fire in Omemee. By an Ontario Act of 1893 all insurance agents had to register, and those doing business in Emily were: P. A. Devlin, Emily; Henry Matthews, Downeyville; Isiah Thornton, Omemee.

Many small accidents happened frequently in farming operations, in lumbering, building, handling livestock, or driving along roads; three rather serious ones reported in the Lindsay *"Post"* might be mentioned here:

"Oct. 14, 1887: A very serious accident occurred Monday last about 2 miles north of Omemee, where E. C. Williamson has a piece of land for potatoes. His 3 sons George, Clarence and Arthur went out to raise the crop and draw in pumpkins . . . Arthur was leaving the field on a load of pumpkins when the end board of the waggon came out, causing the load to roll off which also carried Arthur with it and threw him across the waggon tongue. The noise frightened the horses and they ran away . . . Arthur's leg hit a stump with such force as to break it about 4 inches above the knee . . . and a wound inflicted on the back of his head. After falling off the tongue, he was dragged under the waggon for 50 yards, where he was found by brother George . . . Those who saw where the accident happened say it was a miracle that the leg was not torn off as the stump was quite solid, and had the top broken off it."

"Feb. 22, 1889: The 7 year old daughter of Charles McCaffrey of Omemee met with a terrible accident on Saturday. In running to catch upon a sleigh in company with others, she missed her footing and the sleigh passed over her leg, crushing it so badly that amputation was necessary. Owing to her tender years it is not thought that she can recover." (The habit of spending Saturday mornings hitching rides on farmers' sleighs coming into town to market, and then going out into the country for the afternoon by the same method, was still being practiced around most district towns even 50 years ago, as the writer can remember).

"Jan. 8, 1892: On Wednesday evening Isaac Glenny met with a severe and painful accident, by which he had his right arm completely wrenched off at the elbow. Mr. Glenny was running a threshing machine at Thomas Wilson's farm, in Emily, and was in the act of oiling the pulley at the fanning mill, when his arm was caught in the belt and drawn against the side of the machine. It was a ghastly sight to see the fractured elbow, then the gloveless forearm lying on the barn floor. He was brought to his home in Omemee, where Drs. Cochrane and Thompson were called. They amputated the lacerated stump near the shoulder, and left the unfortunate sufferer as comfortable as could be expected. Glenny is a hardworking man and a large family is depending on his daily toil for a living."

The slowly meandering, sluggish, and weedy Pigeon River (and to a smaller extent Emily and other creeks) was a worry to the businessmen along its banks who wanted to use the stream for navigation; but it was also a continuing pleasure to children and young people who wanted to swim and picnic

Threshing with Horse Power — (Ontario Archives)

First Threshing Instrument — A Flail
(Dr. J. Mannion)

Early Grain Cradle — (Dr. J. Mannion)

Tom Rowan threshing with steam before
1900 (Dorothy Bannon)

Portable Steam Engine about 1900
(Lyle Faulkner)

(a) "Esturion" built 1884

"Greyhound" built 1895, rebuilt as "Kathleen" 1905

(c) "Empress" built 1899
Typical Steamers that came up Pigeon River from Sturgeon and Pigeon Lakes 1885-1910
(H. T. Pammett)

in summer and skate in winter, or those of all ages who liked to fish and trap and hunt. As Omemee had no regular market, it was impossible to arrange a profitable steamer service along Pigeon River for farmers and others, as along the Otonabee or Scugog. In Sept. 1877 the newspapers reported a rumor that Capt. Lewis would put a small steamer on Pigeon River, but this never happened. In May 1878 a steamer excursion from Omemee was advertised for May 24 to Pigeon Lake, with a palace scow attached, and then a moonlight excursion downriver in the same month. M. Boyd of Bobcaygeon, who had the Trent Valley Navigation Company, noted in his diary Sept. 3, 1885: "An excursion to Bobcaygeon from Omemee on str. 'Esturion' on her regular trip today"—the regular schedule was from Chemong to Bobcaygeon. Again in Aug. 1890 the newspapers reported an excursion planned to Bobcaygeon Sept. 2 on str. 'Dominion' with a palace scow and the Citizen's Band for entertainment. Some of the other smaller steamers, especially the newly-built ones with screw propeller instead of paddlewheels, were used on Emily streams for carrying freight or towing small scows, or even taking excursions out to the resorts around Pigeon and Chemong Lakes, or to bring in hunting parties in autumn—the 'Lady Ida' (27 tons), the 'Dominion' (46 tons, the 'Stranger' (28 tons), the 'Eva' (34 tons), the 'Express' (20 tons), the 'Maple Leaf' (26 tons), the 'Greyhound' (20 tons), the 'Waterwitch' (9 tons), or the new 'Lady of the Lake' (19½ tons) built by Kelly at Bridgenorth in 1899. But passage along the Pigeon River became increasingly difficult in the 1890s, as we have seen, due to silting and swampy weedy reaches. Lady Eaton in *Memory's Wall* recalls that church and other groups wanting a steamer excursion usually preferred in the 1890s to go to Lindsay by train and take a steamer from there, down to Port Perry or up to Fenelon or Bobcaygeon.

Another handicap around Omemee was that there was no lake close enough, to hold regattas and to develop serious rowing, canoeing and sailing enthusiasm by organized clubs and races. The newspapers occasionally mentioned swimming races after the May 24 parade, probably in the river (as in 1887 and 1890), and in winter there was skating on the millpond and river. In 1883 and 1886 the papers mentioned Trotting Club races, held in February or March, which were probably on the river ice. The Indians of the Curve Lake Reservation continued to come up Pigeon and Emily creeks to fish and hunt and pick berries each year in season, and to visit the graves of their ancestors, and to visit friends—there were long-standing friendships from pioneer days between Indian families like the Whetungs and Emily families like the Bests, and others along the streams; after 1880 the Indians also acted as guides for tourists, bringing them by canoe or steam launch up the streams to hunt or fish in Emily. Very few Omemee and Emily people had the steam launches so popular after 1875 (before the time of naphtha and gasoline launches), but many people had homemade skiffs and punts, and even an occasional Peterborough or Lakefield canoe, in which to enjoy summer holidays near Cowan's Bridge, or Fee's or Green's or Lowes' or Carroll's Landings. Downeyville and Millersmith people used Emily Creek

Duck hunting in Emily with an Indian guide, c. 1890 (S. Boyd)

Summer sport on Pigeon River, c. 1890 (H. T. Pammett)

in the same way, and those in east Emily on the creeks flowing into Chemong Lake.

In both village and farm homes, the children had regular chores, especially on Saturday: the boys to saw and split firewood and kindling, to pump water and carry it for house and stable, to clean harness and footware, etc.; the girls to help in cooking, to clean house, to make and wash and repair clothing, to clean and fill the lamps, to look after the hens and calves, etc. Then, as Lady Eaton observed, "the same big wooden tub served us for Monday washday and Saturday bath night." Young people were expected by stern parents to stay away from hotels and taverns, which advertised "billiards" and such sports, but the churches busily promoted picnics in fine weather, and concerts, basket socials, glee clubs and social evenings in winter; the Y.M.C.A. in Omemee after 1877 provided healthy indoor games in the old brick church. In Feb. 1879 there was a masquerade skating carnival at Victoria Rink, Omemee, with the band playing for skating; in Sept. 1884 the young people organized a green corn dance in Matchett's woods; in Oct. 1885 a play was performed in Bradburn's Opera House, just opened. Every May 24 Emily people flocked to Omemee for the celebration of the Queen's Birthday—in 1887 there was a parade, a cricket match, footraces, swimming races and a balloon ascension; in 1890 another cricket match, land and water sports, and a concert in the evening, with fireworks. By this date organized cricket was fading in interest, and the first boys' baseball was mentioned in the newspapers, including games with Bethany, Lindsay, etc. However, there were few organized team sports until after the first Great War.

Most entertainment for young people, outside church and school, was unorganized and spontaneous—a picnic to Mount Nebo, a birthday singsong in someone's home, a surprise party (or even a midnight chivaree) for a newly-wedded couple, a swimming or fishing expedition on the river, a visit to the telegraph or telephone office to listen in, a gathering around the general store stove, a back-pasture baseball game, or a buggy race down a concession road. After Edison invented the phonograph in 1877 (with cylindrical records) they were purchased by prosperous farmers and businessmen, and evenings of home dancing were facilitated; the gramophone with its flat disc records appeared in 1897. In the parlour also might be a stereoscopic viewer with a set of views of historic and noted places in Canada or around the world, invented in the 1850s (in the 1890s Eaton's catalogue had viewers at 23c to 55c, sets of 50 views 43c up). Only very enthusiastic amateurs bought the cumbersome cameras developed after 1860, taking pictures by wetplate collodion process, or later the dry-plate glass-negative process, involving long time exposures without movement; but numerous pictures of wedding groups and hunting parties, &c. survive, taken in a town studio or by a travelling photographer in rural Emily. The roll-film folding camera was invented by Eastman in 1889, and within ten years some Emily people were busily taking "snap-shots" on box cameras (early folding cameras were $20 to $30, but by 1900 box cameras were selling for $2 to $5).

The first 'penny-farthing' bicycles appeared in the district in the 1880s, with iron tires and a large front wheel, needing expert riders, but in the 1890s the ordinary bicycle with rubber tires arrived—the *'Post'* correspondent in Omemee reported in August. 1896: "The bicycle fever is pretty well developed here at present, and the number that ride through the village on bikes has a tendency to keep up the contagion. There are now about a dozen of the silent steeds owned about the village . . . The roads in this vicinity are model cinder paths, and we expect that some very fast riders will be developed." The roads of the township were much improved by 1900, ready for a noisier faster steed, the automobile. The machine age gathered momentum in the 1880s and 1890s with its telephones, gramophones, bicycles, typewriters, steamrollers, steam threshers, and other new machinery, all having impact on life in Emily township; and no new invention had more future effect than one just being conceived nearby in the early 1890s by Reginald Fessenden, visiting his uncle Cortez Fessenden (Principal of Peterborough Collegiate) at his summer cottage on Chemong Lake—by watching the spreading waves when a stone or a bird splashed down in the water, he got the fundamental idea for invention of radio transmission and reception equipment, even before Marconi.[10]

Life in Emily improved more in the last 25 years of the Victorian era than in the preceding 56 years since first settlement, in all aspects of farm and village living from home comfort to prosperity, health and longevity. Ontario government pamphlets for British farm emigrants (distributed in 1880 and later) had engravings showing the steady progress from rough small log cabin and stable, with stump-filled fields and primitive tools, through the period of fenced fields, squared or frame buildings, and equipment drawn by oxen or horses, to the latest large stone or brick homes and sturdy timber outbuildings, horse-drawn machinery and carriages, surrounded with an air of comfort and prosperity. Emily homes were still 80% self-contained, though people bought through catalogue or in store an increasing proportion of their machinery, waggons, furniture and fittings, clothing, and even food. Lady Eaton, village-raised, recalled the curing of hams, meat hung on rafters after killing, storing vegetables and preserving fruit, making of butter and cheese, quilting, and other home handicrafts still prevalent in the 1890s. Neighbouring communities still held "bees" to raise a barn, rebuild a school or church, harvest a sick neighbour's crop, make clothes for a bride or quilts and knitted goods for a bazaar, or maple-sugar making in the spring.

In this Age of Taste, village homes became surrounded with lawns and iron deer, croquet courts and formal gardens and arbours within stone or iron fences. But even farm homes now had their hedges or picket fences, vine-covered verandas, fretwork decorations and wooden or gravel walks, and with stables, ice-houses and other conveniences concealed by an arbour, and a hitching-post at the gate. In a shed attached to the "summer kitchen" were placed the sanitary conveniences, including a softwater pump fed from a rainwater reservoir. The cellars were lined with cans of fresh milk and cream, a butter churn, shelves for preserves and bins for vegetables and fruit—few cellars had a furnace yet, since most homes relied on fireplaces, and stoves in kitchen and parlour, with a network of stovepipes through upper rooms to the chimney—also few people yet used coal for fuel, even in town, since it cost more than wood and was dirtier to use. In the parlour, where blinds and drapes were kept drawn tight 6 days a week, factory-made furnishings were appearing—lamps and chandeliers, rugs and tapestries, plush ottoman couches and 'loveseats', sideboards laden with bric-a-brac, and on the walls engraved or embroidered mottos ('God Save Our Home' being most popular) and chromo pictures of solemn ancestors, patient cattle and dogs, and bloody battlefields. There might even be a bookcase with the family Bible, a few moral volumes, an atlas and a few volumes of Dickens or Scott. Parlour organs and pianos were appearing in a few homes, along with violins, trumpets, etc., though the children preferred to play the harmonica or jews-harp. For courting couples, an evening on couch or 'loveseat' with the stereo-scope was something to look forward to all week.

Emily farmers might win no government medals for the latest farming techniques, machinery and under-draining, but their homes were comfortable and happy places to grow up and spend a life of rewarding work. When the family gathered for an evening meal after a long day in field, stable, woods or kitchen, they wished no better life in most cases—and especially on Sunday after church when all the married sons and daughters and their children gathered around the table (extended by 2 or 3 extra leaves), or at Christmas when they all came from town or shanty or construction job to spend the holiday in the surroundings where they had grown up. The background news of distant wars, of exciting train trips, of prairie grain-fields (where a man could plough in a straight line for miles), of Klondike gold fortunes, or even of frantic activities in Toronto streets and factories, seemed far away and unimportant on a quiet Emily farm among all the family. Twentieth century tempo and tensions were still over the horizon in late Victorian Emily.

NOTES

[1]Census figures each ten years were consistently higher in Emily population than county assessment statistics; e.g. 1891: census 2,604, county 2,201; 1901: census 2,304, county 2.051. Possibly the local assessors did not include single men and others not owning property, who might be away at lumber shanties or other jobs.

[2]A list of Emily reeves, councillors and top officials 1850 to 1973 will be found in appendix XXI, as prepared by L. McQuade. Unfortunately, the Council Minute Book for 1885-1902 is missing, with names of Councillors for these years.

[3]Inspector Knight's 1884 report is given in full in Appendix XXII, also his 1888 table of teachers and schools, and his 1891 comparison of Emily schools in 1871-1891.

[4]To end the story, the 1883-84 Directory of Peterborough Town and County gave glowing praise to "our energetic fellow-townsman George Cox" and looked forward to seeing the Midland workshops and head office moved to Peterborough as promised —but Cox in a typical doublecross and doubleplay moved himself and the head office to Toronto, moved the main workshops to Lindsay for a bonus, and left only a dis-patching office at Peterborough; and to cap the scheme, on Jan. 1, 1884 revealed he had acted for the Grand Trunk all along, and arranged the merger of the Midland into the Grand Trunk as its Midland Division, before moving himself on to greener financial and political pastures.

[5]It should be added that the Provincial Board of Health was expressing growing doubts about the accuracy of some local statistics, compiled and sent in by local authorities.

[6]An interesting overview and assessment of agriculture and housing in Emily in 1881 will be found in the Report of the Ontario Agricultural Commission 1881, (Appendix B), of which a summary is given in Appendix XXIII.

[7]These prizelists are faded and fragile, but if possible part of one will be reproduced as an illustration.

[8]This interesting list of Emily people who bought Atlases is found in Appendix XXIV.

[9]The 1890 edition of this Directory had a few changes: DOWNEYVILLE: popul. 85; J. R. Reid, cheese factory; Hanna Tracey, postmistress and general stores; FRANK HILL: popul. 105; Chris Lowes, postmaster; B. Mitchell, blacksmith; KING'S WHARF: popul. 50; J. C. Leary, postmaster and general store; OMEMEE: popul. 850; 52 tradesmen and officials, &c. listed, from J. E. Adams, grocer, to the Windsor Hotel, proprietor Sam. English.

[10]Ormond Ruby: "Radio's First Voice—the Story of Reginald Fessenden" Toronto 1970.

[11]Herbert Streater, born 1880 in England, served in the Boer War 1900-1902 and then emigrated to Canada in 1903; he farmed and operated a rural telephone system in Saskatchewan until retirement in 1939, and from 1951 lived until recently on con. 3, Emily. Mr. Streater was a talented amateur artist, and some of his pictures are preserved in Emily homes; he died Nov. 17, 1973, in his 94th year, and was buried in Emily Cemetery.

PEDIGREE OF THE PURE BRED
SUFFOLK PUNCH STALLION

"TUMBREL"

No. 2608, in the Suffolk Stud Book
Of England.

Color, Chestnut ; Foaled May 26 h, 1895, owned by Mossom
Boyd Co., Bobcaygeon.

SIRED BY DUKE OF THORNDALE (2278), a son of Cross' Invader (2508),
and out of Vanity (1630) by Cupbearer 3rd (566).

Dam Violet (3656) bred by A. Pratt, Chillesford, Suffolk, England, and
Sired by Pratt's Duke (1576). Grand dam Depper by Barne's
Vunwick (73.)

ROUTE FOR 1900.

MONDAY
From Bobcaygeon to Nicholas Tully's, Lot 6, Con. 7, Verulam,
for noon ; thence to John Bell's, Blacksmith, Dunsford for night.

TUESDAY
To Alexander Clarke's, Lot 28, Con. 10, Ops, for noon ; thence
Central House, Lindsay for night.

WEDNESDAY
South from Lindsay to David McMann's, Reaboro, for noon ;
thence to Daniel Wynn's, Lot 2, Con. 8, Emily, for night.

THURSDAY
From Daniel Wynn's north along the east boundary of Ops and
east along the line between the 12th and 13th Con. of Emily, to
Thomas Harrington's, Lot 6, Con. 12, Emily, for noon ; thence south
to Patrick Maloney's, Downeyville, for night.

FRIDAY
From Downeyville east to the middle line of Emily, and north to
John Corbett's, Lot 7, Con. 14, Emily, for noon ; thence northeast
to Joseph Hunter's, on the boundary between Emily and Verulam,
for night.

SATURDAY
North on Peterboro road to Mossom Boyd Co's farm, Bobcaygeon
for noon ; and to Reid House, Bobcaygeon, for the afternoon.

——TERMS :——

TERMS:—To insure a foal, $8.00, to be paid February 1st 1901. Mares
must be returned regularly. Parties disposing of their mares will
be charged insurance whether in foal or not. All accidents to
mares at owner's risk.

THOMAS O'NEILL, Groom.

Bob. Ind. Presses.

Stallion Route through Emily township 1900. (Boyd Records)

Part III: Modern Emily
(1900-1973)

WAR AND DEPRESSION (1900-1939)

Again in this period the simple census figures for Emily population give a misleading first impression—1901: 2,304; 1911: 2,121; 1921: 1,888; 1931: 1,882; 1941: 1,520. Through the forty years the average family remained just about 5 persons; but young people, finding it increasingly difficult or unsatisfactory to marry and settle on an Emily farm, found few other local jobs available except a few tradesmen, teachers, store clerks etc. Many found a solution in a job under city lights, where for girls as well as youths teaching, nursing, secretarial and factory work promised a more alluring and prosperous social life. For young men, a trip to war in Europe, or a harvesting excursion to the prairie wheatfields, or a job in the automobile plants of the United States, held exciting prospects, and from these quite a number never returned to Emily, except a rare visit back to the homestead. The local assessment statistics give a different picture of Emily, and help to explain the above problems which will be described more fully later; while property assessment about doubled in this 40 years, county and township taxes rose sixfold, to provide all the new comforts and amenities—trained teachers and better schools, improved roads with wire fences, telephones and electricity, health services, etc.—which seemed so necessary to meet modern living conditions:

EMILY:	1900	1910	1920	1930	1940
Population:[1]	2051	1854	1809	1651	1546
Ratepayers:	848	779	733	1077	1222
Assessment: (before equalization)					
	$951,743	$1,642,591	$1,622,955	$1,619,200	$1,502,306
Taxes levied: (township and county)					
	$9,909.32	$12,939.62	$34,207.57	$51,439.54	$39,047.00

Emily began the 20th century with William Adams as Reeve. The township officials were: R. J. Grandy, clerk, salary $185.00 a year; W. H. Curry, treasurer, salary $85.00; Charles Corneil, tax collector, salary $85.00; William Patrick, assessor, salary $50.00; Dr. George Cameron, medical health officer, salary $6.00; Wm. Lehane and Wm. Hooper, auditors, salary $6.00 each, per year. There were also 93 pathmasters (who were also fence-viewers) and 14 pound-keepers—the latter charged fees, but otherwise all were unsalaried.[2] The Reeve was not on County Council at that time, due to the strange temporary procedure by which the Council consisted of 2 representatives from each of 6 Divisions—the nearest County Councillors were Thomas McQuade of Omemee and William Switzer of Fowler's Corners. These officials represented as best they could the interests of the population, especially the 845 ratepayers from whose real, business and personal property they collected sufficient taxes to satisfy the county levy, and (with the aid of grants) to maintain highways and bridges, keep the schools operating, guard the safety and morals of the residents and passersby, license all peddlers and auctioneers, and in general keep a fatherly eye on the township, as their predecessors had been doing since the first township council in 1850. The township councillors were unpaid, and in those simple days could provide reasonably efficient local government by meeting 2 or 3 times a year; this job, like those of pathmasters, poundkeepers, school trustees, etc., was a community service that many Emily residents undertook as a matter of course for several decades.

The township started the new century in healthy financial condition. At Jan. 1, 1900, assets were $943, and liabilities $713 (outstanding debentures). Receipts in 1900 totalled $14,376 (of which $10,087 from municipal and school taxes), while disbursements were $13,914, consisting of: salaries, etc. $769, other municipal expenses $80, roads and bridges $5,563, charities $201, county levy $2,590, schools and education $4,459, debenture redeemed $90, interest on loans $29, miscellaneous $133. Next year the provincial auditor found township finances in good shape, with tax rate 8 mills (exclusive of school rates), and added "The Treasurer has been in office 15 years and receives a salary of $90 per annum."

One final vestige of Victorian Emily should be mentioned before going on to the problems of the automobile age. In 1901 Emily Council passed by-law 307, with stringent regulations "for prevention of vice and maintenance of good order" to enforce (1) no work or trade or sale on Sundays except of necessity and charity; (2) no placards, pictures, etc. on any wall or fence or sidewalk or other public place, nor any act of indecency in public; (3) no drunkenness, obscene language, blasphemy, etc. calculated to lead to a breach of the peace, in any public place; no immoral, violent or disorderly conduct; no loitering or vagrancy around house, stable, shed, public highway, etc.; (4) no bathing in waters within the township "without a proper bathing-dress"; (5) no beating or abusing of animals, shooting or destroying any small birds, or other cruelty to animals, etc.; (6) no injury to shrubs, trees or plants in public places, nor any other destruction to public property; (7) no person to lease, occupy, use, operate or employ for "a horse stand" any premises not enclosed and protected entirely from public view, likewise "any occupation, performances and exhibitions therein." Conviction for a first offence was fined $20 and costs. These regulations were perhaps more directed at the growing numbers of gypsies on the roads and tramps on the railways, than at the local young people of the community.

Road maintenance, improvement and traffic were a major problem of the township officials and a tax burden—even with provincial subsidies and county takeover of some main roads; about $1,500 was spent on township roads in 1900, and by 1930 this was $15,000, falling slowly in the depression years to $8,035 in 1939 and $6,764 in 1940. On top of this, the county levied in Emily for county roads sums almost as high in early years; in 1920: $7,047, in 1930: $8,615, and in 1940: down to $5,200. In 1901 Council began granting a bonus of 20c a rod for erection of wire fences along roads, with no conditions of height, etc. specified.[3] Next year one of the last new roads was opened up, on concession line between Con. 5 and 6,

EMILY

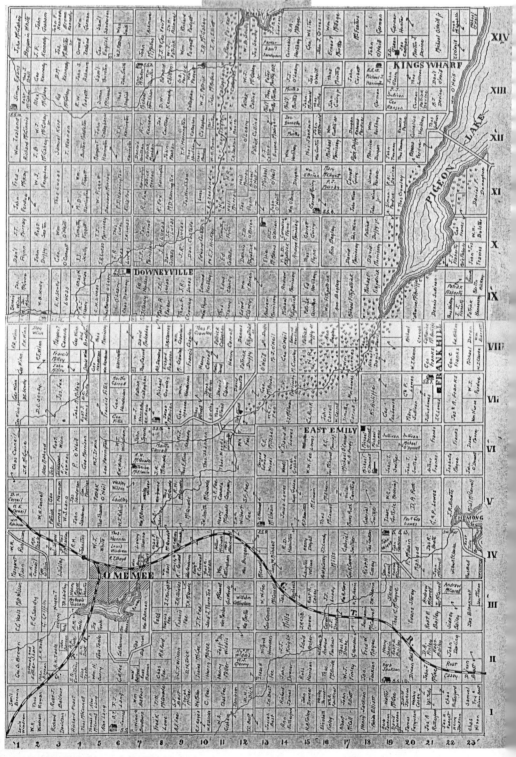

Map of Emily about 1910, showing lot-owners, post offices, rail lines and roads.

opposite lots 9 and 10, to the point where it ran into Pigeon River, and to be 66 feet wide. One of the growing perils of "progress" appeared in Oct. 1904 when Andrew Wilson claimed damages when his horse was frightened by wires (telegraph or telephone) lying on an Emily road, which tangled in his wheels and caused a runaway. By 1907 the "improvement" of Buckhorn and Bobcaygeon dams flooded the Emily Creek marsh in north Emily, making the road impassable. Council in March 1908 "view with alarm the frequency and increasing passage to and fro over roads of this municipality by automobiles at an excessive rate of speed and the consequent increased liability to accidents caused in the frightening of horses and otherwise . . . protests the use of public roads by said automobiles against the interest of the farming community both financially and otherwise . . . to request that legislation be introduced to prohibit the use of said automobiles on the province's highways"—this had about the effect of King Canute ordering the ocean waves to stop rolling in!

Yet the anti-auto feeling was widespread—Victoria County Council, which in 1905 had begun planning a road system, including some stretches in Emily, sent a petition to the Ontario government in 1908 stating "that roads built at the expense and toil of rural residents are no longer open to their free use owing to the dangers arising from frequent use by owners or drivers of motor vehicles. Horses that could formerly be safely driven by women or children are now unsafe for their use and they are deprived of this means of going to church, school or market, (and) prevented from visiting relatives and friends at any distance from home . . . that the use of roads by motorists on Sundays is almost wholly for pleasure and should not be encouraged or permitted at church-going time, if at all . . . that markets in many towns and villages and supplying thereof with produce largely brought in by farmers' wives are seriously affected by fears of meeting with motor vehicles." They requested that it be illegal to operate motor vehicles on Sundays and at least one other day each week, "ensuring the public from one of the greatest dangers that confronts it in rural parts at the present time."

In 1909 Emily adjusted the statute labour of ratepayers—1 day for assessment up to $100, 2 days for $100 to $400, 3 days for $400 to $800, 4 days for $800 to $1,400, 5 days for $1,400 to $2,200, 6 days for $2,200 to $2,700, and one day extra for every additional $1,000. Next year Reeve Charles Corneil and councillor Robert Wilson were paid $2 a day each to supervise a special grant for construction of a roadway over or around Sanderson's Hill on concession 6. In 1911 Council submitted a claim to the federal government "for damages to the public roads especially in concessions 10 to 14 by the raising of the waters of Emily Creek and Pigeon River . . . consequent upon the raising of Trent Canal Waters"; a Commissioner appeared to judge the damage, and Council accepted the award of $1,975 from the federal government, much of it for a raised roadway across Emily Creek marsh on con. 14. By 1914 the Ontario Public Works Department, convinced of the need to help rural areas to meet the dangers of motor traffic, requested a plan of Emily showing "about 27 miles of the most important market roads and an equal mileage of roads of secondary importance" to which the province might contribute money for widening and improvement; they stipulated, however, that their aid was contingent on the township appointing a road superintendent; the province would pay a quarter of his salary, and provide financial aid through the county road system. The Department of Highways by 1916 was also applying pressure on Victoria County to set up a County Road system to prepare for heavy postwar automobile, truck and bus traffic, and by Bylaw 783 Victoria did this for the southern townships (south of the north border of Eldon, Fenelon and Verulam).

In 1918 Emily fixed statute labour commutation at $1.25 a day, if paid before June 1, and $1.50 a day thereafter. Council appointed a committee to work with an Ops committee to improve the boundary road opposite con. 4, Emily, "where automobile accidents have been frequent lately." In Feb. 1920 Patrick Duffy complained that the loop line from con. 10 to 11 known as Begley's Road had been blocked by snow for weeks, stopping mail deliveries, school attendance, etc., and demanded council take action. Few ratepayers were commuting their statute labour (32 in 1918, including the Grand Trunk and Bell Telephone, but only 18 in 1919), and so Council in 1920 raised the commutation rate to $1.75 a day; Council also doubled the wire fence bonus to 40c a rod along public roads, and many farmers took advantage of it, thus causing the disappearance of long stretches of split rail, stake and stump fences.

The 1912 *Official Automobile Road Guide of Central Canada* advised adventurous tourists on safe roads to travel by car; to get from Lindsay to Peterborough they proposed the road from Lindsay to Bobcaygeon, and down through Ennismore; also a trip was suggested from Port Hope to Omemee—"road good all the way, gravel and clay." The 1920 *Guide* included the Port Hope-Omemee route in the same words, but recommended the Lindsay-Omemee-Peterborough road as being safe, provided motorists did not wander off onto swampy, hilly narrow sideroads! The 1925 *Dunlop Trail for the Motorist* was more venturesome, showing car-roads on a map: (1) Omemee north via Dunsford to Bobcaygeon; (2) Lindsay via Reaboro to Omemee, easterly via Fowler's Corners to Peterboro; (3) Ida via Mt. Pleasant northwest a few miles east of Omemee, and northward to Pigeon Lake; it also recommended spots where "fine views can be taken in from the automobile seat"—Dancey's and Sandy's Hills just west of Omemee, near Hog's Back Road, Crawford's Hill just east of Omemee, and another near Fowler's Corners.

Victoria in 1921 launched a massive County Roads programme, levying over $85,000 that year, of which Emily had to pay $9,062.21, and appointing an engineer and road superintendent. The county committee declared "roads are much more important than railways or canals for local traffic", and estimated that road traffic in Victoria was: 50% from farm to town and return, 30% from town to town, and 20% through traffic. In Emily, Crawford's Hill near Omemee was cut down to make a better Lindsay-Peterborough road (no. 41), and two "DANGER" signs were installed in Emily on it. Work was also done on Kelly's Hill on road no. 5 (lot 7, con. 12)—in all,

orse and Cutter, John Sanderson, Sr., in 1916
(H. Jackson)

Horse and Buggy, c. 1920
(Stanley O'Neill)

Model T. Ford of 1920
(W. McMullen)

Model T. Ford of 1914
(Lockhart Wright)

Snow at the Orange Corners in 1960
(H. Jackson)

Snow Plough in 1930 — (W. McMullen)

ROAD TRANSPORTATION

the county was now improving 31.6 miles of road in Emily; the county paid
wire fence bonuses in 1921 to Emily residents: T. Mitchell, lot 14, con. 4;
Geo. Carew, lot 19, con. 4; T. Morrisey, lot 5, con. 10; Jas. Courtney, lots
5 and 6, con. 14; Jos. Smith, lot 6, con. 13; Chester Best, lot 12, con. 1; and
many more in years following. Sums of $200 each were spent in 1922 by the
county on the Emily-Cavan road, no. 5A concession 14 road, and road no. 3
east quarter line; and larger amounts on main roads—Lindsay to Downeyville
nearly $5,000, Omemee to Dunsford nearly $4,500. But the most interesting
county project in 1922 was a traffic census on July 26th on all county roads
7 a.m. to 7 p.m., including the following in Emily:

ROAD NO.	LOCATION lot con.		HORSEDRAWN VEHICLES 1 horse	2 horses	MOTOR VEHICLES Passenger Cars	Trucks	TOTAL NO. VEHICLES
41	(18	3) and (3 3)	38	16	137	10	201
3	19	6	6	11	18	6	41
4	5	11	5	7	18	10	40
5	(7	5) and (7 13)	31	14	86	13	144
5A	7	14	6	26	8	2	42
6	13	2	22	11	29	3	65
			108	85	296	44	533
			193 (36.2%)		340 (63.8%)		

There were two observation-posts on the main highways nos. 41 and 5—on
these the motor traffic was especially heavy; on only one road, 5A, was
horse-drawn traffic heavier.[4]

In three years up to 1923, the county spent $11,645.72 on Crawford's
Hill, lot 9, con. 4, Emily, "previously a rough gravel hill winding through
a ravine which formed a water-course . . . rough and crooked", now reduced
to a 7% grade and straightened. The township in 1922 opened the con. 3 road
west across the old rail line to Pigeon River, and next year set road wages at
30c an hour for a man, or 50c an hour for man and team. Next year the
township refused to pay two claims: a Millbrook man sought $15 damages
"caused by a fallen tree across the road near the farms of W. Herlihey and
E. Madigan", and another motorist asked $10.50 for a broken spring "caused
by a defective bridge opposite the premises of Simon Connell." Again by
1925 a traffic-count showed traffic had increased 2 or 3 times on county roads
and even more on provincially-financed highways like no. 41 Lindsay to
Peterborough; it is worth noting that this July count found one car in every
hundred to be from the United States. The county road superintendent com-

mented "Within 25 years the motor car has revolutionized roads and in itself has grown from an eccentric luxury to a vehicle of necessity in everyday life." Emily Council chose this year to abolish all statute labour, since the commutation at $1.75 a day was not used by more than 12 or 15 ratepayers, and amateur road-workers were no longer satisfactory; roads were from now on paid out of taxes, and machinery purchased or rented—Thomas Rowan contracted at 85c an hour to furnish tractor-power for rock crushing. The road superintendents for the township were: 1925 John McGuire; 1926-31 Chas. Lucas; 1931-33 Chas. Mills; 1934-37 W. Lloyd Boate; 1939 on, Walter Herlihey. Duffy's Hill on the middle road from con. 8 to 9 was to be cut "sufficiently wide to allow two cars to pass", and on other roads old log culverts and swampy stretches were to be filled with stone, and iron culverts where necessary, ditches cleared out, roads widened and gravelled.

On June 22, 1927, the province assumed ownership of the Lindsay-Peterborough road as a provincial highway, and Emily reminded them that the Omemee section was in very bad repair. The county road report that year noted that in 10 years the county had paid bonuses for 131 miles of wire fences (of which about 25 miles in Emily), and that the time was come to test snow-fences at points where snow drifted badly, such as 400 feet on lot 6, con. 12 in Emily, over Kelly's Hill; "the time is rapidly approaching when we will be obliged to keep our main roads open for motor traffic for the convenience of the travelling public." He stated that horse-drawn sleds, with runners about 3 feet apart, could operate on snowy back roads, but motor cars had a width of 4 feet 8½ inches, and could not navigate on icy winter roads. He also remarked that in 5 years horse-drawn traffic had dropped to half, while light cars had increased over 100% and motor trucks even more. Among accidents listed in 1928 was one on con. 13, Emily, when the cars of R. Lough and John Harrington collided, bending axles and fenders. Next year the county road-gang repaired a well dug about 1871 "for the use of the travelling public and threshing etc. at northwest corner of the junction of county road no. 7 and township road at Downeyville, adjacent to the south half lot 6, con. 10, Emily." In Nov. 1930 the county was billed for another accident, on road no. 7, at con. 5, when E. P. Jackson's car hit some loose stone, turned over and burned up.

Road wages on the Emily roads in 1931, early in the depression, were 25c an hour for a man, and 40c for man with team. Three claims for broken car springs (from $2.87 to $3.70) were approved, one on the middle road, one on con. 14, and one on the Ops-Emily boundary near con. 7. The county was cutting down the hills on con. 2 (road no. 12) and grading on road no. 7, in 1932, mostly relief work, and the Canadian Legion was urging county and township councils to give priority to war veterans in all jobs. A petition from 51 Emily ratepayers asked Council to allow voters to decide on reverting to statute labour "as many ratepayers are unable to raise sufficient funds by taxation for road upkeep"—this was done, but in 1934 statute labour was abolished again since provincial and federal relief schedules paid 80% of work under the Highway Improvement Act, but not as statute labour. In 1932

also the Canadian National Railway asked Emily Council to allow removal
of cattle-guards at all rail crossings, and to have no responsibility for keeping
them repaired, since cattle were no longer being driven to market by road,
or allowed to pasture along roads; next year 54 ratepayers petitioned for
amendment of Bylaw 191 to ban all herding of cattle on Emily roads, and
Council complied. Road wages were now down to 17c an hour for a man,
19c-20c for a man on the stone-crusher, and 35c for man and team, working
9 hours a day; in winter roadwork shovelling snow was even lower, 10c an
hour for a man, 20c for a man and team. The county road report noted accidents up 3-fold or more due to heavier traffic, and poorer maintenance of
roads and cars—county road wages were slightly higher: foremen 35c an
hour, labourers 20c, man and team 40c, waterboy 12½c an hour; J. A.
Elliott was maintenance foreman of county roads in Emily, and in 1934 the
gangs graded Knight's Hill on road no. 12, Flynn's swamp on road no. 17,
etc. In Oct. 1935 Emily Council petitioned the Ontario Highways Department for "an electric signal at C.N.R. crossing 2 miles east of Omemee,
where there had been 3 bad accidents in 3 months."

It is interesting to compare with the 1922 traffic census described a
few pages back, another count taken on county roads in Emily on Aug. 14,
1936, from 7 a.m. to 7 p.m. when the totals were 15 one-horse vehicles, 12
two-horse vehicles, 500 automobiles, and 123 trucks; in spite of the depression, total traffic had increased, and now 96.6% was motorized. After again
introducing statute labour when some ratepayers could not pay taxes, and
abolishing it once more, Emily Council in 1937 compromised by allowing
any ratepayer to work out a 3-mill rate on his assessment by road maintenance
and construction; in 1938 a sum equal to 2 mills on assessment was to be
devoted to roads in Emily, and could be worked out at the option of the ratepayer; also road wages were raised to 25c an hour for a man, 45c for man
with team; on winter snow-shovelling 15c an hour or 25c for man with
team; a man with truck was given $1.00 an hour—this is the first mention
of trucks in roadwork. In 1927 the C.N.R. had applied to abandon the
Millbrook-Omemee branch line, and Emily Council had cannily agreed providing the railway gave back part of the bonus Emily had paid when the line
was built (but they received nothing, naturally); now in 1939 Emily Council
petitioned the Ontario government to build a highway along the old rail-line
from Omemee as far as Bethany. The county road superintendent in 1940
recommended replacing old wooden culverts by cement ones along Emily
roads, and improving the gravel road north from Omemee by a "bituminous
surface"—the latter step was not taken for two decades, unfortunately; the
wire bonus of 40c a rod was extended to replacing old wire fences also,
providing they were over 25 years old. The Ontario Highways Department
and the Canada Postoffice were still urging Emily to improve winter road
conditions, by insisting that farms along main roads take down rail fences
which caused snow-drifting, and erect wire fences; it was said the worst drifted
roads were on the Emily-Ops boundary north of V. O'Connell's farm, and
the road from Frank Hill School north near the Franks farm. Each month also

council received several claims from motorists whose cars were damaged by bad roads, but now these were turned over to the insurance company which handled township road claims.

Railways have been mentioned above, and the deterioration of rail service after 1900 irritated Omemee and Emily Councils and residents greatly. In 1907 Emily Council backed Omemee to protest "the shameful and inefficient railway depot & shipping facilities thrust by the Grand Trunk on Omemee & Emily residents and the travelling public, by running trains through said village yet compelling passengers to traverse 1½ miles out to board trains as well as conveyance of freight a similar distance"; finally in 1908 the Board of Railway Commissioners ordered the G.T.R. to build a station at Sturgeon St. crossing in Omemee. Local people welcomed the rumour, in the Peterborough 'Times' in Oct. 1909, that the C.P.R. was considering a Georgian Bay branch to join their main line at Peterborough, which would pass northwest through Emily, and compete with the G.T.R. Midland division for long-distance grain-trade as well as local service, but unfortunately this scheme never materialized. In 1931 the Canadian National (which had absorbed the Grand Trunk and other lines) notified Emily Council of their plan to erect a flag station at McCague's Crossing east of Omemee, especially for loading milk enroute to Toronto, and area farmers found this a convenience. However, by abandoning branch-lines, refusing to mark dangerous crossings, letting cattle-guards deteriorate, and cutting down passenger schedules, the railway lost most of its popularity among local people, especially during the depression years. Automobiles, buses and trucks transported people (as individuals and on excursions) and freight and produce with increasing safety, reliability and cheapness.

Trade and travel by waterway declined even more quickly and completely after 1900, and bridges over the streams gave endless trouble due to heavier motor traffic. In 1900 Emily delegates asked Victoria to help finance a high-level steel bridge "to permit passage of steamers" at Cowan's, but the county instead gave $700 to help repair the old bridge. Then in 1905 Emily asked the Dominion government to send an engineer to survey and estimate Pigeon River "so that the same will be navigable by boats from the Trent Valley Canal back as far as possible through said waters. . . ." Williamson in his *Omemee* has the story from the Lindsay *Post* of May 31, 1907, about a Trent Canal delegation sailing from Bobcaygeon on steamer "Sovereign" on Victoria Day up Pigeon Creek, stopped 3 miles from Omemee since Cowan's Bridge was "not high enough, being only 18 feet above the water, whereas an overhead bridge should be 30. . . ." They were taken on up to Omemee by gasoline launch and given a luncheon, where Superintendent McClellan was optimistic about dredging a 6-foot channel cleared of weeds, promising it would be done that year, a promise not fulfilled. In 1908 Emily Council pressured the Department through Senator McHugh of Lindsay to aid in constructing a causeway across Emily Creek marsh, to supplement an Ontario grant of $2,000 for this—the length was about a mile, on concession 13. Victoria Council also petitioned for federal aid to extend

Shipping milk to Toronto from Carmagner about 1930— Wm. Fife and A. Jackson on wagon. (Harry Jackson)

Train wreck 2 miles east of Omemee—1940. One man killed

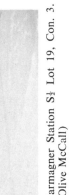

Carmagner Station S½ Lot 19, Con. 3. (Olive McCall)

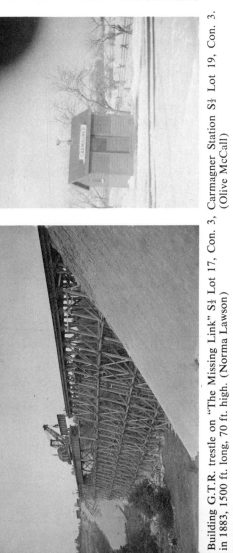

Building G.T.R. trestle on "The Missing Link" S½ Lot 17, Con. 3, in 1883, 1500 ft. long, 70 ft. high. (Norma Lawson)

Timber R.R. Bridge over Pigeon River

Construction on G.T.R. Omemee-Peterborough line 1882-83.

the causeway north into Verulam, since the new Bobcaygeon dam had raised Sturgeon Lake levels; a second county petition stated: "Pigeon River which flows through Emily is a tributary of the Trent Valley Canal . . . at the road between con. 6 and 7 the river for many years was crossed on a low bridge known as Cowan's with a swing portion for steamer passage . . . about 1891 the timber bridge fell into decay and a new one with concrete piers and steel superstructure, high enough to allow steam vessels to pass under, was built with government contributions; this is required to be raised now as the Canal raises water levels, to permit navigation to Omemee; that Emily is burdened with its maintenance, and the government is asked to take this over."

Pigeon Creek Floating Bridge also was troublesome; in 1910 Mr. Sherman claimed damages when his horse went through the bridge and was killed, and Victoria and Peterborough counties each gave him $50 in compensation. In 1911 came the settlement by which the Dominion paid Emily $1,975 for township roads flooded by higher water-levels. In 1912 Father P. McGuire of Downeyville backed the township request for Dominion aid in building the Emily Marsh causeway by a letter to Hon. Frank Cochrane, Minister of Railways and Canals, claiming that the former minister had agreed to match the Ontario grant of $2,000; this $2,000 had been all paid out, and many who worked on the project had not yet been paid; this was backed by a petition signed by nearly 100 north Emily residents, and a neat map of the area,[5] repeating: "by reason of the flat nature of the land along Emily Creek, this has made the width of the swamp on the line between con. 13 and 14 about one mile, the stream itself being about 40 ft. wide. On either side is a good settlement, the King's Wharf postoffice being on east side of creek; the village of Dunsford through which a Canadian Pacific Branch runs is about 5 miles distant . . . the estimate of cost to complete the road across creek and drowned land is about $6,000."

A Trent Canal official reported in 1913 that the bridge, built by Wm. Kennedy in 1911, cost $1,234.82, being of wooden piles about 240 ft. long, and a further $765.18 in 1912 on approaches, using up the Ontario grant; another $1,871.02 had been spent by county and township which they wanted paid by the Dominion; however, he insisted no major change had occured in Sturgeon Lake level between 1881 and 1912. The Dominion capitulated by giving $2,000 in 1913, and next year paid more private flood claims in Emily—Charles Corneil $40; John McMullen $51; James McGahey $37.50; Thomas Harrington $33; Wesley Brown $37.50; Bernice Pogue $23.25; David Boyd $25.50; H. Thurston $21; Joseph Herlihey $24; J. A. Elliott $112.30, etc. Earlier, in autumn 1912, a Canal crew came up the Pigeon River with tug towing a scow, and put log booms around some of the worst floating bogs which impeded boat travel; but within a few years the winter storms and ice carried these away. Even in 1936 the Department of Railways and Canals was receiving claims for damage along Emily and Pigeon Creeks, but was refusing to pay more.

In 1918 the county agreed to make Cowan's Bridge a county respons-

Map and part of list of petitioners accompanying Father McGuire's letter of Dec. 3, 1912, to Hon. Frank Cochrane, Minister of Railways & Canals, asking Dominion aid for Emily Creek Bridge on con. 14. (Trent file RG 43 (B2) vol.135, Public Archives of Canada)

Looking East on bridge.

Emily Creek Bridge (Con. 14) built in 1912 (H. Pammett)

Pigeon Lake Floating Bridge, c. 1910
(H. Flood)

Log Bridge west of Downeyville about
1932, with Emily Council — P. Lowes,
P. McGuire, H. Jackson, H. Endicott,
W. Patrick (Hilda Jackson)

Present dam built by Miller family —
S½ Lot 6, Con. 1, c. 1960 (M. Miller)

Lebanon Dam and saw mill — S½ Lot 6,
Con. 1, before 1900 (E. Connell)

ibility, paying 60% of expenses if the township would pay 40%. Next year Emily urged the county "now that the war is practically over", to memorialize the Dominion government for a new bridge to replace Pigeon Creek Floating Bridge "which structure has fallen into decay and is at present impassable and a serious hindrance to traffic between the two counties". The county complied, and in its petition pointed out that the floating bridge had been built by the two counties about 50 years earlier, 1⅛ miles long, "to foster trade between the town of Peterborough and the northern portions of the counties ... that the present structure has fallen into serious decay. ..." The Dominion refused to help, abandoning the Pigeon channel entirely as a steamer route. The County Warden in his opening address in 1921 said that one important project was the improvement or rebuilding of Cowan's Bridge: "The closing of Pigeon Creek Floating Bridge has again brought the road over Cowan's into prominence as the highway from northern districts toward the city of Peterborough", and council noted that traffic at Cowan's Bridge had doubled and trebled since the Floating Bridge farther north had been closed. Emily in 1923 received its bill for major repairs on Cowan's Bridge, its 40% being $1,132.87, and tried to persuade the county to take over Emily Bridge as a county bridge.

Emily in 1925 again petitioned the Dominion government "that in view of the fact a number of summer resorts, boarding houses and cottages have been erected on Pigeon River between Omemee and Pigeon Lake to provide accommodation for tourists, now frequenting these waters for fishing, and with the object of largely increasing the influx of said tourists ... that the booms installed by the Dominion in 1912 to boom the floating bogs were now disconnected releasing the bogs and rendering navigation quite difficult on said river, sometimes blocking same altogether ... that steps be taken to remedy the present condition and render navigation thereon more feasible than at present"; however, this fell on deaf ears like the proposal to replace the Floating Bridge. Undaunted, Emily sent delegates in 1928 with a large district delegation to Ottawa to promote extension of the Trent Canal System, with improvements down to Lake Scugog, and the Pigeon River to Omemee, and a proposed new bridge across Chemong Lake to replace its floating bridge, also now worn out. Then in 1936 County Council agreed to take over Emily Marsh Bridge on con. 14, Emily, with 100 ft. of approaches at each end, with cost of repairs or rebuilding to be 60% county, 40% township. Waterway traffic was gone from Emily, and road traffic was predominant in future. We will note later something of the recreational, sporting and tourist life along Emily streams which were encouraged by growing use of motorboats and motorcars as other river traffic subsided.

In the year ending June 30, 1906, the Postoffice report listed mail contracts as follows in Emily: Downeyville and Omemee—Bart. Downey contractor, 6 weekly, fee $160 per annum; Ennismore and Frank Hill—C. Lowes contractor, once weekly, fee $70 per annum; Omemee to Rail Station (1½ miles)—W. J. Lamb for 9 months at $150.40, and L. Hayes for 3 months at $49.92 the contractors, 24 times weekly. The 1910 Postal Guide listed 4 postoffices in Emily: *Downeyville* with Henry Matthews postmaster, empowered to issue postal notes; *Omemee* with Richard Grandy postmaster, empowered as postoffice savings bank, and to issue money orders and postal notes; *King's Wharf* with James Leary postmaster, empowered to issue postal notes; and *Frank Hill* with John C. Lowes postmaster; we might also include *Fowler's Corners* in Smith, with Robert Maitland postmaster, empowered to issue postal notes. Later, on March 18, 1910, another postoffice was established at *East Emily,* with M. O'Donnell postmaster. However, in May 1913 rural mail delivery routes were set up in Emily, and the East Emily postoffice was closed, likewise those at King's Wharf and Frank Hill effective July 31, 1914.

One quarrel blew up in Feb. 1913 over the new rural mail delivery, when Lindsay merchants attempted to have all South Victoria mail routes start from Lindsay, which would be good for business; Emily Council vigorously opposed this, pointing out that Postal Inspector Smith had approved two Emily rural routes starting from Omemee and Downeyville postoffices, which was much preferred locally. However, since 1913 R.R.1, Dunsford route, serves the eastern part of con. 14, and R.R.3, Lindsay, serves the northwest, west of the quarterline, where until modern times the drifting snow along rail-fenced roads, and the icy flooded marsh-roads in springtime, caused much trouble and delay to the patient hard-working mail-carriers.

This meant a great increase in volume of mail and parcel-post, since it was now delivered to each property-owner's mailbox on his driveway; mail order business to companies like Eaton's and Simpson's increased tenfold by 1930. The only postoffices left in Emily were at Omemee and Downeyville—at the latter, Henry Matthews became postmaster July 1, 1901; James Guiry Feb. 28, 1917; P. J. Lucas July 1, 1921; Mrs. Lillie Lucas Nov. 8, 1922; Vincent O'Connell July 2, 1944; George O'Donnell March 7, 1945; Mrs. Mary O'Donnell Aug. 27, 1952; James Kirley Oct. 1, 1955 (acting) and Mrs. O'Donnell again from Nov. 16, 1955. The district postal superintendent pressured Emily Council periodically to improve township roads, especially in winter; for example, in Nov. 1927 he said the mailman on R.R.1, Downeyville complained that parts of the road between concessions 9 and 10 were very bad and unfit to travel, and unless they were improved the department would discontinue mail delivery in that area. The rural postmasters of earlier decades, who provided mail service for a minute annual salary, and the rural mail deliverymen who now toured the back roads from postoffices at Omemee, Downeyville, Dunsford, etc., 6 days a week in all weather and seasons, using buggy, sleigh, or the modern "flivver", deserved more reward and appreciation for their hard anonymous work than they ever received, locally or nationally. In many isolated areas, the mailman was often a life-saver, bringing medicines and groceries from town with the mail, and taking letters and messages back with him from all parts of his route.

Electric power came to Omemee in 1907, when the Stephenson Mill installed a dynamo from the mill-dam producing direct current for use in the mill, and contracted to light 300 bulbs along the streets and in a few buildings for evening hours up to 11 or 12 p.m. In Sept. 1911 Isaac Fee was appointed by Emily Council to supervise installation of poles and appliances along township roads by the Central Ontario Power Company, and in the next May the company was given permission to erect a "switching station and operation house" on the east quarter-line just south of the G.T.R. line—however, little more was heard of this project, and it is doubtful whether the company provided any electric power through the neighbourhood, especially as all electric equipment and machinery was then primitive, costly and unreliable. Even earlier, in 1906, the Ontario Hydro-electric Power Commission had been organized by Sir Adam Beck and others to bring low-cost electricity from Niagara to Southern Ontario; Beck was concerned to lighten the burdens of farm labour by encouraging production of electrically-operated farm equipment, powered by inexpensive publicly-produced power, and the Commission launched an extensive farm-electrification programme in 1921. By 1920 Hydro transmission lines came north from Port Hope to Omemee, Lindsay and Fenelon. Some towns and villages (such as Peterborough and Bobcaygeon) had local electricity companies, but in the 1930s the Commission absorbed most of these and the Hydro power-grid connected nearly all Kawartha urban centres. On Sept. 2, 1930, Reeve Ashmore and Clerk Grandy signed for Emily an agreement with H.E.P.C. by which Hydro was to supply, construct and install all equipment along township roads, to deliver "electrical power or energy" to the roadway near each customer, to operate, maintain, repair and insure electric service, to render bills to customers at fixed rates, to keep accounts of all such monies and report annually to Emily Council. In the late 1930s, electricity was brought into East Emily from Peterborough via Ennismore. However, the exigencies of depression and world war prevented the spread of electric-power use in Emily, particularly on the rear concessions, until the 1950s.

Bell Telephone Company in 1904 set up a local Omemee exchange directed by T. A. McPherson, with 13 subscribers—in Omemee the Commercial and Bradburn Hotels, the Stephenson mill, two doctors (Cameron and Keith), Lamb's Tannery, the Grand Trunk Station, two grocery stores and a grain dealer, and S. Grandy's residence; the other two telephones were at Downeyville, in Rev. Bretherton's residence and in Matthews' General Store. By 1906 they had 4 more subscribers tapping into the line, Herbert Jackson and Henry Jackson in south Emily, and J. Stillman and Frank Fowler at Best's Station on the G.T.R., then in 1907 W. Swinton's residence in Emily. As mentioned previously, the telephone line ran along the telegraph line, which in turn ran on poles along the railway. Bylaw 346 in 1907 authorized the Dunsford Telephone, Light & Power Co-operative Association to place its poles, wires and equipment on Emily roads "to transmit messages, light and power . . . maintained so as to prevent injury to persons and public & private property." The Dunsford Company telephone lines were extended in 1907-8 across the west quarter-line and east on con. 14, the first subscribers being W. G. Ashmore, S. G. Sanderson, John McMullen, John Vout, J. A. McGahey, Alex Elliott, and Wm. J. Patrick; soon this line was extended across the west quarter-line and east on con. 13 to serve Thos. English, David Kennedy, Thos. Harrington, etc. In 1909 an independent Omemee Telephone Company was formed (connected with the Bell), and began with 18 customers in the area south to Mt. Pleasant and west into Ops township; Emily Council gave permission for erection of poles and wire along township roads. Up to 1916 only two more telephones had been installed in Emily, in the homes of John J. Magee and J. A. Rutherford, on the Bell exchange no. 531 with the Jacksons, Fowler, etc.—each subscriber had a separate number of rings, as on the later rural lines. Each telephone was "the mecca for people of the area wanting a doctor or in any other emergency", according to Mr. Harry Jackson.

In 1917, when Isaac Fee became local manager for the Omemee and Bell (long distance) lines, the Emily Municipal Telephone System was organized, to extend service through central Emily, supported by Emily Council, and with James Boate as commissioner (succeeded in 1918 by Calvin Mitchell). After a slow start, Bylaw 473 in March 1920 authorized issuance of debentures for construction and installation of the Emily Municipal Telephone System, the money was borrowed from the bank, and each year from 1921 on Emily taxes levied $3,243.57 to pay back the loan, plus maintenance costs (ranging $227, $345, $235, etc. annually); the system was owned by the Emily subscribers, who paid annual maintenance fee of $1 to $1.50 each, plus of course their share of the tax levy. In Sept. 1920 an agreement was signed with Bell Telephone Company to connect with Bell lines at Omemee, covering all long distance calls out of Omemee area. The Emily System spread rapidly, and in 1921 Bylaw 487 approved an extension to 22 Emily subscribers (including Simon O'Connell of south half lot 5, con. 13), plus one in Cavan and one in Ennismore; Bylaw 491 the same year approved extension to the above and another 10 subscribers, with debenture cost $3,663.58—these subscribers were on all concessions from 1 to 13. In 1923 Bylaw 510 approved extension to another 9 or 10 subscribers, and the system built up steadily at very moderate cost, since the Omemee switchboard was operated by Bell. There was some overlapping, since the Omemee (Bell) Company had a line to Downeyville, with its 2 subscribers there, and 2 more on the Bent farms north of Omemee; this was overcome when Bell in 1931 sold its Omemee Company to the Emily System, with all its poles, lines and equipment, and Emily by Bylaw 596 issued debentures to finance the purchase. The same year Bylaw 599 authorized extension of the telephone system into the northern part of the township.

Thus by May 1932, the Emily Telephone System covered all the township, and extended into Ennismore, Cavan, Ops and Manvers, and Bylaw 614 authorized a new debenture of $3,000 to provide improved service. The maintenance levy was now $2 per subscriber, as the number of telephones in the System was over 200. The Omemee switchboard was enlarged several times to handle calls, capably handled by Isaac Fee to 1940, and by his daughter Gladys who served at the switchboard for 40 years until her 1959 retirement. Miss Fee writes of those first decades: "My father secured a building and the switchboard was moved and ready Oct. 1, 1917. The first switchboard had a hanging mouthpiece, and when a signal came in the operator picked up the receiver, answered, then the subscriber put down the receiver while the operator rang by hand, then listened to see if the party called had answered. . . . The office was open from 7 a.m. to 9 p.m. . . . Fire alarms came under the operator's jurisdiction . . . she notified the fire department, then rang a fire alarm on all lines near where the fire was. . . . In early days the local doctors did not employ receptionists and if the wife was out the doctor asked the operator to take his calls. When people were in trouble we tried to give special service; we soon knew most voices as well as the lot and concession where they lived. The people we served were our neighbours and friends, so naturally we had an easygoing relationship with them. . . . We even gave the prices on livestock if the buyer wasn't at home. . . . By 1930 there were 197 Emily M.T.S. subscribers and 71 Omemee T. C. phones. . . . I was acting manager, chief operator, and bookkeeper, also was cashier for the Emily System for many years. . . ."

Doctors have been mentioned above, and this might be the place to list those who served Omemee and Emily in this period. Dr. Cameron moved away in 1906, but Dr. J. Thompson moved back and practiced 1904 to 1917. Dr. Keith (1902-07) and Dr. Sutton (1906-11), and Dr. Snelgrove (1907) had shorter terms in the area, but participated in local church and lodge activities. George Earle, who taught at S.S. 10 for a time around 1900, studied medicine and returned in 1912 as Dr. G. Earle, practicing until his death in 1954 (having been assisted by his son Bill 1945 on). Dr. Carmichael about 1930 and Dr. Montgomery (1938-40) stayed only a short time, finding it difficult in depression years to compete with the older established medical men. Williamson in his *Omemee* gives more particulars of these doctors, who are known to many hundreds in the district, many of whom were brought into the world by them, and later saved during serious illnesses. Like the mailmen, they went out by cutter or buggy on difficult back roads in the worst of weather to perform their duty, and for a low fee that was often unpaid in hard times; Dr. Earle even developed a Ford "flivver" on ski-runners (front) and tracks (back) to carry him over the snowdrifts—an early version of the snowmobile. Rev. Rowland, pastor of Trinity Church in the 1920s, told Mr. Harry Jackson a story about Dr. Earle worth preserving: "Dr. Earle phoned one evening and asked me to accompany him on a night call out among the Franklin hills. Bundled in furs and in a horse-drawn cutter we drove out, and the Doctor explained that the patient was suffering from pneumonia, and this night was the crisis, being the 9th day. Then he said "Ed, this man is very sick and I want you to pray and pray damned hard!" On arrival at the home I was introduced in the kitchen where prayers were offered to the Diety and further prayers in the sickroom for his recovery. We were all happy when the sick man recovered."

Concerning the Emily schools much information was contained in Inspector Knight's reports as reprinted in Victoria county records. In 1901 he noted: "At Orange Line in Emily a new frame schoolhouse has been erected in place of the former building accidentally destroyed by fire . . . an improvement on its predecessor." At this time Omemee High School had 73 pupils enrolled, being 33 boys and 40 girls, over half from surrounding farms, but average daily attendance was only 40 (in 1902); the principal of O.H.S. was Wm. Jardine, B.A., appointed 1898, salary $800, and the assistant Wm. Harvey, appointed 1903, salary $700. A new furnace was installed in the Omemee School in autumn, 1903, which overheated in the severe cold of February 1904 and burned the school down; when the village drew up ambitious plans for an enlarged school, the irate farmers of the Emily portion of the Union School Section threatened to withdraw if the new building cost over $6,000, and carried out their threat later. In 1905 Inspector Knight reported: "The trustees of S.S. no. 13, Emily, about 5 miles east of Omemee, are preparing to erect a new building a short distance south of the present school. It will be of brick with a basement for heating. . . . The public school in S.S. 4, Emily, has been closed . . ." Next year, he continued: "The trustees of S.S. 13, Emily, after planning a new schoolhouse and calling for tenders, found them apparently too high, and patched up the old school. . . . There are no public schools open in sections 4, 6 and 9 in Emily township." By 1909, due to declining population, there were only 9 teachers in Emily, of whom 2 had 2nd class certificates, 6 with 3rd class, and 1 temporary certificate. Inspector Knight on retiring stated that with increased government grants "even the poorest township can now easily pay $400, yet in Emily the average salary is $392, the lowest $350, the highest $425." He compared conditions in schools with that 30 years before when he had begun, and felt the stern discipline of earlier decades "had given place to an easy peaceful manner which encourages neither industry nor business habits", due mostly to the influx of female teachers; "Boys and girls of 14 and over seldom attend where a female teacher is employed."

Next year the new inspector for West Peterborough and East Victoria considered the Victoria schools rather inferior, and found much to criticize. In 1912 he noted that Emily had 9 schools with 296 pupils on the roll but average attendance only 50.8% (ranging from 40 to 64%), which was "most unsatisfactory". That year Emily passed Bylaw 390 to form a new Union School Section no. 16 of Emily and Ops, and Bylaw 391 authorized issue of debentures for $2,600 for this Section "for erection of a schoolhouse and improvements of school property and furnishings and equipment", to be paid back in 20 years, interest being 5%. Also in 1912, S.S. 10 was remodelled with new floors, windows, desks, blackboards, roof, indoor toilets, electric lights, hot-air furnace, and completely redecorated. Next year the new S.S. 16 opened, a modern building costing $1,650, on the southwest corner of lot 1, con. 13, and the first teacher was Miss Lulu Walker. S.S. 8 trustees decided in Dec. 1913 to build a new school, and debentures of $2,500 were issued payable in 15 years at 5%. Obviously most school boards were trying conscientiously to improve the quality of education in their sections in those years.

In January 1914 the Inspector's report on Emily Schools was as follows:

SCHOOL SECTION	Teacher's Certificate	Teacher's Salary	Enrolment	Attendance Average	Attendance Percent
3	2nd	$575	45	30	66⅔
5	3rd	550	31	19	61
7	2nd	600	44	27	61
8	3rd	550	(not given)		
10	2nd	625	17	11	63½
11	3rd	600	26	15	57
12	2nd	550	22	10	46½
13	2nd	550	26	14	51
15	2nd	550	27	17	63
Union 16	None	500	26	18	67
Totals:			264	160	60%

The inspector stated: "There are children between the ages of 8 and 14 who do not attend school at all", and recommended each township to appoint truant officers to enforce the Compulsory Education Act. Gone were the days recalled nostalgically from decades before, when such rural schools were crowded with 70 or 75 pupils (some quite grown up) in winter months, and forced to sit doubled at desks and benches around the walls, while in spring and autumn only 20 or 30 regulars came to school seeking an education. Another well-remembered feature of school before the Great War were the school fairs, which had to be discontinued in 1914 due to lack of funds, but which were revived later.[6] Ontario government reports in 1914 indicated also that there were no fifth or continuation classes in Emily nor any Roman Catholic Separate Schools. At Omemee High School only 15 boys and 31 girls were enrolled, with average attendance 29; of the students, 25 were in lower school and 21 in middle school; their parents were: 36 in agriculture, 2 in law, medicine and church, 1 in teaching, 2 in trades, 3 labourers, and 2 unlisted; through these years only 50 to 60% of those who tried High School Entrance at Omemee passed.

Improvement of Emily Schools continued during the war years, and pupils were encouraged to maintain school gardens to increase food production. In 1916 all Emily teachers had 2nd-class certificates, and school enrolment was up to 287, with average attendance 67.5%, the best in the inspectorate; though this fell off in 1917, S.S. 11 Emily was cited by the inspector as "having a splendid attendance, 75%". He also mentioned S.S. 5, Emily, as one of very few schools in the county having classes in agriculture. However, by 1919 enrolment was down to 237, and average attendance 131, or 55% (the same average as for Victoria rural schools), and this only rose in 1920 to enrolment 278, average attendance 60%; perhaps the rise was linked to an Emily Council motion of Feb. 1920 to appoint 5 school attendance officers, to cover all school sections, each to get $3 a day plus 10c a mile while at work. In any case, township school attendance rose in 1921 to 65%, while teachers' salaries were $800 to $1,000, and by 1924 average attendance in Emily was up to 70%, the best in the inspectorate.

School Interior – c. 1900

15, King's Wharf.

Five sets of twins at S.S.#7 Emily.
L to R back row—Dorothy and Olive Davis, Vera and Marion Franks.
Front row—L to R—Olive and Alma Murray, May and Helen McAuliffe, Loretta and Tom Murray.
(Mrs. A. Franks)

S.S. #16, Emily-Ops Union built c. 1912

St. Luke's S.S., Downeyville

S.S. #11 Emily about 1910.
Back row L. to R. Clara Bannon, Tom Bannon, Bertha Bannon, Victoria Burroughs, Harry Bradley, Beatrice Peacock, Maggie Bannon, Tom Croft.
Front row L. to R. Vera Low, Mary Lang, Terressa Latchford, Vernon Lang, Elsie Bannon, Mina Balfour, Harold Lang, (name forgotten), Teacher Miss Grant.

S.S. #9 (Fee's)

S.S. #10 (Orange Corners)

S.S. #12 (Scully's)

S.S. #13 (Bethel)

SOME TOWNSHIP SCHOOLS

In 1923-24 the S.S. 13 Board planned a new building on land bought from G. Switzer, and next year Emily Council approved debentures of $4,000 repayable in 15 years to pay for it; the actual cost was $4,213.95; the inspector reported: "The trustees of S.S. 13, are to be congratulated on having erected a fine new school, opened early in 1924." That same year Omemee High School had only 56 students (17 boys and 39 girls). Emily schools in 1925 had 1 male and 9 female teachers, with enrolment 257 (129 boys, 128 girls), with average attendance 61%. The cost of operating the schools totalled $12,992, being $50.70 per pupil, the highest in the inspectorate; part of the reason was an upward trend in salaries, as they ranged up to $1,125. Early in 1926 S.S. 9 opened a new school and Council approved a debenture of $3,000 to cover the site and building; but the inspector's report in June, 1927 warned of trouble—with 3 male and 8 female teachers, with salaries ranging $900 to $1,100, enrolment had fallen to 245 (117 boys and 127 girls) with average attendance 67%, yet cost per pupil had soared to $58.81, by far the highest in Victoria County (even higher than in Lindsay).

An interesting event in July, 1927, was the 50th anniversary old-pupils' reunion at S.S. 3, with a crowd of about 750 persons gathered on the spacious school grounds, from all parts of Ontario, the prairies and even a few from United States; after a patriotic march and drill by present pupils, there were numerous speakers, including the present teacher (Hugh Elliott), the County Warden, Rev. Everson of Dunsford, Father Galvin of Downeyville, John McMullen and others; W. J. Patrick was chairman for an enjoyable programme of music, sports, supper and dancing, appreciated by the large crowd of former pupils exchanging reminiscences and memories. Hugh Elliott, who taught for 35 years at S.S. 3, was a real community leader and much beloved by the hundreds of children who received an education from him, then graduated and married and sent their children in later years to study with him. Mr. Elliott was superannuated in 1935 and in that year received a Coronation Jubilee Silver Medal for his whole-hearted contribution to local education; he died Christmas Night, 1941, and was buried in Salem Cemetery.

In 1929 Inspector Downey reported that Emily had 1 male and 10 female teachers, and schools were open 191 days, and had 1,901 volumes in their libraries; 40 pupils had left and 27 new pupils had entered the schools, and total enrolment was 240 (113 boys, 127 girls), with average attendance 70%; but cost per pupil of $56.33 was still the highest in the county. He listed schools with low attendance (1 to 10 pupils) which included S.S. 11, Emily, with an average of only 6 pupils; there were still no 5th or continuation classes in Emily schools. During the 1930s salaries and other school costs fell to half or less, but we have few particulars as the inspectors ended their full reports to county council, and as Emily Council was not asked to approve any new school construction. At S.S. 13 in 1934 Cyril Rice began teaching music one hour a week, and no doubt did the same in other district schools. In 1938 Emily Council minutes mentioned that they had received a list of several dozen Emily students doing high school courses in Omemee, Ennismore, Lindsay and Peterborough, but with no details. That

S.S. #5 (Orange Line)

S.S. #8 (Trotter's)

S.S. #4 (Downeyville)

S.S. #7 (Frank Hill)

S.S. #3 (Millersmith) built c. 1875

S.S. #6 (Guiry's)

SOME TOWNSHIP SCHOOLS

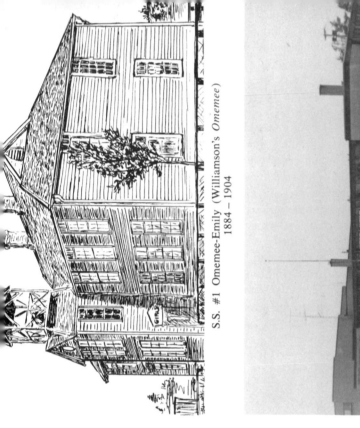

S.S. #1 Omemee-Emily (Williamson's *Omemee*)
c. 1840 – 1884

S.S. #1 Omemee-Emily (Williamson's *Omemee*)
1884 – 1904

Lady Eaton Elementary School
1964

S.S. #1 Omemee-Emily
1904 – 1964

year S.S. 9 was closed and the pupils transported to S.S. 11, but the former school was re-opened 11 years later. In 1939 the only 5th class in the inspectorate was at S.S. 4, Emily. S.S. 13 each year planted several hundred spruce trees around the school on Arbour Day, and doubtless other schools did the same. Most school sections weathered the depression by paring every possible cost and postponing every possible repair or purchase, while trying to maintain high standards of education for the pupils.

As mentioned previously, the schools had small libraries aided by government grants, for the use of all in the community. In Omemee there was the Mechanics' Institute Library, which after 1900 had quarters, partly supported by fees and partly by yearly concerts, over Rehill's store, where newspapers and magazines could be read, and books borrowed. The Omemee 'Mirror' weekly was moved to Millbrook in 1903 and became the 'Millbrook & Omemee Mirror', so that most Emily people preferred to subscribe to a Toronto, Peterborough or Lindsay newspaper. The Ontario Library Inspector reported in 1904 that the Omemee Library had between 1,000 and 1,499 volumes, but made no mention of a government grant. Soon after Coronation Hall in Omemee was opened in 1911, the Library moved to the front second-floor rooms, but had to close soon after for lack of public support, and was revived after the war in 1919. By 1929 the Library had 2,026 volumes, but circulation was static, being only 1,516 in that year. During the 1930s more people in the area had "leisure" time to read, and the library was aided by government grants and a municipal tax of 50c per capita, with Mr. Horace Hill as faithful librarian.

In Jan. 1901 a vote was held on building a County House of Refuge, and it was defeated by 2,895 votes to 2,157; in Lindsay there was a majority in favour (975 to 216), but the township people including Emily still had the tradition of caring for their older relatives at home, and indeed the grand-parents were an important part of many a rural homestead. In 1904 the County proceeded with building of the Home for Aged (or House of Refuge) just outside Lindsay, at contract cost of $29,200; by 1906 the Home had 41 inmates, of whom 4 were from Emily—while the number in the House of Refuge steadily increased, there were never more than 7 from Emily in this period to 1940, and of those usually one or two were partly maintained by their own property. The rules set up by Bylaw 695 in 1910 for inmates seem very severe—rising, meals, workhours and bedtime (9 p.m.) were strictly regulated by bells, there was no leaving of the premises or reception of visitors, etc. without permission, and offenders could be placed in solitary confinement; males and females were even forbidden to converse together without express permission of the matron or keeper, and then only if another female was present! No wonder that Emily old people avoided it if possible—there were 6 from Emily in the Home in 1911, 3 in 1914, 4 in 1917, 3 in 1922, 4 in 1925, 5 in 1929-30, 6 in 1933, 7 in 1935 (out of 66 inmates), and declining afterwards to 2 in 1940 (out of 68). Emily's share of the costs of the Home, included in county levies, rose steadily from $670 in 1905 (for debentures and maintenance), $830.13 in 1911, $943.81 in 1914, $1,351.06

in 1918, $1,573.58 in 1921, $1,728.61 in 1926, $1,443.65 in 1929, down to $382.64 in 1933, up to $1,213.59 in 1938, and down to $520.07 in 1940.

The serious effects of war and depression on Emily are partly reflected in government reports and council minutes, with little dimension in the absence of a local newspaper; but the memories of those who suffered in war and depression years are still vivid, after 40 to 50 years. The Omemee correspondent of the Lindsay 'Post' noted Oct. 18, 1901, that Capt. John McCrea and Principal J. Moffatt of the local public school had received medals for services in the Boer War, but in the next decade there was little local interest in military matters—Emily Council in 1905 noted and refused a request from the South African Memorial Association for a grant toward a monument to Canadian soldiers who died in South Africa. Capt. McCrea drilled his Omemee no. 4 company of the 45th Battalion, and took them yearly to militia camp at Kingston, Ottawa, Toronto, Cobourg, etc. A curious incident in Feb. 1908, immediately connected with war rumours, was reported in the Lindsay 'Post': "Omemee vicinity is to be one of the most important points in the Dominion, so say government engineers and scientists who climbed to the top of Ed. Sheridan's hill, 3 miles east of Omemee, with a view to erecting a tower 100 ft. high, whereon to take views in time of invasion, wireless, observatory, etc. . . . ." However, it is doubtful if anything further resulted, though next year Victoria Council urged the federal government to erect a drill-shed and armoury at Omemee: "that in 1867 Emily Township purchased the site for a drill-shed & armoury in the village and conveyed it to the govt. of Canada; in the same year a drill-shed was erected on the site jointly by Dominion and Emily, each paying half the cost . . . subsequently Emily paid for erection of an addition to be used as armoury. Some years ago said drill-shed collapsed consequent upon snow on roof, and was not rebuilt; that Emily and Omemee have for many years furnished sufficient recruits to form no. 4 company of the 45th Regiment. . . ."

When the energetic Colonel Sam Hughes of Lindsay, M.P. for Victoria, became Minister of Militia in 1911, one of his priorities was the building of armouries for the militia across Canada, and in 1912 the new one at Omemee cost $9,707.00; as Capon states in His Faults Lie Gently (1969): "Hughes felt that the armouries that were to be built should be substantial buildings that would benefit the communities in which they were built and provide, as well as a place for militia training, a public edifice that would serve for other community purposes. The Minister also considered that an armoury should contain a supply of blankets, cooking utensils, pioneering tools and other such apparatus which might be used to make the buildings into relief centres in case of fires, floods, or other emergencies—an Emergency Measure idea far ahead of its time." Unfortunately, the armouries at Omemee burned down in the winter of 1913-14 and Emily Council in March 1914 petitioned the federal government to rebuilt it.

Few details can be given about Emily's contribution to Canada's armies which took a valiant part in World War I (1914-18). According to Kirk-connell's "Victoria", 75 county soldiers went with the First Contingent to

Albert Acreman

Roland Parker

Gordon Harrison

James J. Murtha

Reginald M. McMullen

Victor Callaghan

SOME WORLD WAR I VETERANS

Britain, and over 2,000 Victoria men were in the 21st, 39th, 109th and 252nd Battalions that went to France later; of these 205 died, and many more were wounded; probably there were others in the Canadian navy, airforce and other services, and hundreds of both sexes went to work in munitions plants and other war work. Williamson in his *'Omemee'* gave a partial list of 77 who served in the first war, and the Omemee District War Memorial lists 19 who were killed or died in action. One of these was Harry Brown, V.C., who grew up in East Emily and went to S.S. 7 (Frank Hill) School, living with his step-father, Patrick McAuliffe until 1916, when he went to live with a sister in London and work in a munitions factory. Not yet 18 years old, Brown enlisted in that year and arrived in France in the spring of 1917, reaching the frontline trenches the day before the attack on Hill 70. Brown and another private were given a message to take back after the wires were cut, during an enemy counterattack; after the other man was killed, Brown though wounded continued through a barrage to the support lines, delivered his message, and died shortly afterwards, Aug. 16, 1917. His devotion to duty saved the position and prevented many casualties, and the Victoria Cross was awarded by the King and presented to his mother, Mrs. McAuliffe of East Emily, in Coronation Hall, Omemee; after being held by the family for some years, his medal is now in the Canadian War Museum in Ottawa.

In St. Luke's Church at Downeyville is an Honour Roll of 44 who served in World War I from that parish; and from North Emily went Dr. R. M. Parker, R. M. McMullen, Wm. Smith, S. Cullon, and M. Ashmore. Indeed, it is safe to say that well over 100 from Emily were in the Canadian forces in that war (a list will be found in an Appendix). Council recognized this when in 1916 they made a grant of $500 to the British Red Cross Society, and in Dec. 1918 formed a committee to arrange for the reception of overseas soldiers returning to the township, with presentation of a piece of jewellery to each. Victoria County in 1914 set up a Patriotic Fund with a 1-mill levy of $16,166.25, to which private donations were solicited, to aid in the maintenance and comfort of soldiers' families; in 1915 Emily in addition to regular taxes paid $1,708.12 to the Provincial War Tax, and $427.03 to the Patriotic Fund; these extra tributes rose steadily, and in 1918 Emily paid $2,013.42 Provincial War Tax, and $6,570.76 to the Patriotic Fund. Victoria Council in a Memorial to the Ontario Premier in 1919 urged establishment of a Labour Bureau in Lindsay, pointing out that several thousand from the county had served during the war, and "Many returning soldiers will come to Victoria and seek assistance in obtaining employment in civil life. . . ." At the May 1920 meeting of Emily Council a delegation from Omemee Council attended, to discuss erection of a monument in memory of township and village soldiers who lost their lives in the recent war, and a joint committee was set up; at this War Memorial beside Coronation Hall on Omemee's main street, set up later, services have been held each November 11 (Armistice Day, or later called Remembrance Day).

The other major disaster of the period, the "Great Depression" throughout the 1930s, was especially difficult in rural townships like Emily, when the prices of their farm produce fell to levels making it unprofitable to grow grain and vegetables and to raise livestock, or when it was simply impossible to market them at any price; the one saving feature of their situation was that they never lacked enough food to maintain good health, and enough fuel for comfort in winter, and enough clothing for all seasons, if they were ready to make their own, as their great-grandparents had done so well. The real details of that struggle are still vivid in the memories of all Emily residents over fifty, and the local council records concern only a few of them, those on relief who could not pay their taxes. The children who went to school in worn or patched clothing were no problem to a teacher who received half the salary of the previous decade, and the unrepaired roads were no problem to those who drove around again in a horse and buggy, or even in a Model T 'flivver'. In fact, there are many evidences that people were more neighbourly and friendly and helpful during those years than in any period since pioneer days; there were renewed yet familiar stories of neighbours taking food and home-made medicine to the sick and aged, doing the farm chores, or harvesting the ripe grain, for those 'down on their luck'. Difficult times brought out the best in Emily people.

Emily Council first took notice of the depression in a motion Oct. 1931: "that in view of the extremely serious situation existing as a result of the present depression, Council disapproves of all county and provincial highway construction, except maintenance and repair, until such time as the present depression is ended." Actually, of course, roadwork became a main project to assist the unemployed by giving them some public work to do for small wages.

Despite every effort by Council to reduce taxes, cut township wages and salaries, leave roads unrepaired, and limit all expenses, by 1932 Emily lots were being sold in Lindsay for unpaid taxes—at the May meeting, Emily Council noted 17 ratepayers had not paid 1931 taxes, including East Emily and Maple Leaf Cheese Factories; the Canadian Legion urged Council to give any township jobs to veterans before others, and to ask all employers to do likewise; a petition from 51 ratepayers asked Council to allow electors to vote on reverting to statute labour "as ratepayers are unable to raise sufficient funds by taxation for upkeep of roads." With considerable belt-tightening, the township remained solvent in the worst depression years— for example, in 1932 assets were $25,548.55, and liabilities only $13,896.94, but expenditures exceeded receipts to leave the annual *deficit* at $6,093.55; yet the following year (1933) total receipts were up to $59,076.77, while expenditures were down to $58,986.79 leaving a *surplus* of $89.98 with $213.00 in outstanding cheques, for total surplus $302.98.

In 1933 taxes of 26 ratepayers for the previous year were unpaid, ranging from 98c to $175.34, and totalling $1,254.36; further, unpaid 1931 taxes still totalled $170.89. The Ontario Welfare Department asked council to make lists of lots where reliefees might grow their own vegetables. In 1934 Council listed 61 ratepayers who had not paid their 1933 taxes, and relief was being paid by the township to over 7 indigent families; a bylaw was passed to limit funeral expenses for indigents to be paid by the township; Council also decided to buy some woodlots where those on relief could be employed to cut firewood. In 1935 the list of ratepayers owing 1934 taxes was down to 48, with sums owing from $1.83 to $131.85, and the number of people protesting high assessments in Court of Revision had tripled in five years. Wages paid on winter relief 1933-35 for snow-clearing were: township 10c an hour for shovelling, man and team on plough 20c an hour; county: Foreman 25c an hour, labourer 15c an hour, man and team 30c an hour. In that year, 1935, the depth of the depression, relief was being paid to 5 indigent families in Emily.

Yet in 1936 tax arrears were heavy: 46 ratepayers had not paid 1935 taxes totalling $1,397.03, in sums from $2.21 to $114.00, and another 27 owed tax arrears from earlier years of $1,486.42—some of these people had 2 or 3 properties, having overextended in the earlier years of prosperity; that year also 8 families were on relief in the township before December. Next year, as mentioned, Council allowed each ratepayer to work out a 3-mill tax on assessment by road labour, and in 1938 road wages were raised for winter work to 15c an hour for a man shovelling, and 25c an hour for man and team. But also in 1938 taxes for the previous year were still unpaid on 96 properties, ranging from 61c to $129.82, and were turned over to the County Treasurer for collection; relief pensions were paid by Emily of $10 to $20 a month, depending on size of family, and were used for food, clothing, school-books, medicine, etc. In 1939 taxes for the previous year were unpaid on over 100 properties, and a few were still paid relief, but with rising revenues and prices and employment the problem decreased swiftly and vanished from township council sessions—in 1941 unpaid taxes on 90 properties, in 1942 on 60 properties and dwindling thereafter. No doubt inability to pay taxes hastened the retirement of some older people to a village home, and induced some younger people to obtain war work in town and give up the old family farm; others sold off part of the farm along a stream to cottagers, which helps explain why Emily population fell (in the 1930s) from 1,651 only to 1,546, while number of ratepayers rose from 1,077 to 1,222.

Some other interesting local council matters might be mentioned at this point. A never-ending problem was how to control dogs and prevent them from killing sheep: in 1903 Bylaw 319 abolished the dog tax by popular demand—this negated an 1897 provincial law requiring that each municipality tax each dog $1 a year and each bitch $2, unless 25 ratepayers objected. However, Council then was obliged to recompense ratepayers whose sheep and lambs were harried and killed by roving dogs; at each council session there were few such claims, and it became acute when sheepgrowing became more profitable during World War I; each year it cost the taxpayers over $1,000 to have the dead and injured sheep evaluated, and claims paid. War-time prices inflated the problem, and in 1918 over $1,200 was paid to owners of dead and injured sheep, at $17 to $20 for each sheep, $15 to $17 for each lamb killed by dogs. In July 1926 claims of 5 ratepayers were settled totalling $224.20, at valuation $10 to $12 for each animal killed, $5 to $7 each when injured, and for the first time 3 ratepayers owning offending dogs were ordered to pay part of the claims. By 1929, as a result of growing protests, Council offered a reward of $10 for each dog killed when worrying sheep, but next year even more sheep were killed; but due to the depression the amounts paid fell to $5 to $8 for each sheep killed, and less for lambs and injuries; by 1933 the standard compensation was $5 for a sheep killed, and 50c to $1 for each one injured. In May 1938 Leo Harrington was given $215.00 compensation for 18 sheep and 10 lambs killed by dogs, also 2 sheep and 9 lambs injured. By 1940 there were fewer such cases, since those killing marauding dogs were being paid $10 each, but still the claims being settled at $6 to $8 for each dead sheep, $1 to $2 for each one injured.

In 1903 Dennis Scully of Downeyville and Thomas McQuade of Omemee were on County Council as representing the 3rd Division, but Emily Reeve James Boate of Fowler's Corners was not on Council—by 1907 this unpopular system was dropped, and Emily was again represented on County Council by the reeve and deputy-reeve. In 1912 Emily Council donated $50 toward the proposed new Omemee armouries, in the hope that it could be used for "stock-judging and other exhibitions producing revenue when not in use for military purposes." Through these years Emily Council met in the Farmers' Clubrooms in Omemee, at rental $30 a year; when Coronation Hall in Omemee (a gift of Lady Eaton) was opened in 1911, Emily used it for nominations and other purposes, but did not move its offices and sessions there until 1945. After the wartime decline of the Emily Agricultural Exhibitions, Council in 1922 decided to grant $30 for prizes at the provincial plowing match at Lindsay in October, for Emily residents—3 prizes of $15, $10 and $5; in 1924 the grant was $25 for Emily competitors at the county plowing match—first prize $15 and 2nd prize $10 for boys 18 years of age in the stubble class; these continued with slight variations to 1930. In 1932 $15 was voted to the County Ploughmen's Association for a $10 first prize and $5 second prize open to Emily boys under 20 years of age in any class, and in 1934 $20 was granted for 4 prizes of $5 each to Emily competitors; in 1935 $10 was granted for 2 prizes to Emily residents competing in sod and stubble plowing; then in 1939 $15 was granted, $5 each for Emily winners in sod and stubble, and $5 for winner in stubble with 2-furrow plow; and finally in 1940 the same $15 for prizes, and $5 to aid the Ploughmen's Association.

Emily Council in Aug. 1923 voted to pay an account of $66.00 for burial expenses of "the two Clarke children drowned on or about 23rd day of June last in Pigeon River". Next year a plan was approved for Keneden Park Subdivision on lot 16, con. 7, on Pigeon River, indicating the growing interest in providing accomodation for cottagers and tourists. Perhaps the same impulse persuaded Council in 1925 to obey the Departments of Agriculture and Highways request to have all township road employees "cut down & keep under control all noxious weeds on public highways".

In 1928 Victoria County entered a 30-year agreement with Ontario Lands & Forests Department to purchase lands for reforestation, to improve growth and quality of woodlots, to develop protection techniques against fire, insects and disease, etc. County Bylaw 1087 authorized the first experimental forest, and lot 10, con. 6, Emily was purchased for $1800 from Mr. Weir, also 5 acres of the south half of lot 10, con. 7 "lying south of the travelled road known as the Orange Line" (for which Mr. Chatten was paid $200). This price of $9.75 an acre was rather high and the county bought more land that year in Somerville Township at $2.31 an acre, to which were added thousands more acres in the next 20 years. 193,900 trees were planted in 1928, some of them on the Emily lots, and this forested area just west of Emily Provincial Park has prospered ever since, as an incentive to Emily farmers to develop better woodlots.

The 1940 Financial Statement for Emily showed total receipts $70,968.68, compared to total expenditures of $68,800.22, indicating that the township had come through the depression in sound financial standing. Capital assets were $57,336.33, a surplus of $56,951.80 over capital liabilities; current assets were $22,048.90, surplus of $12,265.52 over current liabilities; the auditors were Harry Jackson and D. M. O'Leary.

The 1900 Federal election, won in Victoria South by Adam Vrooman, Conservative, has already been mentioned. Before the next election, this became Victoria Riding, and it was won in the 1904, 1908, 1911 and 1917 elections by Sam Hughes, Conservative, who became Minister of Militia in 1911 in the Borden government; Hughes was knighted by the King in Aug. 1915 for his fine work in getting the Canadian contingent overseas and trained for battle in France. Emily's 7 polls in 1904 gave Hughes 262 votes, and the Liberal, R. J. McLaughlin, 234 votes—two of the polls were strongly for McLaughlin (97 to 5, and 45 to 6 votes). In the 1908 election, the same pattern repeated: Emily gave Hughes 271 votes, and the Liberal, Archie Wilson, 240 votes, with two polls voting strongly for the Liberal (109 votes to 6, and 49 votes to 6). Sir Sam Hughes died in Aug. 1921, and in that year's first postwar election J. J. Thurston, Progressive, won the Victoria federal seat; in 1925, 1926, and 1930 it was won by Thomas Stinson, Conservative, and then in 1935 and 1940 by Bruce McNevin, Liberal, perhaps partly due to depression reaction.

On the provincial scene, Victoria East was won in 1902 by John Carnegie (Conservative) and again in 1905; in 1902 Emily's 7 polls voted 292 for Carnegie, 252 for L. Heyd, Liberal, then in 1905 they voted 289 for Carnegie, 125 for John Austin, Liberal; it is worth noting that in 1902 Emily also voted in favour of the new Ontario Liquor Act, 231 votes to 95— the vote in the whole district was two to one in favour. In 1908 Carnegie was elected again by acclamation, and when in 1909 he was appointed to an office and had to resign, Robert Mason (Conservative) won by a large majority over L. W. Gordon; Mason won the 1911 election by acclamation, the opposition being demoralized. Then in 1914 the ridings were juggled again, and Emily was again in Victoria South, won by John Carew (Conservative) over Alex. Fulton (Liberal) and Edward Johnson (Socialist—who received 104 votes). One of the postwar phenomena was the rise to power of the United Farmers of Ontario, and in 1919 Victoria South (including Emily) was won by Frederick Sandy (UFO) by a wide margin over John Wood, Conservative.

Sandy was a farmer living a mile west of Omemee, in Emily, prominent in United Church and other community affairs, and a director of Farmers' Union Fire Insurance Company. He was defeated in 1923 by Robert Patterson (Conservative) by a narrow margin, mostly because J. V. O'Connor (Liberal) was a third candidate, but came back to win in the 1926 election over Patterson alone. Then as the U.F.O. party faded, Sandy was defeated in the 1929 election by Wellesley Staples (Conservative), though Emily gave Sandy 434 votes, Staples only 328 (by contrast, Omemee voted strongly in favour of Staples). Mr. Sandy died of a heart attack at age 58 in the same farm home where he had been born. As one Lindsay paper stated "He was always keenly interested in the betterment of the community . . . the district has suffered a great loss. He was honest and fair in all his dealings, and a man of sterling worth and character. Everyone liked him". In 1933 this became Victoria Riding, and was won in 1934 by William Newman (Liberal) over Leslie Frost (Conservative)—Emily in a depression mood voted 624 for Newman, 269 for Frost; but Omemee village favoured Frost. But then in 1937 Frost won by a narrow margin over Newman, and represented Victoria in the Ontario Legislature for over 25 years.

In the period before 1900, most Emily people had been content to invest any extra money in improving homes and buying more farm machinery, with a few savings stored under the mattress or in the postoffice savings bank at Omemee; Rev. B. Coyle of Downeyville had a few bank shares, and a few others invested in mutual fire or life insurance shares. Then in June 1904 the Bank of Toronto opened its branch in Omemee, in time to profit from the growing prosperity of the following 15 years, when Emily farmers were encouraged to deposit their money in the bank. But better roads and automobiles took Emily people also to Lindsay and Peterborough to shop and bank, sometimes with unfortunate results—the Home Bank, organized in Toronto in 1903, had a Lindsay branch in which many Emily investors were attracted by its high interest rates, and when it went bankrupt in 1923 (with its officers arrested for conspiracy and fraud) some lost their life savings. Emily Council in March, 1924, sent a resolution to the Canadian Prime Minister and to Opposition leaders, protesting that the Home Bank had $164,000 of deposits in its Lindsay Branch, "much of which represented the savings of some 700 people of small means in Emily and Omemee". Since the government had known for a decade of the Home Bank's shaky condition, Council claimed the government should take action to ensure that depositors in Home Bank were reimbursed; and in fact in the next year Parliament did make partial restitution to depositors. During the 1930s, of course, few farmers had any spare money to hide away under the mattress or to deposit in any bank, and their off-farm purchases were kept to an absolute minimum.

The decennial Census provides some other useful information about changes in Emily:

EMILY ORIGINS:	1901	1911	1921	1931	1941
English	220	236	230	313	304
Irish	1990	1788	1534	1401	1114
Scots	60	65	86	84	77
Other British	10	9	6	4	8
French	14	7	28	13	4
German	6	—	—	3	2
Dutch	2	2	1	8	4
Indians	—	6	—	12	3
Others	2	8	1	44*	8

(*These 44 included 1 Czech, 4 Hungarians, 29 Italians, 8 Poles, and 2 Ukrainians).

Thus in 1901 the Irish origin accounted for over 86%, which by 1941 had fallen to 72%, as native sons left the township and more immigrants came, especially after World War I. Owing to the growing complexity of census statistics across Canada, printed information about Emily township declined drastically after 1911, but a few facts are clear: (1) In 1901 there were 484 families in 471 houses in the township, and these declined by 1941 well below 400 in each case; (2) There were in 1901—1219 males and 1085 females, which decreased by 1931 to 1057 males and 825 females; (3) Canadian-born in Emily, who were around 80% in 1900, had increased to nearly 95% in 1921, and to about 98% by 1941; (4) The average Emily family, which was 4.8 persons in 1901, was down to 4.5 in 1911, and probably around 4 persons per family in 1941.

There were also substantial changes in the religious statistics in these 40 years:

Emily (without Omemee)	1901	1911	1921		1931	1941
Church of England	435	369	357		381	317
Church of Rome	946	856	792		762	562
Methodists	704	709	596	(United Church)	614	558
Presbyterians	173	152	128		86	53*
Others	46	11	15		39	21*

(*After Church Union in 1925, the United Church absorbed most Methodists and Presbyterians, but in Emily there were (in 1931) 86 continuing Presbyterians, down to 53 in 1941. The category "Others" in 1931 included 21 Baptists, down to 18 by 1941, plus occasional Lutheran, Pentecostal, Greek Orthodox, Salvation Army and other individuals).

The Fifth Annual Sabbath School Convention of Emily Township (interdenominational) was held in Christ Church, Omemee, March 16, 1900;

that same year a new Anglican rectory was built by Pigeon River south of
King Street. In 1900 also the new brick St. James Anglican Church was
opened on the southwest corner of the lot, where it is now. Next year, as
mentioned in the last chapter, Christ Church was moved on rollers to its
present location just east of the rectory. The Rectors of this parish were Rev.
J. Teney (1901-09), Rev. Henry Earle (1909-14), Rev. Edward James
(1914-23), Rev. Alex. Weir (1923-36) and Rev. G. H. Johnson (1936-41).
In 1904 Christ Church installed the first pipe organ in the district, and in
1906 was fitted with electric lights; also in 1926 the first Anglican Young
People's Association was organized. St. James and St. John's were typical
pleasant little rural churches, and started their own A.Y.P.A. and Ladies'
Guild in the 1920s, as community centres. In 1931 Christ Church was
renovated and a large addition added to contain a larger chancel and vestry,
and underneath more room for Sunday School etc, the whole cost of $6000
a gift in memory of Walter Cottingham.

At St. Luke's Church in Downeyville, as mentioned, Father Bretherton
had the church enlarged, veneered with brick, and redecorated, with a vestry
added. When Father McGuire came in 1905, he arranged purchase of the
land for the new cemetery. The next priest, coming to Downeyville in 1916
was Father Galvin, who built the parish hall. During his term, two societies
were organized for the parish, the Catholic Women's League and the Holy
Name Society to promote church and community affairs. The Catholic
Women's League since 1921 has been active in promoting co-operation among
church people and raising funds for parish activities and improvements; since
the same year the Holy Name Society, for men only, has led in church work,
and also the Altar Society organized in 1922 to help in keeping the church
and other parish buildings well-furnished. Father McFadden remained pastor
for almost 20 years (1933 to 1952). One other event should be mentioned,
the Downeyville Homecoming in July, 1925, to celebrate the 100th anniversary of the arrival of the Robinson Immigrants in the area; the committee was
chaired by John O'Leary with Thomas Lucas as secretary, and they arranged
an enjoyable reunion which included a reception and concert in the parish
hall, a garden party, a play by the local dramatic club entitled "Turning the
Trick", and a programme of sports—baseball, horseshoe pitching, and races
of all kinds, as well as booths and games; a fowl supper was served the
second evening to the many hundreds of visitors and parishioners, followed
by an 'Old Time Fiddlers' Contest and square dancing. But the main success
of the event was the opportunity for old-timers to recall their childhood
memories and share with others their recollections of the happy days before
World War I in central Emily.

At Trinity Methodist Church, Omemee, some renovations were made in
1903 and a pipe organ installed in 1907, gift of Mr. and Mrs. John Eaton to
commemorate the Golden Anniversary of Mr. and Mrs. John McCrea. Flora
McCrea's wedding in the church to John Eaton in the summer of 1901 was
of course the social event of the season, with guests from Toronto by special
train, and a large reception after. As a memorial to her father, Mrs. Eaton

First Bethel Church before 1862

Bethel Church — 1862 to 1892

Bethel Sunday School Picnic — 1938

Bethel Church built 1892

Emily Cemetery Chapel

also financed a new parsonage built in 1910, on the old Bradburn Hotel site adjoining the churchyard. In 1918 the church was wired for electricity, and the old gas chandeliers discarded. Trinity Church takes pride in the number of its young people who have entered the ministry or become ministers' wives, including some missionaries in the foreign field. When Church Union came in 1925, it became Trinity United Church when Rev. E. Rowland was pastor; in 1940, due to foundation cracking, it was necessary to remove the church steeple, a landmark since 1876. Salem Church with its new white brick building was part of the Dunsford circuit, and in 1925 became a United Church, still in Dunsford circuit, whose ministers stayed mostly for 3-year terms— Revs. M. Leigh, E. Cooke, M. Wilson, F. Woodger, . . . Webster, W. Smythe, A. Hie, D. Balfour, E. Sexsmith, J. Trumpour, T. Carmichael, J. Everson, P. Gardner, W. Halpenny, H. Wilkinson, and J. Lovelace (the last 1938-41). Bethel Methodist Church also came into the United Church in 1925, and like Salem Church has had an active Sunday School, and a Ladies' Aid Society to maintain and promote church life. Lebanon Methodist Church serving southwest Emily and northwest Cavan was redecorated with new seats in 1901, and in 1912 celebrated its 50th Jubilee; but by 1921 the congregation had dwindled greatly and the church was closed, being sold in 1922 to St. John's Church, Ida; it is still used as a community hall.

Omemee Presbyterian Circuit included the churches in Omemee, Fowler's Corners and Mount Pleasant, served by Rev. Kannawin to 1903, then by Rev. J. Whitelaw to 1907, and by Rev. Horace Peckover, whose health failed under the difficulties of travelling country roads by buggy and cutter to hold 3 services each Sunday; this problem resolved itself after Rev. D. Currie became pastor in 1909, as following a dispute at Lakevale Church (Fowler's Corners) about a new church structure in 1912, that congregation separated and joined with Springville Circuit. When Rev. J. Black was minister in 1925, St. Andrew's in Omemee split over church union, since the pastor and a "large minority" of officials and members favoured Union and joined. Trinity United Church; but St. Andrew's with a small congregation remained Presbyterian, and rejoined Lakevale and Lakefield as a circuit, served by Rev. S. Kennedy, Rev. M. Smart, Rev. H. Kay, and later Mr. Cleveland Robb of Ashburnham, lay preacher.[7]

Emily Presbyterian Cemetery by 1910 was in "a bad state of upkeep", and a committee was set up to make it a fitting resting-place for community pioneers; in 1924 a new fence was built around the grounds, and a fountain installed. At Emily Cemetery, a lovely McCrea Memorial Chapel was opened Sept. 3, 1929, donated by Lady Eaton as a memorial to her family, as well as a new set of entrance gates. One of the last horse-drawn funerals was that of Mrs. James McGahey who had come from Ireland at 9 years of age, and married James McGahey in 1858; her husband had predeceased her 7 years. Mrs. McGahey lived 62 years on the farm, lot 2, con. 13, Emily, and was mother of 10 children; at her death in August 1920 the pall-bearers were her 6 eldest sons, and she was buried in North Emily Cemetery; in this one generation Mr. and Mrs. McGahey spanned the period from pioneer days to

Ancient grave marker in
Old St. Luke's Cemetery

Old St. Luke's Cemetery —
S½ Lot 5, Con. 10

Emily Cemetery east of Omemee on
Highway 7

St. Luke's, Downeyville, begun 1907

Presbyterian — N½ Lot 12, Con. 1

Salem North Emily

TOWNSHIP CEMETERIES

	1911	1921	1931	1941
EMILY FARM STATISTICS (Census)				
Size: up to 10 acres	142	23	—	1
11 to 50 acres	79	70	—	47
51 to 100 acres	249	205	—	165
101 to 200 acres	141	151	—	135
201 acres and over	31	38	—	56
Farm Occupiers:	642	487	452	404
Owners	493	405	357	304
Tenants	129	43	46	53
Both owner & tenant	20	11	49	43
Acres Occupied:	59,676	58,402	56,972	58,242
Owned	47,660	50,507	47,349	49,300
Leased or rented	12,016	7,855	9,623	8,942
Land Improved: (acres):	42,572	38,810	36,985	39,131
Field crops	31,782	26,720	26,996	25,265
Fallow	517	1,737	976	948
Orchard & Nursery	420	265	73	11
Pasture	—	9,628	8,308	11,980

(In this group in 1911 were shown small acreages for vegetables, small fruits & vineyards which were not listed separately in later census statistics).

	1911	1921	1931	1941
Land Unimproved (acres):	17,104	19,592	19,987	19,111
Forest	4,275	6,661	6,553	4,954
Marsh or waste	5,188	2,659	3,430	3,263
Natural Pasture	—	10,272	10,004	10,894

Field Crops:	1911	1921
Fall wheat (bus)	15,596	15,736
Spring Wheat (bus)	7,803	26,751
Barley (bus)	32,301	35,607
Oats (bus)	316,244	328,437
Rye (bus)	3,955	4,800
Buckwheat (bus)	34,769	18,748
Corn (bus)	243	—
Beans (bus)	88	268
Peas (bus)	22,519	19,944
Mixed grain (bus)	10,025	27,823
Potatoes (bus)	33,931	32,688
Turnips (bus)	119,955	51,810
Other field roots (bus)	1,359	256
Flax (bus)	—	71
Hay (tons)	8,932	5,784

(Note: After 1921 field crops are shown only by acreage)

EMILY FARM STATISTICS (continued)

	(Assessment) 1900	(Census) 1931	(Census) 1941
Cattle	3,051	6,669	6,753
Sheep	1,537	3,766	3,943
Hogs	1,162	3,408	3,490
Horses	1,222	1,578	1,529
Hens	—	45,081	46,296
Other poultry	—	6,107	6,004

Miscellaneous Census items:

(1) In 1931 of a population of 1,882, in Emily, 1,687 lived on farms, 195 elsewhere. In 1941 of a population of 1,520 in Emily, 1,349 lived on farms, 131 elsewhere.

(2) Farm mechanization in Victoria County in 1931 (which applies generally to Emily): 76.4% of farms had binders, 74.6% had cream separators, 65.8% had automobiles, 25.1% had gasoline engines, 20.4% had silos, 6.2% had tractors; but only 2.6% had electric motors, 2.4% had trucks, 1.5% had threshing machines, and .5% had milking machines. Other interesting items from the 1931 census (re Victoria County) 62.4% of occupied farms had telephones, 18.3% had radios, 5.6% had electric or gas lighting, and about 4% had water piped to kitchen and bathroom.

(3) In 1941, of the 1,389 living on Emily farms, 665 were classified as farm workers, including hired help: 23 year round, 48 monthly, 26 daily. This hired help earned cash wages that year $20,820, plus $14,430 for room and board. Of the 1,389 on farms, there were 157 males under 14 years, 162 females under 14 years, 592 males 14 and over, 478 females 14 years and over. Farms occupied 404, farms vacant 52.

modern times. Among others who died in this period were Wm. McQuade who died 1931 in his 77th year (a son of Arthur McQuade), and his sister, Sara, who became Mrs. Charles Ivory and died in 1933; Albert Davis of the 8th line, 1858 to 1931; James Jackson, 81 years old, in 1932; Mrs. J. Lowes (nee Sarah Switzer) of 7th line, 1934 in her 87th year; and Samuel Connell, 77 years old, who died in 1934 on the farm where he was born 3 miles south of Omemee—these are only a few scattered examples of the passing of time in rural Emily.

The above tables, mostly from available census information on Emily, show numerous significant trends in agriculture 1900-41. One trend was toward larger farms, at both ends of the scale—small farms up to 10 acres almost disappeared, and those up to 100 acres decreased, while those over 200 acres nearly doubled—in fact, by 1941, of 404 occupied farms, 24 were over 300 acres, and one of those was over 640 acres. Ownership of land remained remarkably stable at about 80% and even rose to 85% by 1941, while number of tenant-farmers fell. As population declined, improved land fell off over 5,500 acres, and then increased during the depression years, though area in field crops (which required more farm workers) continued to decline right to 1941. Marsh and wasteland was cut in half 1911-21, but afterwards grew slowly. Pastureland was about one-third of occupied land throughout, and after a slight drop in 1931, grew rapidly with more emphasis on livestock production after 1921. The census statistics do not show crop production by townships after 1921, unfortunately, but no doubt price fluctuations and market demands helped determine what crops were grown each year, and in the depression years hardly any crops were profitable. The livestock statistics indicate that production of cattle and sheep more than doubled, and hog production tripled, while horses were not yet superceded by tractors on most farms. Though poultry production was not given in the earlier censuses, there was undoubtedly a consistent increase in each decade up to the high 1941 figures—when some farm produce remained unsold in the depression, chickens and eggs could always be sold on local markets or traded at the grocery store for necessities.

An interesting route-card has been preserved for Mossom Boyd's Suffolk Punch stallion "Tumbrel", "color chestnut, foaled May 1895" on its weekly tour in 1900 through the townships. From Bobcaygeon it travelled each Monday to Dunsford, on Tuesday through Ops, on Wednesday to Lindsay and Reaboro, thence to Dan Wynn's (lot 2, con. 8 Emily) for the night; each Thursday the procession went north along the Ops-Emily boundary, then along the 13th Emily line to Tom Harrington's (lot 6, con. 12 Emily) for noon, thence south to Pat Maloney's, Downeyville, for the night; on Friday the tour went east from Downeyville to Emily middle line, and north to John Corbett's (lot 7, con. 14, Emily) for noon, thence northeast to Joe Hunter's on the Emily-Verulam boundary for the night; and on Saturday back to Bobcaygeon for a well-earned rest. Thomas O'Neill was groom, and the list of "services" for May and June include the following Emily names: Dennis Scully, Pat O'Neill, Robt. Wynn, Jno. Sullivan, Michael Crowley, James Kennedy, Jos. Hunter, Pat Callaghan, Bernard Murray, Dan O'Neill, Wm. O'Neill, Jas. Fox, Pat Wynn, Pat Duffy, John Corbett, Michael Callaghan, Edmund Herlihey, Michael Harrington, James Collins, Dan Wynn, Francis Milloy, Timothy Picket, John O'Neill, John Lucas, E. Houlihan, Thos. Harrington and Pat Malloy; some were visited several times; the most were in Downeyville and King's Wharf areas.

Another community project of the early 1900s was the "Beef Ring", formed by farmers in each locality in the days before electricity and refriger- ators, to provide fresh beef once a week to each family. At the annual spring meeting, officers were elected and a 'chart' of 20 members drawn up, each to contribute money to cover the expense of hiring a butcher, rent for the build- ing and equipment; each member also furnished one beast each season, and names were allocated to definite dates so that each would know when his beast was to be turned in. Each member received weekly a roast, a steak, and some boiling beef, weighed and recorded in the book. Records were also kept of the weight of every animal killed, and if any member at the end of the 20 weeks had received more beef than his animal weighed, he paid for the difference; on the other hand, if his beast weighed more than he received in beef, he was paid accordingly. Thus each farm-wife was able to serve fresh beef several times a week to hungry farm-workers and children, through most of the year, especially when other fresh meats were scarce on the farm. In winter salt pork and bacon could be varied occasionally with a chicken or a piece of the frozen deer carcass hanging in the shed, but in warmer seasons the weekly fresh beef from the "Ring" was doubly welcome.

For the produce of Emily farms, prices at district markets fluctuated greatly according to season and supply, so that only a few trends can be detected. Wheat was 65c a bushel in 1900, 85c in 1911, $1.22 in 1914, $2.37 in 1919, fell to 81c in 1921, was around $1 through the 1920s, then fell below 50c again during most of the 1930s; the other grains had a similar path, though lower in price. Wool was 14c per pound in 1900, doubled by 1924, and then fell to its original price in the 1930s. Beef, mutton and pork were 5c-6c a pound in 1900, doubled by 1914, rose to 50c-75c during the first War, fell to 10c-35c in the 1920s (when butchers began selling choice cuts at higher prices), then were down to 8c-15c in depression years. Chickens sold for 20c average per bird in 1900, were 50c by 1911 and $1 by 1914 and $2 by 1919, and then down to 50c during the 1920s, and lower still in the depression; butter and eggs followed parallel paths from their 1900 values (butter 18c per lb., eggs 17c per doz.). Potatoes and carrots were 40c a bag in 1900, up to $1 in 1911 and 1914, up to $3 in 1919, down to 50c in 1921, up to $2 in 1924, down to $1 by 1929, and half that price in the mid-depression years. Hay sold for $8 a ton in 1900, rose to $14 in 1911 and 1914, doubled to $30 during the war and for a few years after, fell to $17 by 1924, and declined further after 1930. The uncertainty of farm income did much to send young people into the towns or westward to the prairies up to 1930, and made many happy young farmers into unhappy urban labourers, both male and female.

Although it would be just as difficult to make any comparative chart through 4 decades of the main goods that Emily farmers bought, some interesting items can be recorded here. Eaton's two 1901 catalogues arrived in every farmhouse, and offered a fascinating display of clothing, furniture, farm tools and equipment, glassware and china, sewing machines, guns and gifts to tempt everyone—the prices can only bring nostalgic sighs now: ladies' summer readymade dresses (from floor to chin to wrist) $7.50 to $20.00; ladies' suits $3.98 to $22.50, ladies' blouses (called 'shirtwaists') 50c to $2.50 (and in silk $2.98 to $7.50); children's dresses 75c to $3.50; ladies' hats $1.00 to $2.25 (and if untrimmed 59c to $1.50); men's & ladies' boots $2 to $4, and low shoes $1 to $3; men's suits (wool) $3.50 to $16 (for full dress-suit with Prince Albert coat); boys' suits $1.50 to $7.50; men's & children's straw hats 25c to $1.00; buggy harness $10 to $18; team harness $20 to $30; steel cooking range $21.50 to $37.50; organ for parlour $29.30 to $75.00; sewing machine $11.75 to $25.50; sideboard $6.50 to $31.00;

Starting for Lindsay, c. 1916
(W. McMullen)

Ploughing, c. 1930 — (Albert Acreman)

Ploughing with four horses, c. 1940
(Stan McCall)

Mr. & Mrs. Wilbert McCall with
horse & buggy, c. 1920 — (Roy McCall)

Ancient sleigh
(Mr. & Mrs. Albert Acreman) 1927

Four-horse hitch, c. 1930
(W. McMullen)

FARMING WITH HORSES

Pumping water with windmill in 1973
(A. Franks)

One of the first tractors used in North
Emily (leased by Dept. of Agriculture)
in 1917 — (W. McMullen)

Stone Machine — 1918
(Marwood McCarrell)

Cutting Wood with Gate Saw in 1925
(W. McMullen)

Cutting Wood with Table Saw c. 1960
(Ed Ruth)

Well-drilling with steam power in 1922
(W. McMullen)

FARM OPERATIONS

upholstered couch $3.95 to $14.75; broad axe 85c; wood or iron plane 75c to
$1.25; scythe 85c; horse rasp 85c; long flannel underwear for children 25c
to 80c, for lady 45c to $2.75, and for men $1.00 to $5.00; men's winter
overshoes $1.50 to $2.00; long rubber boots $3.00; ice skates (to be fastened
on boots) $1.00 to $2.65; child's sled 15c to $1.25; adult's bicycle (rubber-
tired) $25 to $35.00; lawn-mower $2.25 to $4.35, and so on.

There were great changes naturally in the next 4 decades, with more
factory-made products, and new inventions—in 1909-10 a ten-piece rose
toilet set cost only $1.75; a 95-piece "apple blossom" dinner set only $5.15;
a handpower vacuum cleaner only $25.00 (whereas an electrical model was
$100); a fine basswood canoe (16 ft.) $28 to $33; a buggy, a two-seat
democrat or a heavy farm wagon $65-$68; a rotary washer $3.75 to $8.50;
a stereoscope 33c to 45c, with 25 beautiful stereoscopic views 25c; for the
barn a hay-carrier with track for $10.50, and corrugated steel roofing and
siding for 75c to $1.00 a ten-foot sheet; and a steelbeam stubble plow for
$14.50, or a disc-harrow for $28-$40. By 1914 mail-order firms were offering
feed cutters ($9.75 to $33), corn-shellers ($8.75), circular wood-saws
($32.50 up), potato-diggers ($8.75) and many other farm tools.

By 1920 the range of goods and furnishings offered tripled, with endless
variations of size and material to suit every purse—wood-burning box stoves
were $5.25 to $7.80, while coal-burning parlour stoves (with nickle-plate
and mica windows) were $27.00 to $32.25; the latest kitchen range which
burned everything cost $26.75. A combination vacuum-cleaner and carpet-
sweeper was now $5.25; in wartime men's fine suits sold for $7.85 to $15.00.
Eaton's would even sell you the plans and lumber for a stable for $176.00. A
daring wartime innovation were women's overalls (for digging, ploughing,
milking &c) for $2.00 to $3.75. Talking-machines in 1919 were $15 to $25,
with records 90c each (and double-sided at that). For the youth going
courting, a 4-lb. box of assorted chocolates cost $1.50; an elegant cutter for
winter drives was $53.50 to $64. For a paddle on the nearest stream in
summer, a Peterborough Canoe in your choice of colours (red or green, 16 ft.
long) cost $45.00; a cedar skiff with oars was $75.00, and a skiff with square
back for the new outboard motor cost $90.00 (with motor costing $135.00).
An all-weather top for the Ford car cost only $73.50 to $96.50. In the 1920s
the new electric washers cost $85.00, and a crystal-receiving radio was cheap
at $22.50 (to receive radio-transmission up to 25 miles). The newest console
phonographs cost $59.75, with portables at $25.00 for picnics; improved
sewing-machines (some with electric motor) cost $35.00 to $57.50; aluminum
tea-kettles were $3.50, while for the old-fashioned a Universal bread-mixer
cost $3.15 to $4.00. As N. Agnew pointed out: "By 1929 over half the retail
business in Victoria was done by (mail) catalogue and chain-stores who took
money out of the county."[8] The first chain-stores (Loblaw's &c) came to
Peterborough and Lindsay 1927-29; but supermarkets did not proliferate
until after World War II.

In 1904 Victoria County Council, in a resolution to the Minister of
Interior, denied the claim of the labour groups that more mechanics and farm-

workers were not needed in Canada—in fact, they said, thousands of buildings were being planned for the county and needed immigrant labour, and
also the farmers were much in need of farm-workers, due to the movement of
many to the prairies, plus those "who have drifted into the cities." Emily
Council in 1906 added its demand to the Canadian government that farmers
should be protected by higher tariffs for their produce; that same year the
Lindsay *Post* had a comment on the continuing battle of the temperance
forces to cut down liquor outlets by raising cost of hotel licenses—beer would
have to go up to 10c, and whisky to 15c a drink, but farmers could afford
those prices since hog prices had gone up to $7.50! In 1902 there were 50
small cheese-factories in the district which produced 5,756 boxes, selling at
9⅝c a pound; among them were two small ones in Emily—the East Emily
and Maple Leaf (Downeyville) Factories; but by 1911, though the price was
up to 11 5/16 c a pound, the number of these factories was only 25, and they
produced 3,386 boxes. This was due to several factors—the increasing
purchase and use of home milk separators 1905 on, with sale of cream to
ice-cream, butter and condensed milk manufacturers, the growing number of
dairies in the district buying milk and making butter commercially, and the
shipment of whole milk by train to Toronto, as we shall see.

It is perhaps forgotten now that there were small recessions (with falling
farm prices) in 1903-4, 1908-11, and 1914-15, and farmers became more
restless and militant. In March 1914 the United Farmers of Ontario was
organized in Toronto, and one director elected was R. H. Johnston of the
Emily Farmers' Club. The war postponed political action, but in Sept. 1918
Reeve Robert Wilson of Emily was appointed by Council as delegate to a
meeting in Toronto Labour Temple "to further the organization and
protection of farmers". Next year the U.F.O. elected 44 members, and aided
by 11 labour members, formed the Ontario government; Victoria County
elected two U.F.O. members, F. Sandy and E. Watson; then in the 1921
federal election, as mentioned before, J. J. Thurston, Progressive, was elected
in Victoria, as wheat plunged from $2.37 to 81c a bushel 1919-21. But the
U.F.O. faded by 1923 from a variety of causes, though the Lindsay *'Watchman-Warder'* could still say in Jan. 1923: "The typical Canadian is undoubtedly the farmer."

Kirkconnell indicates in his Victoria History that low soil fertility compounded the problems caused by low prices in the 1920s; and that since
1882 production of most crops per acre had fallen 25% to 50%; farmers
needed crop rotation and better seed and fertilizers which since 1920 have
done much to restore crop yields. Thus dozens of uneconomical farms were
being abandoned in Emily, and from 1921 on, Emily young men were among
the 11,000 from Ontario who read the tempting advertisements offering $5 or
$6 a day for harvest-help on the prairies, plus cheap transportation, and set
out for western wheatlands, some not to return. With the closing of Omemee
tannery in 1927, the only industries left in Emily were a few small sawmills,
cheese factories, cooperages and blacksmith shops. New farm machines
replaced much farm-labour, and the tractors which appeared at Lindsay and

Timber Frame Barn Raising — 1910 — S½ Lot 7, Con. 14. (W. McMullen)

Barn Raising — W½ Lot 18, Con. 1 — 1951
(Stan McCall)

Barn under construction in 1920
S½ Lot 19, Con. 2 (Harry Jackson)

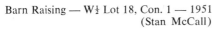

Barn Raising (c. 1928) Lot 18, Con. 3 (Fred Mc

other district fairs on exhibit (1921 on) were purchased by more prosperous farmers—by the 1931 census over 6% of Victoria farms had tractors; and others had threshers, power-saws, etc., to tour around Emily concessions—in Oct. 1919 Thomas Rowan complained to Emily Council that he could not get his threshing outfit over Bannon's Hill on 2nd concession from the railway east, and requested it be repaired promptly. But as roads improved trucks and other large machines moved around Emily more easily. Other threshing outfits recalled by Alvin Franks recently were those of Bob Stinson, George Windrim, Bob Courtney, Pat and Bill Callahan, Michael, Pat and Maurice Dorgan, Billy and Lochart Bell, W. C. Herlihey and Pat Perdue—these operated mostly in north and central Emily.

Two cheese factories flourished in Emily in this period, the Maple Leaf factory at Downeyville operated by John Reid, and after his death in 1906 by his son Cecil until 1912 (when he was killed by a runaway horse while driving in his buggy), then operated by shareholders until 1924; and the East Emily factory, at the northwest corner of the east quarter-line at con. 6, operated by shareholders for about 25 years until it burned down. The East Emily factory made cheese only for a time, then produced butter as well, and ended up producing butter only; the first directors were Eugene Switzer, Pat McAuliffe, Herman Franks, Alonzo Moncrief and Wm. Fee, and over 20 farmers bought one or more shares originally, at $10 per share. Others connected with Emily cheese-making were James Kimble, Deb Junkin, Howard Holmes, Jim Horton and Bruce Shireff. As mentioned previously, these small cheese factories were not a paying proposition by the mid-1920s, and farm milk and cream could be sold elsewhere more profitably; big urban commercial plants were producing cheese and other pasturized dairy products more cheaply for the mass market. In May 1932 Emily Council listed, among ratepayers with unpaid 1931 taxes, the East Emily Cheese Factory, owing $18.24 on a half-acre lot (lot 18, con. 5 & 6), and the Maple Leaf Cheese Factory, owing $22.72 on a one-acre lot (lot 12, con. 12). By the end of the depression the small rural cheese factories (both cooperative and privately-owned) were, with very few exceptions, only a memory in the Kawarthas.

One main reason was the increasing demand of megalopolis Toronto for milk and cream—milk trains by 1920 were picking up hundreds of cans at crossings and sidings all across the district, and taking them via Port Hope and Manilla early each morning to Toronto, at 20c a can, returning the empties later. Farmers even before 1920 brought their milk several miles to Omemee or Best's Station for shipment, and in 1929 they requested the C.N.R. to locate a new stop 1¾ miles west of Best's, where the track crosses con. 3, Emily. The Lindsay 'Post' in a 1969 article noted: "In 1930 some square timbers were laid parallel with the track on the north side . . . and 7 carloads of cinders were dumped. The farmers had a 'bee' assisting the trackmen in spreading them to make a platform. The railway provided a shelter 8 ft. square and also a truck for handling the milk cans. This shelter became a favorite stop for 'knights of the road' in depression days. The Flag Stop was known as McCague's for the first year but on Sept. 27, 1931, was

Perdue's Blacksmith Shop — Lot 18,
Con. 11. Built as a dwelling in 1840's
(S. J. Connell)

Downeyville Blacksmith — Tim Dorgan
c. 1970 — (Dr. J. Mannion)

Early Maple Syrup making with open
kettle, c. 1916 — (W. McMullen)

Maple Syrup making with evaporator
(Harry Jackson)

Sawing lumber in 1951 — (Stan McCall)

Downeyville Store in 1970 — (E. Carroll)

OCCUPATIONS

changed to Carmagner in recognition of the 3 delegates who promoted the idea—Sam Carew, Stan Magee and Elwood Faulkner." Each morning about 30 cans of milk were loaded on the 8:40 a.m. train to Toronto, and empty cans returned on the 8:30 p.m. train. However, by 1947 the township was ploughing township roads in winter, and milk trucks picked up milk right at the farms, and the Carmagner Flag-Stop disappeared in 1955.

At Downeyville Pat Callaghan built a large blacksmith shop about 1898 and turned it over to his son in 1904 when he went to Lindsay to work for Sylvester Machines building gasoline engines &c; while there Pat Callaghan helped design an improved threshing machine that threshed at the stook. The Downeyville blacksmith shop was operated by Jos. Lucas around 1909 then by Lynn Duffey, until in 1915 Tim Dorgan took it over until 1919, when the shop closed; after a few years at other jobs, Tim Dorgan opened the new blacksmith shop at Downeyville in 1922 and carried on for 5 decades. Prices were now higher—removing and repairing a horseshoe cost 15c, and replacing it with a new one cost 30c, but increasingly since the 1930s other types of farm ironwork have been an increasing proportion of the blacksmith's work. There were of course numerous other small business ventures making harness, barrels, boots and shoes, tinsmithing, etc. For example, a Lindsay 'Post' item of Feb. 14, 1902, read: "Shingle and Chopping Mill: Mr. Wm. Callaghan has erected a new shingle mill and farmers were busy hauling bolts until the recent snowstorm. He also has his new engine working in fine order. There is no better place to get your chopping done."

Through most of the first 30 years of this century, the Emily Agricultural Society carried on with its activities, aided in the 1920s by the Farmers' Institute and the Women's Institute, which received provincial grants to bring in speakers and instructors on various farm subjects of special interest such as crop rotation, fertilizers, under-draining, home handicrafts, and so on. Victoria Council in the 1920s gave the Emily Agricultural Society a $100 grant each year that an annual report was submitted, and in depression years this was reduced to $72. The Society continued to function, but instead of holding spring and fall exhibitions it acted as agent for the provincial agricultural department in promoting the work of 4-H Clubs, Junior Farmer activities, and annual school fairs at various township centres.

Mossom Boyd Lumber Company of Bobcaygeon continued to do a lively business in Emily after 1900—in that year he supplied Hamilton Bridge Works with 5256 B.M. planking plus joists and guards at $14 per M, delivered on the railway-cars at Lindsay, for rebuilding Cowan's Bridge. One postcard dated Sept. 10, 1901 in the Boyd records read: "When the Plank for the Pigeon Creek Bridge are ready to be shipped please give Tom Flood *timely* notice by the stage-driver so that he will be at the place of delivery when it arrives. John Belcher, Trent Canal Supt." On Nov. 7, 1900, Mrs. Hannah Tracey, Downeyville postmistress, wrote Boyd complaining that her son who had been bookkeeper in Cresswell's lumber camp (a Boyd camp) came home sick and the doctor now said it was typhoid fever; she asked that his wages be sent immediately, "as I have not means of my own to doctor him, as

I am a widow depending on my children for support." On Nov. 13 Boyd sent $11.41, the amount owing to the son, and March 26, 1901, D. F. Tracey (the son) wrote from Downeyville: "As it is coming near the time for your log-drive to start and knowing you will need a clerk for it, I wish to apply for the position. I clerked for Mr. Cresswell nearly 2 months last fall until I took the Typhoid Fever and was sick nearly all winter, consequently I have a large Doctor Bill to pay."

A note of Jan. 29, 1902, from Boyd to Wm. O'Brien of Downeyville read: "We could take a couple of tons of hay at our private stables here. We are paying $8 a ton and will accept only first-class timothy hay". In 1903 some North Emily and Dunsford men were employed bringing railway ties (for the Lindsay-Bobcaygeon line) by scow to Emily Creek and unloading and carting them from there. In May 1904 a Boyd bill for $959.29 went to Supt. Belcher of Trent Canal "for timber we sent down to Pigeon Creek bridge yesterday", and a June postcard to Peter Murtha of Downeyville acknowledged receipt of $4 "in payment for one service by stallion 'Peavine' (owned by Boyd) on May 23". In April 1905 Boyd was buying timothy hay at $8 a ton from J. O'Brien of Downeyville again "delivered at our farm cattle stables", near Bobcaygeon. There is a sheaf of correspondence 1906-12 with Emily people about stallion service, sale of Boyd thoroughbred cattle, purchase of a sulky plough and a two-furrow walking-plough etc. with P. A. Devine, Jas O'Brien, W. J. McDonnell (King's Wharf), Pat Malloy, Bernard Murray, James Stewart (King's Wharf), and others. Malloy was buying Hereford cattle, and McDonnell the same as well as Suffolk horses. A Boyd letter of March 30, 1908 to McDonnell said: "We would like to draw a few loads of your hay from Forest's as soon as the roads get fit . . . we would also like one or two loads of straw at the same time. The ice is bad at the shores getting on and off and our team is not shod sharp so we will put off going for the straw until we can use the wagon . . ." A letter of April, 1912 to McDonnell told him that the Boyd Suffolk stallion would not be making his tour any more but "you can have the use of him free at our barn for any of your mares." Then on Oct. 24, 1916, the last letter to McDonnell read: "Very sorry indeed to hear of the loss of your barn and contents by fire . . ." Incidentally, McDonnell had acted as a Boyd agent in 1909 and 1911 when he went to Montreal to bring back shipments of thoroughbred horses that Boyd bought while in England for his farm near Bobcaygeon.

The Trent Valley Navigation Company, owned by the Boyds, no longer ran steamboats up to Omemee, but this did not prevent them arranging excursions from Omemee and Dunsford. May 22, 1906, Rev. J. Whitelaw of Omemee, as Grand Master of the Victoria Orange Order, wrote announcing that there would be a "Monster Demonstration" at Lindsay on July 12, and asking for steamboat rates to Lindsay from Simcoe, Kinmount, Lakefield and all other district ports—in a postscript he mentioned that Millbrook and Omemee Presbyterians had an excursion July 20, 1905, on S.S. 'Esturion' from Lindsay to Rosedale. In June 1906 Boyd wrote J. J. Robertson of Dunsford quoting prices by S.S. 'Esturion' for Dunsford Methodist and

Baptist Sunday School Excursions that month—to Fenelon, Rosedale or Ball Lake, adults 40c, children 25c; to Chemong, Buckhorn or Burleigh, adults 50c, children 25c; in either case the guarantee would be $40.00 minimum, and the extra proceeds to be shared 65% to the Company, 35% to the Sunday Schools: "you to advertise, we to furnish tickets". In Aug. 1907 Boyd wrote J. D. Thornton of Omemee concerning an excursion by train to Lindsay, thence by S.S. 'Manita' over Kirkfield Liftlock and back by steamer, or back by train from Beaverton to Omemee. Steamboating became unprofiitable due to roads and railroads and the T.V.N. Company went out of business by 1914.

Overseer Trotter of Bobcaygeon, who worked for the provincial Fisheries Department, reported for 1902: "There is considerable illegal fishing through the ice in Emily Creek. This is a very difficult place to get at and consequently a hard matter to catch anyone in the act . . . It is said the maskinonge[9] are very large and plentiful in that locality." Again in 1903 he reported that Emily Creek was a favourite fishing spot for bass, muskinonge, perch and catfish. On July 30, 1903, Mossom Boyd III (born 1884, grandson of the original Mossom Boyd) wrote in his diary: "This morning Father wished us all to row up Emily Creek in our big boat but the others did not seem very anxious to go, so Laurie, Mose, Thornton and I set out in canoes; the wind got quite strong . . . and we only reached the mouth of the creek by dinnertime; after dinner we paddled about 1½ miles beyond the bridge, the wind being with us, but had a hard time coming back against the wind. We arrived at the mouth of the Creek about 7:30 . . ." Emily Creek continued popular with fishermen, and April 9, 1906, C. Nasmith, Toronto lawyer, wrote the Reeve of Bobcaygeon: "I have learned that about 20 maskinonge a day are being taken from Emily Creek near its mouth. Several of those engaged are the guides who belong to the Protective Association recently formed in your village . . . This sort of thing will probably continue for 3 weeks longer. I suggest that the Inspector at Lindsay be communicated with and asked to send a special man to the creek . . ."

With the coming of greater numbers of cottagers and tourists to the Kawarthas (so named by 1900 in district railway and tourist literature), Emily and Pigeon Creeks acquire new importance. The Indians of Curve Lake Reservation still came up the streams to fish from May to October, and to harvest fruit and berries in autumn, but increasingly they brought fishermen and hunters in their canoes for a day's sport in the streams and marshes of Emily. On Sept. 6, 1901, the Lindsay 'Post' reported: "Duckshooting has been fairly successful, especially on Pigeon Creek." The 'Watchman-Warder' in July 1904 noted that Messrs. Baker and Miller had made the first trip by water from Omemee to Lindsay in their steam-punt. According to Williamson's *Omemee,* the first inboard gasoline launch was on Pigeon River in 1907, owned by H. Beatty of Omemee Commercial Hotel, and soon afterward a dozen others were on the river, navigating through the weedbeds and floating bog-patches past Cowan's Bridge and the Floating Bridge into Pigeon Lake. Fishing trips, duck-shooting, shore dinners and picnics were most enjoy-

able for Omemee and Emily residents who could get out on the water in any
canoe, skiff, punt, or launch; and Green Landing, Lowe's, Carroll's, and
other landings, also Grenadier and Jacob's Island, were popular spots for
camping and picnicking, by young and old alike.

One prominent tragedy on Pigeon River occurred in Sept. 1912, when
Mrs. M. McCaffrey of Omemee, her son William of Toronto and his wife
and two children were all drowned a few miles below Omemee; crowded into
a 16-foot canoe, they upset in deep water when their troll caught a 14-lb.
maskinonge. A search party found them in 12 feet of water late that night,
William still holding the trolling-line; it is believed the chilly water, the tangled
line, and the weedy, marshy shores all contributed to the disaster. Old-timers
can still remember the sad funeral procession when the family were taken
eastward to Emily Cemetery.

We have noted the Keneden Park subdivision approved by Council in
1924, and next year Council's petition to the Dominion government for a
renewed clearing of Pigeon River to aid the "summer resorts, boarding-
houses and cottages erected on Pigeon River . . . for tourists now frequenting
these waters"; but the river remained clogged with weeds, and Pigeon Floating
Bridge was closed as impassable. Outboard motors became popular, and were
useful on the shallow weedy streams of Emily township. Williamson mentions
some of the first resorts on Pigeon River—W. Fee's north of Cowan's Bridge,
Fred Evans near Omemee, George Griffin's at Carroll's Landing (Keneden
Park), and others. The Lindsay 'Post' on Oct. 26, 1929, announced a shooting match (of geese and ducks) at Fee's Landing, on Oct. 29 at 1 p.m., with
riffles and ammunition supplied. Then in April, 1930, Emily Council
petitioned Ontario Department of Game and Fisheries about the Emily Creek
Fur Farm Ltd., asking that fences erected at Emily Creek and marsh be
allowed to remain, since the company was propagating fish and developing
"a profitable and valuable industry"; this company survived for several years,
and Nov. 1934 Emily Council made a special grant of $50 to repair the
company property on the con. 14 swamp "in lieu of the statute labour for
Emily Fur Farm". But the depression slowed down the tourist trade and
most other commercial projects along Emily streams, though they became
more prosperous after 1937 as urban Ontario poured out to cottages and
resorts every summer, on regular annual vacations from factory, store and
office. Often the man who brought his young wife and first children in an old
'flivver' to spend a week camping in a tent by an Emily Lake or stream in
1935, from Oshawa or Toronto, came back 10 years later in automobile or
camper with his family to spend two weeks at a luxury resort, or to build a
cottage by the water, or even to buy an abandoned farm for a vacation retreat
and retirement home—as we have seen, there were 52 vacant farms by 1941.

Fires continued as a menace to isolated farm homes and buildings, though
with improved roads and telephones neighbours could rally to help quell the
flames and rescue stock and furniture more quickly. Wilfred McMullen
remembers a few big fires in north Emily—Ab Padget's barn (lot 9, con. 14);
Geo. and John Vout (lot 8, con. 14); Pat Meehan's barn (lot 8, con. 11)

between 1905 and 1910; Wm. Bell's threshing mill (lot 2, con. 13) in Aug. 1910; Geo. English's house (lot 5, con. 14) 1910 or 1911; the shed behind Guiry's store at Downeyville, Aug. 1918; Ed. McGahey's barn (lot 3, con. 13) in the 1920s, and Alex. McGahey's barn on the next lot a bit later; Wm. Patrick's barn (lot 6, con. 14) in the 1930s; Max Kennedy's barn (lot 7, con. 13) in the 1940s; and Wm. Ashmore's (lot 7, con. 14) in the late 1940s or early 1950s. When Jas. O'Leary's house at King's Wharf burned in 1926, he moved his family back to the old pioneer log house nearby, until he could rebuild. Typical is an undated newspaper clipping from 1931 which read: "LANTERN BLAST DESTROYS BARN: Elmer Henry of Emily township was Preparing to Thrash; Loss about $3500: A large barn containing the season's crops of hay & grain was completely destroyed by fire this morning on the farm of Elmer Henry, 4 miles east of Omemee, on 3rd line of Emily. An open shed and henhouse were also wiped out. The loss, estimated at $3500, was partly covered by insurance. Mr. Henry had arranged for the threshing of his grain on Tuesday, and this morning started to clean out his granary in preparation for the work and to provide storage. He was using a lantern because the morning was dark, and in some way it exploded. The spreading fire quickly ranged beyond Mr. Henry's control; he succeeded in releasing his horses, and the cattle were in the fields. About 100 neighbours were attracted by the smoke & flames, but even the earliest arrivals could do nothing except move the garage beyond the reach of the flames."

We have noted some of the organizations in Emily and district to promote agriculture and temperance and community improvement in general. Some, such as the Children's Aid Society, begun in 1894 in Lindsay, but covering Victoria County, were little needed in Emily where the family ties were strong, and uncared-for or neglected children were very rare; however, one of the C.A.S. County Committee in the years around 1904-5 was Eugene Shine of Downeyville. Another group supported by the provincial government were the Women's Institutes, started 1897, which before 1930 had over 1000 members in Victoria County; at their meetings they took courses in home nursing and hygiene, encouraged local libraries and drama productions, provided literary readings and lectures, etc. By 1905 the Women's Institutes were holding regular meetings at Omemee and Dunsford; they aided the Omemee Library, which developed about 1907 from the Mechanic's Institute, and which after 1911 was set up in the new Coronation Hall under Joseph Sherwood as librarian—this was the only public library in Emily, though most churches and schools had small libraries for their own people; by 1929 the Omemee Library had 2026 volumes and a circulation yearly over 1500. A Peterborough 'Examiner' item of Feb. 3, 1930, reported "OMEMEE WOMEN'S INSTITUTE ARE HOSTESSES TO STUDENTS OF SHORT COURSE CLASSES: Speakers Compare Present Farming Methods with Pioneer Days". The report describes the banquet prepared by the Institute for 120 persons, with Harry Jackson presiding as Toastmaster. Vincent Fee spoke for the Farmer's Club, followed by speeches by Agriculture Representative M. Winter, School Inspector R. Downey,

A Wood Bee — 1899

School Fair at Omemee (1930)

Quilting Bee on Lot 22, Con. 6, c. 1940
(Beryl Clark)
Left: Mrs. Harry Lowes, Mrs. J. L.
Faulkner, Mrs. Albert Davis, Mrs. Robert
Fenwick, Mrs. John Franks, not known,
Mrs. Wilbert Clark, Mrs. Jas. Davis, Mrs.
Lloyd Boate, Mrs. Herman Franks and
Mrs. Vincent Franks.

North Emily W. I. — 1968
Left to right — Front row: Mrs. Wilfred McMullen, Mrs. Milburn Hutchinson, Mrs.
Hector English. Second row: Mrs. Joseph Draper, Mrs. Edward Hone Jr., Mrs. Simon
Connell, Mrs. Carl Montemiglio, Mrs. Bruce Hood. Third row: Mrs. Edward Hone Sr.,
Mrs. Ivan Thurston, Mrs. Thomas Herlihey, Mrs. John McMullen, Mrs. Alvin
McCausland, Mrs. Wm. McGahey, Mrs. Lee Wilson.

Early L.O.L. #41, Orange Corners, before 1900

North Emily W. I. Hall
(formerly L.O.L. #952)

Downeyville Parish Hall

Present L.O.L. #41, Orange Corners

Coronation Hall, Omemee, built 1911, and War Memorial (C. W. Williamson)

Reeve H. Endicott of Emily, and W. Staples, MPP, among others; there were solo songs and community singing, and toasts to the short-course classes, responded to by Arthur Mitchell and Margaret McQuade, who thanked the Institute for promoting the classes. The program ended with dancing to an orchestra.

The Omemee/Emily Farmers' Club was formed 1911, with 9 charter members meeting in Geo. Williamson's harness-shop, and electing Jos. Bradley first President. The Club met once or twice monthly in Coronation Hall, and by 1915 had 70 members; the Club brought in railway carloads of commodities (seed grain, flour, feed, salt, binder-twine, coal, oil-cake, fruit etc.) for the members at lower prices. In 1917 F. G. Sandy organized shipments of livestock from Omemee, followed by Wilbert Fee (1918-20), Wm. O'Neill (1920-23), S. D. Vaughn (1923-44). Clubs were begun at Reaboro and Downeyville, but they soon amalgamated again with the Omemee Club. The Club purchased separate clubrooms in 1920, and weighing scales in 1925, and also for some years operated an egg-grading station at Omemee. Though meeting in Omemee, the Club consisted of members from all parts of the township, and as we shall see is still thriving. At the 1930 banquet mentioned above, the report stated: "Vincent Fee spoke on behalf of the Farmers' Club, giving a short talk on the work of the branch for the betterment of the farmer . . . F. G. Sandy, ex-M.P.P., said the Club . . . had done a great deal for the community . . . The (Agricultural) Society was 52 years old and perhaps older, (and) O. G. Williamson has acted as Secretary for 38 years. The last Fair was held in 1902, but the Society is doing great work in improvement of livestock. Last year 2 standing crop competitions were held. He advised young people to continue in the good work which led to new and greater fields of service."

L.O.L. #41 at Orange Corners, oldest active lodge in the County, continued to flourish throughout this period. Around 1900 the membership list contained pioneer names such as Finley, Hooper, Faulkner, Jackson, Elliot, McCall, Fowler and Magee. Walter Magee, a long-time and highly respected member, was County Master 1926-27, and in 1940 honorary long-term certificates were presented to Isaac Fee, W. Padgett, R. Fowler, L. Calvert, George Low, Fred and Walter Magee. Next year Walter Magee, aided by Harry Jackson and Robert McAdam, wired the Lodge Hall for electricity, at cost $35. King Edward R.B.P. 625 was instituted about 1904 with the first Preceptor Jos. Beatty, Omemee merchant. That year the Lindsay papers announced that Emily Orange lodges would parade on Sunday, July 10, to Omemee Presbyterian church, where a union choir would lead the service; Williamson recalls in *"Omemee"* that either that year or in 1905 the Presbyterian Ladies Guild served dinner on the church lawn after the parade, and "to boil potatoes, the ladies engaged Robert Courtney to bring his steam threshing machine". In the winter 1907-8 most Lorne Lodge records were lost in a fire in the Orange Hall on King St., Omemee, but there were 106 members that year; the lodge met thereafter in rooms over Beatty's store. As numbers declined, L.O.L. 113 and 114 amalgamated in 1932 to form

L.O.L. 3140, and the first Master was Herbert Gardner. Then in 1937 Coronation L.O.B.A. 103 was instituted with the first Mistress being Miss Valerie Hart.

There are other aspects of Emily life which could be described at more length, but a few examples must suffice. A program has been preserved of a concert by the Omemee Choral Society, Oct. 29, 1903 in Bradburn's Opera House, presenting Cowen's "Rose Maiden", aided by Owen Smily, "the popular humerous entertainer", tickets 25c; the conductor was R. J. Mulligan, and there were listed 19 sopranos, 10 altos, 7 tenors and 10 basses (no doubt some from the township). At Downeyville concerts and dances were held in the upper storey of the blacksmith shop, until the Community Hall was built about 1921; other communities in north, east and south Emily had their barn-raising bees, box socials, fowl suppers, corn roasts, strawberry festivals, school Christmas concerts, and Sunday School picnics and excursions.

In Sept. 1928, Mossom Boyd III (who in July 1903 canoed up Emily Creek) wrote at length about a trip by motor to Peterborough, through Downeyville and Omemee and along a road south of the main highway (now no. 7) which was under construction; in June 1929 he mentioned in his diary a police chase after gypsies who were suspected of stealing from homes and shops in Emily and Verulam, and finally caught near Warsaw east of Peterborough; in Oct. 1931 and Sept. 1933 he motored from Bobcaygeon down "the old Peterborough road along Pigeon Lake" to the place where the old Floating Bridge (now closed) had taken travellers across, then south to Cowan's Bridge and on to Peterborough, "a very picturesque autumn drive". The change from a canoe trip up Emily Creek in 1903 to a motor-drive along Pigeon Lake in 1933 to Peterborough symbolizes the great changes in both transportation and entertainment that took more and more young people to the towns, not only for employment but even for shopping and sports, concerts, dances, movies, and other recreation.

In the realm of sports, skating and snowshoeing were still popular up to the 1920s, when skiing spread into the district. As a team game, cricket faded after 1900, when football was growing in popularity in south Emily. Baseball was played everywhere in pasture fields and schoolyards from the 1800s on, with a great boost after 1920 when radio brought in live coverage of professional games, and after 1930 when softball leagues were formed. One undated news-clipping (probably about 1930) tells of a July Sunday at King's Wharf 10 years earlier, when the boys played in Sullivan's cow pasture, dispensing with an umpire and with only a shadowy knowledge of the rules: "it was a long drawn-out affair . . . the lads didn't quit till 'twas milking time . . . just a whale of a good time by all on the one day they had off in a week. They don't play anymore. Some of the younger bucks got married and moved away, some of the older ones passed on, and O'Leary's house burned down (1926) with all the baseball equipment in it . . ." The Downeyville softball team in 1933 played the entire season without a single loss, sparked by two schoolboys: Albert Lucas (14 years old) catcher, and Frankie Shine (16

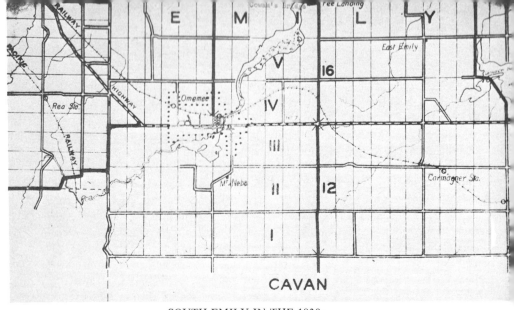

SOUTH EMILY IN THE 1930s
Map of South Emily in the 1930s showing railway, road development, etc.
(H. T. Pammett)

DOWNEYVILLE BALL TEAM 1933
Back Row L. to R.—Joe Shine, Frank Shine, Rev. Fr. McFadden, Charlie Harrington, Jim Carroll.
Front Row L. to R.—Ray Morrissey, Austin Dorgan, Steve Kitson, Bun Lucas, Dan Carroll.

years) pitcher—they defeated the best from the whole district including Lindsay, Peterborough and Oshawa; Frank Shine later played in the Peterborough Senior Baseball League until he joined the Army and went overseas in 1941. In the larger villages like Omemee, tennis, lawn-bowling and badminton were being played soon after 1900, and in winter soon after 1900 there were some indoor games (basketball &c.) in larger community halls.

But the main winter sport was hockey on outdoor ponds and rinks, mostly of church, school and village groups in unscheduled challenge games. The Lindsay 'Post' reported Nov 22, 1901: "Omemee will have a hockey team on the ice this winter. On Saturday the boys had a successful organizational meeting, and with the present extended rink accomodation and the enthusiasm manifested already, Canada's popular winter sport will likely boom here . . ." A poster survives of a game played Mar. 3, 1907, by Omemee Beavers against Bobcaygeon Browns, ending "Skating after the match, band in attendance, admission 15c, ladies 10c"—the Beavers had defeated the Browns the week before in Omemee by one goal. Few rural schools now had enough boys for a team, but many farm boys practiced on the farm pond with homemade stick and puck, and dreamed of fame in the big league, as described so colourfully on the radio. Foster Hewitt's war-cry first echoed out over Toronto radio in 1921 ("He Shoots!!! He Scores!!!") and his narration of hockey action was standard Saturday night entertainment in most Emily homes with radios thereafter.

In closing, we might stop briefly to compare Emily at 1939-40 with Emily (including the village of Omemee) a century earlier. In 1840-41 there were 1851 people, in about 350 households with about 4000 acres cultivated, and assessment totalling less than £15,000—by 1941 there were only 1520 residents in 404 farm households, with nearly 40,000 acres improved, and assessment over $1,500,000. Since Omemee was not included in the 1941 census, the populations were about equivalent, but with an enormous development over 10 decades in farm production, living standards, transportation, communication, education, recreation, and practically every other aspect of life. Yet consider the fact that a century ago the township had 986 children under 16 years of age, while in 1941 there were in Emily only 319 children under 14 years—the average age had shifted upward by a wide margin, and old people now outnumbered children, thanks to better food, healthier living conditions, and superior medical and other facilities; and very probably fewer of the 939 children in 1841 reached adulthood than of the 319 children in 1941.

Who would have dreamed in 1840 of being able to drive to Lindsay in half an hour, or to Toronto in 2 hours? to send milk and other produce to Toronto by train? to pick up a rubber earphone and talk through a wire to Omemee or Montreal or London, England? to turn a dial and hear voices and music brought in a few seconds from a station thousands of miles off? to post an order to Toronto and have clothes, furniture, tools, books &c. delivered a week later to your farm mail-box? or even to turn a switch and get cool electric light, or turn a tap in the kitchen or bathroom and get clean sanitary hot and cold water? Yet in the 1930s most Emily people went about their work along the back concessions without much discernible change from the late 19th century—no oxen now, and not as many horses, but still not many tractors in the wider fenced fields, more fertilizers, more under-draining and crop rotation, and mainly still the same staple crops. The average farm was larger, the farm buildings now of lumber with stone or concrete foundations, the homes of brick or stone instead of logs or square timber; inside much more "store" furniture and furnishings, more magazines and books and newspapers, more fresh food in winter but still the same rows of fruit & vegetable bins in the cellar and shelves heavy with preserves (plus a growing variety of canned goods); much less sickness in bad weather; and many more implements to lighten the workload everywhere on the farm, and many more people living to a ripe old age. The changes were far fewer along the back concession roads than in the township's villages; but still on Sundays there were now more automobiles than buggies or democrats in the church driving-sheds; and people went to church or market, or simply visiting relatives and friends, along wider smoother roads between wire fences around broad fields, instead of along narrow winding dirt roads lined with miles of dense forest, or between rough clearings encircled with stump or split-rail fences. Of the people themselves, an astonishingly high proportion were the grand-children or great-grandchildren of those who had cleared those same farms and travelled those same concession roads in the pioneer decades 1819-49, and having the same objectives in life.

NOTES

[1]Note 1 in chapter eight applies here also, re population figures.

[2]Lists of the pathmasters and poundkeepers in 1900 will be found in Appendix XXV.

[3]Bylaw 358 in 1908 repealed bylaw 189 and regulated height and construction of fences —all were to be not less than 4½ feet high; wooden fences properly based, staked and made solid; wire fences to be not less than 9 strands of wire high.

[4]These County roads, totalling about 32 miles, were: No. 41, east-west through Omemee (now no. 7 Highway); no. 3 north from no. 41 toward East Emily, about 4 miles east of Omemee; no. 4, an extension of the road east from Lindsay, crossing no. 5 a mile north of Downeyville; no. 5, north from Omemee via Downeyville toward Dunsford; no. 5A, eastward from no. 5, just south of Verulam boundary, toward King's Wharf; no. 6, the Emily middle line north from Cavan boundary to meet no. 41, 1½ miles east of Omemee.

[5]If space permits, a sample page of signatures and the map will be reproduced as illustrations.

[6]An essay by Mrs. L. Harrington, on memories of the school fairs 1910-14, is contained in Appendix XXVI.

[7]Mr. Cleveland Robb was a close boyhood friend of the author.

[8]Nelson Agnew "Social Change in Rural Ontario as Reflected in Victoria County 1919-1929", M.A. Thesis, Trent University 1972.

[9]Maskinonge or muskilunge (the word is spelled in about 20 ways, and shortened to muskie or lunge) is an Ojibway Mississauga word meaning "ugly fish".

WAR AND CHANGE (1940-1973)

The population of Emily, for reasons already given, varies according to whether the Dominion decennial census or the local assessment statistics are taken, as below:

	1941	1943	1951	1953	1961	1963	1971	1973
By Census:	1520		1579		1691		2333	
By Assessment:		1503		1433		1660		2572

Assessment in Emily, covering real property, buildings, equipment, livestock &c was either static or rose very slowly until the 1960s; for example, the 1953 assessment was lower than in 1910. Compare with this the astounding increase in township and county taxes (which of course were matched in their swift advance by provincial and federal taxes)—in the 40 years to 1940, local taxes rose almost fourfold, while in the 30 years up to 1973 local taxes rose almost *tenfold:*

	1943	1953	1963	1973
ASSESSMENT (before equalization)	$1,732,727	$1,580,771	$1,875,000	$3,591,828
TAXES (twp. and county)	$37,503	$67,771	$110,511	$360,986

By 1950 the population sank to 1400, and assessment was $1,516,188, but then both began to rise slowly; and by 1959 population was up to 1566, with assessment at $1,704,290—but of this, only about 74% was still farm property and the balance was summer, business and "urban" residential property, mostly owned by city folk for vacations, sports outings or retirement. The township began to undergo qualitative as well as quantitative changes, and some effects on the character and economy of Emily will be outlined in this chapter.

One of the most remarkable trends since 1941 has been the relative decline in the proportion of Emily residents living and working on farms (as revealed in census statistics):[1] 1941: 1,389 or 91.4%; 1951: 1,380 or 87.3%; 1961: 1,257 or 74.5%; 1971: 1.059 or 45.4%—in fact the last 25 years has seen the farm population become less than half the total population, which would have seemed impossible a generation earlier. The township population is now again about equivalent to what it was in 1900, but different in significant ways; yet the average Emily family remained at 4 persons during this whole period, and the balance between the sexes:

	1941	1951	1961	1971
Male:	819	861	894	1209
Female:	701	718	797	1124

These 3½ decades, since World War II began, witnessed a drastic alteration and erosion of township council's powers, as centralization in county control of education, libraries, health, etc. was supplemented by provincial supervision and subsidization of land use, planning, road construction etc. The township council was left to collect greatly increased taxes, to repair its own roads and bridges, to pay bounties for wolves and marauding dogs, to give grants to organizations and bonuses for wire fence construction—and increasingly to be the local agent for the Ontario Municipal Board. Of the $39,047 collected in Emily taxes in 1940, about ⅓ ($13,435) had to be given to the County for its programmes (including roads, house of refuge, patriotic grant &c); of the $360,986 to be collected in 1973, nearly ¾ ($265,881) will have to go to the County for its programmes, including now the County Board of Education, plus another $19,930 for Separate School education. The township is now left with about 20% of the taxes it collects (about $75,000) for its own basic requirements.

The stresses and strains of the machine age, the decline of local community activity, the changing values and priorities of various groups, the increased regulation of all aspects of life by four layers of government, form a complex pattern of wartime and post-war life in rural Emily, which is reflected in county and township council decisions during this period. Unpaid taxes were a depression reminder—in 1941 some 72 owners owed sums from 54c to $100.92 on 90 properties from 1940, and in 1942 a total of $2,726.63 was owing from 1941 on 60 properties, but with wartime prosperity this problem declined as others increased. Emily was paying annual "patriotic grants" collected for the county ranging from $2,600 to $3,465, and in both 1943 and 1944 bought $3,000 in Victory Bonds. Farm and road machinery and workers were difficult to replace, and farm prices were government-controlled while costs escalated. Roads deteriorated as provincial subsidies lapsed, and aging vehicles had more accidents—one unusual example occurred in January, 1940, on the Omemee-Dunsford county road, which was still gravelled; "David Morrissey, R.R.1, Downeyville, reported damage to his car in collision with a building, property of Emery Windrim, Omemee, which had been left overnight partially obstructing the roadway during its removal from one location to another. This claim resulted in a lawsuit between the parties, and judgment given in favor of Mr. Morrissey."

1941 is remembered for a tremendous March snowstorm which closed many township roads especially in east Emily (opened finally by Peterborough snowplows). That July Emily paid the C.N.R. $15 for the abandoned right-of-way in south Emily to be maintained as a township road (as Cavan and Manvers did also). Road wages by 1942 were 35c an hour for a man, 50c for man and team, $1.50 for man and tractor, working a 9-hour day; when Ontario halted its road subsidies, Emily stopped paying wire fence bonuses. Next year the township asked that township boundary roads on its Smith and Cavan sides, connecting to Highways 7 and 28, be taken over as provincial roads, but without success. A similar request in 1944 to "ask the Highways Department to take over the county road from Dunsford south to Omemee, connecting 2 provincial highways, as part of the provincial highway system" was ignored in Toronto. That same year the county replanked Cowan's Bridge for $2,600, and granted Emily $200 to improve the con. 14 road, if the township put up at least $400 for the job. Victoria planned a massive road-building programme for postwar development (with Ontario subsidy), and Emily responded by doubling road expenditures to $15,635 in 1946; when the road superintendent reported that he could not get men at current rates, they were increased in that year, and winter snow-plowing was also expanded. In 1948 the township put up a building for township machinery on the southeast corner of lot 6, con. 6, costing $3,748, and next year road wages went up to 55c an hour for labourers, 75c for man and team, truckdrivers 75c in winter and 65c in summer, snowplow operators 60c, and road superintendent 75c an hour with 6c a mile for his car—by 1950 road expenditures were $24-$25,000, about 40% of all taxes. The county in this period took over maintenance of all bridges over 20 feet span, including the C.N.R. Bridge at lot 5, con. 3, and the Emily Creek Bridge at lot 11, con. 13-14, Emily; county roads in Emily by 1950 totalled 50.9 miles, including 9 miles of 'King's Highway' (provincial) 1.3 miles hard-surfaced, and the balance gravelled or partly-improved—however, in that year Emily had to pay for county roads $6,888.88. Incidentally, Emily had the lowest amount of county hard-surface road in Victoria—as compared, for example, with 13.55 miles in Verulam!

Emily Creek Bridge began to sag in 1953, and in the autumn "failed, being an old wooden structure, under a heavy truck"; but not until 1955 did the county reconstruct it, using an old steel span from the Lindsay Bridge, at cost $10,803.35. By 1957 the township had 53.2 miles of county roads, of which 36.7 miles were still gravel or stone, 6.2 miles bituminous, plus 10.3 miles provincial highway; that year the county took over Emily Middle Line, 3.75 miles, from County Road 17 south and southwest to county road 27 at lot 11, con. 6-7, Emily. Next year the county widened Burley's Bridge on road 7, and put down 5 more miles of asphalt road in the township. Township roads were also being maintained and improved with annual expenditures about $27,000, plus annual Dominion Winter Works Program projects for clearing ditches, underbrushing along roads, etc.—these began in the late 1950s and carried on into the 1960s, a period of mild depression. The county in 1962 gave priority to rebuilding Cowan's Bridge in view of heavy traffic near Emily Park, and spent $43,000 on 15 miles of Pigeon Lake Road north-ward in Emily and Verulam (the pioneer "Bobcaygeon Road"), and more in the next 4 years, to promote the tourist trade. One result was inevitable—Emily spent in 1960 the sum of $34,750 on roads, culverts & bridges, and collected the county road levy in the township for another $15,620.

In 1965 the county began reconstructing the road from Omemee through Downeyville, with branch to Thurstonia,[2] and in 1970 received more Ontario aid by designating it as a Development Road as far as Downeyville. By 1967 Emily had raised the wire fence bonus from 80c to $1.50 a rod, was planning to spend $47,737 on roads, set a minimum wage-rate of $1.50 an hour for its employees, raised all employee wages by 10c an hour, and was paying its road superintendent $1.85 an hour, with other wages graded. But inflation continued, and by 1969 the road superintendent was paid $2.40 an hour, grader operators $2.25-$2.35, truckdrivers $2, labourers $1.85, and they all were increased next year 25c an hour, and in 1971 increased again, and in 1972 another "20c an hour across the board". In 1971 road expenditures were $108,839 and steadily rising; fence-viewers were now paid $10 plus 15c a mile for doing this township job (like the pound-keepers, their jobs had begun as unpaid community work in pioneer times). In the winter of 1972-73 Council applied for $25,000 under the Local Incentives Programme and $4,602 from the Winter Works Programme for removing trees and brushing along township roads and asked the province for aid in building a 5-bay machinery-shed.

County Council also, late in 1972, decided that priority items on the 1973 road programme would be rebuilding (in cooperation with Peterborough) of the road north from Fowler's Corners around the end of Chemong Lake, and also the Causeway Bridge on road 26. But improved roads not only cost much more; they brought many other problems, as we shall see—one Emily Council decision in 1973 was to increase automobile liability policies to $1,000,000, and the same amount for personal injury liability policies, covering all township roads. The Peterborough 'Examiner' Apr. 27, 1973, was told about the dangers of living and driving around Fowler's Corners, where "there have been 7 people killed in the last 5 years". The taxpaying farmer of 1873 could drive his horse and buggy in summer or horse and sleigh in winter along a gravelled winding road at 5 to 10 miles an hour, and get safely to village or church in plenty of time, and home before dark; but now the tourist or subdivision resident (or even the modern farmer) of 1973 wanted to drive his automobile or camper or truck at 60-70 miles an hour from point X to point Y, and must get there in record time. There was no stable point at which road costs and convenience balanced, in spite of endless sheaves of land-use and road-development plans, wafted from Lindsay or Toronto.

The township office during World War II was in the Farmers' Clubrooms at Omemee, until the March 1945 meeting of Council "held for the first time in Coronation Hall". By 1945, Clerk Weir was paid $500 per annum, Treasurer-Collector Laidley about the same, M.H.O. Doctor Earle $5; in 1947 the new Assessor, Thomas Rice, was paid $130. Next year the permanent employees were enrolled under the Unemployment Act—Messrs. Weir, Laidley, Earle, and Walter Herlihey (road superintendent), D. Griffin, C. Lynch and H. Jones. In 1949 T. W. Rehill was appointed clerk at $380 a year, also W. J. O'Neill as assessor, and Ed. Humpage auditor. Next year Herlihey was also appointed building inspector to enforce the new building bylaw requiring permits and establishing rules for all building—after strong protests, Council hurriedly amended the Building Bylaw within a few months "to exempt essential farm residences and buildings on farms comprising 50 acres or more in one parcel of land". That year, 1950, total taxes levied in Emily totalled $62,934. 87, and Mr. Laidley was given $200 plus $30 postage to collect them; next year T. W. Rehill took on the job of Collector, at the same salary, the Medical Health Officer was raised to $200 a year, and

W. J. O'Neill became Assessor at $350 a year. Then in 1953 O'Neill was treasurer ($350) and assessor ($450), while Rehill was clerk ($500) and tax-collector ($200). In 1955 T. H. Laidley returned as Treasurer and Tax-Collector, while Simon Connell was appointed Assessor, for the township. During the 1950s the sanitary inspector, J. M. Lucas, and the relief officer, W. W. Wilson, received only token salaries, like the building inspector, W. Herlihey, since the rush of new building and regulation had not started—for example, in this period there were only 2 or 3 families on relief in Emily. In 1961 the Welfare Officer was given salary $150 per annum, and the others were paid more as their duties increased.

In 1962 a bylaw was passed to regulate hunting in Emily, because of the autumn influx of urban sportsmen, and James Oliver was made special constable to enforce the bylaw at $1.25 an hour plus 10c a mile for his car; the same year the clerk's salary went up to $1,200 a year and the treasurer's to $700, while Council set their own allowances at $12 for each regular meeting and $10 for special meetings. In March the clerk noted in the minutes: "Council met in special session March 19, after the visit of the Prime Minister of Canada (Rt. Hon. John Diefenbaker) to the Coronation Hall, the first such visit since Confederation. Times are tough!"[3] Council that year also granted $500 to the Trent University Founding Fund (and in 1965 added another $200); after hearing a delegate from the Cream Producers' Association, they also passed a motion to protest the colouring of margarine in the likeness of butter. A Bylaw was passed to regulate plumbing and sewage installations in the township, and Esmond Storey was appointed inspector of construction safety at $1.25 an hour plus 10c a mile for his car. Then in 1964 Council raised the treasurer-collector to $1,500 a year, and the assessor to $1,150, plus allowances, in view of escalating duties. Bylaw enforcement officers were named: George Ingle, R.R.3; Stanley Tully, R.R. 2; Gerald Lowes, R.R.1; and Edward Thurston, R.R.1, Dunsford. A plan was begun for permanent township employees' sick leave, 1½ days per month cumulative to 180 days, retroactive to June 1, 1963.

In 1965 Assessor Connell was paid an additional allowance of $1,500 for a complete reassessment of the municipality; the Medical Health Officer was also asked to meet the township solicitor to draw up amendments to the plumbing and sewage bylaw to enforce stricter control on what had become the problem of sewage disposal (Bylaw 940 was adopted in 1966). In 1966 also the clerk's salary was boosted to $2,000 (including the duties of welfare officer), the treasurer-collector's to $1,800, and the assessor's to $1,300, each with usual allowances. After one long and rather dull debate in council, the clerk was moved to add in the minutes a wry comment: "A lot of wind blew around the room for a long time wasting our time." In Centennial Year, 1967, the resignation of Mr. Laidley as Treasurer & Collector was received with regret, and council decided to merge these offices with the position of township clerk, at starting salary $4,500 a year; from 15 applications, Ronald Pogue was selected for the combined post, and one of his first entries in the minutes read: "Council suggested a list of persons to act as a Committee to gather

FENCEVIEWERS' AWARD

(Line Fences Act, section 6, Form 2)

We, the Fenceviewers of the Municipality of _Emily Township_

.... having been nominated to view and arbitrate upon the line fence

between _Joseph Callaghan_ of _Peterborough Ont._

.... and _Patrick Purdue_

of _Emily Township_ .... which fence is to be made and maintained between

_N.½ of N.H._ lot _16_ and _S.½ of N.H._ lot _16_ in the _11th_

concession, and having examined the land and duly acted according to The Line Fences Act, award as

follows: That part of the line which commences at (a) _the East end_

.... and ends at (a) _centre, 58 Rods west_

(a) Describe the points _of east end_ shall be fenced, and the fence maintained by the said _Joseph Callaghan_

.... and that part thereof which commences at (a) _south end of lane_

on west side of N. half S. 16 and ends at (a) _centre, 35 rods north_

of south end .... shall be fenced, and the

fence maintained by the said _Joseph Callaghan_ .... The fence shall be of

(b) State kind of fence, height, material, etc. the following description: (b) _The fence must be all made a lawful_
fence. The one between the lots some of it might be repaired,
and made high enough, without tearing down, but the most
of it will have to be rebuilt. The lane fence could be
properly staked and wired, and raised high enough by drawing
some rails.

and shall cost at least _twenty five cents_ per rod. The work shall be commenced

(c) State by whom, to both in what proportion within _fourteen (14)_ days and completed within _twenty one (21)_

days from this date, and the cost shall be paid by (c) _Joseph Callaghan_

Dated this _21st_ day of _October_ A.D. 193_5_

E. J. Houlihan

Vincent Perdue   FENCEVIEWERS

Jos Flynn

Declaration of Office

Form 19, Municipal Act, section 259 (1)

(a) Insert name of office, or offices in the case of a person who has been appointed to two or more offices which he may lawfully hold at the same time.

I _Vincent Fee_ ....do solemnly promise and

declare that I will truly, faithfully, and impartially, to the best of my knowledge and ability, execute the

office of (a) _Reeve_ ....to which

(b) Elected or appointed. I have been (b) _elected_ in the Municipality of the _Township_

of _Emily_ ....and that I have not received, and I will not receive, any

(c) Where declaration is made by the Clerk, Treasurer, Collector, Engineer, Clerk of Works or Street Overseer, add the words following: "Save and except that arising out of my office as Clerk, or my office as Assessor, Collector, etc., as the case may be"

payment or reward, or promise thereof, for the exercise of any partiality or malversation, or other undue

execution of the said office (or offices), and that I have not, by myself or partner, either directly or indirectly,

any interest in any contract with, or on behalf of the said Corporation (c)..................

....

....

Declared before me at the _Village_

of _Omemee_

in the County (or District) of _Victoria_

this _9th_

day of _January_ 195_8_

W. R. Bell .... J. P.

or Clerk of the said Municipality.

Vincent Fee

(Emily Township Records)

material for a history of Emily Township." Soon after, John A. Bent was recommended to the government for a 1967 Centennial Medal. Council was now meeting every two weeks because of pressure of business, and in 1968 approved Bylaw 970 to hold biennial elections for council, rather than annually, to provide more continuity of experienced administration.

There was also increasing co-operation and merging of services with Omemee, as we shall see later (such as fire protection and subdivision regulation); in 1968 Omemee proposed that Emily council use the offices in Coronation Hall in exchange for village garbage disposal on the township dump. In 1969 the reeve was given allowance of $18 for each meeting, and councillors $16 each, and the salary of the clerk-treasurer-collector was up to $4,900 a year; next year Walter Herlihey resigned after 32 years as road superintendent, and James Farrow took the job at $2.65 an hour. Emily Council, which in 1959 had refused an Ontario Planning Department proposal to join the Otonabee Conservation Authority, now in 1971 informed County Council that "Emily is not interested in planning on a county-wide basis, but is more interested in a township land-use bylaw." The mill-rate on residental property, which in 1947 was 5 mills, was by 1972 up to 20 mills, with commercial property taxed slightly higher. The council still each year made its road inspection trip—the one in March 1973 toured around Jim Johnson's fence, Steve Winn's trees & old pit, the Sumcot road, Stan McCall's culvert, the Cavan boundary roadwork, Lillico's Hill, etc.—but more and more council time was now spent on the modern problems of trailer camps, tourist lodges & marinas, severance of small building lots, sewage disposal and pollution in streams, garbage disposal, fire protection, recreation grants and unemployment projects.

Consider the change from the simple county levy of 1943: Emily was assessed at $1,732,727 on which the county levied general rates $5,198.78, House of Refuge rate $537.21, road rate $3,899.09, and special Patriotic grant $3,465.85—by 1970 this had escalated to the following levies on assessment of $2,870,360: general $27,361.51; welfare $7,665.82; Home for Aged $7,034.18; libraries $3,158.20, and roads $30,146.48. Emily township traditionally had very few on welfare or consigned to the Home for the Aged (later called Victoria Manor); at 1940, out of 68 in the Home for the Aged, 2 were from Emily, in 1944 only 1, in 1950 only 2; in 1954 out of 98 inmates only 1 was from Emily; in 1960, Emily had 4 out of 83; in 1965 only 3 out of 93 inmates; and in 1969 only 3 out of 112. The cost of maintaining each inmate per week rose from $7.57 in 1951, to $22.82 in 1960, and to $59.85 by 1969.

Victoria set up its "library-co-operative" in 1950, which circulated books to 11 public libraries and to high and public schools libraries, including those at Omemee. By 1956, when the county library had 8,237 books (50% juvenile and 25% adult fiction), all 9 Emily schools were receiving books on loan, 3,678 being read by teachers and pupils (and parents) that year. The library report in 1960 listed 11 outlets in Emily and Omemee which circulated 6,104 books that year; by 1965 this had risen to 13 outlets circulating

6,971 books in Omemee and Emily, and still without a county tax levy for the service. But in 1967 the county public library system was set up, covering "areas that had no previous library service . . . at Downeyville, the branch library in the corner store was opened April 13, 1967, and largely due to the amiable & firm guidance of Mr. Joe Kirley the membership has soared to 160, and the local people are making full use of the books provided. Public and high school students are regular attenders to consult the reference material, which . . . had been used on more than one occasion to settle an argument among the local farmers."; that year (1967) Emily people read 23,889 county library books, but for the privilege Emily paid a county levy of $1,184.82. Next year Omemee Public Library was enlarged and re-decorated in Coronation Hall, and open hours increased to 10 a week; but "the fabulous new library quarters in Lady Eaton School" had cut down student use of the public library considerably. In 1968 Downeyville Library circulated 2,053 books—fiction 561, juvenile 768, non-fiction 293, magazines 214, reference 217—and in addition the Emily elementary schools circulated 33,600, indicating far more reading with easier access to a wide range of books.

County Council stopped publishing school inspection reports in the 1930s, and there is little news of the Emily schools during World War II; the schools all participated in war work such as school gardens, buying war savings certificates etc., but inevitably attendance declined with the decline in general population. S.S.9, for instance, which had operated since 1866, was closed in 1938 and the few children transported to S.S.11; then in 1949 the school reopened again, and carried on for 18 years before the final closing. But the future trend became evident after the war, when small high schools (like Omemee) and continuation classes (like Downeyville) could no longer provide the necessary range of courses for the tide of young people who wanted higher specialized education. Emily Council in June 1946 adopted a resolution to the Ontario Education Department asserting that they would regret the closing of Omemee High School as rumoured, since "it made possible for many township children a higher education otherwise denied them". Omemee Public School (which served the Emily area around) was overcrowded and in 1951 a one-room annex was put up across the street, and then in 1956 a new 6-room public school was built on the Athletic Field. The High School used the old school until 1957 when Omemee joined the Victoria County High School Area, closed O.H.S. finally,[4] and bussed its secondary students to Lindsay C.V.S.

In 1954, School Section No. 16 in Emily joined the Victoria High School Area, and in 1956 S.S. no. 6. Then in 1957, when Omemee joined the Victoria Area, the same bylaw took in "all the real property in the township of Emily which composes S.S.1, Emily". In 1958 S.S.12, Emily, joined the Victoria H.S. Area, followed in 1959 by S.S. 5, and in 1960 by S.S.4, Emily; the attraction was the new enlarged composite secondary school in Lindsay to which more senior students were bussed, now that High School Entrance examinations had been abolished. In east Emily the attraction was toward the Peterborough Suburban Secondary School District, with its new Crestwood Secondary School building planned just west of the city limits; in 1958 S.S.13, Emily, joined the P.S.S.S.D., followed in 1959 by S.S.7, 8, 9, and 10; the effective date for bussing students into Peterborough County was postponed from Jan. 1, 1960 to Jan. 1, 1961. This provincial consolidation of secondary education was crowned in 1966-67 by its plans for "Community Colleges", and Sir Sandford Fleming College began courses in arts, trades and crafts on Lindsay and Peterborough campuses soon afterward. These changes in secondary education brought extensive (and expensive) building projects, especially at Lindsay, explaining much of the tax-surge in the early 1960s. In 1963, for example, Emily school levies totalled $52,322.66 for public schools (plus an Ennismore Separate School levy), and including $11,529.25 for Victoria County H.S. Area and $20,510.16 for Peterborough County H.S. District.

In June 1963 Emily Council adopted Bylaw 901 to form a Public School Area in the township abolishing local school boards, but after appeals by 5 school sections, repealed the Bylaw in October. Next year the Ontario Legislature abolished all rural school sections and organized the system of township school areas under township boards. School Inspector Bates met Emily Council in July to explain the procedure for establishing the Township Board effective Jan. 1, 1965; this would include Omemee, as the Act required that each village under 1,000 was to be included in the township school area; there were 3 Emily members and 2 from Omemee; and part of S.S.15 was allowed to join the Verulam School Area, going to Bobcaygeon School, and a few in northwest Emily went to Ops (Lindsay), while a few in north Cavan came up to Omemee School.

S.S.4 (Downeyville) and S.S.6 had been operated as Separate Schools since 1905, and in 1962 were united; by 1964 a Union Separate School Board had been formed to administer S.S.4, 5, 6, 12 and 15, and a new 4-room school was built opposite the Church at Downeyville, with principal Mrs. A Fiorini, which soon had over 100 pupils; the small one-room schools were closed 1965-6 and the pupils all bussed to Downeyville, except for a few in east Emily who went to Ennismore Separate School. S.S.10 at Orange Corners made many improvements after the war—new furnace, toilets, roof, lights and redecoration, and carried on until 1966, the last teacher being Mrs. A. Bailey; at its closing in 1966, Mrs. McCall's article commented sadly: "After 90 years . . . education for this area is to be replaced by a modern central consolidated school in Omemee to which children will be transported in modern buses." Similarly S.S.9, opened in 1866, was newly decorated with new well, lights, furnace etc. in 1960, only to be closed in 1967, the last teacher from 1964 being Mrs. Olga Gall. S.S.3 closed in 1967, the teacher in the last year being Mrs. Ilma Lee. S.S.3 and S.S.16 celebrated their joint Diamond Jubilee in July 1952, and had a reunion at which 247 former pupils recalled their early days there. The last teacher at S.S.16 was Mrs. Muriel McGahey (1956-66) and the building was sold as a home in 1967. S.S. 13 (Bethel School) was unusual in that its attendance was increasing, reaching 45 in 1957, when a classroom was rented at Fowler's Corners and operated for 10 years as S.S.13 East; a new oil furnace was installed at Bethel School in 1957 and a water system in 1961; the school was closed in Feb. 1967 and sold at public auction for $4,000, the pupils like others being bussed to Omemee.

The first Township School Board, elected Jan. 1965, consisted of Dennis Acreman, chairman; Murray Finney, Wilbur Morrison, Robert Scuse and Stanley McCall, members; with Harry Sisson, secretary-treasurer; Ken Harrison, attendance officer; and Dr. J. Sobrian of Omemee, medical officer. In Dec. 1965 Emily Council held a joint meeting with the School Board to plan the proposed 8-room addition to Omemee School, and it was decided to issue debentures for $225,000 to finance 6 classrooms, a general-purpose room and a library. The 1966 School accounts collected and paid out by Emily Council included $21,198 to Emily School Area Board, $6,321.20 to Emily Separate School Area, $18,518.72 to Victoria County High School Board, $10,076.65 to Peterborough Suburban High School Board, and a few other small sums. Lady Eaton Elementary School in Omemee, now 13 rooms, was officially opened in June 1967 as a memorial to an outstanding local graduate.[5] Bussing of children from Emily township to Omemee began in Feb. 1967, and in the first year there were fewer than 300.

1968 was the year that the township realized what was involved in "modern education" as blueprinted in Toronto. It began in a small way when Council concurred in the need for another addition to Lady Eaton School, and approved its small share (less than 1%) of the debenture to build a 10-room addition to Verulam's Bobcaygeon Public School, covering the few Emily pupils who went there. But "the roof fell in" when, in May, Council had before it a 1968 school budget of $202,947.50, up from $164,678.51 in 1967. After grants and subsidies, the Emily P.S. Board wanted $69,785.50, of which Omemee's share would be only $16,008, and this would require (according to a Peterborough 'Examiner' item of May 29, 1968) a 9½ mill tax-increase in Omemee, and a 12-mill increase in Emily. The School Board complained that it had overspent in 1967, by about $20,000, and needed every cent of the estimate, while councillors criticized teachers' salaries, non-teaching employees, and other "frills", goaded by angry enquiries from ratepayers about the higher levy. Some councillors had second thoughts now about the need for more expansion of Lady Eaton School, which they had already approved, and according to the Lindsay 'Post': "Clerk Ronald Pogue had a parting shot when he said he would like to hire the school board chairman to attend at the municipal office and answer the taxpayers' questions." The Emily School Board finally published a long "clarification of facts" which avoided nearly all the financial implications,[6] which finally required a 14-mill increase for Emily ratepayers. Possibly one result was Victoria County's decision by Bylaw 1950, late that year, to establish a County Board of Education to handle both elementary and secondary school for the county, consisting of 13 members on a population basis; on this Board which took over control Jan. 1, 1969, Emily and Omemee together had one member—Paul McGuire, long active in community and school affairs in the district, who still serves in the office.

Emily Council in mid-1969 protested to the County Board of Education that the township was paying more than its fair share of the county school costs, and asked to be supplied with assessment and other relevant statistics on which the levy was based. Principal Ross Brown in Dec. 1969 reported that Lady Eaton School was overcrowded, with enrolment of 506, of whom 50 were in the new kindergarten grade, and about 100 above the previous year. He analyzed the causes: (as reported in the Peterborough 'Examiner' Dec. 18) "Emily township is one of the critical growth areas of the county . . . cottages are being winterized for 4-season living, and new homes springing up in Pigeon and Chemong Lake areas and along con. 3 west of Highway 7 Peterborough bypass . . . Emily will continue to grow rapidly because of its proximity to Peterborough. The municipal council expects development to double in the next two years. Another influence is the improved transportation facilities which make it possible to commute to Oshawa and Toronto . . . this trend is likely to increase . . . The result is the change from a rural agrarian community to a semi-suburban situation. Children from farms are now in the minority. With this change come demands from new families for the extras they enjoyed elsewhere—oral French, industrial arts, home economics and family life education . . . some children are handicapped and await placement in an opportunity class . . . (with) special materials and a teacher with extra training; the school now lacks the resources to assist them . . ." In June 1969 also, Victoria Board of Education was lamenting that it cost $73,197.15 (a year) to send 83 east Emily students to Crestwood Secondary School near Peterborough, only 4 to 24 miles from home, as "they had gone to school in Peterborough for many years . . . and it was not feasible to bus the students to Lindsay . . ."

Six years after the first addition, the second addition at Lady Eaton School was opened in June 1973 with another 6 classrooms, a health room etc., at total cost $252,000. The Ontario Department of Education representative noted that Emily region was one of the few where school attendance was now rising, and mentioned in passing that educational costs were going up 20% a year: "Sometimes it is difficult for parents to know what to think about education". He congratulated Victoria County Board of Education in keeping costs down to $477 per pupil while the Ontario ceiling was $545 per elementary school pupil in 1971; but by 1973 the Victoria average was $556 while the Ontario ceiling was $595 per pupil. Another interesting item (Peterborough 'Examiner' Oct. 6, 1973) outlines the problems of Austin Kirley, transportation officer responsible for getting 4,300 Victoria students to school 5 days a week on 93 buses travelling 5,300 miles a day (and costing $600,000 a year), plus his problems as school attendance officer handling truancy. High School students had to walk up to 2 miles to catch a bus, and elementary students up to one mile; those with serious handicap such as a broken leg were brought to school by taxicab; only once since 1969 have students had to stay at school overnight because of bad weather, but occasionally after a bad storm the buses did not run and the schools closed down. One major problem was pupil-control on the buses, and another was the hundred or so each year who "have no motivation", some of whom should be sent to training school. "We have problems on Highway 7 east of Omemee", he said "We try to stop in the safest places but it is still dangerous." No mention was made of other problems, such as students who had to catch a bus at 7.30 or 7.45 a.m., the conflict of after-school activities and the need to get home before dark to do chores, etc.

Lady Eaton Elementary School now has 531 pupils, of whom 150 are from Omemee and 365 from Emily township; of these, only about 125 or 130 are now from farm homes,[7] indicating the tremendous change in 20 years. In addition, about 20 Emily public school pupils go to more convenient schools in Ops and Verulam, from the township borders, while 6 from Cavan attend Lady Eaton School. Seven buses tour the township roads to bring the pupils to Omemee 5 days a week during school terms. St. Luke's Separate School at Downeyville has 4 classrooms, and its principal is John Gouett; it now has 76 pupils, including a kindergarten for children of 5 years. Pupils are bussed to Downeyville from all parts of Emily at present, and also a few from west Ops and south Verulam. From east Emily about 23 pupils are taken by bus to Ennismore Separate School, as being more convenient. These hundred children are in some ways more fortunate as they are educated in their local rural environment (at Downeyville or Ennismore), not being a minority group in an urbanized environment like the 125 or 130 Emily farm children at Lady Eaton School in Omemee—a comparative study of the two groups over the next decade, analyzing the effects of modern education upon children, would be significant. Although the Separate School Board has jurisdiction over Roman Catholic children up to Grade 10, the children who graduate from Downeyville or Ennismore schools at present continue their education at Lindsay or Crestwood Secondary Schools, being bussed with other children, except for an occasional Emily student who goes to St. Peter's High School in Peterborough or similar district institutions; this also applies to those who continue their training at Sir Sandford Fleming College in Lindsay or Peterborough.

Thus in 1973 all that the ratepayers-parents of Emily, including scores of experienced former school trustees, have to do is to pay in 1973 a tax levy of $212,160 for education (secondary $104,275, elementary $87,955, separate school $19,930); this can be compared with 1951 educational levies totalling $26,693 (secondary $5,100, elementary $18,525, separate school $3,068). This 1973 total takes over 58% of all taxes at the local level, though the taxpayers have lost almost all control over local administration of education, just as they have also lost the local school buildings as community centres. The advantages and disadvantages of modern centralized education can be argued endlessly, but certainly each new encroachment of an outside government authority operating from a distance diminishes local community responsibility and individual involvement, with harmful human results from kindergarten to parenthood, plus a much larger dip into the pocket-book for all concerned. The various effects of 12 to 15 years of schooling for Emily farm children, a minority of about 25% in consolidated multi-roomed schools in urban surroundings, among a majority of town and other children oriented away from farm-life, will no doubt be drastic in the new Emily generation from 1967 on, but they will have to be assessed in the future. To most Emily farm parents, though they have to pay manyfold for this modern education, it is the wrong training for encouragement of young people to undertake a life on the family farm, and will only accelerate the drift to the towns, and the abandonment of the ancestral way of life in Emily, after 150 years.

World War II came to Emily in 1939 as a very disturbing change after ten years of depression, but they responded as in the past to the need to fight Hitlerism and militarism. The Red Cross appealed to residents to collect tinfoil and other salvage for the war effort, and the government quickly mobilized the militia units for active service. In Victoria, according to Kirkconnell, the 45th Field Battery and 56th Anti-Tank Battery, R.C.A., were mobilized first, and distinguished themselves in the invasion of France after June 1944. But local volunteers were in several infantry units, as well as the Air Force, the Navy, the Ordnance Corps, the Ambulance Corps, the Women's Army Corps, and others. The County War Memorial in Lindsay records the names of 112 Victoria County dead, listed in Kirkconnell's appendix, and of these a number were from Emily, Williamson in *"Omemee"* lists the names of those killed in action as recorded on the Omemee District War Memorial: Arthur Boate, Edwin Brenton, Kenneth Brenton, Gordon Fee, Ralph Hanbidge, Leonard Magee, Peter Murray, James Murtha, George Roadhouse, William Stephenson, Clifford Strain, Clifford Veals, and Ernest Wills; he also has lists from Christ Church and Trinity Church and Omemee High School of those who served from their membership.[10]

Emily Council paid annually the patriotic grant as levied by County Council, as mentioned, and subscribed to Victory Loan Drives during the war years, just as individual citizens did. Those who returned were welcomed back late in 1945 when they returned to civilian life and picked up their lives among their relatives and friends in Emily, many of them joining the Omemee Branch of the Canadian Legion. One Peterborough *'Examiner'* item of May 26, 1951, describes a Legion Fair at Omemee on the evening of May 24 which included a softball game against a Mount Pleasant team (won by Omemee), an amateur talent competition in the evening, followed by bingo and other games and dancing in the Legion Hall. In Nov. 1956 Emily Council worked with Omemee Council to plan for the District War Memorial near Coronation Hall, to commemorate all who served, particularly the war dead. The Memorial was formally unveiled at a solemn ceremony on Aug. 25, 1957, and wreaths were laid by the Canadian Legion and other groups, with political and church leaders, school children, and many others attending. Each year since on Armistice Day and other special occasions tributes to the war dead have been held at the Memorial: for example, on the Sunday before Nov. 11, 1970, the Lindsay Salvation Army Band headed a parade of Legion and

Peter Murray

Clifford Strain

Arthur Boate

Gordon Fee

James F. Murtha

Wm. Stephenson

SOME WORLD WAR II VETERANS

Ladies' Auxiliary members, Scouts, Guides, Cubs and relatives from the Legion Hall, in charge of William Acreman; at the Memorial after prayers, wreaths were laid by Reeve Smith of Emily, Reeve Free of Omemee, and several others, and Gordon Bocock read the list of those killed in action.

With a per-capita taxrate which remained fairly stable from 1943 ($24.95) to 1952 ($25.44), and then began zooming up (1953—$47.29; 1963—$66.57; 1973—$140.35), Emily Council had many minor problems, some of which will be described later. County Council in 1943 in Bylaw 1316 provided rules for extension of Bell Telephone lines on highways, streets, bridges and other public places, and Emily Council authorized its road superintendent to supervise any telephone construction in the township, but the big expansion came after 1950. Emily Municipal Telephone levies by Council in 1952 totalled $5,660.70, and in 1956 were $5,267.50, indicating the expense of maintaining and upgrading a municipally-owned system. In 1950 the trustees of the Municipal System met Council to decide its future, and June 3 a meeting of subscribers was held "to decide what to do with the system". Early in 1960 Bylaw 862 authorized sale of the Emily Telephone System—the number of telephones had crept up from over 100 in 1947 to well over 200 by 1960, but costs were becoming prohibitive; the Bell Telephone Company stated that in 1957 it "partly overbuilt" the Emily system, and in 1960 requested Council approval to bury its cables and go ahead with an automatic dialling system. As mentioned, Miss Gladys Fee resigned in 1959 after two decades of service as chief operator of the Omemee exchange, and by 1962 Bell had taken over completely. Bylaw 909 in Dec. 1963 dissolved the Emily Municipal Telephone System. By 1968 Bell had 970 telephones on its Omemee exchange, and the present total is over 1,000, with automatic dialling, though some party lines remain. By the magic of modern technology, Emily residents can dial almost anywhere in Canada and the United States without operator intervention, though annual rates are much higher than in the Emily system.

After the war there was rapid expansion of Ontario Hydro services into rural areas, and by the 1960s reasonably-priced electricity was brought into almost all Emily homes and other farm buildings, for lighting and power to operate furnaces and machines of all kinds; this was particularly useful because of the steady increase in livestock production in Emily, allowing expansion of farm equipment in barns, stables, poultry-houses etc. It also promoted the replacement of wood-stoves by electric stoves and oil-burning furnaces in farm homes. Council in Aug. 1957 approved permission to Consumers Gas Company to built a transmission pipeline across Emily, supervised by the road superintendent, to follow the middle road from the Cavan boundary north to the 3rd line, west on the quarterline, then north to Omemee and on the quarterline to con. 5, and west on the line to the Ops boundary; in 1960 the Company was franchised to install gaslines into Emily buildings and sell its heating services, in competition with electricity and oil.

Through the decades fire protection in Emily consisted mostly of local initiative—fire insurance and lightning rods on buildings, and neighbourly assistance with buckets to put out the fire before the well ran dry (unless one was lucky enough to live near a stream or pond), and to get the livestock and furniture out before the fire consumed them. Omemee had a fire engine and voluntary brigade, but it could not go far out of the village to fight rural fires. But with better roads, alarm systems, telephones and fire-equipment, and with more tourist lodges and non-farm residents who expected services, Emily Council after the war had to consider the problem. Among 1952 expenditures is listed: "Village of Omemee, 1953 Fire Protection rates collected 1952—$910.00". In Oct. 1961 Council decided to pay Omemee the sum of $1,000 as retainer plus $100 for each call answered, for fire protection for the whole township. Three years later Emily made an agreement with Omemee for a joint fire department and to establish the Omemee-Emily Fire Committee to regulate the department. In 1966 Council moved to have the Fire Area Board (for Emily and Omemee) buy a firetruck at value about $18,000, under an Emergency Measures grant; approval was given to appoint a fire chief and deputy-chief, and to pay volunteer fire department personnel $4 for the first hour, $2 an hour thereafter, $1 for each practice meeting, and 10c a mile for their cars in attending fires and meetings. Bylaw 972 in Dec. 1968 endorsed an agreement with Omemee to set up a joint fire department, and next year the township purchased fire protection for the King's Wharf area from the Bobcaygeon Fire Department for $300 a year; this was renewed yearly, as was a similar agreement with Ennismore in 1971 for fire protection for northeast Emily for $300 stand-by pay, plus $100 for the first hour and $50 each additional hour per call. Meanwhile the fires continued to break out—in Jan. 1971, as reported in the Peterborough 'Examiner': "Firefighters battle $25,000 Blaze; Farm Home Razed Near Omemee" when Omemee firemen battled a house fire in temperature 20° below zero for 6 hours at the old Endicott farm near Omemee—"Frequent trips had to be made to Omemee by the tanker to secure extra water, and a pumper was supplied by the Lindsay Fire Department." In Apr. 1973 a barn fire on property owned by Dr. Bishop, half a mile north of Omemee, caused by spontaneous combustion, demolished the barn with $15,000 damage.

The problems caused by residential subdivision, tourist development along lakes and streams, garbage disposal, water pollution, and building, plumbing and sewage regulation, are all inter-related and must be described together; collectively, they have been a major administrative preoccupation in Emily since 1945, and particularly since 1960. Emily Provincial Park, which is related, will be discussed separately. The tourist lodge and summer cottage construction along Pigeon River has been mentioned, and it continued during World War II as urban people came to the peaceful countryside to relax from war-work. Emily Council in June 1944 allowed the proprietors of Ava Lodge at Fee's Landing to operate a dancing pavilion, but when they came back in 1948 for permission to sell beer and wine under license, Council rejected the application after a passionate speech by one of the local clergy; Council decided "the people of the township are overwhelmingly opposed to (such) a harmful influence in . . . a traditional picnic area patronized by young folk", and requested Omemee Council to endorse their stand. In May 1950 Emily Council held a special session to move unanimously a protest at the application of Omemee Lodge for a dining-room liquor license. In 1953 Emily held a vote on local option under the Liquor Control Act of Ontario, and decisively defeated it. Next year a petition was sent to the Department of Transport to have the channel of Pigeon River dredged and cleared of weed-beds and bogs, to help promote tourism, but little was done. There was little regulation as yet of cottage and boathouse construction along lakes and streams, or along township roads, but access roads were constructed. In 1946 the Road Superintendent was instructed to proceed with work to open the Emily-Verulam boundary from the county road east to Pigeon Lake, and in July 1959 Council prohibited any buildings on any road allowance, and also prohibited camping and parking of trailers on any road allowance. By 1959 Emily property was evaluated for taxation purposes as 73.27% farm property, 16.53% summer & cottage property, and 10.2% urban type &c. A few townships had less "summer and tourist" property than Emily (e.g. Mariposa & Ops), but the county average was 33.3% and some northern townships were already over 50% summer and tourist property.

In 1960 Council requested the clerk to notify the provincial police about complaints received re "Sunday dancing and bootlegging at certain summer resorts in the township". But summer property-owners were now more influential, and in Aug. 1962 met with Council to air grievances and promote action to curb blaring radios and motorcycles; an anti-noise bylaw was promptly passed, and the Building Inspector was ordered to require all owners of trailers to remove them within 30 days—in the same category was discouragement of an auto-wrecking and scrap-metal business proposed at Fowler's Corners. Severance of building lots along roads and waterways continued unrestricted—Council approved plans for development of Spenhaven Point Resort on lots 17-18, con. 9 at Pigeon Lake, early in 1966, and inspected reported car dumps at Fox's Corners and C. Hayward's; the same year Bylaw 940 regulated construction and installation of sewage disposal systems in the township. Late in the year Sumcot Development Corporation of Toronto sent a representative to propose a subdivision for retirement homes, cottages and even high-rise apartments on lot 23, con. 11; and Mr. C. Perritt requested permission to operate a stock-car racetrack and garage on the southeast quarter of lot 10, con. 4. Council approved a bylaw to license operation of such racetracks in Emily. Mr. A. Lawrence asked approval to subdivide lot 23, con. 6, and Council agreed to inspect the site.

In Centennial year, 1967, Mr. Perritt received his permit for a racetrack, subject to bylaw regulations. A representative of Bowes & Cocks Realty of Peterborough met Council to discuss a proposed subdivision on lot 23, con. 5, and Council drew up a bylaw to restrict the subdivision plans on this and the adjacent lot 22, owned by A. E. Lawrence, to summer cottages only. Albert Clancy, sanitary inspector, was instructed to clean up and fence the township dumps on south half lot 18, con. 7, and north half lot 6, con. 8. By this year the assessment was only about 56.2% farm property, the balance being:

vacation resort $37,685; commercial and business $6,650; residential
$1,074,330, and telephone, rail & pipeline $13,588. In 1968 the owners of
lots 18 and 19 in con. 10 were refused permission to close part of the road
allowance and sell or lease same, since the public must have access to waterways. The Liftlock City Motorcycle Club was given a license to hold motorcycle races on Joe Knight's farm. The developer of Highview Acres on Pigeon
Lake (parts of lots 22 and 23, con. 10, and part of lot 22, con. 11) was
allowed to install a water-supply system under supervision. Building Inspector
Storey reported that in this year (1968) 163 building permits had been issued
—permanent homes 34, cottages 46, garages 20, boathouses 13, remodelling
39, miscellaneous 11; total cost was $618,664, and permit fees $931.75. In
1969 Council agreed to open the road allowance to the water between con.
13 and 14 on lot 21, at request of F. O'Neill, and gave permission for Chas.
Parker to set up a trailer camp area on lots 22 and 23, con. 14, subject to
Tourism Department regulations of 1960, and Max Edlinger another trailer
camp area on part of lot 23, con. 4.

This was the year when lot severance became very important business,
under provincial regulation—at one meeting Council approved 11 building
lot severances from various farms on concessions from 1 to 14, and dozens
more monthly; some of these were parents deeding a lot to a son on the
farm, but most were building lots for cottages and other residences, sold to
urban families chiefly, or as retirement homes. Early in 1970 the Council
purchased 95 acres of the south half lot 12, con. 8, just north of Emily Park,
costing $18,000, for township use. Another motion permitted Keith Booth
to set up a trailer camp on the north half lot 7, con. 4, subject to provincial
regulations, indicating continued development on roads near Pigeon River.
In September a delegation from Cowan's Bay Cottagers Association brought
a petition signed by 64 property-owners there, protesting mobile homes being
allowed to congregate in the area near Emily Park and Cowan's Bay, and
were informed "The feeling of Council is that if mobile homes are in the
township they should be located in a mobile home area." By 1971, as mentioned, Emily felt no need for Victoria County development-planning, but
more urgently saw the need for a township land-use bylaw, to prevent hap-
hazard ribbon-development along roads and waterways. Next year a delegation
attended Council to object to a trailer camp on part of lot 19, con. 10, but
John Van Gerven was permitted to set up a trailer camp on the north half
of lot 15, con. 8, provided he abided by the provincial regulations, and
deposited a cheque for $1,500 for road construction. During the year (1972)
5 to 8 lot severances were approved each month; and in 1973 the Council
advertised an auction sale of cottage and residential lots held on May 21. Each
year also numerous farms with all equipment and furnishings were being
auctioned as farmers reached retirement age and had no children to carry
on the family farm; some were bought by neighbours for cattle pasture and
a few crops, others by real-estate speculators dreaming of a possible subdivision of "retirement homes" or perhaps a turnover sale for quick profit,
and still others by city people longing for a weekend retreat in peaceful quiet

rural surroundings where they might eventually retire later on to lead the simple life.[8] By 1973, as a result, only about 40% of Emily acreage was still in working farms, and the proportion decreasing steadily.

Although some of the property along waterways was officially listed as "recreation or vacation property" for assessment purposes, the people who had grown up in Emily created most of their own recreation in the local community, with an occasional fishing or hunting trip on lake or stream nearby, and church and school picnics along the waterfront. For decades Emily children had been given a day's holiday on Children's or (later) 4-H Day at Lindsay Exhibition, or to attend the County Plowing Match. Courting couples and anniversary groups occasionally celebrated with dinner or dance at one of the tourist lodges, when they did not wish to drive into town. There were still autumn corn-roasts and square dances and sing-songs on the back concessions, and concerts or card-games in community and church halls. Children near Omemee and Downeyville could join sports teams and other youth groups (including Omemee Boy Scouts and Girl Guides). Reading entertainment could be found in the libraries at Omemee and Downeyville, and Lindsay and Peterborough provided both outdoor and indoor movies, as well as plays, museums, concerts, recitals and other cultural interests—these, however, required automobile transportation, since the railway through Omemee no longer carried anything but freight, and the bus-lines had only service once or twice a day along provincial highways (Travelways Busline as of Oct., 1973, between Cobourg and Orillia, traverses the route Fowler's Corners—Omemee—Reaboro 3 times weekly, while Colonial Coachline has a fall & winter schedule twice daily each way between Peterborough and Lindsay via Omemee).

District newspapers chronicle many aspects of Emily recreation each year. In Oct. 1969 a farewell party was held in Omemee Legion Hall for the Lowes and Roberts families by nearly 100 east Emily friends on their departure to reside in Peterborough; they had been active in the United Church, Canadian Legion, Masonic Order, and other township affairs; "progressive euchre was played and a lunch served to end the evening". In Dec. 1969 Scott Young, eminent Toronto journalist who lives in Cavan just below the Emily boundary, chronicled the joys of snowmobiling "in the great snowmobiling country around Omemee and Mount Pleasant (where) almost everybody drives blue snowmobiles, as I do"; unfortunately, as he relates, snowmobiles also make it much easier to rob isolated farmhouses and cottages that are only inhabited on weekends, in wintertime. In Apr. 1970 Omemee & District Men's Softball League planned a schedule for 10 teams, including Omemee, Fowler's Corners, Old-Timers etc. That year a Downeyville Men's softball team was in the Lindsay League, and was defeated in August by Beaverton 21-9; "4 Downeyville pitchers saw action but were unable to contain the Beaverton batters". Next year in June Downeyville beat Bobcaygeon in 11 innings 3-2; "Dale Cummings was top batter for Downeyville . . . back-to-back doubles by Mike Hadley and Doug McGill in the bottom of the 11th decided the contest."

The Emily Council felt the need to support recreation for its youth, and early in 1970 set up a Recreation Committee with Ray Storey president, given $500 for its work; a grant of $2,000 was offered to Omemee Council for suitable time on arena ice for township children and youths in the year. Near the end of the year a grant of $200 was given to Downeyville Open Air Recreation Committee to help its programmes, and $1,700 to Omemee for 5 hours per week ice time at the arena for children's skating and winter hockey 1970-71. On March 19-20, 1971, the annual Irish Variety Concert was presented in St. Luke's Parish Hall, Downeyville, planned by Rev. F. Mihelich and Miss Betty Dorgan, president of the Catholic Women's League; there were Irish solos, choruses, dances, a pantomime and short skits, including some dancers and players from Douro; "the concert was enjoyed by the large audience . . . music for the dance which followed the concert on Saturday night supplied by Gus Whibbs and his orchestra." Two months later the Downeyville C.W.L. had its 50th anniversary meeting in Lindsay, according to the 'Post', with a banquet attended by several clergy and leaders of district parishes; "Mrs. Harry O'Reilly, historian, read the history of C.W.L. since the 45th anniversary"—as an example of religious co-operation, it is interesting to note that the meeting was in Queen Street United Church.

In Sept. 1971 the Kawartha Invitational Motorcycle races, held at Knight's farm 2 miles from Omemee, and sponsored by the Lift Lock City Club, drew 90 riders from Ontario, Quebec and northern New York, and a crowd of 1,200 spectators; for Emily people this was a noisy spectator event only, with no local winners. Emily Council in November granted $700 to the Recreation Committee for activities that winter and next summer, including an Omemee-Emily hockey schedule including 5 teams from Emily and Omemee, in league with other district teams.

Scott Young, in the 'Globe & Mail' of Nov. 24, 1971, told of reminiscing with a local old-timer who noted that in the area between Omemee and Bethany where he walked through the woods 70 years ago there was rarely a deer or other wild game, but now with so many abandoned farms the deer were much more plentiful, even "with all the chainsawing and snowmobile noise", and the several ski-clubs in the area. "When every farm had a family on it making a living, that was what chased out the deer. Everybody had dogs, and deer don't like dogs or people. There were lots of partridges in those days, more than now; and there were foxes and lots of big jack rabbits, but no deer . . . Now that the people are largely gone, the deer are back." Many local residents in all parts of the township can confirm this, and also the increase in bears and other animals and birds, in the last two decades.

Early in 1972 Emily Council granted $300 to help the Downeyville Open Air Committee with their rink, and granted Omemee $1,250 for ice-time for Emily children and youths on the arena rink. In April a joint meeting of Emily and Omemee Councils discussed construction of a new Arena, and Ennismore was granted $500 for use of their rink by east Emily children during 1972. In May Dr. Jules Sobrian of Omemee came to Council about his private hunting preserve of 200 acres north of the village, which he planned to develop into a business venture, and asked to be allowed hunting on this private preserve on Sunday, but the reeve pointed out that a township bylaw prohibits Sunday hunting in Emily. In May Emily Council granted another $200 to the Emily-Omemee Recreation Committee to promote softball, and appointed Harlan McCarrell to the Committee, also $150 was granted to help the Downeyville Ball Club. Later in the year the Glider Club was given permission to operate on the north half of lot 7, con. 4, but not to plan any building or other development without a permit. After this flurry of activity, the records in 1973 to date are scanty—A Community Centre Committee has been set up to work with Omemee Committee to study the feasibility of a joint Community Centre, and to apply for a $25,000 grant under the Federal-Provincial Winter Capital Projects scheme for construction of this centre, to contain an arena. No doubt the grants for other recreational activities as in past years will also be approved.

In 1954, the same year Emily Council asked the federal government to dredge and clear Pigeon River, they also decided to offer part of lot 12, con. 6, purchased from Mrs. Mildred Fee, to the Department of Lands & Forests for the sum of $1,800, to be developed and maintained as a public provincial park. Another factor was that it was close to the Provincial Forest begun in 1928 and expanded and developed since. A Council motion of Sept. 1955 granted the Department of Lands and Forests the rest of the township park for $1, on condition that they did not obstruct any existing water courses. The park of 67 acres was officially named Emily Provincial Park on June 25, 1957, with a 50-car parking lot, wells, toilets, fireplaces, buildings and a baseball diamond, and by 1960 had an office and gatehouse, dock and beach, and other new facilities, plus over 10,000 new trees planted, and over 400 picnic tables, and parking for 518 cars. The number of visitors rose from 25,113 in 1958 to 169,503 in 1962, the year that Council requested the Ontario Parks Department for tighter controls on the noise and pollution around the park which were disturbing residents in the area. Undoubtedly many of those who came with tent or camper for a holiday at Emily Park came back later to buy an old farmhouse or build a cottage in the neighbourhood.[9] In 1966 Council decided to allow Emily Park to use the dump at lot 12, con. 8, providing they burned refuse regularly, at fee $50 a year; that year the Park covered 167 acres, and had 153,360 visitors and 11,549 campers. Though the number of visitors was down in 1969 to 109,074 (16,372 of them campers) due to poor weather, the officials went ahead with planting 5,200 more trees, both coniferous and hardwood, improving dock and road facilities etc. Wider beaches, new washrooms, underground power and water lines to group camp-areas, indicate the steady improvement of the Park as a holiday centre for urban vacationers.

Council in 1971 boosted the Emily Park fee for use of the township dump to $1,100, and in 1973 to $2,000 for one year. On long weekends especially every provincial park within 150 miles of Toronto became overcrowded by Friday evening, in the summer of 1971; as one Emily Park ranger said: "We put them in the field on the hill back of the general camping area;

it started getting heavy Thursday and by Friday around 3 p.m. all the good sites were gone." One *'Globe & Mail'* page of July 1, 1971 featured a group of ardent fishermen from Ohio camped with their families at Emily Park seeking the famed maskinonge, and a Toronto couple in a camper who had had been coming to the Park for years and were getting tired of erecting and dismantling tent-trailers; on retirement they were going to get a 22-foot "motor home" and spend most of the year on the road. A month later the Peterborough Y.W.C.A. brought 70 children to Emily Park by bus for camping, swimming and crafts, as part of their vacation school programme. In Sept. 1973, Park Superintendent Oscar Irwin reported the park, now 278 acres with 267 campsites, was completely full most weekends, with a great increase in use of beaches and boats in the hotter weather; Emily Park would be open all year round for recreation, with no fees after Oct. 8. The net effect of the Park on Emily Township over these two decades was undoubtedly mostly beneficial, bringing many tourists and campers who spent money in the area, in all types of commercial establishment, and also bringing people who decided to come back later as permanent residents. The small problems of heavier road traffic, more weekend noise, garbage disposal and general pollution, and an occasional troublesome incident involving the police, have been insignificant compared to the many benefits for the township's economy.

Delivery of the mail on the rural routes of Emily (fanning out from Lindsay and Omemee) continued without much change after 1940, 6 days weekly, although the mailman's life has been improved by better roads, more reliable cars, and quicker road snowploughing in winter, as well as higher remuneration. In Omemee, the mail came in from Toronto by train, and by road from Port Hope and Peterborough etc.; an era ended when Robert Grandy retired in 1948, having been Postmaster since 1895 (and his father Richard for 50 years before him). Arthur Weir then became Postmaster, and in 1967 moved the Postoffice into the new building at King and Sturgeon Streets. The Downeyville Postoffice was operated by Mrs. Lillie Lucas until April 1944, then by Vincent O'Connell as acting-postmaster for a year, and by George O'Donnell (the storekeeper) from March 1945 to Aug. 21, 1952; O'Donnell's store was sold to J. J. Kirley in 1955, but except for one brief interlude in 1955, Mrs. Mary O'Donnell was Postmaster from 1952 until Sept. 1962. Downeyville Postoffice was finally closed May 31, 1963, after almost 111 years, but the general store continues as a community centre in the area, even though the postoffice is no longer there.

At the federal level, Bruce McNevin, Liberal, was elected Member of Parliament, in the Victoria Riding in 1940; in earlier days he had been a farmer near Omemee, an official of the Farmer's Union Insurance Company of Lindsay, and a leader of the United Farmers of Ontario; defeated in 1945, he died in 1951. Victoria entered the Conservative fold in 1945 with the election of Clayton Hodgson of Haliburton, who was re-elected in 1949, 1953, 1957, 1958 and 1962; on his retirement in 1963, Charles Lamb of Lindsay won the seat for the Progressive Conservatives; and since Mr. Lamb's death in 1965 the seat has been held for the same party by William Scott of

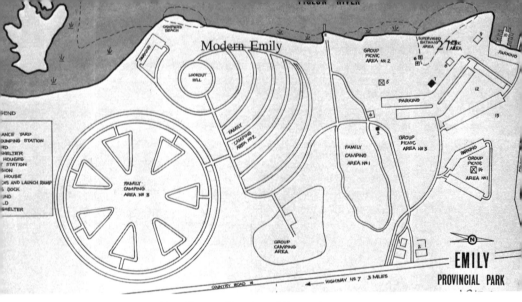

Modern Emily

EMILY
PROVINCIAL PARK

(Ont. Dept. of Lands and Forests)

Haliburton, re-elected in 1968 and 1972. At the provincial level, Leslie Frost of Lindsay kept the Victoria seat in the Conservative camp in 1943, and by increasing majorities in 1945, 1948, 1951, 1955 and 1959; Hon. Mr. Frost was also premier of Ontario 1949-61, and maintained close ties with Emily township and the whole district. On his retirement, the seat was inherited for the Conservatives in 1963 by Glen Hodgson, who was re-elected by decreasing majorities in 1967 and 1971. While the results in the Emily polls are not available for this period, it is probable that they followed the county trend to conservatism since 1945, though the influx of new non-farm residents since 1960 may have altered the previous voting patterns, to some extent; the provincial riding, incidentally, was enlarged to include Haliburton in 1966.

Old-timers in Omemee and Emily still remember Dr. George Earle, who was for many years the only general practitioner in the area; he was joined in his work by his son, Dr. William Earle, and they carried on a joint practice until the father's death, after about 44 years serving the community, during the "Hurricane Hazel" in Oct. 1954. Dr. Wm. Earle carried on until his retirement in 1960 due to poor health, and the area was without a resident doctor until Dr. Jules Sobrian came to Omemee in 1963. Dr. Sobrian has established himself as a skilful, able physician in the tradition of Dr. Earle and his predecessors like Dr. Norris and Dr. Cameron, and he has (like them) become a leader in worthwhile community endeavour.[16] Other professional men were increasingly concentrated in the nearby urban centres like Peterborough and Lindsay; but the Omemee 1973 telephone directory lists the following: Scott & Warner, barristers; G. H. Ward & Partners, chartered accountants; D. J. Warner, barrister; these maintain offices in Omemee as well as elsewhere.

By the 1951 census the religious groups in Emily were: Baptist 21, Church of England 328; Greek Orthodox 5; Lutheran 3; Presbyterian 78; Roman Catholic 536; United Church 598; others 10. Later Dominion censuses unfortunately give religious denominations only by county, but Kirkconnell's history states "In 1965 the parish priest Father F. Mihelich reported his (R.C.) church membership as 90 families and 466 individuals", which may indicate the trend. At St. Luke's Church, Downeyville, major redecoration was carried out by Father V. McFadden, who remained until 1952; Rev. C. Kaye, who stayed only one year (1952-53) organized the Catholic Youth Organization to aid the parish young people, and led in installation of a new heating system. Father Stephen Coffey accomplished further decoration and improvements in the church and the rectory before his sudden death in Dec. 1959. Father Francis Mihelich also improved the church buildings, installed a new electric organ, and led in the building of the new enlarged St. Luke's (Downeyville) Separate School, with a parking lot where the old school had stood for so long. Rev. Mihelich was followed in 1971 by Father Joseph Walsh, the present priest of Downeyville parish.

At Christ Church (Anglican) in Omemee, Rev. A. Johnson was followed in 1942 by Rev. Francis Pooley who stayed 10 years; then in 1951 came Rev. Charles Richmond, formerly a missionary in Africa, rector until 1953, and followed in turn by Rev. A. Smith, Rev. R. Mansfield, and Rev. J. K. Urquhart. In 1950 the former tower with its steeple was taken down, and a Memorial Tower erected to honour the parishioners who gave their lives in two World Wars; a plaque was unveiled on the church's 115th anniversary by Premier Leslie Frost, and Bishop Wells of Toronto spoke at the services. Elsewhere in the parish there were improvements also—at St. John's Church oil-heating was installed in 1960, and the Ladies' Guild has been active in maintaining the church and promoting its work locally. At St. James' Church, electric lights were installed in 1945, in 1950-55 new furnishings, windows, pulpit, organ etc., and in 1960 new seating and a new parish hall; the burning of the mortgage in 1963 was an outstanding event to the parishioners. It was decided that as a Centennial project in 1967 the tombstones in the old St. James' cemetery would be removed and placed around the sides of the church building and the grounds landscaped; a Centennial Memorial Cairn was erected on the lawn, and dedicated in June 1968 by Mrs. Leslie Frost, great-granddaughter of Thomas and Esther Carew who came to Emily in 1825 and lived nearby for 40 years; the plaque on the cairn reads: "In memory of Thomas and Esther Carew of Farrahy, County Cork, Ireland, who with their eight children settled immediately west of this place in lot 21, concession 6, Emily, in 1825 and are buried in this cemetery; and also of the company of over 2,000 men, women and children who settled in this area, helping to found the counties of Victoria and Peterborough."

An Anglican parish letter of July 4, 1973, reads in part: "Sunday, July 1, was indeed a busy day for our new minister, Rev. R. E. Sims. Beginning at 9.30 a.m. in Bridgenorth with Morning Prayer at Christ Church, then down to Christ Church in Omemee for 11.15 a.m., then back to St. James, combining with St. John's, Emily, at 7 p.m. In this way Rev. Sims was able to meet nearly every person . . ." The task of arranging services at 4 churches required help from Lay Readers, though Rev. Sims was kept busy with services each Sunday.

Trinity United Church, Omemee, also removed its spire in 1940, a land-mark for 65 years; in 1953 major renovations were undertaken, with removal of the tower, and a new church front, new heating system, complete redecora-tion, and addition of Sunday-School, kitchen and other rooms. Rev. V. Zufelt, pastor 1946-60, was an unwearying worker for the church—at the annual congregation meeting in Jan. 1948 he reported on his 1947 work, including on the Circuit 17 funerals, 7 weddings, 25 baptisms and visits to 330 homes, as well as a special leadership course, and teaching religious knowledge to 28 public school classes; all church leaders reported progress, and the church had raised about $5,300 in 1947 for its activities. On Sept. 30, 1956, at a special service, a memorial window was dedicated "to the Glory of God and as a grateful tribute to the Presbyterian Pioneers who in 1834 founded a church in this locality, and to her first settled Ministers: Rev. James Dick, 1842-48, and Rev. John Ewing, 1849-93." Linked with Trinity Church is Bethel United Church on the east quarter-line in a lovely rural setting where services have been held since the 1850s, although the 75th anni-versary of the present church was celebrated in 1967. In 1949 a Family Friendship Club was formed which looks after the church building and arranges concerts yearly, and in 1962 the women's group were united into the United Church Women, for other church work. Salem United Church in North Emily, on the Lindsay East Circuit, had a sadder story—it was a part of the Dunsford charge, and services were held until 1969, but with changes in rural communities and the decline in population, the congregation finally decided to close the Salem church and merge with Dunsford United Church, after 112 years of community service. A cairn was erected to mark the site of the church and the lot was given to the Salem Emily Cemetery Company in 1972.

In the last chapter, mention was made of the Presbyterian pastoral charge organized in the 1930s to include Omemee, Lakevale and Lakefield churches; this was served by Mr. C. Robb of Peterborough, (as Lay Reader), for a decade until his death in Nov. 1963. Next spring these 3 churches were joined with Warsaw, Buckhorn and Lakehurst into a mission ministered to by Rev. Gordon Matheson; then in 1965 St. Andrew's, Omemee, was removed from this group and joined with St. Stephen's in Peterborough, served by Rev. K. Wilcox. Lakevale Presbyterian Church, still guided by Rev. Matheson, cele-brated its 100th anniversary in 1966, with M. Deyell as chairman of the Board of Managers and Mrs. Harry Fowler, president of the Ladies' Aid Society; descendants of some of the pioneer families still attend church, where the first "preaching station" was set up in Aug. 1865 in the house of Andrew Fowler, who deeded the lot for the Lakevale Church (opened in Jan. 1866) at the crossroads on the boundary of Smith and Emily townships still called Fowler's Corners.

Emily burial-grounds, from the Presbyterian Cemetery on con. 2 to the Salem Cemetery on con. 13, and from Downeyville Roman Catholic Cemetery to the Emily Inter-denominational Cemetery just east of Omemee, are among the most historic and best-maintained in the Kawartha district—and the Emily Cemetery has one of the finest sites. The Presbyterian Cemetery had its

centenary in 1952 and was enlarged by the purchase of a half-acre to the
south in 1961; in 1963-64 a new well was drilled with an electric pump to
supply the fountain; decoration and remembrance services are held the first
Sunday in August each year. Downeyville Cemetery north of the road west of
the school is full of history, and well worth a visit, especially for the monuments to some of the 1825 Irish emigrants. Salem Cemetery in Millersmith
community, north Emily, has always been interdenominational; the original
half-acre lot has been expanded westward, and now includes also the Salem
church-lot, operated by a Trustee Board led through the last 35 years by
James and Alex McGahey, Joseph Smith, Reid Roadhouse, Hugh and John
Elliott, and others. The Emily Cemetery Board does valuable community
work in maintaining and improving the large cemetery on Highway No. 7;
at its last meeting in May 1973 the Board re-elected C. Miles president and
C. Reeds secretary-treasurer; total expenses for 1972 were recorded at
$5,516.52 and receipts $6,841.41, with Perpetual Care Fund at $1,192. A
community that proudly remembers and appreciates its pioneer ancestors can
always be known by the care its people take in preserving the monuments of
those ancestors.

Most Emily organizations are connected with agriculture or religion; for
example, the Omemee & District Bible Society held its annual meeting Oct.
7, 1973, in St. Andrew's Presbyterian Church, Omemee, and heard com-
mendations of their work "as one of the best rural branches"—the president
elected was Miss Margaret McQuade. L.O.L. #41 in 1952-54 built a new
hall at Orange Corners on con. 2, under supervision of H. Jackson, D. Tully,
W. Magee and H. Franks; this building, fully paid for by 1958, is also a community hall. At Omemee, Lorne Lodge 375 suffered a bad fire which
destroyed their meeting-rooms on King St. in May, 1966; after accepting D.
McQuaid's offer of a site on King Street, it was decided to build a new hall
thereon, and during 1967 (when the lodge had 135 members) several building bees were held, and furniture installed and the hall decorated. On Nov. 8,
1968, the new Masonic Temple was dedicated by the Ontario Grand Master,
D. J. Gunn, and tribute was paid to those who had worked so hard on the
project—A. Bailey, Harry Jackson, Harry Boyd, H. Sisson, W. B. Shaw, J.
Gladding, Dave Lawson and others. Among other worthy township organizations are the Women's Institutes—the Mount Pleasant Institute (in north
Cavan) has some members from south Emily, and the North Emily Institute
draws its membership from all Emily north of Omemee; one of its most
useful endeavours has been the preservation and recording of community
history and achievement over the century and a half since pioneer times, as a
continuing Centennial project. The Institute brings together all community
women for worthwhile projects, such as encouragement of 4-H and other
youth activities, and to provide members with social and cultural interests.
The Omemee and District Horticultural Society has also encouraged community improvement of home-landscaping, as a part of District no. 4 of the
Ontario Horticultural Society; in addition to district picnics and meetings held
each June in some scenic area, the O.D.H.S. has held annual flower and

vegetable shows, often in August at Coronation Hall, Omemee. A news clipping has survived describing the 1951 show, opened by President J. A. Bent,
under the management of Mrs. H. Hill as director, at which the Eaton
Trophy was won by Mrs. C. Best for most points by any exhibitor; other
leading prize-winners were Rev. Zufelt, Mrs. V. Raffin, Mrs. J. Swinson, Mr.
J. Morrison, etc.

We have already noted that during this wartime and postwar period
Emily's population had risen by over 1,000 persons, while the proportion of
these living and working on farms and owning farm property for agriculture
was cut in half; occupied working farms numbered: 1941: 404; 1951: 310;
1961: 308; 1971: 259.[1] Of a population of 2,333 by the 1971 census, the
farm people totalled only 1,059. Of the 259 farms still used for agriculture,
16 were listed as "non-resident"; of the farms, 204 were still owner-occupied,
6 by tenants, and 49 listed as "part-owner, part-tenant". By 1971, farms
were increasingly fragmented: up to 9 acres—7; 10 to 69 acres—27; 70 to
129 acres—85; 130 to 179 acres—37; 180 to 239 acres—48; 240 to 399
acres—44; 400 to 559 acres—9; 569 to 759 acres—1; 760 to 1,119 acres—1;
and none higher. Yet total farm value soared from $2,226,954 in 1941 to
$12,973,800 in 1971;[1] the significant fact is that in 1941 about $\frac{1}{3}$ of this
value was in the land, but by 1971 about $\frac{2}{3}$ of value was the land itself—a
rather artificial speculative value for land development and not for its agricultural productivity.

Similarly, of Emily farmland in 1941, only 39,131 acres was improved: of
this 25,265 was in field crops and 11,980 acres in pasture, with 948 acres fallow
and other small sections in orchard, market gardens, small fruits, etc; in that
year 19,111 acres was unimproved: in woodland 4,924 acres, natural
pasture 10,894, marsh & waste 3,263. In the next 30 years Emily farmland
decreased from 58,242 acres to 43,146 acres, and in 1971 only 25,921 acres
was improved: field crops 15,236 acres, pasture 8,829 acres, fallow 580 acres
and other uses 1,276 acres; while in that year 17,225 acres was unimproved,
of which 5,335 acres was woodland. The obvious trends here are supported
by the following tables based on Emily census statistics:

CROP ACREAGE:	1941	1951	1956	1961	1971
Wheat	1,562	3,011	2,146	1,259	349
Oats	7,120	4,888	3,977	4,736	1,406
Barley	1,100	167	77	127	1,092
Rye	326	65	5	39	12
Mixed grain	3,759	2,194	1,353	1,355	2,254
Tame Hay	10,600	7,894	8,424	8,880	8,131
Corn	—	—	308	163	1,767
Other fodder crops	335	369	201	—	—
Potatoes	227	82	81	31	1
All Field Crops:	25,199	18,677	16,946	16,763	15,236

FARM LIVESTOCK:	1941	1951	1956	1961	1971
Horses	1,529	664	320	248	220
Cattle	6,753	6,726	7,551	8,765	8,892
Sheep	3,942	2,357	2,801	1,531	536
Pigs	3,490	3,537	2,621	3,117	2,908
Poultry	52,300	46,699	43,741	18,500	10,262

(Notes on tables:
1. The 1956 figures are from a special agricultural census that year.
2. Corn and other fodder crops are not listed consistently through the 5 censuses.
3. The cattle figures in 1941 included 3,484 milk cows, 435 beef and 2,834 others, but by 1971 the total only included 1,668 milk or dairy cows.
4. Hens & pullets were ⅞ of the poultry total in 1941, and by 1971 were still ¾, with the rest covering ducks, geese, etc.),

---

The basic trend in this period is away from mixed farming into specialization, mostly in livestock production—wheat and oats acreage fell drastically, with smaller declines in rye and potatoes—the pioneer farmers of 1825 or 1850 would have been incredulous at the thought of only one acre of potatoes in Emily! and only 349 acres of wheat! both staple products on any pioneer farm. Barley production faded and then came back, as did mixed grain. Horses decreased to an average of one per farm, and sheep and poultry decreased steadily, while cattle production rose steadily and swine production fell only a little. The dairy business, producing whole milk to be trucked to dairies and creameries, discouraged ownership of horses, especially as provincial regulations stressed sanitation around stables, and the swing to beef cattle in the last two decades has made horses obsolete on most farms, as oxen were a century before. The profitable working farm in Emily now specializes in one product, beef or dairy cattle, hogs or chickens, etc, and the main specializations are obvious in the above tables. The most important field crops are cultivated hay, corn for ensilage, mixed grain and barley.

With roadside and waterfront farms being subdivided for subdivisions or other residential uses, at the other end of the scale there are now over 100 farms of 180 acres and more each, and increasing mechanization is necessary, especially since "the hired man" had now disappeared except on some large "country estates", or oversize commercial farms; since the war, census statistics have not shown township "hired labour" figures, but have commenced instead to show farm machinery and power (See Table on page 283).

The value of farm machinery and implements, which stood at $226,300 in 1941 census, rose to $732,956 by 1951; then doubled again to $1,526,900 by 1971. Perhaps this helps to explain why food prices, which doubled in the 1940s, were steady in the 1950s and have risen in leaps and bounds since 1960. In 1950 beef was 60c-90c per lb.; pork 49c to 67c; milk 18c a quart;

	1956	1961	1971
All farms	303	308	259
Automobiles	269	269	264
Motor trucks	76	121	154
Tractors	220	265	338
Gasoline engines	36	—	—
Grain Combines	31	54	68
Electric power	253	278	(all?)
Threshing machines	—	33	—
Hay balers	—	66	127
Milking machines	—	—	57

butter 57c per lb.; cheese 29c; flour 7c per lb.; eggs 40c-55c per doz.; dry beans 12c per lb.; potatoes 5c per lb.; bread 10c-12c a loaf; apples 6c to 14c per lb.; fowl 40c-50c per lb.; etc.[11] Few consumers can fail to relate the subsequent rise to the abandonment of district farms and the other costs of modernization, such as more expensive machinery, higher transportation costs, more middlemen and fancy packaging, and changing ways of life both urban and rural. The area which has a local market with direct contact between farmer and consumer, bargaining for fresh farm produce, is becoming, unfortunately, increasingly rare; also the farm family selling eggs, potatoes, or other produce door to door in town, or even bartering at the nearby general store.

County concern in agriculture was reflected in 1944 when the bounty on bearhides was raised by $10, and in 1948 by a bounty of $5 each for destruction of foxes (soon reduced to $3); the county also gave annual grants of $100 (later $200) to Emily Agricultural Society. Emily Council's main problem was compensation for sheep and lambs killed by "dogs or wild animals", which in the war years were recompensed at $6 to $10 for each animal killed, and $1 to $5 for each one injured; the person shooting a marauding dog was paid $10; the price rose rapidly, and in summer, 1944, at one council meeting 12 ratepayers were given about $550 for sheep and lambs killed including one man who had 23 lambs killed. At its next meeting, Council ruled that 10% of sheep must carry bells while on pasture, if compensation was to be demanded. In 1949 the bounty on wolves was raised from $10 to $25, indicating that some marauding dogs were actually wolves, or vice-versa. In 1950 each sheep killed was compensated by $30, each lamb $20, and the annual cost was close to $2,000; another problem that year was the Warble Fly Control Act, requiring all cattle to be treated for warble fly, with an inspector to enforce the township bylaw. In Oct. 1958, 4 taxpayers were paid $1,001 for sheep and lambs killed, of which Timothy Hodgson received $850 for 39 sheep killed. This problem declined somewhat after 1960, as fewer sheep were raised, but by 1965 $200 each was being paid for cows which died after being sprayed for warble fly!

Emily Council for many decades had given small annual grants to farm organizations such as Emily Agricultural Society, Victoria Federation of

Agriculture, and Victoria Plowmen's Association. In 1943 the prizes were $5 each for the best Emily contestants in the County Plowing Match in youth and adult classes. By 1952 this had risen to a grant of $65—$35 toward expenses of the County Plowing Match, plus $30 for prizes—$10 for best Emily man on tractor, $10 for best horse-ploughing, $5 for oldest Emily entrant, and $5 for best girl on tractor. Through the 1960s the grant was usually $50, mostly for prizes to Emily entrants in tractor and horse-plough-ing classes. The 1973 Match is reported in the Lindsay 'Post' of Oct. 4, 1973: "Held Tuesday on the farm of Association president, Harold Millen, north of Fowler's Corners . . . an outstanding success . . . Emily Reeve Stan Smith said in his opinion Victoria County plowmen are among the best in the province . . . He noted good farming begins in the field, and the plow is the first implement used to break up the land." Winning special trophies were Don Franks in "best land with a 3 furrow hydraulic" and Robert Franks in "best utility land with 3 furrow mounted plow"; among prizewinners in some of the 12 classes were Don and Robert Franks, John Harrison, Linda Harrison, Bill Harrison and Ken Harrison.

An interesting example of farm specialization was reported in Peter-borough 'Examiner' on Aug. 25, 1967, concerning East Central Ontario Beef Management Field Day, held at the farm of Don McQuaid, lot 1, con. 1, Emily. About 150 area farmers had a forum addressed by farm experts on the problems of setting up a successful beef feed lot operation—corn-growing, feeding, herd health, buildings, financing and other management matters. Mr. McQuaid talked from experience, having worked as a hired man in the area, in 1948, and come back to buy land for a poultry farm, then in 1960 building a beef-feeder operation. "He has a return of $9.60 per $100 on his invest-ment of $86,000 in land, buildings and equipment." Other speakers talked of the value of good soil drainage, weed control, planned fertilizer program, and "good quality corn silage". The talks by farm experts, "delivered against a backdrop of tall silos and lush fields of corn . . . open fields snuggled up against a big drumlin, 3 miles southwest of Omemee", probably decided other area farmers to go into the profitable beef cattle production. Another example of specialization is an official record reported in Lindsay 'Post', Apr. 22, 1970, of a Dual Purpose Shorthorn female "Marlowemay Aphrodite", owned by Edmund Ruth of R.R.1, Omemee, "2 years old, 10,727 lbs. milk, 405 lbs. fat, 350 days".

The Emily Agricultural Society revived from the depression years, and during World War II began a programme of placing purebred beef and dairy cattle sires, and boars, at strategic points in the township, aided by provincial grants, to improve livestock production; but with the growing use of artificial insemination the above programme was restricted to boars; and in the post-war years the Society began sponsoring field crop competitions, aided by township, county and provincial grants. One such field crop competition was reported in the Lindsay 'Post' Sept. 2, 1970, covering barley and oats, with judge Wallace Thurston; of 10 entrants in barley, the top prizewinners were John Peeters (1st) and Wm. Kennedy (2nd); of 14 entrants in the Rodney

Modern Feed lot in 1973 — (Don McQuaid)

Hauling corn to silo, c. 1935 — (Ed Ruth)

Modern Silo and Corn Harvesting
Equipment — 1970 —- (Stan McCall)

Snow Ploughing, 1970 — (S. McCall)

Building a silo in 1942 — (Ed Ruth)

FARM OPERATIONS

Threshing on Lot 15, Con. 2, c. 1930
(Charlie Mills)

Filling the Water Tank in 1922
(Hilda Jackson)

Barn Threshing about 1965
(Yvonne Lowes)

Cutting with Binder in 1920
(Hilda Jackson)

Modern Harvesting about 1970
(Alton Clark)

Steam Threshing before 1960
(Charles Mills)

FARM OPERATIONS

AUCTION SALE OF
VALUABLE FARMS
—IN THE—
TOWNSHIP OF EMILY.

...and by virtue of the powers contained in a certain Mortgage which will be produced at the time of sale there will be offered for sale by Public Auction, at the

...NSON HOUSE, in the TOWN OF LINDSAY, on
...URSDAY, 21ST DAY OF FEBRUARY, 1895

...T THE HOUR OF ONE O'CLOCK IN THE AFTERNOON, THE FOLLOWING PROPERTY, VIZ.:

...RCEL 1.--The South Half of Lot Number Five, in the 13th Concession of the Township of Emily, in the County of Victoria.

...RCEL 2.--The North Half of the North Half of Lot Number Seven in the Twelfth Concession of the said Township of Emily.

...cel No. 2 is all under cultivation, and also all of Parcel No. 1 except about 6 acres which are well timbered. ...perties are about five miles from Lindsay on a good leading road, and about six miles from Omemee.

...following improvements are said to be on Parcel No. 1: A Frame Barn about 40x52 with Stable under...a Frame House about 22x26, and a second Frame House about 22x28, and a small Orchard; and on Parcel...a Frame House about 20x28 with a Kitchen about 16x18 and a Woodshed attached, and a Frame Barn...0x50, and a small Orchard.

...RMS OF SALE.--Ten per cent. of the purchase money down at the time of sale, and balance within 20 ...ereafter without interest. There will be a reserved bid on each Parcel.

...further particulars apply to

...LE & JOHNSTON,
SOLICITORS FOR THE MORTGAGEE.

or GEORGE McHUGH,
AUCTIONEER.

Auction Sale in 1966
(Harry Jackson)

Auction Sale Poster of 1895
(S. J. Connell)

Auction Sale in 1966
(Harry Faulkner)

Cutting hay about 1926 — (W. McMullen)

Lifting loose hay with hay fork — (H. Jackso

Buck Rake about 1955 — (W. McMullen)

Loading hay about 1925 — (W. McMullen)

Load of sheaves in 1940—(Harry Jackson)

Load of hay bales in 1960s — (Ken Strain)

FARM OPERATIONS

Oats competition, the top winners were James Downey (1st), James Piggott (2nd) and Ken McBrien (3rd). Under the leadership of the late John Bent, the Society also sponsored in 1964 the organization of the Omemee-Downeyville 4-H Club to interest children in raising dairy or beef calves, pigs, ponies, gardens etc. The best of these compete at Lindsay Exhibition, and in 1973 there were 27 boys and girls from Emily among the winners. The 1973 field corn competition winners were: 1st prize—Stanley Smith, 2nd prize—Art Darling, 3rd prize—Don Franks. Presidents of the Society have been: 1920-47—Albert Sanderson; 1948-51—Harold Graham; 1952-56—Wesley Wilson; 1957-59—Elmer Mahood; 1960-64—Victor Williams; 1965-68—John Bent; 1968 to present—Joe Clancy.

The Omemee Farmers' Club still thrives after 62 years, and of the 70 members in 1915 four are still members: Joseph Knight, Wesley Wilson, Leonard Atwell and A. H. Veals. In 1945 the Clubrooms were given up for the building which formerly housed the Cold Storage Plant, and cold-storage lockers for members were installed; unfortunately this building was partly destroyed by fire May 31, 1967, and has been sold, but the Club has continued to function under President Dennis Acreman. The yearly banquets sponsored by the executive have been held in different parts of the township, with the church ladies' groups providing the meals. One outstanding banquet was held to celebrate the 50th anniversary, at St. Luke's parish hall in Downeyville, in 1961, under chairman Alvin Franks; George Veals, 80 years old, who had lived most of his life in the area as a charter member, cut the cake. The officers that year were: President Alvin Franks, Vice-President John Clancy, Secretary-Treasurer Tom McGill, and Directors Victor Williams, Vernon Lang, Alton Clark, Dennis Acreman and Arthur McQuade. The Club still operates its shipping scales at Omemee; in charge have been: 1923-44—S. Vaughan, 1944-52—Wm. Weir, 1953-68—M. McCarrell and his son Harlan, 1968 on—Milton Lacey.

Two incidents reported in Lindsay and Peterborough newspapers confirm the close ties of modern Emily with its pioneer traditions. The first, from the Peterborough 'Examiner' June 28, 1951, is headed "Neighbours Raise New Barn on Emily Township Farm", a few days after concrete foundations had been poured. The barn-raising was on the Stanley McCall farm five miles southeast of Omemee. "25 men began the work early in the morning, and after a stomach-filling dinner the 28 pairs of rafters were erected on Tuesday . . . On Wednesday the volunteers numbering 14 again turned out to begin sheeting the rafters and walls . . . Neighbour women rallied to help (Mrs. McCall) . . . Mrs. A. Jackson, Mrs. A. McCall and Mrs. N. McConnell working industriously both days. While all the commotion was at the barn and the kitchen, activity in the barnyard continued as usual except for one hen; she had adopted 6 fluffy goslings who waddled after her wherever she went." The other event occurred in Feb. 1971; "Destruction last Friday of the old gristmill at Omemee removes a historic landmark. It places local farmers who patronized the mill in an awkward position and forces them to travel greater distances to Dunsford, Lindsay, Peterborough or Millbrook to have their grain ground. The old mill built in 1872 by Wm. Cottingham, an early settler here (was) the third on the site, and his son William Jr. managed it until 1878 when Thos. Stephenson purchased the business . . . Modern machinery has long replaced the old method of grinding grain between 2 mill-stones. Flour had been made from wheat in earlier years at the mill, and in 1940 the Quaker Oats Co. purchased the flour mill . . . There were hundreds of such mills years ago, but modern inventions hastened their obsolescence. Mobile grinding units that travel from farm to farm are becoming prevalent." The old neighbourly "bees" continue after 150 years, but the slow journey with grain to the gristmill has passed into history.

Perhaps it is inevitable that provincial and federal governments, which by their policies and plans play major parts in discouraging life on the farm, are also continually surveying and analyzing the results to plan new "improve-ment" plans and programmes to make agriculture both profitable and attrac-tive as a way of life. The federal rural development authorities completed an Eastern Canada Farm Survey in 1963 which found the average age of Ontario farm operators to be 49 years—Victoria with average age 44 was the young-est. They found generally that the troubles were low productivity, and poor drainage, and few farmers with any off-farm income except some roadwork and carpentry. Other findings: ½ Ontario farmers were making improve-ments, ⅓ were expanding acreage, ⅕ were expanding beef production, ⅛ were expanding their woodlots, and only 1/12 were expanding tourist facilities. But their main needs were found to be a system of machinery rental for specialized jobs, and an improvement in pastures, which could only be "band-aid" medicine for an ailing industry. Similarly, the Provincial Committee on Farm Assessment and Taxation in 1969 after much research found that farms were a special problem, and their property taxes should be "considerably lower" than on non-farm properties, due to their lower incomes and the fact that they benefited less from some municipal services; it was recommended that, in assessing farmland, special consideration should be given to land use, soil types and suitability, and the proportion of arable land vs. wasteland. The real and serious causes of rural decline and farm abandonment have as yet not been seriously studied, and the remedies (to revive a healthy locally-controlled rural community life attractive to young people as a lifetime family endeavour) are still to be discovered.

Although Emily has not had a local newspaper for many years, a file of recent news clippings from district newspapers contains many items on other aspects of Emily life which provide a deeper insight into local activities. Council meetings are of course reported regularly, and we learn that a Bylaw was passed "for stopping up part of township road allowance between lot 18, con. 10 and lot 19, con. 10" (1970), and that "Emily Township Land-use Plan to be reviewed by Consultants" (1971), and "Cottage-owners Protest Trailer Camp Location" (1972). A long article with picture in July 1970 told of a testimonial dinner for Walter Herlihey after 32 years as Emily Road Superintendent; another in Sept. 1973 recorded presentation of an award to the Omemee-Emily Fire Department, won for the 3rd time since 1964.

A MONTAGE OF 1973 EMILY TOWNSHIP EVENTS
(H. T. Pammett)

Emily Council October Meeting

Omemee (PNS) — Emily Mitchell
Council met on Oct. 4, at 1:00
p.m., with Reeve Smith pres
all councillors pre
Messrs.
and L

ible Society Elects Officers

Omemee (PNS) — New of-
cers were elected at the an-
ual meeting of the Omemee
and District Bible Society,
held after the evening service
in St. Andrew's Presbyterian
Church, on Sunday, Oct. 7.
Rev. Rex Norman of Peter-
ough, district president,
dated the local soci-
work and com-
one of the
le also
ville United

TWENTY YEARS AGO

William O'Brien of
Downeyville, who celebrated his
100th birthday had a solemn
high mass (a high honor for a
layman) said for him at St
Martin's Church in Downeyville
in the morning of his birthda
then at noon enjoyed a dinner
his honor at Club Aragon.
On the sly, Mr. O'Brien
his car around the barn
he could say he'd been
drive on his 100th birth
until he was 98 this
gentleman drove reg
was believed to be th
tive licensed d-iver
in Canada.

TOWNSHIP OF EMILY

TO: The Members of Council, Ratepayers and Inhabitant
the Corporation of the Township of Emily.

1972 Financial Statements of the Corpora
My examina

McIntosh-Downey Weddi

St. Luke's Roman Catholic
Church, Downeyville, was decorated with gladioli, carna-
tions and candles on Aug. 4,
1972 for the 2:30 p.m. wed

flower girl wore gowns o
blue flowered voile ove
feta, with rounded neck
stand - up collars, e

Reaches 101 Today

Omemee-Emily Wins Trophy

Oct. 3, Omemee 1973

Mr. Gordon Comby of
Belleville, visited her daugh
tetr Mr. and Mrs. Edgar Fish-
er and Mrs. Evelyn O'Neill has as-
Miss Evelyn O'Neill has assumed the duties of rural mail
Courier
succeeding Harry
Griffin.
Mr. and Mrs. Marwood Mc-
Carrell, Mrs. Vera Ferguson and
John Carew, spent the week-
nell, Mrs. Annie McCon-
A reception was held for the
end in West Virginia.
new rector of Christ Church,
by the congregation, on Wed-
tuesday evening, Rev. Rolar
Sims and Mrs. Sims were
with a hearty welcome, fol
Mrs. Essie Bent
a pot luck supper.
days in Toronto.
ner and fam
Mr. and Mrs.
relatives,
visited her
Mrs. Oswa

y-Omemee embrance Day ice Sunday

mee (PNS) — The an-
Remembrance Day Ser-
or Emily and Omemee,
eld on Sunday, Nov. 11,
0 p.m., with Rev. John
Legion Padre, as
an.

by the Royal Canadian
Cadet Band of Peter-
h, veterans under com-
of Comrade Joseph
Ladies' Auxiliary Wolf
and Brownies, paraded
onation Hall.

on the platform were
Wilson, Past Presi-
the Ontario Command
ad the scripture; Rev.
Pierce who offered
Rev. Alvin Rowselle
Pentecostal Church,
ad the Lesson and Rev

Wreaths were laid by Ree
G. A. Williamson for Omemee
Deputy-Reeve Harold Mitch-
ell for Emily; Ladies' Auxil-
iary, Mrs. Verna Hartin;
Province of Ontario, Donald
Wilson and Branch 497, Clin-
ton Endicott.

Individual family wreaths
were laid by Murray Fee and
Mrs. Olive Acreman; Legion
Color Guard, Comrades Cecil
McGill, Ross Rehill and Lew-
ers Deyell; Ladies' Auxiliary
Color Guard, Mrs. Betty Hart,
Mrs. Evelyn Rehill, and Mrs.
Whalen.

Bugler from the Naval
Band, sounded the Last Post
and Reveille.

9 — Auction Sale
achinery and House-
rniture, Property of
O'NEILL, north. ½ of
nc. 10, Emily Town-
es north of Omemee
Road and 4 miles
11 miles east
ay.
Tractor, stan
halmers r
manu
50
9
AllI
WD
s

Omemee-Downe 4-H Club Banquet

Omemee (PNS) — The an-
nual banquet for the Omemee
Downeyville 4-H Club was
held in the Omemee Legion
on the evening of October 24.
This very important yearly
event for the 4-H members is
sponsored by the Emily Agri-
cultural Society.
Head Table guests included:
Mr. and Mrs. Stan Smith,
Reeve of Emily Township; Mr.
Mr. and Mrs. Ralph Hodgson,
Mr. and Mrs. Lindsay Exhibi-
Reeve and Mrs. Bill Reeve
Agrico
district repre-
Dale Toombs
sentative. Mr. and Mrs. Joe
Clancy, president, and Ira
Omemee
Society, Downe
lub Leader,
the 4-H Club.

No Munici Elections In December 1973

Omemee (PNS)—Municipal
elections will not be held in
Downeyville or Omemee in all
December, owing to the
remain in office for the two-year term
of Emily Township.
Ave, Stanley Smith;
llors, Harold Mitch
Jones and Earl Lo
Hollingst
Reev

ible
De La
machine
chesterfiel
board

Descriptions of the Leahy-Perdue wedding in Aug. 1970 and the McIntosh-Downey wedding in Oct. 1973 are balanced by the numerous golden and diamond wedding festivities: golden for such as Mr. and Mrs. Evans Storey (1950), Mr. and Mrs. Herbert Jackson (1951), Mr. and Mrs. Geo. Henderson (1951), Mr. and Mrs. H. Burke (1970), Mr. and Mrs. Gordon Harrison (1971); diamond for such as Mr. and Mrs. T. H. McQuade (1970), Mr. and Mrs. Herbert Streeter (1970), Mr. and Mrs. Ed. Williams (1972) and Mr. and Mrs. Wallace Downing (1972)—these and many others were feted by church fellow-members, relatives and friends in all parts of Emily.

As we have seen in earlier chapters, much Emily knowledge of pioneer days has been passed down from grandparents to grandchildren in family story-telling sessions, and in every generation there have been a few old-timers bright and active at ages over 90. A news clipping from Nov. 1950 mentions Mrs. Margaret Brooks of Omemee and Emily, entering her 90th year in good health, keeping her own house; "she also loves to visit, entertain friends and talk of old times"; Mrs. Brooks, herself mother of 9 children, now had 77 descendants, including 6 great-great-grandchildren. William O'Brien of Downeyville, born in 1853 and farming in the area until the 1930s, had one of the first Ford Model-T cars and was still at 98 years driving a 1928 Essex in 1951—and probably the oldest active driver in the province, proud that he had never had an accident. Mr. O'Brien gave himself a third car, 1951 model, as a birthday present, "and hoped to wear that one out too"; on his 100th birthday in May 1953, he drove his car around the barnyard to prove he could still do so, and the day were celebrated by a High Mass and a family dinner in his honour.

A few years ago Walter McGee, 97 years old, was interviewed about his long life on lot 19, con. 1, Emily where he farmed until 1950. He talked of going to the log school on the corner of lot 18, con. 2, in the 1870s, when John Dobbin was teacher, and of later years when he cradled 3 or 4 acres of grain a day, binding it by hand and threshing by flail; he said the horse-powered threshing mills came about 1885, and the first steam threshers about 1905. In the depression of the 1890s steers sold at $15 each, and some farmers made a few dollars by cutting maple and other hardwood, chopping it to stove-length, and drawing it to Peterborough to sell door-to-door or on the market at $2.75 a cord; wheat was 75c a bushel, oats 16c, and eggs 7c a dozen. He had no use for tractors, and said oxen were better for ploughing than horses —harder to break in but easier to work with. This staunch lifelong Anglican, Mason, Orangeman and Conservative remembered shooting wolves and wild-cats chasing the sheep, playing football and hockey in the early years, playing the violin at square dances, arranging shivarees for newly-wedded couples, and building the first brick house on the farm. A news clipping of Oct. 1972 tells of Mrs. Elizabeth Fee on her 91st birthday, still in good health; born in Manvers, she came to east Emily on marrying William Fee, and retired to Omemee only about 1935. In Feb. 1972 Cornelius Powers celebrated his birth in Downeyville 100 years ago, where he went to the one-room school; as a young man he headed west by train, farmed in North Dakota for 9 years, then came back to Downeyville, married and farmed in Otonabee; after some misfortunes he moved to a farm near Downeyville where he worked the soil until retirement; Mr. Powers, oldest resident in Victoria County, reached his 101st birthday this year (1973).

Similarly a few examples may be given from surviving news clippings of others who passed on after a long rewarding lifetime mostly in Emily. Mrs. Margaret Gardiner's death was recorded in Dec. 1950, at age 88; she was born in Emily, daughter of Mr. and Mrs. Thos. Jackson. In May, 1951, the Peterborough 'Examiner' noted the deaths of Mrs. William Fitzpatrick (née Leahy, born in Douro), at age 90, and Mrs. Thomas Lucas (née Mary Harrington, daughter of Mr. and Mrs. Thos. Harrington) at age 89—both members of St. Luke's Parish, Downeyville. The same paper in April, 1951 had an article about William Franks of R.R.1, Omemee, member of a pioneer family, who had died at age 85, after retiring in 1942 to live on the farm of his nephew, Alvin Franks, 4 miles north of Omemee. Mr. Franks went west at 19 years with his brother, and they began farming in Saskatchewan; during the Northwest Rebellion of 1885 the brothers freighted beef, biscuit, hay and other supplies from Moosejaw to the army fighting against Riel and his forces, and used the money to expand their farm to 480 acres; William Franks returned to farm near Peterborough in 1911 until retirement. Lady Flora Eaton (née McCrea) died in July 1970 in Toronto at age 91; her close connection with Omemee and Emily, and her lifetime of good works, have already been mentioned. Leonard Atwell, who attended S.S. #5 and farmed most of his life near Cowan's Bridge, died in Bobcaygeon Nov. 1970 at age 84, leaving 4 children, 8 grandchildren and 7 great-grandchildren. Wilfred Jackson, son of Henry and Ann Jackson, farmed all his life in the Bethel area, a prominent member of Bethel United Church; after retirement a few years ago, he passed away in Omemee Sept. 25, 1971, at age 92.

Emily has had few children raised on its farms who went on to adult fame and fortune in the outside world, whether in politics, business, professions, religion, education or entertainment spheres; yet thousands have gone forth from the township to farms on the prairies, to business and industry in the towns of North America, to the professions, and to church and missionary careers in far places. For every Carew or McCrea or Cottingham or McQuade or Sandy or McEvay who was prominent enough in later life to win a paragraph in *"Who's Who"* or *"Representative Canadians"* or *"Canadian Men and Women of the Time"*, there were a thousand exiles from Emily who had peaceful worthwhile lives in British Columbia or Toronto, Lindsay or Dakota—and most passed on to their children the nostalgic memories of childhood days in Emily, fishing in the streams in summer, adventures on the long wooded road to school in winter, ploughing and potato-picking barefoot in the fields, rescuing the newly-born calf from a bear in the back pasture, or listening to grandfather telling stories by the fireplace on winter evenings. If the exiles do not come back to retire in Emily after a life-

time elsewhere, their children and grandchildren often come visiting to find
out more about their family roots on the back concessions, which seem so
enduring and wholesome in a restless modern age.

But more important than those who left Emily are those who grew up
there and stayed to endure the good times and the depressions while raising
their own families, taking part in community activities and township affairs,
and being laid to rest finally in one of the Emily cemeteries. Kirkconnell in
his *"Victoria"*, first published in 1921, stated that of 456 original grantees in
Emily there were 63 male descendants living on the same farm (or 14%),
and 145 male descendants still in the township but not on the original farm
(or 32%), a total of 208 descendants (or 46%); this was the highest in
Victoria county, where the average number of male descendants on the same
farm was 12%, the average number still in the township on other farms 23%,
and the total average 35%. He continued: "Emily was the first municipality
thrown open for settlement, yet it had the highest number of surviving families
. . . The solid nucleus of this survival was the Robinson Immigration of 1825
and settled in the northern concessions of Emily. Most of these families still
persist. It might also be noted that Humphrey Finley, the first settler in Emily
and therefore in the whole county, was still represented on lot 15, concession
1, the original holding." The situation has changed greatly since 1921, but
there are still Jacksons, Fees, McCalls, Connells, Downeys, Dorgans, Foxes,
Lowes, Donoghues, McMullens, and many more, in various party of Emily,
as any recent Voters' List will testify.[12]

One interesting example of this continuity might be mentioned, to
typify many others. Timothy Dorgan was settled by Robinson (and his agent
Huston) on the north half of lot 14, con. 11, in 1825, with his family of
7, and within a year had 4½ acres cleared; by 1833 he had 30 acres cleared.
Born about 1895, another Timothy Dorgan grew up on the farm 5 miles
northeast of Downeyville, and was fascinated by the blacksmithing in Simon
Perdue's shop near the school; from age 7 he hung around the blacksmith
shop and was allowed to start learning the trade at age 11, with wages $3
a month. By age 14 he was an efficient blacksmith and opened his own blacksmith shop at Downeyville, at a time when removing and repairing a horseshoe was 15c, or putting on a new one was 30c. Tim Dorgan throve on the
rugged life, and celebrated his 56th year in the trade at age 70 in 1965;
he finally gave up the full-time job about two years ago but still at age
78 does a little blacksmithing and other iron-work to keep busy. Thus from
Tim Dorgan of 1825 to Tim Dorgan of 1973 the bond stretches nearly 150
years in the Downeyville area. Another example is the Henry Jackson who
came to the south half of lot 18, con. 2, in 1819, and was counted in the
1820 census with his wife and 8 children; Henry died in 1862 at age 95 after
a lifetime as community leader. As a family history states: "At one time
or another almost every farm on 2nd concession from the middle line down
to the boundary has been owned by one of Henry's kin. 154 years later
there are 7 generations of Jacksons, and Henry's property still remains

intact." The family has always led in community activities, as earlier chapters indicate.[13]

Some of the thriving local communities in Emily a century or more ago have vanished, as in all districts—the Lebanon settlement on concession 1 then had its sawmill, blacksmith, store, church, cooper and weaver, and a little group of homes, now all gone; King's Wharf and Frank Hill and Millersmith communities have also faded away as the population shifted. Downeyville remains, as an article in Toronto 'Telegram' March 21, 1961, described it: "This village carries its Irish proudly, like a harp, like a shamrock, or even, if occasion demands, like a shillelagh . . . a village of 90 farming families grouped around a general store, church, blacksmith shop, and, of all things, a chinchilla ranch . . . On the mailboxes the names read like the rent roll in County Down—Fitzpatrick, O'Neill, Shyne, Duffy, Lucas, Connell, O'Connell, Morrisey, Herlihey, Harrington, and of course Downey . . . "A picture shows Mrs. Mary Harrington with the deed for Edmond Piggott's farm dated 1834 "whose descendants still live there". The school then had 34 pupils (it has now increased greatly). "The youngsters may drift off, but when they come back, Downeyville will stand unchanged; there'll still be a cheering pot at the back of the stove and a cheery smile before it."

The Lindsay 'Post' gave a humorous twist to the St. Patrick's Day theme on Mar. 26, 1964, by quoting from Kirkconnell's book the poem "The March on Lindsay, July 12, 1846".

"Bill Parker of South Emily
By Crown and Throne he swore
That the great House of Orange
Should suffer wrong no more . . .

The poem goes on to tell of the manning of the Scugog Bridge by Lindsay Irish led by Father McEvoy, and how a compromise truce was arranged after much loud talk:

"Here in this strange new country
Another day may come
When Irish of the North and South
Will be less quarrelsome."

In truth, of course, as the previous chapters testify, there was a solid basis of neighbourly friendship and co-operation between all religious denominations in Emily, in spite of some early jealousies, and the Cavan Blazers and the Orange and St. Patrick's parades. The frequent stories of St. Luke's parishioners playing in the Orange band, or the Protestants who went each year to the renowned fowl suppers or the St. Patrick's Day concerts at Downeyville church hall, are indications of the real atmosphere of harmony and classless accord that prevailed. It is indicative that through out its history Emily Township had a remarkably small amount of crime, whether feuding and violence between people, or crimes against property; its

MAP OF EMILY TOWNSHIP IN THE KAWARTHA SETTING, 1973

people never forgot the basic lesson of pioneer survival—to help each other and get along together for the benefit of all. Possibly the experiment begun by the Family Compact government of Upper Canada in Emily Township between 1818 and 1830, whether consciously planned or not, was the most successful way of blending all kinds of Irish immigrants into one prosperous community of loyal Canadians in the Kawartha district of central Ontario.

*   *   *   *   *

It is perhaps too easy to become sentimental about pioneer days, to quote reams of reminiscences told by venerable 90-year-olds beside the fireplace or on the farm verandah, and other tales passed down from great-grandparents—and to forget the grim hardships and weary sufferings of those who hacked out homesteads and raised families in Emily in the period of the drafty log cabin, the dawn to dusk toil to keep the family fed, the ox-plough and ox-cart, the rough bush trail with its dangers, the ague epidemics and the barter trade; a period when few farmers ever saw cash money, few women ever went beyond church, neighbour or back pasture, and only half the children born ever reached either school or adulthood. But it is the only way to understand present-day Emily Township, its current crises and its future prospects, and to foresee in what way Emily might survive and evolve for the well-being of this generation's grandchildren, by the time the township is 200 years in 2018 A.D.

One highly respected and cultured lady who has lived in the district since the 1890s told the author a few years ago: "We always thought of Emily as a place where nothing ever happened, a township to pass through as quickly as possible to get to Peterborough or Port Hope." In one sense, this book has been written to revise that opinion. As O. D. Edwards wrote in Conor Cruise O'Brien's 1969 book on modern Ireland: "In Ireland, therefore, the intending traveller needs maps with dimensions, not merely of space but of time." This applies also to Emily Township, where the Irish are still the outstanding element in the population after 155 years.

Therefore, to understand and appreciate Emily and its people fully in 1973, one must not only explore its geography—its drumlins and fields, its woods and swamps, its streams and its back roads—but one must also explore its history through a century and a half since pioneer settlement in the bush. The only difference is that to know Ireland well one must explore 1,500 years of history, ten times the stretch since Emily was first settled. Perhaps the Emily record of individual initiative, family-organized farm industry, neighbourly co-operation, religious harmony and freedom from violence, can provide some worthwhile lessons in 1974 for the Ireland from which Emily's pioneers set sail in the troubled restless depression decades 140 or 150 years ago—and some worthwhile lessons also for the future happiness and progress of Emily Township people, in the difficult uncertain times ahead.

*   *   *   *   *

EMILY COUNCIL 1973-74
l. to r.—Ronald Pogue (Clerk-Treasurer); Earl Herlihey; Stanley Smith (Reeve); Harold Mitchell (D. Reeve); John Hollingshead; Leonard Jones.

EMILY TOWNSHIP HISTORICAL COMMITTEE
Front Row—l. to r.—Alvin Franks; Olive McCall (Secretary); Howard Pammett (Author); Simon Connell (Chairman); Mrs. W. McMullen, Wilfred McMullen.
Back Row—l. to r.—Beryl Clark; Mary Harrington; Ronald Pogue; Lloyd Ashmore; Harry Jackson; John Hollingshead; Yvonne Lowes; Helen Connell.

William Cottingham, County Warden 1861
and 1865.   (Williamson)

Stanley Smith, County Warden in 1974.

Turning first sod of Emily-Omemee Recreation Centre at 10 acre site one mile north of
Omemee, County Road 7, in March 1974. (Lindsay *Daily Post*)

EPILOGUE ON EMILY'S FUTURE

A short summary of recent planning developments may give some indication of what lies in store for Emily in the future. A whole series of provincial government surveys and studies over the last ten years point the way the planners want to "structure" the development of the Kawartha Lakes Region, which is later called "the Lake Ontario Development Region", and then "the Toronto-Centred Region"—this last title is the frankest of all, since it states the main argument that all central Ontario, including Emily Township, is to be deliberately designed totally as a tourist recreation area for the Toronto-centred industrial megalopolis (stretching from Oshawa to Hamilton and north to Lake Simcoe), with a subsidiary use as a residential suburb for the Oshawa-Durham end of the urban sprawl. A 1972 report concludes. "While population concentration was altering cities and towns, the character of the countryside would also be changing as land-use became more specialized. Working farms would be found only on the best land. Much of the rest of the countryside would be 'weekend farms' or the rural residence of people working in the cities . . . To cope with important social and economic changes that are otherwise inevitable, the region needs more planning than has been necessary in the past."[14]

One of the latest and glossiest studies, "The Rideau-Trent-Severn: Yesterday, Today, Tomorrow", released by the Ontario Economic Council in 1972, forecasts that this whole area of waterways from the Rideau to the Kawarthas, up to Lake Simcoe and Georgian Bay, will be an all-year recreational playground for the toiling millions from Metro-Toronto and its suburbs, plus tourist millions from the rest of the continent. Just to make the point crystal-clear as to what interests are supporting this planning, and will profit from such development, the Peterborough 'Examiner' of Oct. 23, 1973, headlined: "Reveal $100,000,000 Plan for Pigeon Lake Development"—concerning one company's plans for a 2,000-acre recreational resort on Pigeon Lake near Gannon's Narrows. This would be reached by a new wide expressway coming up the provincial bypass route to Fowler's Corners, thence north along Emily's east boundary to Pigeon Lake, and curving northeast through Ennismore to Gannon's Narrows, bringing the rushing tens of thousands from Toronto Super-City and other urban hordes for weekends and vacations.

Tied in with this provincial planning are Ontario Municipal Board "reforms" planned for the 1970s; since the taxpayers will bear most of the burden for such development, the province recommends standardized assessment, with all financing and taxation first administered by counties, and then later by regional "governments", as has already begun in such fields as education, health, libraries, and care of the aged. The theory on which plans are built is that by centralizing all programmes for land use, roads, unemployment relief, drainage aid, etc, the tax-load on working farms can be reduced. But since every new shift in taxing-power to a distant centralized bureaucracy not only destroys local community involvement and control but also increases the personnel required for endless computerized paperwork (studies, plans, programmes, reports, permits and receipts), for supervision and subsidization payments, the inevitable result is that costs multiply (as already in such spheres as education). Local participation at all stages (except paying taxes yearly and voting every 4 years) vanishes, and people at the community level feel helpless and dependent increasingly on "handouts" from the central government "Authority", while their children more and more find the only profitable and "attractive" careers are in the urban office or factory, or at least in the nearby recreational commercial enterprises. There is a certain irony in this, since exactly the same fate was meted out to the Mississauga Indians after their lands and livelihood were taken away in the Treaty of 1818; perhaps rural Emily will end up as an Irish "reservation", just as Curve Lake became an Indian "reservation" 140 years ago, where the natives can practice their simple farm handicrafts and sell souvenirs and services to the passing tourists, while "the Great White Father" in a distant capital doles out annual subsidies (to those who conform and obey).

The Lindsay '*Post*' of Dec. 29, 1971, quoted Lindsay Mayor Eakins: "There are too many people governing too few people", and he issued a call for "sensible amalgamation of municipalities . . . Emily township and Omemee should be united . . .", with a stronger Victoria County Council over only 6 or 7 municipalities. In June 1973 by the same paper, Deputy-Reeve Stewart of Lindsay urged a Victoria County Region amalgamating about 8 municipalities, before the province forced a multi-county region: "Would a larger region give us a better way of life or a better quality of life? I really don't think it could improve anything." The Peterborough '*Examiner*' of Sept. 18, 1973, editorialized about the threats from the provincial government to cut subsidies for areas which did not co-operate in amalgamation: "CO-OPERATE OR LOSE MONEY: . . . It will reward those counties that do restructure themselves but not others, if we correctly understand Provincial Treasurer White . . . The province will accomplish what it set out to do all along—streamline Ontario's archaic and unwieldly municipal structure into new larger units that can hope to be able to pay for the services the province says it must have". In simple English, the province will pay back more subsidies, from the money it takes away in escalating taxation, if the region restructures itself to allow stronger centralized control of all administration in order to collect the (necessary) higher taxes more easily. For the residents of Emily Township, especially those whose ancestors for 150 years administered their own affairs in a democratic local township council, and even for the newcomers of the past 20 years, the future presents problems (both real and imaginary) which will take even more wisdom and industry than the people of Emily ever required before.

NOTES

[1]From the decennial Dominion census; after 1941 the Dominion census gives less and less information about rural townships, except farm statistics.

[2]The Lindsay '*Post*' of Aug. 13, 1969, had a very illuminating and humorous letter from "Mick McGilligan of Downeyville" about the difficulties of driving his donkey around the potholes and other road hazards of this section.

[3]At the Dominion election in April, 1963, the Diefenbaker government was defeated.

[4]As a fitting end to its "fire-lit" career, and to the end of an educational era, the old building in Omemee, used for overflow classes from Omemee P.S., burned down in 1964. Williamson's *"Omemee"* gives a fitting tribute to Omemee High School, and has pictures of some graduating classes, including Emily students.

[5]Williamson's book also has a picture of Lady Eaton School 1967. Lady Eaton died in 1970 after a lifetime of community service.

[6]This letter, published June 5, 1968, will be given in Appendix XXVII.

[7]According to a recent survey by Principal R. Brown of Lady Eaton School.

[8]One Emily farm about a mile north of Omemee was purchased by Ontario Water Resources Commission recently, and according to the Lindsay *'Post'* of Oct. 10, 1973, will be the site of the lagoons for Omemee sewerage system as now projected, the system to cost about $1,200,000 and to be completed by Sept. 1974. Another "smelly" example of Omemee-Emily co-operation is the town's use of the township dump for garbage disposal.

[9]Others as they became more affluent came back to the tourist lodges and marinas along Pigeon River—Pigeon River Camp, Cap's, Cedar Grove, Beaver Park, Riverview, Omemee Lodge, Bob's Camp, Sportsman's Lodge, Longfellow Lodge, Pinewood, Cedarville, Fee's Landing Lodge, etc.; also the Emily Creek Club, which in 1964 had 1,260 acres on Con. 13-14; and the lodges and resorts along Chemong and Pigeon Lakes.

[10]A list prepared by the Historical Committee of Emily people serving in World War II will be found in Appendix XXVIII.

[11]Statistics on food prices issued monthly by Dominion Bureau of Statistics.

[12]Patrick Shenick came with the 1825 Irish emigrants, and later changed his Gaelic name "Shenick" to the English "Fox"; Fox's Corners is named for the family. Lists of 1825 Irish settlers with descendants on the same farm, and lists of Century Farms in the same family since 1867, prepared by the Committee, will be found in an Appendix.

[13]Tim Dorgan is shown in a couple of illustrations wielding pioneer farm implements near his blacksmith shop at Downeyville. Harry Jackson, who served in school and church and council activities, as well as various societies, is now in retirement a member of the Emily Historical Committee.

[14]The quotation is from "Design for Development: Prospects for the Lake Ontario Region" June 1972, which in turn builds on "Design for Development: A Status Report on the Toronto-Centred Region", (Aug. 1971), issued by Hon. W. Darcy McKeough, Prov. Treasurer & Minister of Economics.

[15]At the end of 1973 Ontario Department of Agriculture released a report, lamenting that "old-fashioned neighbourliness, once a trademark of the farm community, is becoming a thing of the past . . ." Though based on a survey 1963-70 in east Ontario, its findings are an omen for all Ontario unless the tides of centralization and urbanization are checked and reversed. Significantly, the demoralizing causes are those mentioned in this chapter. The newspaper item states: "This breakdown in rural cohesiveness is blamed on the mechanization of farms, the consolidation of schools and churches, and the continued urbanization of rural areas . . . the lack of personal contact with neighbors . . . Modern machine technology has eliminated the need of help from neighbors, and television entertainment has replaced visiting . . ." What such reports do not stress is that the continuing decline in rural initiative and "neighborliness' has been promoted for over 40 years by government urban-oriented policies toward rural education, economy and life.

[16]Dr. Sobrian in January, 1974, as a member of the Canadian team at the Commonwealth Games in New Zealand, won a gold medal and a silver medal in pistol-shooting competitions, and is expected to be a leading Canadian contender in these events at the World Olympic Games in Montreal in 1976.

LIST OF APPENDIXES

APPENDIX I

ARTICLES OF PROVISIONAL AGREEMENT BETWEEN THE DEPUTY
SUPERINTENDENT GENERAL OF INDIAN AFFAIRS AND CHIEFS
OF THE MISSISSAUGA BRANCH OF THE CHIPPEWA NATION

Smith's Creek (Port Hope), November 5, 1818

(Canada: Indian Treaties and Surrenders, 1680-1890,
Vol. 1, No. 20, pp 48-49, Ottawa, 1891.)

Articles of Provisional Agreement entered into on Thursday, the Fifth day of
November, 1818, Between the Honourable William Claus, Deputy Superintendent
General of Indian Affairs, in behalf of His Majesty, of the one part, and Buckquaquet,
Chief of the Eagle Tribe; Pishikinse, Chief of the Reindeer Tribe; Pahtosh, Chief of the
Crane Tribe; Cahgahkishinse, Chief of the Pike Tribe; Cahgagewin, of the Snake Tribe;
and Pininse, of the White Oak Tribe, Principal Men of the Chippewa Nation of Indians
inhabiting the back parts of the Newcastle District, of the other part, witnesseth:
That for and in consideration of the yearly sum of Seven Hundred and forty pounds
Province Currency in Goods at the Montreal Price to be well and truly paid yearly, and
every year, by his said Majesty to the said Chippewa Nation inhabiting and claiming the
said Tract which may be otherwise known as follows: A tract of Land situated between
the Western Boundary Line of the Home District and extending Northerly to a bay at
the northern entrance of Lake Simcoe, in the Home District, commencing in the western
division line of the Midland District at the north-west angle of the Township of Rawdon;
then north sixteen degrees west thirty-three miles, or until it strikes the line forty-five;
then along the said line to a bay at the northern entrance of Lake Simcoe; then along
the water's edge to the entrance of Talbot River; then up Talbot River to the eastern
boundary line of the Home District; then along said boundary line south sixteen degrees
east to the northwest angle of the township of Darlington; then along the Northern
Boundary Line of the Townships of Darlington, Clarke, Hope and Hamilton to the Rice
Lake; then along the southern shore of said Lake and of the River Trent to the western
division line of the Midland District; then north sixteen degrees west, to the place of
beginning, containing about one million, nine hundred and fifty-one thousand acres.
And the said Buckquaquet, Pishikinse, Pahtosh, Cahgahkishinse, Cahgagewin and
Pininse, as well for themselves as for the Chippewa Nation inhabiting and claiming the
said tract of Land as above described, Do freely, fully and voluntarily surrender and
convey the same to His Majesty without Reservation ór Limitation in perpetuity.
And the said William Claus, in behalf of His Majesty, does hereby promise and
agree to pay to the said Nation of Indians inhabiting as above mentioned, yearly and
every year forever, the said sum of seven hundred and forty pounds Currency in goods
at the Montreal Price which sum the said Chiefs and principal people parties hereunto
acknowledge as a full consideration for the Lands hereby sold and conveyed to His
Majesty.
In witness whereof the parties have hereunto set their Hands and Seals on the day
first above mentioned in the Township of Hope, Smith's Creek, Signed, Sealed and
Delivered in the presence of
W. Claus, Dy. Supt. Genl. i. A. on behalf of the Crown.

Buckquaquet	(totem)	Cahgahkishinse	(totem)
Pishikinse	(totem)	Cahgagewin	(totem)
Pahtosh	(totem)	Pininse	(totem)

Witnesses:
William Gruet)
J. Givens   ) of the Indian Department.
William Hands)

ARTICLES OF PROVISIONAL AGREEMENT BETWEEN THE DEPUTY
SUPERINTENDENT GENERAL OF INDIAN AFFAIRS AND CHIEFS
OF THE MISSISSAUGA BRANCH OF THE CHIPPEWA NATION

The manner in which the yearly payment was to have been made to you, for the lands which you had ceded to the crown on the fifth day of November 1818, not having been sufficiently explicit and defined in the Provisional Agreement; in order to obviate any difficulty or misconstruction which might hereafter arise I have called you together for the purpose of explaining to you the manner in which it is intended that the payment shall be made, and in order that you may subscribe your names on the back of the Provisional Agreement as acquiescing and approving of the same as follows, viz. Every Man, Woman and Child to receive to the amount of ten dollars in goods at the Montreal prices, so long as such Man, Woman or Child shall live, but such annuity to cease and be discontinued to be paid in right of any Individual who may have died between the respective periods of payment, and the several individuals then living, only, shall be considered as entitled to receive the yearly payment of ten dollars in goods as above stated.

(Endorsed) No. 20 Provisional Agreement with the Rice Lake Chippewas for the surrender of 1,951,000 Acres, signed the fifth of November 1818.

APPENDIX II

SAMUEL WILMOT'S SURVEY DIARY FOR EMILY TOWNSHIP 1818:

Some excerpts: (Crown Lands Papers, Ontario Archives)

Monday October 26: "I found myself placed in a bad situation, the canoe that I had for use all summer was taking to the Carrying Place by the Indian traders, and a Boat that I occasionally used was sold to the English Emigrants settling in Smith who were employed in moving their baggage & Families. I then hired a small Birch Canoe & sent three men to the Carrying Place in Smith for the large Canoe."

Monday November 2nd: "Transported the Provisions to Mr. Dicksons in Smith on lot no. 1, and made a Scaffold near the House to secure my provisions. I then proceeded along the Boundary line between Smith and Monaghan 3 miles with very heavy packs."

Tuesday November 3: "Arrived at the new Township to be surveyed in the rear of Cavan and commenced opening the 2nd Con. line . . . and laid off lots of 29c. each which I also divided into 100 acres, continued to no. 18."

Friday November 6: "Raining very hard all night, opened to the East Boundary of Manvers & returned 4 lots planting posts at the corner of each 100 acres on each side of the allowance for a Road as pr. Instructions from Thomas Ridout, Esquire, Surveyor-General dated the 8th Oct. 1818."

Wednesday Nov. 11th: "Produced the western Boundary of this Township from the N.E. corner of Manvers n.n.w. to the 5th concession alowing 70c.40L. including Roads for each Concession & opened 5th Con.N.74°E. 4 lots."

Saturday Nov. 14th: "Completed the 5th Con. to the East Boundary and produced this Boundary N 16°W. through the marsh to the high ground for fear of Rains would raise the water over the marsh which would make it impossible while frozen."

Tuesday Nov. 17: "Completed the 4th Con. & produced the western Boundary to the 6th Con. in a bad Swamp."

Thursday Nov. 19: "All day in Swamp opened 5 lots—one lot & four chains to the River

APPENDIX II (cont.)

SAMUEL WILMOT'S SURVEY DIARY FOR EMILY TOWNSHIP 1818:

impassable, which I was obliged to make a floating bridge about 10c. below the line, from this plan I continued the line without Chaining."

Saturday Nov. 21st: "Continued to the termination of no. 23, & produced the Eastern Boundary from the marsh to the intersection of the 6th Concession line."

Saturday Nov. 28th: "Continued the East Boundary 16c. in the 12th Con. terminating at a River in a very large marsh at present impassable. I then returned to the 9th Con. which I opened 74°W.21.50 in no. 19 to the River impassable."

Thursday December 3rd: "This morning the Ice being just sufficient for to cross by laying poles thereon we cross(ed), but one of the pack men fell in—opened this line to no. 4. Clear and cold."

Tuesday Dec. 8th: "Continued the 11th Con. 6 lots—it will appear singular to the Settlers of this Township to see the Trees from 50 to 60 feet high with their tops loped off which was bent down by the weight of Snow."

Friday Dec. 11th: "Continued to the River which not being sufficiently frozen . . . by the fall of Snow, I proceeded to the 9th con. at the River & continued 2 lots to the high land."

Tuesday Dec. 15th: "Opened to the western Boundary, No. 1 fell short, from chaining over such immense windfalls in Swamps which we return to correct by Chaining."

Friday Dec. 18th: "Proceeded to the 8th Con. & continued this line across the lake(?) Much(?) for fear of heavy Rains that would raise the water over the lowland; I then proceeded to the 6th Con. to chain it from the River which could not be done when the line (was) run."

APPENDIX III

NEWCASTLE DISTRICT LAND BOARD GRANTS IN EMILY TOWNSHIP 1819-25
(from Ontario Archives Records)

Name	Where born	Age	How long in U.C.	Lot allocated
1819 (June)				
Samuel Peacock	USA	33	14 years	north part lot 19, con. 1
Silas Johnson	USA (Vermont)	23	9 years	south half lot 19, con. 1
John Percy	USA	37	9 years	south half lot 20, con. 1
Nathan Moore	USA	22	10 years	south part lot 18, con. 1
Whitney Grant	USA	20	10 years	north part lot 18, con. 1
John Callender	Upper Canada	20	— —	south part lot 17, con. 1
Zeenos Ross	Upper Canada	20	— —	north part lot 17, con. 1
William Moore	Ireland	40	1 year	south half lot 8, con. 1

Nathan Moore allowed to change from above to rear half lot 23 in con. 1
Whitney Grant allowed to change from above to front half of lot 23, con. 1
Zeenos Ross allowed to change from above to front half of lot 23, con. 2
John Callender allowed to change from above to front part of lot 22, con. 1
Silas Johnson allowed to change from above to north part lot 22, con. 1

Name	Where born	Age	How long in U.C.	Lot allocated
(July)				
Hiram Ash	USA	28	20 years	south half lot 13, con.
(August)				
David Best	Ireland	51	6 weeks	west half lot 12, con. 1
David Best 2nd	Ireland	49	6 weeks	east half lot 12, con. 1

APPENDIX III (cont.)

NEWCASTLE DISTRICT LAND BOARD GRANTS IN EMILY TOWNSHIP 1819-25
(from Ontario Archives Records)

Name	Where born	Age	How long in U.C.	Lot allocated
(September)				
Thomas Quay	Ireland	30	Month or two	south half lot 19, con. 2
William Winrowe	England	40	Month or two	south half lot 13, con. 1
William Parts	Ireland	60	3 months	north half lot 23, con. 3
John Parts (son of William)	Ireland	26	3 months	north half lot 22, con. 3
Robert Mahary	Ireland	above 40	week or two	south half lot 19, con. 1 (cancelled above)
Robert Baity	Ireland	21	1 month	north half lot 20, con. 1
William Henderson	Ireland	22	3 months	south half lot 23, con. 4
Francis Henderson	Ireland	21	1 year	north half lot 20, con. 4
John Pogue	Ireland	21	1 year	south half lot 19, con. 4
George Sherry	Ireland	23	week or two	front half lot 23, con. 5
William Jones	Ireland	25	1 month	south half lot 22, con. 5
James Jones	Ireland	30	1 month	north half lot 22, con. 5
(October)				
Thomas Webb	Ireland	22	14 months	north half lot 23, con. 5
William Emerson	Ireland	71	14 months	south half lot 23, con. 6
Isaiah Merriman	USA	23	19 years	north half lot 23, con. 6
Humphrey Finley	Ireland	33	1 month	south half lot 15, con. 1
Henry Jackson	Ireland	40	1 month	south half lot 18, con. 2
James Moore	Ireland	21	1 month	south half lot 21, con. 2

(December)

Catherine Smith (daughter of a United Empire Loyalist) lot 14 (all), con. 2 (subject to the settlement duties being done within 18 months)

John Marshall	Germany	33	18 months	south half lot 10, con. 1
Hugh Collum	Ireland	23	several months	north half lot 12, con. 2
Richard Taylor	Ireland	22	several months	north half lot 11, con. 2

John Pogue is allowed to change south half of lot 19, con. 4, it being a swamp, for south half lot 12, con. 2

Francis Henderson is allowed to change north half lot 23, con. 4, being short of 100 acres, for north half lot 23, con. 2

Robert Mitchell	Ireland	21	3 months	south half lot 8, con. 1
Edward Macammus	Ireland	25	3 months	south half lot 16, con. 2
William Hall	Ireland	23	3 months	north half lot 16, con. 2
William Lees	Ireland	60	3 months	south half lot 18, con. 3
Nathan Lees	Ireland	27	3 months	north half lot 17, con. 3
James Taggart	Ireland	21	4 months	south half lot 12, con. 3
John Boyd	Ireland	22	2 or 3 weeks	north half lot 12, con. 3
James Laing	Scotland	28	3 weeks	south half lot 19, con. 1
Patrick O'Bryan	Ireland	23	6 weeks	south half lot 18, con. 3
William Best	Ireland	21	5 months	rear half lot 14, con. 1
Henry Best	Ireland	21	5 months	rear half lot 13, con. 1
William Harkness	Scotland	39	2 years	rear half lot 18, con. 2

1820 (February)

Thomas Stapleton	Ireland	26	8 months	rear 50 acres of lot 23, con. 2

APPENDIX III (cont.)

NEWCASTLE DISTRICT LAND BOARD GRANTS IN EMILY TOWNSHIP 1819-25
(from Ontario Archives Records)

Name	Where born	Age	How long in U.C.	Lot allocated
(April)				
James Jones	Ireland	21	6 months	northeast quarter lot 19, con. 2

(June)

William Lee and Nathan Lee, having returned their tickets for whole of lot 17 in con. 3 and proved it to be a swamp, allowed to exchange these lots for lot 18 in 1st concession, Nathan Lee the east half, William Lee the west half; settlement duties to be performed in 1 year.

Name	Where born	Age	How long in U.C.	Lot allocated
Thomas Cleff	England	29	1 year	southwest quarter lot 20, con. 3
William Nicholson	England	34	1 year	southeast quarter lot 19, con. 3
William Holroyd	England	45	1 year	southeast quarter lot 20, con. 3
(July)				
Hugh Jones	Ireland	22	2 months	southeast quarter lot 11, con. 2
William Wright	Ireland	45	2 days	southwest quarter lot 11, con. 2
George Dixon	Ireland	30	3 weeks	northeast quarter lot 10, con. 1
James Fallis	Ireland	31	3 weeks	southeast quarter lot 7, con. 1
Alexander Robertson	Scotland	23	5 months	north half lot 21, con. 2
William Mason	England	36	6 weeks	southwest quarter lot 13, con. 7
(August)				
Joseph Porter	Ireland	22	24 days	northeast quarter lot 19, con 3
James Phair	Ireland	42	8 days	southeast quarter lot 13, con. 3
Thomas Mitchell	Ireland	—	1 month	northwest quarter lot 13, con. 3
John Mitchell Sr.	Ireland	56	1 month	northwest quarter lot 15, con. 1
John Mitchell Jr.	Ireland	23	1 month	northeast quarter lot 15, con. 1
Robert Henderson Jr.	Ireland	21	1 month	southwest quarter lot 14, con. 3
Thomas Henderson	Ireland	24	1 month	southeast quarter lot 23, con. 3
David Armstrong	Ireland	23	1 month	southwest quarter lot 13, con. 4
Christopher Marshall	Germany	28	1 week	north half lot 17, con. 1
Andrew Henderson	Ireland	34	3 weeks	southwest quarter lot 13, con. 3
David Henderson	Ireland	21	3 weeks	southeast quarter lot 21, con. 4
John Richell	Ireland	24	This season	northeast quarter lot 8, con. 1
John McGee	Ireland	37	This season	northwest quarter lot 8, con. 5
Robert Henderson	Ireland	46	This season	southeast quarter lot 12, con. 4
James Henderson	Ireland	24	This season	southeast quarter lot 13, con. 4
George Mitchel	Ireland	21	This season	northeast quarter lot 12, con. 4
George Dixon	Ireland	28	This season	southeast quarter lot 11, con. 4
Thomas Dixon	Ireland	25	This season	southwest quarter lot 11, con. 4
John Dixon	Ireland	30	This season	northeast quarter lot 11, con. 4
William Gray	Ireland	26	This season	southeast quarter lot 22, con. 3
Joseph Porter	Ireland	33	This season	southwest quarter lot 19, con. 3
James McCarthy	Ireland	22	3 years	southeast quarter lot 13, con. 4
Richard Coxon	England	28	This season	east half lot 19, con. 11
George Ingle	Ireland	44	This season	southwest quarter lot 19, con. 10
Benjamin Barris	Ireland	50	This season	southeast quarter lot 8, con. 2
Robert Sanay	Ireland	33	1 month	southwest quarter lot 9, con. 2
Robert Macammus	Ireland	22	1 month	southeast quarter lot 10, con. 3
John Thornton	Ireland	23	1 month	west half lot 10, con. 3

APPENDIX III (cont.)

NEWCASTLE DISTRICT LAND BOARD GRANTS IN EMILY TOWNSHIP 1819-25
(from Ontario Archives Records)

Name	Where born	Age	How long in U.C.	Lot allocated
Andrew Holmes	Ireland	60	1 month	southeast quarter lot 7, con. 2
James Holmes	Ireland	30	1 month	southwest quarter lot 7, con. 2
Henry Sharp	Ireland	60	1 month	northwest quarter lot 8, con. 2
Thomas Elliot	Ireland	21	1 month	northeast quarter lot 7, con. 2
John Hall	Ireland	50	1 month	northeast quarter lot 8, con. 2
William Hall	Ireland	28	1 month	northwest quarter lot 9, con. 2
Royal Collum	Ireland	56	1 month	northeast quarter lot 8, con. 4
James Rutledge	Ireland	24	1 month	southeast quarter lot 10, con. 5
Francis Taylor	Ireland	21	1 month	southwest quarter lot 10, con. 5
Morris Cottram	Ireland	41	July last	northwest quarter lot 6, con. 3
Samuel Cottram	Ireland	21	July last	southwest quarter lot 6, con. 4
Thomas Trotter	Ireland	24	1 month	northwest quarter lot 12, con. 4
Henry Jones	Ireland	23	1 month	southwest quarter lot 7, con. 1
David Balfour	Ireland	23	1 month	northwest quarter lot 7, con. 1
James Ladley	Ireland	21	July last	southwest quarter lot 21, con. 4
William Fee	Ireland	36	July last	south half lot 12, con. 5
Thomas Fee	Ireland	23	July last	north half lot 12, con. 5
Mark Robison	Ireland	21	1 month	southeast quarter lot 9, con. 2
Samuel Dancey	Ireland	22	1 month	southwest quarter lot 8, con. 2
Robert Jackson	Ireland	51	1 month	northwest quarter lot 13, con. 5
John Jackson	Ireland	—	1 month	northeast quarter lot 13, con. 5
Henry Thorsden	Ireland	25	1 month	northeast quarter lot 9, con. 2

(September)

Henry Fee	Ireland	26	2 months	north half lot 7, con. 3
Adam Thornton	Scotland	21	This season	southeast quarter lot 9, con. 4

William Jones (located last Sept. on south half lot 22 in 5th con.) is allowed to exchange it for north half lot 9 in 4th concession

Joseph Porter (located last month as above) is allowed to exchange it for southwest quarter lot 22, con. 3

Samuel Plant	Ireland	25		northeast quarter lot 7, con. 1

(having lost his recommendations in the "Richmond" schooner which was wrecked)

Frederick Hinds	USA	37	6 years (or more)	southwest quarter lot 7, con. 4
William Bradley	England	36	2 months	southeast quarter lot 7, con. 4

James Henderson, having drawn southeast quarter of lot 13 in con. 4, which proves to be a swamp, is permitted to exchange for northwest quarter lot 19, con. 2

James Layng	Ireland	35	This season	north half lot 7, con. 5
William Allen	Ireland	22	This season	northwest quarter lot 7, con. 4
William Cottram	Ireland	21	This season	northeast quarter lot 6, con. 3
Andrew Holmes	Ireland	25	2 months	northwest quarter lot 7, con. 2

George Sherry (located September 1819) produced proof that his land was not good, and is allowed to exchange same (south half lot 23, con. 5) for north half lot 6, concession 4

(October)

John Blackstock	Ireland	25	4 months	northeast quarter lot 6, con. 1
Humphrey Jones	Ireland	26	3 months	southeast quarter lot 6, con. 4
Robert Jones	Ireland	22	3 months	northwest quarter lot 8, con. 4

APPENDIX III (cont.)

NEWCASTLE DISTRICT LAND BOARD GRANTS IN EMILY TOWNSHIP 1819-25
(from Ontario Archives Records)

Name	Where born	Age	How long in U.C.	Lot allocated
Adam Jones	Ireland	22	3 months	southwest quarter lot 8, con. 4
Samuel Ferguson	Ireland	27	3 months	southeast quarter lot 6, con. 1
Edward Lemon	Ireland	21	1 year	northeast quarter lot 8, con. 3
William McIndoo	Ireland	56	3 months	southeast quarter lot 4, con. 2
James McIndoo (son of William)	Ireland	21	3 months	southwest quarter lot 4, con. 2
John Toole	Ireland	31	3 months	northeast quarter lot 4, con. 2
James Follis	Ireland	21	1 year	southeast quarter lot 6, con. 3
Mihil Jackson	Ireland	40	3 months	south half lot 13, con. 5

(November)

Name	Where born	Age	How long in U.C.	Lot allocated
James Balfour	Ireland	26	6 months	southeast quarter lot 6, con. 2
William Fard	Ireland	30	6 months	southwest quarter lot 8, con. 3
Edward Baily	Ireland	34	9 months	southeast quarter lot 7, con. 3

James Follis (given land grant in July 1820) allowed to exchange for southwest quarter lot 16, con. 4

Name	Where born	Age	How long in U.C.	Lot allocated
Andrew Haw	Ireland	25	2 weeks	northeast quarter lot 1, con. 3
Alexander Stewart	Ireland	35	3 weeks	northwest quarter lot 1, con. 3
Francis Bainbridge	Ireland	21	2 months	northwest quarter lot 10, con. 1

David Henderson (having proved the land he drew is not fit for cultivation) is allowed to exchange it for southeast quarter lot 14, con. 3

Name	Where born	Age	How long in U.C.	Lot allocated
William Mitchel	Ireland	23	5 days	southeast quarter lot 13, con. 6
John Mitchel	Ireland	21	5 days	southwest quarter lot 13, con. 6

(Oddly enough, the father of William and John was given a lot in Smith township)

Name	Where born	Age	How long in U.C.	Lot allocated
Francis Bonask	France	—	7 years	northeast quarter lot 13, con. 6

(a discharged soldier from the Royal Scots)

Name	Where born	Age	How long in U.C.	Lot allocated
Robert Allen	Ireland	60	3 months	northeast quarter lot 7, con. 4
Thomas Macammus	Ireland	60	3 months	northeast quarter lot 10, con. 3

John Burn of Hope Township (one of the Land Board) by special Order-in-Council, allowed to locate the following lots in Emily—nos. 1 and 3 in con.1; nos. 3 and 5 in con. 3 (800 acres)

(December)

Name	Where born	Age	How long in U.C.	Lot allocated
James Best	Ireland	25	2 weeks	southwest quarter lot 14, con. 5
Samuel Mitchel	Ireland	—	1 week	southwest quarter lot 6, con. 1

(a discharged private from Royal Marines)

Name	Where born	Age	How long in U.C.	Lot allocated
Robert Shearn	Ireland	27	5 months	northwest quarter lot 6, con. 1
John Moore	Ireland	26	1 month	southeast quarter lot 5, con. 1

1821 (February)

Name	Where born	Age	How long in U.C.	Lot allocated
Robert Dixon	Ireland	25	Few months	southeast quarter lot 14, con. 5
Samuel Orr	Ireland	33	2 years	northeast quarter lot 14, con. 4
Michael Dingan	Ireland	30	8 months	southwest quarter lot 18, con. 5
Timothy McPherson	Upper Canada	26	— —	northwest quarter lot 11, con. 4
George Casseman	England	22	2 years	southeast quarter lot 5, con. 5

James Laidley (formerly given southwest quarter lot 21, con. 4) allowed to exchange it for southeast corner of lot 4 in concession 4

APPENDIX III (cont.)

NEWCASTLE DISTRICT LAND BOARD GRANTS IN EMILY TOWNSHIP 1819-25
(from Ontario Archives Records)

Name	Where born	Age	How long in U.C.	Lot allocated
(April)				
David Kelly	Ireland	22	2 years	southwest quarter lot 14, con. 6
John Goodin	Ireland	42	2 years	southeast quarter lot 14, con. 6
James Moore	Ireland	25	11 months	northwest quarter lot 23, con. 4
Morris England	Ireland	27	2 years	northeast quarter lot 14, con. 5
William Coon	USA	36	17 years	northwest quarter lot 14, con. 5
James Maccamus	Ireland	30	3 months	northwest quarter lot 20, con. 3
James Kelly	USA	36	— —	southwest quarter lot 16, con. 6
John Barnes	USA	35	— —	southeast quarter lot 16, con. 6
Thomas Barnes	USA	60	11 years	northwest quarter lot 16, con. 6
David Barnes	USA	22	11 years	southwest quarter lot 18, con. 6
(May)				
Ephraim Farrar	USA	28	11 years	southwest quarter lot 15, con. 5
John Moore (formerly given southeast quarter lot 5, con. 1, which is found unfit for cultivation) is allowed to exchange same for northwest quarter of same lot				
Francis Sheridan	Ireland	23	6 months	northeast quarter lot 12, con. 6
John Creighton	Ireland	22	9 months	northeast quarter lot 18, con. 5
William Swain	Ireland	23	9 months	southeast quarter lot 18, con. 5
Caleb Coon	USA	26	14 years	northeast quarter lot 16, con. 6
(June)				
James Staples	Ireland	24	10 months	southeast quarter lot 15, con. 5
Henry Bennett	Ireland	27	13 months	northeast quarter lot 13, con. 3
John Jackson	Ireland	42	12 months	northeast quarter lot 16, con. 4
Henry Moore	Ireland	21	11 months	northeast quarter lot 20, con. 3
John Bulford (of Hope Township)				south half lot 19, con. 4
Gardner Gifford (of Hope Township)				north half lot 19, con. 4
William Swain permitted to exchange his former location for northeast quarter lot 15, con. 5				
John Deyell	Ireland	21	7 months	northwest quarter lot 9, con. 6
Robert Deyell	Ireland	55	7 months	northeast quarter lot 9, con. 6
Owen Curren	Ireland	25	7 months	southeast quarter lot 9, con. 6
Henry Argua	Ireland	21	21 months	southwest quarter lot 9, con. 6
(August)				
John Swain	Ireland	30	1 year	southeast quarter lot 7, con. 7
Henry Fisher	USA	28	21 years	northeast quarter lot 7, con. 6
Andrew Jamieson	Ireland	49	1 month	northwest quarter lot 8, con. 3
John Vent	Ireland	24	1 month	southwest quarter lot 9, con. 6
John Brisbin	Lower Canada	26	4 years	southwest quarter lot 8, con. 7
Rufus Beevie	USA	40	20 years	southeast quarter lot 8, con. 4
(September)				
Israel Sammes	USA	31	12 years	southeast quarter lot 20, con. 5
Benjamin Sammes	USA	40	11 years	southwest quarter lot 20, con. 5
Ebenezar Sammes	USA	21	12 years	southeast quarter lot 19, con. 5
James Sammes	USA	36	13 years	northeast quarter lot 20, con. 5
Morris Jaynes	USA	28	22 years	northwest quarter lot 20, con. 5

APPENDIX III (cont.)

NEWCASTLE DISTRICT LAND BOARD GRANTS IN EMILY TOWNSHIP 1819-25
(from Ontario Archives Records)

Name	Where born	Age	How long in U.C.	Lot allocated
John Sockshaw	— —	30	This season	northeast quarter lot 19, con. 3
Archibald Collum	Ireland	32	1 year	southwest quarter lot 4, con. 4
Lothrup Smith	USA	39	30 years	northeast quarter lot 5, con. 1
Edward Sutton	Ireland	52	This season	southeast quarter lot 8, con. 7
Richard Sutton	Ireland	25	This season	southwest quarter lot 7, con. 7
Edward Sutton Jr.	Ireland	23	This season	northwest quarter lot 8, con. 6
James Sutton	Ireland	21	This season	northwest quarter lot 7, con. 6
Thomas Kelley	Ireland	26	This season	northeast quarter lot 7, con. 7

(October)

William Thornton	Ireland	50	This season	southwest quarter lot 2, con. 4
Nathaniel Belch	Ireland	21	This season	southeast quarter lot 1, con. 4
Elias Burbanks	USA	70	22 years	northwest quarter lot 19, con. 5
Thomas More	USA	33	26 years	northeast quarter lot 19, con. 5
Caleb Coon	USA	60	15 years	southwest quarter lot 19, con. 5
John Coon	USA	39	15 years	northeast quarter lot 18, con. 4
William Ladely	Ireland	60	3 weeks	southeast quarter lot 2, con. 4

John Mitchel (with certificate from John Huston of Cavan that his lot s.w. quarter 13 in 6th concession unfit for cultivation) allowed southeast quarter lot 5, con. 1

Robert Mitchel Sr.	Ireland	44	3 months	northeast quarter lot 7, con. 5
James Mitchel	Ireland	26	3 months	northwest quarter lot 7, con. 5
(son of above)				
Robert Mitchel Jr.	Ireland	24	3 months	southwest quarter lot 7, con. 6
Patrick Crawford	Ireland	27	2 years	northeast quarter lot 13, con. 6
James Allen	Ireland	25	2 years	northwest quarter lot 13, con. 6
John Birney	Ireland	36	This season	northwest quarter lot 6, con. 2
Abraham Henderson	Ireland	21	2 years	southwest quarter lot 12, con. 4
David Fleming	Ireland	24	This season	southeast quarter lot 13, con. 7

William Mitchel (given s.e. quarter lot 13, con. 6, which is unfit for cultivation) is allowed to change to southeast quarter lot 12, con. 6

Francis Goodden	Ireland	21	5 months	northeast quarter lot 14, con. 6
Owen Goodden	Ireland	22	5 months	northwest quarter lot 14, con. 6

(December)

Joshua Mulligan	Ireland	28	4 months	southeast quarter lot 14, con. 7
Anthony Hunter	Ireland	35	2 years	southwest quarter lot 14, con. 7

1822 (January)

Richard Morgan	Ireland	22	18 months	southwest quarter lot 6, con. 3

(February)

Harden Eddy	USA	27	15 years	northwest quarter lot 6, con. 2
Benjamin Purdy	USA	29	20 years	northwest quarter lot 13, con. 7
Joshua Ross	USA	30	21 years	northeast quarter lot 13, con. 7
Daniel Kelly	Ireland	25	8 months	southeast quarter lot 13, con. 6

(March)

Samuel Anderson	Ireland	23	6 months	southwest quarter lot 1, con. 4

APPENDIX III (cont.)

NEWCASTLE DISTRICT LAND BOARD GRANTS IN EMILY TOWNSHIP 1819-25
(from Ontario Archives Records)

Name	Where born	Age	How long in U.C.	Lot allocated
(April)				
Russel Belnap	USA	33	16 years	northwest quarter lot 1, con. 4
Joseph Belch	England	29	2½ years	northwest quarter lot 4, con. 2
John Belch	England	21	7 months	northwest quarter lot 2, con. 4
Adam Thornton	Ireland	28	7 months	northeast quarter lot 1, con. 4
(May)				
William McElvey	Ireland	42	5 months	northeast quarter lot 2, con. 4
Samuel John Best	Ireland	21	2 years	southeast quarter lot 8, con. 3
Christian Elsworth (by special Order of Lt. Governor)				lot 6, concession 7
Irena Vaublascom (by special Order of Lt. Governor)				lot 6, concession 6
(July)				
Barbara Preston (by special Order of Lt. Governor)				lot 5, concession 6
(September)				
Robert Mitchell Sr.	Ireland	70	18 months	northwest quarter lot 8, con. 5
Jeremiah Mitchell	Ireland	21	18 months	southwest quarter lot 7, con. 6
William Elliott	Ireland	24	2 years	northeast quarter lot 6, con. 5
Henry Sherin	Ireland	28	This season	southeast quarter lot 17, con. 3
(October)				
William Potts	Ireland	26	This season	southwest quarter lot 17, con. 2
(No applicants in rest of year)				
1823 (January)				
James Ross	Haldimand, U.C.			southeast quarter lot 1, con. 3
Benjamin Burdy	Haldimand, U.C.			southwest quarter lot 1, con. 3
(July)				
Edward McCall	Ireland	35	1 month	southwest quarter lot 15, con. 3
Lancelot Welwood	Ireland	35	1 month	southeast quarter lot 15, con. 3
John Hawe	Ireland	54	This season	southwest quarter lot 5, con. 5
James Jones	Ireland	57	2 years	northwest quarter lot 14, con. 3
John Jones	Ireland	—	2 years	northeast quarter lot 14, con. 3
Hugh Mitchel	Ireland	21	3 years	southwest quarter lot 5, con. 1
Samuel Robson	Ireland	35	2 years	southeast quarter lot 19, con. 4
Alexander Swain	Ireland	—	This season	northeast quarter lot 15, con. 3
John McCall	Ireland	—	This season	northwest quarter lot 15, con. 3
(September)				
Robert Shearn	Ireland	34	This season	southwest quarter lot 8, con. 6
James Corbett	Ireland	40	This season	southeast quarter lot 3, con. 5
James Riddle	Ireland	40	15 months	southwest quarter lot 3, con. 5
John Riddle	Ireland	23	15 months	northwest quarter lot 3, con. 5
Robert Riddle	Ireland	21	15 months	northeast quarter lot 3, con. 5
(October)				
William Walker	England	22	15 months	northwest quarter lot 2, con. 2

APPENDIX III (cont.)

NEWCASTLE DISTRICT LAND BOARD GRANTS IN EMILY TOWNSHIP 1819-25
(from Ontario Archives Records)

Name	Where born	Age	How long in U.C.	Lot allocated

(November)

Simeon Wright (by special Order of Lt. Governor, a son of a United Empire Loyalist)
lot 1, concession 2

1824 (February)

Name	Where born	Age	How long in U.C.	Lot allocated
Richard Morgan	England	45	— —	northeast quarter lot 21, con. 4
Thomas Aukson	Ireland	45	— —	southeast quarter lot 16, con. 4

1825 (March)

Name	Where born	Age	How long in U.C.	Lot allocated
John Mitchell	England	33	1 year	southeast quarter lot 7, con 1

(In 1823 to 1825 most individual settlers in District were referred to Smith, Otonabee, Ops and
Mariposa, especially in 1824-5).

APPENDIX IV

HISTORY OF THE BEST FAMILY

(By Squire William Best, Emily, 1876)

Three of the Bests came to Ireland with King William in 1690 and served with him,
afterwards receiving grants of land. In the next century several descendants came out to
settle in the United States, as well as one in Chile, and then three brothers came to
Canada (probably around 1800) and settled in Frontenac County back of Kingston.
David Best and family came to Canada in 1819 and settled in Emily. They were
composed of seven children, Nancy and Anne Jane, William, Thomas, Samuel, John and
David, and his family are all dead except the writer of this brief sketch. His grandchildren
are comfortably settled and connected with the church of their fathers.

1876—A SHORT HISTORY OF THE EMIGRATION AND EARLY
SETTLEMENT OF THE BEST SETTLERS IN THE TOWNSHIP OF EMILY

On May 19th, 1819, two David Bests and their families sailed from Belfast for America
in a small brig. of 300 tons that was scarcely fit to go to sea and, after a tedious and
tempestuous voyage of seven weeks and three days, we arrived at Quebec on July 10; from
there to Montreal by steamboat, 172 miles. There we had to hire teams to take us to
Lachine, 9 miles—there was no canal made then. From there to Brockville was 116 miles
by Durham boat. This was a tedious, uncomfortable passage, night and day in an open
boat, without covering, exposed to all the changes of weather.
    This boat was propelled by men with long poles. They placed one end on the bottom
of the river bed and leaning on the head of these and with their feet, shoved the boat
forward. Sometimes it was drawn by horses and sometimes by oxen, passing rapids. This
boat had no deck, but a plank along each side for a footpath for the boatmen to walk on.
    From Brockville we sailed to Kingston by steamboat, 97 miles, from there to Port

APPENDIX IV (cont.)

HISTORY OF THE BEST FAMILY

Hope by schooner, 98 miles. This took several days because of adverse winds, then we were put ashore by a small boat. There was no wharf or harbour there then. Thus we spent about four weeks from Quebec, arriving in Port Hope the first week in August.

Here I might say the knowledge of this country was very limited. Having no fixed destination, information was gleaned by the way. One kind friend in Quebec, finding our object was farming, advised us not to stop short of the Township of Darlington, where he said land was good. Hearing a good report of the Township of Cavan and the country around it, we stopped, and in September we selected land in Emily Township where we settled. In the last of October four of us left Port Hope for Emily to build some huts to live in, each carrying as much provisions as he could, together with his blankets and his axe.

After reaching our destination we built shanties and cut down a few trees around each shanty, leaving a place we could return to with our families. As soon as sleighing would permit, we returned to Port Hope, where we stayed until March. Having provided a stack of provisions to last until we could raise our own, we employed teams to move us to our new homes in the woods. This was no small job, for there was only a track where the brush was cut out of the way. The snow covered most of the logs and frost bridged the creeks.

Having reached our new home, our outfit was a year's provisions, two cows, two steers, a yoke and chain. Browse kept the cattle alive until the snow was gone, then wood and feed was plenty and the cattle got fat. We had plenty of milk, butter and maple sugar. We chopped and cleared two or three acres that we planted with corn and potatoes that yielded plenty for our use and some to spare for others coming in requiring seed.

The first year there were only four families in the Township, the two Bests, Finley and Jackson. The second year a few more came in, Henderson, Cottingham, Fee, Laidley. This year we raised a little wheat, but there was no mill within 30 miles of us until 1822, when John Deyell built a small mill at what is now called Millbrook, but they had no bolt and for a time wheat was ground without bolting.

This part was a wilderness until 1818. The settlement was only five or six miles wide along the north short of Lake Ontario. Then a few settled in the Township of Cavan and when we passed through there was no one who could sell us any food except potatoes, corn and milk. Everything we required for food must be carried on men's backs thirty miles. There were no teams on the settlement, only oxen. Our only chance to get a team was in winter, when the roads and streams were frozen and covered with snow. Oxen were then used for all purposes. They were essentially necessary for the early settlers. They were cheaply kept and harnessed, only requiring a yoke and chain to hitch them to a plough or harrow or draw logs, and also ready for cart or wagon or sled and after using them a few years, fatten them up for beef.

The early settlers suffered many privations. Money was scarce and all imported goods were dear. Many of the luxuries of life had to be dispensed with and everyone had to manufacture for himself or to exchange work with someone to work for him. We had to make our own shoes and boots and some people had to use wooden soles for their shoes when leather could not be got. We built our own houses and made such furniture as we could, but sawed lumber was scarce. Boards were sawed by hand, we had no sawmill within thirty miles of us (Port Hope).

Schools and meeting houses were few and far apart. Politics was then little known. The law was then very deficient and badly administered. There was no party feuds to disturb the harmony that existed among the first settlers.

Steam was little use in those days, there were but two steamboats on the lakes and rivers. The lake was navigated by sailing vessels. There were no steam mills, no railroads, no telegraph lines. Post Offices were few and postage dear—25 cents on a letter to

APPENDIX IV (cont.)

HISTORY OF THE BEST FAMILY

Montreal, 60 cents to Ireland, and only carried by sailing vessels; no ocean steam ships then.

Toronto was a small place then, called Little York. It was the seat of what government we had. If we had business with the government we had to go on foot and make the journey in two days if we could, spending five days on the round trip.

We had no machine shops. Implements now used were then unknown. Ploughs and harrows were of the rudest kind. The irons of the first plough that was ever in Emily, I carried home 30 miles on my back. The sickle, scythe and the flail were the best implements then invented. Those who could get a cart or wagon were well off, either for pleasure or marketing. Oxen and sled were commonly used on the farm to draw grain or the like. Steel plows, grain seeders, reapers, mowers, threshing machines, stone and stump lifters are of late invention. Land is now being cleared of stumps and stones, roads and bridges improved, schools and churches built, railroads made, telegraph lines by land and sea. News is sent everywhere in a very short time . . .

(NOTE: Some deletions have been made in the original longer text prepared by Mr. Best)

APPENDIX V

THE FIRST TWELVE SETTLERS TO RECEIVE DEEDS FOR THEIR LANDS: 1821-22

1821: Hiram Ash—100 acres, south half of lot 13, con. 2
Catherine Smith (U.E.L.)—200 acres, lot 14, con. 2
1822: John Mitchell Jr.—50 acres, northwest quarter lot 15, con. 1
John Mitchell Sr.—50 acres, northeast quarter lot 15, con. 1
James Holmes—50 acres, southwest quarter lot 7, con. 2
Benjamin Barris—50 acres, southeast quarter lot 8, con. 2
Robert Savey—50 acres, southwest quarter lot 9, con. 2
James Jones—50 acres, northeast quarter lot 19, con. 2
James Moore—100 acres, south half lot 21, con. 2
William Holroyd—100 acres, east half lot 20, con. 3
Thomas Cliff—50 acres, southwest quarter lot 20, con. 3
Roswell Belnap—50 acres, northwest quarter lot 1, con. 4.

APPENDIX VI

ROBINSON'S LIST OF VACANT AND RESERVED LOTS IN EMILY, OCT. 1825

Vacant   1, 2, 4, 11, w½ of 12, n½ of 18 ⎱ 5th Con.
Reserves 3, 5, 10, 15, 17, 20, 22 ⎰
Vacant   1, 3, 10, 12, 15, 18, 19, 20, 22, 23, n½ of 8 and 17 ⎱ 7th Con.
Reserves 2, 4, 9, 11, 16, 21 ⎰
Reserves 3, 5, 10, 15, 17, 18, 19, 20, 22 in 8th Con.
Reserves 2, 4, 9, 11, 16, 21 in 9th Con.
Reserves 3, 5, 10, 15, 17, 20, 22 in 10th Con.
Reserves 2, 4, 9, 11, 16, 21 in 11th Con.
Reserves 3, 5, 10, 15, 17, 20, 22 in 12th Con.

APPENDIX VI (cont.)

ROBINSON'S LIST OF VACANT AND RESERVED LOTS IN EMILY, OCT. 1825

Reserves   2, 4, 9, 11, 16, 21 in 13th Con.
Reserves   3, 5, 10, 15, 17, 20, 22 in 14th Con.
[Robinson placed a bracket around the last 7 concessions, with the note "It would appear by the Sur. Genls. Return that the remaining lots in these Concessions are vacant (viz. 8, 9, 10, 11, 12, 13 and 14 Cons.)"]
(NOTE: On another list with a letter of Sept. 26 to Huston, Robinson gave a short-list of "Good land", containing *the two lots underlined above,* and also: Con. 8: east half lot 8, lot 7, lot 6, north half lot 1, north half lot 2; Con. 9: south half lot 1, west half lot 3, east half lot 6.)

(from Huston Papers, Trent University Archives)

APPENDIX VII

PLACEMENT OF IRISH ON LOTS IN EMILY TOWNSHIP 1825-26
BY ROBINSON AND HUSTON
(Robinson Papers, Peterborough Museum, and his Report 1826 to Brit. Parl. Committee)

Name	No. in Family	Lot	Concession	Robinson's Comments in 1826 Report
John Blackwell	10 (11)	s.half 17	1	
John McCarroll	11	s.half 18	3	
Adam Shouldess	10	s.half 22	3	
Michael Lowes	4	n.half 23	3	
Daniel Finnegan	7	n.half 4	4	Working at his trade (black-smith)
Robert Gordon	10	s.half 14	4	Sick during summer
Samuel Gordon	—	s.half 18	4	Living on brother's lot
George Miller	4	n.half 18	4	Sick during summer
Jeremiah Driscoll	—	n.half 21	4	Mason by trade, living with John Lancaster
Timothy Cronin	7	n.half 23	4	Keeping a school
Timothy Leary	8	s.half 1	5	Sick & late on his land
John Leary	—	n.half 1	5	Living with his father
Andrew Ormsby	4	w.half 3	5	Shoemaker, living on son's lot
David Mulcahy	—	e.half 3	5	Living with his father
John Callaghan	7 (8)	n.half 5	5	
George Ormsby	—	s.half 6	5	Shoemaker, working at trade
James McCarroll	—	s.half 10	5	Living on father's lot
Richard Lowes	—	n.half 17	5	Sick during summer
Tobias Swytzer	9	s.half 18	5	Wheelwright
John Lancaster	11 (9)	s.half 22	5	Sick during summer
James Boate	7	n.half 22	5	
John Sliney	11	s.half 23	5	Sick during summer
James Rochfort	4	n.half 23	5	
William Mulcahy	7	w.half 1	6	
Edward Shea	4	e.half 1	6	
Richard Sullivan	8	w.half 2	6	
Michael Sullivan	—	e.half 2	6	Living with his father

APPENDIX VII (cont.)

PLACEMENT OF IRISH ON LOTS IN EMILY TOWNSHIP 1825-26
BY ROBINSON AND HUSTON

Name	No. in Family		Lot	Concession	Robinson's Comments in 1826 Report
Jeremiah Boland	7		e.half 4	6	Mason by trade, sick all summer
Jer. Callaghan jr.	8		n.half 6	6	Living with father, John C.
John Hogan	7	(6)	n.half 11	6	Sick during summer
James Cunningham	4		e.half 18	6	Sick during summer
Samuel Carew	—		s.half 19	6	Living with his father
Thomas Carew	10		s.half 21	6	Recovering from ague
John Geary	8		n.half 21	6	
Edmond O'Donnell	—		s.half 23	6	Living on father's lot
Thomas Hennessy	9		n.half 23	6	
John Shouldess	—		n.half 19	6	Living with father, Adam S.
John Murphy	—		n.half 3	7	Labourer, living with R. Sullivan
Daniel Scully	5		s.half 3	7	Labourer
Thomas Groves	5		n.half 17	7	Labourer
William Russell	9		w.half 18	7	
John Carey	7	(6)	e.half 18	7	Ague during the summer
John Brien	6		n.half 19	7	Ague during the summer
William Cotter	9		s.half 22	7	
John Clancy jr.	—		n.half 22	7	Living with Pat Clancy
Edmond Sullivan	8		s.half 23	7	
John McGrath	4		n.half 23	7	
Robert Wynne	—		n.half 1	8	Living with his father
Henry Wynne	—		n.half 2	8	
William Fitzgerald	4		s.half 6	8	Shoemaker working at trade in Cavan
Maurice Fitzgerald	7		w.half 7	8	Ague all summer
Edmond Callaghan	4	(5)	w.half 8	8	Alias Edmond Lynes
Patrick Callaghan	4	(0)	e.half 7	8	Alias Patrick Lynes
Denis Fitzpatrick	6	(8)	n.half 12	8	Labourer, living with father, Daniel F.
Patrick Shea	6		w.half 16	8	
Patrick Dawson	4		n.half 19	8	
Thomas McCarthy	5		w.half 21	8	
Martin McAuliffe	8	(7)	e.half 21	8	Living on son Michael's lot
William Doran	—		s.half 23	8	Living with his father
Martin Doran	7		n.half 23	8	
Richard Wynne	8	(7)	s.half 1	9	Living with son Henry
Richard Wynne jr.	—		n.half 1	9	Living with brother
Timothy Connors	7		w.half 3	9	Prevented from going on his lot by illness
George Connell	—		e.half 3	9	Living with father, Daniel C.
James Hargrove	3		w.half 5	9	Sick all summer
Patrick Baragy	3		e.half 5	9	Living with an old settler
John Leary	6	(7)	w.half 6	9	
Bartholomew Downie	6		e.half 6	9	
Daniel Donoghue jr.	—		n.half 7	9	Living with his father
John Nagle	4		n.half 8	9	Very ill

APPENDIX VII (cont.)

PLACEMENT OF IRISH ON LOTS IN EMILY TOWNSHIP 1825-26
BY ROBINSON AND HUSTON

Name	No. in Family	Lot	Concession	Robinson's Comments in 1826 Report
Patrick Nagle	—	s.half 8	9	Living with his father
Michael Flynn	5	s.half 10	9	Sick during summer
Daniel Flynn	—	n.half 10	9	Living with J. Flynn
Patrick Walsh	8	n.half 12	9	
Jeremiah Ahearn	3	n.half 13	9	
John Morrisey	8	n.half 14	9	
William Barrett	8	s. half 15	9	Ill with the ague
Patrick Clancy	8	n.half 15	9	
Michael McAuliffe	—	w.half 20	9	
Martin McAuliffe jr.	—	e.half 20	9	Living with brother Michael
James Flaherty	9	n.half 22	9	Living with son Patrick
James Flaherty jr.	—	s.half 22	9	
Patrick Flaherty	—	s.half 23	9	
Michael Flaherty	—	n.half 23	9	
Daniel Donoghue	9 (10)	n.half 1	10	Family sick during summer
Denis Donoghue	—	s.half 1	10	Living with father
Maurice Donoghue	—	s.half 2	10	Living with father
Daniel Connell	9 (8)	s.half 4	10	
Edmond Pigott	—	n.half 4	10	Living on Daniel P's lot
James Hurley	5	s.half 6	10	Carpenter working in Peterboro
Michael Collins	—	n.half 6	10	Living with father
Patrick Ryan	7 (11)	s.half 7	10	Schoolmaster
Patrick Shenick	3 (4)	n.half 7	10	
Denis Houlihan	7	w.half 8	10	Sick all summer
William Houlihan	—	e.half 8	10	Living with his father
Edmond Brislane	—	w.half 9	10	Living with his father
John Brislane	9	e.half 9	10	
John Flynn	—	s.half 11	10	
William Flynn	6 (5)	n.half 11	10	Living on son's lot
Jeremiah Dwyer	6	s.half 12	10	Recovering from ague
Edmond Dwyer	—	n.half 12	10	Living with his father
John McCarthy	8	w.half 13	10	Ague all summer
Jeremiah Callaghan	7 (8)	e.half 13	10	Sick all summer
Daniel Fitzpatrick	8	w.half 14	10	
William Halloran	5	e.half 14	10	Sick during summer
Moses Begly (Bigley)	2	s.half 16	10	Blacksmith in Peterborough
Michael Buckly	6	n.half 16	10	
John Hartnett	10 (11)	s.half 23	10	Sick all summer
John Hartnett jr.	—	n.half 23	10	Living with father
Bartw. Kennelly	—	s.half 1	11	Tailor
Benjamin Maddigan	—	n.half 1	11	Living with Kennelly
Bartholomew Pigott	—	w.half 5	11	Living on Daniel's lot
Daniel Pigott	7	e. half 5	11	
Timothy Collins	—	w.half 6	11	Labourer, living with father
James Shenick	3	e.half 6	11	Worked all summer at Welland Canal
Thomas Shenick	4	w.half 7	11	

APPENDIX VII (cont.)

PLACEMENT OF IRISH ON LOTS IN EMILY TOWNSHIP 1825-26
BY ROBINSON AND HUSTON

Name	No. in Family	Lot	Concession	Robinson's Comments in 1826 Report
John Ryan	—	w.half 10	11	Living with Patrick R.
Timothy Ryan	—	s.half 12	11	Living with Patrick R.
Florence McCarthy	—	w.half 13	11	Living with father, John
John Sheehan jr.	5	e.half 13	11	
Daniel Mahony	—	s.half 14	11	Came out as Daniel Dorgan; living now with J. Sheehan
Timothy Dorgan	7	n.half 14	11	
Owen Keily	7	s.half 15	11	
Daniel Sheehan	—	s.half 17	11	Living on father's lot
John Sheehan	7 (9)	n.half 17	11	
Callaghan Connell	5	s.half 18	11	Sick during summer
John Connell	6	n.half 18	11	
Jeremiah Murphy	4	w.half 19	11	
John Collins	10	e.half 19	11	Recovering from ague
Cornelius Lynes	6 (5)	n.half 20	11	
Denis Maddigan	—	w.half 1	12	Living with James
Owen Maddigan jr.	—	e.half 1	12	Worked this season at Welland Canal
Owen Maddigan sr.	—	w.half 13	12	*
James Maddigan	9	e.half 13	12	Recovering from ague
Patrick Herlehy	8	s.half 14	12	
Patrick Herlehy jr.	—	n.half 14	12	Living with father
Richard Owens	—	s.half 18	12	Carpenter, living with father
John Owens	—	w.half 19	12	Living with father
David Owens	9	e.half 19	12	Family sick all summer
Thomas Stack	7	s.half 21	12	
John Sullivan jr.	2	n.half 21	12	

(* When Owen Maddigan Sr. died, this lot was given to Matthew Maddigan; there were several other shifts later also—for example, Jeremiah Boland was given the west half 6 in 12th concession, and Cornelius Callaghan given his former lot, east half of 4, con. 6. In a number of cases, when the father died, the deed was issued to his widow—Widow Walsh, Widow Daly, Widow Groves, Widow Sullivan, Widow Dawson, Widow Gordon, Widow Lowes, Widow Sliney, etc.)

(NOTE: The total placements in 1825 were stated as 142, with 575 persons, and in the 1826 report this had grown to 604 persons—but births, marriages, deaths, sons given separate lots, and other movements, make the total variable. Where a family total varied from 1825 to 1826, the 1826 figure is given in a bracket.)

APPENDIX VIII

EMILY CENSUS AND ASSESSMENT RETURNS
(U.C. LEGISLATIVE ASSEMBLY APPENDICES)

	1832	1835	1838	1841	1844	1847
Males 16 & over	305	382	364	465	——	549
Females 16 & over	234	319	315	397	——	487
Males under 16	284	395	375	462	——	594
Females under 16	272	422	432	527	——	634
TOTAL POPULATION	1095	1518	1486	1851	——	2226
Persons Assessed	236	302	277	312	380	397
Uncultivated Land (ac.)	22365	26470	23929	27278	29850	28041
Cultivated Land (ac.)	1413	2686	3290	4133	5376	7781
Horses	50	63	109	140	195	281
Oxen	173	207	210	250	298	309
Young Cattle	78	146	149	180	207	146

	1832	1835	1838	1841	1844	1847
Assessment	£7704/8	£11654/16	£13186/16	£14673	*	*
Total Rates	£39/17/7	£58/19/2	£119/4/1	£131/8/5	£201/6/6	£210/0/0¼

*(Assessment not quoted after 1842, but probably close to £20,000)

APPENDIX IX

INSPECTION REPORT OF THOMAS DENNEHY DPS
JULY 1840 ON TOWNSHIP OF EMILY

(Newcastle District) (approximately 100 lots) (Survey Records, Ontario Archives)

Following are examples:

Con. 1:   *south half lot 10*—6 acres cleared; occupant John Marshall; clay land, very uneven hilly lot; maple, beech, basswood; 1½ miles to Best's Mill in Cavan; value 12/6 an acre; John H. Marshall the younger has got the deed, his father being dead.

north half lot 19—35 acres cleared; occupant John Magee; locatee Samuel Peacock; clay soil; maple, beech & basswood; 2 miles to Best's Mills; value 15s. an acre. I understand that Magee sent up the money for deed last winter & that it has been said he bought from Peacock.

east half lot 18—40 acres cleared; occupant Nathan Lee, locatee the same—has his deed (other particulars much same as last).

Con. 2:   *northwest quarter lot 8*—50 acres, none cleared; original locatee Harry Sharp; most excellent loam, part peaty; maple, beech, elm, bass and cedar; 1 mile to Cottenham's Mills; value 10s. an acre. On northwest corner some very good land; more than half swamp but situation good, increasing value; nothing ever done on land or cutting out concession line. However, it is said one David Armstrong is striving to sell it. George Morton on adjoining lot proffered 10s. per acre: it would be useful to him as it joins his own land.

north half lot 12—50 acres cleared: Hugh Collum occupant & locatee; clay soil; maple, beech, bass and pine; 3 miles Cottingham's and 2 miles to Best's Mill; value 15s. an acre.

north half lot 16—40 acres cleared; occupant L. Wallwood; locatee Wm. Hall;

APPENDIX IX (cont.)

INSPECTION REPORT OF THOMAS DENNEHY DPS
JULY 1840 ON TOWNSHIP OF EMILY

clay soil, part swampy; maple, bass, elm, cedar; 2¼ miles to Best's Mill; north
half hilly and swamp; value 12s. 6d. an acre; has sent up money to Toronto
for his deed.

Con. 3: *west half lot 10*—30 acres cleared; John Thornton locatee (dead); occupant
his son Wm. Thornton who resides with mother and family on lot; clay
soil; maple, beech and cedar; 1 mile to Cottenham's Mills (Williamstown);
value 17s.6d. an acre.

north half lot 17—40 acres cleared; Henry Sheering occupant and locatee;
sandy loam soil; maple, beech, bass and cedar; 4 miles to mill; Robt. Sheering
owns n.w. quarter; value 10s. an acre.

northeast quarter lot 15—5 acres cleared; unoccupied lot; original locatee John
McCall or Wm. Wilson; it is stated that an Alexander Swann owns this; Wm.
Wilson occupies by location the northwest quarter and has up to 40 acres
cleared; clay soil; maple, beech and pine; 3¼ miles to mill; value 10s. an
acre.

Con. 4: *southwest quarter lot 4*—none cleared; no occupant; locatee Arch. McCollum;
loam soil; maple, beech and bass; concession line has been cleared, some
alledge by statute labour; 1 mile to Williamstown mills; 15s. an acre. This
man is away.

south half lot 18—20 acres cleared; occupant Charles Chambers; original
locatee Sam. Gorden, then Charles Chambers; clay loam sandy soil; maple,
beech, bass, elm, cedar; 4¼ miles to Cottenham's; south part of lot all swamp
and drowned with old dam of Tiger's mill; value 8s.9d. an acre.

north half lot 18—60 acres cleared; George Miller occupant and locatee; clay
soil; maple, beech and bass; 4¼ miles to mill; value 11s.3d. an acre.

north half lot 21—15 acres cleared; occupant Alex. Brennan; original locatee
Jeremiah Driscoll; afterwards the widow of Adam Hewitson now Mrs. Lochart;
about ⅓ clay soil, the rest swamp; hemlock, cedar, maple & beech; 5¼ miles to
mill; this is a very bad lot; value 5s. an acre; the respective claims of Brennan
and the present Mrs. Lochart (who lives at Mud Lake) require investigation.

Con. 5: *southeast quarter lot 5*—5 acres cleared; occupant Francis Tailor; locatee
George Casemore; clay soil; maple, beech, pine, cedar; 1 mile to mill; value
12s.6d. an acre.

Con. 6: *part lot 11 west of Pigeon Creek*—about 100 acres of which 30 cleared;
George *Cowan* occupant and locatee; sandy soil; pine, hemlock, maple and
beech; 4 miles to mill; value 7s.6d. an acre. He has an Order-in-Council for
another 100 acres in lieu of waste on this lot caused by Pigeon Creek and
swamp.

southwest quarter lot 12—none cleared, not even a stock cut on concession
line; no occupant; locatee Thomas Mitchell deceased; part good clay land, rest
swamp; maple, beech, bass, elm, cedar, hemlock; 5 miles to mills; 10s. per acre
value; Mitchell's sons claim this, but regulations to settlement duty has been
non-complied, so their claim is dubious.

north half lot 19—none cleared; no occupant; locatee John Shouldis afterwards
James Reed; about ⅓ good hardwood land, rest swamp; tamarack, hemlock and
some hardwoods; 6 miles to Cottenham's Mills; Pigeon Creek cuts it up and a
tamarack swamp; value 3s.9d. to 4s. per acre; the respective claims of Shouldis
and Reed require investigation; settlement duty partially done as regards the
road allowance on concession line.

north half lot 21—40 acres cleared; occupant and locatee John Geary; clay

APPENDIX IX (cont.)

INSPECTION REPORT OF THOMAS DENNEHY DPS
JULY 1840 ON TOWNSHIP OF EMILY

land with large tamarack swamp; maple, beech, hemlock and tamarack; 3 miles to Baldwin's Mills and 7 miles to Cottenham's Mills; value 8s.9d. per acre.

Con. 7:   *north half lot 7*—45 acres cleared; occupant and locatee Patrick Callaghan; clay soil; beech, maple, elm and basswood; 4 miles to mill; 10s. an acre value.

west half lot 12—12 acres cleared; occupant and locatee Edward McDonell; sandy soil; part swampy; pine, cedar, tamarack and hemlock; 5 miles to mills if road made passable; knolly rough bad lot, drowned in south with marsh and Pigeon Creek, perhaps as bad a lot as there is in the township; value 2s.6d. an acre.

north half lot 17—40 acres cleared; occupant and locatee Thomas Groves; clay and sandy loam soil; maple, hemlock, bass and cedar; half-mile to Baldwin's Mills; value 8s. an acre; Groves says he will not have northwest quarter it being bad and marshy, but wants instead the southeast quarter which is an excellent 50 acres mostly hardwood land.

west half lot 18—about 15 acres cleared; occupant Widow Russell with children; locatee William Russell deceased; sandy loam soil; bass, maple, oak and elm; half-mile to mill; value 10s. an acre; Cornelius the eldest son is said to be of age.

south half lot 23—about 80 acres; 10 acres cleared but growing wild again; unoccupied; locatee Edward Sullivan, is away; clay soil; maple, beech, basswood and elm; 4 miles to mills; value 10s. an acre; about 60 acres excellent land, rest marsh and indifferently good.

Con. 8:   *west half lot 8*—30 acres cleared; Edmund Callaghan occupant and locatee; clay and sandy loam soil; maple, beech, elm; 4 miles to Mills; value 11s.3d. an acre.

west half lot 16—2 or 3 acres cleared; occupant Wm. Barret (squatter); locatee Pat Shea deceased; nearly all marsh; hemlock, cedar, tamarack; 1 mile to mill across creek and marsh; about 5 acres of hardwood valued 10s. an acre; Pat Shea previous to death, not liking this lot, went upon Clergy Reserve lot adjoining (west half 16 in con. 9) and cleared there about 25 acres; his eldest son Cornelius and wife, their claim requiring investigation.

Con. 9:   *north half lot 7*—10 acres cleared; unoccupied; locatee Daniel Donoghue; clay soil; maple, beech, basswood, cedar; 6 miles to mill; value 11s.3d. an acre; it is stated by Donoghue's mother and others that Michael Collins (Dan's brother-in-law) pays the taxes and takes care of the lot for him.

south half lot 13—nothing done in clearing; no occupant; locatee Robert German; clay soil; maple and beech; 8 miles from mills; value 11s.3d. an acre; it is said German sold this to Kelson; but none of them complied with regulations re settlement duty; it is a level lot.

north half lot 14—10 acres cleared; occupant Edward Morrissey; locatee John Morrissey deceased; clay soil; maple and beech; 8 miles Cottingham's Mills and 2¼ miles Baldwin's Mills (if bridge made over Pigeon Creek); excellent lot; value 12s.6d. an acre.

south half lot 17—none cleared; no occupant; locatee Matthew Connor; nearly all swamp; cedar and tamarack; 1 mile across creek to Baldwin's Mills; about 20 acres at 10s. an acre; Connor threw this up and I think got a lot in Verulam township.

Con. 10:   *south half lot 6*—8 acres cleared and settlement duty done; unoccupied; original locatee James Hurley, now resides in Peterboro; clay soil; maple, beech and basswood; 6 miles to Mills; value 12s.6d. an acre.

INSPECTION REPORT OF THOMAS DENNEHY DPS
JULY 1840 ON TOWNSHIP OF EMILY

south half lot 9—20 acres cleared; unoccupied; locatee John Brislane; maple, beech, elm, basswood; 7 miles to Cottenham's Mills and 3½ miles to Baldwin's; clay soil; value 13s.9d. an acre; the widow Margaret Brislane claims this lot.

north half lot 12—12 acres cleared; occupant E. Dwyer's father takes charge of lot for locatee Edmund Dwyer; sandy soil, part swamp; maple, beech, hemlock, cedar; poor lot value 8s.9d. an acre; Dwyer away.

south half lot 23—80 acres, of which 20 cleared; occupant and locatee John Hartnell; clay soil; maple, beech, elm and hemlock; 2 miles to Baldwin's Mills; 10s. an acre value.

Con. 11:   *south half lot 1*—35 acres cleared; occupant and locatee Barth. Kenelly; clay soil; maple, beech, elm, tamarack; Purdy's Mills 6 miles; 8s. an acre value; a tamarack swamp on this lot decreases its value.

north half lot 1—none cleared and no occupant; locatee Benjamin Madigan; clay soil; basswood, beech and elm; 6 miles to mills; good lot; value 11s.3d. an acre; it is said Madigan sold it to Denis Connor, but none did settlement duties on it.

south half lot 12—6 acres cleared; unoccupied; locatee Timothy Ryan; part clay; rest swampy; maple, beech and cedar; 4 miles to Baldwin's and 8 miles to Cottenham's Mills; value 8s.9d. an acre.

north half lot 17—15 acres cleared; John Sheehan occupant and locatee; clay on north half, swampy on south half; maple, beech, elm, tamarack; Verulam Mills 2 land carriage miles but 10 by water; poor lot; 7s.6d. an acre value.

Con. 12:   *east half lot 13*—30 acres cleared; unoccupied; locatee James Madigan; clay soil; maple, beech, basswood and elm; 9 miles to mill; value 10s. an acre; Madigan away.

south half lot 16—15 acres cleared, growing wild again; unoccupied; locatee Robert Fox is away to States this long time; sandy soil; cedar, tamarack, maple and beech; mill at Bobcaygeon is 10 miles by water and 4 miles land; value 7s.6d. an acre.

Con. 13:   *east half lot 1*—30 acres cleared; occupant and locatee John Clarke; clay soil; maple, beech and elm; Purdy's Mills 8 miles; good lot; value 15s. an acre.

south half lot 5—35 acres cleared; occupant James Callaghan; locatee John Maher (who sold to Callaghan); clay soil; beech, bass and maple; 10 miles to either Purdy's or Cottenham's Mills; good lot; value 13s.9d. an acre.

east half lot 7—12 acres cleared; occupant and locatee Thomas Cullen (who lives on next lot); ½ clay land, rest swamp; cedar, maple, beech; 10 miles to mill over bad road; value 2s.6d. an acre; a very bad lot.

north half lot 8—25 acres cleared; occupant and locatee Christopher Bentley; light clay soil intermixed with gravel; maple, beech, elm; 10 miles to mills; value 11s.3d. an acre.

Con. 14:   *west half lot 4*—occupant and locatee Peter Gannin; light clay, limestone and gravel intermixed; hemlock, maple and beech; 9 miles to Ops Mills; value 10s. an acre.

east half lot 8—about 8 acres cleared; occupant and locatee John McMullin; clay upon limestone gravel; maple and beech; 10 miles Cottenham's or Purdy's mills; value 10s. an acre.

west half lot 8—18 acres cleared; occupant and locatee John Dwyer; clay soil; maple, beech and basswood; 10 miles to Cottenham's or Purdy's Mills; value 10s. an acre; this farm is growing up wild again.

south half lot 9—12 acres cleared; occupant and locatee Thomas Magher;

APPENDIX IX (cont.)

INSPECTION REPORT OF THOMAS DENNEHY DPS
JULY 1840 ON TOWNSHIP OF EMILY

light clay soil; maple, beech; 10 miles to Cottenham's or Purdy's Mills; value
10s. an acre.

south half lot 12—none cleared; no occupant; locatee Michael Brennan; clay
soil; but over ⅔ swamp; tamarack, cedar, maple and beech; 12 miles to mill;
drowned land along creek and bad tamarack swamp; very poor lot; value
2s.6d. an acre.

south half lot 16—12 acres cleared; unoccupied; locatee Jeremiah Connell;
sandy loam; maple, beech and cedar; about ⅓ swampy; over 12 miles to mill;
value 5s. an acre.

APPENDIX X

TORONTO 'EXAMINER', APRIL 17, 1844

MEETING OF THE REFORMERS OF EMILY: A meeting of the friends of Responsible
Government in the Township of Emily, Colborne District, was held at Murray's Inn on
Monday 25th March and a Branch Association formed. From the well-known patriotism
and energy of the Reformers in that quarter, we feel satisfied that they will not allow the
good cause to languish for want of support. Mr. John Lane being unanimously called to
the Chair, and Mr. P. Ryan appointed to act as secretary. The following Resolutions were
carried unanimously—

Moved by Mr. J. Dwyer, seconded by Mr. D. Paquette—That this meeting deeply
deplores the course of policy pursued by H. E. Sir Charles Metcalfe which has cast a
deep and extended gloom over the brightening prospects of Canada, the land of our
adoption. That we fully concur in the principles contended for by the late Executive
Council, and are fully determined to sustain them, by every constitutional means in our
power.

Moved by Mr. Lehane, seconded by Mr. Connell—That Responsible Government
is the most effectual means of maintaining our connection with Great Britain, and secur-
ing peace and tranquility in Canada. And if there was ever a moment that demanded
firmness and exertion it is at this crisis when our rights and liberties as British subjects
are going to be wrested from us.

Moved by Mr. David Owen, seconded by Mr. D. Houlihan—That we fully agree
with the Reform Association of Toronto, in carrying out the measures of Responsible
Government in conformity with the Resolutions of 1841, and are fully determined to
support the same. For which purpose we form ourselves into a Branch of the said Association under the title of the Reform Association of Emily, Colborne District.

Moved by Mr. Michael Collins, seconded by Mr. Michael Lehane—That the thanks
of the meeting is due to Dr. Smith, for his able explanation of Responsible Government,
so essentially necessary on the present occasion.

APPENDIX XI

PART 1—J. G. Hodgins *"Documentary History of Education in Upper Canada"* (1894)

(Reminiscences of an anonymous former teacher)

TOWNSHIP OF EMILY. The first Public School opened, in what is now the County of Victoria, was held, or opened, in the Township of Emily on the south east corner of Lot number 10, Concession 3, then known as the Clergy Reserve Lot. The School House, or building used as such, was an old log shanty about 20 by 12 feet, covered with Elm Bark, a flat roof, it had neither window, floor, or fire place, or stove, consequently could only be used in summer, there was an opening in the roof, and the original occupants, (who were Brickmakers, imported in the early twenties of this century), used it while making a kiln of Brick for an English Cabinet Maker, who did not think wooden house healthy residences. The School was opened in June, 1834, and lasted three or four months, until the days got too cold for the pupils to sit without a fire. The Teacher, (like nearly all of the early Teachers, in this new country, then) was an old British Soldier, named, Hamilton, an Irish Man and a graduate of Trinity College, Dublin. Six feet two inches in height, and of fine appearance, and of very Gentlemanly manners. Poor fellow, he had an old Soldier's failing,—a great fondness for drink. He drifted to Emily, where he took up the land granted him, as a discharged soldier, but being not used to manual labour, he did not stay long on the land. The Settlers, being desirous of getting their children as much of an education as the resources of the country, and their limited means could afford, held a meeting and concluded to endeavour to make an arrangement, with Mr. Hamilton, to open a school. The result was, that he was engaged to teach, while the weather kept fine, at the rate of eight dollars per month. Each farmer paying a fixed sum for each child, sent, or promised to the School, there were from sixteen to twenty children which commenced attending. Some of them, (those large enough to assist in harvest), went the first two months, as the days grew cool; the smaller ones dropped off—and the school came to a natural stand still, but the poor old splendid British Soldier, was found lying dead, by the roadside, not far from the school house, one cold morning early in the fall, after the school closed. The School furniture and fixings consisted of two benches made by the two largest scholars, felling a Basswood tree, splitting it up the centre, and fitting two legs on each end,—these making two benches for use to sit on. The Desks consisted of rough boards, resting on long pins, or stakes, driven into two inch auger holes, bored into the side logs of the building,—no trouble in sweeping floor, as it was Mother Earth. The Books and equipment consisted of the Bible; Carpenter's and Mavor's Spelling Books, and such old Arithmetics as the parents of the children had brought from the old country. We had very little paper, some slates; one which now costs 13 cents to 15 cents then costing as high as 80 cents (or four shillings Halifax Currency). The pupils had to use quill pens— (there were no steel pens then,) and they learned to make them, for their own use. If a boy got handy at the work, not only then, but for years afterwards, he had to assist others, who did not possess the mechanical skill, to make pens for themselves. Slate pencils cost two pence each (4 cents). Ink was made by the parents, by boiling soft maple bark in rain water, for a couple of hours, straining or filtering it, and putting into it sufficient copperas, or sulphate of iron, to get the required colour—black. No blotting paper was to be had and "if you wanted a Ruler, make one."

Pupils of the present day would not even think of a school with such school supplies, as we, sixty years ago, were thankful to possess. If there is one thing more than another in which Ontario shews her material and social growth, it is in her schools. Then there was no School Fund, or School Law. No educational assistance of any kind, in the rural parts. Now the country,— (then an endless wilderness, dotted here and there with the small trough-covered shanties, and small clearing openings in the woods), is well provided with comfortable, (mostly brick,) School Houses, having all the modern appliances, to assist

APPENDIX XI (cont.)

PART 1—J. G. Hodgins *"Documentary History of Education in Upper Canada"* (1894)

the pupil and Teacher; but in some cases, no doubt, the Teacher get the greatest amount of benefit, or help, of such assistance so provided.

OMEMEE. The next School in that neighborhood, was taught in the Village then known as "Williamstown," now "Omemee." The Teacher was Mr. William Bamford, Son of a retired Methodist Preacher; he was a well educated man, and a good teacher. The School was opened late in the Fall, and was kept open six months. The House was the Bar-Room of an old Tavern, previously kept by one of the Original Settlers, named "Morris Cotnum,"—his sons afterwards changed their name to "Cottingham." There was a good floor, and a large open fire place in this old House. The Benches and Desks were similar to the first mentioned; the School opened in 1835, and continued in operation until the spring of 1836. The School Books were about the same as were used in the first school.

The next school in Omemee was taught by another old ex-British Officer, Captain Handcock, a most kind-hearted, gentlemanly individual. It was also kept in the Bar-Room of an unused Tavern belonging to a member of the same family of "Cotnum." The school furniture and appliances were about the same, except that Walkingame's Arithmetic had come into use. This poor old man had like tastes and habits, with the first Teacher. He is long since dead, but his memory is still green in the memories of his surviving pupils. This School lasted until 1837. The next School in the Village was held in a one storey frame Building, only clapboarded outside; no ceiling or chimney. The stove pipe was secured through the roof by pieces of sheet iron. The House was built on uneven ground, and one side stood on posts, about two feet above the ground, which made it cold in winter. The Teacher also an old soldier, who had been Band Master of one of the West India Regiments during the French Wars,—ended by Waterloo. He was a splendid Musician; no instrument came amiss, or awkward, to him. We had lots of fun and enjoyment at his School; and if we did not learn a great deal, many of the pupils, at least, acquired a decided taste for music. One day, the Violin, then the Bagpipes, Cornet, Clarionet, Flute, or any other musical instrument, which happened to be handy. His name was Mr. John Henderson, and, as nearly all the old settlers were either related to or connected with him, he was called "Uncle Johnnie" by every one—pupils and all. He was teaching when the McKenzie Rebellion broke out, and nothing could keep the gallant old soldier from the front—so there was no school time for about a year.

After attending other Schools and Teachers for two or three seasons more, the writer obtained a certificate of fitness to teach,—(there having, by this time, been a School Law enacted, and School Regulations made),—and taught schools in rural School Sections for the following three years in the neighborhood. The School Houses, being, in all cases, not only where he was employed, but all through this part of Ontario, of rough logs, shingled, and with a couple of small windows in them, and an open fire place. For all these Schools, the larger boys had to provide the fuel, and cut it ready for use;—but the Teacher had to do the sweeping, cleaning and lighting the fires, bring in his own wood, make all the pens, set Head Lines in Copy Books, and teach, (if able) all the branches required by Parents. The wages had risen to ten dollars a month, (and board round with the pupils), and $13.00 to $14.00 a month, and find your own board and lodging.

Teachers of to-day would greatly object to such offers, or pay and treatment; then, we considered ourselves fortunate to get a six months' engagement, on such terms. Where the Teacher got his board, he boarded a week in each house,—(no matter how far away), for each pupil sent to his school—and the parent paid from 20 cents to 40 cents per month, to make up the salary. In all cases the Teacher had to go round, and collect the school fees himself, and what he could not get, he had to lose, as the Trustees were not responsible to him for anything.

APPENDIX XI (cont.)

PART 2—Hodgins *"Establishment of Schools in Ontario"* (1910)

THE FIRST ESTABLISHMENT OF SCHOOLS IN OMEMEE IN 1837

A Correspondent of the Editor of this Volume writes as follows:

"In the year 1837 Mr. George Hughes settled in Omemee and opened a School for his grandchildren, the sons of Mr. J. L. Hughes and William Cottingham, and other Pupils, and he taught until the year 1843, when, owing to a fire and family affliction, Mr. Hughes discontinued his Classes. Soon after a Log School House was built on what was called the Distillery Road, and a man named Captain Handcock, who had been in the Army, became Master of the School. After a time Mr. R. Grandy (Father of the present Richard Grandy, Postmaster at Omemee) was chosen to succeed Captain Handcock, and for many years taught the Public School. About 1860, a new School House was built, nearer the centre of the Village, and, notwithstanding much opposition, Mr. Cottingham and Doctor Irons succeeded in having a Grammar School established in Omemee and Mr. John Wood, B.A., of Toronto University, was, I think, the first Head Master, and was succeeded by Mr. John Shaw, who, for many years, kept the School in a flourishing condition. Pupils coming from Millbrook, Lindsay, and other places adjacent to it."

APPENDIX XII

"THE CHURCH": JAN. 20, 1838: Journal of Rev. C. T. Wade, "On the following day (Nov. 26, 1837) accompanied by Mr. Hughes, I proceeded to the 2nd concession of Emily where in a convenient schoolhouse I read prayers and preached to a tolerably good congregation. A 'raising bee' in the neighborhood prevented many from attending—a species of friendly association which, whatever may be its value to the new settler, is generally accompanied by demoralizing effects—arrived in Williamstown, where I experienced a most kind welcome from Messrs. Cottingham and Josiah Hughes. In the evening read prayers and preached to a large and attentive audience. In this township is a large Protestant population and many firm and attached adherents of our invaluable Church. A very anxious desire was expressed for the ministrations of a regular clergyman . . . and a considerable sum was subscribed towards the erection of a church.

Nov. 27 This day in company with Messrs. Hughes and Cottingham, I proceeded to Ops. . ."

"THE CHURCH": FEB. 4, 1840: Journal of Rev. Geo. Street, travelling missionary "On the 26th Oct. (1839) I reached Emily, and the next day being Sunday, preached in the village in the morning, and in the afternoon in Ops . . .

Monday morning found me again in Emily, and on the next evening I rode through a pitiless snowstorm to Mr. Armour's (in Cavan) . . . (About Dec. 1st) . . . I reached St. Paul's church in Cavan . . . having preached for Mr. Armour, I proceeded in company with him to his house, and remaining till Wednesday, went on to Emily . . . I made the most of my time by forwarding as far as I could the plans for completion of the Church at this spot. On Thurs. I rode round accompanied by Mr. Hughes to call on the members of the Building Committee, a meeting of which was called for Saturday. On the evening of that day, Rev. R. Taylor arrived from Peterborough, and having been aware I was in the neighborhood, on the following morning I assisted him in the service at the village . . . he returned to Peterborough, officiating at a station about 5 miles on the road . . . (From Eldon), I returned on Friday to Emily . . . the contract for completion of the church was given out by the Building Committee . . . I preached the following day at the village, in the morning, and in the afternoon at Braden's on the Peterborough road . . . The members

APPENDIX XII (cont.)

of the Church in this quarter are only waiting for the appointment of a resident minister in Emily, to erect a suitable building for divine worship. (Late December) . . . (from Brock twp) drove to Emily on the following day. There I ministered private baptism to an infant, and married a couple; after which I proceeded to Mr. Armour's (Cavan) . . . thus ended my third tour of 280 miles . . ."

APPENDIX XIII

Rev. Wm. Shaw's letter to the Governor concerning the situation in Emily
(Ontario Archives)

Emily, Colborne District
22d April 1844

Sir

I have taken the liberty to request your kind interposition in representing to His Excellency, the Governor General, the circumstances connected with the appropriation of a valuable lot of land in this Township for the purpose of a Glebe. The lot in question N° 10 on the 4th Concession was surveyed by the Major Wilmot about 20 years ago, and at his recommendation was entered on the Council Books as a Glebe. Prior to the appointment of a resident Clergyman to this Township, the guardianship of the property was exercised by the Revd Joseph Thompson, the late Rector of Cavan; and the Revd Saml. Armour, the present Incumbent of that Parish. My predecessor, the Revd. G. C. Street, rented a small portion of it consisting of 6 acres, and reserved the remainder at his own disposal. Shortly after my arrival here, about 2½ years ago, I rented it to four different individuals in shares of 50 acres each.

My principal object in addressing you is to ascertain whether His Excellency after an investigation of the title of the church to the above property, would be graciously pleased to grant me a regular license of occupation for any term of years which he might consider expedient. I am not prompted to make this request from any selfish motives, since it is my full intention to appropriate the whole of the proceeds arising from the lease or rental of the lot, to the exclusive advantage of the church in this Parish.

I beg, Sir, to remain
Your most obedient humble Servant

The Private Sect. to His Excellency   William Shaw
             Kingston   Minister of Emily

P.S.

I am sorry to add that my present Tenants after having exercised my patience for upwards of two years, manifest a real indisposition to satisfy my claims against them, and that such indisposition is not attributable to any lack of ability to discharge the respective amounts of those claims. In one case particularly the property itself has sustained considerable damage, owing to the perverseness of its occupant. If therefore I could obtain a Title of Occupation, such annoyances would be effectually prevented in future instances, as I should in that case, during my Incumbency, transfer the management of the business to the Churchwardens with a view to the promotion of the interests of the Church.

I beg to state that the lot is *not a Clergy Reserve,* and therefore cannot be affected by the arrangements recently made with regard to the sale of Lands of that description. It has always been understood by the inhabitants of this place to have been specially set apart by the Government for the benefit of the church, in consequence of the recommendation of the gentleman already mentioned.

W. S.

APPENDIX XIV

From Sam'l Strickland "27 Years in Canada West" London 1853

Volume I (Undated but perhaps around 1840)

. . . People who lose themselves in the Bush seldom persevere long enough in any one direction. They fancy they are going wrong, and keep changing their course; till probably, after four or five hours' walking, they find themselves near the spot whence they started. This has occurred to me more than once, and I shall relate a melancholy incident which happened only a few years ago, and which proves what I have just stated.

The person to whom I allude, resided in the township of Emily, and had been all the summer working at his trade in the village of Bowmanville, to earn money sufficient to pay for his land, which he had succeeded by the fall in doing. As the cold weather had set in, he determined to return home, and chop all the winter on his farm. He knew that by crossing the township of Darlington and Manvers in an oblique direction, twenty-five or six miles in length, he could reach his own house in half the time, the distance by the road being more than double that by which he proposed to travel. He therefore determined to try the short way, although he was well aware that the last eight or ten miles of his road was through the Bush, with not even a blazed line to guide him. He was, however, young and active, and moreover considered himself a good backwoodsman. He started one fine frosty morning early in December, expecting he should be able to reach his own house sometime before sundown.

For the first ten or twelve miles he got on pretty well, as he had a sleigh-track to follow, and as long as the sun shone out he made a good course. Unfortunately for him, a snow-storm came on and obscured his only guide. He, however, struggled on manfully through cedar-swamps and over ridges, with the snow half-way up to his knees, till the approach of darkness compelled him to look out for some place to shelter him from the storm, where he might best pass the weary hours of the coming night.

He selected a dry spot beneath some spreading cedars, and busied himself as long as daylight lasted in collecting as much fire-wood as would last till the morning. He then gathered a quantity of hemlock-brush for his bed, and by breaking off some large limbs from the surrounding evergreens, succeeded at last in forming a temporary shelter. For a long time he despaired of getting a fire, till he at length found some dry cedar-bark, which he finally succeeded in igniting with a piece of punk, which every backwoodsman carries with him for that purpose. Though the poor fellow had only taken with him provisions for a day's journey, he made a hearty supper, merely reserving a portion for his breakfast, not suspecting that he should fail in reaching his destination. He fully expected he should see the sun in the morning, which would enable him to correct his course; for he knew that he was in the township of Manvers, and not more than seven or eight miles from his own home.

Wearied with his day's journey, he slept the greater part of the night, although awakened occasionally by the cold. At such times he would heap fresh fuel on the fire, and again compose himself to sleep.

To his infinite joy the morning beamed brightly—the sun shone out. With a light heart and renewed confidence he again shaped his course eastward, following the direction in which his house lay; and there is no doubt, had the day remained clear, he would in a few hours have extricated himself from the dilemma into which he had fallen. His disappointment was great when he again beheld the sky overcast, and the snow falling thickly around him. He pushed on, however, bravely, till at length a thick cedar-swamp lay before him. For some time he travelled along its edge, in the hope of finding a narrow spot to cross, but in this he was disappointed, so he determined to attempt the passage. He fully believed, once on the other side, he should know the face of the country, from his having so often hunted game, or searched for his cattle in that direction.

For fully an hour he pressed on through a complete thicket of cedar; but it was all

APPENDIX XIV (cont.)

From Sam'l Strickland "27 Years in Canada West" London 1853

random work, for the evergreens were so loaded with snow, that it was quite impossible to go one hundred yards in a straight course. At last he saw the tops of hard-wood trees before him, which again revived his sinking spirits, for he thought he had crossed the swamp. Alas, poor fellow! he was mistaken. He had come out on the very side by which he had entered it, but of this he was not aware at the time. He, however, wondered that he did not recognize any part of the ground he was travelling over.

At length, to his great joy, he came upon the fresh track of a man, which he had no doubt belonged to some person, who was then out from the settlement, still hunting; for he knew that Manvers was the most celebrated township for deer in the Newcastle District. As he observed that the footprints were going in a contrary direction to what he was, this circumstance gave him increased confidence. Two or three times, however, he thought some of the small swamps and ridges looked vastly like what he had traversed in the early part of the day. At last, about an hour before dark, he saw a thin wreath of blue smoke in a thicket before him. Judge of his disappointment and dismay, when, on his nearer approach, he found he had actually followed his *own track,* which had brought him back to the spot where he had passed the night. To describe his feelings on this occasion would be difficult and painful. He thought of his wife and his young children, who were hourly expecting his return, and who had, no doubt, prepared some little treat to welcome the wanderer home.

Bitter were his reflections during the waking hours of that long night! Hungry, tired, and unrefreshed, the morning's light saw him struggling through the snow, but whither he knew not; for though it had ceased snowing, the sky was still overcast, and continued so till the middle of the afternoon, when the wind suddenly veered round to the north-west, attended with intense cold. He now renewed every effort; for once or twice he thought he heard the sounds of civilized life—the distant supper-horn or cattle-bell—but the fierce howling of the wind, which blew half a gale, rendered his hearing indistinct.

As long as daylight lasted he dragged on his wearied limbs, till utter exhaustion and coming darkness rendered his further progress impossible. To add to his misfortune, on attempting to kindle a fire, he found that his punk was damp, from the snow having come in contact with it when pressing his way through the swamp. He now gave himself up for lost, for the night was extremely cold, and he had neither fire to warm him, nor roof to shelter his head. To sleep thus he knew was certain death. He therefore paced up and down as long as he was able to stand, but his boots were frozen stiff, and his feet numb with cold. After great difficulty he managed to pull off his boots, and having wrapped up his feet in his woollen cap, he lay down on the path he had beaten in the snow, for he could no longer resist the inclination to sleep.

While in the act of lying down, he distinctly heard a cock crow at no great distance. By a great effort he roused himself, and called as loudly as he was able. Once he thought he heard an answer to his cry—again the horn seemed to ring in his ears,—and then all was blank.

At daylight he was found by some of his own neighbours, one of whom was up early in the morning feeding his oxen, preparatory to a journey to the front, when he heard the shouts, which sounded to him like those of some person in distress. He immediately blew his dinner horn, that the sound might guide the lost person, and having collected three or four of his neighbours, they started into the woods in the direction from whence the shouts of the lost man had proceeded. Half a mile from the clearing, they came across his track, which they only followed for a few yards, when to their surprise they found their poor neighbour, whom at first they concluded to be dead. It was some time indeed before they could wake him, so overpowered was he with fatigue and the death-like sleep he had fallen into.

His friends lost no time in carrying him home; but unfortunately they placed him near

APPENDIX XIV (cont.)

From Sam'l Strickland "27 Years in Canada West" London 1853

a large fire, instead of rubbing his hands and feet with snow. The too sudden reaction of the blood caused him the most excruciating agony, for both his hands and feet were badly frozen. At length Dr. Hutchinson was sent for from Peterborough, who found mortification had commenced, and that there was no chance of the poor fellow's recovery, which proved too true, for he expired the next day, a week from the morning he was found.

He, however, died in the arms of his afflicted wife, and was surrounded by his family, a privilege purchased at the expense of severe pain, but still one to the husband and father—even though he had been snatchd from his pangless death-sleep to possess it, poor fellow! . . .

(In a footnote Strickland stated that he heard this story from Dr. Hutchinson, but he probably elaborated on the original.)

APPENDIX XV

JOHN HUSTON OF CAVAN
(Newcastle District)

(a) SOME BIOGRAPHICAL NOTES ON THE HUSTON FAMILY:
  (1) Huston was born in Ireland 1790 and entered Masonic Lodge no. 953 in April 1812.
  (2) His wife, Martha Middleton, was also born in Ireland 1787; the date and place of marriage are unknown. Martha's brother William wrote Huston 1818-20 from Coraghy in Ireland, which may have been the birthplace of both John and Martha.
  (3) The Hustons emigrated to New York State, but after a short period came to Upper Canada, probably 1813-14, and settled in Cavan Township.
  (4) Their children: Mary Anne, born in New York State, married John Fair in Cavan and died at Linden Hill, Oct. 1891; Jane, born in Cavan in 1814, married Wm. Cottingham, and died at age 16 and was buried in the Cottingham family plot in Emily Cemetery; Eliza was a spinster (no other facts known); Joseph married a Miss Graham, and died at an early age.
  (5) John Huston was licensed as Deputy Provincial Surveyor Oct. 1820; after aiding Robinson in settling the Irish emigrants in Emily 1825-26, he was given numerous government surveying jobs for roads, reserves and bridges all over Newcastle District, as well as undertaking many private surveying jobs; after appointment as Surveyor of Highways for Newcastle District, he laid out main roads such as the Port Hope-Peterborough and Peterborough-Lindsay roads. In Nov. 1843 Huston was appointed Inspector of Clergy Reserves for Colborne District.
  (6) Huston was commissioned as Adjutant of the 2nd Company, Durham Volunteers, in June 1826, then promoted Captain Nov. 1838, and Major Oct. 1844; he was responsible for the militia in Emily, Ops etc.
  (7) Huston was also a Justice of the Peace and Coroner, and held other district offices.
  (8) Huston continued his Masonic and Orange Order membership in the Port Hope-Cavan area, and was a leading force in smoothing out religious and factional friction in the district.
  (9) John Huston died in Cavan, May 18, 1845; his wife Martha died there in April, 1867.

APPENDIX XV (cont.)

JOHN HUSTON OF CAVAN
(Newcastle District)

(10) Like Peter Robinson and Dr. Hutchison, John Huston died early in the pioneer period of the district, but they were always remembered with esteem and affection by the people of Emily as benefactors.

(b) HUSTON'S FIELD NOTES ON THE CLERGY RESERVES IN EMILY, surveyed in Dec. 1844 as mentioned in the text, are too long to be included here, but a few interesting extracts follow:

"LOT 3, Con. 2 (200 acres): David Rown 70 A(cres) cleared, log house and barn. Land broken, a large hill, hardwood, Soil sandy, 3m. to Mill. N.W. Quarter: Richard W. Marmon log house and barn, 12 A(cres) improved. Some swampy and flooded by Wm. Cottingham's Mill-dam (;) the flooded land Mr. Cottingham has purchased from Mr. Marmon and expects Government will protect him in the purchase. N.E. Quarter: Wm. Copeland 25 A(cres) cleared, rough land, hemlock, pine and hardwood (;) soil sandy, house and barn erected thereon—3½ M. to Mill. Mr. Cottingham expects to receive a patent for the portion of land that he purchased from the Government, of the aforesaid N.E. Quarter."

"LOT 10, Con. 4 (200 acres) Revd. M. Shaw preferd a claim of 17 years by decendancy of occupation first by the late Revd. Jos. Thompson, from him to the Revd. S. Armour, from him to the Revd. Street, from him to the beforenamed M. Shaw who offers 20s. per acre for the whole lot, which he says he will present to the Church for an indowment as originally intended by the beforenamed clergymen. Geo. Dixon wants the N½, land slow descending (;) some pine balsam & hardwood, 21 A(cres) cleared, ½ mile to Mill. Edward Davidson wants the w½ for which he offers 25s. per Acre. Widow Dixon wants the S.E. quarter."

"LOT 3, Con. 8 (200 acres) S. half Thomas Clerke 14 A(cres) cleared, House and barn (;) Land some swampy level wood hemlock and pine hardwood (;) Soil Sandy loam 5 M. to Mill. N. half Nicholas Mulkahy 16 A(cres) cleared a dwelling house (;) Land and wood the same as the South half."

"LOT 3, Con. 10 (200 acres) Timothy Connell 6 A(cres) improved on south half (;) Level land generally clay and hardwood, 7 M. to Mill. North half George Connell offers for land level 40 (Acres) swamp, wood and soil as the south half."

"LOT 17, Con. 12 (200 acres) Francis Duffy 25 A(cres) improved, house and barn on s½ of the lot which is all the hard land on the said 200 A. The remainder is swamp and pond-holes (;) Wood black ash cedar and Tammerack, soil sandy."

"WEST HALF LOT 2, Con. 13 (100 acres) Revd. James Moor 7 (Acres) improved, a small house and barn (;) level land, about 25 A. hard land on the part lot, wood generally hard with pine and hemlock (;) soil sandy, the remainder a Cedar Swamp."

APPENDIX XVI

An Emily Child Sentenced To Death 1849-50

FROM—"FAMOUS CANADIAN TRIALS"
by Albert R. Hassard—Toronto—(Carswell)—1924
(by permission of Carswell Co. Ltd.)

EXCERPTS:

. . . A boy of whom the trial Judge wrote the unusual words, "apparently eleven years of age," was once placed in the charge of "twelve good men and true" in the ancient County of Peterborough and was found guilty of a cruel murder. When the moment for sentence had arrived, the lad, more terrified by his surroundings than by his wickedness, lifted his small and quivering figure up, peered across the wooden railing of the criminal dock, and listened while a kind-hearted Judge, voicing the terrible and inflexible mandate of the law, said to the child, "You must be hanged by the neck until you are dead." . . .

. . . The Township of Emily is one of the many townships of the large county of Victoria devoted almost exclusively to the pursuit of agriculture. In 1849 it was connected judicially with the County of Peterborough. The exigencies of an increasing population, and perhaps some political pressure, caused the separation of a tract of territory from the original parent county. Emily passed with the separation into the newly constituted County of Victoria. Part of Victoria is still a wild, but other sections fringe closely upon the margin of great industrial activity. Indeed, only a few miles to the east of Emily throbs the mighty commerce of fast advancing Peterboro city, and in the heart of that township also abides the little but prosperous and contented community of Omemee. A creditable population has long occupied Emily township. A high respect for the laws of the land has kept its people much out of the pages of history. . . .

. . . Towards the close of the month of October in the year 1849, the people of Emily township were filled with consternation at hearing of the brutal murder of a tender little five-year-old child named Margaret O'Connor. Margaret had been adopted by a kind-hearted farming couple named Thomas and Eliza Rowan. The little creature who thus passed into the new home was the daughter of a "widow woman," who was in rather straightened circumstances and who had other children left by her recently deceased husband for her to support. In the new habitation the little visitor was well nourished. She speedily became a great pet. . . .

. . . The men passing on their tasks to the barn, or along the road, would call to her a cheery greeting, and although, because of her tender years, these greetings drew not so boisterous a response from her, still they never failed to bring the bright colour to her innocent cheeks, and the happy smiles to her ruddy lips. She rapidly became a general favourite, and was loved by nearly everyone who knew her. . . .

. . . Beneath the same roof which sheltered Margaret dwelt a lad of about eleven years of age. He too had been adopted into the household of the Rowans. His juvenile experience had been varied, and he, like her, had been denied a parent's care. Still, he had been far from neglected. Some years previously he had been placed in the home of the Reverend Mr. Dick, the Presbyterian minister of the locality, and in the year 1847 he had been taken from the manse and placed in the home of the Rowans. School was some distance away, and its benefits were not extensively shared by the youth. The farmer and his wife were thoughtful of him, however, and some learning was occasionally imparted to him. His time was principally occupied about the house and the barn. And yet besides his daily duties this lad had discovered another occupation. That occupation was to conceive a jealous dislike, a murderous hatred of little Margaret, the delight of every heart, the joy of every soul. What was it that made this boy envy where others cherished; what was it that made him loathe where others loved?

APPENDIX XVI (cont.)

An Emily Child Sentenced To Death 1849-50

. . . On the twenty-sixth of October, 1849, Mr. Rowan prepared to leave home to attend a plowing "bee," at the farm of Samuel Hannah, who lived nearly a mile away from the Rowan homestead. Mrs. Rowan was to accompany her husband a part of the distance, and stop for some hours with a neighbour. The two children were to remain at home.

"George," said Mr. Rowan to the lad, whose name was George Green, "while I am away I want you to go to the potato field just to the south of the house, and 'raise' ten or twelve rows of potatoes."

"Yes, sir," answered George obediently.

"And," added Mr. Rowan, "when Margaret goes out to you, you may have her help you to pick the potatoes, and place them in the wheelbarrow."

The farmer and his wife then drove away. Half an hour before sunset, farmer Thomas Rowan was surprised to see George Green hurrying towards him across the Hannah acres where Rowan and a number of other men were at work at the plowing "bee." George passed quickly by the other men, and approached to where Mr. Rowan stood in the furrow behind the plow awaiting the lad's coming.

"Mr. Rowan," began the terrified youth.

"What is it?" queried the astonished farmer.

"Margaret has been eaten by a bear," shrieked out the blanche-faced lad.

. . . Hurriedly men brought their horses to a standstill. Hurriedly horses were unhitched from the plows. Hurriedly the animals were driven to their stables. Hurriedly the men set off with the boy in the direction of the Rowan premises.

Arriving there, they went to the potato field, and, directed by the lad, commenced their search for traces of little Margaret. Marks were examined. Footsteps were followed.

"There is where the bear seized her," said George Green. The men looked. But no traces of a dragged body or of a struggle marked the spot.

"There is where the bear jumped over the fence, carrying Margaret with him," continued the boy. The men went thither, and examined the fence, and the ground around it. But they could find no traces of body or bear. The sun had long since dipped behind the purple horizon. . . .

. . . On the morrow the resolute men were early at their sorrowful task. The boy arose after a comfortable night's rest, and ate that hearty breakfast which, amidst good report or ill, invariably characterizes short-visaged youth. With the others he resumed the investigation about the potato field. He professed to be as eager and as diligent as the others. Several times, there at the scene of the tragedy, he was accused of having slain the missing girl. On each occasion he repudiated the charge, and reiterated his story that the bear had borne her away into the depths of the adjoining forest. Noon came, but with it no reward to the searchers. Early in the afternoon, however, one of the men observed newly turned mould near the root of a spreading tree. Digging there, the body of the little girl was discovered. Her face had been pitifully cut with a sharp instrument. The back of her head had been shockingly lacerated. Her arms and other parts of her body had shared a similar fate. Many deep cuts and bruises mutely told of the frightful treatment she had received. Near by was the hoe, which the boy had been using. Blood and hair upon its edge and back testified all too truly of the dreadful manner in which Margaret had met her death. A doctor was summoned. Right there in the field, he held an inquest. The doctor found that death had been caused by the savage treatment inflicted on the little girl. The boy, still protesting innocence, was taken into custody. He was removed to Peterborough jail, and charged with the wilful murder of Margaret O'Connor.

The investigation before the Police Magistrate was brief. It resulted in George Green being sent to the assizes for trial. In jail he remained during the short remainder of the Autumn, the whole of the terrible Winter of eighteen hundred and forty-nine, and well on

APPENDIX XVI (cont.)

An Emily Child Sentenced To Death 1849-50

into the Spring of the year 1850. On Wednesday, the first day of May of the last named year, opened the Spring assizes for the county. . . .

. . . George Green entered the dock on Friday, the third day of May, 1850, to take his trial for murdering Margaret O'Connor. Mr. Burnham, a lawyer of soundness of judgment and distinguished legal experience, was assigned to assume the boy's defence. He made a manful battle on behalf of his youthful client. A jury was empanelled. The Crown Counsel opened with a brief outline of the crime. . . .

Thomas Rowan was the first witness called by the Crown.

"I am a farmer," he began, "and I live in the Township of Emily, in this county. I have dwelt there for eighteen or nineteen years. My wife and I have never had any children. I have known George Green for six years. He was born in Ireland. His father died four years ago. This boy lived with the Reverend Mr. Dick, the Presbyterian minister, for a year. He was 'bound' to me until he reaches the age of twenty-one years. He attended to the cattle, and did many things around the house. . . .

"I asked him to tell me about it. He said they were out in the field, and a bear suddenly appeared and came towards where Margaret was standing. She was not frightened, but thinking it was a calf, held out her hand to it, and called it a 'suckey bossy.' The bear caught her dress in its teeth and dragged her away out of the field, across a rail fence dividing it from the adjoining woods, and soon was lost in the depths of the forest.

. . . "I was suspicious of the story at once," the witness informed the Court, "and I said to the boy, 'You have done something with the child.' He denied that he had done so, and still persisted that she had been eaten by the bear. . . .

. . . Mr. Rowan said that into the rapidly darkening forest the men went, pausing at every sound, searching eagerly for any indication which might mark the path taken by the mythical animal. But it was all in vain. Darkness had descended while they were still patiently endeavouring to discover some faint traces of the missing little girl.

"Who were with you in the search?" inquired the Crown Counsel.

"Samuel Hannah, David Rowan, James Copeland and Robert Abraham," was the reply.

"Eventually," said Mr. Rowan, "I gave up the search, and decided to go for a magistrate. I called at the residence of Squire William Cottingham, but he was not at home. Then I returned, and on the way to my own dwelling I was told that Margaret's body had been found. I had to stop at the store to get some things. Then I came on home. I learned when I arrived that an inquest had been held on the body. The face was covered with cuts. There were cuts over both eyes. I couldn't look any more. The body was buried that same evening. I saw the prisoner standing at the end of the house. He was in custody. I ask him why he had killed Margaret. He said that she was a dirty little thing, and that she would not leave him alone. . . ."

. . . David Rowan, brother and neighbour of the last witness, gave evidence for the Crown. He had been at the "bee" at Samuel Hannah's. He corroborated his brother's story, but went a little more into detail regarding the search which had been made for the murdered girl.

". . . James Copeland said to the boy, 'You have killed the child.' This accusation the boy denied. I went for the Coroner, and he came back. An inquest was held at the foot of the tree. The body then was lying on its back. There were many cuts on the temples. One great gash appeared on the back of the head. The arms were badly cut. The head had seven cuts in all, one of which went through the skull. The earth over the body was only one and one-half inches deep. Leaves were scattered around. We found the hoe at the place where the potatoes had been dug. Only a barrowfull had been 'raised.' Some clay from around the tree was on the hoe, also some of the little girl's hair." . . .

. . . A youth named William Adams, who lived about half a mile from the Rowan

An Emily Child Sentenced To Death 1849-50

farm, gave evidence. He said that between one and two o'clock on the afternoon of the murder, the prisoner had come to the Adams field, and said that Margaret had been carried off by a bear. The boy was on his way to the farm of his uncle, James Copeland, to get him to come with his gun and hunt the bear. . . .

. . . Eliza Adams had heard Margaret singing between ten and eleven in the forenoon of the fatal day, as she was on her way to the potato field. She hadn't seen the prisoner, however. . . .

. . . Doctor Francis Henderson, a Coroner for the county, said that Margaret had been killed close by her superficial grave near the tree. Her death had been occasioned by the hoe. He added that he had heard the prisoner announce that the little girl had annoyed him considerably at the table. . . .

. . . Eliza Rowan was the last person who testified. She was the wife of Thomas Rowan, the first witness in the case. She corroborated many of the facts already presented in evidence. She had been away from home on the fatal Friday, when her husband had gone to the plowing "bee." She had gone part of the way with him. The children, always affectionate to one another, had been left behind. It was nearly dark when she had returned to her home. On her arrival she was surprised to learn that little Margaret was missing, and that the men were searching for her. This witness had asked George Green where the child was, and the boy had bluntly averred that "the bear had her in his belly."

"After the body had been found," continued Mrs. Rowan, "the boy had confessed his crime, and explained how it had been done. He said that Margaret had come out to the field before noon, and that she had not been there very long before he had 'taken the notion of killing her.' He had not invited her out into the field; but when once there, he had resolved to kill her. He struck her with the hoe. She cried, but there was no one near to hear her. Beneath repeated blows she had fallen to the ground. He had kept on striking her until she had ceased to cry. He then had dragged her to the tree, and had dug for her the shallow grave in which next day the body found. There still was some life left in the tiny frame, for when being buried she had faintly moved. In a little while all was still, and Margaret had ceased to breathe." . . .

. . . No witnesses were summoned for the prisoner. Just what his counsel felt to be the prisoner's real defence can scarcely be surmised after this long lapse of nearly three-quarters of a century. The newspapers of the time are silent upon the question. Perhaps the defence was that the affair was an accident in which the culprit admitted the slaying of the little girl. Frightened at his unintentional deed, he, with a natural effort to conceal his guilt, proceeded to hide the evidence of the crime. Then, of course, followed the customary falsehoods to avert the consequences. . . .

. . . Justice Sullivan's charge, delivered with his customary kindliness and eloquence, cannot have failed to make a profound impression. In his notes of the case appears the following brief observation:- "I left the case to the jury and explained what was necessary to constitute the crime of murder, and the law of accountability of infants above the age of seven and under the age of fourteen." . . .

. . . All that remains is a brief entry in the Judge's book, in these significant words:- "Verdict—guilty, the jury recommends the prisoner to mercy on account of his youth." Some pages further in the same notebook appears the tragic yet inevitable disposition of the matter:- "George Green, convicted of murder; sentenced to be hanged on Wednesday, the twenty-sixth of June, 1850."

. . . On the fourth day of June, 1850, an Order in Council of Canada was passed granting him a commutation of the death sentence to one of imprisonment in Kingston Penitentiary for life. Thither the child was taken, as many, not much older than he have been taken, at intervals during the long span of the intervening years. Behind the great grey

APPENDIX XVI (cont.)

An Emily Child Sentenced To Death 1849-50

stone walls of that mighty living sepulchre the boy spent the short remainder of his life. It was not a long one. Soon after his admission his face grew pale, and his pulse slackened. In a little while the murderer of little Margaret O'Connor was a corpse. . . .

APPENDIX XVII

EVENTS IN THE LIFE OF ARTHUR McQUADE 1817-1894

Extract from *"The Irishman In Canada"* by Nicholas Flood Davin, published 1877

"In Emily Township and the Village of Omemee, one of the first names that occur is that of McQuade. Mr. McQuade is the member for the South Riding in the Dominion Parliament. He is a very large property holder in real estate. He is from Cavan, where he was born in 1817. His father, Henry McQuade, died in Ireland; his mother, whose maiden name was Mary Curran, came to the United States with a large family. Thence the family removed to the Township of Emily, where they arrived in 1837. Most of the brothers and sisters are dead. One sister is still alive in West Durham, where she is married to a Mr. Henry Gibson, an Irishman from the North of Ireland. Arthur McQuade, when he first came to Canada, "hired out" to a farmer for ten dollars a month; he worked with the same man for a second year at eleven dollars per month. He then purchased from his employer one hundred acres of land. He married Susan, a daughter of Thomas Trotter, who came from Fermanagh, and was one of the oldest settlers of that section of the country. Mr. McQuade has seven children living, all well to do; five died. He at present owns one thousand acres of land, and has considerable investments in stocks, mortgages, and the like. He is probably worth $100,000. He has for years resided in Emily Township; he was for twenty years collector of taxes there, deputy-reeve for eleven years, being frequently returned by acclamation. He was school trustee for fifteen years, and can look back on a career of usefulness and success. He is a hale, hearty, open-hearted man; a Conservative in politics. He is a Protestant, and has been County Master of the Loyal Orange Society in the County. The wise liberality of the Roman Catholics in Victoria could not be more strikingly shown than in the election of Mr. McQuade. Mr. McQuade is a great man at agricultural associations."

APPENDIX XVIII

SUMMARY OF THE FIRST 90 EMILY BYLAWS, 1850-59
EMILY TOWNSHIP COUNCIL

1850:
(1) Appoints series of highway overseers by divisions, also pound-keepers and fence-viewers.
(2) Sets twp. clerk (Robt. Grandy's) salary as £5 per year, payable half-yearly.
(3) Sets twp. treasurers salary to be 3% (of what not said).
(4) Sets salary of twp. superintendent of schools at £5 per annum payable half-yearly.
(5) Pound-keepers to set up enclosure(s) for animals straying and if not collected by owner within 48 hours paying fees of 3d., notice to be posted in 3 public places for 15 days, and then animals sold to highest bidder, returning any surplus to owner if

APPENDIX XVIII (cont.)

SUMMARY OF THE FIRST 90 EMILY BYLAWS, 1850-59
EMILY TOWNSHIP COUNCIL

known. Poundage for horse 1s. a day, Oxen 9d. a day, cow 7½d., young cattle 6d., swine 3d., sheep 1d. (food & water per day same amount). Advertising and selling 2/6 each, appraisers 2s. each.

(6) Statute labour to be commuted by paying 2/6 for each day's labour, if desired. Road overseers may spend such commutation money on local roadwork.

(7) All "intire" horses, bulls, boars, rams and breachy cattle not to be allowed to run at large April 1 to November 1, and each animal so found the owner to be fined 2/6 for first offence, 5s. for second, and so on—height of fences to be 4½ feet of good material.

(8) Duties of overseers of highways defined. Statute labour to be assessed on property on roads—if value less than £25—2 days, £25 to £50—3 days, £50 to £75—4 days &c. up to 12 days for £400-450, and for every £100 above £500 another day. Any owner with a wagon, cart or team of horses or oxen &c. liable to work on roads not less than 3 days. Roads newly made to be from 40 to 60 feet wide. More details about lists to be kept &c.

(9) Duties of twp. assessor defined.

(10) Salary of tax collector to be £10 per annum. Sureties required to be approved by council. Report to be made to Council on monies collected before Jan. 31 each year. Collector to proceed against persons refusing or neglecting to pay rates after 14 days' notice. Rules also for seizure and advertising sale of delinquent property. Collector to accept in payment of taxes any certificate for killing of wolves at rate of 30s. each wolf.

(11) Twp. Treasurer empowered to demand and receive from County Treasurer all monies belonging to township.

(12) Bylaw to provide for regulation of line fences and water courses. Duties of fence-viewers.

(13) To provide for raising sum of money for municipal and school purposes on rateable property. Sum of £130 to be levied for schools—sum of £70 to be levied for paying twp. officers and other expenses—*total tax to be collected £200.*

(14) Bylaw to appropriate labour at rate of 8 hours a day to amount of £51 granted by County Council to pay local inhabitants along main roads to open up same— boundary line on con. 1 between Cavan and Emily, road between 1st and 2nd concessions, boundary line between Emily and Smith, 8th concession line, road from Cowan's Bridge to 10th con. line (Middle Line), &c. 6th concession line (including through Carey's swamp), Scully's road through swamp, &c.

(15) To raise sum for repairing school in section 13—sum of £5, 7s. 10½d. "for following repairs viz. for laying and jointing the upper floor, building chimney, making seats and desks. For providing 500 feet of lumber, 15 lbs. nails, 250 brick, 2 elbows for stove, drawing of said lumber and for paying George Miller the sum of 27/6 due to him by said school section (for the building work)".

(16) Repealing No. 11 above.

(17) To repeal part of No. 14 above.

(18) To spend £18 on middle line through 9th, 10th, 11th and 12th concessions.

(19) To establish a line of road between lots 15 and 16 in 11th concession.

(20) To add to collector's roll the sum of £2 10s. in favour of Wm. Laidley . . . "to be collected off the inhabitants resident within s.s. no. 2 Union School (and no. 10 Ops) . . . to remunerate Wm. Laidley in part for loss sustained in the burning of the schoolhouse in said section."

(21) To define mode for altering, laying &c. site of any new or existing road or bridge & to prescribe duties of surveyors of roads.

APPENDIX XVIII (cont.)

SUMMARY OF THE FIRST 90 EMILY BYLAWS, 1850-59
EMILY TOWNSHIP COUNCIL

(22) To provide payment of wages to members of council, and for remuneration for use of the Council Room, fire, candles and attendance to David Harkness. Each council member to be allowed 5s. per diem for services performed. Sum of £3 10s. to Harkness.

(23) To define place of twp. meeting . . . "the township meeting for Emily shall be held at the Inn of David Harkness in village of Metcalfe for the ensuing year." (Dec. 10, 1850)

1851

(24) Bylaw 24 repeals no. 23!!! *Jan. 21, 1851* and provides "that township meetings in future be held at the Inn of Edward Blackwell in Metcalfe" (same reeve, Wm. Cottingham, and same clerk, Robt. Grandy)

(25) For appt. of township officers, on same plan as no. 1 above. 56 highway overseers, 9 pound-keepers, 18 fence viewers (incl. a Connell & a Jackson) also 3 town wardens, and 2 auditors.

(26) To limit number of inns and houses of public entertainment within municipality "where spiritous or malt liquors shall be sold"—not be exceed 7—each to have a "comfortable dwelling house with at least 3 furnished bedrooms exclusive of those required for use of the innkeeper's family."—rules for reception of travellers— provision of stable stalls for horses, water supply—forbid any exhibitions of "slight of hand, tumbling, rope dancing, card playing or any kind of gambling whatever" . . . lock up at 11 p.m. with no more drinking, "no profane swearing, immodest or disloyal songs or tales shall be allowed"; innkeeper shall not sell liquor to any person intoxicated—fine of 5s. ɩo £5 for breaking. FEES: £4 in village of Metcalfe or within 1½ miles of same; £3 at "DOWNEY'S CROSS", and £3, 10s. on boundary line between Emily and Smith.

(27) Amends no. 26, each inkeeper licensed must post bond £40 as security—himself £20 and 2 sureties of £10 each for keeping his rules as above. Prohibition of selling intoxicating liquors on Sabbath except to travellers—fine 10s. to £5. Prohibition on selling drink to any person under 16 years of age, penalty 5s. to £2.

(28) Inspectors authorized to grant inn licenses to Francis Best, David Harkness, Edward Blackwell, Robert Henderson, Isaac English, James Collins and Mary Ann Davidson.

(29) Prescribes duties of Inspectors of Licenses (incl. breakers of rules above, and any selling intoxicating liquors without license).

(30) Bylaw 26 amended to allow 9 inns &c. to sell spiritous liquor in Emily, the two new ones to be Michael Lehane and David Armstrong. Lehane licensed for "house of public entertainment at Downey's Cross" . . . David Armstrong not located . . . each to pay £3 for his license.

(31) To repeal bylaws 2, 3, 4 and 10 of 1850, and to determine salaries of municipal officers—Collector £13, 15s.; assessor £13, 5s.; clerk £7, 10s.; treasurer £5, 5s.; inspectors each £1; auditors each 10s.

(32) To raise money for municipal and school purposes—£81 for schools; £194 for municipal purposes. Total twp. rates £275.

(33) Renew appt. as overseer of highways, amending earlier bylaw in part.

(34) Repeal of bylaw 32, and to raise £80 for schools and £120 for municipality. TOTAL NOW ONLY £200 AS IN 1850.

(35) To raise money to build a schoolhouse in s.s. no. 6 in Emily—sum of £17 be assessed and levied in the said school section for the purpose . . . "materials necessary for the erection of the said schoolhouse shall be received by the Trustees at a fair

APPENDIX XVIII (cont.)

SUMMARY OF THE FIRST 90 EMILY BYLAWS, 1850-59
EMILY TOWNSHIP COUNCIL

and current price delivered by any of the inhabitants compelled to assist by law in the erection of the same." (July 8, 1851).

(36) To provide for protection of sidewalks in village of Metcalfe . . . "any person or persons riding or driving any horse, mare, gelding, oxen or other cattle along the said sidewalks except where same may cross some street, lane or entry, the same shall be liable to such fine as shall be hereafter provided"—also any person or persons cutting, destroying or carrying away any part of said sidewalk—fine not less than 2/6 nor more than 20s.

1852 (Wm. Cottingham still reeve, Grandy clerk).

(37) To annul a road between lots 2 and 3 in 7th concession and angling through lot 2 in 8th con.

(38) Bylaw to assess and levy on lands of non-residents in twp. for municipal purposes the sum of £40 in addition to the sum of £120 already authorized for resident landowners.

(39) To provide for appt. of twp. officers for current year—lists of names for highway overseers, pound-keepers and fence-viewers.

(40) To appt. township officers and their salaries: Robt. Grandy, clerk £8, 5s. per annum; Thomas Matchett, treasurer, £6, 7s. 6d. per annum; James English, assessor, £12, 15s.; Arthur McQuade, collector, £15; Thomas Crawford and Henry Sherin, auditors, 10s. each per annum. Clerk and treasurer required to give bonds. (Each of above to retain office during pleasure of Council, so annual appt. not required).

(41) To convey powers to Reeve out of council to give necessary directions.

(42) To license *temperance hotels* within twp. and define rules &c. . . . not to exceed 7, license fee £1, 5s. for each. Prohibition against selling or giving to drink any spirituous or malt liquor under penalty £10. Each must have at least 3 rooms with beds for travellers above those used for innkeeper's family, and stables &c. Prohibition against exhibitions, profane swearing, immodest or disloyal songs or tales &c.

(43) To limit number of Inns and Houses of public entertainment, & licensing &c. not to exceed 7. (cf. 1851)

(44) To authorize Hardis Alwill to sell spirituous liquors & keep a house of public entertainment, thus increasing number to 8, amending no. 43. Alwill's Inn in Metcalfe village. To comply with all other regulations as above.

(45) To provide for raising money for county and twp. purposes. . . . For county the levy to be £50, 15s. 3d. on all rateable property; For township the further sum of £140 assessed & levied "for the improvement of roads and bridges," salary of twp. officials & contingent expenses.

(46) To raise money for school purposes—£85 on all rateable property (Oct. 5, 1852).

(47) To establish a new line of road through the 7th con. of twp. Emily—commencing between lots 16 and 17 in front of 7th con. thence northwest &c . . . to rear of said concession bet. lots 17 and 18. Width of road to be 50 feet.

1853

(48) To repeal bylaws 26 and 27 re rules & regulations of Innkeepers—Each tavern in Metcalfe village to have (in addition to their private rooms) 4 well-furnished bedrooms, 1 sitting-room and 1 dining-room besides the bar-room, plus good stabling for 8 horses, with sufficiency of provender and water, sheds for 6 teams, & good enclosed yard. Along Smith-Emily boundary line road, and at Downeyville (first time name used) to have 3 bedrooms for travellers well furnished, 1 sitting-room beside the bar-room, with stabling for 6 horses, together with provender & water, sheds for 4

APPENDIX XVIII (cont.)

SUMMARY OF THE FIRST 90 EMILY BYLAWS, 1850-59
EMILY TOWNSHIP COUNCIL

teams & an enclosed good yard. Innkeepers in all Emily to be accountable for safety of travellers and baggage, and shall not allow in premises immoderate drinking, or gambling, or lottery of any sort, nor profane swearing, immodest or disloyal songs, and no exhibitions of "shows, slight of hand, rope-dancing, tumbling or any immoral conduct whatever". Employees and innkeepers forbidden to give drink to persons intoxicated, or under 16 years of age, or on Sabbath day,—bar-room closed on that day. Nor to allow any person to leave his "House" in state of intoxication but shall "take care of him until he becomes sober"—closing at 11 p.m. when all persons to be put out, (and travellers to rooms). Fines listed for breaking the regulations— recognizance of £20 himself and two sureties of £10 each before getting license . . . "good moral character" for each innkeeper.

(49) To limit no. of taverns within munic. and to fix amount to be paid for licenses for same. Number limited to five—license fee in villages of Metcalfe and Downeyville £4, exclusive of 'Imperial Charge'—on the 4th con. fee to be £2, 10s., & tavern at F. Best's to pay £1, 1s. 3d. Following licensed—F. Best, Robert Henderson, Edward Blackwell and David Harkness, and a new one to Michael Guiry at Downeyville. Each tavern-keeper also to pay to one of the Tavern Inspectors the sum of 15s. on receiving his certificate.

(50) To establish a new line of road between lots 13 and 14 through 12th con., in n.w. direction and to be not less than 50 feet wide.

(51) Raising sums of money for county, township, lunatic asylum & debenture bylaw purposes. Sum of £74, 3s. 8d. assessed & levied on all rateable property for county purposes. Sum of £90, 5s. 8d. be assessed and levied for improvement of roads & bridges, twp. salaries &c. Sum of £19, 9s. 8d. be assessed and levied for paying amount imposed on twp. by County bylaw passed in June 1853 (re lunatic asylum?). Sum of £46 be assessed and levied on all rateable property for paying amount imposed on twp. by County bylaw passed in June 1853, entitled Debenture Bylaw.

(52) To levy money for school purposes in Emily £70 to be assessed & levied. (Total of above tax levies for 1853 about £300).

(53) To establish new road through 7th concession of Emily—commencing in front of 7th conc. at limit between lots 17 and 18, then northwest to allowance for road in rear of concession—not less than 50 feet wide—a public highway, on which overseers to use statute labour.

(54) To establish new line of road through lot 18 in 6th concession—40 ft. wide—a public highway, on which overseers to use statute labour.

(55) To establish new line of road in 7th concession—commencing west of post planted between lots 9 and 10, then northeast turning southeast, then northeast again to middle road at Cowan's Bridge—then commencing between lots 9 and 10 in said 7th concession intersecting road leading to Cowan's Bridge northwest to east bank of the Creek, thence southwest across creek on lot 9—not less than 40 ft. wide and a public highway for statute labour &c.

1854 (Wm. Cottingham, reeve; Robert Grandy, clerk).

(56) To unite s.s. 10 and 14 in Emily into one school section—"it having at the annual school meetings in the year 1854 (January) held in each of said school sections been unanimously agreed upon by the ratepayers thereof." Jan. 17, 1854 Council mtg.

(57) Appt. of certain twp. officers—Wm. Matchett issuer of licenses—3s. 9d. for each license. Thomas Crawford and Alex. Beaton auditors—10s. each.

(58) To set license fees for Innkeepers, stores and alehouses to retail wine, spirituous or malt liquors—(Exception for Francis Best who shall pay same as last year)—£3, 10s.

APPENDIX XVIII (cont.)

SUMMARY OF THE FIRST 90 EMILY BYLAWS, 1850-59
EMILY TOWNSHIP COUNCIL

to treasurer plus £2, 3s. 9d. 1 farthing for Imperial Charge—15s. to Inspector of licenses and 9d. to issuer of Licenses . . . this is for Inns and taverns. For store-keepers seeking license to retail wine & liquors—treasurer £7, 10s., to issuer of license 1s. 9d., plus any Imperial charge &c. Those selling only ale or beer—to treasurer £2, 10s. and to issuer of license 3s. 9d.

(59) To regulate auctioneers or others selling goods, wares, effects and merchandise by public auction—to treasurer a deposit of £2, and to issuer of licenses his usual fee (3s. 9d.?). Penalties provided for contravention.

(60) Appointment of certain township officers—52 highway overseers, 23 fence-viewers, 8 pound-keepers.

(61) Payment of councillors—6s. 3d. a day to attend meetings.

(62) Raising of moneys for county, township and other purposes—£700 required—£81, 3s. assessed and levied for county purposes. £323, 17s. 4d. for township salaries and expenses, £19, 9s. 8d. to meet asylum tax imposed by County Council—£70 for school purposes. £45, 10s. to be levied to pay County debenture tax. £160 levied to meet an equivalent granted by County Council for "improvement of boundary lines adjoining Emily and other roads, cutting down hills and repairing bridges."

(63) Amount to be paid each person licensed to keep a saloon—£10 per year to treasurer —each person keeping saloon to be allowed to sell wines and spirituous liquors by wholesale or retail. No profane swearing, card playing or gambling of any kind shall be allowed—shall close same at hour of 10 p.m. Penalty to be forfeiture of license.

1855 (Cottingham still reeve, Grandy Clerk)

(64) Amount to be paid for statute labour and repealing bylaw no. 6 Feb. 1850— All persons assessed for statute labour allowed to commute same by paying 5s. for each day. All commutation money paid to highway overseer in area who is em-powered to spend same on roads of area, from May 10 to July 24 each year. Those neglecting or refusing to do statute labour or commute to be fined 5s. a day collected by Collector and paid over to treasurer. Highway overseers to make out list of all liable to statute labour and of labour done and performed by each, of comm. money collected and expenditures of same—on statutory oath, and delivered to Council clerk on or before Sept. 1 each year—after which Clerk to place delinquents on Collector's roll for amounts owing. Overseers neglecting or refusing duties as above to be fined 5s. to £1 collected by J.P. and to Treasurer.

(65) To grant licenses to Robert Henderson, Richard Owens and Benj. Madigan to keep public houses and sell wine and spirituous liquor—Henderson to pay £3, 5s.; Richard Owens at King's Wharf to pay same amount; Benj. Madigan to pay same amount. Last two to be exempted from regulation about number of bedrooms and stabling for horses.

(66) Appt. of twp. officers: 53 highway overseers, 21 fence-viewers, 9 pound-keepers. Robert Grandy reappointed clerk, salary £20 per annum; Thos. Matchett reappt. Treasurer £12, 10s. James English, assessor, appointed, salary £20; Arthur McQuade, collector, salary £20. Thomas Crawford and Alex. Beaton, auditors, salary of each 10s. per annum.

(67) Raising sums for county, twp. and other purposes include erection of town hall and courthouse—£173 levied (for county?), also £155 for asylum, paying municipal officers and other municipal expenses; also £100 for school purposes; and "£250 to assist in erection of a town hall and courthouse in Metcalfe village in said Munici-pality of Emily"—TOTAL taxes levied £678.

(68) To prevent Horses, Cattle and Hogs from running at large—from Dec. 1st to April

SUMMARY OF THE FIRST 90 EMILY BYLAWS, 1850-59
EMILY TOWNSHIP COUNCIL

1st. To be impounded if found so doing and fine of 2s. imposed plus lawful costs and charges of pound-keeper for care—to come into effect Jan. 1, 1856.

1856 Cottingham, Reeve and Grandy, Clerk.

(69) To provide for township officers—highway overseers &c.

(70) Fines or imprisonment for disorderly person(s) or intoxicated who disturb municipal Council meetings, fines 5s. to £5 with costs—anyone refusing to pay fine to be collected from their goods and chattels—if this impossible, to be imprisoned for term not less than 1 day or more than 1 month. No person allowed to address Council at sitting until motion adopted by Council to allow same.

(71) To permit Pathmasters to demand statute labour by ratepayers or their hired men with or without teams and tools.

(72) To raise sum of £620 on all rateable property for following: £219, 3s. for county purposes; £43, 15s. for payment of debenture rate to County; £100 for school purposes; £26, 6s. for asylum tax; £230, 16s. for township purposes.

(73) To establish the travelled road through swamp in 4th concession commonly called Middle Line. Road to be 66 ft. wide.

(74) To repeal bylaw passed Dec. 10, 1850, to define place for holding township meetings. Township mtgs. in future to be held in the *TOWN HALL.*

1857 Cottingham, Reeve and Grandy, Clerk.

(75) Appointment of certain twp. officers for year and continued in office until replaced by Council. Robert Grandy, Clerk; Thos. Matchett, Treasurer; James English, Assessor; Arthur McQuade, Collector. Salaries to remain as last year. Thos. Crawford and Wm. Lehane, auditors; Chas. Hartley, Gabriel Balfour and John Colum, Inspectors of License—salaries £2 each—these now to remit all fees to the Treasurer. Also appointing 21 fence-viewers and 8 pound-keepers for indefinite term (rather than yearly as before).

N.B. This bylaw signed by C. & G. at "Council Chambers, Omemee, Emily twp."
April 14, 1857.
(First time the name "Omemee" used in this minute-book.)

(76) To establish a new line of road around the hills on the 1st, 2nd and 3rd concessions, Middleline, agreeable to the Engineer's Report for the contemplated Gravel Road through this twp. from the boundary line of Cavan to the boundary line of Ops.—crossing Middle Line beyond 2nd con. and following it in places . . . land required 6.28 acres—from Hamilton Best over 2 acres, Wm. Kells less than two, and small bits from James Fee and John Story.—66 feet wide.

(77) To authorize Reeve to sign a quit claim deed of piece of land now occupied for a school site, number 4 at Downeyville—to Bartholemew Downey—part of n. half lot 6 in 9th conc. in lieu of another piece of ground purchased from B. Downey of said lot, for a new school site. (School to be built on the new site).

(78) To provide for 1857 current expenses—to raise £625 on all rateable property: for general township rate—Treasurer's salary £12, 10s., Clerk's salary £20; Assessor's salary £20; Collector's salary £20; £20 to remunerate councillors for attendance; £2 for auditor's salaries; £6, 10s. for insurance on the town hall; £107 for school rate; £30 for asylum rate; £256, 5s. for County rate; £6 for inspector of licenses; £124, 5s. for roads and bridges and sundry township expenditures.

1858 Cottingham, Reeve and Grandy, Clerk.

(79) To define duties of Inspector of Licenses, sureties of £100 himself, and another

APPENDIX XVIII (cont.)

SUMMARY OF THE FIRST 90 EMILY BYLAWS, 1850-59
EMILY TOWNSHIP COUNCIL

person £50; to visit all inns, saloons, wholesale, beer and temperance houses—inspect and report quarterly on their state, if they are conducted in orderly manner &c. His salary to be "40 dollars per annum payable half-yearly," (first time dollars mentioned). (No bylaws passed between Sept. 1857 and March 1858).

(80) For appt. of certain township officers for current year—60 overseers of highways, who are also fence-viewers—11 pound-keepers.

(81) To raise and collect the sum of £1,000 on all rateable property—£288, 10s. for county tax; £107, 10s. for school purposes; £200 for township salaries and expenses; £404 to assist in repairs of roads and bridges in township.

(82) Bylaw to repeal bylaw No. 41.

1859 Cottingham, Reeve and Grandy, Clerk.

(83) To repeal part of bylaw for appointment of township officers for 1857 and continue them in office till replaced by Council. Auditors Thos. Crawford and Wm. Lehane to be continued, at salary 20s. each per annum.

(84) Bylaw to fix amount paid for licenses to keep taverns, saloons, shops, beer houses and "houses of public entertainment" . . . in Omemee and Downeyville to keep tavern $40 incl. imperial and provincial duties; elsewhere tavern licenses $30, inc. charges; beer license $12; temperance house and any other houses of public entertainment $4. Saloon or shop license $40.

(85) Following to be appointed during pleasure of council (not yearly as previously)— Robert Grandy, clerk; Thomas Matchett, treasurer; James English, assessor; Arthur McQuade, collector; and salaries to remain as last year. On same terms bylaw appointed 63 overseers of highways, also appointed fence-viewers. On same terms 9 poundkeepers appointed.

(86) To raise and collect sum of *$3,200* on all rateable property for municipal purposes: $1,008 for county tax; $438 for school tax; $303 for payment of county debenture tax; $480 for payment township officers and expense; $971 for "improving the public highways and bridges and other township contingencies."

(87) To amend bylaw 48 defining rules and regulations of innkeepers Feb. 26, 1853. No innkeeper shall permit barkeeper or any other servant to sell wine or liquors to any intoxicated person, nor to any person under 17 years of age, nor after 7 p.m. Saturday until 8 a.m. Monday—during said period barrooms to be closed except to travellers lodging at or ordinary boarders lodging at the place—only exception "a requisition for medicinal purposes signed by a licensed medical practitioner or by a Justice of the Peace." No innkeeper to allow any person to leave his inn in a state of intoxication but "he shall take care of him until he becomes sober." On every other night (except Saturday and Sunday as above) no person to be allowed to remain drinking, and premises to be closed. Penalties provided for infractions.

(88) To divide township into 5 rural wards: WARD ONE: part of first 3 concessions from lot 1 to 9 inclusive. WARD TWO: from line between lots 9 and 10 on concession 1 north to intersect Pigeon River, then north along river to sideline between lots 16 and 17, then southeast between said lots to front of first conccssion. WARD THREE: from con. 1 between lots 16 and 17 northwest to intersect Pigeon River, then northeast along river to east boundary of Emily at Ennismore, then east to front of first concession. WARD FOUR: from front of 4th concession between lots 9 and 10 along front of concession to Ops boundary then northwest along boundary to front of 10th concession, then northeast along concession line to Pigeon River and southwest along river until it intersects sideline between lots 9 and 19, then south to place of beginning. WARD FIVE: on west boundary in front of lot 1, concession 10, then north-

APPENDIX XVIII (cont.)

SUMMARY OF THE FIRST 90 EMILY BYLAWS, 1850-59
EMILY TOWNSHIP COUNCIL

west along boundary to boundary of Verulam, then northeast along boundary to Pigeon River, then southwest along river until it intersects 4th con. line, then northwest along con. line to place of beginning.

(89) Places for holding elections and to appoint returning officers, in each ward.
WARD 1: at Old School House near David Balfour's—Ret. Officer Robert Grandy.
WARD 2: at School House No. 8—Ret. Officer Arthur McQuade.
WARD 3: at School House No. 13—Ret. Officer David Storey.
WARD 4: School House No. 5—Ret. Officer William Curry.
WARD 5: at House of Michael Walsh—Ret. Officer Michael Walsh.

(90) To divide S.S. No. 6 into two separate sections—north part to be known as S.S. 15 and composed of all part of 13th and 14th concessions and also north half of 12th concession from Emily Lake Marsh easterly to Pigeon River Marsh, and that schoolhouse be erected for purpose on rear of lot No. 19 in 13th concession.

APPENDIX XIX

EMILY FARM STATiSTICS FROM CANADIAN CENSUS 1851 TO 1881

	1851	1861	1871	1881
WHEAT: acres	3,713	7,899	7,398	11,173
WHEAT: bushels	56,045	133,460	72,294	95,122*
BARLEY: bushels	884	3,235	27,113	64,839
RYE: bushels	730	160	475	2,698
OATS: bushels	47,753	107,698	78,942	165,166
PEAS: bushels	5,042	29,874	21,017	26,396
BUCKWHEAT: bushels	105	138	158	472
INDIAN CORN: bushels	398	156	568	2,270
POTATOES: acres	395	642	685	484
POTATOES: bushels	17,147	73,785	72,620	60,860
TURNIPS: bushels	4,365	27,340	38,444	28,826
OTHER ROOTS: bushels	— —	1,450	5,350	17,474
CLOVERSEED: bushels (timothy &c)	47	57	505	36
BEANS: bushels	27	144	257	— —
CARROTS: bushels	234	5,208	— —	— —
HOPS: pounds	286	406	— —	— —
HAY: tons	1,219	1,920	3,991	3,136
FLAX & HEMP: pounds	40	156	— —	— —
WOOL: pounds	10,341	12,223	— —	— —
MAPLE SUGAR: pounds	16,806	26,940	— —	— —
CIDER: gallons	700	502	— —	— —
FLANNEL: yards	5,371	6,615	— —	— —
BUTTER: pounds	43,420	89,850	— —	— —
CHEESE: pounds	919	1,442	— —	— —
BEEF: (barrels of 200 lbs.)	92	296	— —	— —
PORK: (barrels of 200 lbs.)	603	1,515	— —	— —

(*—in 1861, ¼ of wheat was winter wheat, and ¾ spring wheat; in 1871, ⅔ winter and ⅓ spring; in 1881 the crop was all spring wheat except 699 bushels).

APPENDIX XX

SOME RECORDS OF EMILY FRAME, STONE AND BRICK HOUSES IN EMILY
TO 1861 (prepared by Simon Connell for the Historical Committee)

FRAME 1851 census — 35 1861 census — 92

First recorded—John Mitchell, in 1839, a 1½ storey frame house on north half lot 15, con. 1.

1847—W. Brady, 1 storey, on lot 19, con. 2.

Others built by 1851, though definite dates unknown:

Rev. James Ewing—2 storey, lot 12, con. 1.

Harry Best—2 storey, north half lot 13, con. 1.

William Best—2 storey, south half lot 13, con. 1.

Margaret Finley—1 storey, south half lot 15, con. 1.

Francis Hudson—1½ storey, lot 13, con. 2.

Isabella McColl—1 storey, lot 16, con. 2.

John McCarroll—1 storey, lot 18, con. 3.

L. Galbraith—3 storey, lot 8, con. 3 (as he was a merchant, probably a hotel or store).

E. Hannah—1 storey, north half lot 7, con. 4.

James Reid—1 storey, lot 21, con. 5.

Tobias Switzer—1 storey, lot 18, con. 5.

John Hayes—size unknown, lot 6, con. 7.

STONE 1851 census — 8 1861 census — 11

First recorded in 1842—James Evens—a 1 storey stone house on south half lot 9, con. 2.

1846—Henry Moore—1 storey, north half lot 22, con. 1.

Francis Best—2 storey, south half lot 23, con. 2.

1850—S. Magee—1 storey, south half lot 10, con. 2.

Others built by 1851, though definite dates unknown:

W. Workman—2 storey, lot 17, con. 1.

Hugh Jackson—1 storey, south half lot 18, con. 2 (Mr. Jackson, born in 1763, was at age 88 in 1851 probably the oldest white settler in Emily township).

Thomas Trotter—1 storey, north half lot 12, con. 4.

Albert Groves—2 storey, lot 20, con. 7.

Stone houses built 1852-61, known:

S. F. Best—size unknown, south half lot 12, con. 1 (built 1858).

George Harkness—size unknown, lot 17, con. 2 (date unknown).

Joseph Lowes—2 storey, lot 20, con. 7 (date unknown) (he and Groves apparently each had half this lot).

BRICK 1851 census — 0 1861 census — 4

(1) The definite date 1856 can be placed on Harry Best's 2 storey brick house on north half lot 13, con. 1; he already had a frame house on this lot.

(2) James Storey by 1861 had a 2 storey brick house on south half lot 20, con. 3.

(3) William Fowler by 1861 had a 1 storey brick house on south half lot 23, con. 3.

(4) John Scully by 1861 had a brick house, size unknown, on south half lot 2, con. 7; this was the first brick house by a Robinson settler, and was made from a pottery clay deposit on the farm; the hand-made bricks were rather larger than modern bricks. The Scully family made their own bricks and in the next 20 years built other brick houses in the area.

APPENDIX XXI

EMILY TOWNSHIP COUNCIL
(Reeve each year in Capitals) (surnames only used in years after first year)

1850 WILLIAM COTTINGHAM: William Best, Thomas Fee, Christopher Knowlson, Michael Lehane
1851 COTTINGHAM; Best, Fee, Knowlson, Lehane
1852 COTTINGHAM; Best, Fee, Knowlson, James Laidley
1853 COTTINGHAM; Best, Fee, Knowlson, Edward Hanna
1854 COTTINGHAM; Fee, Knowlson, Robert Ford, Isaac English
1855 COTTINGHAM; Fee, Ford, English, Edward Blackwell
1856 COTTINGHAM; Wm. Best, Thos. Trotter, Chris Knowlson, Michael Lehane
1857 COTTINGHAM; Trotter, Knowlson, Blackwell, Robert Ford
1858 COTTINGHAM; Ford, Trotter, John Bailey, Thomas Stephenson
1859 COTTINGHAM; Knowlson, Bailey, Stephenson, Wm. Best
1860 COTTINGHAM; Best, Lehane, Bailey, Stephenson
1861 COTTINGHAM; Best, Bailey, Stephenson, James Kelly
1862 COTTINGHAM; Kelly, Bailey, Stephenson, Arthur McQuade
1863 COTTINGHAM; McQuade, Lehane, Bailey, Stephenson
1864 COTTINGHAM; McQuade, Bailey, Stephenson, Thomas Brenan
1865 COTTINGHAM; McQuade, Brenan, Bailey, Stephenson
1866 COTTINGHAM; McQuade, Brenan, Bailey, Stephenson
1867 JOHN BAILEY; McQuade, Ford, Stephenson, Wm. Best
1868 COTTINGHAM; McQuade, Stephenson, Thomas Evans, Frances Adams
1869 COTTINGHAM; McQuade, Evans, Stephenson, David Storey
1870 COTTINGHAM; McQuade, Storey, Evans, Stephenson
1871 COTTINGHAM; McQuade, Storey, F. Adams, Stephenson
1872 COTTINGHAM; McQuade, Adams, Stephenson, James Kelly
1873 THOMAS STEPHENSON; McQuade, Kelly, Adams, John Mitchell
1874 ARTHUR McQUADE; John Bailey, Michael Lehane, Dennis Scully, John Mitchell
1875 THOS. STEPHENSON; Robert Ford, Wm. Adams, William Mills, William Mitchell
1876 STEPHENSON; Bailey, Adams, Dennis Scully, John Mitchell
1877 STEPHENSON; Bailey, Adams, John Mitchell, Scully
1878 STEPHENSON; Bailey, Adams, Wm. Miller, Scully
1879 STEPHENSON; Bailey, Adams, Scully, Miller
1880 STEPHENSON; Adams, Miller, John Mitchell, William Graham
1881 JOHN BAILEY; Miller, J. Mitchell, Scully, Julius Lowes
1882 BAILEY; Miller, Lowes, Scully, Thomas H. McQuade
1883 BAILEY; Scully, Stephenson, McQuade, Wm. Graham
1884 BAILEY; Miller, Graham, Scully, Garrell Guiry
1885 THOMAS H. McQUADE; re-elected each year to 1891   )
1892 WILLIAM C. SWITZER; re-elected each year to 1896   ) (Record Book lost and
1897 J. R. BOATE   ) names of Councillors
1898 WILLIAM ADAMS; re-elected each year to 1901   ) unavailable)
1902 J. R. BOATE   )
1903 BOATE; James Courtney, William Lowes, William Herlihey, Isaac Fee
1904 BOATE; Courtney, Lowes, Herlihey, Fee
1905 BOATE; Courtney, Herlihey, Fee, Wm. Cottingham
1906 BOATE; Cottingham, Courtney, Herlihey, Fee
1907 WILLIAM LOWES; Cottingham, Herlihey, Fee, Robert Wilson
1908 BOATE; Cottingham, Herlihey, Courtney, Wilson
1909 BOATE; Cottingham, Herlihey, Courtney, Wilson
1910 CHARLES CORNEIL; Cottingham, Herlihey, Wilson, I. Fee
1911 CORNEIL; Fee, Wilson, Herlihey, Samuel Carew

APPENDIX XXI (cont.)

EMILY TOWNSHIP COUNCIL
(Reeve each year in Capitals) (surnames only used in years after first year)

1912 ISAAC FEE; Herlihey, Wilson, Carew, Martin Carroll
1913 FEE; Carew, Carroll, Wilson, Herlihey
1914 FEE; Carew, Carroll, Wilson, William J. Patrick
1915 FEE; Carew, Carroll, Wilson, Patrick
1916 ROBERT W. WILSON; Carew, Carroll, Wm. Lowes, Patrick Meehan
1917 WILSON; Carew, Carroll, Lowes, Wm. Herlihey
1918 WILSON; Carew, Carroll, Lowes, Herlihey
1919 WILSON; Carew, Carroll, Lowes, Herlihey
1920 WILSON; Carew, Carroll, Herlihey, Jeffers Ashmore
1921 SAMUEL CAREW; Ashmore, Carroll, Thomas Rice, Thomas McConnell
1922 FEE; Ashmore, Carroll, McConnell, Rice
1923 FEE; Ashmore, Carroll, Rice, McConnell
1924 FEE; Ashmore, Carroll, McConnell, Rice
1925 FEE; Ashmore, Carroll, Rice, George Griffin
1926 MARTIN CARROLL; Ashmore, Rice, Griffin, David W. Wilson
1927 CARROLL; Ashmore, Griffin, Rice, Wilson
1928 CARROLL; Ashmore, Herbert Jackson, D. J. Guiry, Parmenio Lowes
1929 JEFFERS ASHMORE; Lowes, Jackson, Guiry, David Wilson
1930 ASHMORE; Lowes, Guiry, Wilson, Harry Endicott
1931 HARRY ENDICOTT; Jackson, Rice, Guiry, Wm. J. Patrick
1932 ENDICOTT; Guiry, Jackson, Rice, Patrick
1933 ENDICOTT; Jackson, Patrick, P. A. Lowes, Paul J. McGuire
1934 ENDICOTT; Lowes, McGuire, Jackson, Patrick
1935 D. J. GUIRY; Jackson, McGuire, Lowes, Patrick
1936 GUIRY; Patrick, McGuire, Wilson, F. Wilbert Fee
1937 GUIRY; Patrick, McGuire, Fee, Wilson
1938 GUIRY; Patrick, McGuire, Fee, Wilson
1939 WM. JAMES PATRICK; Fee, McGuire, Wilson, Harold Dick
1940 PATRICK; McGuire, Dick, Wilson, Thomas Morrissey
1941 PATRICK; McGuire, Morrissey, Wilson, Vincent S. Fee
1942 PATRICK; Fee, McGuire, Morrissey, Wilson
1943 PAUL McGUIRE; Fee, Morrissey, George Magee, J. Milton Thurston
1944 McGUIRE; Fee, Magee, Morrissey, Thurston
1945 McGUIRE; Fee, Magee, Morrissey, Thurston
1946 McGUIRE; Fee, Magee, Morrissey, Thurston
1947 McGUIRE; Fee, Magee, Morrissey, Thurston
1948 McGUIRE; Fee, Magee, Morrissey, Thurston
1949 VINCENT FEE; Magee, Pete Perdue, Elmer Mahood, Elwood Faulkner
1950 FEE; Perdue, Magee, Mahood, Faulkner
1951 FEE; Perdue, Magee, Mahood, Faulkner
1952 FEE; Perdue, Magee, Mahood, Faulkner
1953 FEE; Mahood, Faulkner, Edward Lowes, Lloyd Ashmore
1954 PETE PERDUE; Lowes, Ashmore, Nelson McConnell, Victor Callahan
1955 PERDUE; Ashmore, Lowes, McConnell, Callahan
1956 PERDUE; McConnell, Lowes, Ashmore, Callahan
1957 PERDUE; McConnell, Ashmore, Elmer Mahood, Alvin Franks
1958 LLOYD ASHMORE; Franks, Lowes, Mahood, Faulkner
1959 ASHMORE; Franks, Lowes, Faulkner, Mahood
1960 ASHMORE; Lowes, Mahood, Faulkner, Albert O'Neill
1961 ASHMORE; O'Neill, Franks, Lowes, Mahood

APPENDIX XXI (cont.)

EMILY TOWNSHIP COUNCIL
(Reeve each year in Capitals) (surnames only used in years after first year)

1962 ASHMORE; Lowes, Franks, Mahood, Nelson McConnell
1963 ASHMORE; McConnell, Lowes, Franks, Albert O'Neill
1964 ALVIN FRANKS; McConnell, Lowes, O'Neill, Stan Smith
1965 FRANKS; Lowes, O'Neill, McConnell, Smith
1966 FRANKS; McConnell, Smith, Lowes, O'Neill
1967 FRANKS; Smith, L. Ashmore, Harry Jackson, John Hollingshead
1968 STAN SMITH; Ashmore, Jackson, Lowes, Earl Herlihey
1969 SMITH; Ashmore, Lowes, Jackson, Herlihey
1970 SMITH; Ashmore, Lowes, Jackson, Herlihey
1971 SMITH; Ashmore, Jackson, Herlihey, Harold Mitchell
1972 SMITH; Ashmore, Jackson, Herlihey, Mitchell
1973 SMITH; Herlihey, Mitchell, Leonard Jones, John Hollingshead (elected for two year term 1973-74)

EMILY TOWNSHIP CLERKS (1850-1974)	EMILY TOWNSHIP TREASURERS (1850-1974)
Robert Grandy 1850-1898	Thomas Matchett 1850-1877
Richard J. Grandy 1899-1929	William Curry 1878-1924
David Weir 1930-1948	David Weir 1925-1930
T. W. Rehill 1948-1967	Arthur McQuade 1932-1941
Ronald Pogue 1967-present	Thomas Laidley 1942-1967
	Ronald Pogue 1967-present

WARDENS OF VICTORIA COUNTY FROM EMILY

1861 William Cottingham, also in 1865
1890 T. H. McQuade   1896 William Switzer   1920 R. W. Wilson
1939 D. J. Guiry   1953 Vincent S. Fee   1974 Stanley Smith

APPENDIX XXII

SCHOOL INSPECTOR KNIGHT'S REPORTS 1871-91

(a) Inspector Knight's Comparison of Emily Schools 1871 and 1891

	1871	*1891*
Schoolhouses:	5 brick, 1 frame, 7 log	9 brick, 3 frame (plus 1 in Omemee)
Schoolhouses (Condition):	2nd class—4	1st class—3
	3rd class—1	2nd class—7
	4th class—8	3rd class—1
		4th class—1
School sites:	13 less than ½ acre	12 with ½ acre or more
Fences, trees &c.:	4th class—13	1st class—1; 2nd class—11
School Desks:	3rd class—1	1st class—6
	4th class—12	2nd class—5
		3rd class—1

APPENDIX XXII (cont.)

SCHOOL INSPECTOR KNIGHT'S REPORTS 1871-91

(a) Inspector Knight's Comparison of Emily Schools 1871 and 1891 (cont.)

	1871	1891
Blackboards & Maps:	1st class—1	1st class—1
	2nd class—3	2nd class—11
	3rd class—5	
	4th class—4	
Teachers' Certificates:	1st class—1	2nd class—3
	2nd class—3	3rd class—9
	3rd class—8	
	Permits—1	
Average Teachers' Salary:	$210.92 a year	$322.08 a year
Attendance (when school visited):	On register 924	On register 615 (down 33%)
	Present at school 354 (38%)	Present at school 317 (51½%)

(b) Inspector Knight's Annual Report, June 1884

TOWNSHIP OF EMILY

Number Three — M'Mullin's

Good brick school house, fairly furnished. Attendance generally good. Teaching fair.

Number Four — Downeyville

Good brick school house. Has been badly used, showing carelessness on the part of teachers and trustees or very rough behaviour of pupils. Owing to the frequent change of teachers and want of care in their selection the school has never been a high rank. The section is large, and the attendance generally good.

Number Five — Orange Line

Good frame school house. Supply of blackboard insufficient. Attendance small, teaching fair and discipline good.

Number Six — Guiry's

Brick school house of ugly design. Seats uncomfortable. Teacher's desk horrid. Attendance small. Teaching as good as can be expected under the circumstances.

Number Seven — Frankhill

Frame school house. Rather too small for the number of pupils in the section. Supply of blackboard sufficient and of fair quality. Teaching fair.

Number Eight—Trotter's

Brick school house of inferior design; placed close to the road and parallel to it. Trustees usually engage a new teacher every year. For 1884 they have made an exception.

APPENDIX XXII (cont.)

SCHOOL INSPECTOR KNIGHT'S REPORTS 1871-91

(b) Inspector Knight's Annual Report, June 1884 (cont.)

Number Nine — Best's

Brick school house of inferior design; placed close to the road and parallel to it. The site was probably selected before play-grounds were invented, as it would be very difficult to adapt the ground for that purpose. The attendance varies very much, and generally in direct ratio to the quality of the teaching.

Number Ten — M'gee's

Good brick school house, well equipped. The teaching and discipline have been uniformly good for some years.

Number Eleven — Lang's

Brick school house, fairly constructed. Desks of inferior pattern. Attendance generally good. Teaching and discipline have been good of late.

Number Twelve—Scully's

Brick school house, out of repair. Site should be enlarged, and a new school house built on higher land adjoining. Good work can hardly be expected under present circumstances.

Number Thirteen — Switzer's

Good brick school house. Desks fair, but not of the best design. Playground inferior. The attendance is much less than it used to be. Teaching fair and discipline good.

Number Fifteen — Crimmon's

Frame school house, poorly built. Difficult to make comfortable in winter. Desks inferior. Attendance, discipline and teaching fair.

APPENDIX XXII (cont.)

SCHOOL INSPECTOR KNIGHT'S REPORTS 1871-91

(c) Teachers and Pupils in Emily, East Victoria, 1888

Number of Section	Teacher's Name	Certificate	Salary	Has Taught Total Yrs.	Mos.	Here Yrs.	Mos.	Teacher Re-engaged	Changed	Pupils on Roll	Present 1st Visit	2nd Visit	Average 1st Half	2nd Half
EMILY 3	Gertley, Eliza	II	$350	8		4			1	79	23	15	31	25
EMILY 4	Matthews, Henry	III	450	9		5			1	86	54	49	45	44
EMILY 5	Marr, May	III	250	3		1			1	48	14	19	16	14
EMILY 6	Maloney, Paul J.	II	390	4		1		1		80	26	35	31	37
EMILY 7	Moreland, May	III	275	2		1		1		56	19	26	25	27
EMILY 8	Cullon, Lemmie	III	275	3		2			1	48	20	5	18	15
EMILY 9	Widdis, Jeffrey	III	300	2		1		1		43	21	19	17	25
EMILY 10	Blackwell, William S.	III	375	2		2		1		60	21	32	25	33
EMILY 11	Robinson, Francis W.	III	265	1		1		1	1	35	18	5	13	7
EMILY 12	O'Boyle, Francis W.	I	450	19		0	4	1		66	23	37	25	27
EMILY 13	Heaslip, Charlotte	III	250	3		1		1		41	19	17	19	19
EMILY 15	Sullivan, Johanna	II	300	4		0	5	1		46	26	24	16	21
OMEMEE	Sheppard, Joseph H.	II	525	10		7		1						
OMEMEE	Lough, Hattie	III	235	2		2			1	203	102	128	111	—
OMEMEE	Stephenson, Daisy	III	200	1		1			1					

APPENDIX XXIII

REPORT OF THE ONTARIO AGRICULTURAL COMMISSION 1881

Appendix B (based on county statistics and on questionnaires
sent to hundreds of farmers for reply)

"VICTORIA COUNTY: Sandy and clay loams predominant soils, with increasing rockiness toward northern part; mostly well watered, many beautiful lakes and streams, and fine drainage. Land prices: Emily $60 to $70 an acre, Mariposa $60, Ops $65, and to north $2 down to 20c an acre. Many pine stumps still remaining, even in southern townships. In south 27% of houses are of brick, stone or 1st-class frame, remainder log or inferior frame—outbuildings 28% average or better, the rest inferior. Markets for southern townships are Lindsay, Omemee, Bobcaygeon, Fenelon Falls; most of the thoroughbred cattle raised in Mariposa and Ops. There are 6 cheese factories and 1 creamery in Victoria, several saw, shingle and grist mills, but no other industries.

EMILY TOWNSHIP: The first settlers in 1819, now about 80% settled; an average soil for agricultural purposes, 12% heavy clay, 50% clay loam, 5% sandy loam, 5% sand, 20% gravelly, 8% black loam. No areas are too rocky to cultivate, but 2% is too hilly to cultivate, 20% rolling but cultivable, 3% low, flat, bottomland, 3% swampy, 5% wet springy land. 50% is 1st-class agricultural land, in first 4 concessions mostly; 30% is 2nd-class, from 4th to 13th concessions; 20% 3rd-class, mostly toward north boundary. Farm prices—1st-class $60 to $70; 2nd-class $40 to $50; 3rd-class $20 to $30, per acre. About two-thirds is clear of stumps, and about a quarter of remainder are pine stumps. About 40% of dwellings brick, stone or 1st-class frame, 60% log or inferior frame structure. Fences are average, mostly split cedar; 50% outbuildings 1st-class, 50% inferior. About 80% of farmers use improved farm machinery—reapers, mowers, seed drills, sulky rakes, etc. A very small proportion of farms are underdrained, and with tile used. Salt, plaster, and other artificial fertilizers are used by a small proportion of farmers in Emily. Proportions of acreage: fall wheat—25 bushel an acre; spring wheat 14 bushel an acre; barley—25 bushel; oats 30 bushel; rye—15 bushel; peas—20 bushel; potatoes—100 bushel; turnips—500 bushel; one-tenth of acreage is in hay and 15% in pastureland; orchards are very few. Township is well adapted to graingrowing, especially spring wheat, also for stockraising; the cattle mostly native breeds with few thoroughbreds; horses mainly general purpose; sheep are common breeds. About 5,500 acres still timbered, mostly hardwood and cedar, used for fuel and fencing. Market facilities: Omemee or Lindsay on Midland Railway; only one local industry, a cheese factory at Downeyville. (The only creamery in the county is at Woodville). Acreage in Emily: 59,299 acres; cleared acres 34,425; population in 1880—2,434. Livestock: cattle 856, horses 771, sheep 1,633 and hogs 838."

APPENDIX XXIV

1881 ATLAS — VICTORIA COUNTY

EMILY TOWNSHIP SUBSCRIBERS

Adams, Thomas, farmer. Is owner of S.¼ Lot 4, Con. 2, and N.W.¼ Lot 5, Con. 1—together, 150 acres. Was born in the township in 1849. His father was one of the first Justices of the Peace. P.O. address, Omemee.

Adams, James, farmer. Lives on Lot 1, Con. 1, and owns 130 acres. He has lived in the township since birth (1853). P.O. address, Omemee.

APPENDIX XXIV (cont.)

1881 ATLAS — VICTORIA COUNTY

EMILY TOWNSHIP SUBSCRIBERS

Adams, William, farmer and Deputy Reeve. Is owner of W.½ Lot 5, Con. 6, and S.E.¼ Lot 4, Con. 7, 150 acres. Was born in Ireland in 1835. Came to the county in 1841. P.O. address, Omemee.

Allport, J. S., millwright at Collingwood. He owns village property in Omemee. Born in Birmingham, England, in 1838. Settled in this County in 1880.

Boates, William, farmer. He has 300 acres of land, being whole of Lot 22, Con. 5, and S.½ Lot 22, Con. 6. Born in Ireland, 1809. Settled here in 1825. P.O. address, Frank Hill.

Best, S. H., farmer, on Lot 11 and 12, Con. 1. He owns 165 acres. Has lived in the township since 1841. Is a Canadian. P.O. address, Mount Pleasant (Cavan).

Best, Valentine, farmer. Is owner of 187½ acres in Lot 14, Con. 1, and Lots 14 and 15, Con. 2. Was born in the township, 1840. P.O. address, Mount Pleasant.

Burnett, Alexander, farmer, on Lot 4, Con. 14, of which he owns 100 acres. Was a Township Councillor and Collector. Born in Ireland in 1834, and settled here in 1861. P.O. address, Dunsford.

Collins, John, teacher, S.S. No. 7. He has lived in the county since 1838, and was born same year. P.O. address, Frank Hill.

Deyell, Samuel, farmer. He owns 200 acres, situated in Lot 1, Con. 3. Was born in Cavan Township, Ontario, 1819, and settled here in 1857.

Doyle, B. J., teacher in Village of Downeyville. He was born in Brock Township, Ontario, in 1857. Settled here in 1880.

Elliot, George, farmer, on Lot 18, Con. 1, of which he owns 100 acres. He settled here in 1865. Born in Durham County, 1842. P.O. address, Mount Pleasant.

Finlay, Alexander, farmer. He owns S.½ Lots 15 and 16, Con. 1, 200 acres. He was born here in 1826. His father was the first settler in the township. P.O. address, Mount Pleasant (Cavan).

Fowler, David, farmer. He has 300 acres, situated in Lot 20, Con. 3, and Lots 19, 21, 22 and 23, Con. 4. He settled in the county in 1850. Born in Scotland, 1816. P.O. address, Fowler's Corners.

Hickson, William, teacher at Mount Pleasant, Cavan Township, Durham County. Was born in Canada in 1850.

Howden, Robert, farmer. He owns 113 acres, in Lot 23, Con. 3. Born in Cavan Township, Ontario, in 1852. Settled here in 1877. P.O. address, Fowler's Corners.

Hill, W. H. insurance agent at Omemee. Is Village Councillor. Was born in York County, Ontario, 1840. Settled in Victoria County, 1850.

Harrington, M. F., teacher, S.S. No. 3. Has lived in the township since 1859. Was born same year. P.O. address, Downeyville.

Heenan, Patrick, carpenter at Downeyville. Came to the county in 1875. Born in Ireland in 1845.

Jackson, W. J., farmer. He owns 100 acres in Lots 19, 20 and 21, Con. 1. Has lived in the township since his birth (1855). P.O. address, Fowler's Corners.

John, Thomas, farmer. Is owner of N.W.¼ of Lot 6, Con. 10, and W.½ Lot 6, Con. 11— 150 acres. Born in Pembrokeshire, Wales, in 1818. Settled here in 1861. P.O. address,, Downeyville.

Lang, Alexander, farmer. He owns 100 acres of Lot 5, Con. 1, and 25 acres of Lot 5, Con. 1. Came to Victoria County in 1839. Born in Ireland in 1819. P.O. address, Omemee.

Lowe, Joseph H., farmer, on Lot 8, Con. 1, owning 100 acres. Born in Durham County, 1843. Settled here in 1873. P.O. address Mount Pleasant.

APPENDIX XXIV (cont.)

1881 ATLAS — VICTORIA COUNTY

EMILY TOWNSHIP SUBSCRIBERS

Miller, Charles, farmer, on N.$\frac{1}{4}$ Lot 18, Con. 4. Owns 100 acres. Is Township Auditor. Born in New York State in 1834. Came to Victoria County in 1856. P.O. address, Omemee.

Morrison, William, waggon-maker at Omemee. Came here in 1879. Born in Canada 1848.

Mason, Thomas A., proprietor of Windsor Hotel at Omemee. Born in Devonshire, England, in 1826. Came here in 1880.

McLeary, D., blacksmith at Downeyville. Was born in the township in 1852.

Magee, Thomas, farmer. Is owner of 300 acres, situated in Lot 19, Con. 1, and Lots 18 and 21, Con. 2. He was born in the United States in 1824. Settled here in 1830. P.O. address, Omemee.

Meagher, P. J., teacher, S.S. No. 12. Born in the county. P.O. address, Downeyville.

McFeeters, John, farmer. Lives on Lot 17, Con. 14, and owns 400 acres. Born at Kingston, Ontario, 1830. Came to Victoria County in 1836. P.O. address, Bobcaygeon.

Ruth, George, farmer, and owns 150 acres of Lot 20, Con. 5. Was born in Ireland in 1823, and came to this country in 1833. P.O. address, Fowler's Corners.

Smyth, J. C., teacher, S.S. No. 10. Came here in 1877. Born in Durham County in 1854. P.O. address, Omemee.

Switzer, Gabriel, farmer and stock-breeder. He owns the S.$\frac{1}{4}$ Lot 18, Con. 5, 100 acres. Was born in Canada in 1843. Settled here in 1870. P.O. address, Omemee.

Storey, David, farmer, on Lot 20, Con. 3, of which he owns 100 acres. Has also 100 acres in Ops Township and 100 in Smith Township. He came to Victoria County in 1831. Born at Bowmanville, 1828. P.O. address, Fowler's Corners.

Sherin, J. W., farmer, on N.$\frac{1}{4}$ Lot 17, Con. 3, owning 100 acres. Born in the township in 1855. P.O. address, Omemee.

Thompson, J. W., shoemaker, Omemee. Came here in 1878. Born in Canada in 1840.

Weir, Robert, farmer, on Lots 18 and 19, Con. 8. He owns 200 acres, and settled here in 1862. Born at Otonabee, 1836. P.O. address, Frank Hill.

APPENDIX XXV

LISTS OF PATHMASTERS (and of POUNDKEEPERS)
as in Bylaw No. 299 of March 19, 1900

PATHMASTERS (who were also fence-viewers) with no. of road division for which responsible:

Louis Windrem 1	Robert J. Hayes 2	William J. Finley 3
James Ferguson 4	John Bannan 5	Charles Fee 6
Walter J. Boyd 7	William J. Jackson 8	David Toole 9
Francis Fee 10	David Mitchell 11	Robert Bailey 12
William Bannan 13	Isaiah Thornton 14	Thomas Mitchell 15
William McCarrell 16	John Sanderson 17	George McQuade 18
William Deyell 19	Robert Adams 20	Henry McQuade 21
Robert McElwain 22	John Switzer 23	John O'Donnell 24
Joseph Davis 25 & 26	Adam Spence 27	John Gillis 28
Isaac Moore 29 & 30	John Garvey 31	Michael Crowley 32

APPENDIX XXV (cont.)

LISTS OF PATHMASTERS (and of POUNDKEEPERS)
as in Bylaw No. 299 of March 19, 1900

PATHMASTERS (who were also fence-viewers) with no. of road division for which responsible:

Francis Kearns 33	Daniel Carmody 34 & 35	Thomas Crowley 36
Michael Fitzpatrick 37	Leonard McAuliffe 38	George Connell 39
Eugene Shine 40	Edmund Herlihey 41	Thomas Lucas 42
Joseph Houlihan 43	John Winn 44	Thomas Harrington 45
Charles Meehan 46	Timothy Morrissey 47	Robert Perdue 48
William Padget 49	James Courtney 50	Martin Dorgan 51
Patrick Herlihey 52	George English 53	William Thurston 54
Cornelius Herlihey 55	Isaac Hodge 56	John Graham 57
Richard Padget 58	Charles Millage 59	George S. Brown 60
Matthew Wilson 61	Charles Corneil 62	George Winn 63
John Murray 64	William J. White 65	Richard Connell 66
George B. Fee 67	Thomas Shannin 68	George Henderson 69
George Connors 70	Joseph Lucas 71	Martin Harrington 72
Thomas H. Wilson 73	William Martin 74	William McQuade 75
David Vannatte 76 (or Varmcotte)	Dennis Fitzpatrick 77	James D. O'Brien 78
James Jackson 79	John W. Sherin 80	William Switzer 81
Thomas Twomey 82	Michael O'Donnell 83	Michael Harrington 84
James Blackwell 85 & 86	Patrick Flaherty 87	John Travis 88
Joseph Meehan 89	Alexander Mahood 90	Francis Scully 91
Arthur Franks 92	George Franks 93	

POUNDKEEPERS:

1. George B. Fee	2. James H. Best	3. Henry Jackson
4. Thomas Bell	5. Francis Kearns	6. John Sanderson
7. Thomas W. Blackwell	8. Jacob McBrien	9. Daniel Winn
10. Eugene Shine	11. Michael Flynn	12. Robert Perdue
13. James C. Leary	14. James F. Kennedy	

APPENDIX XXVI

"THE SCHOOL FAIR — (1910-14)"

by Mrs. Mary Harrington

As September came each year, the dread of returning to school was lessened by the delight the children had in preparing for the annual School Fair.

School Fairs were organized and conducted by the Department of Agriculture with four school sections combined for each fair held in the County. During the winter months a representative of the Department of Agriculture visited each school to arouse the interest of the students in agriculture and home economics. He distributed circulars to the pupils which gave all the information about what seeds, eggs, etc. could be obtained from the Department. Each pupil was allowed one package of vegetable seed, one of flower seed and enough seed to plant a small plot of grain, the size of which was stipulated in the circular (approximately 16 x 20 feet). The seeds were supplied by

APPENDIX XXVI (cont.)

"THE SCHOOL FAIR — (1910-14)"

the Department of Agriculture free of charge. They were delivered to the school in the spring and distributed to the children, giving each the variety he had chosen.

During the summer the plots were inspected by a representative of the Department and points given for correct size, neatness in planting, if the plots were free of weeds and stones, quality of grain, etc. The vegetable and flower gardens were also inspected and points given for neatness, quality, etc. The girls were given the opportunity to display their sewing talents and many aprons and hemstitched handkerchiefs were proudly exhibited.

Weed and seed collections were considered of great importance and any student who was going to show a weed collection looked for choice plants, pressed them between newspapers and put them under a weight for a few weeks until they were thoroughly dried. Then each plant was carefully mounted on a large sheet of white paper, with its common name, botanical name, kind of flower, leaf and root neatly written under each plant.

The seeds were collected in little bottles which were supplied by the Department of Agriculture and labeled with the name of each variety of weed.

Insect collections were also important and all sorts of butterflies, moths, flies, beetles and bugs were captured and put in jars or bottles until they died. A large box was made with a velvet bottom on which the insects were carefully mounted with long black pins. The largest butterfly was usually placed in the centre and the smaller insects artistically arranged around. Under each insect was a label giving its common name and name of the species whether "diurnal lepidopterous" or to the order of "Coleoptera." The box usually had a glass top, and an attractive box added a lot to the appearance of the collection.

Leaf collections were always popular. Leaves were pressed in the same way as weeds and were taken from all varieties of trees, weeds, vegetables and flowers. The collection which was the most difficult to assemble and arrange was the "Wood Collection." The wood was cut in small uniform pieces about 4 inches long and 1 inch wide. Each piece was sandpapered and polished to bring out the grain. A large board with rows of tiny hooks was used to display wood collections. Each piece had little screws placed in the end and hung on the hooks. A large collection, neatly arranged and labeled, was quite attractive when completed, and it took a great deal of effort to get each piece the required size and finish.

A story of the School Fair would not be complete without mentioning the Poultry Division. The Department of Agriculture gave out hen eggs of different kinds in the spring to pupils interested in going in to the poultry business. A "setting" of eggs (12 or 14) was given free of charge and the eggs were set under a hen. This hen and her chickens were carefully looked after during the summer and the best birds from each flock were shown at the School Fair in September. The following year eggs were also shown. The most popular breed was the Plymouth Rock—a large grey bird. There were also other varieties—the White Rock, Leghorn, Buff Orpington, New Hampshire and Rhode Island Red. That first setting of eggs which was obtained from the school was the start of many large flocks of highest quality.

Programs were sent to each school giving the topics for the Public Speaking Contest and a timetable for drills, entertainment of different kinds such as songs, recitations, group singing, dances, etc., and also a program of sports.

For a few weeks before the fair, the pupils had great pleasure in practicing for the different races—such as sack race, three-legged race, egg-and-spoon race, wheel-barrow race, different kinds of relay races, and only the best from each school participated when the great day arrived. There was always a tug-of-war in which all students took part.

APPENDIX XXVI (cont.)

"THE SCHOOL FAIR — (1910-14)"

This was the time when the "School Yell" was really heard as the students let the world know to which one of the School Sections they belonged.

The fair was held in the school grounds or some suitable field which was located nearest the centre of the area. A large tent was placed on the grounds with a "Union Jack" flying on top. Long tables were placed within, along the sides and down the centre on which the various arrangements of flowers, fruit, vegetables and grain—(in sheaves as well as grain)—also the sewing and weed, seed and insect, leaf and wood collections were attractively displayed. When all the exhibits were properly placed, the tent was closed in order to allow the judges time to choose the winning entries. At this time the entertainment program was carried out and the Public Speaking Contest was held. In this contest two young orators from each school were allowed to participate and judges were selected who were not supposed to know any of the contestants. The program of sports was held next and provided lively entertainment for all the people who attended.

When the judging was completed, the pupils were allowed to re-enter the tent to see whose entries received the red, blue and white ribbons. Generous cash prizes were given and at the final ceremonies the lucky winners received a "fair-sized" pay envelope from the representative of the Department of Agriculture who was in charge of the fair.

The representative of the Fairs for a few years was a Mr. D. MacKenzie and he was followed in 1913 by Mr. A. A. Knight. Mr. Knight will be remembered as well for the manner in which he displayed his patriotism by standing erect and singing in a voice loud and clear the national anthem "God Save The King."

The School Fairs were of benefit to the children in both the educational and social areas. Shortly after World War I started in 1914, the fairs were discontinued for lack of Government funds.

APPENDIX XXVII

A CLARIFICATION OF FACTS BY EMILY TOWNSHIP AREA SCHOOL BOARD
(Letter in *Lindsay Post* — June 5, 1968)

Dear Sir:-

It is with great regret that so many erroneous and ill-informed statements have been made regarding the School Board and Teaching Staff at Lady Eaton School. A combination of misinterpretations by press reporters (not Lindsay Post) and a failure on the part of a very few individuals to understand and interpret some very simple data have helped to cause a deterioration in the educational atmosphere of this township. Irresponsible statements by two municipal servants have been nothing but a disservice to our community.

In fairness to the principal, the teaching staff and the general public the school board wishes it to be known that the following information is factually correct:

1. There are no reading rooms in the school as has been suggested.

2. The audio-visual room (not rooms) is no more than a small storage room for supplies.

3. There is a serious crowding situation at present and more space is desperately needed whether the enrolment increases or not.

4. An analysis of past and present enrolment increases suggest a sharp and steady increase in the school population that is far in excess of the repeatedly reported and incorrect figure of 12 pupils.

APPENDIX XXVII (cont.)

A CLARIFICATION OF FACTS BY EMILY TOWNSHIP AREA SCHOOL BOARD
(Letter in *Lindsay Post* — June 5, 1968)

5. School plans for an addition are "tardy" rather than "premature".

6. The increase of teachers' salaries was caused by the fact that seven teachers have increased their qualifications since the beginning of 1967 sufficiently to enter a higher category. Secondly a full-time librarian was hired in January 1968. Five teachers have been given extra raises to place them on the proper position in the salary schedule, and fourthly there has been an addition to the teaching staff of three members for September 1968. This will make for 12 teachers in the present classrooms, 2 teachers in the gymnasium and one teacher in the staff room plus a librarian equalling sixteen teaching areas —not twelve as again it was so erroneously stated by a public official. With or without an addition we will be operating as a 16 room school next September. In any case, the actual average increase in teachers' salaries is far below the figure quoted in a newspaper on May 28.

7. The principal is presently relieved of teaching duties each afternoon by a relief teacher. In the mornings he teaches science and health to all grades 7's and 8's on a semi-rotary basis. Next year he has chosen to teach some units of work at all grade levels. The complexity of school organization continues to increase the duties of principals all over this province. For such an onerous task his present salary is $2,000 below that quoted in a paper, is below provincial averages for equally qualified personnel.

8. The statement made by our principal William MacKillican to the Home and School on April 9 was no more than basic information available to any member of the public. At that time the School Board being unable to attend the meeting authorized the principal to state next year's plans to fulfil a request for information made by a group of interested parents. The printed copy (available to anyone) of that report is completely free of implication and merely states an alternative proposal previously suggested, out of necessity, by this Board. Mr. MacKillican was within his jurisdiction and the facts of his statement, made on April 9, are supported by the members of the Emily T.S.A. School Board. At that meeting the following statements were made:

(a) A regular Auxiliary Class of 16 pupils will be established in one of the present classrooms.

(b) A kindergarten-grade one classroom for six and seven year old children with readiness difficulties will be placed in the staff room.

(c) Two classes placed here in the G.P. room will benefit from the open area teaching principle. This will involve such advantages as team teaching, cross grouping—a step toward nongrading.

(d) The plans for a kindergarten program have been dropped.

(e) All indoor Physical Education will be cancelled.

(f) The implementation of Oral French appears to be too difficult to pursue at this time.

(g) The present Remedial Reading Program will be discontinued because there will no longer be a single corner of space where it could be carried on satisfactorily.

The principal was by no means placed on "the carpet" or "reprimanded"—again false statements. As well how can it be logically said that Mr. MacKillican could influence the graduating class of LCVI when he has not yet been in our school for two years? In addition, inspector's reports made to the Board have clearly pointed to the success and improvement of programs in our school. For this we owe our staff appreciation and due consideration.

9. The school secretary's services are used by the principal, the librarian and all teachers.

10. By Provincial Regulation, school boards are required to receive approval for

A CLARIFICATION OF FACTS BY EMILY TOWNSHIP AREA SCHOOL BOARD
(Letter in *Lindsay Post* — June 5, 1968)

building programs from the Department of Education before approaching any municipal organization. After receiving this approval through the proper channels, the board called a joint meeting of the two councils to inform them simultaneously of carefully prepared plans for the addition in question.

11. It is ludicrous to say our school contains unnecessary frills.

12. Our Board Chairman merely stated, in reference to Ops teachers, that "could make no comparison", meaning that he was in no position, and no desire, to make any comparison of the teaching staffs of any schools.

It is, and will remain, the policy of this board to encourage teachers to continue the improvement of their qualifications. We well realize that the costs involved in being away for a summer probably exceed $500. This is paid by the teachers and we are proud to say that 50% of our teachers are qualified beyond category one and that nearly 90% are continuing their own personal education during the summers. Hiring well qualified personnel is a sound investment. For this type of person we must offer a salary schedule that is competitive with other areas of the province. Some parts of our schedule are better than other areas while other sections are not as good.

Emily Township Area School Board

APPENDIX XXVIII

EMILY AND OMEMEE PEOPLE WHO SERVED IN TWO WORLD WARS

(* Those killed or died during wartime)

(Prepared by members of the Emily Historical Committee)

(a) WORLD WAR I
(1914-18)

Charles Banks	Albert Acreman	Mansel Ashmore
Robert Bestor*	William Balfour	Stewart Bannon
George Boulds	Frederick Birchall	John Best
Harry Brown V.C.*	Peter Brady	T. J. Bradley
Fred Bradley	Albert Brooks	Lowery Brooks
Victor Callaghan	William Brockley	
John Carey	Lawrence Carroll	William Carroll
Norman Clarke	Ormond Carroll	Louis Clancy
John Clemett	Noel Clarke	Ted Collins
Albert Clemett	James Clemett	Lloyd Clemett
Percy Crawshaw	Fred Corneil	Ernest Corneil
Hilliard Cunningham	Harry Crecy	Joseph Crowley*
Ambrose Donoghue	Harold Cunningham	S. F. Cullon
Alfred Eggleton	Walter Eggleton	Frederick Evans
Elwood Faulkner	Havelock Fee	Cecil Fletcher
John Flynn	Leo Flynn	Hubert Fox
James Gall	William Gallagher*	M. A. Germain
Charles Gerard	John Gilliece	George Gilliece
William Godfrey	Alphonse Gosselin*	Albert Green*
Kenneth Griffin	John Groves	George Guyaine

APPENDIX XXVIII (cont.)

EMILY AND OMEMEE PEOPLE WHO SERVED IN TWO WORLD WARS

(a) WORLD WAR I

George Haliday*	Harold Harrison	Gordon Harrison
Leah Hayes	Edward Herbert	Walter Harris
William Herlihey	Leo Herlihey	Alphonse Herlihey
Robert Hetherington	James Hopkins*	Cyril Houlihan*
Leo Houlihan	Joseph Houlihan	
Charles Johnson	Victor Johnson	Thomas Jones
James Kennedy	Albert Kenmore*	
Norman Laidley	Stanley Laidley	Fred Lang
Francis Lucas*	Cyril Lehane	Burton Lewis
James Madigan	Leonard Marsh*	E. Marsh
Victor McAuliffe*	John McCrea	Joseph McLaughlin*
Charles McCaffrey	R. M. McMullen	Charles Mellar
Cecil Mills	Walter Mitchell	Fred Mills*
C. V. Mulligan	James Murtha*	
William Neal	Clayton Nurse	William O'Neill
Daniel O'Brien	Francis O'Brien	Eugene O'Brien
George O'Donnell	Cyril O'Neill	Peter Overholt
R. M. Parker	Stanley Parker	Arthur Peck
William Percival	Michael Perdue*	Peter Perdue
John Palmer	George Pollet*	Roy Post*
Joseph Poyser		
Jessie Rix	George Raines	Reuben Reeds
Charles Scully	John Scully	Wilfred Scully
Walter Scully	William Scully	Walter Scholfield
William Shine	Herman Shaw	Frank Smith*
James Stewart	John Sullivan	William Smith
Harry Taylor	W. J. Thorne	Charles Toole
Joseph Trott*	Harold Underwood	George Werry
George White	William Whitehead*	W. Wilkinson
Harry World*	John Wylie	

(b) WORLD WAR II

(1939-45)	William Acreman	Albert Acreman
Denis Acreman	Allan Adams	Lewis Adams
Rae Ashmore	Douglas Armstrong	
Albert Ball	Alden Bailey	Melville Bannon
John Bannon	Joseph Black	Burret Ball
Fred Birchell	Roland Blackburn	Roger Blackwell
Harry Boyd	Arthur Boate*	Jackson Boate
Arthur Brenton	Edwin Brenton*	Kenneth Brenton*
Edgar Brenton	Edwin Brackman	Mons Brooks
Arthur Brockley	Gilbert Brockley	Arthur Burnett
Wilfred Byres		
Alvin Casey	Earl Casey	Fred Casey
Victor Caton	Roy Crawford	Harold Crawford
John Crawford	Vincent Cornwall	Leslie Curtis
Arthur Darling	Gordon Darling	John Deyell
Lewers Deyell	Martin Devine	Francis Dorgan
Paul Downey		
Betty Eggleton	Clifford Elliot	Ernest Eggleton

APPENDIX XXVIII (cont.)

EMILY AND OMEMEE PEOPLE WHO SERVED IN TWO WORLD WARS

(b) WORLD WAR II

James Eggleton	John Eggleton	Harry Ellis
Clinton Endicott	Meryle Endicott	Hubert Elliott
George Fair	Bruce Fairfield	Nelson Faulkner
Gordon Fee*	James Fee	Kenneth Fife
Cecil Finley	Frank Fitch	Ross Foster
Raymond Foster*		
Alphonse Garvey	Charles Gerard	Joseph Gosselin
Harold Gray	David Guiry	Norman Graham
Earl Hanbidge	Ralph Hanbidge*	Arthur Hart
Charles Harrington	Francis Harrington	Eldon Harrison
Jay Hayes	Douglas Hayes	Robert Hayes
John Herlihey	Fergus Houlihan	George Hendry
Neil Henderson	Arthur Hives	James Hoskin
Garnet Howden	Douglas Hughes	Vernon Hunt
Harry Irwin		
Arthur Jamieson	Herbert Jones	James Johnson
Clarke Kennedy		
Harry Lathan	William Laidley	Daniel Leith
John Lee	George Linsdale	Edward Lowes
Albert Lucas	Donovan Lucas	Keith Lucas
Urban Lucas		
Earl Magee	John Magee	Leonard Magee*
Neil Magee	Norman McBain	Earl McCarrell
Russell McCarrell	Clarence McFarlane	Ross McConnell
Elzina McQuade	Larry McQuade	David Metcalfe
Clifford Miles	Raymond Miles	Garnet Mitchell
Helen Moyer	George Moyer	Earl Morrissey
Leo Morrissey	John Murray	Peter Murray*
J. P. McGinnes	James Murtha*	Raymond Murtha
Vernon Nelson	Eldon Northey	
Austin O'Leary	Gerard O'Neill	Lorne O'Neill
Leo O'Neill	Patrick O'Neill	Ralph O'Neill
Harley Overholt		
Sidney Palmer	Ruth Paul	Thomas Parsons
Clare Parkes	Reginald Pattenden	Alfred Perkins
Milburn Perritt	Garnet Pogue	Ronald Pogue
I. H. Pollard		
Hugh Rehill	Ross Rehill	George Roadhouse*
William Riley	Robert Reeds	Arthur Renoult
Ford Rowan	Thomas Rowan	
Lawrence Sandy	Claude Scully	Clement Scully
Parnell Scully	Burton Shaw	Francis Shine
Joseph Shine	Leo Shine	Richard Skuce
Robert Skuce	John Smelt	Edward Spencer
Clifford Strain*	George Stephenson	William Stephenson*
James Stone	Stephen Sullivan	Urban Sullivan
Earl Tracey	Lionel Tracey	Norman Thorne
Lorne Tracey		
Howard Vaughan	Richard Vaughan	Clifford Veals*
Arthur Weir	Fred Weir	Burton Weir

APPENDIX XXVIII (cont.)

EMILY AND OMEMEE PEOPLE WHO SERVED IN TWO WORLD WARS

(b) WORLD WAR II

Russell Weir	Charles Weir	Ernest Wells*
Deane Wellman	Donald Wellman	Stewart Wellman
William Wedlock	Bertram Werry	Harold Welch
Francis Whalen	Ross Widdis	Howard Wilson
Russell Williamson	Neil Windrem	Wilson Windrem

APPENDIX XXIX

FARMS IN SAME FAMILY SINCE CONFEDERATION

(Those in same family since Robinson settlement 1825 marked with *)

(List prepared by Simon Connell and Harry Jackson)

LOT	CON.	1825	OWNER 1867	OWNER 1973
Pt. 9 & 10	1		Robert Hays	Bessie Hays
Pt. 11	1		Charles Fee	Reginald Fee
Pt. 19	1		Thomas Magee	Mildred (Magee) McBain
Pt. 13	2		James Fee	Murray Fee
S½ 18	2		William Jackson	Arthur Jackson (estate)
W½ 20	3		David Storey	Ray Storey
Pt. N½ 22	3	*John McCarroll	David McCarrel	Mansel Burley
Pt. 22	3		John Bailey	Olive Bailey
Pt. 4	5		Joseph Sanderson	William Sanderson
N½ 5	5		Morgan O'Neill	William O'Neill
N½ 7	5		Samuel Wilson	Alma Wilson
N½ 20	5		James Ruth	Edmund Ruth
NE¼ 8	6		Thomas McBrien	Orville McBrien
W½ 4	7		Thomas Garvey	Garvey Estate
N½ 7	7		Michael Callaghan	Victor Callaghan
SE¼ 8	7		Jacob McBrien	Orville & Kenneth McBrien
Pt. 21	7		Julius Lowes	Gerald Lowes
N. pt. 22	7		Thomas Franks	John Franks
N. pt. 3	8		John Milloy	Earl Milloy
S. pt. 3	8		Patrick Milloy	Steven Winn
S½ 10	8		Martin Carroll	Yvonne Carroll
N½ 12	8	*Denis Fitzpatrick	Denis Fitzpatrick	Patrick Fitzpatrick
S½ 22	8		William Franks	Gilbert Franks
N½ 22	8		Patrick Hickey	Elmer Hickey
Pt. 23	8	*Martin Doran	William Doran	John Doran
W½ 3	9		Denis Scully	Velma Scully
N½ 4	9		John Connors	James D. Lucas
NW¼ 5	9		Charles Lucas	James D. Lucas
E½ 6	9	*Bartholomew Downie	Bartholomew Downey	Eugene Downey
N½ 8	9		Charles Lucas	James S. Lucas
N½ 12	9		Owen O'Brien	Edward & Bernice Herlihey
Pt. 22	9		Patrick Hickey	Clair Hickey
N½ 3	10		William O'Neill	Albert O'Neill

APPENDIX XXIX (cont.)

FARMS IN SAME FAMILY SINCE CONFEDERATION

LOT	CON.	1825	OWNER 1867	OWNER 1973
N¼ 4	10	*Edmond Pigott	Edmond Pigott	James Pigott
Pt. 6	10		Charles Lucas	Joseph Lucas
SW¼ 14	10	*Daniel Fitzpatrick	Patrick Fitzpatrick	Patrick Fitzpatrick
E½ 14	10		Edward Morrissey	David Morrissey
S½ 16	10	*Moses Begley	Denis Begley	Annie Begley
S½ 17	10		Timothy Morrissey	John Morrissey
N½ 17	10		Timothy Morrissey	Gerald Morrissey
S½ 23	10		David Travis	David Travis
W½ 5	11	*Bartholemew Pigott	William Pigott	Adriene Pigott
Pt. 7	11	*Thomas Shenick	John Fox	Richard Fox (indirect descent from Thomas S.)
Pt. 8	11		Martin Harrington	William Harrington
N½ 13	11		Michael O'Neill	Parnell O'Neill
N¼ 20	12		Patrick Herlihey	Kevin Perdue
N½ 21	12	*John Sullivan	John Sullivan	Steven Sullivan
S½ 4	13		Henry Padget	Clifford Padgett
N½ 4	13		William Ashmore	Lloyd Ashmore
NW¼ 7	13		Patrick McMullen	Wilfred McMullen
Pt. S½ 13	13		Patrick Murtha	Paul Murtha
S½ 7	14		William McMullen	John McMullen
SE¼ 8	14		James Patrick	William Patrick

NOTES

1. In cases where the name is different in 1973, descent was through a daughter who married.
2. This list can be correlated with the list given by Kirkconnell in his Victoria History (p. 272) of 63 Emily pioneers whose farms remained in the same family at 1921. More farms have passed out of the ownership of the original pioneer families in the 50 years since, than in the 100 years before.

APPENDIX XXX

BEGINNINGS OF THE MILLERSMITH COMMUNITY IN NORTH EMILY

(Provided by Mr. and Mrs. Wilfred McMullen)

Emily, March 9, 1934

This is the account of the first settlers to come to this part of the Township of Emily, 13 and 14 Concessions on the west Quarter Line known as Miller Smith, named after two of the first settlers on the corner.

I have heard this story many times from my Grandmother and my Father and Mother.

"John McMullen"

"In the year 1831 on June 2nd my grandparents and parents set sail from Liverpool for Canada and sailed for 6 weeks before landing in Quebec. From there they came up the St. Lawrence River to the Trent River, by Rice Lake to Peterboro and Mud Lake then to Pigeon Lake to Kings Wharf in the Township of Emily, where they stopped for 6 weeks, living in brush tents in September and October. It was a very wet fall, then they

BEGINNINGS OF THE MILLERSMITH COMMUNITY IN NORTH EMILY

took Ague. The women and children stayed in the tents while the men came here to the 14th concession to build their shanties.

There were five of them: William Smith located Lot 6, Con. 13 of Emily. John Kennedy on Lot 5, Con. 13, Christofer Bentley on Lot 8, Con. 13 and his grandson John Cullon then a small boy of 4 years. Sergeant John Miller on Lot 7, Con. 14 which was a grant of land from the British government for his service in the Peninsular war, now occupied by his great-great-grandson. John McMullen, Sr. on Lot east ⅓ 8, Conc. 14. They had only a short time to build all the shanties but some men from Downeyville who had settled there 6 years before helped them and brought with them a yoke of oxen. My Grandfather Miller's (house) was the last to be built, and the family got into it on November 2nd, and only half the roof was on. It snowed that night and didn't leave until spring. They lived for some time without floors, with a blanket hung in the doorway.

To get their groceries they had to go to Port Hope for them, and walk both ways and carry their flour on their backs. Later on when they had wheat they had to carry it to Peterboro to get ground and maybe they had no bread for their breakfast. They had no roads just a blazed trail. The load for a man was 60 lbs. of wheat and a woman 30 lbs. They often had to stop on their way home at some person's shanty and bake a flap-jack to eat on the way, and the family had to go without their supper till it was cooked after the father came home. The woods were full of wolves so had to get home if possible before dark. If not they had to have a torch to scare the wolves away and Father said they could hear them snarling behind them. After while Christofer Bentley got a yoke of oxen and the five families used them and got along nicely.

Roads were cleared out so they could get wheat to the mill and with the oxen and a jumper (a homemade sleigh). After a year or two they got horses. The Miller boys were the first to get horses. Then all the wheat to spare was taken to Port Hope by the Miller's team. All the hills were in their natural state so they couldn't take very big loads. They all worked together logging and clearing the land. When they dug their potatoes they sowed fall wheat.

Money was very scarce then and when they got their crops in some of them would go out to Cavan and work until their crops were ripe. When the harvest was over they would underbrush whatever they were going to chop the next winter. They would chop all day, get their supper and thresh what straw would feed the stock that night and the next day. When spring came they burned their fallows and had logging bees with lots of whiskey to make the sawers frisky. These bees would last for weeks. About 1835 they started to build better buildings and shortly they all had good buildings.

About this time a very sad thing happened. William Smith was killed by a falling tree while chopping in the woods, leaving his wife and four children. Her son John kept the farm; it is in the Smith family still, one hundred and three years. They all got along as a community until fever and ague broke out and some families were wiped out completely. Just 3 of the Miller family survived—the father and two daughters, Mrs. William McMullen and Mrs. John Murdoch. That was the forties.

About this time a school was built on the south west corner of Lot 6, Con. 14. Before this, school was held on Lot 8, Con. 14 by a farmer named Dwyer. I, John McMullen, went to the second school which was built on southwest corner of Lot 6, Con. 14. It was roofed with basswood troughs and half of it was floored. The seats were small logs split in two and 4 legs put in them. There were 4 of them set in a square and a stove in the centre. There was school only about half time. The teacher taught one week at the Scotch Line, the next at Dunsford and next in Emily. The teachers were untrained, not knowing very much about teaching.

Then there came a minister named Rev. Rogers from Peterboro and held services

APPENDIX XXX (cont.)

BEGINNINGS OF THE MILLERSMITH COMMUNITY IN NORTH EMILY

in John Miller's house, and also another man from Port Hope held service in Miller's house. He was English Church minister. Mr. Rogers was Presbyterian. A man named John Moore held regular service from house to house until they built a church at Sheriff's Corner now Dunsford. Rev. Mr. Moore lived on Lot 2, Con. 13, Emily, which was a clergy reserve. Rev. John Ewing who ministered in Omemee from 1849 to 1893 made many visits to North Emily.

A sad thing happened to one of the early settlers. John Kennedy went to work on the Welland Canal to get some ready money. He was not long there till he took "Colery" and died, leaving his wife and 4 children who were unable to work, but the wife managed to get along with her children at home.

Lone Grave At Pioneer Cemetery For Omemee Veteran

Omemee (PNS) — Unknown by many inhabitants of the village, there is a lone grave in the first Anglican pioneer cemetery, behind the Shell Service Station, that few have heard about or seen.

Amid the tall grass and barricaded by snow fence, to protect its consecration during recent construction work, lies the grave of a man who carried the King's Colors in the War of 1812-1814. This cemetery was used until the nondenominational cemetery (Emily) was opened in 1872.

The remaining tombstones were removed but the heavy bronze plate covering the entire length of the grave, still remains.

The inscription reads:

"In memory of Matt. W. Hancock, Late Lieutenant in the 59th Regiment of the Line.

"A Native of Maryborough, Queen's County, Ireland, he served with distinction in the War of 1812 and was present at the Battle of Lundy's Lane and carried the King's Colors the entire of that eventful day. He also served at the siege of Fort Erie, and died Feb. 26, 1858," age 74 years.

Erected by the Orangemen of Emily.

(Harry Jackson)

(Lindsay "Post", June 19, 1974.)

INDEX

TANNERIES 79, 121-4, 132.

Taverns (see Inns)

Taxes (Township, County, District) 20-1, 95-7, 101, 146-8, 192-3, 222-3, 255-6, 269, 290, 322, 340-6.

Teachers (see Education)

Telegraphy 126, 158.

Telephone Services 176, 178, 208-10, 269.

Temperance Movement (agitation, regulation) 102-5, 138, 154, 159, 162, 225, 239, 270-1, 342-6.

Threshers (see Farm Machinery, Industries, Steam Machines)

Tourists (and Tourist Trade) 196, 198, 206, 224, 245-6, 257, 270-1, 300, 302.

Township Administration 20, 47, 68, 95-9, 146-8, 192-3, 255-9, 298, 300-1, 339-47, 349-51

Township Records (Assessment, Census) 15-6, 20-2, 39, 43, 51, 59, 94, 101, 115, 146, 192, 322.

Township School Board 263-4, 360-2.

Trails (Indian, pioneer) 4, 7-8, 35, 82.

Trains (see Railways)

Trent Valley Navigation Company (see Boyd Industries)

Trent Waterway (canal, river) viii, 2, 7, 39, 66, 124, 127-8, 156-7, 201-6.

UNITED CHURCH (see also Methodists, Presbyterians) 227, 230, 279.

United Farmers of Ontario (UFO) (see Farm Organizations, and Elections)

Universities (see Education, Secondary & Higher)

VEGETABLES (production, use) 134, 232, 280, 347.

Verulam Township 11, 17, 69, 196.

Veterans, War (and Canadian Legion) 199, 221-2, 267-8, 362-5.

Victoria County (council, organization, bylaws, taxes &c) 69, 99, 127, 147, 153, 195-6, 221, 258-61, 264-5, 301, 351.

Victoria County Atlas (1881) 15, 20, 41, 69, 128, 176-7, 335-7.

Victoria Library (see Libraries)

Victoria Magazine (1847-8) 61, 63.

WAGES (farm help, township employees) 82, 95-8, 137, 146-7, 192-3, 198, 201, 222-3, 256-9, 339-47.

Wagons and Carriages (manufacture, price, use) 82, 132, 137, 143, 316-7, 357.

Wardens, County (from Emily) 95, 351.

War Memorial 221, 249, 267-9.

Wartime Activities & Services 219-21, 267-8, 362-4.

Water Transport (see Steamers, Kawarthas, Boating &c)

Waterways (see Kawarthas, Pigeon River, Trent &c)

Weavers (and Weaving) 82, 132, 134.

Welfare (for Indigents) 111, 222-3, 259-61.

Wild Life (animals &c) (hazards, hunting) (see also Recreation) 3, 6, 36, 86, 148, 274, 283, 336-8.

Williamstown (see Omemee)

Women's Activities (Institutes &c) 82, 134, 138, 160-3, 169-71, 184-6, 228, 230, 243, 247-50, 278-81.

Wool Production (see Sheep and Weavers)

World Wars I and II (see Wartime Activities)

Writers (about Emily) 44, 49, 60, 79, 86, 94.

YOUNG MEN'S CHRISTIAN ASSOCIATION 140, 186.

Youth Activities (see also Church Denominations, Recreation, Sports & Games) 160, 162-3, 184-7, 228, 243, 273-5, 278.

HISTORIC SITES AND SIGHTS TO VISIT IN EMILY TOWNSHIP

(as marked on end map)

1. Site of the murder of the Rowan child by a young boy, 1849.
2. Good view point.
3. Site of early Lebanon settlement. Old mill pond restored by Miller family.
4. Presbyterian Cemetery—1832, registered in 1852.
5. Site of one of Emily's first brick houses, built by Harry Best, 1856.
6. Site of Emily's first frame house, built by John Mitchell, 1839.
7. Farm of one of Emily's earliest settlers, Humphrey Finley.
8. Log house built before 1840.
9. Stone part of house built about 1850.
10. Henderson pioneer burial site.
11. Orange Corners, with St. James's Church, LOL #41, S.S. #10, and Timber House built 1847 by W. Brady.
12. Stone house, former stage coach inn, built 1846.
13. Good view point.
14. Site of Cottingham's first mill in 1830s.
15. Rectory Farm—Anglican Glebe lot with century-old stone house.
16. Pioneer frame house built 1851, still in use.
17. Lakevale Presbyterian Church built 1866.
18. Emily Cemetery, 1874.
19. Third Bethel Methodist Church, 1892.
20. Site of Tiggert's Mill, 1830's.
21. Site of Lancaster's Bridge.
22. Original stone house, 1850, with a later brick addition.
23. Good view point.
24. Site of early East Emily Post Office and hamlet.
25. Site of East Emily Cheese Factory about 1900.
26. Second St. James Anglican Church, 1900. Cairn erected on site of pioneer cemetery.
27. Brick house built in 1850s by John Scully. First Robinson settler to build a brick house (note Rose window).
28. Fitch's log house built about 1840.
29. Cowan's bridge, County Forest and Emily Park.
30. Site of Colonel Baldwin's Mill in early 1830's.
31. Site of pioneer hamlet (Frank Hill)—Post Office, school and blacksmith's shop.
32. Downeyville timber frame church built 1858. (European custom of burying clergy beneath church was practised here in early times.)
33. Site of Downey's Cross—pioneer hamlet with Roman Catholic Church, stores, inns, Post Office and blacksmith's shop.
34. Flynn's log house about 1830, once a halfway house on the Bobcaygeon-Port Hope trail.
35. Site of pioneer cemetery and first Roman Catholic church about 1835.
36. Downeyville Cemetery, 1907.
37. Site of Maple Leaf Cheese Factory.
38. Sullivan house—used as stage coach inn in pioneer times.
39. Entrance to Pigeon Lake floating bridge and site of William (Captain) King's ferry dock.
40. Old log house site of Callaghan's steam powered saw mill in late Victorian times.
41. Site of former North Emily United Church and North Emily Salem Cemetery.
42. Site of Millersmith School, built about 1875.
43. Good view point.
44. Site of King's Wharf hamlet—Post Office, school, store and blacksmith's shop.

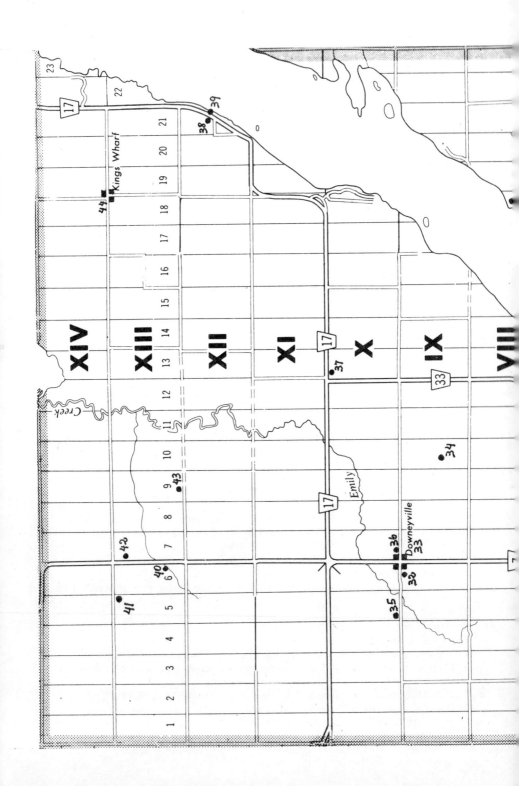